Personal Computer Secrets®

Personal Computer Secrets®

Bob O'Donnell

IDG Books Worldwide, Inc.
An International Data Group Company

Foster City, CA ♦ Chicago, IL ♦ Indianapolis, IN ♦ New York, NY

Personal Computer Secrets®

Published by

IDG Books Worldwide, Inc.

An International Data Group Company

919 E. Hillsdale Blvd., Suite 400

Foster City, CA 94404

www.idgbooks.com (IDG Books Worldwide Web site)

ISBN: 0-7645-3133-6

Printed in the United States of America

10 9 8 7 6 5 4 3 2 1

1B/QW/QW/ZZ/FC

Distributed in the United States by IDG Books Worldwide, Inc.

Distributed by CDG Books Canada Inc. for Canada; by Transworld Publishers Limited in the United Kingdom; by IDG Norge Books for Norway; by IDG Sweden Books for Sweden; by IDG Books Australia Publishing Corporation Pty. Ltd. for Australia and New Zealand; by TransQuest Publishers Pte Ltd. for Singapore, Malaysia, Thailand, Indonesia, and Hong Kong; by Gotop Information Inc. for Taiwan; by ICG Muse, Inc. for Japan; by Norma Comunicaciones S.A. for Colombia; by Intersoft for South Africa; by Le Monde en Tique for France; by International Thomson Publishing for Germany, Austria and Switzerland; by Distribuidora Cuspide for Argentina; by Livraria Cultura for Brazil; by Ediciones ZETA S.C.R. Ltda. for Peru; by WS Computer Publishing Corporation, Inc., for the Philippines; by Contemporanea de Ediciones for Venezuela; by Express Computer Distributors for the Caribbean and West Indies; by Micronesia Media Distributor, Inc. for Micronesia; by Grupo Editorial Norma S.A. for Guatemala; by Chips Computadoras S.A. de C.V. for Mexico; by Editorial Norma de Panama S.A. for Panama; by American Bookshops for Finland. Authorized Sales Agent: Anthony Rudkin Associates for the Middle East and North Africa.

For general information on IDG Books Worldwide's books in the U.S., please call our Consumer Customer Service department at 800-762-2974. For reseller information, including discounts and premium sales, please call our Reseller Customer Service department at 800-434-3422.

For information on where to purchase IDG Books Worldwide's books outside the U.S., please contact our International Sales department at 317-596-5530 or fax 317-596-5692.

For consumer information on foreign language translations, please contact our Customer Service department at 800-434-3422, fax 317-596-5692, or e-mail rights@idgbooks.com.

For information on licensing foreign or domestic rights, please phone +1-650-655-3109.

For sales inquiries and special prices for bulk quantities, please contact our Sales department at 650-655-3200 or write to the address above.

For information on using IDG Books Worldwide's books in the classroom or for ordering examination copies, please contact our Educational Sales department at 800-434-2086 or fax 317-596-5499.

For press review copies, author interviews, or other publicity information, please contact our Public Relations department at 650-655-3000 or fax 650-655-3299.

For authorization to photocopy items for corporate, personal, or educational use, please contact Copyright Clearance Center, 222 Rosewood Drive, Danvers, MA 01923, or fax 978-750-4470.

Library of Congress Cataloging-in-Publication Data

O'Donnell, Bob, [DATE]

    Personal computer secrets / Bob O'Donnell.

      p. cd.

    ISBN 0-7645-3133-6 (alk. paper)

    1. Microcomputers. I. Title.

QA76.5.O32   1999

004.16--dc21   99-27352

                                              CIP

In addition to the five parts, a glossary includes extensive definitions of over 500 terms, and the appendix explains the useful software you'll find on the CD-ROM included in this book.

All told, I hope you find this book to be the only computer book you ever really need. I thoroughly appreciate your interest and investment in this labor of love, and I hope you enjoy it.

Bob O'Donnell
www.everythingcomputers.com

Conventions

To help you find what you want as quickly as possible, I use a number of conventions throughout the book to denote specific types of information.

Secret

Secrets signify little-known facts and a few undocumented techniques.

Tip

Tips indicate how to do something useful or interesting.

Note

Notes offer a little more background information on a given subject.

Caution

Caution warns you to be careful with certain information and procedures because without taking the proper precautions, you can cause serious damage to your PC's data.

Cross-Reference

Cross-References provide an easy way to find information on a particular subject within another section of the book.

CD

CD signifies that a product is available on the CD-ROM disc included with this book.

Acknowledgments

Many thanks are due to the people who helped make this book a reality, but none is more heartfelt than my thanks to Jim Sumser, acquisitions editor at IDG Books Worldwide for believing in me and this book, and pushing the concept through. Thanks Jim, I owe you one. I want to thank the development editors who helped guide me through the process and put up with many long delays: thank you to Tracy Thomsic, BC Crandall, Jennifer Rowe, and, in particular, Kevin Shafer. Thank you to the copy editors, Nancy Crumpton, Karyn DiCastri, And Lauren Kennedy. Thanks and appreciation are also due to technical editor, Sean Dugan.

I also want to thank Marissa Manheimer at Dell and Kate Paisley at Krause-Taylor Associates (Micron's PR firm) for loaning me the equipment I used to write the book. A huge thank you is also due to Greg Botto and his staff at Global Network Services for their undying efforts on behalf of my Web site. Another huge thank you is owed to all my *O'Donnell on Computers* radio show listeners, whose problems and questions inspired me to write this book in the first place.

Many companies contributed software to the CD-ROM and I am grateful to them all.

Thank you also to the various family members and friends who listened to my ideas and read early drafts as the book progressed. Finally, I owe an enormous thank you to my children, Ryan and Kelsey, who started to wonder if their daddy ever did anything except sit in front of a computer, and most important, to my wife, Jennifer. Without her sacrifice, support, guidance, pushing, and love, I never would have made it. Thanks honey, I love you.

Contents at a Glance

Part I: Buying a PC 1

Chapter 1: How to Buy a New Computer 3
Chapter 2: Microprocessors and Memory 43
Chapter 3: Hard Disks and Removable Drives 81
Chapter 4: Video Cards and Monitors 121
Chapter 5: Sound Cards, Speakers, and Modems 155
Chapter 6: Printers, Scanners, and Digital Cameras 195
Chapter 7: Input Devices and Power 231

Part II: Enhancing Your PC 251

Chapter 8: How Your Computer Works 253
Chapter 9: Adding, Upgrading, and Removing Software 307
Chapter 10: Adding and Removing Hardware 361
Chapter 11: Upgrading Your PC 397

Part III: Connecting Your PC 437

Chapter 12: Setting Up a Small Business or Home Network 439
Chapter 13: Connecting to and Using the Internet 503

Part IV: Using Your PC 587

Chapter 14: Working with Documents and Files 589
Chapter 15: Working with Pictures and Video 623
Chapter 16: Working with Audio and Music 655

Part V: Fixing Your PC 695

Chapter 17: Troubleshooting Techniques 697
Chapter 18: Solving Common PC Problems 755

Appendix A: What's on the CD-ROM? 807

Glossary 815

Index **905**

End-User License Agreement **930**

CD-ROM Installation Instructions **936**

Contents

Preface...ix

Acknowledgments xii

Part I: Buying a PC 1

Chapter 1: How to Buy a New Computer 3

Computer Concepts 4
    Digital data 7
    Memory and storage 8
    Basic operation 10
PC Components 11
    A system of systems 14
    Connecting external devices 18
Reading the Specs 19
What to Buy 21
    System cost 26
    Desktop versus notebook 27
    Expandability 32
User Profiles 33
    Home office/basic productivity 33
    Creative work 34
    Games and entertainment 35
    Web browsing/e-mail 35
When to Buy 36
    Planning and research 37
    System type 38
Where to Buy 39
    Retail versus direct 39
    Service 41
    Refurbished PCs 41

Chapter 2: Microprocessors and Memory 43

The Processor 44
    How it works 44
    Processor types 45
    Speed 47
    L1 and L2 cache 48
    Architecture 52
    Processor alternatives 56

Notebook processors 57
Multiprocessor systems 59
Physical connections 60
Logical connections 62
Chipsets and BIOS 64
Recommendations 66
Memory 68
SIMMs, DIMMs, SO-DIMMs, and RIMMs 69
Memory types 71
Virtual Channel Memory 76
Error correction 77
Recommendations 78

Chapter 3: Hard Disks and Removable Drives 81

Hard Drives 82
How it works 82
Drive specifications 87
Hard drive interfaces 93
Recommendations 104
Removable Drives 105
Floppy drives 107
CD-ROM and DVD-ROM 107
Removable storage options 112
Recommendations 117

Chapter 4: Video Cards and Monitors 121

Video Cards 121
Resolution 123
Color depth 124
Video memory 126
Refresh rates 130
Video card interfaces 131
Acceleration 133
TV inputs 139
Video recording 140
Recommendations 143
Monitors 144
Monitor sizes 145
Monitor resolutions 146
Dot pitch, interlace, and dots per inch (DPI) 147
Display Data Channel (DDC) 147
Built-in features 148
Liquid crystal display (LCD) 149
Recommendations 153

Chapter 5: Sound Cards, Speakers, and Modems 155

Sound Cards 156
Digital audio versus synthesized sound 158
Digital audio 159

Synthesized sound 162
Audio processing 167
Audio outputs 169
Other connections 171
Recommendations 173
Speakers 174
Satellites and subwoofers 175
Speaker technologies 175
Multispeaker systems 176
USB speakers 177
Recommendations 177
Modems 178
Modem speeds 179
Analog modems 181
ISDN modems 187
Cable modems 190
DSL modems 191
Recommendations 193

Chapter 6: Printers, Scanners, and Digital Cameras 195

Printers 196
Inkjet versus laser versus other options 196
Specialty printers 206
Printer connections 210
Recommendations 216
Scanners 217
Resolution: Optical versus interpolated 217
Color depth 218
Interface type 219
Size and speed 219
Specialty scanners 220
Bundled software 221
Recommendations 221
Digital Cameras 222
Resolution 223
Compression 224
Storage 225
Camera issues 226
Other digital imaging devices 226
Recommendations 228

Chapter 7: Input Devices and Power 231

Input Devices 232
Keyboards 232
Mice 235
Graphics tablets 238
Game controllers 239
Recommendations 240
Power 241

Power supplies 242
Power management 244
Surge protectors 245
Line conditioners 245
UPSes 247
Recommendations 248

Part II: Enhancing Your PC 251

Chapter 8: How Your Computer Works 253

The Basics 253
Hardware and software 254
Input and output 255
General operation 257
How the Hardware Works 260
Structure 260
Buses 261
Bus speeds and bandwidth 263
Processor and memory 264
Peripheral buses 266
Resources 275
How the Software Works 281
Basic connections 281
Software layers 282
Inside Windows 283
In Action 287
Booting 288
Windows Startup 298
Running an application 302
Printing 305

Chapter 9: Adding, Upgrading, and Removing Software 307

Installing New Programs 308
Downloading programs off the Internet 311
Installation example: Publisher 2000 319
Upgrading applications 323
Reinstalling 326
Installing Operating Systems 328
General issues 328
Using multiple operating systems 329
Installing Windows 95 or 98 332
Reinstalling Windows 95 or 98 335
Updating Windows 98 345
Installing Windows 2000 347
Installing Linux 348
Removing Software 354
Standard techniques 355
Additional steps 357

Chapter 10: Adding and Removing Hardware **361**

    Connectors and Resources 362
      Resources 364
      What uses resources? 367
    Adding External Hardware 371
      Getting ready 371
      Special considerations 372
    Adding Internal Hardware 378
      General precautions 378
      Making the connection 380
      Notebook PC Cards 383
    Installing Drivers 384
      Upgrading drivers 385
      Removing drivers 389
    Removing Hardware 393

Chapter 11: Upgrading Your PC **397**

    To Upgrade or Not to Upgrade,
      That Is the Question 398
    Adding Memory 399
      Opening the case 400
      Installing 402
      Reconfiguring 404
      Testing the memory 405
    Adding a New Hard Drive 406
      Configuring drive settings 407
      Connecting the cables 407
      BIOS settings 411
      Testing the connection 412
      Partitioning, formatting, and copying software 413
      Large drive problems 417
    Adding or Upgrading Your CD or DVD-ROM Drive 418
      IDE interfaces 418
      SCSI interfaces 419
      DVD-ROM 419
      Installing drivers 419
    Upgrading Your BIOS 420
    Other Hardware Upgrades 423
      Firmware updates 424
      Printer memory 425
    Upgrading Your Processor 425
      Determining processor types 425
      Installing the processor 428
    Replacing Your Computer's Motherboard 431
      Getting organized 431
      Removing the old motherboard 432
      Installing the new motherboard 434

Part III: Connecting Your PC 437

Chapter 12: Setting Up a Small Business or Home Network 439
Basic Networking Concepts 440
  Network data 441
  Network structures 442
  Network architectures 446
  Network protocols 448
  Network types 449
  Network operating systems 451
  The OSI network model 452
Putting Together a Simple Network 455
  The pieces 455
  Direct cable connection 458
  Installing the network software 459
  Other network considerations 467
Creating a Home Network 474
  Phone lines 476
  Power lines 476
  Wireless 477
Taking Advantage of Your Network 478
  Sharing files 479
  Sharing drives 482
  Mapping drives 483
  Sharing printers 485
  Sharing scanners 487
  Sharing an Internet connection 488
  Playing games 491
  Building an intranet 492
  Remote access 496
  Other network applications 499

Chapter 13: Connecting to and Using the Internet 503
How the Internet Works 504
  Connecting with a Web site 505
  Setting up your connection 510
Customizing Your Web Browsing Experience 518
  Plug-ins 520
  Bookmarks and favorites 524
  Using applications on the Web 525
  Optimizing your Web connection 536
  Finding information on the Web 540
Setting Up an E-mail Account 541
  Editing an existing e-mail account 543
  Making the most of e-mail 546
Other Ways to Communicate via the Internet 556
  Newsgroups 557
  Live chat 563
  Internet phone calls 565

Videoconferencing and application sharing 568
Building Your Own Web Site 570
Site strategy and structure 571
Creating Web pages 572
Obtaining a Web address 581
Posting your pages 582
Updating your site 584
Publicizing your site 584

Part IV: Using Your PC 587

Chapter 14: Working with Documents and Files 589

Applications and Documents 590
File extensions 592
Editing file types 594
Creating new files 598
Opening existing documents 602
Converting Documents 606
Sharing Your Documents 608
Specialty printing 609
Electronic documents 609
Managing Your Files 611
Backing up 612
Freeing up disk space 615
Taking care of your disks 618

Chapter 15: Working with Pictures and Video 623

Digital Pictures 624
File formats 625
Digital picture sources 626
Scanning your own images 629
The details on resolution 631
Scanning tips 635
Cropping and resizing 637
Editing images 638
Special effects 642
Printing tips 643
Using the pictures in other programs 645
Using images on the Web 646
Digital Video 647
Making the connections 648
Capturing the video 650
Editing 651
Titles, graphics, and special effects 652
Finishing the program 653

Chapter 16: Working with Audio and Music 655

Getting Started with Sound 656

Playing back sound files 657
Digital audio basics 658
Recording your own CDs 663
Digital Audio Recording 664
The hookup 664
Recording and editing 666
Processing 666
Special effects 668
Making Music 668
Audio remixing 669
MIDI basics 670
MIDI sequencing 672
Music notation 688
Other MIDI software 689
Putting Sound Files on the Web 692
Converting files 692
Adding them to your pages 693

Part V: Fixing Your PC **695**

Chapter 17: Troubleshooting Techniques **697**

Troubleshooting Strategies 698
Define the problem 698
Narrow in on the specifics 699
Use available resources 700
Keep track of what you do 702
Test your solution 703
Basic Troubleshooting Checks 703
Physical connections 703
Updates and upgrades 704
Hardware Troubleshooting Concepts 705
Drivers 706
Resources 711
Software Troubleshooting Concepts 718
Shared files and DLLs 719
Software conflicts 720
Bugs 723
Viruses 724
Troubleshooting Tools 724
Boot disk with CD or DVD-ROM driver and utilities 725
Diagnostic programs 730
Windows 98 utilities 730
Windows 95 diagnostic tools 741
Starting Over 749

Chapter 18: Solving Common PC Problems **755**

Fixing Startup Problems 756
BIOS setup 757

Startup files 759
Shutdown problems 771
Fixing Hardware Problems 771
Video display problems 772
Hard drive problems 773
Mouse, keyboard, and joystick problems 776
Printer problems 778
Modem and Internet connection problems 780
Sound card/audio problems 786
Power management problems 788
USB problems 790
SCSI problems 792
Network problems 793
Fixing Software Problems 793
Uninstalling software 793
Consistent and random crashes 794
Running out of memory 794
DOS games 797
Web browser/Internet problems 801
E-mail problems 802

Appendix A: What's on the CD-ROM? **807**

Glossary **815**

Index **905**

End-User License Agreement **930**

CD-ROM Installation Instructions **936**

Part I

Buying a PC

Chapter 1: How to Buy a New Computer

Chapter 2: Microprocessors and Memory

Chapter 3: Hard Disks and Removable Drives

Chapter 4: Video Cards and Monitors

Chapter 5: Sound Cards, Speakers, and Modems

Chapter 6: Printers, Scanners, and Digital Cameras

Chapter 7: Input Devices and Power

Chapter 1

How to Buy a New Computer

In This Chapter

▶ You will learn what a computer is and how it basically works.

▶ You will learn what components go inside a modern PC.

▶ You will learn some of the terminology that you need to know to make sense of PCs.

▶ You will learn how to read and understand computer system specifications.

▶ You will receive advice on what type of system to buy, when to buy it, and where to buy it.

Computers are the tools and toys of the modern age. They are the defining symbols of our era, the workhorses of our time, and, arguably, one of the most important developments in the last few hundred years.

Even more importantly, computers are useful. And they're fun — usually, that is. Because they can also be incredibly frustrating, vexing, confusing, frightening, and costly, you may wonder if they are worth the time, money, and effort they require. The answer is: absolutely. Owning a personal computer (or even a few of them) will forever change how you do certain tasks, how you communicate with friends, family, and associates, and even how you view certain aspects of the world around you.

But buying a computer isn't always a straightforward process. There are a lot of potential potholes along the way. First of all, with the exception of homes and cars, personal computers — along with their various extras — are some of the biggest ticket items that consumers purchase. The typical purchase price for a consumer computer system, including the monitor and other accessories, is well over $1,000, so it's a big decision.

Furthermore, buying a computer is a decision fraught with a seemingly overwhelming list of possibilities and options. Not only do you need to figure out computer terminology to understand your choices, you need to decide what kind of system is right for you. On top of this, you need to figure out where and when to buy a system; this can be confusing as well.

Computer Concepts

First things first: Before you can buy a computer, you need to know what one is. Now, a dictionary will probably tell you that a computer is an electronic device that processes data (whatever "processes data" means — I never did get that). But, while this may be a perfectly reasonable, concise definition of a computer, it doesn't really tell you what computers are all about. To figure this out, you need to understand what a computer is *conceptually*.

I like to think of a computer as essentially an electronic desk; it provides a place for you to do work or any number of other activities. Figure 1-1 illustrates this concept.

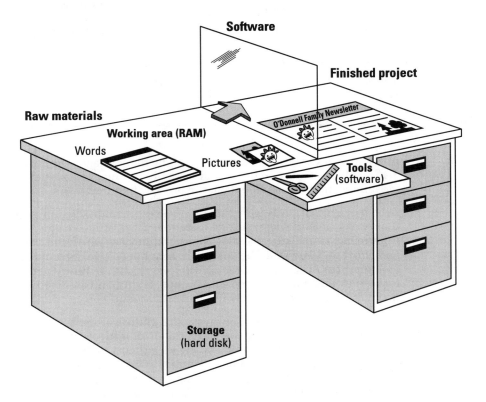

Figure 1-1: Why your computer is like a desk
In many ways, a computer is like a desk. It provides a place where you can do projects, and provides tools you can use to get those projects done. In its basic operation, a computer lets you take various types of raw materials, including words, pictures and more, and through the magic of software, generate finished results that would be difficult or impossible to achieve without one.

You bring raw materials, such as letters, words, numbers, and even pictures or sounds, to a computer, just as you would bring pens, pencils, and paper to a desk. Then you use computer software — sometimes called *programs* or *applications* — to perform various operations on this raw material, just as you would use the tools you find located in the drawers of the desk to manipulate the words and drawings you might create while you work there.

One of the primary challenges in getting computers to do what you want them to do is to figure out which type of tool is necessary to perform the required task. As with desk tools, you can often make do with simple instruments — a scissors, tape, a stapler, and so on, but certain jobs, such as cutting 50 sheets of paper into squares, are much easier with the addition of a new tool, like a paper cutter. With a computer, some tasks, such as faxing your creation to someone else, require the purchase and installation of a new tool. In this example, a fax machine has the capability that your existing tools lack.

So, too, with computers, you can often use basic hardware and software tools to perform most tasks, but some tasks are made easier with the addition of new software or hardware and some tasks are impossible without the addition of a new piece of software or hardware.

It is also important to remember that with regard to computers and how they operate, there's not necessarily one right way to do something. Just as there are numerous ways to use different desk tools to create, for example, a homemade calendar, you can use any of a number of different pieces of software to, say, create a newsletter on your computer. You might use specialized publishing software that's specifically designed to create newsletters, or you might just use fancy formatting in a word processor. Either one is fine, as long as you are able to achieve the end result you want.

Some of the activities you can perform on a computer include:

- Connect to the Internet
- Send e-mail to friends, relatives, and acquaintances
- Write letters (or the Great American Novel)
- Manage your finances
- Play computer games
- Create a family history complete with old and new photos
- Compose and record your own music
- Edit home, or even professional, videos
- Create a newsletter or flyer for an organization you belong to
- Make videophone or regular voice phone calls over the Internet
- Create your own greeting cards
- Help your children use educational software

Not all desks are alike and, similarly, not all computers are alike, but there are qualities that all desks share — a certain *deskness* as Plato might have said. When it comes to selecting a desk, you need to consider how much working space it provides, how much storage it offers, and things of this sort. So too, when you buy a computer, you need to worry about how much working space the computer provides, how much storage it offers, how much of your work you can see at once, and other related issues.

Too much information

The raw material that computers work with is referred to as *information*, but the information is not a specific fact or bit of knowledge. Ironically, in this "information age," information has become any object, idea, or action that can be described in the language of computers — that is, the 1s and 0s of digital data. So, for example, as far as your computer is concerned, your mouse pointer moving across the screen is just as much a piece of information as the fact that 2 x 4 = 8, or that Abraham Lincoln was the 16th president of the United States of America.

One of the biggest challenges with computers is to figure out how to translate different types of raw material into digital "information" that a computer can use and manipulate. In fact, one way to view and understand development and progress in the computer industry is to see this development as a continuous effort to make more and more different types of information part of the normal computing experience.

Early versions of what we consider modern computers couldn't do any translating. They started out with punch cards that essentially contained strings of 1s and 0s (in the form of small holes punched in the cards at certain points

or not) in literal form. Then, regular keyboards with text-only screens were added to computers; this was the first abstraction away from these literal strings of 1s and 0s. A computer took input from the keyboard, "translated" those letters into a form it could understand and use, then "re-translated" them back into a form that people could understand when it displayed them on the monitor.

Subsequent development has refined computers' original capabilities. Color displays with graphics and other pictures, as well as entirely new types of translations such as sound inputs and speakers for adding music and audio, and video inputs for adding video are examples. And even now, new developments to enable people to use their handwriting and spoken commands reflect the continued efforts in this continuum.

As computers progress, it has becomes easier to add each type of "information" into the computer's vocabulary of capabilities. It is, however, often a challenge to add on these capabilities to existing or older computers. This is one of the primary reasons why computers become outdated — or are updated — on such a frequent basis.

Digital data

All the raw elements you work with on a regular desk come in a form that our eyes and ears can understand. We can see and recognize the shapes of letters we draw, for example, or hear the sounds of our voices or music being played. Before a computer can "see" or work with those raw materials, they all need to be translated into a form that a computer can understand.

The form, or language, that computers use to work with information is called *digital data*; this simply means the information has been translated into the 1 and 0s of binary math (that's base-2, you know, 2, 4, 8, 16, 32, and so on for all you math flunkies). Each individual 1 or 0 is called a *bit* and eight bits placed together form a *byte*.

Note

By the way, you will never, *ever* need to know anything about bits and bytes and binary math to operate a computer, but I would be seen as remiss if I didn't include this information in a computer book; so here it is.

The conversion from a physical to a digital form can be nearly invisible; it happens when you type letters on a keyboard attached to a computer to form words. It can also be very obvious and deliberate, such as when you use a device called a *scanner* to translate a photograph or other image into a form the computer understands. Regardless of how the translation occurs, and whether it's a simple note, a recording of Beethoven's Fifth Symphony, or pictures of your Aunt Gladys, the computer sees all the information, or raw material, exactly the same way. The information appears as a bunch of numbers made up of nothing more than 0s and 1s.

Computers work their magic by manipulating those binary strings of numbers mathematically. In essence, a computer is like a big, very fancy calculator. When you and I use different programs on the computer, we assume the computer does different things for each program. In truth, the computer just performs various types of calculations on different strings of 1s and 0s. (Kinda takes the magic out of it, doesn't it?)

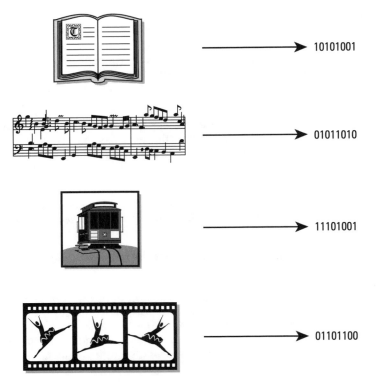

Figure 1-2: Nothing more than 1s and 0s
Computers break down everything they work with, whether it's a letter, song, picture, or video, into binary, or base-2 numbers. This essentially lets everything inside a computer work like a simple set of on-off switches (although there are millions of them working at extremely high speed).

Memory and storage

Computers need room to read and manipulate these numbers and that working area is called *Random Access Memory*, or RAM. Think of RAM as the available space on your desk. The more of space you have, the better off you are (and the more things you can be working on at once).

Units of RAM measurement in most computers are referred to as *megabytes*, or MB. You may also see memory measured in *kilobytes*, or KB, or even bytes or bits. As you might suspect from the similarity in the measurement names, there is a logical and numerical correspondence between them, and they're all related to multiples of the number two (there's that binary math again). All you really need to know, however, is that a computer's main memory is measured in megabytes, and the more megabytes a computer has, the better.

Do the math

For those of you who are mathematically inclined, here's a quick breakdown of the different storage measurements commonly used in computers.

A megabyte is equivalent to 1,024 kilobytes or KB, which in turn is equivalent to 1,024 bytes, and each byte is made up of 8 bits. So, there are 8 bits x 1,024 bytes x 1,024 kilobytes = a lot of bits per megabyte (8,388,608 to be exact). Many computers these days come with 64MB of RAM, although it's not uncommon to see systems with 16MB or 128MB or more.

Hard drives are typically measured in gigabytes, or GB, which is equivalent to 1,024 megabytes. Many hard drives are in the 2-20GB range, although again, both larger and smaller versions are not at all uncommon.

Table 1-1 shows the relations between the various measurements, including a hypothetical translation into lengths.

Table 1-1   Making Sense of Measurements

Measurement	Number of Bits	Number of Bytes	Number of Kilobytes	Number of Megabytes	Approximate length if one bit = 1 mm
Byte	8	1			Pencil tip on a sharpened #2 pencil
Kilobyte	8,192	1,024	1		Height of a two-story building
Megabyte	8,388,608	1,048,576	1,024		A 5-mile run
Gigabyte	8,589,934,592	1,073,741,824	1,048,576	1,024	Distance from San Francisco, California to London, England

In addition to a working area, computers need storage space to save the fruits of their (and your) labor. Storage space is particularly important on PCs because, for the most part, they don't keep automatic records of what you do on them. It would be nice if they did, so that, as with paper, the very process of creating something generated a record of it, but they just don't.

What this means is you could be writing the Great American Novel for three days and three nights, non-stop, pouring your heart out, but if little Johnny comes and trips over the power cord before you've saved — or made a record of — your work, it will all be gone. This is one of those tough lessons that virtually every computer user, experienced as well as novice, finds out on his or her own (hopefully only once). The bottom line is no matter what kind of work you do on a computer, save often.

On a computer, storage is handled by a mechanism called a *hard drive*, and *storage space*, like memory, can be measured in megabytes. However, most hard drives these days are at least 1GB (1,024MB) or larger.

One very common misconception made by computer novices is to confuse memory with storage, and think that they are one and the same. They aren't. RAM is where the programs and files are temporarily stored while you're using them, but the hard drive is where all your computer's files are stored, whether they're in use or not. Again, think of the desk analogy: the computer's RAM is like the desktop and the hard drive is like the file drawers.

When you look at the specifications of a computer system, you can differentiate between memory and storage because the bigger number (keep in mind that 1GB=1,024MB) is the storage space on the hard drive and the smaller number is the working space, or RAM. (The reverse is possible, but highly unlikely.)

Basic operation

On a fundamental level, a computer copies information from storage into memory, manipulates this information in memory, updates the display based on that information, and then writes the revised information back into storage space.

Figure 1-3 illustrates the process.

In other words, a computer *reads* information stored on the hard drive into RAM, performs various operations in RAM, and then *writes* the revised version back to the hard disk. Think of it as pulling a file out of a drawer in your desk and, in the process, automatically making a copy of your work. You then make revisions to the version on your desk, quickly make a copy of those revisions, and put the new copy in the file drawer in place of the version you began with. It sounds tedious, but it happens quickly on a computer.

The software installed on your computer, and in particular the operating system, control all of these operations. An operating system, such as one of the many versions of Windows, provides the basic instructions that enable a PC to operate. Individual application programs, such as a word processor, work on top of the operating system and provide a means to perform specific functions or complete particular tasks.

Cross-Reference

For more details on how your computer works, see Chapter 8, "How Your Computer Works."

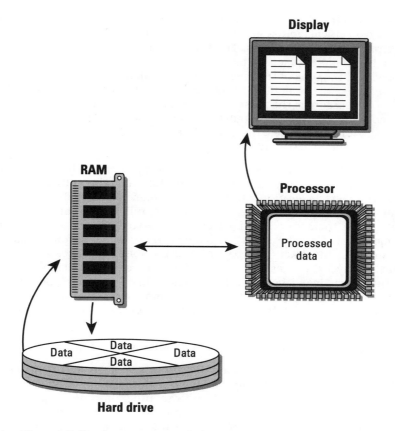

Figure 1-3: How a computer works
In a nutshell, your PC first reads data, or information, off the hard drive into RAM, or memory. Then the processor performs calculations on the data while simultaneously updating the display and the contents of the RAM. Finally, the revised data is stored again on the hard disk when you save the file.

PC Components

Most computers are made up of several different elements, including the main computer unit (also called the CPU or Central Processing Unit), the monitor, the keyboard, the mouse, and so on. Inside the main box are numerous components that, working together, create a functioning PC. As you probably suspect, each computer model features its own unique set of components.

In addition to this unique combination of features and components, one of the most critical factors in differentiating among PCs is how quickly they can perform various operations. The speed of operation is determined by a variety of different factors, but one of the most important factors is the speed and the type of the *microprocessor*, which is the number-crunching powerhouse that functions as the computer's brain. Intel's Pentium line of microprocessors is the most well-known and most widely used type of processing chips. Other popular options include Intel's Celeron line, the AMD K6 and K7 families, the Cyrix MII and MXi, the Rise Technology MP6, and the Centaur/IDT WinChip.

Different types of microprocessors, or simply *processors*, have different inherent capabilities; today's Pentium III chips are inherently more powerful than previous generation Intel Celerons because of internal structural differences. In addition, different processors run at different speeds, which also affects their overall performance. Processor speed is generally measured in megahertz (MHz for short), or millions of cycles per second. This refers to how quickly the timer chip that controls the speed of processor's operation runs. Really fast processors — none of which are even available quite yet — are measured in gigahertz (GHz), or billions of cycles per second. As you would expect, the higher the number, the more operations it can perform in a given amount of time; hence, the faster the processor (and the faster the computer — usually, that is).

Cross-Reference

For more on processors, see Chapter 2, "Microprocessors and Memory."

Of course, none of this means anything unless you can see the results of your work. Computers display information via a TV-like monitor. What you see on the screen is dependent on which software programs you happen to be running. The actual video signal is often generated by a video card, one of many different components that are at work inside a computer's case.

Cross-Reference

For more on video cards, see Chapter 4, "Video Cards and Monitors."

A *video card* is one of several small circuit boards attached to a larger circuit board, called the *motherboard*, or *mainboard*, inside the case of the computer. The motherboard holds the processor, memory, other circuitry the computer needs to operate, as well as a variety of different connectors for hooking together the various pieces of a computer system.

Figure 1-4 shows the inside of a typical PC.

Plug-in cards, such as video cards, enable the computer to do certain things its processor and motherboard can't efficiently do alone. In theory, the computer's main processor can actually do everything necessary to run a computer, but you can make a computer run faster by offloading certain tasks to video cards and other devices that essentially work as coprocessors. (Ironically, though, as computer systems evolve, more and more of the functions that used to be handled by separate components or plug-in cards, including the video signal, have begun to be integrated onto the motherboard itself.)

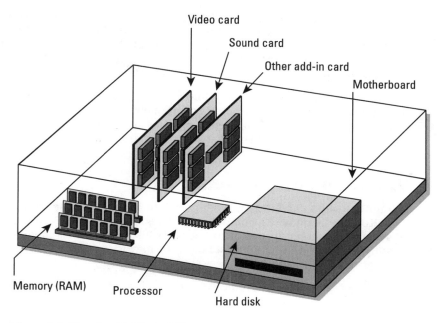

Figure 1-4: The ghost in the machine
The heart of every computer system, desktop or portable, is the motherboard. It either holds or connects to all the main components in a computer. These components include the processor, memory, hard drive, video card, and more.

Typically, if you buy a complete system, you never see the video card or any number of other cards located inside your PC because the majority of them are pre-installed at the factory. But it is important to know that your computer system is a sum of many different parts working together; in fact, it's not only important, it's critical to know this, because this concept forms the whole basis for understanding how computers work.

Secret

Essentially, computers are a conglomeration of different specialized pieces that work with each other (hopefully) to form a single functioning unit.

You want to keep this in mind if you're trying to solve a problem with your computer, or if you're thinking about upgrading your computer. Sometimes you only need to upgrade a single component to get the performance improvement or features capability that you want. It's a lot cheaper than buying a whole new computer.

If you are buying a new computer, it's also important to think of the computer as a group of components because you can choose the types of video cards and other plug-in cards that are best suited to your needs.

Cross-Reference

I explain each of the different components that make up a typical PC in more detail in Chapters 2-7.

While PCs derive a lot of their flexibility from the capability to be put together in pieces, their structure can also be problematic. Think of the internal working of a computer like a party at the United Nations; all the different country's ambassadors are speaking in their native tongues while many interpreters run around translating between the various languages.

Secret

Each component within a computer, in essence, speaks its own language, and a good number of any computer's components and software are required to "translate" between the different languages so that meaningful communication can occur (and you and I can get some work done).

A system of systems

Another way to understand what goes into a computer and to start to get a better handle on how a computer operates is to look at a PC as a system of systems. Different groups of components inside a PC work together as subsystems and those subsystems, in turn, work together to create a functioning PC.

Figure 1-5 graphically outlines what these different subsystems generally look like.

The boundaries between different subsystems are not always as clean as the figure shows because some devices belong to several different subsystems. But, the figure does give a good overview of the general principles. The core of any computer system is the microprocessor and memory, or RAM. This is where the real "computing" occurs, and this core system is fed by the main storage device, typically your PC's hard drive. The hard drive, in turn, is also part of the storage subsystem; this includes the hard drive, floppy drive, CD or DVD-ROM drive and other removable storage devices (such as Zip drives).

Removable storage devices, such as floppy drives and Zip drives, are also known as input/output, or I/O, devices. They enable you to bring data into the computer and take data from it by either copying information from the disk into the computer, or by copying information from the computer onto the disk. A CD-ROM or DVD-ROM drive is similar to a floppy in theory, but most CD-ROM and DVD-ROM drives can only read data off of a compact disc (the ROM in both names stands for read-only memory); you cannot copy data or information onto them.

Figure 1-6 illustrates the difference.

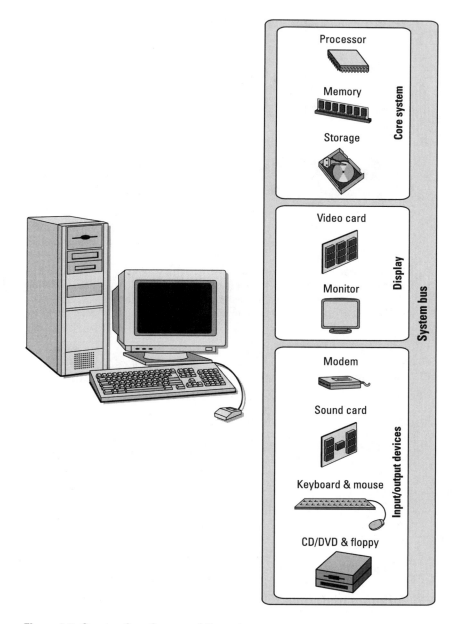

Figure 1-5: Greater than the sum of its parts
A working computer system is the sum of many distinct parts that can be understood both individually and as part of several groups, or subsystems. At any computer's core are the processor, memory, and storage. The display subsystem converts the digital data computers manipulate back into something you can see and understand. The input/output devices enable you to bring material in or take it out of your PC. All of these various components are linked together by a computer's system bus, which routes data around all a computer's components.

Figure 1-6 illustrates the difference.

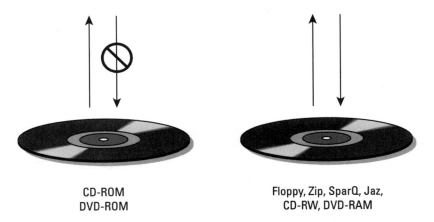

CD-ROM
DVD-ROM   Floppy, Zip, SparQ, Jaz,
CD-RW, DVD-RAM

Figure 1-6: Read-only vs. read-write
Any devices with the word ROM in their name only enable you to copy information from them. Rewritable drives, on the other hand, such as regular floppies, Zip Disks, and others enable you to copy information from them as well as write information to them.

A computer's display subsystem is typically made up of a video card and a monitor. Monitors are also referred to as *output devices* because they display the results, or output, of the computer's internal work. Another example of an output device is a sound card, which plays back music or any other kind of sound that the processor instructs it to play. (The processor, by the way, is told what sounds to play by the software application it is running.)

But having output devices isn't very useful if you can't get any data into the computer in the first place. The most common *input devices* are the keyboard and mouse; both enable you to enter different types of information into the computer (remember, even a mouse clicking on one area of the screen is a form of information as far as your PC is concerned).

Another increasingly common input device is a scanner; it translates photos or printed pages into a digital format that the computer can understand. Video cameras attached to your PC offer a similar capability for moving images. Like a lot of different computer peripherals, scanners come in many forms. Some are external devices that attach to your computer via various types of cables and connectors, and others are built into the main computer unit, somewhat like a floppy disk drive.

Cross-Reference

See Chapter 6, "Printers, Scanners, and Digital Cameras," for more on scanners and video cameras.

Yet another type of input/output device is a modem; it lets you connect your computer to the rest of the world via an ordinary phone line. Figure 1-7 shows you how.

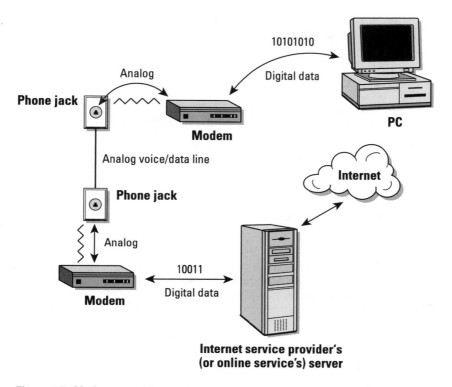

Figure 1-7: Modems provide your Internet connection
Most personal computers connect to the Internet through analog modems (short for
modulators/demodulators). Modems are devices that connect, through a process called
modulation, the 1s and 0s of computer data into audible analog signals that can be sent over
phone lines. On the other end of the connection is another modem that demodulates, or
converts, the analog signal back into a digital form that the computer can understand. These
messages are then passed along to another computer that, in turn, is connected to the
Internet.

A modem translates the 1 and 0s of digital information into audible sounds
(more like screeches, actually) that can be sent over a phone line, and then
translates the incoming screeches back into digital information. The process
is virtually identical to how a fax machine works and, in fact, most modems
can also send and receive faxes. The exception to this rule is that cable
modems, DSL (Digital Subscriber Line) modems, and other types of modem-
like devices that use digital connections don't support faxing directly, but
they do offer tremendously high-speed connections.

Cross-Reference

For more on various types of modems, see Chapter 5, "Sound Cards,
Speakers, and Modems."

Early computer modems were primarily used as output devices — to send computer files between one computer and another. With the phenomenal growth of the Internet, however, most modems today are used more like input devices; for example, they retrieve information from the World Wide Web and display it on your screen.

Connecting external devices

Ports are used to hook up various types of external computer peripherals, or extra components, that sit outside your computer, to your PC. These ports, or connectors, enable you to use these external devices as part of your computer system. The ports differ in the physical size and shape of the connectors, as well as the manner in which they communicate between the computer and the external devices.

Virtually all PCs include one serial port and one parallel port; most machines include Universal Serial Bus (USB) ports and a game port, and some include the new IEEE 1394 (also sometimes referred to as a FireWire or i.Link) port. The greater the variety and the larger the number of different connection options a computer has, the better equipped it is to grow with you as your needs increase (and believe me, they *will* increase).

Figure 1-8: Computer ports
The quantity and variety of ports on your PC directly determines the quantity and variety of extra components you can hook up to your system.

The *serial port* is typically used to connect external modems to your computer, but it can also be used to connect many other components. They include a mouse, a printer, a joystick for playing computer games, a drawing tablet for creating artwork, a MIDI (Musical Instrument Digital Interface) sound module for recording and playing back music, a little handheld computer or even another full-size (or notebook) for transferring files between computers, and more. *Parallel ports* are commonly used to connect printers, though they're also used for removable storage drives, to transfer files between computers, and more.

With the help of operating system software, particularly Windows 98, Windows 2000 and later versions of Windows 95, USB ports can be used to connect a wide variety of different peripherals to your PC: monitors, modems, scanners, video cameras, printers, and more. Dedicated gaming ports, or *Joystick ports* are typically used for connecting joysticks and other gaming peripherals to your machine. Finally, IEEE 1394 *ports*, a high-speed connection, can be used with digital camcorders, hard drives, video cameras, and more.

Reading the Specs

OK, now that you've got the basics down, you can look at real computer configurations and specifications, and start making sense of them. First, I'll cover overall system specs, and then I'll look at each of the components individually. Don't worry if you see a few numbers or terms in the system section that don't make sense; trust me, they'll all be explained in subsequent chapters.

**Cross-
Reference**

If you really feel lost, you can refer to definitions in the Glossary at the end of the book.

Keep in mind that computer system specs are often listed as a series of numbers and/or abbreviations, each of which refers to the individual capabilities of pieces that make up the system. (Remember, a computer is just many different specialized parts working in tandem.) I'll break down a hypothetical system configuration, which is a listing of the primary components in a computer, to explain exactly what I mean.

Imagine your Sunday paper includes a nice flyer from your local computer superstore that advertises a:

PIII 500 with 128MB/12GB/4xDVD/8MB VRAM/56K

Typically, this type of specs lists the type of processor first, then the amount of RAM, the size of the hard drive, the type and speed of removable drives, the amount (and sometimes type) of memory on the video card, and the speed of the modem.

So, this means in English that this computer has:

- A 500MHz Intel Pentium III processor
- 128 megabytes of RAM
- A 12 gigabyte hard drive
- A Digital Video Disk drive that runs at four times the standard speed (this is about as fast as a CD-ROM drive that runs at 32-40 times the normal speed)
- A video card with 8 megabytes of video RAM
- A modem that runs at 56 kilobits per second

The computer may also have other features or other plug-in cards installed (such as a sound card), but they won't necessarily be listed in the main system specifications. There is no real standard as far as specification listings, so sometimes the system specs included in an ad provide more details than the example I've given and sometimes they include less. Read the fine print to see what else the system offers, and make sure you find out which types of ports the system has.

The most prominent specification that companies list (and most people look for) is the speed of the processor. Generally speaking, the processor speed, as well as the processor type, tells you how fast the computer operates. In addition, the processor you choose typically has the biggest impact on the price of the system you buy. You may see support for MMX (MultiMedia eXtensions), 3DNow, or Streaming SIMD Extensions (SSE) listed along with the specification. All three marketing names are used to describe extensions to the capabilities of the main processor, and to most people, they aren't terribly important.

Cross-Reference

See Chapter 2, "Microprocessors and Memory" for more details on processor instructions.

Other critical specifications are the amount of memory, or RAM, that the computer has, and the size of the hard drive. More is always better in these areas. Frankly, the most important specification in relation to a computer's memory is how much the system can be upgraded.

The choice between a CD and a DVD-ROM drive is important because it determines the types of discs the system can use (DVD-ROM can read both CDs and DVDs, whereas CD-ROM can only read CDs). Quite honestly, though, the speed of the drive you purchase isn't that big of a deal.

Cross-Reference

See Chapter 3, "Hard Disks and Removable Drives," for more.

Similarly, although you probably will want to look for a video card with accelerated 3D graphics, the amount of memory above 8 megabytes is only important for computer games. You'll see some video cards listed with support for AGP (or Accelerated Graphics Port). This is a high-speed internal connection that can typically improve the video card's (and therefore your computer's) performance.

Cross-Reference

See Chapter 4, "Video Cards and Monitors," for more.

Lastly, most new computers come with a 56K analog modem that complies with the V.90 specification so there isn't much differentiation here. If you happen to live in an area where you have access to cable modems or DSL (Digital Subscriber Line) services — both of which provide high-speed access to the Internet — then you'll probably want to find a system that includes a modem that works with those types of connections.

Cross-Reference

See Chapter 5, "Sound Cards, Speakers and Modems" for more.

What to Buy

Knowing, in general, what a computer system offers is certainly worthwhile information but, for many people, it's not really enough. Most people want to know what's right for them. This, of course, depends.

Determining the type of computer system for you should really begin with a period of self-analysis where you probe your deepest soul and determine what it is you want to do with your life. Well, actually, just a quick list of what you think you'd like to do with the computer will suffice. (But it may not be as meaningful an experience . . .)

The important thing to remember when you scope out computer systems is not only what you plan to do right away, but also, which activities you might want to try down the road. For example, if you're a closet musician who's always dreamed of cutting your own CD, be sure to think about which capabilities the computer you buy today will need in the future, even if you don't plan on starting the project for six months or so. (What you need in this example, by the way, is a very high-quality sound card, probably a MIDI interface, a CD-Recordable drive, and a SCSI adapter card to attach the CD drive to because most, though not all, recordable CD drives are SCSI-based. If you don't understand half of what you just read, don't worry, it is covered in the next few chapters.)

Now, some people go to the extreme and buy a system equipped to do anything and everything under the sun when, in reality, they end up using very little of its capabilities. You can save hundreds of dollars if you make at least a semi-honest assessment of your aspirations and you will be able to keep up with the computer industry if you purchase a system that conforms to the PC 98 or PC 99 specifications.

PC 98 and PC 99

One easy way to determine if a system you're interested in is up-to-date is to see if it conforms to the PC 98 or PC 99 specifications. These are two guidelines created primarily by industry leaders Microsoft Corp. and Intel Corp. Check if the system comes with a Designed for Windows 98 and Windows NT 4.0 (or Windows 2000) logo. Systems (or peripherals) that conform to the spec and are tested by Microsoft's Windows Hardware Quality Lab are the only ones permitted to use those identifiers. If you look for a PC 98 or PC 99 logo, you won't find one (though you may come across ads or other marketing materials touting the fact that a particular product conforms to one or the other of the specs).

The PC 98 specification, a several hundred-page guideline for computer vendors to match suggested sets of technical requirements to their computer hardware, was actually finalized in 1997, but it is expected to be the standard for PCs released in most all of 1999. (If you want to, you can find it on the Internet at `http:// developer.intel.com/ design/pc98/ index.htm`) The document describing the specs goes into great detail, but it does enable companies to differentiate their computers from their competitors because it only offers recommendations in some areas. The PC 99 spec is similar, but is geared for systems introduced toward the end of 1999 and into 2000. (You can find it at `http://developer.intel. com/design/desguide.`)

The idea behind the PC spec, which was originally created in 1995 to coincide with the launch of Windows 95 and updated in 1997, was to offer a base level of performance and capabilities users and software vendors could depend on.

The PC 98 specification describes an overall Basic PC 98, and breaks it down into Consumer and Office systems, as well as an Entertainment PC 98, a Mobile PC, and a Workstation PC. It then details what type of capabilities each type of system should have.

Table 1-2 offers a summary of the recommendations for each type of system.

Table 1-2   PC 98 System Requirements

Computer Component	Consumer PC 98	Office PC 98	Entertainment PC 98	Mobile PC 98	Workstation PC 98
Processor	200MHz or faster Pentium-level performance; support for MMX recommended	200MHz or faster Pentium-level performance; support for MMX recommended	200MHz or faster Pentium-level performance; support for MMX recommended	166MHz Pentium with MMX	Pentium Pro or 266MHz Pentium II-level performance; support for MMX recommended
Memory	32MB	32MB	32MB	24MB; 32MB recommended	64MB
CD/DVD	8x or faster CD-ROM; DVD-ROM recommended	8x or faster CD-ROM	8x or faster CD-ROM; DVD-ROM recommended	Optional; 8x or faster CD-ROM recommended	8x or faster CD-ROM; DVD-ROM recommended
Video	2-D hardware acceleration, 3-D software acceleration required; 3-D hardware acceleration recommended; AGP recommended	2-D hardware acceleration required; 3-D software acceleration recommended; AGP recommended	AGP video card, 2-D hardware acceleration, 3-D hardware acceleration, TV tuner required; video capture recommended	2-D hardware acceleration; 3-D software acceleration recommended	2-D hardware acceleration, 3-D software acceleration required; 3-D hardware acceleration, AGP recommended
Audio	Optional; wavetable synthesis and digital audio output recommended	Optional; wavetable synthesis and digital audio output recommended	Wavetable synthesis, digital audio output, 3D sound	Optional; wavetable synthesis recommended	Optional; wavetable synthesis and digital audio output recommended
Network Card	Recommended	If no modem is present, required	Recommended	Recommended	If no modem is present, required

Continued

Table 1-2 PC 98 System Requirements *(continued)*

Computer Component	Consumer PC 98	Office PC 98	Entertainment PC 98	Mobile PC 98	Workstation PC 98
Modem	33.6 (V.34) analog modem	Optional; 33.6 (V.34) analog modem recommended	33.6 (V.34) analog modem	Optional; 33.6 (V.34) analog modem recommended	33.6 (V.34) analog modem recommended
Input Devices	USB-based keyboard and pointing device; game pad recommended	USB-based keyboard and pointing device	USB-based keyboard and pointing device; game pad recommended	1 USB port; IEEE 1394 port recommended	USB-based keyboard and pointing device

PC 99 has the same categories as PC 98 and a similar — though more advanced — set of requirements. Table 1-3 shows the basic specs.

Table 1-3 PC 99 System Requirements

Computer Component	Consumer PC 99	Office PC 99	Entertainment PC 99	Mobile PC 99	Workstation PC 99
Processor	300MHz Celeron A level performance; support for MMX recommended	300MHz Celeron A level performance; support for MMX recommended	300MHz Celeron A level performance; support for MMX recommended	233MHz Pentium-level performance	400MHz Pentium II-level performance
Memory	32MB; 64 recommended	64MB	64MB	32MB; 64 recommended	128MB

Computer Component	Consumer PC 99	Office PC 99	Entertainment PC 99	Mobile PC 99	Workstation PC 99
CD/DVD	8x or faster CD-ROM; 4x DVD-ROM recommended	8x or faster CD-ROM; 4x DVD-ROM recommended	2x DVD-ROM; 4x recommended	Optional; 8x or faster CD-ROM or 2x DVD-ROM recommended	8x or faster CD-ROM; 4x DVD-ROM recommended
Video	2-D hardware acceleration, 3-D hardware acceleration required; TV tuner and video capture recommended	2-D hardware acceleration required; 3-D hardware acceleration, TV tuner and video capture recommended	AGP video card, 2-D hardware acceleration, 3-D hardware acceleration, TV tuner required; video capture recommended	2-D hardware acceleration required; 3-D hardware acceleration recommended	2-D hardware acceleration, 3-D hardware acceleration required; TV tuner and video capture recommended
Audio	Optional; wavetable synthesis and digital audio output recommended	Optional; wavetable synthesis and digital audio output recommended	Wavetable synthesis, digital audio output and 3D sound	Optional; wavetable synthesis recommended	Optional; wavetable synthesis and digital audio output recommended
Network Card	Recommended	Required	Recommended	Recommended	Required
Modem	56K (V.90) analog modem	56K (V.90) analog modem	56K (V.90) analog modem	56K (V.90) analog modem	56K (V.90) analog modem
Input Devices	USB-based keyboard and pointing device; game pad; support for IEEE 1394 and Device Bay recommended	USB-based keyboard and pointing device; game pad recommended; support for IEEE 1394 and Device Bay recommended	USB-based keyboard and pointing device; game pad; support for IEEE 1394 and Device Bay recommended	1 USB port required; IEEE 1394 and Device Bay recommended	USB-based keyboard and pointing device; game pad recommended; support for IEEE 1394 and Device Bay recommended

Not all the requirements or recommendations in the PC 98 or PC 99 specifications are cutting edge, but they do define a reasonable level of overall system performance and capabilities. The specs also outline specific requirements for all of the major components within the PC, including video cards, sound cards, and more. I will describe some of the specific requirements for each type of computer component in Chapters 2-7.

Secret

PC 98 and PC 99 were specifically designed with Windows 98 and Windows 2000 in mind; a PC that meets either of the two standards should be able to take advantage of all the important features and functions included in those operating systems.

System cost

One of the first questions you have to answer — or at least consider — when you buy a computer system is how much are you willing to spend? More often than not, the amount of money you've budgeted for a PC purchase determines the type of system you are able to buy. Many excellent desktop computers are available for well under $1,000 these days, but if you want a really powerful system with a lot of built-in capabilities, you'll probably end up spending around $2,000 or more for a complete desktop system. You can spend less, or more, of course, but $2,000 has been a computer price threshold for many years.

When you budget, don't forget to include all the pieces you need for your computer system:

- The computer itself
- The monitor
- The keyboard
- The mouse or other pointing device
- The printer

While most systems come with a keyboard and mouse, many are priced without a monitor, and very few come bundled with a printer; make sure that you compare prices of similarly equipped systems.

Note

Some people think they can get by without a printer, or they don't give one much thought, but it's critical for doing anything useful with a computer, so don't leave it out.

Desktop versus notebook

Another important factor to consider when you decide which computer to purchase is the *form factor*, or shape, of the computer you'd like to buy. The most obvious choice is between traditional *desktop* computers and portable *notebook* computers, also called *laptops*. Until recently, only business people or folks who travel a lot and need to have a computer with them purchased notebook computers.

Recently, though, portable computers have become a viable and popular option for people who do little or no travelling. Notebooks are convenient and offer you the freedom to take it wherever you go. Many home users, for example, want to be able to easily move a computer from room-to-room. And many businesses provide their employees with notebooks so they can do work at home.

The increased popularity of notebooks can, in part, be attributed to the fact that they have become more powerful and lighter in weight. Again, until recently, notebook users typically had to compromise on features and capabilities that were available with desktop computers, but this is no longer true. The era where notebooks can match desktops in features and offer nearly equivalent performance has definitely arrived. In fact, these high-powered notebooks are even referred to as desktop replacements. And, as notebooks shrink to four- and five-pound packages, computing power becomes easier and easier to tote around.

However, this convenience does come at a price; specifically, it is the price. Like desktops, notebooks have come down in price significantly over the last few years, but you still pay a premium for the notebook packaging. The cost differential between equally configured desktops and notebooks is still fairly large, so if you want the convenience and flexibility of a notebook, be prepared to fork over some extra cash.

Secret

A rarely considered cost difference between desktops and notebooks is that peripherals and upgrades for notebooks are a lot more than their desktop counterparts. Depending on what you plan to do with your computer, this can be a significant amount of money.

Additionally, portable notebook computers are harder to upgrade than desktop machines, so keep this in mind if you plan to buy a computer that you want to upgrade in the future.

On a positive note, notebooks typically integrate everything you need, including the keyboard, monitor, and mouse (or equivalent pointing device), into a single package, and most notebooks now offer sets of ports similar to desktops; this means it's relatively easy to add external peripherals.

Table 1-4 summarizes some of the main pros and cons when considering a notebook computer vs. a desktop computer.

Table 1-4 Notebooks vs. Desktops: Pros and Cons		
	Pros	*Cons*
Notebook		
	Convenience	Expensive
	Mobility	Expensive Add-Ons
	Integration	Difficult to Upgrade
Desktop		
	Easy to Expand and Customize	Bulky
	Low Cost	Difficult to Move
	Low Cost Upgrades	

Of course, there are times none of this matters. Sometimes people just make a connection with a laptop and decide that it's the computer they have to own.

Notebook choices

If you do decide to purchase a notebook, you still have more decisions to make. In addition to comparing features and performance between various models (don't forget battery life; it's critical if you'll be on the machine a lot without a power source nearby), you still need to consider different types of laptops.

The computer industry enjoys making up different names to distinguish different size and different weight notebooks, but rather than play this game (no one seems to completely agree on the naming conventions anyway), I'll simply tell you that not all notebooks are the same. Recently, a new category of tiny, two-pound notebooks has appeared, as have some new ultra-slim models, which shave a half-an-inch or more off the standard height of most notebooks. If you're really concerned about size and portability, you'll want to give these machines a look.

Figure 1-9 illustrates some of the different notebook form factors.

Keep in mind, however, that the general rule of thumb with notebooks is the smaller the package, the more the machine costs. Although this may sound backwards, the reality is, you pay more for the extra miniaturization involved in making machines smaller and smaller.

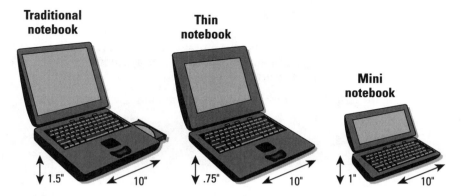

Figure 1-9: Notebook sizes
Notebook computers come in many shapes and sizes. The smaller-sized computers offer more portability than their larger counterparts, but many have cramped keyboards, or cost significantly more than other models.

Windows CE

Another issue to be aware of when buying a notebook is that some of the low-cost systems you may come across in computer stores, mail-order catalogs, or on-line shopping sites may not be "real" PC notebooks. What I mean is, many mini-notebook-like devices are powered by the Windows CE operating system which, while similar in basic look-and-feel to Windows 98 and Windows 2000, is very different.

Windows CE-based computers generally do not have a hard drive and cannot run standard Windows applications. Instead, most CE devices have cut down or "pocket" versions of popular Windows applications stored inside a ROM chip inside the device. You can do some of the same work on them as you can on a standard notebook (such as writing letters, sending and receiving e-mail, and browsing the web), but you can't install other Windows applications on them. You can only install Windows CE applications — which are significantly fewer in number.

A good way to think of the Windows CE devices is as companions or partners with a regular desktop or notebook PC. Thanks to the built-in synchronization features of Windows CE, you can typically share basic Microsoft Office files between a standard PC and the Windows CE devices. But, because most Windows CE devices lack any type of significant storage room, you can't use them as a replacement for a standard PC because you'll quickly run out of space to store your files.

Desktop choices

Not all desktop computers are created equally either. The traditional box-shaped computer that sits horizontally, underneath a monitor, used to be the primary desktop configuration, or form factor, but in recent years, the tower and mini-tower configurations have become more popular.

Figure 1-10 shows some popular desktop configurations.

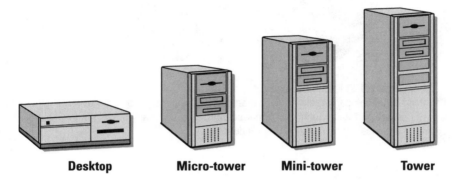

Desktop   Micro-tower   Mini-tower   Tower

Figure 1-10: Different desktops
The differences between most desktop computer configurations, such as the traditional under-the-monitor model, and different types of PC towers, are almost entirely cosmetic. A few towers offer more room for expansion, but the guts of most desktop computer form factors are very similar.

The only real difference between traditional desktops and most tower configurations is the shape and orientation of the box. Inside, it's all the same. (In fact, many people create their own towers by turning traditional desktops on their side.) The only exception to this rule is that some tower configurations offer more expansion slots than other machines, but this is becoming increasingly rare.

Another form for desktop computers is an all-in-one unit where the monitor is incorporated in to the computer itself. Apple's Macintosh computer first popularized this shape and Apple used the basic idea in many other subsequent models, including the popular iMac line. Several PC-compatible vendors have also offered all-in-one-style computers. The benefit of these devices is that they're easier to set up and move around than regular desktop computers. The downside is that you are locked into a fixed monitor size. If you decide later that you don't like how the built-in monitor looks or that you want a bigger screen, you're stuck. Also, many of these computers are very difficult to upgrade.

Operating system choices

When most people think of computers, they think of Windows, which is the operating system software created by Microsoft Corporation. In fact, many people refer to today's PC-compatibles as Wintel machines because they usually run a version of the Windows operating system on a processor from Intel Corp. (inventor of the x86 family of processors, which includes the Pentium III line).

An operating system, or OS, is a critical piece of software that takes charge of your computer as soon as it starts up and controls its overall operation once it's up and running. The operating system also determines which applications can be used on your computer.

The operating system is so critical, and such an integral part of the PC, that many people don't even realize it's independent of the computer hardware. Similarly, they aren't aware that, because it is separate, you can run operating systems other than Windows on your PC.

Although Microsoft would probably like us all to think otherwise, there are actually several viable options available for non-Windows operating systems. The most well known alternative is the Apple Macintosh and the MacOS. Current versions of the MacOS don't run on PC hardware, so using a non-Windows operation system is not an option for PC owners. However, it is an option for people who have not yet bought a computer, but are interested in creating computer graphics or other professional-quality creative work.

Well-known options for PC-compatible computer owners are IBM's OS/2, the BeOS and, particularly, a version of the UNIX operating system designed specifically for PCs called Linux. Linux is available in several different forms from several different vendors, including a company called Red Hat. Both OS/2 and Linux are full-featured, very capable operating systems (OSes) and some PC users prefer them (often vehemently) to Windows. The problem with OS/2 and Linux, however, is that they cannot run Windows 95, 98, NT, or 2000 applications. And while there are high-quality applications specifically available for these alternative OSes, there is nowhere near the number and variety as there is for Windows. With the number of the different flavors of Windows (3.1, 95, 98, NT, or 2000), most users can find an operating system that is a good fit. But, if you're looking for something different, it's good to know that other options are available. One of the attractive features of Linux, for example, is that it is basically free (although some companies charge for utilities that they bundle with it to make it easier to install or use).

Be aware, though, that it's very difficult to buy a new computer with one of these alternative OSes pre-installed on it; the different versions of Microsoft's Windows have a nearly complete lock on that market. If you want to use an alternative OS, you probably need to build your own system and install it yourself. Or you can buy a new machine and a copy of the OS you want, erase the PC's hard disk, and then install the new OS. The final option, which I recommend, is to use one of several utilities, such as PowerQuest's PartitionMagic or V Communications' System Commander Deluxe. They enable you to install and boot from one of several different operating systems every time you turn on your machine. This way you can keep a version of Windows installed on the machine, as well as one, or even several, alternatives.

For more on how to install and use multiple operating systems, see Chapter 9 "Adding, Upgrading, and Removing Software."

**Cross-
Reference**

Expandability

Regardless of whether you decide to purchase a desktop or a notebook, you want to bear in mind that you may be expanding or upgrading at a later date. As I discuss earlier, the number of available ports on either type of computer has a large impact on how easily you can expand its capabilities.

Expansion card upgrades

You should also look at the overall room for expansion, but don't just count the open expansion slots — that won't tell you the real story.

The only way to really find out how much internal expansion a desktop computer system permits is to find out how many available IRQs (Interrupt ReQuest Lines) it has. IRQs are mechanisms used by computers to communicate with their internal components. It's not at all uncommon — though it is very unfortunate — to find brand new computers that have only one or even no available IRQs despite the fact that there are several open expansion slots. In many instances, those slots are completely useless without available IRQs.

Secret

To find out more about IRQs, see Chapter 8, "How Your PC Works."

**Cross-
Reference**

Finding out whether or how many IRQs are actually available isn't easy. Most salespeople that you speak with won't know off the top of their heads, and many won't even know what you're talking about at all. But if you're concerned with expandability options, make sure you get an answer before you make a purchase. Otherwise, you might end up with a very unpleasant surprise somewhere down the road when you go to add a new peripheral to your PC, only to find out that you can't (at least, not without taking something else out).

As the computer industry moves away from internal card expansion and more towards usage of new external connections, such as the USB (Universal Serial Bus) port and USB-based peripherals as well as IEEE 1394 devices, some of these concerns regarding IRQs may go away. In the mean time, however, it's a very serious problem that very few people know about. Consider yourself forewarned.

To find out more about adding new internal (or external) peripherals to your PC, see Chapter 10, "Adding and Removing Hardware."

**Cross-
Reference**

Memory upgrades

Find out how much memory the system can support. Notebooks, in particular, generally have fairly low limits on maximum memory, but you'll often find desktops that are somewhat cramped by limited memory expansion. Again, this is one of those issues that won't necessarily affect you right away, but it can come back to bite you down the road when you want to upgrade your system.

Secret

Some notebooks only include one memory expansion connector. In some cases this means you have to take any already installed extra memory out when you try to add new memory. For example, if the notebook comes with 32MB of RAM, but 16MB are installed on the motherboard and the other 16MB are actually in the form of a memory card, when you try to upgrade that computer to 48MB (or any other amount), you may need to purchase a 32MB memory upgrade, instead of just a 16MB upgrade.

Another way to put it is, if you buy a 32MB memory upgrade for this machine, you'll only get 48MB of total memory instead of 64MB when you complete the upgrade because you'll have to take out the 16MB module that came with the notebook. Not all machines have this problem, some offer the capability to include two different memory upgrades in a single machine, but you need to find out first. You probably won't find this information in a product brochure or on a Web page; you may have to ask a knowledgeable salesperson to get the answer.

As a general rule, make sure the system can support up to four times its base memory. So, for example, if a computer comes with 64MB of RAM, you should be able to expand it to at least 256MB.

Cross-Reference

To find out more about upgrading memory, see Chapter 11, "Upgrading Your PC."

User Profiles

To give you a foundation for which type of computer system to look for, I've put together four generic profiles of different types of computer users and included recommendations on features and specifications. I have not included detailed descriptions of the various specifications here, but they're covered in the next six chapters. So, if you want more details at this time, you may refer to those chapters.

If you see yourself reflected in one of these profiles, feel free to consider my recommendations as a starting point for your search. Remember too, in the case of computers, more is better; if the specs for something you're interested in are better (or larger) than what's listed below, that's fine.

Home office/basic productivity

Many people want the basic, general-purpose home computer. If you'll be doing any word processing or spreadsheet work at home, or plan to do typical personal projects, such as track your finances, file your taxes electronically, publish a church or school newsletter, run educational software for your children, and more, this is the type of machine to get.

I recommend you look at a system with some of the following specifications:

- Mid-range Pentium II processor (350-400MHz for 1999, and faster in consecutive years)
- 64MB of RAM
- 8GB or larger hard drive
- 2x DVD-ROM drive
- 100MB removable storage drive
- 3-D accelerated video card with 8MB of SGRAM
- 16-bit wavetable sound card
- 56K V.90 modem
- 17" monitor
- 600 dpi or greater, 4-color inkjet printer

Creative work

If you plan to do creative work on a computer, such as sophisticated print or web publishing, recording your own music, or editing video, you need a more powerful, better-equipped computer.

I'd start with:

- High-end Pentium III processor (500-600MHz in 1999, and faster in consecutive years)
- 64-128MB of RAM
- 10-20GB hard drive
- 4x DVD-ROM drive
- 1GB or larger removable storage drive, or rewritable CD or DVD drive
- 3-D accelerated video card with 12MB of SGRAM
- 16-bit wavetable sound card with digital audio input/output jacks and MIDI interface (for music)
- 56K V.90 modem
- Video capture card
- 19" monitor
- 1,200 dpi optical, 30-bit color scanner
- Graphics tablet
- 600 dpi or greater, 4-color inkjet printer

Games and entertainment

Computer games are some of the most demanding applications you can run, so dedicated computer gamers need very powerful machines with a lot of storage space. They also need high-quality sound systems and dedicated input devices, such as a force feedback joystick, to truly immerse themselves in the experience.

Here's a starting point:

- High-end Pentium III processor (500-600MHz in 1999, and faster in consecutive years)
- 128MB of RAM
- 10-20GB hard drive
- 4x or greater DVD-ROM drive
- 100MB removable storage drive
- 3-D AGP video card with 16MB of SGRAM
- 16-bit wavetable sound card with large speakers and sub-woofer
- 56K V.90 modem or cable modem
- Force feedback joystick
- 17" monitor
- 600 dpi or greater, 4-color inkjet printer

Web browsing/e-mail

If you're primarily interested in getting a computer to have access to the Internet and e-mail, a simple, low-cost system will be fine. (A low-cost system like the one I've outlined below is also a great choice as a second computer for the kids.)

I'd look at systems that include:

- Intel Celeron, AMD K6, or Cyrix MII processor (virtually any speed will do)
- 32-64MB of RAM
- 2-4GB hard drive
- 24x or faster CD-ROM drive
- 3-D accelerated video card with 4MB of SGRAM
- 16-bit wavetable sound card
- 56K V.90 modem or cable modem
- 15" monitor
- 600 dpi or greater, 4-color inkjet printer

Non-computer product for Internet access, such as a Web phone or a Web TV device, are also options.

What about WebTV?

With the phenomenal growth of the Internet and the enormous popularity of e-mail, many people are starting to view computers as communication and information appliances. In some instances, people want their computers to do only a few specific functions such as browse the Web and send/receive e-mail. In this case, the computer acts as a simple appliance instead of being a multi-purpose machine.

Not surprisingly, the computer industry is responding to these demands by building some lower-cost devices that are designed specifically, and solely, for these purposes. For example, there are many iterations of television set-top boxes that enable you to surf the Web with your TV, and there are screen-based telephones with simple Web browsing and e-mail features.

Nevertheless, the best choice for people who want to just simply browse the Web and send and receive e-mail is a low-cost, general-purpose PC. This is because the Internet is changing so rapidly that you constantly need updated software, such as browser plug-ins, to be able to view and fully enjoy different Web sites. The easiest type of machine to add software to is a PC. Upgrading software built into dedicated devices, such as a set-top TV Web box, is often difficult and sometimes, even impossible.

Also, despite many technological improvements, it's still hard to look at Web sites on normal TVs. Most Web sites were designed on, designed for and look best on real computer monitors.

When to Buy

One of the great (or frustrating, depending on when you bought your computer) things about computer technology, is that with the never-ending march of technological progress, the same $1,000 to $3,000 investment you made last year buys a better and better computer each passing year.

Some people react to this situation by buying new computers on a regular basis and replacing their older machine(s) with a newer one(s) — sometimes as often as once a year or less. Most of us, however, can't afford the luxury of upgrading to a new computer every year, and even if we could, the hassles involved with moving over all our files and applications are enough to discourage the practice, or greatly reduce its frequency.

So, given that you may only purchase a new computer every few years, you want to consider the timing of the purchase. The reason for this is that computer technology is constantly evolving, so you want to try and make your purchase at a point on that evolutionary cycle that makes sense.

Now many would argue that you shouldn't really worry about the timing of a computer purchase — just get one when the need arises. The reasoning behind this philosophy is that no matter when you buy something, another model that's better, faster and cheaper than what you bought is right around the corner, so you might as well just dive in now. Sadly (or happily — again, it all depends on your perspective), this is all too common when it comes to computers and their peripherals.

Moore's Law

Computer technology and the computer industry change so rapidly that there are very few "rules" or guidelines that have any relevance even a year after their proclamation. One startling exception, however, is Moore's Law, which has proven to be remarkably accurate and prescient since it was first uttered over twenty years ago by Gordon Moore, one of the founders of microprocessor giant, Intel Corp.

According to Moore's Law:

Computer processing power will double every eighteen months.

It's simple, easy-to-remember, and surprisingly useful. What's particularly interesting is that Moore's Law holds true not only for processors,

but all aspects of computer technology because hard drives, video cards, memory, and more have a large impact on a computer's overall performance. And true to his prediction, these developments have kept pace along with processors to maintain the doubling in performance every year-and-a-half.

The question of how long Moore's Law can continue to be an accurate forecaster for the future is often raised, and there have certainly been times when it didn't look like the computer industry could live up to it. But somehow, some way, a development has occurred to keep the industry on track. So, at least for the foreseeable future, Moore's Law is safe. Keep this in mind when you plan a PC purchase.

As a result of these constant upgrades, many people fall into the trap of continuously waiting for the next big thing and they end up never getting anything. They waste time and lose potential productivity by waiting, instead of just purchasing something immediately and getting to work. If you need to do something now and you either don't have a computer yet, or your current system isn't capable of doing what you need to, then you should take the plunge and not worry about what's coming next.

Planning and research

Still, there are times when it is better to hold off on a computer purchase, at least for a brief period of time. For example, many people who bought (or received) new computers around Christmas 1996 were very disappointed when Intel introduced their first MMX-enhanced processors — a technology that was widely touted as a critical development in their product line — in early 1997, less than two weeks after Christmas. This was a particularly clear demonstration of the benefit to waiting for certain key developments.

Secret

Computer technology may be constantly evolving, but the evolution isn't continuous. It occurs in fits and starts. Important innovations, such as the introduction of new processors, or faster, cheaper versions of existing processors, occur on specific dates. The trick is to try and time your purchase around one of these introductions.

Your challenge (should you choose to accept it) is to find out when these type of major introductions are scheduled to occur — a task that really isn't as hard as it may first sound. Your best resources are computer magazines, preferably the World Wide Web versions of them, since they're always more up-to-date. Traditional computer magazines, such as *PC World* (www.pcworld.com) and *PC Magazine* (www.pcmag.com), are a good starting point, but sometimes you'll find better, more far-reaching information on trends and technology announcements in computer industry magazines, such as *InfoWorld* (www.infoworld.com) and *PC Week* (www.pcweek.com).

Once you have the date of an introduction that's important to you (not all of them will be, after all), you need to decide if it occurs within a time frame that's acceptable to you. In general, I don't recommend waiting more than a month or two or you'll start to drive yourself crazy. Once this decision is made, I recommend that you plan a purchase around the time of the intro, both to reduce your wait and to maximize the amount of time you can enjoy using the latest developments.

If you aren't able to find the specific launch dates of new processors by searching around the Web, you can also sometimes tell by looking at PC system prices. If you see some fairly dramatic price drops from several different PC manufacturers, this may be a good sign that something new is coming.

Secret

By the way, the buying process shouldn't end when you walk out of the store. Many computer retailers and other types of stores have 30-day price guarantees. So, make sure you watch the prices for the month after your purchase. Because computer price cuts are so frequent, there's a good chance you can get some money back. (Or buy something else for your system with the difference.)

System type

In addition to figuring out the right time to buy a system, you should sit down and try to figure out, in general, what category of computer system you'd like to purchase. Many people believe that you should always buy the current top-of-the-line, arguing (usually correctly) that it will last longer and won't become obsolete as quickly as less expensive, less powerful computers do.

The only problem with this reasoning is that you typically pay quite a premium to own a top-of-the-line system. A better bet, for most people, is to go just one notch down the performance and/or feature scale. This is sometimes referred to as the *sweet spot*. For example, if the latest processor runs at 600MHz and the second fastest runs at 500MHz, you'll probably get a much better deal going with the 500MHz model — not only in absolute price, but also in performance and feature value for your dollar.

Where to Buy

Once you decide on the type of computer you want, as well as when to buy it, where you choose to spend your money might seem like a trivial afterthought. However, if you're a smart shopper, you want to spend a fair amount of time considering your options. Buying a computer is no longer a process of driving down to your local computer store and plopping down your credit card. There is a wealth of possible places to make a PC purchase.

Consider some of these choices:

- Local computer store
- Computer superstore
- Department store
- Consumer electronics store
- Mail-order catalog
- Direct from the manufacturer
- Company Web site
- Retail store Web site
- Online auction

Retail versus direct

Most of these options boil down to dealing with a retail store, or ordering a computer direct, either via a paper catalog or an electronic catalog found on the Web. The question of going retail vs. mail order/electronic has been a long-standing issue in the computer industry and many strong opinions have been expressed over the years. To be fair, there are good arguments to be made on both sides of the issue.

On the one hand, buying locally from a store often makes it easier to get service and support for your computer because you can quickly go back to the source. Also, many people feel strongly about supporting their local economy.

On the other hand, buying mail order usually gives you a better price and, if you buy out of state, can even save you a bundle on state sales tax. The reason being, if you purchase a product from an out-of-state vendor and have the product shipped to you, you often don't have to pay sales tax. On a $2,000 computer, this can amount to $160 or more.

Secret

If you purchase a system via the Web, you can sometimes save even more money. To encourage customers to overcome the fear of sending their credit card number over the Internet, some companies offer a several percentage point discount just for ordering electronically.

Electronic commerce is generally much cheaper per sale than traditional phone operator ordering, so these companies may pass some of their savings onto you.

Also, many of the larger mail-order operations actually offer better support and faster turnaround times on service and repair calls than local retail operations. So, don't presume that just because a retail store is nearby, you'll be better off in the service and repair departments.

Finally, most retail stores only offer a very limited number of predefined configurations. If you want to build a custom computer system with a specific amount of memory, size of hard disk, type of video and sound card, and more, then you'll be much happier going directly to the manufacturer where you can, typically, create a system to your liking. Another option is to go with smaller retail stores, many of which specialize in building their own systems.

Table 1-5 summarizes some of the pros and cons of buying retail vs. buying direct.

Table 1-5   Buying Retail vs. Buying Direct: Pros and Cons

	Pros	*Cons*
Retail	See and touch equipment before buying	Prices are higher
	Easy to return for service or repair	Tech support hours may be limited
	Can develop personal relationship with technicians for support questions. Helps local economy	Predefined configurations only available in certain stores
		Uninformed sales people
Direct	Lower prices	Buying blind
	No sales tax (often)	Returns for service or repair more difficult
	Customized configurations	Takes money away from local economy
	24 hour x 7 day Tech Support (usually)	

Service

Virtually all computer purchasers, whether they're beginners or advanced users, at some point call upon the technical support services for the computer system they've bought. Consequently, it's very important to find out whatever you can about the quality of that service.

Of course, first of all, you need to find out who is actually providing the support. Sometimes the answer to this question isn't as obvious as it first appears. In some instances it's the computer maker; in others, it's the store from which you purchased the machine; and it can also be a third company contracted by the store or the computer vendor to provide the service.

To get a rough idea of the quality of technical support before you buy a system, try calling the tech support number with a question you already know the answer to. See if they get it right and how they treat you.

The sad truth of the matter is that tech support quality can vary tremendously, even within the same company, so this isn't always the most accurate test, but it's certainly better than nothing.

Refurbished PCs

Whether you ultimately decide to buy retail or direct, you'll undoubtedly be looking for the best deal you can get. If so, I've got a word of advice for you: think "refurbished."

Secret

The best way to get the most bang for your computer buck as possible is to buy a refurbished computer.

Refurbished computers, which you can find both at retail stores and direct from computer manufacturers, are typically machines that were purchased by a customer and then returned within the 30-90 day money-back guarantee period. In some instances they were unboxed and setup, while in others they may not have been opened at all. In every case, the computers are rechecked at the factory, reboxed and generally returned to "like-new" condition.

Regardless, because they were returned, most companies sell refurbished machines at a fairly substantial discount (often several hundred dollars) versus similarly configured new systems. As long as you can get past the stigma of buying what is, technically speaking, a "used" computer, you can get a great deal. Most, though not all, companies even provide a warranty for refurbished computers that is equal in length to ones that come with a brand new product, so you usually have nothing to lose. Occasionally you hear stories of computer companies trying to resell some of their "lemons" as refurbished machines, but I believe this is more of the exception than the rule.

The only catch to buying refurbished is that there is a fairly limited supply of computers. After all, companies can only refurbish merchandise that is returned. If you can find a refurbished system that meets your requirements (and has a long enough warranty), I say go for it. You'll be glad you did.

Summary

In this chapter, I explained some of the basic terminology of computers and provided advice on which type of PC to buy, when to buy it, and where to buy it.

▶ Computers are essentially fancy calculators that enable you to use and manipulate things we're all familiar with — such as letters, numbers, pictures and sounds — by converting it all into the digital language of 1s and 0s.

▶ The basic components in any computer system are the processor, memory (RAM), and storage (hard disk). Other important pieces include the video card, sound card, modem, and various types of removable drives, such as floppies, CD/DVD-ROM, and Zip drives.

▶ One of the first decisions you have to make when buying a PC is whether you want a notebook or desktop. Then you should figure out what kind of notebook or what kind of desktop you want to purchase.

▶ To make sure your system is current, you may want to compare it to the PC98 or PC99 specifications, which are valid for the years 1999 and 2000 respectively.

▶ In addition to getting the right mix of included features, another important thing to look for when buying a computer system is expandability.

▶ Different types of applications place different demands on a PC so you should base your buying decision on which computer is best suited for the things you want to do.

▶ You can buy computers from many different places, but the choice may boil down to buying retail vs. buying direct. Each option has benefits and drawbacks.

Chapter 2

Microprocessors and Memory

In This Chapter

▶ You will learn what a processor is and how it works.

▶ You will learn the importance of cache to computer performance.

▶ You will learn the differences among processors.

▶ You will learn how different types of memory work.

▶ You will receive recommendations on processors and memory.

Most people think of computers as single, monolithic entities, but the reality is, they're actually made up of many different components doing many different things. In this chapter, and the remaining five chapters in Part I, I dive into the details of the different components used in today's computer systems. My goal is to provide you with all the answers you need to make intelligent PC purchasing and upgrade decisions, as well to give you some background on how the various pieces work—both by themselves, and in conjunction with other components.

In each chapter, I focus on the main features of each of the different components, and explain what they are, what they do, and why they're important. As a result, by the end of Part I, you should be able to completely decipher just about any computer-related ad or spec sheet that you come across. And more importantly, you should be able to figure out which features or specifications are important and which ones aren't. The first components I cover, the microprocessor and memory, form the central core of any computer's operation. The processor, of course, is the most important part of any computer. It is the workhorse that drives a PC's operation. But memory also plays an important role, because memory provides a processor with the raw materials and the working area it needs to perform its computational magic. In fact, working together, these two pieces enable a computer to "compute."

Practically speaking, the speed at which the processor and memory do their work has the most dramatic impact on how fast a computer operates. In addition, the type of processor you have can affect the type of software your computer is capable of running. So, knowing about different processors and types of memory, as well as how they interact, gives you an excellent idea of how powerful a particular computer system really is.

The Processor

The heart and/or brain of the computer — depending on your perspective — is the *central processing unit* (CPU), also known as the microprocessor or simply processor for short. The processor performs the major number crunching that drives any computer's operation. Processors play such an important role that computers are often defined and described based solely on the type of processor they have; for example, "I've got a Pentium III computer" or "I've got a K7."

Processors used to be a single chip that connected to different-sized sockets on your computer's motherboard, which is the main circuit board inside your computer. In fact, some still are, but many newer processors come on a separate circuit board — sometimes called a daughterboard (because of its relationship to the motherboard) — that plugs into a special processor slot on the motherboard.

Cross-Reference

See the section on physical connections later in this chapter for more.

The most important features to look for in a new processor are:

- The type of processor it is (for example, Pentium III vs. K7)
- The speed at which it operates
- The amount and type of L2 cache (a special type of high-speed memory) it includes
- Any additional processor instructions it supports
- The type of physical connector it uses

How it works

Processors work by performing calculations based on specific instructions that software running on the computer provides. These instructions, which are loaded into the processor when an application runs, tell the processor how to manipulate chunks of data stored in the computer's memory (RAM). This, in turn, produces the desired result, whether it is adding boldface to text in a letter, changing the color of a background in a scanned digital photo, or what have you. In other words, processors are constantly churning through instructions and data that are loaded into it from the computer's memory.

In addition to working with the main memory, processors also work with a special type of high-speed memory referred to as *cache* (pronounced cash). In fact, most of the time processors work directly with various types of cache memory and this cache memory, in turn, works with the main memory. Essentially, the cache memory acts as a high-speed buffer in between the processor and main memory, shuffling data into the processor as it needs it, or requests it. As a result, the processor takes advantage of the high-speed cache memory and therefore works faster, which, in turn, makes the computer that the processor drives, operate faster. Figure 2-1 illustrates the concept.

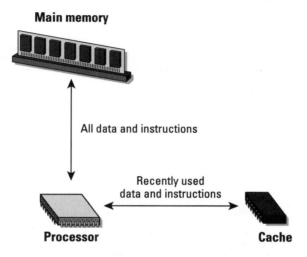

Main memory

All data and instructions

Recently used
data and instructions

Processor   **Cache**

Figure 2-1: Cache helps make processors more efficient
Cache is a special form of high-speed memory that stores instructions and data the processor has recently used. Thanks to its proximity to the main computing engine inside the processor, and the fact that the processor often needs to reuse those instructions and data, cache keeps the processor busy and speeds up a computer's performance.

Processor types

Microprocessors come in different types and different speeds. The most popular processors are Intel's Pentium family, which includes the standard Pentium, the Pentium with MMX Technology, the Pentium Pro, the Celeron, the Pentium II, the Pentium II Xeon, and the Pentium III. (MMX, which is sometimes referred to as MultiMedia Extensions, but according to Intel doesn't really mean anything, is a set of additional processing instructions chips that support MMX can perform.) Other processors you may hear about are the AMD K5, K6, K6-2, K6-3, and K7; the Cyrix 5x86, 6x86, 6x86MX, MediaGX, MII, and MXi; Centaur/IDT's WinChip, WinChip 2, and WinChip 3; the Rise Technology MP6; the Motorola/IBM PowerPC; and the Digital Alpha.

Table 2-1 is a list of some of the more common processors.

Table 2-1 Common Microprocessors	
Manufacturer	*Models*
Intel	Pentium
	Pentium with MMX Technology
	Pentium Pro
	Celeron (and Celeron A)
	Pentium II
	Pentium II Xeon
	Pentium III
AMD	K5
	K6
	K6-2
	K6-3
	K7
Cyrix (A division of National Semiconductor)	5x86
	6x86
	6x86MX
	MediaGX
	MII
	MXi
Centaur/IDT	WinChip
	WinChip 2
	WinChip 3
Rise Technology	MP6
IBM/Motorola	PowerPC 603 and 603e
	PowerPC 604 and 604e
	PowerPC 750 (aka G3)
	G4
Digital/Compaq	Alpha

Speed

Many people think processors differ only in speed. They figure a 500 MHz processor from Company A is bound to be faster than a 400 MHz version from Company B, for example. But this is not always the case.

Secret

While a processor's rated speed is a critical factor in determining how fast it performs calculations (and hence, how fast the computer housing the processor runs), there are other important differences in how various processors work their magic internally. These differences impact how fast various microprocessors perform real-world tasks, such as checking a document for spelling mistakes, recalculating the numbers in a spreadsheet, or removing imperfections from a digital photograph.

For example, many processors can perform several calculations at once; the technology that supports this technique is called *pipelining*. In addition, some jump ahead to perform extra calculations they think the running program will ask for, before the program actually does. This is called *speculative execution*, and it is another one of several very complex operations occurring inside today's processors. In addition, different processors implement these techniques, along with other technology, in different ways, which accounts for many of the differences in overall chip performance, independent of the chip's rated speed (in MHz).

For example, future versions of the Pentium III (or perhaps IV) family of processors, which have the codenames Foster and Williamette (using product codenames is a common high-tech industry practice) are expected to include new internal refinements to make the chips faster than today's Pentium IIIs.

Another critical factor in overall chip performance is how efficient various processor designs are. Processors are capable of performing continuously, and cranking out results as quickly as they are given problems to work on. Ideally, therefore, you want to feed the processor a steady stream of data so it can keep crunching away at maximum speed. The reality, however, is that — for a number of different reasons — data is not fed into the CPU on a steady, consistent basis. In fact, most processing occurs in fits and starts. This, in turn, slows a computer down.

Figure 2-2 shows the principle in action.

One of the many ways processor designers attempt to compensate for this is by using the technologies, such as speculative execution, that I mention above. Another even more important way is by adding a special high-speed cache memory into the processor's or computer's overall design. In both cases, the goal is to make the processor work as much as possible because this translates directly into faster computer performance.

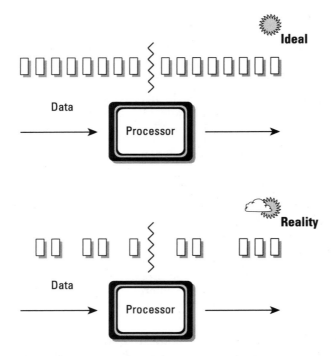

Figure 2-2: Feeding the CPU

In an ideal environment, a computer's processor runs at its maximum rate because it is fed a steady stream of data. In reality, however, various delays that occur throughout a computer system often force a processor to sit idle for brief periods of time, waiting for the next chunk of data to arrive.

L1 and L2 cache

Cache memory, in its various forms, plays a particularly important role in a processor's performance. Cache can dramatically improve a processor's efficiency by offering it access to the data it needs more quickly than regular memory would. Not only are cache memory chips (typically Static Random Access Memory, or SRAM) faster than regular memory chips, but they also have a faster connection to the processor, as I explain in just a bit.

The way cache works

Because of the way most software works, processors tend to spend a lot of their time either performing the same operations over and over or performing several different operations on the same set of data. Well, one day, somebody realized that if a processor could access used instructions and data more quickly, it could run much more efficiently. So, a clever designer came up with the idea to create a special "work area" right alongside the processor, called a cache, that temporarily stores the data and instructions the processor used most recently.

The idea was (and is) that once the processor finishes what it is working on, it can "fetch" what it needs next from this nearby area instead of getting it from regular memory, which is further away and takes longer to get to.

Processors aren't the only computer-related component to use a cache. Many software programs, such as Web browsers, also use a cache. While a processor's cache and a browser's cache are not the same thing, they are conceptually similar. For both components, a cache speeds up access to recently used information.

Web browsers, for example, set up memory and/or disk caches (which use RAM or space on the hard disk, respectively) to store recently used files. The thinking is that you probably will want to use the files you've accessed recently again. If they're stored either in RAM, or on disk, the browser will be able to get to them much more quickly than if it had to go out to the Internet again. For example, when you hit the Back button on your browser, the Web page loads almost instantly because the files the browser needs are nearby. If there wasn't a cache (or if you empty or clear the files in the cache), going back to the previous page would take just as long as when you called it up in the first place. This is similar to what happens with processors and their specialized cache; if the information the processor needs is close by in the cache, the processor operates quickly without waiting, but if the information isn't close by, the processor has it to request it from main memory. (The main memory isn't as slow as the Internet, of course, but it is a lot slower than getting it from the cache.)

The process of going out to main memory to get more data and instructions also forces the cache to become "flushed," or emptied out. During the process of running programs, the processor regularly flushes the cache. This is important to know because it explains why it's possible to have too much of a good thing; that is, too much cache. Beyond a certain amount, extra cache doesn't help the computer's performance very much because the cache's contents are often flushed before it's full. So, if you have too much cache, a certain portion will consistently go to waste. And a cache is a terrible thing to waste . . .

When the processor finds what it needs in the nearby cache, it's called a *cache hit* and if it doesn't, well, it's a *cache miss*. Some utility programs, such as Symantec's popular Norton Utilities, can track the percentage of cache hits and misses that your processor has while it's running various applications. If you really want to impress your technical friends, you might want to start talking about your computer's cache hit percentages while running certain applications. Then again, maybe you shouldn't . . .

The two most common types of cache are referred to as L1, or Level 1, and L2, or Level 2 cache. (It is possible to have Level 3 caches, but they are not very common.) Although technically speaking caches are a type of memory, in most cases the L1 and L2 cache are actually built into the processor chip or processor card itself. Thus, they're really more a feature of the processor than of memory.

Each level of cache is a separate chunk of memory and is treated independently by the processor. The two levels refer to how close the cache is physically located to the main number-crunching section of the processor. Figure 2-3 shows how the different caches work together with main memory.

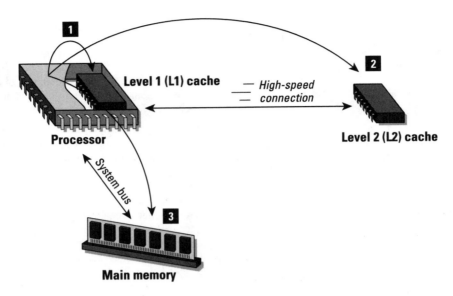

Figure 2-3: Multiple caches
They way a processor works with a system that has multiple caches is that the processor checks the L1 cache first, then the L2 cache, and then, finally, the main memory.

Traditionally, L1 cache, which is usually the smaller of the two, has been located on the processor itself and L2 cache has been located outside, but near the processor. (The physical location on a computer's motherboard does make a difference because when you shuttle data back and forth to different places, the further away something is, the longer it takes to get there and back. And when it comes to computer processing, nanoseconds — billionths of a second — really do count.)

Recent processor designs have begun to integrate L2 cache onto the processor card or into the CPU chip itself, much like L1 cache. This speeds up access to the larger L2 cache which, in turn, speeds up the computer's performance. Figure 2-4 demonstrates the differences.

Another traditional difference between L1 and L2 caches has been the speed at which the processor can access the different types of memory. Because L1 cache is integrated into the core of the microprocessor, it typically runs at the same speed as the CPU; so on a 500MHz processor, the connection speed to L1 cache is usually 500MHz. On older systems, the L2 cache often connected to the processor at the same speed as main memory. This speed is determined by a connecting route, called the computer's *system bus*, and typically runs at 66, 100, or 133MHz (although faster speeds are possible).

Cross-Reference

For more on system buses, see the "Logical connections" section later in this chapter.

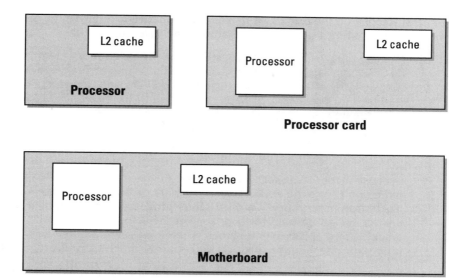

Figure 2-4: Cache locations
The L2 cache is located in different places on different processors. Some processors have the L2 cache integrated into the main chip itself, others have L2 cache on the circuit board that holds the processor, and still others work with L2 cache that's separate from the processor on the computer's motherboard.

On newer systems, however, where the L2 cache is located on a daughtercard, such as most Pentium II and Pentium IIIs, or in the processor itself, as with the Celeron A, K6-3, and some mobile Pentium IIs (sometimes called Pentium II PEs, for performance enhanced) and Pentium IIIs (those designed for notebooks), communication between the processor and the L2 cache occurs much more rapidly. On the Pentium II and III, for example, the processor-to-L2 cache connection is often via a *backside bus*; it runs faster than the system bus, but at half the speed of the processor. (This is sometimes referred to as a 1:2 ratio.) Again, with a 500MHz Pentium III processor, the processor-to-L2 cache connection speed is 250MHz. Additionally, systems that incorporate L2 cache on the chip itself feature a 1:1 ratio between the speed of the processor and the speed of the processor-to-L2 cache connection. So with a 500MHz processor, the connection to the L2 cache also runs at 500MHz.

The faster your processor is, the more important it is to have a reasonable amount of L2 cache. In fact, without the proper amount of L2 cache, a processor often sits idle, "wasting cycles" as they say, which means your computer is not running as fast it can.

This lack of L2 cache explains why some of the early Celeron-based computers had relatively poor performance. The original Celeron essentially wasted a great deal of its processing power. The upgraded Celeron A chip and all current Celerons (including the mobile versions), however, incorporate some

L2 cache on the processor itself, and dramatically improve the performance of computers using the "A" version of the Celeron.

You can tell whether or not a system uses the Celeron or Celeron A because all Celerons faster than 300MHz are Celeron As and all processors slower than 300MHz are original Celerons. (The only exception is that all Celerons designed for notebooks have the integrated L2 cache, regardless of speed.) Unfortunately, desktop PC-oriented 300MHz chips were available in both Celeron and Celeron A formats, so the only way to tell 300MHz Celerons apart is to look at the computer's documentation (or use a diagnostic program that lists the processor's type and speed).

Because most processors incorporate L2 cache into their basic design, you often don't have the option to choose more or less cache in the system you'd like to purchase or put together. (Older processors with standalone L2 cache are the one exception.) Instead, you get the amount of L2 cache a particular model of microprocessor includes. Therefore, when you decide which type of processor to get, make sure you find out how much L2 cache it includes.

Remember, though, you can have too much of a good thing — in other words, it's possible to have too much cache (believe it or not . . .). Depending on the type of applications you plan to use, you can reach a point of diminishing return, and additional cache won't improve your performance very much. Also, cache memory tends to be very expensive, so you need to balance the price vs. performance.

Computers that operate as *servers*, machines that sit at the center point of computer networks, typically need more cache than normal desktop machines because of the type of work they do. Due to this fact, several versions of the Pentium II and Pentium III Xeon, which is designed for servers, include 2MB (or more) of expensive L2 cache, as opposed to most desktop-oriented Pentium IIs and IIIs, which include only 512KB.

Architecture

In addition to their rated MegaHertz (MHz) speed, and the amount and type of cache, processors can be categorized by their internal structure, or *architecture*; it basically determines the language software programs must use to work with them. The vast majority of IBM-compatible PCs use what are called x86 processors because they are derived from Intel's 8086 processor — the same processor found in some of the earliest IBM PCs. The very first IBM PC, however, used Intel's 8088 processor, a predecessor to the 8086.

The 8086 and 8088 are often confused because the later chip used a lower number as its product name. The reason for this is that the 8088 was an 8-bit processor, while the 8086 is a 16-bit processor (a distinction I explain below), and hence the difference in the last digit.

The x86 family of processors share a common set of instructions that software programs use to run on the chip. These instructions are the basic "language" of the processor and determine what types of calculations the processor is capable of doing.

Faking it with software

When is an x86-compatible processor not really an x86-compatible processor? When it's a Motorola processor (or one of several other types) pretending to be an x86-compatible via trickery, commonly called software emulation. Software emulation basically fools an application into thinking it's running on the type of chip that the application was originally written, even though it really isn't. The processor does this by translating one set of instructions to another.

So, for example, Insignia Solution's SoftWindows 98 or Connectix Corp.'s Virtual PC, which are programs for the Apple Macintosh, enable Mac users to run Windows programs on the Motorola processor inside the Macintosh, even though those Windows programs were written for Intel processors. Basically, the instructions the Windows program (and even Windows itself) calls for are translated into a form that the Motorola processor understands through the software emulation program. Then the Motorola processor performs the necessary calculations, and finally, the software emulator takes those results and feeds them back to the Windows application. As far as the application is concerned, it's running under Windows on an Intel processor, as normal. Performing these translations back and forth takes time and processing power, however, and software emulators are much slower than running the same programs on PC hardware.

Other processors use different instructions. This is why programs written for the Macintosh, for example, won't work on PC-compatible machines; Mac programs use instructions that are specific to the PowerPC family of processors. If you try to run a Mac program on a computer with an x86 chip, the x86 will think you are speaking to it in a foreign language. (Not to confuse matters, but it is possible to run applications written for one type of chip architecture on another via a technology called *software emulation*.)

Each generation of x86 chips has added to the original set of core instructions that previous generations could understand, thereby expanding the capabilities of the processor. This explains why some newer applications, written to work with the latest generation of processors, won't run on older computers, even though they use the same type of chip. In other words, some applications require a Pentium or Pentium-class processor to work and won't run, for example, on a 486.

MMX, 3DNow, and Streaming SIMD Extensions

One of the most well-known extensions to these core instructions is MMX technology, which chip leader Intel introduced several years ago as the Pentium with MMX Technology (the "official" name for the Pentium MMX processor). MMX consists of 57 new instructions that processors that support the technology understand and execute. The new instructions were primarily designed to improve the performance of multimedia applications, such as computer games and entertainment titles.

In 1998, AMD developed a different set of instructions called 3DNow. It was designed not only to improve 2D games, but also to improve 3D gaming performance. The 3DNow instructions are found in AMD's K6-2 and later processors, as well as some processors from other third-party manufacturers, such as Cyrix and Centaur (makers of the IDT WinChip).

Most recently, Intel has added Streaming SIMD (Single Instruction, Multiple Data) Extensions, or SSE, technology to its newest Pentium III processors. Streaming SIMD was designed to improve the performance of 3D games as well as improve speech recognition and other advanced applications, and it brings an additional 80 new instructions to the core language of processors that support it.

Note

SIMD refers to a technique for performing the same operation on multiple bits of data at the same time. This can be helpful for things like making all the pixels, or individual dots, in a digital photograph all a bit darker. The original MMX instructions perform SIMD on integer data and the Streaming SIMD instructions in the Pentium III extend this to floating point data. (Integer refers to whole numbers and floating point refers to decimals where the decimal point floats.)

As great as these new additions can be, they also raise important and potentially problematic issues. On the positive side, if software programmers take advantage of these new instructions, they can make certain features in their programs run faster. But if the programmers don't provide an alternative method to perform the same operation using a non-MMX, non-3DNow, or non-Streaming SIMD set of instructions, the program won't work on machines that don't support the special extensions. Given that many of these extensions are only supported in relatively new computers, this limits their potential audience. Additionally, now that there are three different sets of extensions, figuring out which chips support which extensions and which applications work most efficiently with which processor can be very confusing. For the record, though, virtually every CPU now supports MMX. Brand new Intel chips support MMX and Streaming SIMD Extensions (SSE). AMD K6's and K7's, as well as the Cyrix' MXi and later IDT/Centaur WinChips, support MMX and 3DNow.

Thankfully, many applications that support these technologies (programs that are said to be MMX- or 3DNow- or SSE-enabled) will run on older machines because programmers provided an alternative "backdoor" capability. Programs using older instructions on a machine that doesn't support new extensions won't run as fast as they would on a computer with a chip that supports MMX, 3DNow, or SSE, but at least they'll run. The only time you run into a problem is if the program actually *requires* MMX, 3DNow or SSE. If this is the case, then this program will only run on computers with processors that support the appropriate extensions. (Whew!)

Word size

Processors also differ in the size of data chunks they can work on at any given time. The 8086 processor and the subsequent 80286 processor (often shortened to 286) are 16-bit processors, which means they can munch on 16 bits of data, sometimes called *16-bit words*, at once. The 80386, or 386, was the first 32-bit processor which, you guessed it, means it can deal with 32 bits of data at once. Not surprisingly, the capability to read in and process twice as much data simultaneously made the 386 a much faster chip than its predecessor. The 486s, members of the Pentium family, and the most current x86-compatible chips, are 32-bit processors as well.

The next major generation of Intel processors, including the forthcoming Merced and McKinley chips (those are the code names for its seventh generation processor line) will be the company's first 64-bit processors. They won't be the first 64-bit processors on the market, however. Digital's Alpha family of chips already owns that distinction.

The reason you should care about all of this — in case you were starting to wonder — is that, like the instruction set, the size of data chunks a processor can handle affects how software runs on the chip. In the case of data word size, it doesn't necessarily mean older software won't work on newer processors, as is the case with instructions that aren't supported. Existing software will work (usually) on newer processors, but applications won't run as fast as they could.

So, older 16-bit software can run on 32-bit hardware and today's 32-bit operating systems (such as Windows 95, Windows 98, Windows NT, and Windows 2000), and 32-bit applications should run on 64-bit processors. To really take advantage of the new hardware, however, they will need to be rewritten to feed the processor 64 bits at a time. (You'll often hear that computer hardware is way ahead of computer software, and this is one of many examples that support this claim.)

CISC vs. RISC

Another important difference between Intel's seventh generation processors and previous generations of x86 processors is that the Merced chip is more heavily based on RISC (Reduced Instruction Set Computing) technology, while all previous Pentiums are primarily based on CISC (Complex Instruction Set Computing). Centaur's IDT WinChip family of processors are some of the only x86-compatibles that take advantage of RISC technology. In a nutshell, this change affects the size and type of instructions that the processor can handle at once (this is different — although similar in theory — to the size of the data chunks described in the previous few paragraphs).

In RISC processors, such as the PowerPC chips that power all current Macintoshes, all the instructions are the same size, whereas in CISC processors, the instructions vary in size. Figure 2-5 illustrates the difference.

The primary benefit of RISC technology is that the processor can run more efficiently because it always knows how big the instructions are going to be. As an end user, this isn't anything you'll ever have to worry about — it's just how the processor works — but it's good to know.

CISC versus RISC

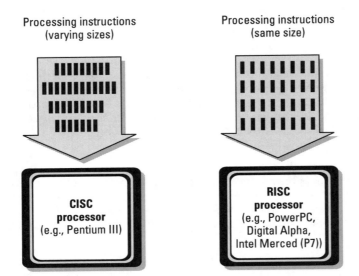

Processing instructions
(varying sizes)

Processing instructions
(same size)

Figure 2-5: Comparing CISC and RISC processors
Processors differ not only in the size of data chunks they can handle at one time, but in the
size of the instructions they use to process that data. Most x86-family processors, including
the Pentium III, use CISC (Complex Instruction Set Computing) technology, which permits
instructions of different sizes. In RISC (Reduced Instruction Set Computing) processors, such
as Intel's forthcoming seventh generation processors, as well as Digital's Alpha and
IBM/Motorola's PowerPC, all instructions are reduced to a single size.

Processor alternatives

While Intel is by far the biggest player in the x86-compatible processor
market, they aren't the only game in town. AMD and Cyrix, in particular —
and several other smaller companies as well — offer solid x86- or Pentium-
compatible alternatives for folks who would rather save a few bucks, or who,
for philosophical reasons, would prefer to buy a non-Intel computer. These
x86-compatibles don't have the exact same instruction set as Intel chips, but
they have functional equivalents that enable them to successfully run virtually any software that's designed to run under Intel x86 processors.

So, if you're wondering whether or not it's safe to buy a PC with a non-Intel
processor, the answer is yes. Software designed for the x86 architecture,
whether it's for any of the versions of Windows, Linux, BeOS, OS/2 as well as
any other operating system that runs under x86, will function just fine on x86-
compatible processors because these compatibles include all the instructions
necessary to run x86-based programs.

As mentioned above, most AMD and Cyrix chips will support extensions to
the core x86 instruction set, such as the 57 MMX instructions Intel first added

to their line with the Pentium MMX processor. Some will even support the Streaming SIMD Extensions (SSE). Just to be safe, if you buy a non-Intel chip, check to make sure that MMX and SSE are, in fact, supported.

Note

Occasionally you hear about problems with systems that use an x86-compatible processor, but they are often due to an incompatible BIOS (Basic Input/Output System) or improper voltage settings on the motherboard. (See the section, "Chipsets and BIOS" later in this chapter for more.) Some early users of the K6 and 6x86MX/MII ran into problems with the chips overheating and eventually failing, but most of these were due to incorrect voltage settings on the motherboard. If there is a problem, most BIOSes can be easily updated to support the processors, and voltage settings can usually be changed via tiny switches on the motherboard or in the BIOS or CMOS setup program.

Cross-Reference

See Chapter 11, "Upgrading Your PC," for more on processor and BIOS upgrades.

There have been a few documented cases of x86-compatibles not working with some software, but in virtually all cases, software upgrades quickly fixed the problem.

To get a better idea of how all the Intel and alternative processors relate to each other, take a look at Figure 2-6, which shows an x86 processor family tree.

Notebook processors

The processors used in most notebook computers are similar though not identical to their desktop counterparts. The primary difference is that mobile processors designed for notebooks run at lower voltages than their desktop equivalents. (Some desktops actually use these lower-power chips as well for power-saving purposes.) The lower voltage is critical because when processors work, they generate a lot of heat and, in the small enclosure typical of a notebook PC, this heat can translate into overheating problems. By lowering the voltages, mobile chips generate less heat than their larger desktop counterparts and they can run on batteries for longer periods of time.

Caution

Some companies sell portables that use desktop chips, partially because the latest, fastest processors tend to appear in desktop versions first and because they're usually a bit cheaper for the computer makers to buy, but I strongly recommend against these portables. Desktop chips tend to run hotter than their portable equivalents and they don't include the battery-saving features built into notebook varieties. Thus, portables can get too hot (which can hurt the chip or cause other problems) and will not have a very good battery life. This is not a good combination.

So, if you're shopping for a notebook, be sure the model you buy uses a processor specifically designed for notebooks. You can usually tell quite easily because, in most instances, an ad or a data sheet for the computer says it uses a mobile processor, such as the mobile Pentium II or mobile Pentium III processor. Also, find out if the processor can be upgraded or not.

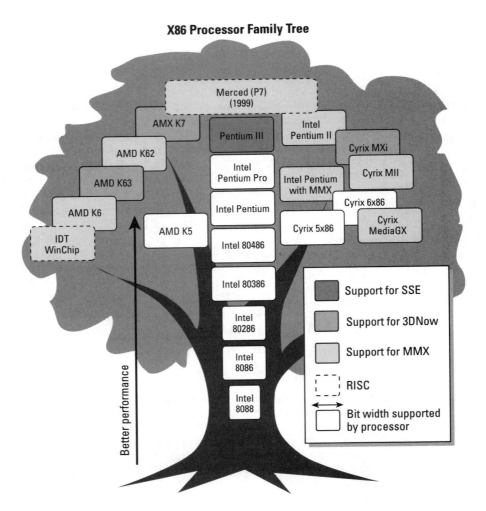

Figure 2-6: x86 processor family tree
Most of the processors used in today's computers all stem from Intel's 8086 processor, which was actually a follow-on to the 8088 — an 8-bit processor that was used in the first IBM PC. As you would expect, later processors offer better performance. In the diagram, processors that support the MMX instruction set are shaded light gray, those that also support 3DNow are medium gray, and those that also support SSE are dark gray. In addition, those that use RISC instructions are in a box bordered by dashed lines. The size of the instructions supported by each processor is notated by the width of the box. Consequently, the 8-bit 8088 features a narrow box, while the forthcoming 64-bit Merced (P7) processor is very wide.

Upgrading notebook processors

If you plan to add a notebook computer to your arsenal of equipment—or even use it as your primary machine—you want to check if the processor is upgradeable. Starting in 1997, Intel began to offer some of its processors packaged on *Mobile Modules*, which are small circuit boards that can be removed and upgraded.

Prior to the Mobile Module-based computers, most notebooks couldn't be upgraded to a faster processor. With the advent of the Mobile Module, however, some systems enable you to pull out the older, slower processor and put in a new, faster version; this is a very nice option to have. Because of the way certain notebook cases are designed, however, not all systems with Mobile Modules can be upgraded. Plus, there are actually several types of Mobile Modules in slightly different shapes and sizes. Also, even if they can, it's almost never a DIY (do-it-yourself) project, so be prepared to take it to a computer dealer or authorized repair center to have the upgrade done.

Secret

One power-saving trick some notebook processors use is they run at slower speeds when working off a battery and run at full-speed when powered by an AC adapter attached to an electrical outlet. If you want to turn this feature off and always run at the fastest possible speed, you'll usually need to make changes to your notebooks' BIOS Setup program. (See the section on Chipsets and BIOS later in this chapter for more.)

Multiprocessor systems

If you're someone who absolutely has to have the fastest personal computer known to humankind, then you probably going to want to investigate computers that have more than one processor. Primarily the domain of computer workstations and servers, multi-processor systems, are available for some desktop systems (albeit at the high end). In a multi-processor system, sometimes referred to as SMP, for Symmetrical Multi-Processing, two or more processors share the number-crunching capabilities, under the direction of an operating system that knows how to divide the duties. Neither Windows 95 nor Windows 98 is multi-processor enabled, however, so if you want this kind of system, you'll have to run Windows NT, Windows 2000, Linux, BeOS, IBM's OS/2, or another multiprocessor-enabled operating system. (If you do try to run Windows 95 or 98 on a machine like this, one of the processors will simply be ignored and you will get no performance benefit whatsoever.)

The level of performance that you can expect from a multiprocessor system varies according to the operating system you choose to run on it, as well as the applications you use. Just because an OS supports multiple processors doesn't mean that, for example, two processors will run two times as fast, or four processors will run four times as fast. Due to the time involved figuring out how to divide the instructions between the processors, there's always going to be at least a small amount of overhead detracting from performance. However, most of the newer SMP-enabled operating systems are approaching

95 percent or better performance per processor, which is much better than the 50 percent or so that older operating systems typically feature.

Physical connections

In addition to internal structural differences, processors differ in physical and electrical specifications. The Pentium III, for example, looks much different than AMD's K6-3. Further, the two chips differ in the way they connect to a computer's motherboard.

This is because the desktop version of the Pentium II and III actually house the processor and L2 cache memory on a single circuit board. This processor card connects to the computer's motherboard via a 242-pin connector that's commonly called Slot One. The K6, on the other hand, like the original Pentium and many x86-compatibles, consists of just the processor itself and connects to a computer's motherboard via a standard connector known as Socket 7.

Slots vs. sockets

Believe it or not, the type of connector used to attach a CPU to a motherboard is a somewhat controversial issue. The problem is that when Intel introduced the Pentium II processor, they switched from what used to be a standard connection known as Socket 7, to a proprietary connection called Slot One. This made it much more difficult — though not impossible — for other x86-compatible microprocessor companies to develop alternatives to the Pentium II that would take advantage of the Slot One connector and all the motherboards that were built to support it.

Figure 2-7 shows what the two connectors look like.

With the introduction of the Pentium II Xeon family, Intel also introduced the longer Slot Two, another proprietary design that will only accept cards designed for that slot. (You can't put a Slot One processor into a Slot Two slot.) In addition, Intel's 64-bit Merced processors will use yet another proprietary connection called Slot M.

Just to add to the confusion, AMD's K7 uses something the company calls Slot A, which is similar to, but not completely compatible with, Slot One. In other words, you can't put Slot A processors into Slot One motherboards and vice versa. And, of course, you can't put any Socket 7-based processors into any kind of system with a CPU slot connector.

Thankfully, CPU socket connections are a bit more straightforward, although there's still some variation there. Some of the later K6 and MII systems use connectors referred to as a Super7 (the name Super7 is meant to distinguish systems that support a 100MHz system bus versus those that support a 66MHz bus, which is explained in the Logical Connections section just below), but the physical connector is the same as a standard Socket 7. In addition, some later versions of the Celeron use a Socket370 connector that currently only works with these specific Celerons (though other companies are expected to produce Socket370-compatible processors as well).

Socket 7 versus Slot One

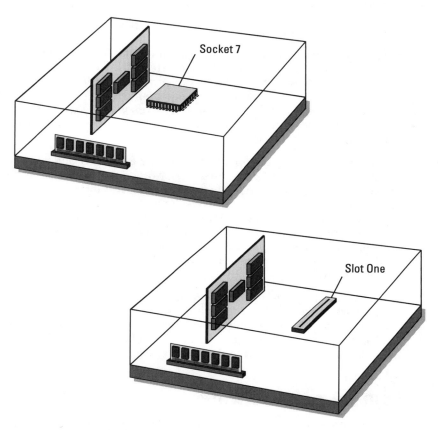

Figure 2-7: Comparing Slot One and Socket 7
Both Socket 7 and Slot One are connectors for attaching a computer's processor to the
motherboard. Beyond this functional similarity, however, the two are very different. In
addition to the obvious physical differences between the two, there are major structural
differences. Socket 7 is an open industry standard that accepts multiple different processors,
including older Intel Pentium MMX family chips, Cyrix MII-family chips, AMD K6-family chips,
and IDT Winchip-family chips. Slot One, on the other hand, is a proprietary Intel connector
that only works with Celeron and Pentium II- and III-family processors.

Secret

If you build your computer from scratch, or replace your computer's motherboard, finding out what type of processor connector is on the motherboard
you purchase is absolutely critical. Without the proper connector, you won't
be able to plug the processor in (and you'll be pretty upset with yourself for
not checking first).

If you're simply buying a prebuilt system, you generally don't have to worry about what type of CPU connector it has, although you're bound to see it listed in the spec sheets.

Electrical specs

Microprocessors are electrical devices and different chips operate at different voltages, both internally and externally. You only have to worry about this if you want to upgrade your processor, or if you decide to build a computer system from individual components. But it's important to be aware of because it explains why certain processors won't work in certain motherboards and why there are different chips for notebook computers than there are for traditional desktops.

Most desktop CPU chips operate at 3.3 volts externally and a lower voltage, such as 2.8 volts or 2.6 volts, internally. Notebooks, on the other hand, also have 3.3-volt external connections, but even lower internal voltages. Not all microprocessors match these levels, however, so if you plug in a chip with certain voltage requirements into a processor connector that's set to or only supports other voltages, you can fry the CPU. In other cases the voltage mismatch might simply cause the CPU not to work (and thus, the computer not to boot) or worst of all, it may partially work but then cause random problems over time.

So if you do decide to upgrade your processor or build your own system, make sure the motherboard you have supports the voltages required by the processor or processor upgrade you plan to use. Again, check for both external and internal voltages. Your processor and motherboard's documentation should include references to the voltages that are required.

Logical connections

In addition to functioning as the primary "calculator" inside a PC, the processor also sits at the logical center of the system. As I mention in Chapter 1, computers consist of a number of separate components that are connected together to make a coherent whole. The processor serves as the point through which most of the data inside a computer flows.

The connections between the processor and other components inside a computer are called *buses*. Buses essentially act as data highways, enabling chunks of data to be sent from one point to another inside your PC. The most important among the various buses is the one that connects the processor to memory—the system bus.

The system bus is the primary mechanism for moving data around to different parts of the computer. When it connects the microprocessor to memory, as well as to other buses, they, in turn, connect to the various input and output devices attached to your computer. Figure 2-8 shows how the system bus works.

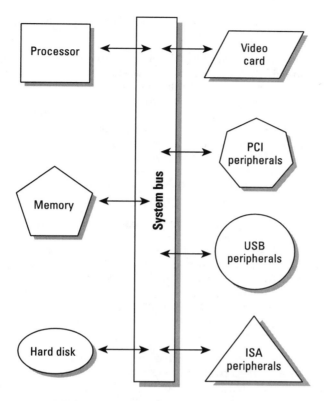

Figure 2-8: The system bus
A computer's system bus connects the processor, memory, video card, hard drive and all the other internal components together in a computer system.

If you think of a computer as a living organism, the microprocessor would be the brain and the system bus would be the central nervous system, connecting together all the various pieces of the computer/body to the processor/brain. And while, like the brain, the processor gets all the good press, it wouldn't be anywhere without the system bus.

In addition to its central functional role, the system bus also plays a role in determining a system's overall performance. The speed at which data gets shuffled around the system, in fact, has a very large impact on normal operations. It is visible when you see how fast your word processor launches or how quickly an image editing application removes the red eye from one of your scanned photos.

For several years, most personal computers were limited to 66 MHz system bus speeds; this proved to be a big bottleneck, particularly as processor speeds got faster and faster. Part of the reason for the bottleneck is that processors run at multiples of the system bus speed. For example, a 333MHz processor runs at 5 times the speed of a 66 MHz system bus.

However, with the introduction of Intel's 440BX chipset in early 1998, computers became able to support 100MHz system buses; this translated to a modest increase in performance. With the introduction of the 820 chipset (and others) in mid-1999, system bus speeds jumped to 133MHz and higher. More important than performance increases, the jump to faster system buses prevents PCs from becoming completely overloaded and actually slowing down because of large multiples of the system bus necessary to drive the processor. These multiples place increased demands on all other aspects of the computer, and can eventually slow it down. Even faster system bus speeds, such as 150 and 200MHz, will soon be commonplace in desktop PCs. This, in turn, will support even faster processor speeds.

The subject of buses can get confusing because in addition to the main, or host, bus, other buses are used by a computer's peripherals, such as the hard disk, video card, and sound card, to talk to the processor and the rest of the computer. The most common of these are the PCI (Peripheral Connect Interface) bus, the AGP (Accelerated Graphics Port) video bus, the redundantly named USB (Universal Serial Bus) bus, and the ISA (Industry Standard Architecture) bus. Each of these buses function at their own speed and talk to the main host bus via some bridging chips (think highway on-ramps and off-ramps), called the *chipset*.

So, for example, while a computer's video card may plug into the AGP bus, the processor can send data to the video card. It first sends it out along the host, or system, bus through the chipset to the AGP bus, and then once the data's on the AGP bus, to the video card itself. To demonstrate this principle, Figure 2-9 displays how the AGP bus connects to the main system bus.

Cross-Reference

For more details on how buses and other connections inside your PC work, see Chapter 8, "How Your Computer Works."

Chipsets and BIOS

The processor is the primary component on a computer's motherboard, but there are two other critical pieces found on there that also play an important role in a computer's overall operation: the chipset and the BIOS.

Chipsets, sometimes called *core logic*, provide the genetic map for PCs, determining what kind of technologies they are capable of supporting. For example, it's the chipset that determines whether or not your computer can support multiple processors, RDRAM memory, the AGP 4x video standard, or the ATA/66 hard disk interface. Because of this critical capability, chipsets can be an important differentiating factor between computers. The type of chipset is also one of the primary distinguishing features between different types of motherboards; this is important to remember if you're interested in upgrading your computer's motherboard or building a computer on your own.

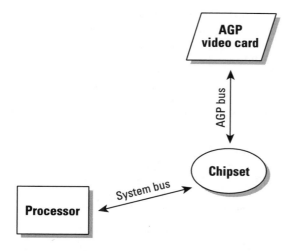

Figure 2-9: The AGP bus

In addition to the main system bus, a computer features several smaller buses, such as the AGP bus, that attach to the system bus. In this example, a video card attaches to the AGP bus, which connects to the system bus via bridging chips called the chipset. So, communications between the processor and video card go over the system bus, through the chipset, onto the AGP bus, and eventually end up at the video card (that is, unless they somehow end up at grandmother's house).

The chipsets also serve as translators between the processor and the computer's various peripheral buses, and allow the processor to communicate with PC add-in cards, such as a modem or SCSI controller. In this role, chipsets are often referred to as *bridge chips*, because they provide a bridge between the main system bus and the various peripheral buses, such as PCI, AGP, ISA, and USB.

Intel and several other chipset vendors have also started to add even more capabilities to recent chipsets, including incorporating the functions of a graphics accelerator.

Secret

When researching a new computer system, very few people try to determine what chipset a computer houses, but most everyone looks for features such as the type of memory it supports, the type of video card, and so on, all of which are directly determined by the chipset. So, while the process may require some extra work on your part (tracking down info on chipsets isn't always easy), I highly recommend you find out what chipset a system you are interested in includes.

The type of chipset used in a computer is very rarely mentioned in ads for computers because most marketing people apparently see them as too obscure. You'll be able to tell if one is mentioned, however, if you see names like 82440BX, 82440ZX, 810, or 820, which are popular chipsets created by Intel. In the case of the first two, you may also see or hear them referred to with their shortened names: the 440BX or the 440ZX.

Another critical motherboard component that's directly related to the processor, as well as lots of other systems components, is the BIOS, or Basic Input/Output System. The BIOS is a piece of software that's stored in hardware—specifically a chip that sits on the computer's motherboard—and takes control of your PC when you first turn it on. In fact, it's the BIOS that initially "talks" to all the components inside a PC and enables certain settings.

The BIOS can affect what types of CPUs the system can support, as well as memory types and other peripherals, particularly hard drives. Like most other software programs, you can adjust how the BIOS software operates. To do this you need to open up a built-in utility called BIOS Setup. (It can also be called CMOS, which stands for Complementary Metal Oxide Semiconductor—the type of material that's often used to store BIOS settings or CMOS Setup.) The utility is typically only available as soon as you turn your computer on. Look for a message along the lines of Hold down the Esc key to enter Setup.

The BIOS or CMOS Setup program provides control over a number of important low-level system settings that can affect how your processor, memory, and other PC components operate. In notebook computers, the BIOS also has settings that affect power management and other battery-related functions.

Cross-Reference

For more details on the BIOS and BIOS Setup, see Chapter 8, "How Your Computer Works."

Recommendations

The type and speed of the processor is unquestionably the most widely quoted computer spec there is, but while it certainly is important, the microprocessor's role in a computer's overall performance can be over-rated.

Secret

The little-known truth of the matter is that the speed of the processor does not necessarily determine the speed of the computer.

As I've mentioned already, a computer is a sum of many parts and correspondingly, a computer's overall performance is the result of several different factors.

It's not at all uncommon to find that a computer with a faster processor will take longer to finish common real-world tasks than a computer with a slower version of the same chip. When you throw in the fact that two different types of processors, such as a Pentium III and a K7, rated at the same speed will perform differently due to internal design differences, you realize the possible permutations in performance become enormous. On the other hand, two identically configured computers that differ *only* in the speed of their processors will give you the results you expect: the system with the higher-rated chip will perform faster.

Why is it that the computer equipped with the faster processor could run more slowly overall, you ask? Well, the differences may be on account of a number of different factors, but the primary reason is that other components, such as the hard drive or video card, in the computer with the faster chip might be slower than their counterparts in the other system. A fast hard drive and/or video card, extra memory, and better performing system components can (and do) often outweigh the performance benefits of a faster processor.

How do you compare?

Given all the possible combinations in computer components and given the complex interaction between the various components, how do you tell if one computer is faster than another? Glad you asked. The answer is benchmarks. Computer benchmarks are applications that typically perform a series of operations on a computer system and time how long it takes the system to complete those operations. The idea is that by running the same benchmark tests on different computers, you can see which one is fastest by looking at which one finished the tests in the least amount of time.

The problem is, no one seems to agree on which operations should be measured and, as a result, there are thousands of different benchmarks measuring thousands of different things. Even worse, because different operations are measured, one benchmark test might show System A being fastest, System B being in the middle, and System C being the slowest, while another benchmark could show the complete opposite, and they'd both be right! In fact, it's been said (and proven in real-life) that benchmarks can be used to prove just about any point somebody would like to make.

Now, this is not to say that benchmarks are worthless. They do have real value. The trick, however, is to make sure the benchmarks you use measure things that are of importance to you.

The two primary varieties of benchmarks are called *synthetic benchmarks* and *application benchmarks*. Synthetic benchmarks typically isolate the performance of a single component of a computer system, such as the processor, video card, or hard disk, and run it through a series of operations that are designed specifically for the benchmark. This is handy if you're just thinking about upgrading a certain component of your computer system and want to know how the theoretical performances of different products compare. Application benchmarks, on the other hand, use real functions from real applications to test the performance of either certain components, or the system as a whole. Though this is subject to intensive debate, I think these types of benchmarks are the most informative and the best indicator of real-world performance differences you'll see between two computer systems.

Within these two types of benchmarks, there are many variations. Different application benchmarks, for example, use different applications and/or different processes or functions within those applications. The popular WinStone benchmark, for example, which is created by the Ziff-Davis Benchmark Operation, has a version that uses business applications, such as Microsoft Word and Excel, and another that uses graphic applications, such as Adobe PhotoShop and PageMaker. Running the two versions on several machines will typically generate very different results, even comparatively, because most computers perform some operations better than others. In other words, the fastest system on the Business WinStone test may only be the third fastest in the Graphics WinStone test, and so on.

So, while I encourage you to use benchmarks to compare different systems, make sure you know what the benchmark is comparing. And don't presume that when one system beats another in one performance test it's the fastest overall or the fastest at what you want the computer to do. Not only do you need to compare apples to apples, you need to make sure the apples you compare are ones you want to eat.

Still, my recommendation is to purchase a system with the fastest processor you can afford because there's no such thing as a computer that's too fast (and don't let anyone tell you otherwise). The PC 98 spec calls for a minimum of 200MHz Pentium performance (and support for MMX), while the PC 99 spec calls for a minimum of 300MHz Celeron A-level performance with 128KB (or more) of L2 cache.

If you really want to zip along, and you're willing to run something other than Windows 95 or 98 as your operating system, you may even want to consider a computer system with multiple processors. But, try not to go overboard.

Secret

In general, you want as fast a processor as possible, but don't overspend on the processor at the expense of getting more memory, a faster hard drive, or a speedier video card. You really need to keep a balance to get the best-performing computer for the money.

Also make sure that your system has plenty of L2 cache (preferably 512KB) so that your processor can run as efficiently as possible. I specifically do not recommend computers with processors that don't have and don't support L2 cache.

Memory

After the processor, one of the most important components of any computer is its memory. The computer's memory is its working area, where it temporarily stores all the files it needs to run. Memory is typically referred to as RAM, or Random Access Memory (random access refers to the fact that every location in memory can be accessed as quickly as the others — the computer doesn't have to go through points A and B to get to C). It's usually quoted in megabytes, or MB.

Memory comes in different physical shapes and sizes. In some of the first PCs, memory came in the form of individual chips, each of which was capable of storing a certain number of bytes of digital data. Memory add-ons often took the form of add-in boards, not completely unlike today's video and sound cards. Then, as chip design circuitry became more sophisticated and manufacturers were able to squeeze more memory into a smaller space, memory took the form of tiny circuit boards called SIMMs, or Single In-line Memory Modules. This, in turn, led to the development of other types of memory packages, including DIMMs (Dual In-line Memory Modules), SO-DIMMs (Small Outline DIMMs), and RIMMs (Rambus In-line Memory Modules).

The most important features to look for with memory are:

- The physical package it comes in
- The type of memory technology it uses
- The speed at which it operates
- Whether it supports any type of error correction

SIMMs, DIMMs, SO-DIMMs, and RIMMs

SIMMs consist of several memory chips on a single card that connect to the computer's motherboard via an edge connector. Early SIMMs have 30 discrete connection points on the edge connector and are referred to as 30-pin SIMMs; later SIMMs have 72 different connectors and are called 72-pin SIMMs.

Memory was condensed further still with the introduction of DIMMs, or Dual In-Line Memory Modules. One DIMM is essentially equivalent to two SIMMs and uses a high-density 168-pin connector. As you might suspect, physical differences in the connectors prevent you from trying to use say, a 30-pin SIMM in a DIMM slot. RIMMs, or RamBus In-Line Memory Modules, are a new type of memory chip that's specifically designed to work with computer systems that use Direct RDRAM, a new type of computer system memory that I explain below. Like DIMMs, RIMMs come in packages with 168-pin connectors, although the connectors are spaced differently so as not to confuse the two types and so you can't use one in place of the other.

Figure 2-10 shows different types of memory chips.

Notebook computers often use yet another type of memory packaging called SO-DIMMs (Small Outline DIMMs), which have another type of 72-pin connector. As their name suggests, SO-DIMMs are more compact than their desktop equivalents and, therefore, are better suited to the compact quarters inside a notebook's case.

Secret

Some notebooks use proprietary memory connectors, and this can make it tough (or expensive) to add extra memory. So, if you're buying a notebook, be sure to find out what type of memory it uses.

Some desktop computer motherboards actually include both 72-pin SIMM and 168-pin DIMM slots, in deference to customers who start with some existing 72-pin memory, but eventually decide to move to the newer DIMM format. Similarly, some newer systems have both DIMM and RIMM slots, for similar reasons. In either instance, some systems let you use both types of memory at the same time, while others only let you choose one or the other. The settings for this choice are typically found in the computer's BIOS or CMOS Setup program.

Secret

If you do set a system to use both types of memory, it will typically slow the faster memory down to the speed of the slower memory; this can have a minor impact on your computer's overall performance.

Note

As with many issues that I discuss in this section, you usually don't need to worry about the type of physical connectors your memory uses until it comes time to upgrade your machine. It is important, however, to be aware of the physical connectors when you make a purchase because you always need to think about the future when it comes to computers. Buying a PC is the beginning of a process, not the end of one.

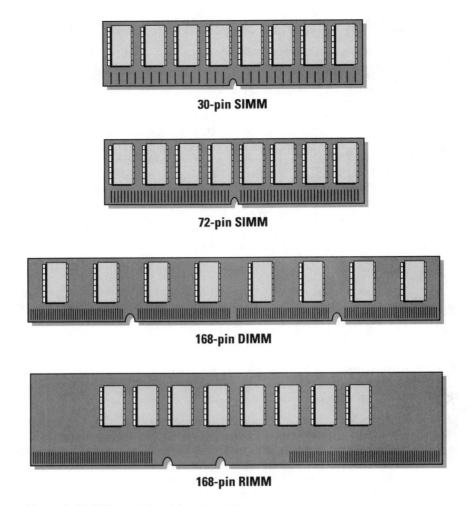

30-pin SIMM

72-pin SIMM

168-pin DIMM

168-pin RIMM

Figure 2-10: Different sizes of memory
Computer memory comes in several shapes and sizes, but the most important difference has to do with the connector at the bottom of the memory module and the number of discrete connection points, or pins, it has. The most common types are 30- and 72-pin SIMMs and 168-pin DIMMs. The newest type of memory is RDRAM, created by RamBus, which uses 168-pin RIMMs.

In addition to physical differences, there are important functional differences between SIMMs, DIMMs, SO-DIMMs, and RIMMs (not to mention that first letter, of course) that have to do with how different generations of computers operate. Memory sends data back and forth from the processor in discrete chunks. This communication occurs over the system bus which, as explained earlier in this chapter, is like a computer's main highway, attaching the processor to memory, add-in peripherals and more. The size of chunks that are sent back and forth is determined by the "width" of the system bus, which in turn, is related to how large a chunk the processor can munch on at once. (See, this stuff is all related!)

Early 32-bit processors, such as the 386 and 486, used system buses that were 32-bits wide and required 32 bits of data at once. Because SIMMs could provide 32 bits at once, each SIMM could fulfill the processor's needs individually and you could add SIMMs to your computer one at a time.

With the introduction of the Pentium family of processors, computers began using 64-bit wide system buses because the Pentium was capable of receiving two chunks of 32-bits at once. SIMMs could only provide one 32-bit chunk at a time, however, and this meant you had to add memory to Pentium machines two SIMMs at a time. (Hence the common practice of buying SIMMs in pairs.)

DIMMs and RIMMs work with 64 bits of data at once. A practical benefit is that you can install DIMMs or RIMMs one at a time in any Pentium family-based computer (that is, as long as it has DIMM or RIM slots — not all do). One limitation of SO-DIMMs versus real DIMMs is that they can only transfer 32-bits of data at a time, which makes them more like SIMMs than DIMMs. Eventually, computers will move to 128-bit buses and we'll probably be back to adding memory in pairs (that is, until 128-bit memory chips come along, and the cycle will begins again).

Another benefit of DIMMs and RIMMs (or pairs of SIMMs) is that some computers can take advantage of a process known as *interleaving*, where two separate banks of memory can be treated as a single entity. The processor can send a chunk of data to memory or request one from this unified bank of memory, and the task can be split between the two individual banks. This results in a faster completion of the request and, in turn, eventually leads to an overall boost in the computer's performance.

Memory types

In addition to different sizes, memory also comes in several different types. The most common is Dynamic RAM, or DRAM. It is found in virtually all desktop and notebook computers, and requires power to maintain its contents. This means if you pull the plug, or the power goes out, the contents of the memory is wiped out. In concrete terms it means everything you were working on at the time disappears and all the memory in your computer is empty again.

Static RAM, or SRAM, another major type of memory, can actually maintain its contents with a tiny trickle of a charge from a simple battery. It's used in handheld PCs and other small electronic devices that you turn on and off (or that turn themselves on or off) all the time. Flash RAM, which is also used in portable organizers, is a specialized form of SRAM. SRAM's capability to keep everything in memory is what enables you add an address or phone number to your organizer, for example, turn it the organizer off, and still have that address or phone number in memory when you turn the organizer back on. In a way, it's like a combination of memory and a miniature hard drive all in one. SRAM is much more expensive than DRAM, however and this is why it isn't used as the main memory in traditional PCs.

Interestingly, SRAM is also much faster than DRAM, and is commonly used for a computer's L2 cache.

Within the DRAM genus, there are several different species. They include the following, and are discussed in this section:

- FPM (Fast Page Mode) RAM
- EDO (Extended Data Out) RAM
- SDRAM (Synchronous) DRAM
- DDR (Double Data Rate, also called High Data Rate) RAM
- RDRAM (RAMBus) DRAM.

For the most part, the type of memory is not determined by the physical form factor it comes in and vice versa. So, for example, SDRAM comes in SIMM and DIMM varieties, but not all DIMMs are SDRAM; some may be EDO or another memory type. It's even possible to find SDRAM in RIMMs, although those types of memory are typically called S-RIMMs. The bottom line is there's a confusing array of choices that you generally can't distinguish among visually. However, you'll know what you're dealing with if you find out both the type and form the memory a specific computer system requires. Another confusing issue with regard to memory modules of all varieties is specifications for the amount of memory on a particular module. (The sidebar "Reading memory specs" explains this issue in detail.)

Reading memory specs

Buying memory ought to be straightforward. You should just be able to say I need 16 megabytes or 64 megabytes, or whatever figure you want. Instead, however, when you go to order memory you may find yourself confronted with confusing specifications describing the amount of memory on a particular DIMM, SIMM, or RIMM, such as 16Mx32, or what have you. What these specs refer to is the depth and width of the individual DRAM chips that go into a particular SIMM, DIMM, or RIMM module. Many memory modules have eight individual chips, while modules that support a basic type of error checking called *parity* have nine. (See the "Error correction" section later in this chapter for more.)

So, in this case, each of the individual chips on the module is 16 megabits (16Mbits) or 2 Megabytes deep, and 32 megabits (32Mbits) or 4 bytes wide. This translates into a total capacity of 8 Megabytes per chip. With eight chips on the module, this means the SIMM has a capacity of 64MB.

Most chips will be listed as x32 but parity memory will be listed as x36. Another way of saying this is if you see a memory module listed as some number x36, then it's a parity module.

The performance puzzle

One of the real tricks in putting together a high-performance computer system is trying to balance the different components that go in to the computer, particularly the processor, memory, hard disk, and video card. As I've said elsewhere, a computer is nothing more than a series of specialized components working together and the computer's overall performance is dependent on how efficiently each of these components work with each other. The problem is, each component has the potential to be a bottleneck that slows down the entire computer — it's a classic example of how one weak link can negatively impact an otherwise solid system.

The challenge is to find a group of components and/or technologies that work together efficiently. This doesn't necessarily mean you need to have the fastest component of each variety, however. When you shop for a system, the compatibility of various components depends on where in the technological development curve each particular component happens to be. For example, an older form of memory may work better with the current generation of processors, or vice versa.

Throughout the history of personal computers, various components have been bottlenecks in overall system performance. However, as soon as the next iteration of that component, or the next technological development in that specific area reached the market, that specific bottleneck was removed and another one appeared in a different area of the computer.

In fact, in many ways, the entire history of the personal computer industry is a series of leapfrog moves, with different components becoming stuck at the tail end of the performance curve. It's a never-ending cycle that promises to drive the computer industry's development well into the twenty-first century.

In practical terms it's also just another illustration of how, no matter how well you plan and time your purchase, there's going to be something better coming along soon. The new systems may have the same type of processor or same type of memory as something that you've already bought, but somewhere inside the new system, there's bound to be an old bottleneck removed (and a new bottleneck started).

Each particular DRAM species works in a slightly different way and their method of operation determines their overall speed. As with the processor (and every component of a computer, for that matter), you want the memory to be as fast as possible to keep the computer running at an optimum level, and the trick with memory is to move data into and out of it as quickly as possible.

FPM RAM

Fast Page Mode (FPM) RAM, is an older type of memory that is typically referred to as plain old RAM. In fact, if a system specification doesn't mention what type of memory a computer uses, it's probably FPM RAM. (Actually, the very first type of memory used in personal computers was called Page Mode RAM, but it's no longer available. Fast Page Mode was an improvement over Page Mode RAM.)

To understand what Fast Page Mode as well as all the different RAM types are, you need to know a little bit about how memory works. The purpose of memory is to store bits of digital data that can be written to or read from the computer's processor. The computer keeps track of where everything is by giving each piece of memory an address, and memory chips are essentially like big square grids. An address consists of both a row number and a column number, and all the various squares in a particular row are collectively referred to as a page.

When the computer's processor requests a chunk of data from memory, it seeks out the specific address of the data it needs, requests that data be sent, and then starts looking for the next address. Oftentimes the processor needs contiguous bits of data, all of which are located in the same row, or page, of the memory chip. With Fast Page Mode RAM, the computer can reduce the amount of time it takes to find the next address by simply sending the next few bits in a row; it doesn't waste time looking up the address. Eventually the processor needs a chunk of data in a different location, and so the process starts anew.

EDO RAM

EDO RAM provides even faster access to the data in memory by seeking out a new address at the same time it's sending data from the previously requested address. Though the incremental improvement might seem tiny compared to FPM RAM, because of the number of times that this process occurs each second, your computer's overall operation improves about 10 to 15 percent. In other words, the same computer with EDO RAM should run about 10 to 15 percent faster than one with FPM RAM.

Another factor that can influence how fast your FPM or EDO memory works is the memory's rated speed typically quoted in nanoseconds, (See "What about RAM speeds?" for more.) The lower the number, the better because the quoted numbers refer to how long it takes a bit of data to be delivered to the processor after it has been requested. So 60-nanosecond memory requires sixty nanoseconds to deliver the necessary info.

What about RAM speeds?

One commonly quoted, but usually misunderstood memory specification, is the speed of the RAM, often given in nanoseconds. For example, memory that requires 60 nanoseconds to deliver the necessary info is called 60-nanosecond RAM. This speed refers to the time it takes to send a requested chunk of data from memory out to the system bus and on its way to the processor. The lower the number, the faster data can move around your computer, and hence, the faster your computer will be. Not surprisingly, then, the lower the speed within a given memory type, the more expensive it is. FPM RAM is often found at 60- to 70-nanosecond speeds, EDO RAM tends to run in the 50 to 70-nanosecond range, and SDRAM runs as fast as 10 to 15 nanoseconds.

To put this into perspective, a 100MHz system bus moves at the pace of one new event or new clock cycle, or every 10 nanoseconds. So, SDRAM rated at 10 nanoseconds can theoretically supply the bus with a new chunk of data every time it needs one. And to give you even more of a perspective, a 300MHz processor performs an operation, and wants a new chunk of data, about every three nanoseconds. This is one of the primary reasons why computers, particularly those with faster processors, need cache memory so they do not sit around wasting their processing power.

SDRAM

Synchronous DRAM or SDRAM (not to be confused with SRAM) expedites the process of delivering and receiving data to and from the processor even more. Thanks to the addition of additional circuitry that functions as a timing mechanism, SDRAM can operate at speeds of 10–15 nanoseconds and to run at the same speed as, or synchronously with, the computer system's bus (hence the name).

This means that once the first data location in a memory chip is found, subsequent bits of data can be read out at every tick of the system clock. FPM RAM and EDO RAM, on the other hand, do not run at the same speed as the system bus, but at several multiples slower. As a result, they are just as fast at finding the first bit of data to be read, but are much slower at delivering subsequent bits. EDO RAM can deliver the subsequent bits at every other tick of the system clock, while FPM RAM can only do so at every third tick of the system clock. Thus, the processor is forced to wait even longer for data and, in turn, your computer does not run as fast as it could. With SDRAM, however, the memory feeds the system bus almost as quickly as it requests it and this translates to better performance.

Because of its relation to the system bus speed, SDRAM is typically paired with the type of system bus it can support. So, for example, PC133 SDRAM is for systems with 133MHz system buses, PC100 SDRAM is for systems with 100MHz system buses, PC66 SDRAM is for systems with 66MHz system buses, and so on.

DDR DRAM

Double Date Rate DRAM, or DDR DRAM, is a relatively new specialized type of SDRAM that can transfer two bytes of data in the same time frame that a normal SDRAM can transfer one. This is important in computer systems with very fast system buses, such as those running faster than 100MHz, because it can feed data to the CPU at a faster rate, and the CPU no longer sits around waiting to be "fed." As with most memory types, support for DDR RAM has to be in the computer's chipset in order for it to be available.

RDRAM

RAMBus RAM, or RDRAM, uses a new, proprietary, high-speed connection between the processor and memory that enables data to be shuttled back and forth, to and from, the processor at rates that are several times faster than previous technology, including SDRAM. Developed by RAMBus Technology, and licensed by Intel and many other memory manufacturers, RAMBus breaks away from previous designs by providing a separate bus for the RAM (a RAM Bus . . .get it?) that's separate from the main system bus.

With all the other types of memory, communication between the processor and memory occurs over the system bus, but with RAMBus memory, the communication occurs over a dedicated, high-speed bus. The RAMBus bus, called the Direct RAMBus Channel, is only 16 bits wide, but it offers transfer rates of up to 1.6 Gigabytes/second, versus 800 Megabytes/second for SDRAM on a 100MHz system bus. If you combine several channels, you could theoretically get 3.2 or even 4.8 Gigabytes/second, which should translate into much better overall system performance because it can keep the processor busy.

Unfortunately you can't just add RDRAM to any system and see this big boost in performance. Support for this technology has to be added at the lowest level of the system, specifically the chipset and its embedded memory controller — a special component that "talks" directly to the memory.

Secret

Beware of SDRAMs in RIMM clothing. To help computer makers and users in the transition from SDRAM to RDRAM, Intel developed a specification for S-RIMMs. S-RIMMs basically put SDRAM technology into a RIMM package. While S-RIMMs are cheaper than true RDRAM RIMMs, they don't offer the speed and technology benefits of the real McCoy.

Virtual Channel Memory

Up until now, I've primarily focused on how quickly various types of memory can transfer their contents to the L2 cache and onto the processor, but there's another equally important aspect to memory performance that's been over-looked. The issue is called *latency* and it refers to how long it takes to get the first chunk of data that the processor requests. As it turns out, latency times haven't changed much since the introduction of FPM RAM because of the way in which the memory core works. Even RAMBus and SDRAM often take five clock cycles in order to get to the first memory address they need.

Depending on the types of applications you use, latency problems can have a fairly big impact on overall performance. Technologies like RAMBus are great for streaming large chunks of data from memory to the processor, such as when you play multimedia titles. But they aren't really any better than older technologies when it comes to working with small chunks of data at time, such as when you're writing in a word processor.

To address the latency issue, NEC developed a technology called Virtual Channel Memory (VCM), which can theoretically be used in conjunction with any type of main memory, including SDRAM or RDRAM. Basically, Virtual Channel Memory adds the equivalent of a small amount of fast

SRAM to each memory chip; it's almost like having a baby L2 cache on each piece of memory. By using technology that guesses what to load into that baby cache, you can effectively reduce the latency problem to almost nothing — theoretically, that is. Practical results weren't ready at the time of writing, but when Virtual Channel Memory support is added into chipsets, and systems start to support it, we should start to see even better memory performance.

Error correction

Another issue that you may need to worry about is the type of error correction memory uses, if any. Believe it or not, computers really can make mistakes, but those mistakes are extraordinarily rare and usually so subtle that we never notice them. For example, one pixel on the screen might be drawn the wrong color momentarily. Never the less, as a result of a sudden surge in electricity, or even because of the minute radiation generated within a memory chip or any electronic device, the number stored at a particular memory address can change. (Remember that computers store everything in binary form — ones and zeros, so we're talking about changing from a zero to a one or vice versa.)

Now, the likelihood of such a soft error occurring is, according to information released by IBM, about once every three years in a 16MB memory module that's used 600 hours a month. Meticulous computer designers want to get rid of this possibility, however, so they developed mechanisms for error checking and correction that are included in some types of memory. The most common type is referred to as *parity checking*, and memory that incorporates it is called *parity memory*. Not surprisingly, memory that doesn't incorporate parity checking is called *non-parity memory*. (See "Parity vs. non-parity" for more information.)

Parity vs. non-parity

Parity memory, which costs a few dollars more than an equivalent amount of non-parity memory, adds up all the numbers in memory and stores the results in an extra chip located next to the main memory chips. (The extra chip — typically there are nine located on parity memory vs. eight on regular, non-parity memory — along with the circuitry required to perform the calculation, account for the extra cost for parity memory.) Before a bit of data is retrieved, parity memory can add up the numbers again to make sure that they still have the same total. If they do, then no soft error has occurred and things can proceed as normal. If they don't, then parity memory raises up a flag to the computer's BIOS, which in turn passes it to the operating system, which ultimately leads to some kind of dialog box or error message saying that a parity error has occurred.

Secret

If your system generates parity errors on a regular basis, it's almost a sure sign that your memory has begun to go bad (which can happen), or that there's a problem with your motherboard.

The other type of error correction is called ECC, or *Error Correcting Code*. ECC is a more complex, more thorough error-testing scheme that is able to identify more types of possible soft errors in memory (it's also used to verify information is read correctly from CD-ROM and DVD-ROM drives). For example, if two memory addresses in a memory chip suffer from soft errors at the same time (a rare, though not impossible occurrence), parity checking may not notice the error, but ECC would.

As with the type of memory, support for parity and ECC memory is determined by the chipset. This means if a computer's chipset doesn't support these types of memory, there's no point in spending the extra money for them because they won't do any good. There are some practical issues, too. You cannot get EDO memory that supports parity, for example, because it's not made.

Frankly, whether or not you need parity memory is more of a philosophical question than a technical one. Some people strongly believe that a computer should have error correction mechanisms for memory and other people believe that such errors are so rare and so often benign, it's not worth worrying about.

Recommendations

The two critical issues with regard to a computer's memory are what type it is and how much of it the PC contains. The type of memory determines how quickly information can be transferred to and from the processor; this has a big impact on how fast the computer runs in day-to-day use. The amount of memory determines how much working room your system has and it, too, has a large impact on a computer's speed.

Intel and many other vendors have made it clear that RDRAM is the memory format for the future, so if you can find a system that uses RDRAM, I recommend getting it — although you will pay for the privilege. In addition to a speed boost, because it incorporates technology of the future, the system is bound to give you a few more years of useful life than it would otherwise.

If you don't want to spend the premium for RDRAM, however, I suggest you go with SDRAM or DDR SDRAM in DIMM format. SDRAM is a speedy format that works well with computers that have 100MHz or faster system buses. DIMMs are preferable because they can be added individually, which makes it easier to increase your memory at a later date. Instead of having to buy two 32MB SIMMs, for example, you can buy and add one 64MB DIMM to one slot, and then, say, a 128MB DIMM at a later date.

The amount of memory you need in a computer is a constantly increasing. My recommendation (and the one listed in the PC98 specification) is to get at least 32MB of memory, but to ideally make it 64MB (the recommended amount in PC 99) or more if you can afford it. There's really no such thing as too much memory because even if you get a system that has more than you think you'll use initially, within a year or less, I virtually guarantee that you'll be glad you have it.

Summary

In this chapter, I described the important characteristics of microprocessors and memory, which are at the core of any computer system, as well as offered recommendations on what type of processor and memory to look for in a new computer system.

► Processors work by performing mathematical calculations on data and instructions that they receive from the computer's memory.

► High-speed cache memory, such as L2 cache, makes processors work more efficiently; it makes data and instructions readily available and acts as a buffer between the processor and main memory.

► Processors differ not only in how fast they run, but also in how they perform their calculations internally and the size of the data chunks they can process.

► MMX, 3DNow, and Streaming SIMD Extensions (SSE) are all extensions to the internal language that a processor can understand, and support for them in a particular processor can determine what type of software applications a processor can run.

► Processors connect to a computer system's motherboard via slots or sockets.

► Chipsets and the BIOS play a critical role in determining a computer's overall capabilities.

► Memory types differ in both their physical package and the technology used for them.

► Different types of computer memory transfer data to the processor at different rates and that, in turn, impacts how fast a computer system works.

► Parity and ECC are two types of error correction built into certain memory modules that can help computers avoid certain types of errors.

Chapter 3

Hard Disks and Removable Drives

In This Chapter

▶ You will learn how a hard drive works and what distinguishes one drive from another.

▶ You will learn the factors that affect a hard drive's performance.

▶ You will learn about the different types of hard drive interfaces, including IDE, SCSI, and IEEE 1394.

▶ You will learn about various types of removable storage.

▶ You will learn the differences between CD-ROM, DVD-ROM, CD-R, CD-RW, DVD-RAM, DVD+RW and DVD-R.

▶ You will get recommendations on hard drives and removable storage devices.

A computer's capabilities and personality, (if you can call it this) are defined by the software that resides within its system. But software doesn't just suddenly appear — it needs to be stored and loaded from somewhere before it adds usefulness and sparkle to the otherwise dormant circuit boards buried inside your PC.

The job of storing and loading software is handled by several different components, the most well-known of which are the floppy disk drive, hard drive, and the CD- or DVD-ROM drive. Collectively, they are referred to as a computer's storage devices because, well, they can store things (like programs, files, movies, sounds, pictures, and so on).

Storage devices are the real workhorses and unsung heroes of today's PCs. Their job isn't glamorous, but it's absolutely essential to the successful operation of your computer and makes a big difference in how fast your computer works.

Hard Drives

Most of the software used on a particular computer is stored on the *hard drive*, or *hard disk*, as it is sometimes called. The hard drive (or drives — computers are capable of working with more than one) is like the electronic filing cabinet for your PC. It's the place where you store all your work. All the software that your computer needs to start up properly, including the operating system, the software that essentially controls how your computer works and runs (for example, Windows 98), is also stored there, so the hard drive is a really critical part of your PC.

Drives are typically classified according to their storage capacity, which is usually quoted in GB (or gigabytes), although older, smaller drives may be quoted in MB (or megabytes). As you would expect, the larger the capacity, the more data a drive can hold.

Secret

A gigabyte (GB) is technically equivalent to 1,024MB, although many hard drive vendors skimp and actually make it equivalent to 1,000MB. So, don't be surprised if you discover that your new 16GB drive only measures out to 16,000MB instead of 16,384MB.

In addition to storage capacity, the most important specs to look for in hard drives are:

- The type of connection, or interface, the drive uses to connect with the rest of the PC

- The time the drive takes to retrieve a chunk of data, called the access time

- How quickly the drive can send large blocks of data to the processor, called the sustained throughput

- How quickly the platters inside the disk move, or the drive's rotation speed (this has a dramatic impact on the throughput)

- The shape and size of the drive, which determines the type of system it can fit into

How it works

Hard drives work by reading and writing data from and to specific places, or addresses, on the hard drive. In hard drive parlance, these addresses refer to the track and sector at which a particular data chunk resides. All hard disks are actually made up of several disks, or platters, stacked on top of one another. When a drive is formatted, each platters is divided into tracks, or cylinders, much like the grooves on phonograph records (remember those?), and these tracks are further divided into sectors.

Data is read from the disk by a group of read/write heads. These tiny devices are attached at the end of a positioning arm that moves the head across the disk, and there is one for each side of every patter. In many ways, the process can be compared to a high-tech version of a turntable.

Figure 3-1 shows the different sections of a typical hard disk.

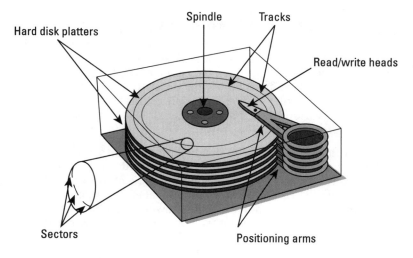

Spindle Tracks

Hard disk platters

Read/write heads

Sectors

Positioning arms

Figure 3-1: Hard disk dissection
Hard disks consist of several different platters, each of which is broken up into tracks and sectors. Each track and sector has a particular address, and your computer stores files to and reads files from the hard disk by looking up these particular addresses.

Hard disks work in a manner that's analogous to how memory works. That is, they both retrieve chunks of data from and put chunks of data into specific addresses. Unlike memory, however, hard drives cannot necessarily get to the address where the data they need is located as quickly as any other address or drive location. There are timing differences dependent on the physical location of the data on the drive. The time required to get to a specific location of data is commonly referred to as the drive's *access time*, and it is usually quoted in milliseconds. Note, however, some vendors use access time and seek time interchangeably, even though, technically speaking, they are different. (*Seek time* refers to how long it takes the drive's read/write heads to move into place.)

Drive connections

Hard drives connect to your PC system via one of several different types of controllers; a controller is a device that serves as an intermediary, or interface, between the drive and the rest of the computer system. The most common type of hard drive connection is via an IDE (Integrated Drive Electronics) controller, but SCSI (Small Computer System Interface) and, increasingly IEEE 1394 (sometimes called FireWire or i.Link) controllers and their associated connections, are also used. The type of controller used to connect between a hard disk and the rest of the PC can have an important impact on the drive's and the computer's overall performance.

See the section "Hard drive interfaces" later in this chapter for more.

Cross-
Reference

Partitioning and formatting

Before a hard drive can hold any data, it needs to be partitioned and formatted. The partitioning process breaks a drive up into logical chunks, like individual file drawers within a file cabinet. The formatting process goes a step further and provides additional order to the drive so that your computer's operating system and applications know how to find the locations of various files; it's somewhat similar to putting folders and dividers into individual file drawers.

The partitioning process can divide hard disks into several different partitions, or volumes. Under the various Windows operating systems, each volume on your hard drive is assigned a name starting with the letter C: and is treated by the computer as an individual entity. Again, this can be compared to creating individual file drawers in a filing cabinet. Under other operating systems, such as Linux, you won't see individual drive letters; instead, these operating systems address partitions with other types of naming conventions, such as `hda1`.

If you prefer, you can generally keep your hard drive as a single partition or volume. Due to several factors, hard drives must occasionally be broken into a few partitions in order to take advantage of all the space on the drive. This explains, for example, why a new computer system with a single 6.4GB hard disk may appear to have three different hard drives (C:, D:, and E:) that are just over 2GB each. In reality, these are simply separate volumes, or partitions, but they are all part of a single physical drive.

Size limitations

Partitions affect not only the organization of a hard drive, but also how much data a particular drive can hold. The maximum partition size is determined both by the type of partitioning used by an operating system as well as the capabilities of a PC's BIOS, or Basic Input/Output System. (See Chapter 8, "How Your Computer Works" for more.) The partition size, in turn, determines the size of a volume that your operating system can "see." For example, veteran PC users will recall the 504MB (or 528MB, depending on whether you multiple by 1,000 or 1,024) limit that used to confine hard disks to nothing larger than just over half a gigabyte. (Seems tiny now, doesn't it?)

The problem was that on some older computers, the system BIOS, which used to negotiate all conversations between the computer operating system and the hard disk, couldn't recognize any more individual addresses beyond the hard drive's 504MB capacity. In other words, it couldn't work with partitions larger than 504MB. As a result, the computer couldn't "see" anything past 504MB and ignored any additional space that may have been available on a larger drive.

This problem was solved by later versions of BIOS software, which feature a capability called BIOS translation. (Another way around the problem is to have a BIOS that supports Logical Block Addressing, or LBA.) BIOS translation and LBA enlarge the number of possible addresses on a hard drive that a computer system can see. The practical result is that computers build around a BIOS that supports BIOS translation (sometimes called a translating BIOS or an enhanced BIOS) or LBA can take advantage of hard drives up to 8GB.

Well, actually, let's make that most computers. In reality, some earlier versions of translating BIOSes only did a partial job and were limited to supporting drives of up to 2.1GB.

Tip

If you have an older computer limited by either the 504MB or 2.1GB limit, you can solve it by simply upgrading or replacing the BIOS on your computer's motherboard. Partitioning the drive into smaller volumes will not solve BIOS-based size limitations. See Chapter 11, "Upgrading Your PC" for more on how to upgrade your BIOS.

Fortunately (or unfortunately, depending on your perspective), many PC systems now ship with 8GB or larger hard drives. However, even with support for BIOS translations, many of today's modern BIOSes cannot work with individual drives larger than about 8GB. To get around this problem your computer's BIOS, hard disk, and the operating system must support Int13h extensions. (Int13h refers to the BIOS interrupt address used to access the hard disk. It's something only programmers need to worry about, but you're bound to hear it tossed around when the subject of large hard disks is discussed.)

Thankfully, most modern operating systems, including all versions of Windows 95, 98, NT and 2000, support Int13h extensions. Not all applications do, however. As a result, some applications, particularly older ones that communicate directly with the hard disk, such as disk utilities, won't work with BIOSes and hard drives that use them. So, be careful if you upgrade a system with a drive larger than 8GB. New computers that ship with hard drives larger than 8GB won't be a problem because they already have a BIOS that supports the Int13 extensions.

FAT16 vs. FAT32

Now, there's actually a much more common 2.0GB hard drive limit that can affect Windows 3.1, 95, 98 and 2000 users. This limitation has nothing to do with BIOS limitations; it's a factor of the file system the operating system software uses. (The file system is a method for storing and organizing files on a hard disk.)

The BIOS limitations I've discussed are hardware limitations. That is, they are limitations that are determined by your PC's hardware, and they exist regardless of what operating system software your computer runs. The file system-based 2.0GB limitation I just referred to, however, is related to the operating system software loaded onto your computer.

The most popular file system in use on PCs is called FAT, or File Allocation Table. FAT, or FAT-16, as it is sometimes called, is at the heart of DOS, Windows 3.1, and early versions of Windows 95. Windows 98, Windows 2000, Windows NT, Linux, and virtually all PC operating systems also support it. The FAT file system imposes limits on how many separately addressable sections, or clusters, the file system can see. (A cluster is made up of several hard drive sectors, and the specific number is dependent on the type of partitioning system used by the operating system. FAT-16, for example, can use as many as 64 sectors per cluster.) The practical result is that FAT-based hard disk volumes are limited in size to 2GB.

Note

By the way, because the problems with the FAT file system are based in software, this limitation can affect hard drives that use any type of IDE-, SCSI- and even IEEE 1394-based controllers.

While this concept is very similar to the BIOS limitations discussed previously and the practical results are essentially the same, the two concepts are different in reality. Though logically you might presume otherwise, there is not a one-to-one correspondence between individual hard drive sectors and the clusters that a file system uses to store files. Again, clusters consist of multiple sectors. This can be very confusing, but it's important to remember that one is more of a hardware problem and the other a software problem.

To get around the 2GB volume limitation imposed by FAT, you can break up a larger hard drive into several individual volumes, or partitions, each of which can be no larger than 2GB. The other option for Windows users is to take advantage of the FAT32 file system, which is supported by Windows 98, Windows 2000 and later versions of Windows 95. If your operating system uses the FAT32 file system, your computer can see and work with drive volumes up to 2TB, or 2,048GB (although drives anywhere close to this size will run into the same inefficiency problems that led to the development of FAT32).

Secret

Even FAT32 has certain issues with hard drives over 8GB. A little-known extension to FAT32 called FAT32X helps later versions of Windows 95, Windows 98, and Windows 2000 work with these big drives, but FAT32X can cause big problems for disk utilities, back-up programs and other applications that work with the hard disk's basic structure. Again, as with the 8GB BIOS-related hardware problem solved with Int13h extensions described above, the practical results are similar, but the concepts differ in reality. The bottom line is, if you want to work with partitions that are larger than 8GB, you need to make sure your disk-related programs support FAT32X.

If you're using Linux, BeOS or other alternative operating systems, the native file systems for those OSes (such as Ext2 for Linux) do not have the 2 or 8GB partition limitations, so you don't have to worry about these particular types of problems.

Drive specifications

No single component inside your PC has been more debated and boasts more dubious specifications than the hard drive. There are many ways to measure the activities that go on in the hard drive, and manufacturers in the drive arena seem to go out of their way to pick the spec that makes their drive look the best (not surprisingly). As a result, you need to take certain drive specs, particularly access times and throughput (both of which are explained a bit later) with a grain of salt. Unless two drives are measured identically, their measurements may not provide an apples-to-apples comparison. Nevertheless, there are a number of specifications you can look for in your hard drive or complete system shopping.

Drive speed

The most important specification to look for in a hard drive, other than the type of connection it requires, is the drive's speed, or overall performance. Unfortunately, this isn't always very easy to determine because there are a number of factors that affect a hard drive's performance. They include: how fast the disks inside the drive mechanism rotate, the amount of cache memory built into the drive, the type of controller mechanism and interface used to "talk" to the drive, and more.

Secret

Many specifications used to describe a hard drive's speed are confusingly similar and can be used to manipulate you into thinking one drive is faster than another, when in real-world performance, the opposite may be true.

Your efforts to decipher it all are definitely worth it, though. Virtually all computing activities begin and end at the hard disk, and the hard drive's speed plays a critical factor in a computer's overall performance.

Secret

In many instances, the hard drive can have a larger impact on the overall speed of a computer system than the processor.

When the computer starts up, or when you start an application, the data is read off the hard drive and into working memory, and when you create and save a file, the results are saved from memory back to your disk. In addition, there are thousands and thousands of small dialogues between your hard disk and memory while your computer is running. So, if these communications happen quickly, your PC is fast and responsive and if they don't, well, it's part of the reason those spinning clock icons that you can look at while you wait for your computer to finish working were developed.

Access time

The time it takes a hard disk (or any other storage device) to get to the next chunk of data it needs is called the *access time*. The most important access time measurement, and the one you should use to make comparisons between drives, is officially called the *average access time*. It consists of averages of the fastest and slowest possible access times for a given hard drive and, consequently, offers the most realistic view of hard drive performance. Unfortunately, some vendors don't quote the average access time in their product brochures or specification sheets; instead, they show best-case scenarios so it can be difficult to track this number down.

The differences in access time, by the way, result from differences in the physical location of the data being accessed. If the next bit of data or next available open location happens to be situated right in front of the read/write head's current position, then the access time to read this bit of data is tiny. But, if the data happens to be just behind the head, or on the other side of the cylinder from the head, the disk has to do a full revolution before the head can read it; this results in a much slower access time. The average access time is an approximation of how long it will take to read a chunk of data that is 180^0, or half-way around the disk, and half way across the platter.

Figure 3-2 shows the different issues involved with accessing data on a hard drive.

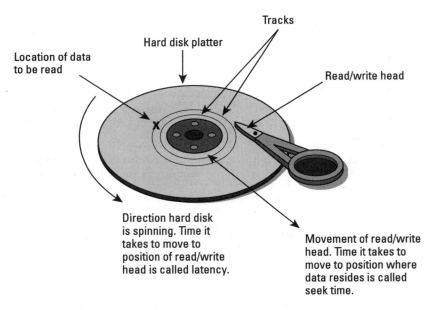

Figure 3-2: Getting access
Finding and reading a bit of data off of a hard drive involves several steps. First, the disk must rotate into position so that the section of the disk where the file is located is under the drive's read/write head. At the same time, the read/write head moves laterally to ensure that it is also properly lined up to reach the specific address on the hard drive where the requested data is located.

The access time measurement to the specific sector on the track is determined by two factors: the drive's latency, or delay and its seek time. The delay is how long the disk takes to spin around to where it needs to go, and seek time is how long the disk takes to move the read/write head across the appropriate cylinder to the correct track. Again, however, access time and seek time are sometimes used interchangeably. Some vendors will quote minimum access or seek times in their literature, which, while perhaps technically interesting, is virtually meaningless to real-world performance. Feel free to ignore it.

Many newer drives offer access times of less than ten milliseconds. While this certainly seems fast to you and me, remember that memory and processors work in nanosecond increments, which is a million times faster. In the real world, a difference of a few milliseconds in access time between two hard drives can mean a relatively big difference in performance.

Rotation speeds

The drive's rotational speed, which is given in revolutions per minute (rpms), is a commonly quoted specification that signifies how quickly the disks inside the drive are spinning. Common numbers you may see listed are 4,500; 5,400; 7,200; and, even 10,000 rpms or higher. Generally speaking, the higher the revolutions, the faster the drive. The reason for this is simple physics: the faster a drive is spinning, the shorter the time it takes to get to a piece of data located somewhere else on the disk. And because hard drives spend a lot of time looking for new data, this rotational waiting time can really start to add up.

Another related factor that affects a hard drive's performance is how quickly the hard drive's head, which is the part that actually reads and writes data, can move across the individual platters that make up a hard disk. Like the needle on a turntable, a hard drive's read/write head is moved across a platter by a device inside the drive called an *actuator*. Unlike a turntable, though, the read/write on hard drive never actually touches the surface of the drive; instead, it floats above it on a tiny cushion of air. A tiny motor drives the actuator, which, in turn, moves the read/write head to a specific location on the disk where the data it wants is located.

Drive cache

The process of finding a requested chunk of data on a hard drive takes a certain amount of time, and during this time, the processor often sits around idly waiting for something to do. As a result, hard drive makers have had to come up with a number of different tricks to try and feed the computer's memory (which, then, feeds the processor) as quickly as possible. One of the most important is borrowed from the world of RAM and is called a *buffer*, or cache.

As with RAM, often times the computer needs to reaccess some of the same data that it just read off the disk. To make this process faster, hard drives include a small amount of their own memory (typically less than one megabyte, though the amount can vary widely), which is built into the drive mechanism. This onboard memory functions as a disk cache. Like other types of cache, this memory stores recently accessed data.

If the CPU requests the same data from the hard disk a second, third, or even a greater number of times, the drive can simply send it out from its cache memory, which is an order of magnitude faster than reading it from the disk itself. (A drive's advertised maximum throughput figure often refers to how quickly data is read from the cache, which just goes to show you how deceptive a specification that can be.) Again, as with memory, larger disk caches typically translate into better performance, but you can meet a point of diminishing returns.

Note

Not that you'll ever have to worry about this, but just so you know: the hard drive cache typically does not consist of the special SRAM used for processor caches, but instead uses some form of DRAM.

Most operating systems, including Windows 3.1, Windows 95, Windows 98, Windows 2000, Windows NT, and Linux also create a disk cache in software by setting aside a certain amount of your computer's memory to function similarly to an L2 cache for your hard disk. The operating system stores data recently retrieved from the hard disk in its own disk cache. In the case of hard drives, the operating system usually checks its own software disk cache for the data it needs first, checks the disk's own cache, and then, if it needs to, reads the data from the disk itself.

Throughput

All of this theoretical gobbledygook actually translates into a meaningful specification that you need to be aware of when you compare hard drives; it is the drive's sustained throughput. Throughput is how fast the drive can pump out a long string of data in a single session. Launching programs or opening big files often entails loading a large chunk of data into memory at once, so the sustained throughput (which is typically measured in MB/second) has a big impact on real-world performance. The higher the throughput, the faster the hard drive (and thus the computer) can start an application or load a file, and the faster you can get something done.

As you might suspect, a drive's rotational speed has the biggest impact on this number because the faster a drive spins, the more quickly it can read new bits of data. However, getting drives to work reliably at speeds such as 10,000 rpm or faster isn't easy, and this is why these fast drives tend to be expensive.

Density

Another factor that impacts a hard drive's performance and storage capacity is how tightly the data is packed onto the disk, which is sometimes referred to as the *areal density*. In the early 1990s, IBM developed a new method for cramming more data onto a typical disk by improving the accuracy of the disk drive head, which reads and writes the data.

Note

Reading and writing the data, by the way, consists of nothing more than creating a magnetic orientation — or not — and reading the presence or lack of magnetic orientation at a particular point on the disk. Remember that computers deal only with ones or zeros, or frankly just on or off signals, and hard drives simply record very long strings of these magnetic orientations at a blindingly fast pace. It takes software to turn these Morse code-like signals into something meaningful to you and me.

IBM's Magneto-Resistive, or MR, technology, which is now included in drives of several different vendors, enables hard drives to squeeze more data into the same amount of space, thereby increasing hard drive capacity. Large chunks of the tightly packed data can also be accessed more quickly, which helps boost performance.

Dimensions

Hard drives come in many different sizes. Most drives found in desktop computers fit the $3^1/2$ inch form factor, which measures the depth of the hard drive mechanism. (The mechanism is the case that actually holds the hard drive inside it and attaches to the computer's motherboard via a ribbon cable — a flat, wide, typically gray cable that consists of numerous individual wires all wrapped in plastic.) Some older drives were $5^1/4$ inches deep and thus were called $5^1/4$ inch drives. Today's notebooks typically boast $2^1/2$ inch drives, and some devices feature drives that are even smaller. Figure 3-3 shows some examples.

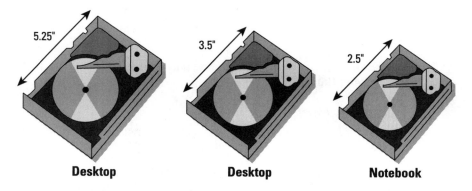

| 5.25" | 3.5" | 2.5" |
| **Desktop** | **Desktop** | **Notebook** |

Figure 3-3: Hard drive sizes
Hard drives come in a lot of different sizes, for different devices. In general, physically larger drives designed for desktops offer more storage capacity than smaller drives geared towards notebooks.

In addition to drive widths, there are also different drive heights. Full-height drives (or drive bays that can hold them) are about 3 inches high, half-height drives are about $1^1/2$ inches, and one-third-height — which is probably the most common size — are about one inch. In order to use smaller height drives in larger drive bays, you generally need to use adapters inside your PC's case.

The drive's physical size can have an impact on its storage capacity and speed; for example, $3^1/_2$ inch drives usually have larger capacities and somewhat better performance than smaller drives, although there's no direct correlation. You can certainly find $2^1/_2$ inch notebook drives that offer larger capacities and faster speeds than $3^1/_2$ inch drives.

The main reason $3^1/_2$ inch drives typically perform better has more to do with economics than technology. Desktop computers, the largest segment of the computer market, use $3^1/_2$ inch drives as their primary drive. As a result, technological innovations, such as increases in capacity and improvements in speed, often happen for $3^1/_2$ inch drives first. As more people begin to buy and use notebooks, the roles will undoubtedly change—just as they did between $5^1/_4$ inch drives and $3^1/_2$ inch drives—and then, perhaps, innovations will happen for smaller drives first.

Drive size is important if you replace your existing hard drive or add an additional drive to a computer because your computer's case may only have room for certain size devices. It is important to look at the type of drive bays your computer has; this is the place where the new drives will be physically located. Computers with two $3^1/_2$ inch drive bays and one $5^1/_4$ inch bay are common, but the larger $5^1/_4$ inch bays are becoming increasingly rare. However, if you have any $5^1/_4$ inch hard drives or other devices you want to use in a system, be sure to find a system with a case that supports it.

Notebook users who replace their existing hard drives most often need $2^1/_2$ inch drives, although sometimes other sizes will fit into their notebook's casing.

Cross-Reference

For more information on upgrading hard drives, see Chapter 10, "Adding and Removing Hardware."

Device Bay

While most storage devices, such as hard drives, install inside a computer's case, the new Device Bay specification, found in some new PCs that conform to the PC 98 and PC 99 specifications, enables fixed hard drives, as well as removable hard drives and other computer peripherals, to slide into a special slot inside the computer's case. (See Chapter 1, "How to Buy a Computer System" for more.) Best of all, it can usually be done while the computer is turned on and running, thanks to a technology called *hot-plugging*. As its name implies, hot-plugging enables devices to be plugged in and recognized while the system is still hot, or turned on.

On computers equipped with Device Bay-compatible expansion slots, you simply slide a Device Bay device into this slot, install the necessary driver software (or let the system install it for you), and then you can immediately put it to use. (In theory, that is—as with Plug and Play, it may not work every time.)

Inside the Device Bay slot are connectors for both the USB bus, as well as the faster IEEE 1394 bus. The device will connect to and use whichever bus it was designed for. In the case of most hard drives and removable storage, it is the IEEE 1394 bus, although some removable storage drives use USB.

Secret

You need Windows 98 Second Edition or Windows 2000 in order to use Device Bay (and IEEE 1394-based storage devices) on a Windows-based PC.

Device Bay comes in three sizes: DB32, DB20, and DB13. The numbers refer to the height of the opening in millimeters, and as you might suspect, smaller devices can fit into larger bay (with an adapter), though the reverse is not true.

Hard drive interfaces

The other critical factor in hard drive performance and compatibility is the language the drive speaks to the rest of the computer. The language is determined by the type of interface and the controller that the computer attaches to. A *hard disk controller*, which is typically built into most motherboards (but can be purchased and added to a computer separately), is one of many translating or bridging devices inside a computer.

Like other bridging devices, the controller takes messages and data from one part of the PC (in this case, the microprocessor and memory) and converts them into the native form of another part of the PC (in this case, the hard drive). A hard disk controller takes a request for certain data from the CPU and then issues the appropriate commands to the hard drive to find the physical location on the drive where the specific data is located. In addition to hard drives, a PC's controller often communicates with CD-ROM, DVD-ROM, and removable drives. A separate controller is normally used for the much-slower floppy disk.

Most computers today come with IDE- (Integrated Drive Electronics) based hard disks, and two IDE controllers (typically called the primary and the secondary controller). It's not uncommon, however, to find computers that also have SCSI (Small Computer Systems Interface — pronounced scuzzy) controllers and hard disks. In addition, some newer systems offer IEEE 1394 connections. In many cases, the IEEE 1394 hard drive connections are made through Device Bay slots, which, as I discussed previously, enable you to simply slide a hard drive into your PC without making any internal connections.

Each type of controller offers benefits and capabilities, including different numbers of devices, such as hard drives, that can be connected to a chain, different maximum transfer rates, and more.

IDE vs. SCSI

Many a philosophical debate has raged over the merits of IDE controllers vs. SCSI. The reality, however, is much more mundane. In today's iterations of the two technologies, the two are not very different in terms of their performance in basic productivity applications. The difference may be apparent, though, when large amounts of audio or video are digitized; in this case, some version of UltraSCSI is better suited to the task.

Functionally, however, there are some important differences between the two controllers. First, today's ATA-2 (commonly, but mistakenly, called EIDE controllers) and UltraATA-based IDE controllers can handle a maximum of four devices. Due to severe restrictions on cable length, the devices are internal — that is, located inside the PC's case. SCSI host adapters, on the other hand, can handle at least seven devices, in virtually any internal or external combination, and some SCSI controllers can even address up to fifteen devices. (Groups of interconnected SCSI devices are called SCSI chains.)

Also, SCSI's command set is much more sophisticated than the various types of the ATA standard; this enables SCSI's command set to work with a larger variety of devices, including scanners, some printers and more. If you plan to add other SCSI peripherals to your computer, you may want to consider a SCSI hard drive because you're going to have to have a SCSI controller anyway.

As mentioned previously, SCSI drives perform more efficiently than IDE drives in certain situations, particularly when they read and write large chunks of data, or do multiple things simultaneously such as record and/or edit audio or video, or do some other type of multimedia work. This is because SCSI controllers have their own processor and the SCSI bus is able to perform multiple actions simultaneously without waiting for the processor (as the ATA-based drives must sometimes do). As a result, SCSI drives are commonly used in computer servers or other environments where a great deal of disk activity occurs.

Some IDE drives have a capability somewhat similar to what SCSI offers. It is through a technology called *PCI IDE bus mastering*. Bus mastering refers to the capability of a peripheral — in this case, an IDE controller that's part of the PCI bus — to perform certain actions, such as take control of the bus, without intervention from the processor. In other words, the drive transfers data to and from the computer's memory without bothering the CPU. This results in a minor improvement in your computer's performance because the processor doesn't have to stop what it's doing to get involved with every activity occurring on the PCI bus.

Note

On some systems, turning on PC IDE bus mastering can cause problems, so make sure you have the latest drivers for your system's IDE controllers and check to make sure that your hard drives support it.

The reality is, IDE controllers are standard on virtually every computer you buy today, which means they're less expensive than the typically optional SCSI controllers. Also, because IDE controllers are built-in and simpler, they tend to be much easier to set up and troubleshoot than more sophisticated SCSI controllers.

However, with the introduction of Device Bay and the support for IEEE 1394 hard drives that simply slide into your PC like big floppies, even IDE-based drives seem difficult to use.

Interface categories

In addition to the main categories of controllers, there are sub-categories within each type. For example, you may not see IDE referred to as IDE. In many cases you'll see references to EIDE (or Enhanced IDE), or UltraDMA (sometimes called UltraATA). The sub-categories refer to the type of interface the hard drive uses to attach to an IDE-based controller. Both EIDE and UltraDMA are based on the ATA-2 standard, which defines how the hard disk talks to the controller. ATA stands for AT Attachment — a reference to the old IBM PC AT computer on which this type of interface first appeared.

An even newer version based on the UltraATA spec is called ATA/66; the 66 refers to the 66MB/second transfer rates that these controllers are capable of supporting. Previous versions of IDE controllers only supported maximum transfer rates of 16.6MB/second and UltraDMA, sometimes referred to as UltraDMA/33, maxed out at 33MB/second.

See the "EIDE, UltraDMA, and ATA/66" section later in this chapter for more.

In addition, there are multiple types of SCSI, including Fast SCSI, Wide SCSI, UltraSCSI, Ultra2 SCSI, Ultra3 SCSI and various combinations, such as Fast and Wide SCSI, UltraWide SCSI, and so on. Each offers different transfer rates and a few other types of enhancements. UltraSCSI connections, for example, support up to 15 devices and, in some instances, support hot-swapping, or hot-plugging, devices. With hot-swapping, you can plug devices into the controller while the computer is on, instead of first having to turn the computer off, as you need to with connections that don't support hot swapping.

See the "Flavors of SCSI" section later in this chapter for more on UltraSCSI.

The most recent type of hard drive connection is based on the IEEE 1394 specification, which is sometimes called FireWire, i.Link or just 1394 for short. Some initial implementations of IEEE 1394 support transfer rates of 100Mbits, 200Mbits, and 400Mbits per second, or 12.5MB, 25MB, and 50MB per second. Later versions offer 800Mbits and 1.6GB per second, which equal 100MB and 200MB per second, respectively. Other benefits of IEEE 1394 are that it supports up to 63 devices on a single chain (versus two devices per IDE channel and seven devices for most versions of SCSI) and it provides both data and power over a single cable. It also supports hot-plugging devices while the computer is turned on, much like USB (Universal Serial Bus).

See the "IEEE 1394" section later in this chapter for more.

Types of controllers

Most hard drive controllers in today's PCs are part of the computer's chipset—the core set of chips attached to a PC's motherboard. In some instances, the hard drive controller, or host adapter, may come in the form of an add-in board. This is often the case with SCSI drives but it can also be true with hard drive controllers using the newer IEEE 1394 specs. IDE, SCSI, and IEEE 1394 controllers use different types of commands to tell the connected hard disk how and where to write or read a certain chunk of data. As a result, the different types of controllers are not compatible with one another; in other words, you can't connect a SCSI controller to an ATA/EIDE or IEEE 1394-compliant hard disk or vice versa.

You can tell different drives apart by looking at the connectors on the back of them. IDE drives have a 40-pin connector (ATA/66 drives use a new 80-pin connector), SCSI drives usually have either a 25-, 50-, 68- or a different type of 80-pin connector, and IEEE 1394 drives have a 6-pin connector.

Although various controllers work differently, there may be multiple types of controllers and disks in a single system. You can certainly copy information back and forth between the disks; the computer simply treats each drive as an independent entity. There is one important limitation, however.

You cannot set a SCSI or IEEE 1394 drive to be your main boot drive in a system that also has an IDE controller attached to EIDE or UltraDMA drive unless the system's BIOS specifically supports it (and many do not). This is because support for the IDE controller and attached drive is built into the computer's BIOS and, in many cases, cannot be overridden.

Transfer rates

Probably the most important difference between different controllers is the transfer rate that each supports. This specification can be very misleading, however, because the speed only refers to how fast the bus is capable of moving data between the controller and the rest of the computer—not how fast the drive is capable of transferring data.

Secret

The transfer rates for the various connection methods need to be considered in light of the hard drive's own transfer rates. For example, if a hard drive's maximum sustained throughput is only 6MB/second, it doesn't matter if you attach it to an original ATA-based IDE controller (or any type of SCSI or IEEE 1394 host adapter, for that matter) because the drive can't run as fast as the "pipe" it's connecting to.

In this example, the drive is capable of running at a maximum speed without the artificial bottlenecks or slowdowns due to a slow controller connection; this is because the IDE controller runs faster than the drive. The only time there is a problem (and a situation you definitely want to avoid) is when the drive's throughput is faster than the controller it's connecting to.

Be aware that if you have multiple devices attached to a controller, regardless of their types, the effect is additive — that is, if the connected drives or other devices are all in use simultaneously. (If they're not, then it isn't as much of an issue.) For example, if you have two drives that are each capable of transferring 8MB/second and they are both reading or writing data, then you are transferring up to 16MB/second. This means you need to use a faster transfer mode, such as PIO Mode 4, or Fast and Wide SCSI (both of which are explained later in this chapter), in order to avoid slowing down the performance of the different drives.

Most drives, however, can't move data at rates anywhere close to the speeds the controllers support. So, practically speaking, increasing the bus speed can be compared to increasing the speed limit on a road traveled only by Model Ts in anticipation of high-speed cars. In other words, without faster hard drives, bus speeds really don't make much of a difference.

EIDE, UltraDMA, and ATA/66

As mentioned previously, there are several different types of IDE-based hard drives and several flavors of SCSI. Original IDE controllers used the ATA standard for interfacing with IDE hard drives, but because the ATA standard had a number of limitations, particularly with regard to performance, the ATA-2 standard was developed.

The ATA-2 standard outlines two protocols, or methods, to communicate with hard drives, and each has several variations. They are the PIO (Programmed I/O) modes, which are numbered zero through four, and the two DMA (Direct Memory Access, a method for transferring data directly into memory without any assistance from the processor) modes, which are labeled single word 0-2 and multiword 0-2.

The PIO modes specify different transfer rates, and the fastest mode (PIO Mode 4), supports up to 16.6MB/second. Similarly, multiword DMA mode 2 supports transfers up to 16.6MB/second. (Again, the ultimate rate of transfer is determined by the hard drive itself, however, not the pipe it's connected to.)

Most hard drive and system vendors don't use the name ATA-2 as part of their products; they prefer instead to use their own creations, which includes Fast ATA, and the most common variety, EIDE.

EIDE is generally synonymous with ATA-2, except that EIDE calls for double the number of devices you can attach to the IDE bus (it goes from two to four). EIDE also adds support for the ATAPI (AT Attachment Packet Interface) standard, which enables IDE controllers to work with devices other than hard drives, such as CD-ROM, DVD-ROM, and removable storage devices.

Another variant to ATA-2 is called UltraATA, UltraDMA/33, ATA-33, or DMA-33, depending on whom you ask. UltraDMA adds an additional multiword DMA mode (called multiword DMA mode 3) to the standard that doubles the theoretical performance limit of IDE from 16.6MB/second to 33MB/second. This means an UltraDMA-enabled drive can theoretically transfer data twice as fast as an EIDE drive (though no drive really transfers data anywhere near the "theoretical" limit). The most recent addition to the standard is Ultra ATA/66, or just ATA/66, which doubles the theoretical performance again to 66MB/second.

Table 3-1 lists the different ATA or IDE-based hard drive interfaces with their maximum theoretical transfer rates. Real rates are always much lower.

Table 3-1   ATA Interfaces

Type of Hard Drive Interface	ATA Specification	Maximum Transfer Rate	Maximum Number of Attached Devices	Types of Devices Supported
IDE	ATA	8.3MB/Second	2	Hard Drives
EIDE or Fast ATA	ATA-2	16.6MB/Second	4	Hard Drives, CD-ROM/DVD-ROM, Tape Drives, Removable Drives
UltraDMA or ATA-33	Ultra ATA	33.3MB/Second	4	Hard Drives, CD-ROM/DVD-ROM, Tape Drives, Removable Drives
ATA/66	Ultra ATA	66.6MB/Second	4	Hard Drives, CD-ROM/DVD-ROM, Tape Drives, Removable Drives

As with many technologies in a computer, the support or lack of support for the various transfer modes in a particular machine is determined by the chipset (which integrates the functions of the hard disk controller). If the computer's chipset supports UltraDMA or ATA/66 drives, the controller built into the chipset will be able to take advantage of the drive's faster performance. If it doesn't, it's still generally okay because most newer hard drives that support these standards are backwards-compatible with normal ATA/EIDE controllers. A hard drive advertised as supporting ATA/33 or ATA/66 will still function in a machine that doesn't support the UltraDMA or ATA/66 standard. However, it will work at the slower ATA-2 transfer rates (up to 16.6MB/second). Another option is that you can purchase a standalone controller that supports the latest standards and plug it into your existing system.

Flavors of SCSI

In virtually all cases, SCSI drives require a separate plug-in card called a SCSI host adapter. Some machines come bundled with a SCSI adapter, which means it's been pre-installed at the factory). This is important to consider because if the machine does not have a preinstalled SCSI host adapter, it will undoubtedly cost $100 - $200 or more to add one. Like an IDE controller, the SCSI host adapter accepts requests from the processor and communicates directly with attached SCSI devices after it has translated messages into the appropriate commands.

Like ATA or IDE-based drives, SCSI drives and controllers come in a wide range of types. In most cases there's a standard SCSI version that delivers the data in parallel over an 8-bit channel, and a wide SCSI version that delivers the data at the same speed over a 16-bit channel.

Table 3-2 lists the most common SCSI formats, with their theoretical (and not necessarily real-world) transfer rates.

Table 3-2   Flavors of SCSI

SCSI Type	SCSI Specification	Maximum Transfer Rate	Maximum Number of Attached Devices	Types of Devices Supported
Normal SCSI	SCSI-1	5MB/second	7	Hard Drives, CD-ROM/DVD-ROM, Tape Drives, Removable Drives, Scanners, Printers
Fast SCSI	SCSI-2	10MB/second	7	Hard Drives, CD-ROM/DVD-ROM, Tape Drives, Removable Drives, Scanners, Printers

Continued

Table 3-2 *(continued)*

SCSI Type	SCSI Specification	Maximum Transfer Rate	Maximum Number of Attached Devices	Types of Devices Supported
Wide SCSI	SCSI-2	10MB/second	7	Hard Drives, CD-ROM/DVD-ROM, Tape Drives, Removable Drives, Scanners, Printers
Fast/Wide SCSI	SCSI-2	20MB/second	7	Hard Drives, CD-ROM/DVD-ROM, Tape Drives, Removable Drives, Scanners, Printers
UltraSCSI	SCSI-3	20MB/second	15	Hard Drives, CD-ROM/DVD-ROM, Tape Drives, Removable Drives, Scanners, Printers
UltraWide SCSI	SCSI-3	40MB/second	15	Hard Drives, CD-ROM/DVD-ROM, Tape Drives, Removable Drives, Scanners, Printers
Ultra2 SCSI	SCSI-3	40MB/second	15	Hard Drives, CD-ROM/DVD-ROM, Tape Drives, Removable Drives, Scanners, Printers

SCSI Type	SCSI Specification	Maximum Transfer Rate	Maximum Number of Attached Devices	Types of Devices Supported
Wide Ultra2 SCSI	SCSI-3	80MB/second	15	Hard Drives, CD-ROM/DVD-ROM, Tape Drives, Removable Drives, Scanners, Printers
Ultra3 SCSI	SCSI-3	80MB/second	15	Hard Drives, CD-ROM/DVD-ROM, Tape Drives, Removable Drives, Scanners, Printers
Wide Ultra3 SCSI	SCSI-3	160MB/second	15	Hard Drives, CD-ROM/DVD-ROM, Tape Drives, Removable Drives, Scanners, Printers

The original SCSI standard supports transfers of 5MB/second, and SCSI-2 supports transfers of 10MB/second, which is why it's sometimes called Fast SCSI. The SCSI-2 spec also defines the option for 16-bit or two-byte transfers, which is called Wide SCSI. Putting the two together, you have Fast and Wide SCSI (no, I'm not making this up), which offers transfer rates of up to 20MB/second. Yet another flavor of SCSI, typically called UltraSCSI, or Fast20, also supports up to 20MB/second with single byte messages and, you guessed it, UltraWide SCSI enables two-byte transfers at this rate for a maximum transfer limit of 40MB/second.

The most recent additions to the SCSI family are Ultra2 SCSI, or Fast40, and Ultra 3 SCSI. Ultra2 SCSI supports 40MB/second in standard mode and 80MB/second in a wide mode; Ultra3 SCSI supports 80MB/second in standard mode (though no one uses this), and up to 160MB/second in wide mode. Practically speaking, these high-speed rates are much higher than you will ever need with a single hard drive on a desktop PC, but they can be useful on servers that use multiple hard drives at once in a configuration called a RAID (Redundant Array of Inexpensive Disks).

It's a RAID

In applications where speed and ultra-high data transfer rates are important, such as large network or Web servers, and professional level digital video editing, single hard drives just don't cut it. Instead, the notion of multiple hard drives working together in unison — a concept known as a Redundant Array of Inexpensive Disks, or RAID — was developed. RAID is important not only for performance, but also for critical applications that can't afford to lose data. These applications are typically found on servers. (The capability to maintain data even in the event of one hard drive — or other component — breaking down is known as fault-tolerance.)

There are several different types, or levels, of RAIDs; each use various numbers and combinations of drives, as well as different techniques for storing the data. The most common types include:

Level 0 supports striping; data is written across two (or more) drives as if they were one.

Level 1 supports mirroring; data is written simultaneously to two (or more) hard drives at once. This type of RAID doesn't offer any performance benefits, but it has obvious reliability benefits.

Level 3 supports both striping for performance and an additional dedicated drive for storing error correction information in the event that one drive breaks down.

Level 5 supports striping and stores error correction data across multiple disks.

An important wrinkle added with Ultra2 SCSI is the use of Low Voltage Differential (LVD) signaling. It is different from the single-ended signaling used by all previous types of SCSI, and a benefit is that it increases the total length of SCSI cables that you can run.

It is generally recommended that Standard SCSI chains be no longer than about ten feet total (this includes the cable length of all attached devices combined), but the LVD signaling permits cable lengths of about 35 feet. However, the capability to use long cable runs and maintain high speeds is dependent on all the SCSI devices attached to a chain using LVD. In other words, if you add a standard SCSI device to a chain of LVD-equipped devices, you'll reduce the length the chain can be as well as the performance of the chain and all the devices attached to it.

One thing that's shared across all SCSI types is the need to have termination at each end of the chain (and no termination in the middle). Conceptually speaking, termination is a means to denote the beginning and the end of the SCSI chain, and to prevent messages from bouncing back across the chain and interfering with data transfers. All controllers and most newer SCSI devices have termination built-in that you can turn on and off manually. Most SCSI devices, in fact, have automatic termination that first senses whether the termination needs to be on or off and then takes the appropriate action. Some older devices do not have termination, however, and require the use of an external terminator, which looks kind of like a standalone jack from a SCSI cable.

Cross-Reference

See Chapter 17, "Troubleshooting Techniques" for more on dealing with SCSI termination issues.

Generally speaking, as with IDE-based drives and controllers, the speed of the SCSI controller determines the maximum transfer rate of any connected devices. So, for example, if you attach an Ultra3 SCSI drive to an UltraWide SCSI controller, the drive's top transfer rate is limited to UltraWide SCSI's 40 MB/second transfer rate. In addition, because of the differences between LVD signaling and normal single-ended signaling, if you attach, for example, a scanner that supports Fast SCSI-2 to a chain that includes an Ultra2 SCSI controller, the whole bus drops down to the slower rates. Everything still works, however, because except for a few rare occurrences, SCSI devices are backwards-compatible. In other words, old devices will work with newer controllers and vice versa.

To get around these issues, some companies sell controllers that have an LVD Ultra2 SCSI connection that's distinct from the standard Ultra SCSI connection; this is so that each type of device can be connected to the most appropriate type of connector and can run at its highest rate. As a result, these type of controllers let you maintain two separate SCSI chains.

IEEE 1394

The most current option for hard drive connections is the IEEE 1394 standard. Some computers come with support for IEEE 1394 built into the motherboard, either through the chipset or a separate controller chip that's part of the motherboard. Other systems have an IEEE 1394 controller on an expansion card, like a SCSI controller, to which devices such as hard drives connect. Many hard drives that connect via IEEE 1394 do so via Device Bay slots, which are open bays that accept devices that conform to the Device Bay standard.

As with the other types of hard disk interfaces, there are several different types of IEEE 1394 with support for different transfer rates. Table 3-3 lists the transfer rates supported by the IEEE 1394 specification.

Table 3-3   IEEE 1394

IEEE 1394 Type	Transfer Rates	Maximum Number of Attached Devices	Types of Devices Supported
1394a (or 1394-1995)	12.5, 25 or 50MB/ second (these are commonly noted as 100, 200 and 400 Mbps)	63	Hard drives, digital camcorders, removable storage
1394b	100 or 200MB/ second (commonly seen as 800Mbps/ and 1.6Gbps	63	Hard drives, digital camcorders, removable storage

As with IDE and SCSI controllers and drives, faster IEEE 1394 drives work with slower controllers, but they only work at the rate supported by the controller. So, a drive that supports 400Mbits, or 50MB/second, that's plugged into a controller that tops out at 200Mbits, or 25MB/second, may be limited by the controller's speed. Remember, however, individual hard drives rarely hit the limits imposed by modern controllers.

Another feature offered by the IEEE 1394 standard is support for *isochronous data transfer*, the delivering of data of a time dependent nature, even if it means dropping small bits of it. Typical examples of isochronous data are streams of audio and/or video. For normal hard disk storage usage isochronous data transfer would be disastrous, but for audio and video playback, which need to maintain a steady rate, it can be very beneficial.

Recommendations

The easy answer regarding hard disks is to purchase the biggest, fastest hard drive you can afford. One immutable law of computing, however, is that no matter how big your system hard disk is, you will eventually fill it. So, there's no such thing as too much hard disk space (though it may appear that way at first).

But while size is easy to quantify, speed isn't. Two critical factors to consider when you try to determine a hard drive's speed are the drive's access time and its sustained throughput. You want the lowest access time possible and the highest sustained throughput. As you do comparison shopping, you'll undoubtedly notice that the two aren't necessarily related. Just because a disk has a fast access time doesn't mean it has the fastest possible throughput. In situations where you need to make a choice, opt for the faster access time, because the day-to-day operation of a computer involves constantly grabbing bits of data from the hard disk and improved access time has a bigger overall impact on performance than the sustained throughput.

In some computer systems, you will not be able to choose the controller. But if you are able to choose, the decision is more philosophical and economical than performance-related — that is, if you are only using standard applications. UltraATA and UltraSCSI drives perform similarly for typical productivity applications, but if you want the flexibility of attaching multiple devices to your computer (such as a removable drive and/or a scanner), SCSI may be a better choice — albeit more expensive. If you're interested in digital audio or video applications that move large amounts of data to and from the hard disk, then you should also go with SCSI. IDE controllers and UltraATA drives, on the other hand, are generally easier to configure and cost less.

IEEE 1394 is the interface of the future; it offers both excellent performance and convenience, particularly in conjunction with Device Bay. If you can find an IEEE 1394-based drive that meets your needs, it should be the best choice.

Removable Drives

Hard drives are great for storing programs and information that you create on your computer, but they don't provide the physical means to take your data with you.

This is where removable drives, or *removable storage devices*, come in. The simplest removable storage device is the good old floppy drive, which enables you to bring information to or take information from your computer via lightweight, transportable disks.

Many of today's computers also come with some type of removable storage device, such as a Zip drive, that provides an easy means to move large files into and out of the computer. The typical floppy drives, with a 1.44MB capacity, simply aren't big enough for the large files and applications used nowadays.

A floppy drive (like other removable storage devices) can move data into or out of the computer because the media — which is the physical entity that holds the data can be written on and read from. In other words, floppy disks receive bits of data and store them, as well as provide a means to retrieve data that has previously been stored. A high-tech definition for this capability is that floppies are read/write media.

Figure 3-4 shows the basic concepts involved in removable storage, such as a floppy drive.

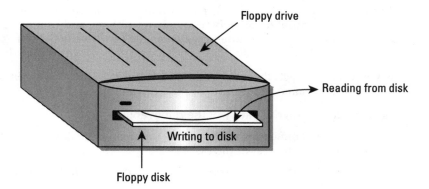

Floppy drive

Reading from disk

Writing to disk

Floppy disk

Figure 3-4: Read and write
Floppy drives, like other types of removable storage devices, permit you to both read from and write to individual pieces of media — in this case, a floppy disk that is inserted into the drive.

Other common removable storage drives that use read/write media are Iomega Zip and Jaz drives, and CD-ReWritable (CD-RW) drives. There are also various types of recordable DVD drives, such as DVD-RAM and DVD+RW, tape drives, and any of a host of similar devices.

As with hard drives, removable storage devices differ from one another in the amount of data each fits on a single disk or similar media, and the speed each transfers data.

Table 3-4 lists the storage capacity and sustained transfer rates of several common removable disk varieties.

Table 3-4   The Details on Removable Storage Devices

Removable Drive	Storage Capacity per Single Piece of Media	Approximate Sustained Transfer Rate
Floppy Drive	1.44MB	62KB/second
Iomega Zip250 Drive	250MB	1 MB/second
CD-RW	650MB	600KB/second
Iomega Jaz2 Drive	2GB	5.4 MB/second
DVD-RAM	5.2GB (2.6GB per side)	1.4MB/second

Conspicuously absent from this table are regular CD-ROM and DVD-ROM drives, which are also commonly referred to as *removable drives*. They are absent because the *ROM* in their names refers to *read only memory*. This means that a computer can only read data from them, and cannot write data to them. (You can consider the acronym as *read only media*.) Technically, this is why CD-ROMs and DVD-ROMs are not called removable storage drives.

As you would expect, the most important features to look for in removable devices are the same as they are for hard drives:

- The total storage capacity of the removable device

- The type of connection, or interface, the removable device uses to connect with the rest of the PC

- The time the removable device takes to retrieve a chunk of data, called the access time

- The removable device's *sustained throughput* (how quickly it sends large blocks of data to the processor)

- The removable device's rotation speed (how quickly the platters inside the disk move); this has a dramatic impact on the throughput

- The removable device's shape and size (this determines the type of system it will work in).

Floppy drives

Virtually all of today's machines either come with floppy drives or another means of reading floppy disks because floppies are still the most ubiquitous way of sharing information with other computers. However, several companies have come up with some interesting alternatives to floppies.

The Imation LS-120, or SuperDisk, for example, is a clever device that can read and write regular 720KB and 1.44MB floppy disks, as well as special 120MB floppies. *Flopticals*, such as the LS-120, are drives that work like floppies, but use optical lasers — similar to those found in CD-ROM and DVD-ROM drives — for more precision. This is an interesting option for folks who need the capability to read and write standard floppies (as we all still do), but also want something more efficient. The beauty of this device, which offers transfer rates many times faster than traditional floppy disks, is its complete backwards compatibility with existing floppy disks.

Sony's HiFD drives work in a similar manner, but offer up to 200MB on a single disk. In addition, like LS-120 drives, HiFD drives can read and write standard 1.44MB floppies.

Secret

The one critical issue to be aware of with these next-generation floppies is that your system's BIOS generally needs to be upgraded in order to be able to work with them properly.

Several other technologies have been touted throughout the years as the next-generation floppy device (including the popular Zip drive), but most of them lack this crucial compatibility, and without it, they stand little chance of becoming the new floppy.

CD-ROM and DVD-ROM

Virtually all machines come with either a DVD-ROM or CD-ROM drive because these types of drives offer the easiest means for installing today's large applications. Without a CD-ROM or DVD-ROM, you could end up having to feed 50, 100, or even more floppies into your computer — one at a time — just to install a software program!

CD-ROM drives were the original multimedia enhancement to PCs, offering about 650MB of storage for large audio and video files, in addition to programs and data files. DVD-ROM is a next-generation storage media for computers that is completely backwards-compatible with CD-ROMs, as well as the digital video disks you can buy for your TV or home theater system. This means DVD-ROM drives can read and playback virtually any kind of shiny silver 5-inch disc , whether it's a CD-ROM, an audio CD, a digital video disc movie, a DVD-ROM title, or a software program.

You can use many DVD software disks with just a DVD-ROM drive attached to your PC. But a decoder is required to view DVD movie disks, or any DVD-ROMs that take advantage of the high-quality MPEG-2 video and Dolby Digital (sometimes also called AC-3) audio support that's part of the DVD standard. A decoder, which is available both as a hardware plug-in card, or in software form, takes the MPEG-2 and Dolby Digital data streams off the DVD disc and converts them into standard video and audio signals that can then be passed along to your system's video and sound cards. When they were first introduced, most DVD-ROM drives were bundled with hardware decoders, but as processors have become faster and faster, software-only decoders that use the CPU to do the decoding work are becoming viable options.

The first generation of DVD-ROM disks can hold over four 4GB (about seven times that of a normal CD) and later generations can hold and read about 17GB (four times the capacity of the original disks). Virtually all DVD-ROM players can read both the lower and higher capacity DVD disks, although disks with more than 9GB of data take advantage of DVD's capability to hold data on both sides of the disk. Such disks may need to be turned over (unless you've got a drive that can read double-sided disks without flipping them).

Table 3-5 offers a comparison of the different CD and DVD media.

Table 3-5   Storage Capacity of CDs and DVDs

Drive	*Storage Capacity*
CD-ROM	650MB
DVD-ROM (first generation)	4.7GB
DVD-ROM (second generation)	17.0GB

DVD-ROM drives are clearly technically superior to CD-ROM drives; they can read existing CD-ROMs as well as DVD-ROM and DVD video disks, whereas CD-ROM drives can only read CD-ROMs. Yet, some computer vendors sell computers with the less expensive CD-ROMs. This is because there aren't many DVD-ROM disks available to take advantage of the new format, and because some CD-ROM drives can play existing CD-ROMs faster than the multipurpose DVD-ROM drives.

Rotation speeds

A major difference between CD-ROMs and DVD-ROMs is the speed at which the drives read the data. The speed is the result of how fast the drive spins (and the resulting data transfer rate), its access time, and the type of controller used to connect to the drive. If you're feeling a sense of déjà vu right now that's because yes, these are the same factors I just wrote about when distinguishing hard drives. In fact, any type of storage device — including the removable storage devices discussed later in this section — is affected by these same basic principles.

The most commonly quoted specification for CD-ROM and DVD-ROMs is the rotational speed of the drive (given as 24×, for example). In the case of CD-ROMs, this number represents the multiple of how many times faster than a regular CD-audio drive the disc is spinning (and how much faster data is transferred from the drive as a result). Because CD audio discs were the prevailing standard when CD-ROM was first developed, the rotational speed of audio CD players has become the benchmark against which all other CD-ROM drives are compared.

So, in our CD-ROM drive example, a 24× CD-ROM drive spins discs 24 times faster than your stereo's CD player. (Of course, to be able to playback normal audio CDs and not have them sound like ultrasonic chipmunks, all CD-ROM players also need to work at the more leisurely pace of 1×.)

With DVD-ROM drives, the rotational speed is a multiple of how fast digital video disc players spin. A standard DVD player spins its discs about eight times faster than CD audio players do, so the first generation of 1× DVD-ROM players can play CD-ROMs at about the same speed as 8× CD-ROMs. Today's 2×, 5×, and faster DVD drives work two times, fives times, or whatever times faster, offering in the case of a 5× DVD drive, up to 40× playback speeds for CD-ROMs (and, of course, 5× playback for DVD-ROM disks).

Variable speeds

Unlike hard drives, some CD-ROM and DVD-ROM drives do not spin at a consistent rate; they speed up or slow down depending on where on the disc the data they're reading is located. However, the speed at which the data is read from the disc on these types of drives and transferred out to the computer's system bus remains constant. And because we're talking about computers here and moving data quickly from one place to another is job numero uno, this is what really counts.

The standard 1× CD audio rate converts to a mere 150Kbps transfer rate (which is not much faster than a $3^1/_2$-inch floppy drive's snail-like transfer rate of 62Kbps), whereas a 32× drive works at a more respectable 4.7Mbytes/second. In other words, a 32× CD-ROM drive can read and transfer up to 4.7MB of data off of a CD-ROM disc over the computer's system bus to the processor in a period of one second—a rate that is as fast or even faster than some hard disks.

Figure 3-5 illustrates the process of moving data off the disc and into the processor.

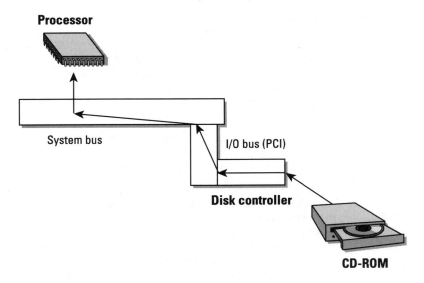

Figure 3-5: From shining disc to speedy processor
Programs, files, and other data are read off the CD-ROM or DVD-ROM disc, sent to the IDE, SCSI or 1394 controller to which the drive is connected, and passed onto one of the computer's I/O buses, such as the PCI bus. The data then travels from the I/O bus to the system bus before eventually making its way to the processor. The faster the CD-ROM drives spins and moves its laser light-based read head over the spot on the disc, the faster the data is transferred to the processor. In real world terms, the faster the CD-ROM drive spins, the faster programs, movies, and games load and run.

Now, you may notice that I say some CD-ROM and DVD-ROM drives work this way. Other drives break the rules and spin the disc at a consistent rate. This results in a variable data transfer rate, such as CD-ROM drives that are quoted as being 20-40×. When a drive like this reads data located at the inner part of the disc, where the individual data sectors are closer to each other, it can transfer data at its higher rate. But, as soon as it needs to read something on the outer edges of the disc, the transfer rates dip down to lower speeds.

Note

By the way, hard drives avoid variable rate differences by altering the size of the sectors on different parts of the disk. The sectors on the inner portion of the disk are larger and the ones on the outer portion of the disk are smaller; thus, enabling a drive spinning at a consistent speed to maintain a consistent transfer rate.

The best way to determine how variable speed CD-ROM drives compare to other fixed-rate drives is to simply split the difference between the two. So, in the example of a drive listed as 20-40×, it would be roughly equivalent to a 30× drive. But, be forewarned: this transfer rate range is frankly more of a marketing ploy than anything else because 20-40× somehow sounds better than 30× (especially when it's quoted as up to 40× or 40× Max, as transfer rate ranges typically are).

Access times

The other critical specification for CD-ROM and DVD-ROM drives is their access time, which is quoted in milliseconds. As with hard drives, the access time for a CD-ROM measures how long it takes (on average) to reach a particular location on the disk (and then start reading the data located there). The access time typically relates to how fast the drive is spinning, but there isn't a one-to-one correlation. So, while a 32× drive usually offers faster access times than, say 24× drives, that needn't always be the case. More importantly, not all 32× drives offer the same access time, and this is why some offer better real-world performance than others. The lower the access time (under 100 milliseconds, for instance), the better.

CD-ROM and DVD-ROM drives' real-world performance — that this, how fast they are in day-to-day use — is determined by a combination of the drive's rotational speed and access time. (As with hard drives, a CD-ROM or DVD-ROM's rotational speed is directly related to its transfer rate.) In general, rotational speed plays a more important role than access time, but there are exceptions. When you install software, which typically entails reading large chunks of data at once, faster transfer rates make a big difference. On the other hand, with an electronic encyclopedia or another reference title, where you are searching for data on the disc, faster access times are more important.

Physical connections

As with hard drives, another potential factor in a drive's performance is the type of connection between the drive and the computer itself. Most CD-ROM and DVD-ROM drives use either IDE or SCSI connectors; that is, they connect to the computer via either an IDE controller (which supports the ATAPI standard) or a SCSI controller, although there are some external drives that use a parallel port or USB connection. And some newer CD-ROM and DVD-ROM drives support the IEEE 1394 specifications, and connect either to a controller on the motherboard, or take advantage of the Device Bay specification.

Tip

Removable storage device performance, such as with CD- or DVD-ROM drives and various types of cartridge-based drives, is not nearly as critical as it is for hard drives. The speed of the connection shouldn't be a big factor; instead, you should focus more on convenience in relation to the types of connections your system offers.

Some applications do demand high-performance removable storage devices, but they are an exception. Most larger format (1GB and up) removable drives will handle anything you throw at them with aplomb.

If you happen to purchase a notebook that doesn't come bundled with a CD- or DVD-ROM drive and you want good quality performance, you may want to consider a SCSI or an IEEE 1394-based drive.

In either case, you'll probably need a dedicated controller (unless your notebook already has built-in support for IEEE 1394). The notebook format for such plug-in devices is called a *PC Card*. In some instances, it's still referred to by its old name: a PCMCIA (Personal Computer Memory Card Industry Association) card. PC Cards are credit card-sized add-ons that are used to upgrade notebooks in a manner exactly analogous to how larger plug-in circuit boards are used to expand the capabilities of desktop PCs. In fact, PC cards are generally shrunk down versions of desktop plug-in cards.

Removable storage options

As essential as floppy and CD-ROM/DVD-ROM drives are to any computer system you buy, ultimately, they're not that exciting; it's the choices available in alternative storage products that are really interesting. Many computers come with at least one and even several of these devices built-in, but alternate storage products can also be easily added onto a computer system at a later date.

Tip

Because running out of hard disk space is a nearly universal problem, adding an alternative storage device is one of the best upgrades you can make to a computer.

Zip, Jaz, and other cartridge drives

The most popular alternative storage device is undoubtedly Iomega's wildly successful line of Zip drives. The Zip drive looks and functions like an oversized floppy, although it cannot read traditional floppies; this is why the Zip drive is not a true floppy alternative. Like floppy disks, Zip disks basically consist of a magnetic platter encased in a plastic housing. A metal *shutter* protects the disk and enables the drive heads to get access to the platter when the disk is inserted into a drive. You can easily insert and remove Zip disks from your PC's Zip drive and store up to 250MB of information on a single disk.

Zip drives come in several varieties, including versions that come with different storage capacities. Zip drives also differ in the types of connectors and connection schemes used to attach to the PC. Early versions were parallel port and SCSI versions, but the company later added an ATAPI version for internal drives on desktop computers and another version that fits into many notebooks. The Zip Plus drive is capable of automatically sensing and adapting to either a parallel port connection or a SCSI connection. The USB version connects via the USB bus. The Zip's only drawback is that it isn't particularly fast.

A larger, faster alternative from Iomega is the Jaz drive (available in 1GB and 2GB versions). Jaz drives use cassette-tape-sized cartridges to store large amounts of data, yet can move data around at speeds that are close to the speed of many hard disks, and are SCSI devices, meaning they use SCSI connectors.

Other companies offer similar types of removable storage devices, all with different amounts of storage, different transfer rates, different connection methods and different types of media. But because the media is different between drives, you cannot share disks between them.

Recordable CDs and DVDs

Recordable CDs and DVDs are another removable storage option. Unlike their read-only brethren, CD-RW (CD-ReWritable), CD-R (CD-Recordable), DVD-RAM (DVD-Random Access Memory), DVD+RW (a slightly different DVD+ReWritable), and DVD-R (DVD-Recordable) drives can also write data to special recordable CD and DVD discs (see sidebar "The many faces of recordable DVD" for more on recordable DVDs).

CD-RW, and the various flavors of recordable DVD, can read and write a single disc many times over, much like a floppy drive. CD-R drives can write data to a disc, but cannot erase or write over existing data. Similarly, DVD-R is an archival format for DVD only. So, if you need a rewritable storage device, get a CD-RW, opposed to a CD-R, or a rewritable DVD and not just a drive that supports DVD-R.

CD-R vs. CD-RW

Though they share the capability to write data to CDs, there are important differences between CD-R and CD-RW drives. CD-R drives were developed first, and were designed for archiving applications. This is very different than normal reading and writing of data off a floppy or hard disk. CD-RW, on the other hand, does what most people expect a recordable drive to do: permit you to copy data to it, erase the existing data, and re-record new data.

The many faces of recordable DVD

At the time of this writing, recordable DVD drives are in quite a state of flux; several proposed standards are being put forth by different groups of companies. Among the proposals are two types of rewritable DVD: DVD-RAM offers 2.6GB per side and DVD+RW offers 3.0GB per side. (There's even been talk of a DVD-RW, which is different still.) Additionally, there already exists a single DVD-R standard that offers 3.9GB per side. All three standards, like DVD-ROM, offer support for double-sided disks, which doubles their potential capacity. However, because DVD-RAM, DVD+RW, and DVD-R are in flux, these capacity numbers are subject to change.

Unfortunately, the two rewritable standards are incompatible with one another, and you can't use DVD-RAM discs interchangeably with DVD+RW discs. Each format is only guaranteed to work on its respective recorder.

Even worse, it's not clear which of these standards will be capable of being read by regular DVD-ROM drives. As a result, the recordable DVD arena is probably something you should avoid until there's a clear consensus on a single standard.

Now, if you're wondering why anyone would ever want a CD-R drive instead of a CD-RW drive, there are many good reasons. CD-R is perfect for recording data that you don't want to write over, such as a collection of photographs, a music CD, a permanent backup of certain files. Recording on a CD-R is like making a video or audiotape and then breaking out the tab that prevents you from ever recording over what's on the tape. (One important difference is that if you make a mistake with a CD-R, you need to toss the disc and start over again.)

CD-R discs are also much cheaper than CD-RW media, and this makes them attractive to people who plan to use a lot of discs.

Secret

You are able to use the less-expensive CD-R media to create CD-R discs on many CD-RW drives. So, if you own a CD-RW but occasionally want to make an archive disc, just use a piece of CD-R media instead of a CD-RW disc. Similarly, some rewritable DVDs permit you to create a DVD-R archival disk by using DVD-R media.

Occasionally you may hear a CD-R or DVD-R device referred to as a WORM (Write Once, Read Many) drive, because they create a master disc that can then be read on any CD-ROM (or DVD-ROM) drive.

Secret

You should be aware that some early DVD-ROM drives are unable to read discs created by CD-R and CD-RW drives. In addition, most older CD-ROM drives cannot read CD-RW discs (though most can read CD-R discs).

Disc formats

One of the most confusing aspects to these types of drives is figuring out which drive reads which format. As a rule, recordable drives can also read their respective read-only discs; DVD-RAM drives can read DVD-ROM discs, for example, and CD-RW drives can read CD-ROM discs, but not DVD-ROMs.

Compatibility among the drive types is a different story, however. CD-R discs can be read by most CD-ROM or DVD-ROM players, although, as noted previously, there are some exceptions. Similarly, DVD-R discs can be read by most DVD-ROM players. CD-RW discs are generally readable (though not writable) on DVD-ROM and recordable DVD drives, but they are only readable on CD-ROM drives that support the MultiRead standard. MultiRead support, which is typically only found in more recent CD-ROM drives, means the mechanism can read both CD-R and CD-RW discs, as well as normal CD-ROMs.

This means, if you record a disc full of material using a CD-RW or CD-R drive and give it to a friend who only has a CD-ROM or DVD-ROM drive (but your friend's drive supports the MultiRead standard), your friend's computer should be able to read the disc without a problem.

Because of current fluctuations in standards, the same cannot be said for DVD-RAM and DVD+RW. Discs recorded with these drives may or may not be viewable by standard DVD-ROM. It depends on who made the drive. (See the sidebar "The many faces of recordable DVD" for more)

Table 3-6 summarizes which discs can be used on which drives, including which formats can be read and which formats can be written to.

Table 3-6   CD and DVD Disc Compatibility

Drive Type	Formats It Reads	Formats It Writes
CD-ROM	CD-ROM, CD-R, CD-RW*	None
CD-R	CD-ROM, CD-R	CD-R
CD-RW	CD-ROM, CD-R, CD-RW	CD-RW, CD-R
DVD-ROM	DVD-ROM, DVD-R, CD-ROM, CD-R, CD-RW*	None
DVD-R	DVD-ROM, DVD-R, CD-ROM, CD-R, CD-RW*	DVD-R
DVD-RAM	DVD-ROM, DVD-R, DVD-RAM, CD-ROM, CD-RW, CD-R	DVD-RAM, DVD-R
DVD+RW	DVD-ROM, DVD-R, DVD+RW, CD-ROM, CD-RW, CD-R	DVD+RW, DVD-R

*MultiRead-compatible drives only

Generally speaking, the rewritable drives are an attractive choice for users who only want a single device for reading and writing large chunks of data. They aren't always the perfect choice for all cases, however, because their transfer rates are often much slower than those of other removable storage options. Also, rewritable drives' read-only rates (which are almost always different from the rate at which they can write data to disc) also tend to be slower than the read-only rates of standalone CD- and DVD-ROM drives. For example, a CD-R drive that writes at 6x- or 8x-speed may only read CDs at 12x- or 16x-speed, which is much slower than standalone CD-ROM drives. Rewritable drives are a very good solution for backup purposes, though, because the speed at which the backup is made isn't critical.

Tape backup

If you're interested in a removable storage device primarily for backup purposes, you may also want to consider a tape drive. A tape drive, as its name implies, is a drive that uses magnetic tapes, such as DAT (digital audio-tape), or QIC (quarter-inch cartridges) to store computer data. Though tape drives have fallen out of favor in recent years (primarily because of their slower transfer rates), they offer cheap, high-capacity storage, which is great if you have to back up a lot of files (such as your entire 8GB or larger hard drive, for example). Different tape drives use different size tapes, offer different amounts of storage capacity, and feature different transfer rates. Tape drives generally come in IDE versions, although external SCSI versions are also available.

Many tape drives also use some type of data compression to store more data on a single cartridge. (Compression isn't limited to tape drives — it can be used with any kind of storage device, including hard drives — but it happens to be built into many tape drives as a standard feature.)

Note

Data compression squeezes files into a more compact format by using very sophisticated mathematical algorithms — like little software programs unto themselves — that look for redundancies in the data and then remove those redundancies.

As a result, you can often fit 3GB of data onto a 2GB tape cartridge. When the files are restored, which means copied back off of the tape, they are decompressed, using the same algorithms in reverse, and written to the hard drive in their original format. If they weren't, your software programs wouldn't be able to read the files.

Note

The reason why all files aren't compressed in the first place is because the compression process takes a certain amount of time. When you're working in a program and constantly have to save the file you're working on, you may not want to wait for the compression and decompression process every single time.

As I mentioned before, transfer rates are not important for backup, so I wouldn't worry about comparing the performance of tape drives. In fact, because tapes access data stored on them in a linear fashion, as opposed to the random fashion available with hard drives and other storage devices, tape drives are incredibly slow. Storage capacity per tape is certainly important, but the type of media used to create the backup is even more important. You're generally better off selecting a tape drive that uses common tape formats than one that uses a proprietary design.

Media costs

When shopping for a tape drive or any type of removable drive, make sure you look at the cost of the media, as well as its availability. It's not unheard of to have three or four pieces of media (such as cartridges) cost more than the drive itself or to discover that additional cartridges for your removable drive are very hard to find. As a point of reference, figure out how many cartridges or tapes would be required to back up your entire hard drive and then factor the cost of that media into the total cost of the system or the upgrade to an existing computer. You may find it changes your perspective on the drive you want.

Table 3-7 breaks down the costs of two hypothetical removable drives.

Table 3-7   Comparing Costs

Type of Drive	Cost of Drive (and One Cartridge)	Cost of 5 Media	Total Cost	Total Storage Capacity	Cost per GB
2GB Removable	$500	$750 ($150 × 5)	$1,250	12GB	$104
1GB Removable	$350	$375 ($75 × 5)	$725	6GB	$121

Now, if you don't ever intend to backup your entire hard drive with a removable drive, you don't have worry about this expense. It's still good, though, to think about cost breakdowns when you're making comparisons.

Cross-Reference

For more on file backup and other important disk care tips, see Chapter 14, "Working with Documents and Files."

Finally, as with hard drives, if you buy a removable storage drive that you plan to install inside your computer — that is, an internal drive — you need to make sure the drive will fit into one of your computer's drive bays. Most drives sold these days come in $3^1/_2$-inch form factors; this shouldn't pose any problems for your computer case, but you need to be sure your computer has an available place for it.

Recommendations

Removable storage devices are evolving so rapidly that it's hard to make recommendations I'm confident will be valid by the time this book reaches your hands. Still, there are some general principles to use as guidelines.

First, make the plunge and go with a DVD-ROM drive. It's unquestionably the technology of the future and you'll regret not having one if you decide to stick with a CD-ROM. Even if you buy a used system or are working on upgrading your own computer, I'd recommend upgrading to DVD-ROM because you will not lose anything in the process. You get complete compatibility with any existing CD-ROMs, as well as the capability to read newer DVD-ROM disks. (And hey, the capability to watch digital movies on your computer is thrown in for free!)

Second, be sure to get some kind of removable storage device, either internal or external, as part of your PC system. The type you opt for should be determined by the capacity and speed you want, which, in turn, is related to what type of applications you'll be doing and how often you'll be sharing files with other computer users (as well as the size of those files). If you'll be working with digital photographs, or video, or audio, you'll want a high-capacity, high-speed device. If, on the other hand, you'll only be writing a few letters, surfing the web, and tracking your personal finances, a smaller, less-speedy device will be just fine. Everyone should be backing up his or her critical files, so some type of backup system is important.

If you want to keep your life simple, you may want to consider a floppy alternative, like the LS-120 or HiFD drives, which permit you to read and write standard floppies as well as high-capacity disks. Another option is a recordable CD or DVD drive so you are able to read your CD-ROM/DVD-ROM discs, as well as store data on rewritable discs. In either case, you'll be working with only two drives, which makes things a bit easier. Remember though, until a standard is established in the area or recordable DVDs, things may be very confusing, particularly if you plan to share your recorded discs with anyone else. My recommendation is to avoid recordable DVDs until things shake out.

I think the best overall solution for most people is to have three single-purpose drives (a floppy, a CD/DVD-ROM, and a removable storage of some type). You get the best possible performance from each of the respective drives and you can upgrade or replace each one individually if you decide to do so down the road. If you purchase external drives, try to make sure you get models that support hot plugging, either through the dedicated USB or IEEE 1394 connectors, or through Device Bay-compatible slots.

Summary

In this chapter, I described the important characteristics of hard drives, CD- and DVD-ROM drives, and various removable storage options. I also recommend what type of drives to look for when you buy a new system or upgrade an existing one.

▶ Hard drives differ according to their storage capacity, the speed at which they operate, and the interfaces they use to connect to the rest of your system.

▶ Before hard disks can be used, they must be partitioned and formatted. There are several different types of partitioning schemes; the most well-known are FAT16 and FAT32.

▶ The size of individual hard drive volumes can be affected by a PC's BIOS as well as the type of partitioning system used on the drive.

▶ The most important specifications for determining a hard drive's performance are its average access time and sustained throughput levels. Unfortunately, finding numbers you can compare in an apples-to-apples way can be very difficult.

▶ The three most common types of hard drive interfaces are ATA/IDE, SCSI and IEEE 1394; each type has several different sub-types.

▶ There are several types of floppy disk alternatives that combine both backwards compatibility with existing floppies and high-capacity storage on specialized disks.

▶ CD- and DVD-ROM drives have similar specifications and concerns to hard drives, although they operate more slowly and performance is less of a concern.

▶ Recordable CD and DVD drives are an attractive solution for many applications, but not all drives can read all disc formats. Recordable DVDs, in particular, are not all compatible.

▶ When considering any removable storage option, you should also factor in the cost of the media.

Chapter 4

Video Cards and Monitors

In This Chapter

▶ You will learn how a video card works and what distinguishes one card from another.

▶ You will learn the factors that affect a video card's performance, including 2D acceleration, 3D acceleration, and motion video acceleration.

▶ You will learn about the features to look for in video cards if you want to add TV and video signals to your computer.

▶ You will learn important specifications to look for in both tube-based and flat-panel computer monitors.

▶ You will get recommendations on video cards and monitors.

A picture may be worth a thousand words, but when it comes to PCs, a picture is actually worth millions and millions of bits. Not surprisingly then, generating and displaying the graphical images that come from the heart of any PC operating system's interface requires a lot of work. Several different components, in particular the video card (or the computer's built-in video circuitry) and the monitor, contribute to this effort.

Together, the video card and monitor make up your computer's display subsystem; they make the interesting stuff happening in the guts of your computer visible. Each component has unique characteristics. Video cards, for instance, are complex beasts that perform many different functions and many monitors include more than just a tube or flat panel to display an image. At their core, however, the two components need to work together to enable an image to appear on your desktop or notebook PC screen.

Video Cards

A video card, sometimes called a video adapter, has one primary job: to generate a signal that a monitor can display. To do this, it takes instructions from the processor, performs its own calculations, and translates the results into a video signal. It temporarily stores the signal using the card's onboard memory (called a *frame buffer* because it buffers, or holds, a complete frame, or screenful, of data), and it passes the screen image along to a monitor, where the image is ultimately displayed.

Most of today's cards also have ancillary capabilities, such as decoding video streams off a DVD (digital video disc or digital versatile disc) disc or accelerating 3D graphics, but the basic capabilities are the first thing to consider when understanding and comparing video cards.

Most basic of all is the format the video circuitry comes in. While most PCs still use a standalone video card, some computers have the equivalent of a video card incorporated into the motherboard or the chipset. For example, Intel's 810 chipset includes a 3D graphics accelerator as part of its basic package. This means that computers based around this chipset don't need a separate video card.

Secret

If you want to later upgrade a system like this, you can turn off the video circuitry in the computer's BIOS Setup program and then install a new card. This principle generally holds true for any component that's built directly into the computer's motherboard.

Video cards (or built-in video circuitry) determine the monitor's resolution, which is the degree of detail that your monitor can display, the number of colors it can display simultaneously, and the rate it refreshes or updates the screen (the refresh rate affects whether or not you notice any screen flicker). Other than refresh rates, the monitor has no impact whatsoever on these various characteristics; it simply displays what the video card gives it. (The one exception is that some LCD (Liquid Crystal Display) monitors, such as those found in notebook computers and flat panel monitors, are limited in the resolution and number of colors they can display, regardless of what the video card's capabilities are.)

Video cards have a big impact on a computer's day-to-day performance, because the faster an image appears on screen, the faster the computer seems to be working. You may compare two computers with the same processor and the same amount of memory and notice that one feels faster than the other does; there's a good chance this is because the faster computer has a higher performance video card.

The following specs are important to look for in video cards:

- The resolution of the card, which is determined by the amount and type of memory the card has
- The refresh rate of the card at different resolutions, or settings
- The type of connection/bus the card uses to attach to the computer
- The types of acceleration the card provides
- The card's extra features, such as TV input and video recording

Resolution

The most common specification for video cards is the amount and type of memory used on the card. As I will explain in a bit, this directly relates to a card's maximum resolution. Generally speaking, video card memory is distinct from the memory inside the rest of your computer and only briefly stores the contents of your computer screen right before it's displayed on your monitor. The amount of memory, typically quoted in MB, determines what resolution (given in pixels, the tiny dots that make up a computer display on your monitor) the video card is capable of supporting and the number of colors that can be displayed as part of that image.

In real-word terms, this means the video card affects how much you can see on your screen at once, both in size and color. As examples, you may see part of a page or a full page, and you may see photographs that are blotchy and messy or smooth and beautiful.

Common resolutions, in pixels, include:

- 640 × 480
- 800 × 600
- 1,024 × 768
- 1,280 × 1,024
- 1,600 × 1,200
- 1,920 × 1,080

Typical color support is 256 colors (or 8-bit color), 65,536 colors (or 16-bit color, called *Hi-Color* under the various versions of Windows), and 16,777,216 colors (or 24-bit color, called *True Color* in Windows).

Secret

Some video cards operate in a 32-bit mode but offer the same amount of colors for display as 24-bit. Because of the way these 32-bit cards work with memory (8 bits at a time), the extra 8 bits are simply ignored. Other 32-bit cards use the extra 8 bits to handle something called an *alpha channel*. 3D graphics programs, games, and some high-end image editing programs such as Adobe PhotoShop use the alpha channel to determine the transparency or opaqueness of an image.

On a traditional tube-based monitor, adjusting the resolution on your video card can't change the physical size of the image you see. This is determined by the dimensions of your monitor. Instead, think of the different settings as different levels of magnification. At the lowest setting, typically 640 × 480, all the dots on the screen are larger and fewer of them fit on the screen because each one takes up more space on the monitor. At a higher setting, say 1,024 × 768, the dots are smaller, and the screen display appears zoomed out, because each one takes up less space on the monitor.

Figure 4-1 shows a comparison of these two resolutions on the same screen setting.

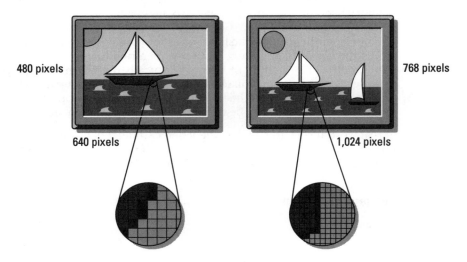

Figure 4-1: Screen real estate
At different resolutions, the amount of information you see on your monitor varies because the pixels are larger or smaller. At lower resolutions, the image seems magnified because the pixels are larger and take up more space, and at higher resolutions, the screen image seems zoomed out because the pixels are smaller and take up less space.

On flat-panel monitors, the pixel sizes are usually fixed. What this means is that selecting a lower resolution, such as 640 × 480, often does change the size of the image because the monitor uses just a portion of the screen to display the image.

Color depth

The number of colors that a card supports at a particular resolution is sometimes called the *bit depth* because it determines the range of colors available for each pixel on the display. To make sense of this analogy, think of your monitor as a cube with only one side facing you. The cube has an available range of colors that determines its depth; the more colors there are, the deeper it is.

With a given amount of video memory, there's a tradeoff between how large (in pixels) the screen resolution is and how many different colors you can see at once. For example, four megabytes of memory on a video card support up to 24-bit color at a resolution of 1,280 × 1,024 pixels and 16-bit color on resolutions up to a HDTV (high definition television) resolution of 1,920 × 1,080. Two megabytes of memory provides 24-bit support at 800 × 600 pixels, or 16-bit color up to a resolution of 1,024 × 768 pixels, or 8-bit color at a resolution of 1,600 × 1,200 pixels. Eight megabytes, on the other hand, enables you to see 24-bit on virtually any resolution.

Table 4-1 lists popular resolutions and color depths and shows both how much memory (in megabytes) is actually required to hold that signal and how much memory your video card needs to support these resolutions.

Table 4-1   Video Resolutions and Color Depths Chart

Screen Resolution	8-bit (256 colors)	16-bit, Hi Color (65,536 colors)	24-bit, True Color (16,777,216 colors)
640 ×480 (VGA)	.29/512KB	.59/1MB	.88/1MB
800 × 600 (SVGA)	.46/512KB	.92/1MB	1.37/2MB
1,024 × 768 (XGA)	.75/1MB	1.5/2MB	2.25/4MB
1,280 ××1,024 (SXGA)	1.25/2MB	2.5/4MB	3.75/4MB
1,600 ×1,200 (UXGA)	1.83/2MB	3.66/4MB	5.49/6MB
1,920 × 1,080 (HDTV)	1.98/2MB	3.96/4MB	5.93/6MB

You'll notice from the table that certain resolutions waste a lot of video memory. This is because memory can typically only be added in even MB increments; most video cards offer 2, 4, 6, 8, 12, 16, or 32MB of video memory. As an example, 24-bit color at a resolution of 1,024 × 768 requires exactly 2.25MB of memory to maintain, but in order to get this resolution, you need to buy a 4MB video card, even though you'll only use a little over half the available memory. The one exception to this rule is that some cards that use a little-known type of memory known as MDRAM (Multibank DRAM) offer memory in 1/4 MB, or 256Kbyte, chunks.

There's not really much you can do about this; it's just a fact of life in the world of computer video cards. It is important to know, however, that all unused memory may not go to waste. Some video cards set aside a portion of their memory to use for 3D graphics acceleration (I explain this in detail later in the chapter.) In fact, demanding 3D games and the technology used to support them can quickly quadruple your video memory requirements; in some cases it can go much higher than that!

If you plan on working with digital photographs or video, make sure you have at least 16-bit color at the screen size, or resolution, you want to work at, though 24-bit color is preferable. In other words, if you want to work with photos at a setting of 1,024 × 768 pixels (which provides a very nice amount of workspace, or screen real estate, on your screen), your video card should have four MB of memory. Similarly, most Web sites look better in 16-bit color, so even if you plan to browse through the Internet, you want to have the ability to display 16-bit color.

By the way, just because your video card supports higher resolutions, you might not be able to take advantage of them because your video card works as a team with your monitor. If your monitor only supports a maximum resolution of 800 × 600 or 1,024 × 768, then that's all you'll see, regardless of how much your video card can support. You want to try to match the capabilities of your video card and monitor. So if your monitor supports 1,280 × 1,024, and you plan to work in 24-bit color, you need to make sure your video card can support 24-bit color at a resolution of 1,280 × 1,024. If you look back at Table 4-1, you'll see that this means you will need a video card with 4MB of memory.

Video memory

The memory on a video card, which is often referred to as local memory, is generally divided into two main sections: the frame buffer, which briefly stores the image that's passed along to the monitor, and additional memory, which stores textures for 3D applications. In some cases, the extra memory is even referred to as texture memory, although it has other uses, such as buffering.

Cross-Reference

See the section on 3D acceleration later in this chapter for more.

Video card memory can be expensive (comparatively speaking), and not all 3D graphics calculations require the use of fast memory designed specifically for video cards — it's overkill in a lot of cases. To address the need of providing the video card with access to more memory, and to reduce the overall cost of building fast systems, Intel Corporation developed the *accelerated graphics port* (AGP). It enables a video card to work directly with a portion of your computer system's main memory, and it provides a faster connection to the processor and the computer's system bus.

Main memory is less expensive (and slower) than the type of memory found on most video cards, but it usually works just fine for storing textures and performing 3D graphics calculations. By using AGP, a video card can use a smaller amount of RAM for its frame buffer (which reduces the cost of the video card) and provide access to system RAM for the 3D graphics work it needs to do.

Cross-Reference

See the section on Video card interfaces later in this chapter for more.

Note

Some very inexpensive computer systems, such as those based on the original versions of Cyrix' MediaGX processor, as well as those that include Intel's 810 chipset, use the idea of a Unified Memory Architecture (UMA), in which the system's main memory is used for the frame buffer. The end result can be fairly anemic video performance compared to a standalone video card, depending on how quick the connection between the video circuitry and memory is. It's important to note that AGP is different from UMA in that it doesn't use main memory for the frame buffer — only for the extra memory needed to store 3D textures, perform 3D calculations, and so on.

Memory types

Another critical issue for video cards is the type of memory used on the card. Video cards have to move a lot of data very quickly to keep the screen display up to date.

Note

Not that you'll ever need to know, but just to give you an idea, at a setting of 24-bit color and a screen resolution of 1,024 × 768 pixels, the card moves 1,024 × 768 pixels × 3 bytes / pixel = 2,359,296 bytes just to refresh the screen. Plus, at a typical refresh rate of 75Hz, it does that 75 times a second, which works out to a transfer rate of 176,947,200 bytes/second or 168.75MB/second. This is sometimes referred to as the video card's bandwidth. When you realize that hard disks commonly move data at less than 10MB/second, you see that this rate is very fast.

The type of memory used by a video card has a big impact on how quickly these transfers occur, which translates into a real-world increase in how fast the screen is redrawn and how responsive the computer feels when you use it.

Many video cards use the same kind of memory as the working RAM inside your PC. For example, it's not uncommon to find older video cards with 2MB of EDO (extended data out) RAM. Many higher performance cards use special kinds of memory that, while based on the familiar RAM types, are specifically designed for graphics cards and work somewhat differently than their regular RAM counterparts. Memory called Video RAM (VRAM), for example, and SGRAM (Synchronous Graphics Random Access Memory), are based off of FPM and SDRAM, but can work at a much faster rate.

Cross-Reference

See Chapter 2, "Microprocessors and Memory," for more details on common memory types.

VRAM, and a variant called WRAM (Windows RAM), are referred to as dual-ported memory because they have two ports, or two separate means of getting data into and out of them — kind of like a front door and a back door. Figure 4-2 illustrates the concept.

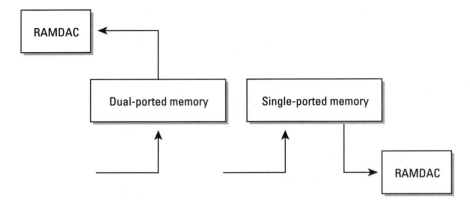

Figure 4-2: Dual-ported memory versus single-ported memory
Video cards that use VRAM take advantage of the fact that data can enter in from one direction, or port, and then be sent off through another. The practical result of this is better overall video performance and higher refresh rates than those systems that use older, single-ported memory.

With regular memory, data is sent to a particular location in memory through a front door and is read from that location through the same door — in other words, data goes into and out of the memory location through a single port. On dual-ported memory, data is sent through the front door and out through the back door, avoiding any potential slowdowns, for example, if data trying to get in the front door had to wait for the previous bit of data to exit first. Because video cards are constantly refreshing the contents of their memory, or frame buffer, to update the screen, this dual-ported memory scheme works very well in video cards.

SGRAM and RDRAM (Rambus DRAM), which are single-ported, avoid potential problems by simply running at a much faster rate than older single-ported memory. The end result is that they typically match and even sometimes outperform some systems with dual-ported memory.

Memory width

One of the most commonly quoted specifications for video cards is their bit width: for example, a 64-bit card, a 128-bit card, or even 256-bit video. What these numbers refer to is the size of the data path on the card itself and between the card's onboard processor/accelerator, the dedicated video memory, and, on traditional analog video cards, something called the RAMDAC (Random Access Memory Digital-to-Analog Converter), which is what actually generates the analog video signal that your monitor displays.

Note

Cards that offer a direct digital connection to a flat-panel monitor don't need RAMDACs, although some include one, along with a standard 15-pin VGA analog video output, for backwards compatibility.

Figure 4-3 shows the architecture of a typical graphics, or video card.

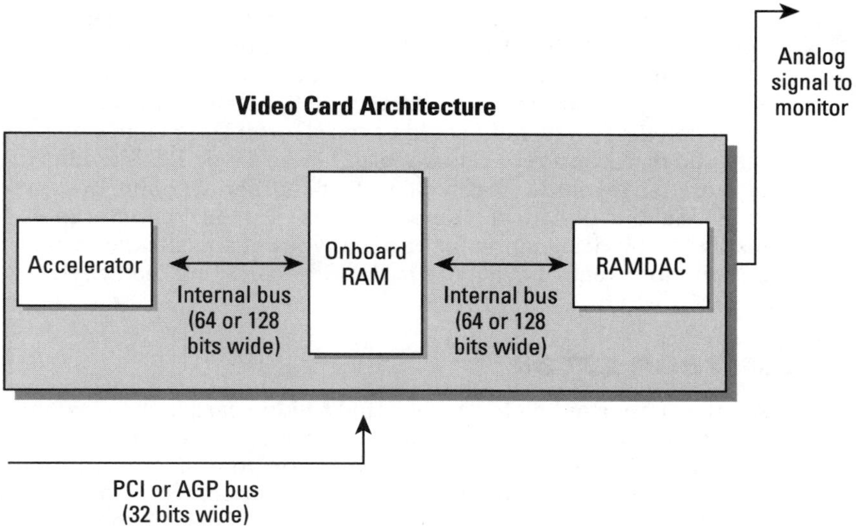

Video Card Architecture

Analog signal to monitor

Accelerator

Internal bus (64 or 128 bits wide)

Onboard RAM

Internal bus (64 or 128 bits wide)

RAMDAC

PCI or AGP bus (32 bits wide)

Figure 4-3: Inside a graphics card
Virtually all modern video cards, whether they are based on the PCI (Peripheral Component Interconnect) spec or the AGP spec, connect to the computer via a 32-bit connector; however, some cards communicate in 64-bit chunks, while others use a 128-bit wide path. These wider connections occur between the video card's accelerator chip, its onboard memory, and the digital-to-analog converter, or RAMDAC.

Secret

Though many people presume otherwise, the bit width of the card does not have any impact on the connections between the video card and the rest of the computer. Regardless of whether a video card bills itself as a 64-bit or 128-bit card, all external communications between the video card and the processor occur on a connection whose width is determined by the bus to which it attaches. While PCIs both support up to 64-bit wide connections in theory, PCI video cards still only use 32 bits.

In other words, a 128-bit video card is not necessarily twice as fast as a 64-bit card (though it's easy to unwittingly presume that is the case). In fact, a 128-bit card may not be any faster at all when it comes to real-world performance; it simply moves more data across its own circuits. Faster memory types (such as dual-ported VRAM) on a 64-bit bus can even outperform slower memory types (such as single-ported EDO RAM) on a 128-bit bus, so you can't rely on the specs to determine how fast or slow a video card may perform in the real world. As with systems in general, your best bet for making fair comparisons is to get the results of popular application-based benchmarks. The WinStone benchmark from Ziff-Davis Benchmark

Operations (`www.zdbop.com`), for example, has a separate graphics score that specifically rates how well the video card performs.

Note

By the way, the bit width of video cards is one of many examples of computer specsmanship. In other words, it's a case where the companies who build these products chose the largest number they could to tout their capabilities. Even though computers and video cards typically work with data in byte-sized chunks (sorry, but I couldn't resist) which are eight times larger than bits, the manufacturers choose to call them 64- or 128-bit video cards instead of 8- or 16-byte cards. Technically speaking, serial connections work with individual bits of data at a time, which is why the computer industry can justify the bit designation for various types of specifications; however, these designations really have more to do with marketing than anything else.

Refresh rates

Another important factor in selecting a video card is the maximum refresh rate it supports at various resolutions. Though the ultimate refresh rate you see is actually determined by your monitor, your video card's refresh rate is directly related (remember, the video card and monitor work together as a team to actually generate the image you see.) This is important because at low refresh rates, a CRT-based monitor can appear to flicker, which will quickly aggravate you and tire your eyes. Most people recommend that your video card and monitor run at a refresh rate of at least 75Hz, although some people prefer at least 85Hz. Ultimately, only you and your eyes can really decide.

On flat-panel monitors, everything is much easier. Flat panels are generally optimized to work with 60Hz refresh rates and have no flicker whatsoever, but some also support other refresh rates to remain compatible with existing video cards. (Using the higher refresh rates on flat panels will *not* give you a better picture.)

The refresh rates that an analog video card supports are determined by the speed of the RAMDAC, which is typically quoted in MHz. What the RAMDAC MHz rating refers to is how often data is read from the card's frame buffer and sent along to the monitor. The higher the number, the larger the screen resolution and the higher the refresh rates that a particular card can support. For example, a video card whose RAMDAC runs at 220MHz can support refresh rates up to 85Hz on resolutions up to 1,600 × 1,200 pixels, but a card whose RAMDAC runs at 180MHz can only support a refresh rate up to 60Hz on the same resolution; this would create an unacceptable flicker.

Note

In case you're curious, the equation you use to figure this out is: Refresh rate × Total number of pixels to display (1,600 × 1,200 in our previous example)/1,000,000 ×1.32 = RAMDAC speed (in MHz) required to support the desired resolution at the desired refresh rate. The 1.32 figure is a constant that's used to offset the amount of time the monitor is temporarily unable to draw pixels on the screen because the electron gun inside the monitor's tube—which is what generates the video signal we see—has to move from the lower right corner back up to the upper left corner.

Video card interfaces

Other than RAM, a computer's video card has the highest requirements for bandwidth of any other device in the system. In other words, it needs to have a fast connection to the processor and the system bus in order to be able to function efficiently and keep us from twiddling our thumbs as we wait for the screen to redraw. Today's fastest video cards use the AGP bus, but you still find many cards that use the Peripheral Component Interconnect (PCI) bus.

AGP

One of the most important developments in the world of video cards was the introduction of the Accelerated Graphics Port (AGP) in 1997. AGP is actually several different things rolled into one. Physically, it appears as a separate new connector on the motherboard of systems that support it. Functionally, it provides a new, dedicated high-speed means for communications between the processor, system bus, and the video card. Logically, it is capable of allocating a certain amount of main system memory, which is cheap and plentiful, as working area for certain types of graphics operations, particularly 3D graphics.

The AGP bus (actually, it's technically just a port because it only connects two devices instead of several) is based on Version 2.1 of the PCI bus and so shares a number of similarities with its predecessor. Like the PCI bus (see farther on for more info on PCI), AGP is an input/output bus that attaches to the computer's main system bus through the chipset, or AGPset as Intel likes to call its latest versions. (Note that you can only use AGP video cards in systems that include chipsets that support AGP.)

The AGP bus is 32-bits wide and runs at a speed of 66MHz. This translates into a theoretical data transfer rate of 266MB/second (32 bits/8 bits per byte × 66 million cycles/second), which is twice as fast as the PCI bus—which typically runs at 33MHz. In other words, even the base level of AGP bus is faster than the PCI bus for video cards. The real-world differences are nowhere near the theoretical differences, however. In many cases, AGP versions of video cards are only 10 percent faster than their PCI-based counterparts.

In addition to its base mode, the AGP bus also supports 2x and 4x modes where it can essentially transfer two bytes or four bytes at once. (The video card, its driver, and the chipset all need to support these modes in order to get the faster transfers.) This provides transfer rates, or bandwidth, of 533MB/second and a staggering 1.06GB/second respectively (at least, in theory—all bus speeds are listed at their theoretical maximum). Even better, the AGP bus is dedicated to the video card and doesn't have to share its bandwidth with other peripherals, as the PCI bus and other I/O buses do.

Note

In some ways, this makes AGP like an updated version of the old VESA Local Bus or VL-Bus standard found on older computers based on the 486 processor.

And in addition to the speed increases, AGP is also capable of setting aside a certain amount of system RAM for use with 3D graphics. What this means is that while the 2x and 4x AGP modes offers better performance for computer users across the board, those interested in playing sophisticated computer games and other entertainment titles may particularly benefit from AGP.

Secret

Not all AGP-based 3D video cards take advantage of this capability. You specifically need to look for support of AGP texturing, which is sometimes also called Direct Memory Execute.

The reason for this limited support of AGP texturing is that most local memory connections on the video card run much faster than even AGP 2x mode. As a result, for the best possible performance, it still makes sense to put more local memory on the card and use it instead; however, with the introduction of AGP 4x and the increasing demands of video games, this situation is bound to change.

PCI

The PCI (Peripheral Component Interconnect) bus, which is sometimes referred to as a local bus because it offers relatively direct, or local, connections to the processor, is at the heart of most of today's PC systems. It is now the primary bus for connecting different components inside your computer to the main system bus. In most systems, the PCI bus typically runs at 33MHz and is 32-bits wide, which translates into an effective throughput of 133MB/second.

Version 2.1 and later of the PCI specification calls for twice the width and twice the speed of the regular PCI bus: from 32-bits wide and 33MHz to 64-bits and 66MHz, which would be a four-fold improvement over most existing implementations. A PC's chipset and the plug-in cards and their respective drivers all need to support these faster speeds in order for the faster and wider PCI speeds to work. Sixty-four-bit PCI cards have started to appear, and there has been some movement towards 66MHz PCI buses on high-speed computers, called servers, that are used on networks, but it will be awhile before they become a primary standard, particularly on desktop computers. (Note that you can have one without the other: 64-bit PCI cards can run at 33MHz, and a 66MHz PCI bus can use 32-bit cards.)

Even with this increase, PCI is not as fast as AGP accelerated modes (2x and 4x), which is why AGP is still a better choice for video cards.

Cross-Reference

See Chapter 8, "How Your Computer Works," for more on buses and bus speeds.

Acceleration

Virtually all current video cards and most of those created in the recent past include some type of hardware accelerator that helps it keep up with the demands of today's fast systems. In many ways, the accelerator chips found on video cards are like coprocessors, working in conjunction with your system's main processor to generate the graphic images we see on our monitors.

Hardware accelerators work by performing common operations, such as drawing a window on the screen or moving a particular shape from one area of the screen to another. What this means is instead of the processor having to figure out exactly where all the pixels in an image of a window need to go, it can simply pass along a message to the video card that there needs to be a window drawn in a particular location. The video card's accelerator chip takes the instructions that are prestored on the card, and it calculates exactly where the individual pixels need to be drawn.

Not all accelerators are the same or work the same way. Some are capable of performing more and/or different instructions, and some cards are better at performing certain types of operations than other types of operations.

There are three main types of acceleration: 2D graphics acceleration (sometimes just called graphics acceleration), 3D graphics acceleration, and motion video acceleration. Each one of these is distinct from the other and requires special support on the video card. In other words, just because a card is advertised as having an accelerator doesn't mean it can accelerate every different kind of graphic that may appear on your screen.

2D graphics acceleration

The most common type of acceleration is 2D graphics acceleration, which affects all the standard shapes and screen elements that you'll find in most applications, including dialog boxes, icons, still photographs, and more. Today, it's virtually impossible to find a video card that doesn't have at least some amount of graphics acceleration. (Note that even though most video cards are commonly referred to as accelerated video cards, they really accelerate computer graphics, not the video signal you're used to seeing on your TV; that's a different kind of acceleration.)

The amount of 2D acceleration varies between cards, depending on the efficiency of the chips that perform the task, as well as the type and amount of memory in use.

Note

One feature you may want to look for in 2D video cards (or any other type, for that matter) is whether or not you can use more than one at a time (for working with multiple monitors). Windows 98 and Windows 2000, for example, offer support for multiple monitors, but not all video cards will work in that configuration. The cards and their respective drivers have to be specifically written to offer multiple monitor support.

3D graphics acceleration

Most newer video cards support 3D acceleration, although the amount and type of support varies widely. In fact, one of the most important differences among newer video cards is the type of 3D acceleration the cards provide. Any card is capable of displaying 3D graphics — fundamentally, a 3D graphic is, after all, nothing more than a collection of pixels on the screen, just like any photograph or your word processor's main window — but cards that tout themselves as having 3D features all have different types of accelerators that speed up different types of operations. The specific part of the acceleration process that 3D video cards tackle is referred to as *rendering*, which is the process of drawing pixels on the screen.

Cards that support 3D acceleration come in two basic types: those that include 3D acceleration in addition to standard 2D acceleration and those that only support 3D acceleration. The first type functions as your system's main video card and as a 3D accelerator, while the second type functions only as a 3D accelerator and works in conjunction with (and requires) a standard video card. These 3D-only accelerators often connect to a system's primary video card through a special feature connector or through a special video pass-through connector that connects the video card's output to the 3D card's input. The feature connector provides a high-speed bus between the video card and the 3D card. Not all video cards have a feature connector (or the right kind of feature connector), so before you buy a 3D-only accelerator, make sure it can work in conjunction with the video card you already have (or are planning to get). Because of these types of problems, stand-alone 3D graphics accelerators are becoming increasingly rare.

3D cards are used both for the display of static 3D images, such as complex 3D models or CAD (Computer Aided Design) drawings, as well as animated 3D images, which is what you'll often find in today's computer games. In computer games, 3D images, such as finding your way through a tunnel or driving a car along a racetrack, need to be constantly redrawn on the screen as you move through the game — so the video cards need to be able to generate many complicated images as quickly as possible.

The mathematics involved in generating these effects is fairly intense, which is why specialized hardware chips have been developed to perform them. As with 2D accelerator chips, the 3D accelerators differ in the types of operations they perform and the manner in which they perform them. Unfortunately, this has led to some incompatibilities between certain computer games and video cards. (See the sidebar, "3D game grab," for more).

3D game grab

If you're dead set on running a particular game, you may need to find out what 3D accelerator chip your video card uses. (You can't tell by just knowing who made the video card because some video card makers have used several different types of 3D accelerator chips. Conversely, the same chip may be at the heart of 3D accelerators from several different manufacturers.) Some game developers have chosen to only support certain chips, which means some games will only run on video cards that use those chips. If you try to run a game on a card that has a different chip, it simply won't work.

Part of the reason this unfortunate situation arose is that there was no standard way for games to talk to 3D accelerated video cards and so game developers took matters into their own hands and wrote directly to the hardware (a similar problem sometimes occurs with old DOS games that write directly to the hardware on older sound cards.) What this means is that instead of communicating through a layer of software that could generalize the requests made by the game and pass it along to any 3D chip that could fulfill those requests, those games send messages straight to the hardware. While this process sounds okay in theory, the end result is that many people get locked out of playing a particular game.

The growing popularity of common programming interfaces for 3D graphics, such as DirectX and OpenGL, means that this problem is starting to go away. Now, many game developers are working with these standards, called APIs (application programming interfaces), and letting the APIs pass along the requests for generating 3D images to whatever hardware accelerator is found on the video card. The end result is that more people will be able to play the games on a wider variety of hardware.

To ensure that you get the widest possible support, make sure any video card you're interested in has drivers that support DirectX and OpenGL.

3D Image Basics

To understand the benefits and differences between various types of 3D video cards, you need to understand how most 3D graphics are created. Most 3D images are made up of thousands and thousands of simple triangles or other polygons joined together to form complex shapes. The smaller the polygons, the finer the resolution of the completed image is. The trade off is that higher resolutions require more polygons that need to be drawn onscreen and manipulated in memory. A compromise solution is to blend the edges of side-by-side polygons to produce a more realistic, smooth image with fewer polygons. Common blending techniques for achieving this affect include Gourad shading, anti-aliasing, and various types of dithering.

To give the objects a sense of depth, various types of lighting effects can be applied to them, often through technologies such as ray tracing, which traces where rays of light from a given point would go and the shadows and lighting that would result.

Even with some of these shading techniques, most 3D graphics objects don't look very realistic. To add a new level of realism, many 3D graphics use texture mapping. With texture mapping you can apply any type of graphical pattern, or texture, onto a 3D object, much like covering a wireframe model of, say, a car with a sheet of colored plastic. Texture mapping is a very efficient way to generate high-quality 3D graphics, and most technologies now applied to 3D graphics have something to do with texture maps.

In fact, there are numerous technologies that affect how large or realistic the 3D textures can be (and how quickly the 3D video accelerator can manipulate them). Mip-mapping, for example, lets you store several different versions of the same textures at different sizes and resolutions and enables you to use whichever version the game requires at a particular point, depending on the size of the object on the screen. Bi-linear filtering, by applying a blur to the texture, helps avoid the blockiness and pixelization problem that can occur when lower-resolution texture maps get too big. Tri-linear filtering combines the techniques of mip-mapping and bi-linear filtering into one. Fogging effects involve blurring textures through the use of an alpha channel, which affects the textures' degree of transparency. This can be used to create a misty-looking atmosphere, for example. Finally, there are several different types of texture compression techniques for squeezing the highest-quality, highest-resolution textures into the smallest amount of space.

Speed

Frame rate is the specification commonly used to distinguish the speed of 3D graphics. The frame rate determines how many different images can be drawn per second. An NTSC (National Television Standards Committee) television video signal, the type used in the United States and Japan, runs at a rate of about 30 frames per second (fps), and most video cards run at rates of at least 30 (fps), while many go much higher. In fact, it's not uncommon to see video-card rates of over 100 fps.

3D graphics speed, like 2D acceleration, is affected by a number of different factors, including the efficiency of the graphics chip at the heart of the card and the type and amount of memory in use. The amount of memory is particularly important because many 3D graphics operations occur in local memory, which is the memory on the video card itself. AGP cards that support AGP texturing can also take advantage of the AGP bus to store the large textures used to generate complex 3D images.

Other factors that affect 3D graphics speed include support for various types of buffering, such as double, triple, and z-buffering. In double buffering, the video card sets aside an amount of memory equivalent to the frame buffer to store the already-rendered frame, or image, so that it can output one frame while working on another. With triple buffering, there are two drawing buffers storing frames in progress and one buffer that stores the next frame. The upside of this approach is that you can get much faster frame rates, but the downside is you have to use a lot more memory on the video card to do so. For example, to support 24-bit color at 1,024 × 768, you normally need 2.25MB of memory, but with triple buffering you need 6.75MB.

Z-buffering involves maintaining a record of all the z-coordinates, or depth, of each pixel in a 3D image in yet another separate area of memory. Then, as graphics are rendered, the video card can look to see if a particular pixel is in front of or behind the other elements in the image, based on its z coordinates. If it's behind, the card won't have to draw it, which can speed up performance. Different cards support different resolutions of z-buffers, such as 16-bit or 32-bit, which affects the depth resolution of an image.

Image Quality

The speed and frame rate of 3D graphics aren't the only important issue. The other important factor is the quality of the image in each frame. On 2D graphics accelerators, image quality isn't an issue because all the cards draw the same pixels. With 3D accelerators, however, the image is actually generated by the card, which leads to differences in image quality.

Early 3D cards only supported a limited amount of 3D functions and the result was that the images seemed relatively crude — it wasn't that the cards couldn't create more detailed images, they just couldn't do it quickly enough to maintain realistic game play. Most newer cards support a wide range of 3D functions in order to improve their image quality, such as tri-linear filtering, mip-mapping, texture compression, and more. In addition, many cards offer high amounts of memory for storing higher-resolution textures, or take advantage of technologies such as AGP in order to have quick access to large textures.

Tip

Even with support for these types of features, different 3D video cards still produce different image qualities based on how they implement the features. As a result, the best way to compare image quality is simply to look at images that different types of cards have created.

Motion video acceleration

In addition to 3D-acceleration, many video cards offer some type of motion video acceleration — faster playback of video signals such as you're used to seeing on your TV or from your VCR or camcorder. In fact, what these cards are really doing is speeding up the video decoding process, which basically means they are translating some precompressed video signals into a form that looks like a television display on your computer's monitor.

Let me give you a bit of background. Video is essentially made up of a series of full-screen still images presented very rapidly (approximately 30 times a second), which gives the illusion of continuous motion. To translate that into computer terms requires generating and handling a large amount of data. In fact, in its uncompressed, raw state, today's standard definition video signals require bandwidth of about 27MB/second, which is still a bit too fast for many of today's PCs to handle. As a result, video files used in games, references titles, and other applications need to be compressed to work properly.

Compression reduces the size of the image files by essentially throwing away certain bits of information. As drastic as this may sound in theory, clever engineers have figured out ways to do this — and produced mathematical algorithms which do the dirty work — in such a way that there's usually little visual difference between completely uncompressed video and a compressed version.

Software applications which use video typically store it in a compressed form. These compressed files must be decompressed, or decoded, in order to be viewed. The decoding process is fairly intensive, so some specialized video cards incorporate video accelerators that offload some of the work that the main processor would otherwise have to do.

Most video acceleration is tied to a particular kind of file format: the most common are MPEG-1 (which stands for Motion Picture Export Group, a trade association that developed the file format standard) and MPEG-2. MPEG-1 is an earlier, lower-resolution format, and MPEG-2, which is included as part of the DVD standard, is a newer, higher-resolution standard. MPEG-2 decompression is backwards compatible with MPEG-1, which means MPEG-2 decoders can also decode any MPEG-1 format files, but the reverse is not true; older MPEG-1 accelerators cannot do anything with MPEG-2 files.

Table 4-2 shows the differences between the MPEG-1 and MPEG-2 formats.

Table 4-2 Computer Video Formats		
Characteristics	*MPEG-1*	*MPEG-2*
Playback Rate	Approx. 1.5Mbits (or 200K)/second	Approx. 4-15Mbits (or 500K to 2.1MB)/second
Approximate Video Quality	VHS	DVD, HDTV

Because the processing requirements for decompressing MPEG-2 are so high, it's not uncommon to see dedicated MPEG-2 decompressor cards that work alongside regular video accelerator cards. In fact, many DVD-ROM drives come bundled with an MPEG-2 card that doesn't replace but works in conjunction with a computer's video card. As with standalone 3D accelerators, they often connect to the video card through a special connector on the video card (although some simply communicate through the PCI bus). Again, you need to find out whether or not the MPEG-2 decoder you want works with the video card you have (or want). Other video cards have MPEG-2 decoding built-in or enable you to attach a small daughtercard that handles this function to the main video card.

For notebook computer users, the connection comes through the Zoomed Video (ZV) port (see sidebar, "Zoomed video," for more).

Zoomed video

Because the video adapters built into notebook computers don't have room for a video feature connector, computer engineers needed to come up with a way to use MPEG decoders, as well as TV tuners, video cameras, and any other high-bandwidth video devices on a notebook.

Their answer was the development of a new bus (or port, because it only connects between two devices) called Zoomed Video (ZV). What Zoomed Video does is enable any device that's inserted into a notebook's PC card slots to communicate directly with the notebook's video memory, without having to take up any bandwidth on the PCI bus. In other words, it talks straight to the notebook's internal video card. Functionally, it works identically to the feature connector on many of today's desktop video cards, but it does so in the space-restrained confines of a notebook PC.

Not all notebooks offer Zoomed Video-enabled PC card slots, but most newer notebooks do.

Some DVD drives come with software that uses the computer's main processor to decompress the MPEG-2 video, but it only works on Pentium II-level or faster systems. While this is cheaper, because it doesn't require an additional piece of hardware, software-based decompression doesn't always work as smoothly or effectively as hardware. Plus, it puts a big load on the processor, which makes it hard for the computer to do anything else while it's decompressing the video. For an interactive DVD-based program or game, this could be a problem and may slow down the program or game's performance.

TV inputs

The capability to watch regular television programs or view video requires a few more pieces of dedicated circuitry (as well as a few new connectors) on a video card.

As with a television set or a VCR, a PC requires either a TV tuner card or a video card that incorporates a TV tuner in order to display TV channels on your computer's monitor. Both of these cards offer typical coaxial cable TV connections that simply plug in a dedicated cable TV line. For standalone TV tuner cards, the connection to the video card, once again, is typically through a feature connector found on the video card.

Figure 4-4 shows a typical connection.

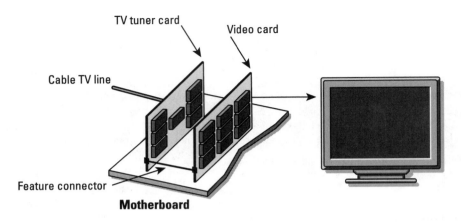

Figure 4-4: The TV-PC connection
Watching television on your PC involves connecting a cable TV line or antenna into the TV tuner card inside your PC. From there, the signal is sent to the computer's video card and then onto the display.

To watch your favorite shows or special digital TV broadcasts, you'll typically use an application that comes bundled with the card, although Windows 98 includes support for TV viewing directly in the operating system. In either case, you select channels, adjust the volume, and so on, through the TV viewer application. Some card/software combinations are capable of scanning through the close-captioned text incorporated into TV signals and notify you if a particular word or phrase comes up. This is a handy tool for serious investors who want to closely watch news developments surrounding their favorite companies or for anyone who wants to follow a particular subject.

Video recording

To watch and/or record existing video you need a video card with dedicated video inputs. Typically, this means RCA and S-Video jacks, which are the same types of connectors you'll find on VCRs and camcorders. As with the TV tuners, you simply plug the output of your VCR or other video device into these inputs, and use the bundled viewing application to watch it on your PC's screen.

Tip

By the way, if you don't want to invest in a TV tuner card but you do have an old VCR, you can use the VCR's tuner to feed live television channels into a video card's video inputs.

If you're working with a DV (digital video) digital camcorder that supports the IEEE 1394 standard (sometimes referred to as FireWire or i.Link) for direct digital transfer, you'll need access to an IEEE 1394 port, either built into your PC or via a separate 1394 controller.

Inside a video card that records incoming analog video signals onto your hard disk is circuitry that can capture and convert the incoming video signal into a digital form. While that may sound trivial, it's not.

The process of digitizing standard video is essentially like creating a 16- or 24-bit color scan of an image, 30 times a second. Figure 4-5 shows how the process works.

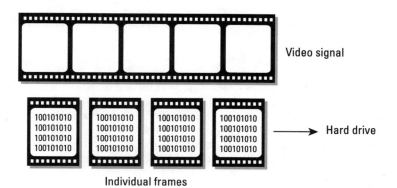

Video signal

Hard drive

Individual frames

Figure 4-5: Recording video to disk
The video digitization process converts each individual frame of video into a separate digital image. Once the images are created they are typically compressed before they are sent to the hard disk.

Given that a full-screen video image is approximately 640 × 480 pixels, capturing thirty 24-bit scans of that size requires a data transfer rate of 27MB/second — as well as 27MB of storage for every second of video you digitize. (For those of you who are interested, the math is 640 pixels × 480 pixels × 24 bits/frame × 30 frames/second/1,048,576 bits/MB = 27MB/second.)

This can get even more complicated because each frame of analog NTSC video — the kind used for normal TV — is actually made up of two separate fields, each of which displays half the picture. Broadcast-quality TV signals contain 525 lines of resolution (480 of which are actually visible), and, for 1/60 of a second each, one field displays the odd-numbered lines while the other displays the even-numbered lines. Because it happens so quickly, our eyes are fooled into thinking that the two interconnected fields are actually one image. On computers, however, each field needs to be digitized separately and then combined to create a single frame.

Secret

Some video recording devices only capture one field per frame, which negatively impacts the quality of the digitized video. Make sure you look for cards that digitize 60 fields per second.

Cross-Reference

For more on how use video recording for things such as editing home videos, see Chapter 15, "Working with Pictures and Video."

While the data transfer rates, or bandwidth, required to move data around the computer that quickly are now achievable, most hard disks are still not up to the task. (RAID, or Redundant Array of Inexpensive Disks, systems generally are up to the task, but they're usually quite expensive.)

Cross-Reference

See Chapter 3, "Hard Disk Drives and Removable Media," for more on RAID systems.

Consequently, most video digitizing cards use some form of compression to shrink down the digitized files and reduce the overall transfer rate required to handle those files. Some use industry-standard compression methods, such as MPEG-1, MPEG-2, or MJPEG (Motion JPEG), while others use their own proprietary compression schemes. This is important if you'll be working with particular video editing programs — you'll need to make sure the video editing programs can read files generated using the compression methods that your hardware digitizing card uses.

Today, virtually all cards with video inputs are capable of recording, but that wasn't always the case. When video input cards were first made available for PCs, they often only enabled you to view the incoming video signal on your PC and combine it with some computer-generated graphics — a process called video overlay.

Some external video editing peripherals use this technique to provide a low-cost way to edit videos on your PC. They offer low-resolution video capture but perform their final editing by remotely controlling VCRs and camcorders and then processing their video signal output with video overlay techniques.

By the way, don't presume that just because a video card offers video recording that it will also include the capability of outputting a video signal from your PC either to a TV or back to a VCR for recording. Some cards are designed just to input video for creating digital movies on your PC, and they make no provision for sending the signal back out to be recorded on videotape.

Tip

Frankly, you can't presume anything when it comes to video cards and video recording capabilities — you really need to double check to make sure that it has all the features you want.

Often times a single card won't have all the features you need, so check to see if the computer system you're interested in has the combination of video-related boards you'll need. Most current video cards that offer video recording include all the features you'd expect in a single board: video input, overlay, recording, and output — all of which you'll need if you plan to do something such as edit home or business videos on your PC. But again, it pays to double check.

Table 4-3 has a list of the important functions you'll want to consider when it comes to viewing and/or recording video on your PC.

Table 4-3   Video Recording Functions

Application	TV Tuner	Video Input	Video Recording	Video Output
Watching TV on your PC	x			
Watching other video sources	optional	x		
Creating and editing movies for playback on computers	optional	x	x	
Creating and editing movies for playback on VCRs	optional	x	x	x

Recommendations

Video cards have the most wide-reaching capabilities of virtually any peripheral included as part of your PC. They have evolved from the early days of display adapters, where they simply produced a string of text on your monitor, to the center of a cornucopia of visual possibilities. Whether it's accelerating the 3D graphics at the heart of today's fast-paced computer games, giving you the option to record your own video footage, or simply speeding up the display of a big spreadsheet, video cards make a big difference in the overall experience with our computers.

In addition to providing access to a lot of cool stuff, they also include many features that, to many people, are unnecessary bells and whistles. You need to decide for yourself which of the many capabilities a video card offers that you'll really need (or think you're going to need at some point during the time you own the computer) and which aren't really that important to you. There's certainly nothing wrong with getting a video card that does everything just because you want to — hey, it's your money, after all — but it might be worthwhile to sit down and think out what types of applications you plan to run and whether those will require a TV tuner, video recording capability, or what have you.

Computers that fit under the category of Entertainment PCs in the PC98 and PC99 specs (see Chapter 1, "How to Buy a New Computer," for more) are very likely to have these kinds of capabilities (they're strongly recommended in that specification), but they aren't a necessity for the typical home office PC.

3D acceleration, for example, is really only useful for computer games — if you don't plan on playing any games, it will do you little good, at least for a while. 3D graphics are starting to be incorporated into other software products and will eventually become a regular part of our everyday computer interfaces, but that's probably still a few years off — nearly an eternity when you're talking about the normal life span of a desktop PC!

As for features that are important, everyone needs good-quality 2D acceleration, and I believe that nearly everyone would benefit from at least 4MB of memory on their video card (8 is even better). By having 4MB of memory you can see 16- or 24-bit color even at high screen resolutions. If you're interested in computer games, 8MB provides room for at least some 3D textures for games or other entertainment-based CD-ROM or DVD-ROM titles. Purchasing a video card with 16MB or more is a bit luxurious, but as with regular RAM, it's hard to have too much memory — your system's performance will probably benefit from the extra video memory, particularly if you plan to play any graphics-intensive 3D games.

The type of memory on your video card also has a big impact on its performance. I'd recommend trying to get a card that uses dual-ported VRAM; fast, Synchronous Graphics RAM (SGRAM); or even Rambus RDRAM. Also be sure to get a card that uses the AGP connector, preferably 2x or better, because it will offer a boost over cards that use the slower PCI bus.

Monitors

Computer monitors display the signals sent to them by the computer's video card. Because they are what we look at and interact with when using a computer, they are one of the most important components in a computer system.

Most of today's monitors are based on Cathode Ray Tubes (CRTs), much like televisions, but flat-panel monitors which use LCD displays, which is the same technology used for notebook computers, are becomingly increasingly common. Flat-panel displays are more expensive than traditional tube-based monitors are, but they're much smaller, lighter, and more energy efficient than the older tube designs. (And hey, let's face it, they look a lot cooler too.)

The most important features to look for in a monitor are:

- The size and type of screen it uses
- The amount of detail it is capable of displaying, or its resolution
- The speed at which it can update the screen or its refresh rates
- The type of other components, such as speakers, built into it
- For flat-panel displays, the type of connector it uses to connect to the video card

Monitor sizes

Monitors are typically categorized according to their size. In a traditional tube-based monitor, the size actually refers to the dimensions of the tube diagonally from corner to corner. Unfortunately, this measurement is virtually meaningless because a portion of the tube is hidden behind the monitor's case. As a result, the specification you really need to look for is called the maximum viewable area. The maximum viewable area measures the visible portion of the tube.

Secret

Even knowing a monitor's maximum viewable area doesn't tell you the real story, however, because very few monitors take up the entire viewable area. Most leave a black border around the edge of the actual image. As a result, a 17-inch monitor with a 16.1-inch maximum viewing area may very well have only a 14.5-inch image area.

Figure 4-6 shows how all the various measurements relate.

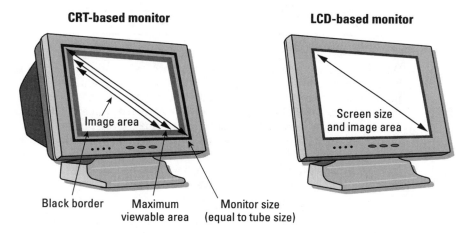

CRT-based monitor

LCD-based monitor

Image area

Screen size and image area

Black border   Maximum   Monitor size
viewable area   (equal to tube size)

Figure 4-6: Measuring monitors
To really find out how large the image area is on a particular monitor, you need to find out not only its maximum viewing area but also its standard image area, which you will never find quoted in any specifications. You have to look at the monitor and measure it yourself.

On flat-panel monitors and notebook displays, life is much simpler. Because LCD monitors use every inch they have to display the image, the monitor size is the same as the maximum viewing area and the standard image area. So, if you're comparing the size of a CRT-based monitor with that of an LCD monitor, make sure you measure the actual image area of each.

Secret

In general, you get equal image sizes from LCD monitors that, at first glance, appear to be much smaller than tube-based monitors. For example, a 14.1-inch LCD monitor offers nearly the same image area as many 17-inch monitors.

Monitor resolutions

Another important characteristic of monitors is the maximum resolutions that they support. Table 4-4 lists common CRT-based monitor sizes along with the recommended resolutions for those various sizes.

Table 4-4   Common Monitor Sizes and Resolutions

Monitor Size	Typical Maximum Viewable Area Measurement	Preferred Resolution	Other Common Resolutions
14″	13.1″	640 × 480	800 × 600
15″	13.7″	800 × 600	1,024 × 768
17″	16.1″	1,024 × 768	1,280 × 1,024
19″	18″	1,280 × 1,024	1,600 × 1,200
20 and 21″	19.7″	1,600 × 1,200	1,920 × 1,080 (HDTV)

While there's usually a correspondence between a monitor's size and its maximum resolution, there doesn't have to be. As discussed previously, a monitor's size refers to its physical dimensions, whereas the resolution refers to how many pixels it can display on the screen at once. So, for example, one 17-inch monitor may have a resolution of 1,024 × 768 pixels (that is, it can display up to 1,024 pixels across and 768 pixels down), and another one might be capable of displaying 1,600 × 1,200 pixels. The same principle holds true for notebook displays and flat-panel desktop displays. You can't presume that similar-sized displays will support the same resolutions. (Refer back to Figure 4-1 for more.)

The reason for this is that individual pixels on the monitor that supports the small resolution are actually larger and take up more space per pixel. While this sounds like it might be helpful, it's not. Generally speaking, the smaller the dots, the finer the resolution and the easier a computer monitor is on your eyes. Large pixels usually make the screen harder to read and cause annoying eye fatigue.

Secret

There is a limit to how small you want the dots to be. Some monitors can technically support very high resolutions, but trying to view the image at those sizes is virtually impossible.

All newer monitors can display images at several different resolutions, but they're usually compared at their highest resolutions. For example, a monitor that supports resolutions up to 1,024 × 768 pixels could also display images at 800 × 600 pixels or 640 × 480, but it won't work at a resolution of 1,280 × 1,024.

Dot pitch, interlace, and dots per inch (DPI)

Dot Pitch is commonly used to determine the resolution of a CRT-based monitor's display. The dot pitch is the space, measured in millimeters, between similarly colored phosphors, which are the elements that make up each pixel on the screen. The dot pitch generally recommended for monitors is .28 or smaller. Some less expensive monitors offer a much larger dot pitch (as high as .39), but you want to avoid those at all costs; the fuzziness of the image will be enough to keep you away from your computer, and we wouldn't want that to happen, now would we? So, when you're shopping for a monitor, make sure it offers a .28 dot pitch or less. In fact, many people use .25 or less.

Another image quality issue to look for in CRT-based monitors is interlaced versus noninterlaced operation. If you'll recall from the section earlier in the chapter on recording video, analog NTSC video consists of two fields per frame that are interlaced to create a complete image. Translating that subject to monitors, an interlaced monitor (like a TV) draws every other line of an image and then goes back and fills in the lines that are left. The result is an image that isn't sharp and is hard to view up close. Most computer monitors are noninterlaced, which generates a much higher-quality image by drawing all the lines consecutively.

Note

By the way, this is why video cards need to have a separate NTSC output and/or why you can use external NTSC converter boxes to connect a computer's video signal to a TV. The primary role that these outputs and devices fulfill is to generate an interlaced signal.

Like printers, flat-panel monitors use a dot-per-inch (dpi) rating to describe their resolution and overall image quality, although monitors actually have pixels per inch. Generally speaking, you want to get a dpi rating of 90 or better on flat panels, but it's not unheard of to have 110 dpi or higher. In fact, IBM has prototyped flat panel monitors with resolutions of about 300 dpi. As you would expect, the higher the dpi, the smaller the pixels, and the smaller the pixels, the sharper the picture.

Display Data Channel (DDC)

Virtually all CRT-based monitors sold today are referred to as multisync monitors because they are able to run at any one of several synchronization, or refresh, rates. Similarly, most video cards can drive monitors at one of several different refresh rates. The trick to getting the best quality picture from your computer is to make sure the two are working together and using the highest refresh rate that they both can support.

While some older systems require you to make these adjustments manually, most newer monitors and video cards automate the process through support of the Display Data Channel (DDC), which essentially brings Plug and Play support to monitors. What a DDC-capable monitor can do is basically tell the video card what types of resolutions and refresh rates it supports, and then the video card can automatically select the options that best fit it's own capabilities.

Some implementations of DDC also enable a monitor to control centering, resizing, and generally adjusting the size of the image you see via software; this can be handy for saving specific settings.

Built-in features

Because monitors play such a pivotal role in an overall PC system, and because they're centrally located, many companies are starting to integrate other components into them. Some are including audio speakers and/or a microphone. In addition, some companies are incorporating easy-access connectors, such as USB (Universal Serial Bus) ports, for peripheral devices. Others have even started to include video cameras.

Cross-
Reference

For more on video cameras, see Chapter 6, "Printers, Scanners, and Digital Cameras."

Speakers

As sound has become an increasingly important part of the PC experience, monitor makers are choosing to integrate these audio elements for two primary reasons:

First, because you tend to sit very close to computer monitors, having speakers built-in can help localize the sound to the screen, which is particularly important when you're viewing video clips or playing games. If sound that accompanies onscreen activity appears from too far a distance, it reduces the overall impact of what's being shown.

Second, built-in speakers can reduce desk clutter and help simplify the process of setting up a computer because you don't have to worry about the extra connections you need to make with separate pairs of speakers.

A third, less important reason is that well-designed monitor speakers avoid the problem of magnetic interference, which can impact the image quality of older, nonshielded monitors. See the sidebar "Audio interference" for more details.

Cross-
Reference

See Chapter 5, "Sound Cards, Speakers, and Modems," for more.

Audio interference

Most speakers that are used in conjunction with computers contain magnets inside them and generate a magnetic field. If the speakers are not properly magnetically shielded, this magnetic field can negatively impact your computer monitor's display if it, too, isn't properly shielded. If you bring unshielded speakers too close to an unshielded monitor, you'll end up seeing strange rainbow-like alterations in the monitor picture. The only way to avoid this situation is to move the speakers far enough away from the monitor.

Most modern monitors and computer speakers all have some level of shielding to prevent this from happening, but it's not unheard to run into problems if the shielding in one or the other is inadequate. The only way to ensure that monitors with built-in speakers won't have display problems is to crank up the volume because the magnetic field increases in strength as the volume gets louder (particularly with low frequencies).

Newer speaker technologies, such as that found in flat-panel speakers, don't use magnets; therefore, they don't suffer from this problem.

USB hubs

As USB peripherals start to proliferate, the need for additional connector ports has grown with it. Devices that provide extra USB ports are called hubs, and while you can buy them as standalone devices, many monitors are starting to integrate USB hubs into the monitor case. Monitors offer an excellent solution to the problem of obtaining easy access to open USB connectors because your monitor is always right in front of you and, hence, easy to get to. In addition, they typically have room for the ports.

Secret

It is important to be aware that some monitors include what's called a bus-powered USB hub, but what you really want is a true powered hub. The phrase bus-powered is very misleading, but what it actually means is that the device itself — in this case, the hub — is powered by the bus. A powered hub, on the other hand, not only has its own power supply, but it can also provide power to each of its individual ports. Many USB devices require power and will not work properly if they don't have adequate power. As a result, they won't work with a bus-powered hub built into a monitor. Instead, those devices need to be connected to and powered from either the USB ports on your PC or a powered hub.

Cross-Reference

See Chapter 18, "Solving Common Problems," for more on dealing with USB-based problems.

Liquid crystal display (LCD)

Whether it's part of the notebook you own or that sleek, new flat-panel display you've been lusting after, the LCD panel that sits at the heart of many of today's computer display systems has a unique set of characteristics you need to be aware of when comparing different models side-by-side.

Of course, the best piece of advice anyone could ever give you when it comes to monitors of any kind, is to just look at it and decide whether or not you like what you see. After all, the monitor is what you're going to be staring at whenever you use the computer, and you must like it and feel comfortable with it, no matter how cool all the stuff inside the CPU may be.

The need to look at and compare screens is particularly true for LCD displays, however, because the differences between various types of LCDs is even more pronounced than the differences between various types of tube-based monitors.

Often times, the reason for these large differences has to with the technology driving the screen. The two most popular types are referred to as active matrix (sometimes also called Thin Film Transistor or TFT) and passive matrix, which is available in one of several varieties, the most well-known of which are dual scan (sometimes also called Dual Super Twisted Nematic or DSTN) and High Performance Addressing (HPA).

Active matrix

In active matrix screens, which is the more expensive technology to implement, each individual pixel on the screen is addressed individually by three transistors: one each for the colors red, green, and blue. The result is a bright, sharp, crisp picture that can be easily seen both straight on and from an angle and which holds up well in bright light and sunlight. (Note, however, that even active matrix screens typically do not have as good a viewing angle as a CRT.)

Active matrix screens also have very fast response times, which means they adapt quickly to rapidly moving images on the screen. This is important when you're trying to display digital video or other moving images (such as 3D animations), and it's also important for following your cursor around the screen.

One common problem with some passive-matrix screens is that if you move your cursor around quickly, it can seem to temporarily disappear. This phenomenon, which is called submarining or ghosting, is due to the fact that the slower response times of some passive-matrix screens can't keep up with the movements of the cursor. To compensate for this, computer systems are capable of setting a mouse trail, where multiple images of the cursor follow the main cursor, so you won't lose track of where it is. Generally speaking, however, you don't need to worry about mouse trails with active matrix screens.

The one potential problem with active matrix screens is that if one of the transistors doesn't work correctly, you can get a bad pixel that looks miscolored or that appears to stay lit when the other parts of the screen look dark. Unfortunately, there's nothing you can do about this, short of replacing the whole screen at a very costly expense. The reason this occurs is that manufacturing large active matrix displays is extremely difficult, and it's very hard to make a large batch of displays that are all perfect.

Secret

In fact, the manufacturing process is so hard that it has become standard practice for manufacturers to accept LCD displays with as many as seven or ten errant pixels as *good enough*. Many companies won't replace notebook or flat-panel displays unless they have five or more bad pixels in prominent positions on the screen.

Personally, I have a big problem with this. Thankfully, it appears that as manufacturing processes improve, vendors are starting to move away from the policy of not replacing screens with multiple bad pixels, but don't be surprised if you come across this issue. By the way, this is yet another good reason to look at an LCD display before you buy it.

Passive matrix

Passive matrix screens of all varieties generate their images by addressing entire lines of pixels (both horizontally and vertically) on a constant basis. The result is a screen that isn't typically as bright or as crisp as an active matrix but is usually acceptable and costs much less. The two main types of passive matrix technology are dual scan and HPA (High Performance Addressing).

In dual-scan screens, the screen is essentially cut in half and both halves are refreshed simultaneously, which helps response times and increases brightness and contrast. Similarly, HPA-based screens refresh the lines more quickly than older technologies, which can improve the brightness and contrast of the display. In fact, later versions of both technologies — Toshiba calls their refinement Fast Scan — can generate displays that are quite good.

Still, it's a case of you get what you pay for. In addition to the slower response times, other down sides to the various passive matrix screens are that you generally need to look at them straight on (which usually isn't a problem unless multiple people are looking at the screen simultaneously), and they are harder to read in sunlight. On the other hand, because of the way the technology works, they don't suffer from bad pixels, as active matrix screens can.

Color and resolution limitations

One potential issue for LCD displays of either variety is that some are limited to a potential color palette of only 262,000 colors, versus the 16.7 million available on any CRT-based monitor. This means that some LCD-based monitors or notebook displays cannot display true 24-bit images, regardless of the capabilities of the video card driving the system. Caveat emptor.

In addition, flat-panel monitors have a specific number of pixels; therefore they have a fixed resolution at which they are designed to operate. So, for example, a screen that supports 1,024 × 768 has 1,024 pixels going across and

768 pixels down and each pixel corresponds with a specific dot in the resolution. If you set that monitor to work at, say, 800 × 600, what often happens is that the pixels outside that range are not used, and you end up with a smaller picture in the middle of your monitor. In some cases flat-panel monitors can support lower resolutions at the full screen size, but they have to use various types of interpolation techniques to do so, which don't always look that great.

This is very different than how CRTs work because there is no resolution dot-to-pixel correspondence in monitor tubes. The CRTs just adjust the size of the dots based on the resolution you select. On the other hand, because of the way flat-panel monitors work, you can find out the specific dpi that they support, which you can't do with CRT-based monitors.

Connection method

Flat-panel monitors come in both analog and digital versions, with analog models offering the standard 15-pin VGA connector. Digital flat-panels use a variety of different, incompatible connection schemes, so if you want a digital flat-panel monitor — which generally offers the sharpest, brightest colors — you need to find out what type of connector it uses and whether the video card you're interested in connecting to it supports that standard.

(Another option — one that flat-panel manufacturers often use — is to bundle a compatible video card with the monitor. This guarantees that the two will work well together, but then you're stuck with the video card chosen by the monitor vendor. If it doesn't support the features you want or need, then you may be out of luck.)

The four main types of digital monitor connection mechanisms are the P&D (Plug & Display) standard, the DFP (Digital Flat-Panel) standard, the LDI (Low-voltage differential signaling Display Interface) or OpenLDI standard and the DVI (Digital Visual Interface) Standard. There are actually several different types of P&D, which commonly uses a 36-pin connector, but the basic format supports not only a straight digital video connection, but also USB, IEEE 1394, and analog video. The USB and IEEE 1394 support can be handy for monitors that incorporate speakers, video cameras, and other add-ons. By using P&D, you can reduce all the various connections that would normally be necessary to a single cable.

DFP, which commonly uses a 26-pin connector, is essentially a simplified version of P&D without the USB, IEEE 1394, and analog video. The digital video signal is similar to P&D, because they are both based on PanelLink technology, or Transition Minimized Differential Signaling (TMDS).

The various types of LDI, which often use a different type of 36-pin connector, are based on the digital connection used in laptops to connect their video circuitry to their screens (which are usually digital, by the way). Finally, the DVI standard, developed by the industry organization known as the Digital Display Working Group (DDWG), is also based on PanelLink technology, but uses yet another variation. Eventually the computer industry (or the market) should settle on a single standard, but in the mean time, things are a bit messy.

Recommendations

The first decision you have to make when it comes to monitors for desktop computers is whether you want to go with a traditional CRT-based model or one of the newer, flat-panel displays. The LCD-based devices weren't a realistic option for most users until recently, because of the enormous disparity in prices between them and traditional monitors, but now that their prices have dropped to reasonable levels, you should at least consider them.

You'll still get more screen real estate per dollar with a tube-based monitor, but the difference may not be as large as the specs lead you to believe. Remember to compare the actual image area (and resolution) of each before you make a decision. In the case of CRT monitors, make sure it supports the DDC (Display Data Channel) standard.

If you go with a CRT-based monitor, take a look at the relatively new 19-inch category of monitors. These displays offer a fairly large improvement in actual image area versus 17-inch monitors, but the cases (and prices) aren't that much bigger (or higher) than the more common 17-inchers. 21-inch monitors are great, but they tend to be significantly more expensive, bigger, and heavier than either 17-inch or 19-inch monitors, so they're a lot harder to deal with.

If you decide to go with a flat-panel display, or if you're looking at notebooks, I would go for an active matrix screen despite the extra cost. Over time, you'll really appreciate its sharp, bright, fast display. If your budget is a bit limited, you should certainly consider dual-scan or HPA-based screens (at least for notebooks), but make sure you take a look at the screen before you buy. Again, there are large differences in quality between various types of passive matrix technology, and you need to see the screen before you can really make a good decision.

In general, built-in speakers are fine for most applications, but they may limit your options in monitor sizes; however, if sound is really important to you, I would go with stand-alone speakers and a speaker-free monitor. You'll have more (and better) choices in speaker systems that way.

Cross-Reference

See Chapter 5, "Sound Cards, Speakers, and Modems," for more on speaker choices.

Summary

In this chapter, I described the important characteristics of video cards and monitors.

- A video card's resolution and the color depths it can support are determined by how much memory is on the card.

- Video cards use a wide variety of different memory types, including EDO RAM, SDRAM, SGRAM, VRAM, WRAM, and RDRAM.

- High refresh rates are important when connecting to a tube-based monitor to avoid flicker but they don't matter for LCD displays.

- The two main interfaces for video cards are the Accelerated Graphics Port (AGP) and the PCI bus. AGP offers performance benefits, but they aren't really that noticeable in real-world applications unless the video card uses the AGP 2x or 4x modes.

- Most video cards include several different types of acceleration including 2D graphics, 3D graphics, and full-motion video.

- Some features on 3D graphics cards are geared toward improving the speed at which images are displayed, and others are focused on improving the image quality.

- Cards that support video capture enable you to do video editing on your PC, but some only digitize either a tiny version or a small amount of video, while others enable you record the entire signal to disk.

- Monitor resolution does not determine your monitor size but determines how large the image is on your screen.

- In addition to the display, some monitors also include speakers, USB hubs, and more, which can be handy for keeping your desk tidy.

- Active matrix LCD displays, such as those in notebooks and flat-panel monitors, offer the brightest, sharpest picture, but newer types of passive matrix screens, such as some dual-scan and HPA-based models, offer reasonably good picture quality at a better price.

- Digital flat-panel monitors may use any one of several different, incompatible connection types, so you need to make sure you have a video card that can work with your monitor.

Chapter 5

Sound Cards, Speakers, and Modems

In This Chapter

▶ You will learn how a sound card works and what distinguishes one card from another.

▶ You will learn the differences between digital audio and MIDI, as well as the difference between FM synthesis, wavetable synthesis, and physical modeling synthesis.

▶ You will learn the specifications that are important to look for in computer speakers.

▶ You will learn how various modem technologies work, including 56K cable and DSL (Digital Subscriber Line) modems.

▶ You will learn what features are important to look for in modems.

▶ You will get recommendations on sound cards, speakers, and modems.

In the early days of personal computers, a machine's sound capabilities were typically limited to the simple, though gut-wrenching, beeps that often signified a problem with a piece of the system's hardware — not exactly something people looked forward to hearing.

And when it came to communications with other computer users, things rarely got more sophisticated than copying files from one computer onto a floppy disk and then walking that disk over to another person's computer and having them copy the files onto their computer — a technique jokingly referred to as *sneakernet*.

Today, however, sophisticated sound features and high-speed connections to computer users around the world have become the standard. Computer sound has moved beyond the days when it was merely associated with special multimedia computers and has become an integral part of the entire computing experience. As a result, sound cards and speakers are no longer considered a frill but rather a primary component of any modern computer system.

Similarly, the wide-reaching range and appeal of the Internet has brought the importance of high-quality, high-speed connections into the spotlight. Today's modems, many of which incorporate some audio circuitry of their own (hence their inclusion here), not only provide a way to connect to other computers, but make personal computers the most important and most powerful communications tool we have at our disposal.

Sound Cards

The sound-generating capability of a computer system is typically handled by a separate circuit board, or plug-in card, called a *sound card* that attaches to one of your computer's expansion slots. On older computers, this card attached to an ISA (Industry Standard Architecture) connector, while in most newer systems, it attaches to a PCI (Peripheral Component Interconnect) connector.

Note

On some systems, including virtually all notebook computers, the sound-generating circuitry doesn't take the form of a card but instead is integrated onto the computer's motherboard.

Regardless of the physical form it takes, a sound card's job is to generate sound. But this is not always as straightforward as it appears. There are actually several different kinds of sounds that today's applications use, and they all have to be handled by separate components of the sound card.

And in addition to playing back sounds, virtually all sound cards can convert existing audio signals, either from a microphone, an attached CD audio player, or any other audio source, into digital form. Once that's done, the sound can be recorded on your hard disk (for music or other audio-related applications) or sent through a modem or other Internet connection (for real-time phone calls, videoconferencing, or any of a host of communication-based applications).

The most important features to look for in sound cards are:

- The card's sampling rates for digital audio recording
- The type of synthesis methods, such as wavetable synthesis, it supports
- The amount of synthesized voices it can play (called it's *polyphony*)
- The type of processing effects, such as 3D audio, it includes
- The type of connections it provides, both to external devices and to various types of speakers

What is MIDI?

MIDI, or *Musical Instrument Digital Interface*, is essentially a control language that sends commands to MIDI-equipped devices that are capable of receiving and responding to those commands, such as electronic musical keyboards. Originally developed in the 1980s by manufacturers of professional musical instruments, MIDI sends messages to these types of instruments and tells them how to play a particular passage of music — almost like a form of digital sheet music. MIDI messages include information on what notes to play, how hard to play them, and how long to hold a particular note.

MIDI messages also include information on what particular sound to use to play those notes, but they don't include anything regarding the specific qualities or characteristics of that sound. MIDI simply says something along the lines of "Use sound #1." As a result, the exact same set of MIDI messages sent to two different sound cards (or two different sections of the same sound card) can sound very different. This is because sound #1 on one sound card may sound very

different than sound #1 on another (even though sound #1 might be called Acoustic Piano in both places). The notes are the same, but the actual sound is determined by synthesizer's specific characteristics and capabilities.

In its most basic form, MIDI serves as a method of remote control. You can play a note on an instrument — a MIDI controller — that generates MIDI commands and the messages pass over a MIDI cable (or through an internal MIDI connection) and the receiving unit (sometimes called a MIDI slave) responds to those messages by playing the note requested. The accompanying figure shows a typical example.

A whole series of MIDI messages can be recorded and saved as a MIDI sequence, or Standard MIDI File (SMF). The SMF, which typically consists of a complete piece of music, can then be played back on any sound card or MIDI device. When you play the MIDI sequence, all the previously recorded MIDI messages are sent out and the sound card or MIDI device plays back those messages in real time.

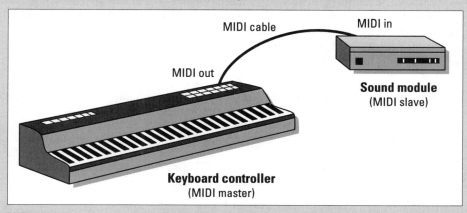

MIDI control
In a basic MIDI setup, when you play notes on a MIDI keyboard (also called a controller), you generate a series of MIDI messages that are sent from the keyboard's MIDI output to the sound card or other MIDI device. Upon receiving those messages it generates the actual sound that you hear.

Digital audio versus synthesized sound

The two most common types of computer sound are digital audio and synthesized sound. *Digital audio*, sometimes called *wave audio*, consists of any sound, whether it's a speaking voice, sound effect, or piece of music, that has been previously recorded and stored in a digital form. (It is stored as a .wav file — hence the name wave audio.) On the other hand, synthesized music, sometimes called MIDI (Musical Instrument Digital Interface) music, consists of music (and sometimes sound effects) that has not been previously recorded but is generated dynamically by special circuitry, called a *synthesizer*, on the sound card. This can be confusing because MIDI helps generate audio, and it's certainly digital, but it's not digital audio. (See the sidebar "What is MIDI?" for more.)

To understand MIDI and how it is different from digital audio, imagine a piece of piano music. Digital audio would be like an audio CD recording of that music. It's an exact record of a particular moment in time. MIDI, on the other hand, would be like a player piano roll that would get the piano to play back that same passage in real time — it is essentially a set of instructions regarding what notes to play, how loud to play them, and so on.

The digital audio version of that music would always sound essentially the same (except, perhaps, for differences in speaker quality — just as audio CDs can sound slightly different on different stereo systems), whereas the quality of the synthesized MIDI version would vary tremendously, depending on the type of player used.

Note

Don't presume that synthesized MIDI music sounds worse than digital audio — the sound quality depends entirely on the quality of the sound card's synthesizer circuitry. In fact, MIDI itself doesn't sound like anything at all — it's just a set of instructions used to play back sounds on MIDI synthesizers. Some of the synthesizers sound good and others, well. . . . On older, less sophisticated cards, the music generated by MIDI files is almost laughably bad, but on newer, high-quality cards the exact same files can sound quite good.

Distinguishing aurally between digital audio and MIDI can be difficult because there are many instances where a certain piece of audio, such as the soundtrack for a game, can be either digital audio, synthesized MIDI music, or even a combination of both. Luckily, as a user you never need to worry about deciding which is which — that's the job of your sound card — but it's important to understand that there are differences so that you can better understand how sound cards work and the features they offer.

If you look at the size of the different types of files, however, it's easy to distinguish between digital audio and MIDI. Audio files are an order of magnitude larger than MIDI files. A three-minute song, for example, could take up as much as 30MB if it was recorded as digital audio at CD-quality standards (16-bit stereo, recorded at a 44.1kHz sampling rate — see the following section for an explanation), whereas a MIDI version of the same song could easily be under 100KB.

Digital audio

In order to handle the various types of audio used on computers, a sound card consists of several different parts, each of which has different specifications. The basic digital audio playback and audio recording capabilities are often signified by a bit rate. While older sound cards, such as the original Sound Blaster, were 8-bit cards, most modern sound cards are 16-bit cards. (Some cards designed for professional audio recording applications offer 18-, 20-, or even 24-bit audio.) Offering a higher bit rate means they are capable of dealing with audio in higher resolution, 16-bit chunks, which is the same size used on audio CDs. The increase in bit size allows for a larger dynamic range, which translates into audio which sounds much more lifelike.

Sampling rates

Another important factor in the digital audio portion of the sound card is the sampling rates that a card supports. The sampling rate, which only affects the recording of sounds — not playback, refers to how many times per second a sound signal is digitized, or sampled. The process of digitizing audio basically involves taking a snapshot of a continuously varying analog audio signal many thousands of times per second and then converting each of those snapshots to a digital number. Figure 5-1 shows a typical audio waveform and illustrates how the digital audio recording, or sampling, process works.

The higher the sampling rate, the more accurate the digital representation and the better the sound.

Secret

Even if your sound card supports CD-quality 16-bit, 44.1kHz sampling rates, it can only play back files at the rates at which they were recorded. So, a sound recorded as an 8-bit, 11kHz audio file won't sound very good on any computer system, regardless of the type of sound card on which it is played.

So before you presume that your speakers or sound card aren't any good because a particular digital audio file doesn't sound good, find out first what the sound's sampling resolution and sampling rate are. Under Windows, you can do this via the file's properties. (See Figure 5-2 for more.)

The sampling rate is directly related to the frequency range of the digitized signal. Lower sampling rates create sounds with a lower frequency range, and higher sampling rates create sounds with a higher frequency range. Sonically, audio files created with lower sampling rates don't sound as crisp and bright or rich as the original but instead will be somewhat dull and muted.

The way the math works out, sampling rates needs to be twice as high as the frequency range of the sound we want. Because the human hearing range, in terms of frequencies, is approximately 20Hz to 20,000Hz — 20,000Hz = 20kHz — to create a full range sound, the audio needs to be sampled at a rate above 40kHz. This is why CDs are recorded at a 44.1kHz sampling rate.

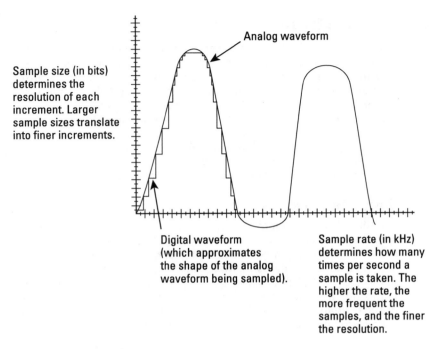

Sample size (in bits) determines the resolution of each increment. Larger sample sizes translate into finer increments.

Analog waveform

Digital waveform (which approximates the shape of the analog waveform being sampled).

Sample rate (in kHz) determines how many times per second a sample is taken. The higher the rate, the more frequent the samples, and the finer the resolution.

Figure 5-1: Recording digital audio
The process of recording a sound with a computer's sound card is called *sampling* or *audio digitization* because it converts a regular analog waveform into its digital equivalent. The sample size, measured in bits, affects the dynamic range of the sound, and the sampling rate, measured in kHz, affects the frequency range of the sound.

Sounds that are recorded at 11kHz or 22kHz, which are commonly used for different types of computer sounds, have frequency ranges up to about 5.5kHz and 11kHz, respectively. You can typically tell when sounds have been recorded at these rates because they sound muted, kind of like the audio quality you hear over a telephone.

Of course, as with virtually all computer specifications, there's a trade-off. Higher sampling rates create more data, which means sounds recorded at higher rates take up more space (stereo sounds, by the way, take up twice as much space as single channel mono sound files). Even if you never record anything with your computer, this is good to know because it explains why some program developers choose to use slightly lower-quality sounds — they take up a lot less space.

If you're interesting in playing computer games, another digital audio feature to be aware of is the number of separate audio streams, or channels, that the card is capable of playing at once. Many games have multiple sounds going on simultaneously, and some cards can support more of those independent streams than others can.

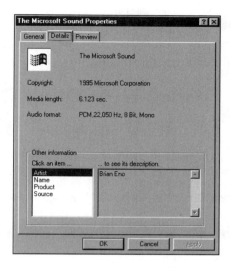

Figure 5-2: Digital audio properties
You can find out the sampling resolution and rate of any digital audio .wav file under
Windows by right-clicking the file, selecting Properties from the context menu, and then
clicking the Details tab.

Duplex

Though virtually all sound cards can both play back and record sounds, not
all of them can do both at the same time. The capability to record (or at least
digitize) and play back sounds simultaneously is called *full duplex*. Sound
cards that can only do one at a time are called *half duplex*. Walkie-talkies and
many speakerphones, for example, only support half-duplex operation and
this is the reason why you must wait for one person to stop talking before
another person can begin.

Secret

Full duplex support on sound cards is critical for music recording
applications, where you need to be able to listen to one part as you record
another. It's also very important for telephony applications, such as Internet-
based phone calls, where you want to be able speak and listen simultaneously without one cutting off the other.

As you'll discover in the modems section of this chapter, full duplex support
on voice-enabled modems is also critical for telephony-based applications
when you want to call another person directly through your modem, as
opposed to doing it over the Internet. When you use your modem as a phone
and place a call to another person, the audio is handled by the modem
instead of the sound card, whereas phone calls and videoconferencing that
occurs via the Internet use the sound card for audio.

Cross-
Reference

See Chapter 13, "Connecting to and Using the Internet," for more.

Synthesized sound

The other type of sound generated by sound cards is synthesized MIDI music. Unlike the digital audio section of most cards, there's a lot of variation in the synthesis section of today's sound cards. The reason for this is that there are several different types of synthesis — the most common are FM synthesis, wavetable synthesis, and physical modeling synthesis — and within these types there are many different implementations. In addition, many sound cards actually support several types of synthesis.

Unifying characteristics among these different types and implementations is that they're all capable of generating, or synthesizing, a wide variety of sounds, and all generate music (and sometimes other audio elements — such as sound effects in computer games) in response to MIDI messages that are sent to the sound card.

Cross-Reference

See Chapter 16, "Working with Audio and Music," for more on using MIDI and MIDI software.

One of the important differentiating factors between various sound cards, regardless of which synthesis methods they support, is the number of voices that they are capable of playing. This is also called the card's *polyphony*, which is the number of different musical notes that can be played at once. The more voices, or notes, a card supports, the more complex a musical arrangement it is capable of playing.

Note

In many cases, there's a one-to-one correspondence between voices and notes. In other words, one note requires one voice; however, some complex sounds actually use two voices per note played, which reduces the number of notes a card can play at once in half.

Many cards now offer 128-voice polyphony or more, split between some of their different synthesis methods. For example, some cards can play 64 wavetable voices at once and 64 physical modeling voices at once.

Another specification that some sound cards use to distinguish themselves is the number of different sounds (sometimes called *patches*) that their onboard synthesizer is capable of creating. The General MIDI specification calls for at least 128 different, specific sounds, but some cards include support for even more. This is important if you ever plan to create your own music and want to have a wide variety of options to choose from.

General MIDI

By their very nature, the synthesizers built into sound cards (as well as professional synthesizers used by musicians) are designed to generate as wide a range of sounds as possible. But to ensure that all MIDI files created for one sound card will sound approximately the same on a different one, regardless of the synthesis method used to create the sounds, a standard was needed that identified a core group of sounds. That standard is called *General MIDI*, or GM, and is supported by most sound cards.

General MIDI defines 128 different sounds organized into 16 groups of 8. The groups identify different general categories of sounds, such as pianos, guitars, woodwinds, strings, and so on, and the individual sounds represent certain instruments, such as nylon-string guitar, flute, and violin. By codifying both the type of sound as well as its particular sound number, General MIDI enables music composers to create music that they can be sure will sound relatively consistent across different types of sound cards.

Cross-Reference

For more on the specific patches supported by General MIDI, see Chapter 16, "Working with Audio and Music."

If you happen to run across a sound card that doesn't support General MIDI and try to play a game or other program that uses music on the General MIDI standard, you can get pretty hilarious results. Parts designed to be played by a piano may actually be played with a woodblock sound, and so on.

Occasionally you may also come across sound cards (and some games) that claim to offer support for extended formats called GS or XG. These two standards are actually proprietary extensions to the General MIDI standard created by Roland Corp. and Yamaha Corp., respectively. Both GS and XG add additional capabilities that sound designers and musicians can take advantage of, but it is not necessary to have a sound card that specifically supports them. As long as your sound card supports General MIDI, it will work just fine. The only things you may not hear are some additional manipulations of the sound that are commonly referred to as audio effects. One common example of such an effect is reverb, which is an echo-like effect that adds a realistic-sounding ambience to a sound.

FM synthesis

Most original sound cards — and all those that claim to be true Sound Blaster-compatibles — take advantage of a technology called FM (frequency modulation) synthesis. In FM synthesis, which was commercialized by Yamaha Corp., sounds are generated by mathematically combining a number of basic waveforms in interesting ways.

Note

Sound cards that support FM synthesis often refer to the OPL-3, which is the name of the Yamaha chip that actually generates the sounds. If you see a card that offers OPL-3 support, this means it is capable of doing FM synthesis. OPL-4, which is the successor to the OPL-3, supports both FM synthesis and wavetable synthesis (explained later in the chapter).

When it was first introduced in the professional music market, FM synthesis was a revolutionary breakthrough, and it was widely admired for its capability to create striking bell-like timbres. Unfortunately, it was never very good at emulating traditional instruments, such as acoustic pianos, guitars, strings, and drums. As a result, FM synthesis is still capable of generating interesting synthetic sounds, but it's not very successful at replicating the sounds of normal instruments. And because a lot of the music we're used to hearing contains parts designed for traditional instruments, FM synthesis doesn't sound very good playing back many types of music.

Wavetable RAM

The amount and variety of different sounds that a wavetable synthesizer on a sound card generates is directly related to the amount of wavetable samples to which it has access. As a result, most companies try to include a nice selection of samples in their sound ROM. But no matter how good the selection is, it can never completely satisfy all the potential sounds that say, a computer game designer, may want. To address this concern, several sound card manufacturers now include a certain amount of RAM (or the capability to add your own RAM) on the sound card into which new wavetables can be temporarily stored. In addition, some cards enable you to set aside a certain amount of main system memory for storing custom sounds.

With all these various types of wavetable RAM, a computer game, or any other software title, can load its own wavetables into the available memory and then use those sounds as easily as any sounds built into the sound cards' ROM. This technology is sometimes called *Sound Fonts* or DLS (DownLoadable Samples), and is a recent addition to the MIDI specification. DLS and the updated DLS2 are supported by Microsoft's DirectMusic technology (part of the larger DirectX software platform built into Windows).

The end result is that a particular program can define its own unique sound, which results in a more captivating experience (at least, in theory). Users can also take advantage of this basic expandability to create a wider palette of sounds that they can use for musical applications and other artistic endeavors.

Some of the first audio cards that included slots for adding or upgrading a sound card's RAM used industry-standard SIMM slots that enabled you to use normal computer memory; however, other cards use proprietary connectors that require special (in other words, more expensive) RAM. So, if you're interested in adding wavetable RAM, be sure to find out what format the memory needs to be in.

Wavetable synthesis

The next generation in music synthesis for sound cards is called *wavetable synthesis*. Wavetable synthesis is much more effective at re-creating traditional instruments than FM synthesis because it generates sounds by starting with short recordings, or samples, of real instruments. These digital samples are stored in ROM (Read Only Memory) on the sound card as wavetables (hence the name). Some wavetable sound cards also have access to RAM for storing additional samples. (See sidebar, "Wavetable RAM," for more.)

Cross-Reference

See Chapter 16, "Working with Audio and Music," for more on using music applications on your PC.

In wavetable synthesis, when a request for a particular note is received, the synthesizer looks up the specific sample it needs in the wavetable and then processes the recording through several bits of specialized circuitry to generate the sound.

Ideally, a wavetable synthesizer would have a recording of every instrument playing every note so that the process of generating sounds could be as simple as just looking up the right sample and playing it back. But for a variety of different reasons, and primarily because of the enormous amount of storage it would take to hold all the samples, it is not possible. As a result, wavetable synthesizers have to perform a number of different tricks on the raw samples to generate lots of different sounds at different pitches.

For example, on one card, a synthesizer's tuba sound may actually be a recording of a trombone or even a trumpet played back at a slower rate. (Think about what it sounds like when you record your voice and then play that tape back at a slower or faster rate, and you'll get the basic idea.) On another card, a synthesizer's tuba sound may actually be a tuba, but it might be a much shorter recording that, in its raw form, doesn't sound very much like a tuba.

For reasons such as these, different wavetable synthesizers can sound very different. Usually, the more samples a sound card has access to (a factor that is determined by the size of the wavetable ROM included as part of the sound card) the better it will sound. That is not always the case, however. A wavetable sound card that contains a well-chosen, well-recorded set of samples that takes up 4 or even only 2MB of ROM can sound better than a card with 8MB of ROM.

Secret

The most critical factor in the quality of a wavetable sound card is the quality of its wavetables (typically found in ROM). The better the original samples sound, the better the card's overall sound quality will be.

Unfortunately, there's no easy, objective way to compare sound ROMs. The only way to really to differentiate between sound cards is to listen to them — preferably side-by-side. If you have a chance, play back several different types of MIDI sequences on several different sound cards; you'll undoubtedly be able to hear the differences between them. Some will sound better with some types of music, and some will sound better with others — a fact which is due, in large part, to differences in their sound ROM (or the samples that they've loaded into RAM).

If you still aren't happy with what you hear (or if you have an older sound card that doesn't offer wavetable synthesis), you may also want to look at wavetable upgrades. Wavetable upgrades are little daughterboards that include additional sound ROM that you can attach to certain sound cards. Unlike RAM upgrades, the sounds in a ROM upgrade are fixed — you cannot add your own sounds to them.

Several different companies offer these wavetable upgrades. You don't have to get a wavetable upgrade from the same manufacturer as your sound card (though they do, obviously, need to have the same kind of connectors). Once it's attached, this wavetable upgrade gives your sound card access to all the samples included in the daughterboard's ROM, as well as the samples in its original ROM.

Physical modeling synthesis

As great as wavetable synthesis may be for many applications, it does have a few drawbacks. Most noticeably, because its sounds are based on prerecorded samples, it can be difficult to add expression to them. The problem is, as music aficionados well know, the heart of any great musical performance is in the expression that a performer can provide. Consequently, it can be difficult to create a convincing musical performance using wavetable synthesis alone, particularly on solo instruments. This is why, intuitively, you can often tell when a piece of music is made with a wavetable synthesis-based instrument; it just doesn't sound (or feel) right.

To address this concern, sound card manufacturers have begun to incorporate a new synthesis method called *physical modeling*, sometimes also called *waveguide*. With physical modeling, sounds are generated mathematically through a series of equations that model how sound waves move and change through various musical instruments. In essence, these models attempt to digitally recreate how various instruments create sound.

So, for example, to model an acoustic guitar, you would need to have equations that describe the initial pluck of the sound, the characteristics of the different types of guitar strings (steel or nylon), the size of the sound hole, the resonance of the guitar's body, and so on. By combining the results of these equations, you can begin to emulate the sound of an acoustic guitar. (Even better, you could manipulate some of the equations to create instruments that don't exist, such as a guitar with a four-foot-wide sound hole whose body has the same resonance as glass.)

In addition, by making alterations to the different equations, you can create minor differences in expression, such as adjusting how a string vibrates after it's been plucked by the back of your fingernail instead of your finger tip or a plastic guitar pick. In many cases these differences are quite subtle, but taken together they can emulate the expressiveness of acoustic instruments.

Now, as good as all of this sounds in theory, the reality is, most physically modeled sounds generated by sound cards don't sound that realistic (at least, not yet). They're certainly better than FM synthesis–generated sounds, but they're not as good as wavetable. The problem is, processing the complex equations required to create very realistic sounding physically modeled sounds in real time is just too demanding.

As a result, most cards that offer physically modeling also include wavetable synthesis so that, for example, you can use wavetable sounds to play back most parts of a piece and use waveguide only for a single solo instrument.

Hardware vs. software synthesis

One of the interesting characteristics of physical modeling is that most implementations of it are done in software, which means the computer's processor is actually doing the hard work of generating the sound, instead of the sound card. In fact, with software synthesis and speakers that offer a direct digital connection, you don't even need a sound card at all.

Note

What actually happens with software synthesis is that the processor generates the digital waveform using physical modeling equations and then sends that digital waveform to the sound card's Digital-to-Analog Converter (DAC). The DAC then translates the digital data into an analog audio waveform that's passed along to your speakers and converted into sound waves that we can hear. If you don't have a sound card, but instead use speakers with digital connections, such as USB, then the DAC resides inside the speaker.

The benefit of this software-based approach is that it allows for easy upgrades.

Secret

In fact, many existing wavetable sound cards can be upgraded to offer 32 voices of physical modeling synthesis (in addition to whatever wavetable voices they already provide) simply by installing a piece of software.

In addition to physical modeling, some computers also do wavetable synthesis in software. The benefit of this is that software-based wavetable synthesis can typically take advantage of wavetables stored on a computer's hard drive, which are much easier to update and expand than those in a fixed ROM.

The downside to software-based synthesis, of course, is that any additional processing power that the CPU expends generating sounds takes away from other activities that it could (or may need to) be doing. Most of today's fast processors can typically handle the load required by real-time synthesis software, but it's still a factor to bear in mind.

Audio processing

In addition to generating sounds, many sound cards can manipulate sounds through various types of audio processing effects, including reverb and 3D, or positional, audio effects.

If you've ever had the opportunity to go inside an anechoic chamber (a special room designed for testing audio equipment in which there are absolutely no echoes of any kind), you know how strange it is to hear sounds in their raw form. Every sound that we hear is affected and shaped by the room that we're in and the subtle echoes and reverberations that the environment creates.

Digitally generated synthesizer audio doesn't naturally have those characteristics, so to make it sound more lifelike, many sound cards also include effects, such as reverb and echo. These audio effects, which are similar to what you find in many home stereo systems, add the ambience that our ears are used to hearing. Your sound card doesn't have to support audio effects to play MIDI files, but if it does, it can make the synthesized music sound more lifelike.

3D audio

In addition to these standard types of effects, many sound cards also include 3D audio effects. These types of effect are sometimes also called *positional audio*, because they can alter the position of where our ears think a sound is coming from. The basic issue is this: Two- and three-speaker sound systems are great for playing back music, but they aren't the ideal solution for creating a movie-theater-like environment where sound seems to come at you from all directions. The problem is simple physics: if you've got two speakers sitting in front of you, it's hard to create sounds that come from behind you.

What 3D audio effects do is perform some sophisticated alterations, often referred to as Head-Related Transfer Functions (HRTFs), on a sound source and then combine that altered version with the original. The result is that you can fool your ears into thinking that a sound that comes from the front of you is coming from the side or even the back of you.

You'll probably never really be fooled into thinking that there's a separate set of speakers sitting behind you, but these positional audio effects (such as SRS — Sound Retrieval System — technology) can certainly create a sound perspective that sounds wider than what you'd get if the effect was turned off.

Secret

The best way to enjoy 3D audio is through headphones because this can produce the most realistic effects.

In most cases, these types of effects can be applied to any type of signal, but things can get very interesting when you specifically take advantage of technologies that can produce and alter these effects dynamically. Computer games, in particular, can benefit if the sounds from the game not only seem to come from all around you, but also dynamically change depending on how you move around the game. If the effect is done well enough, it can go a long way towards creating a very realistic environment that really pulls you into the game.

There are several types of dynamic 3D audio effects in use and being developed, but for Windows users, the Microsoft DirectSound 3D programming interface should provide a standard way for game developers and game players to take advantage of them. So, make sure your 3D sound card's drivers support DirectSound 3D.

Most of these 3D audio effects are very sensitive to where the listener is sitting in relation to the main speakers. But because computer users typically sit in one spot that's directly centered between and closely located near the main speakers, these effects can work very well with computer systems.

3D audio effects don't just work with two or three-speaker systems. In fact, they're much more realistic when you have a set of rear speakers behind you.

To support that kind of application, many sound cards now include four or more speaker outputs. (See the section, "Multiple outputs," for more.)

Audio decoding

In addition to playing games with 3D audio, many people are now viewing movies on their PCs via DVD. And just as the video portion of the signal needs to be decoded before it can be viewed, so too must the audio signal be decoded before it can be heard.

Cross-Reference

For more on DVD Video decoding, see Chapter 4, "Video Cards and Monitors."

The standard audio encoding method for DVD is Dolby Digital, sometimes also called AC-3. What Dolby Digital does is compresses up to six channels of audio into a single stream of data, which you can then decode and pass along to your speakers. An older version, Dolby Pro Logic, uses slightly lower quality sound and only a mono signal for the rear speakers. Some sound cards include a Dolby Digital or Dolby Pro Logic decoder in hardware or come with a software-based decoder. Others provide a digital audio output, which you can connect to an external audio decoder.

The ideal speaker configuration for Dolby Digital (and most surround-sound-type systems) is 5.1, which means there are five main speakers (front left, front center, front right, rear left, and rear right) and one subwoofer for handling the low frequencies. If you can't afford or don't want to bother with that many speakers for your PC, most sound cards can also provide a simple stereo signal.

Note

Unlike 3D audio for games, which has to be created dynamically, encoded audio for DVD has the 3D positioning already built into the signal. All the sound card, or external decoder, has to do is decode it and then send each signal out to the appropriate speakers

Audio outputs

Sounds generated by a sound card aren't audible until they leave the card via one of several different types of audio outputs. The most common type is a stereo analog signal, typically available through a 1/8-inch stereo mini-jack (the same kind typically found on portable audio devices). Before the various types of audio can get there, however, they need to be combined into a single signal through a device built into the sound card called a *mixer*.

A mixer mixes all the different audio sources from a sound card down to a single, stereo pair that connects to your computer's speakers. In addition to the digital audio and various music synthesis sections of a sound card, many sound cards also include internal audio connectors for CD- and DVD-ROM drives as well as voice modems. In many cases those connectors are analog, but some CD- and DVD-ROM drives offer a digital output that can be connected directly to certain sound cards.

Secret

A related, but somewhat different, feature offered by some CD- and DVD-ROM drives is *audio extraction*. Drives that support audio extraction enable certain types of applications to have direct access to the music tracks on audio CDs as if they were data files. This can be important for audio editing and CD recording—where you create your own CD.

Cross-Reference

See Chapter 16, "Working with Audio and Music," for more on digital audio-editing applications.

By offering these various connectors, a sound card's mixer can become the complete control center for all the various audio components included in a computer. Figure 5-3 shows how the Volume Control panel applet bundled with Windows can control a typical setup.

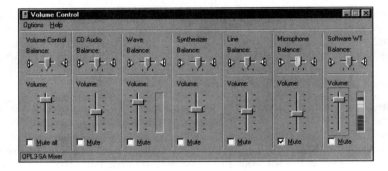

Figure 5-3: Mixing the sound
The mixer built into sound cards can control the volume levels and left-right panning for all the different audio components inside a PC, including the various synthesizers built into the sound card. Most sound cards include an internal ribbon cable connector for CD- and DVD-ROM drives, and can control their volume as well.

Multiple outputs

3D audio effects can provide fairly decent simulations of an audio environment with only two or three speakers, but to really get the best effect, you need to have a separate pair of rear speakers as well. Also, if you want to get a real home-theater-like experience from your PC, you'll need those extra speakers as well.

To help in this regard, many sound cards include connectors for four or even more separate speakers. Note that you don't have to use all of them in order to use the card. You could, for example, just start out with two speakers and then add two more later on.

Digital outputs

In addition to the standard analog audio outputs, some newer sound cards have a digital audio output (some music-oriented sound cards have digital inputs, as well). A digital output offers the possibility of greatly improved audio quality, because it avoids the degradations that occur when you convert the digital audio signal to analog inside the computer.

The problem is, the inside of a computer is not conducive to high-quality audio because of all the electrical noise that occurs while the PC is running. By moving that conversion process into a more friendly environment outside the PC, you can get much higher quality sound and free yourself from annoying hiss (among other audio problems). The latest development in this regard is digital speakers — speakers that accept a digital signal and then perform the conversion process to analog internally. Digital speakers are really a misnomer and more of a marketing term, however, because all sound that we are capable of hearing has to be in analog format. Consequently, even digital speakers generate analog audio.

Most of the digital outputs you'll find on sound cards use the S/PDIF (Sony/Philips Digital Interface Format — commonly pronounced spidif) format. S/PDIF is typically used on professional recording equipment, such as DAT recorders, as well as high-end stereo systems. The only way you can hear the signal generated from this port is to attach to an S/PDIF-compatible set of digital speakers. Or, if you really want to go upscale, you can get a stand-alone digital-to-analog converter (DAC) and then connect the analog output from that to standard speakers.

As mentioned previously, some sound cards also use a S/PDIF output to connect directly to a Dolby Digital decoder or other device that offers this feature.

The other type of digital audio connection that some computers provide is through the USB (Universal Serial Bus) port. In this case, there's usually not a dedicated sound card present in the computer. Instead, software is used to generate the sounds and the results are sent out the PC's USB connector to a set of USB-based speakers.

Other connections

Most sound cards have other types of connections besides audio inputs and outputs, including microphone input and a MIDI/joystick port.

Microphones

Virtually all sound cards enable you to input data into your computer by way of a microphone. With the increased interest in telephony applications, such as Internet-based phone calls and videoconferencing, as well as the growth in voice recognition software, microphones are becoming increasingly important.

Most computers come with simple omnidirectional microphones, which you plug into an input on the back of the card. In addition, some monitors include microphones built into their casing. While these are fine for most uses, such as simple voice recordings, they can be problematic for things such as voice recognition because they typically pick up all the extraneous sounds that occur in any environment (omnidirectional means it can pick up sounds coming from all directions).

As a result, some applications actually come with their own headset microphones, which have a more directed pick-up pattern that only hears sounds spoken straight into it. This can greatly improve the accuracy of voice recognition software and is also very convenient for telephony applications. These headset microphones simply replace the one that comes with your sound card.

If you're interested in better audio fidelity, you may also want to consider an electret microphone (sometimes called a *condenser microphone*). Electret microphones offer a higher-quality audio signal, but require a small amount of power to work. The power is often supplied by the sound card itself, which may have a jumper or other setting that turns the power to the microphone input on or off.

Caution

Do not turn on the electret microphone power setting (if your sound card even has one) unless you actually have an electret microphone that requires it plugged in. If you plug in a normal microphone that doesn't require power, it could be damaged.

MIDI/Joystick port

The final feature to look out for when shopping for a sound card is a *MIDI/joystick port*, or *game port*. You'll use this connector to attach joysticks and other game controllers to your PC, as well as a MIDI interface (if you plan to use the PC for musical purposes). Joysticks typically attach straight to this connector, but to use it for MIDI, you'll usually need to buy a MIDI adapter cable (although some cards include the cable). Most MIDI adapter cables have pass-through connectors for joysticks, so you can keep both connected if you like to play games and create music on your PC.

The standard MIDI adapter cable usually has one MIDI input and MIDI output, which you can use to attach to an external MIDI sound module and a MIDI controller (such as a keyboard). If you do connect an external MIDI sound module, you can direct all MIDI messages used within any application through it to take advantage of the sound module's (usually) better sound quality.

Figure 5-4 shows how you would make this type of connection.

If you're at all interested in playing computer games, you're definitely going to want to invest in a joystick or other dedicated game controller. A joystick essentially takes the place of your mouse and keyboard and enables you to play many games in a more intuitive way.

Cross-Reference

See Chapter 7, "Input Devices and Power" for more on joysticks and other game controllers.

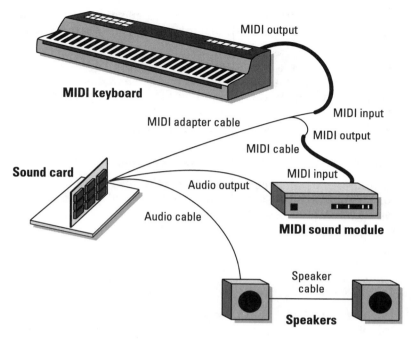

MIDI output

MIDI input

MIDI keyboard

MIDI adapter cable

MIDI output

MIDI cable

Sound card

MIDI input

Audio output

Audio cable

MIDI sound module

Speaker cable

Speakers

Figure 5-4: Make mine MIDI
If you really want high-quality MIDI music, attach an external MIDI sound module to your sound card's MIDI port and have the module play back all the MIDI files. The wiring can get a bit complicated, but it's worth it.

Recommendations

Sound is a frequently overlooked and highly underrated part of the overall computing experience. (I often call computer audio the "bastard child of multimedia.") But, because sound can make a critical difference, I recommend that everyone get a high-quality wavetable soundcard, preferably in PCI form.

On the digital-audio side of the card, you'll want to make sure the card offers full-duplex 16-bit operation and recording rates of 44.1 or 48kHz. On the music side of the equation, even though you may not be interested in FM synthesis, you may get it anyway if you buy a SoundBlaster-compatible card (which many older games require). You'll definitely want to get as many voices of wavetable synthesis as you can, a large amount of good-sounding ROM samples, and, most important, some expandability for add-on wavetables in RAM through support of the DLS (DownLoadable Samples) standard. I also recommend that the wavetable synthesis occur in hardware.

Despite the capability to perform synthesis in software, my experience has been that most implementations of hardware synthesis sound much better. In a manner somewhat analogous to accelerated video cards, sound cards that perform wavetable synthesis in hardware act, in a sense, as sound accelerators.

If you're looking toward the future, investigate the card's physical modeling sounds (if it offers them), and be sure to listen to them before you make any decisions. In fact, that statement holds true for any audio-related component, whether it's sound cards or speakers.

Find out if the card offers internal connectors for both the CD- or DVD-ROM drive, and a voice modem, and see whether or not they're analog or digital. The convenience these connections offer is worth money.

Serious computer gamers and DVD movie buffs will want to get a card that offers 3D, or positional, audio processing, as well as support for multiple speakers and Dolby Digital decoding.

Another factor you may need to consider is that some sound cards can use up several IRQs (Interrupt Requests), which are critical computer system resources. On older systems (and even many newer systems) where free IRQ addresses are extremely rare, this can be a big problem and may prevent the card from working properly within a particular system.

Cross-Reference

See Chapter 17, "Troubleshooting Techniques," for more on dealing with IRQ problems.

To get the best possible audio quality for recording applications, go for a card and set of speakers with support for digital audio inputs and outputs. The digital audio connection that this provides should guarantee pristine, CD-quality audio from your PC.

Finally, to ensure compatibility with all the latest games, make sure the card has drivers that support Microsoft's DirectX technology, which is the company's new standard for low-level multimedia operation. Specifically, sound cards should have DirectSound, DirectSound 3D, and DirectMusic drivers bundled with them or available from the sound card manufacturer.

Speakers

To actually hear the sounds being generated by your computer's sound card or sound-generating circuitry, you need to connect speakers to the sound card's output (although virtually all notebook computers and even many desktops now incorporate speakers into the computer's case).

The speakers' job is to create as accurate an audio signal as they can, just as with speakers for your stereo or home theater system.

The important specs you need to look for in speakers include:

■ The frequency range they support

- The amount of power they support
- The number (and type) of speakers included in a set
- The type of connections they provide.

Satellites and subwoofers

Computer speakers are generally much smaller than stereo speakers, which makes it much harder for them to create full-range, high-quality sound.

Many speaker manufacturers have addressed this issue by creating three-part computer speaker systems that include two smaller satellite speakers and a subwoofer. The satellites handle the mid- and high-frequency range signals, and the subwoofer handles the low-frequency signals. In many cases, the result is extremely high-quality sound in a small, space-efficient package (which is an important issue for computer speakers).

Secret

If your computer system came with only two speakers, but you want to upgrade the sound system and get more pulse-pounding bass frequencies, check to see if your speakers offer a subwoofer output. Many do, which enables you to simply add a subwoofer and saves you from having to buy a complete new speaker system.

You can also upgrade the built-in sound systems on some notebooks and speaker-equipped desktops, though in many cases the external speaker output essentially shuts off the existing speakers and requires a complete set of external speakers instead of just a subwoofer.

Speaker technologies

Though speakers may seem like the lowest-tech devices you have connected to your PC system, there are actually several technology-related features you need to consider.

Powered vs. unpowered

First of all, although some sound cards have tiny amplifiers that can be used to drive small, unpowered speakers, the amplifier isn't usually enough to generate even moderate-quality audio. As a result, most computer speaker systems include their own power amplifier, built into one of the speakers, that drives all the speakers in one system. On three-piece speaker systems, it's typically built into the subwoofer.

This is an important difference from most stereo and home theater speakers, which are usually unpowered and derive their signal from a receiver or separate power amp. It also explains why you can't just hook up an extra pair of old stereo speakers to your computer's sound card and expect to hear anything.

Because of this built-in power amp, when you compare computer speakers you should not only check their sound quality, but also look for any types of volume controls or other adjustments that might expect to see on a stereo system, such as tone controls, balance controls, and so on.

Finally, as with stereo and home theater systems, you also need to check the wattage of the amplifier built into the speakers. If you want gut-wrenching sound for computer games, you're going to need as much power as you can afford.

Traditional vs. flat panel

Traditional stereo speakers use cones that vibrate to generate sound waves. Cones take up a fair amount of space, which means that speakers using them are also relatively large and deep. With the ever-increasing interest in small computer peripherals — particularly after the proliferation of flat-panel monitors — several speaker companies have started to use other technologies that enable them to create much smaller (at least depth-wise) speakers.

Flat-panel speakers, which are available in several different types, use completely different means of generating sound than traditional speakers. Some of them take advantage of a new technology called NXT that vibrates a tiny panel in a pseudo-random fashion and enables the speakers to generate sound. Best of all, they do so in such a way that the sound radiates everywhere around a room — without the usual sweet spot.

Other flat-panel speakers take advantage of thin drivers and other, older technologies that are cost-reduced to use in inexpensive computer speakers. Ultimately, the differences between any of them boil down to sound quality, and you have to listen to them to distinguish that.

3D speakers

Just as some sound cards provide 3D audio effects, some speakers do as well. In the case of speakers, the type of processing is more of a constant effect that widens the soundfield of the speakers. It cannot provide the dynamic processing found in sound cards. In fact, if you have a sound card that supports 3D audio effects, you're better off with a standard set of speakers than with one that supports 3D; otherwise, the two effects could conflict with each other.

Multispeaker systems

One of the larger developments in computer sound systems is multichannel audio, in which the sound card supports up to six or more different speakers. This is exactly analogous to the home theater phenomenon that may have invaded your living room, where the extra center and rear speakers are used to provide a more realistic soundscape. With the proliferation of DVD-ROM drives capable of playing back digital movies on your PC and increased interest in higher-quality sound for computer games, this was probably an inevitable development. (Although, I have to wonder how many computer users are going to be able to find a good place to hold their rear speakers — sitting here at my PC, there's nothing but empty air behind me right now.)

The speaker requirements for this type of arrangement are not much different than they are for home theater, except that most PC-based systems include a power amplifier inside one of the speakers (as opposed to connecting to a separate receiver). Several companies are now offering various configurations and combinations that vary greatly in quality and price.

USB speakers

Some speaker companies also offer USB speakers. With USB-based audio, your PC no longer needs a standalone sound card because a digital audio signal passes from the PC's USB port straight to the USB port of the speakers. Once inside the speakers, a digital-to-analog converter (DAC) takes the digital signal and converts it into sound waves that the speaker can then amplify. In order to use USB speakers, you need to have a software-based synthesizer because, in most cases, there's no hardware card to synthesize MIDI-based audio.

Note that not all speakers that include USB ports are actually equipped with a DAC and thus cannot accept audio over the USB port. Some early implementations of USB speakers simply used the USB port to control certain settings remotely, such as volume and tone controls, and still use traditional analog connections for the audio. Just to confuse matters, some speakers that do have a DAC and can accept digital audio via USB also have analog connections for backward compatibility with traditional sound cards.

Secret

Some early USB audio configurations have been plagued with dropouts in the audio signal, which you hear as pops and clicks. In some cases these problems can be fixed with updated USB drivers and speaker drivers, but in some instances it cannot be fixed (short of buying an upgraded motherboard) because it has to do with problems with the PC's USB controller.

Recommendations

Speakers are one of the most subjective items there are, so the most important thing you can do is to listen to a set you are interested in. Many retail computer stores have set up listening stations just for this purpose. As with stereo stores, they have switches that enable you to quickly choose among several different pairs of speakers.

Tip

One thing to be aware of is that louder speakers always sound better to our ears; so try to make sure that the volume is the same for all the speakers you listen to. (That may mean turning up or turning down the volume slightly for different sets of speakers.)

If you want to try USB speakers, or others that offer a digital connection, make sure you try them on your system and check for possible dropout problems.

Modems

Computers are powerful devices on their own, but they take on a whole new dimension when they are connected to a network of other computers. In the recent past, most personal computers were isolated devices. Fortunately, the notion of a single, disconnected computer is now almost as foreign as the notion of someone who hasn't heard of the Internet. The primary impetus for this increased level of connection between computers is the rapid growth and proliferation of modems (although the popularity of the Internet sure hasn't hurt). As with sound cards, modems are now considered standard equipment on virtually all new computers.

The word modem is a contraction of the words modulator and demodulator. The way a standard analog modem works is by taking the digital data inside a computer and converting it into an analog form that can be sent over a normal phone line (which can only work with audible analog signals, such as your voice). The conversion process is done through a technique called *modulation*. The modem at the receiving end of a connection takes the modulated analog signal and demodulates it to convert it back into a digital form that the computer can understand.

Note

Some higher-speed digital modems, such as cable, ISDN (Integrated Services Digital Network), and DSL (Digital Subscriber Line), don't need to convert the signal to analog; they keep it digital the entire time. As a result, these high-speed devices are officially called *terminal adapters*, but they're still commonly referred to as modems.

A modem's basic function is to provide a means through which one computer can talk to another over a long-distance (that is, compared to within the confines of your workspace or office) connection: typically a phone line. Early modems, in fact, only worked over traditional telephone lines. However, because of both the limitations on how fast connections over traditional phone lines can go and the huge demand for higher-speed connections, additional types of modems that work over different types of lines (such as cable and ISDN) or that use new technologies to transfer data over existing copper phone lines (such as DSL) have become increasingly popular.

Modems can be used to connect one computer to another, so that, for example, you can send a file directly to another person, but they're most commonly used to connect to an Internet Service Provider, or ISP, or an online service, such as America Online. Both ISPs and online services (which, frankly, are ISPs as well) offer large banks of modems to which individual users can connect. These banks of modems, in turn, are connected to computers that are connected directly to the Internet or, in the case of online services, to the service's dedicated computers.

Cross-Reference

For more on connecting to the Internet, see Chapter 13, "Connecting to and Using the Internet."

The most important features to look for in a modem include:

- The type of connections it supports
- The transfer rates it supports
- If it's an analog modem, the type of voice and fax features it includes

Modem speeds

The most important factor in differentiating between modems is the speed at which they operate. A modem's speed determines how quickly it can transfer data between your computer and the one you connect to. The speed is often measured in kilobits per second (Kbps), although faster options offer transfer speeds in the range of several megabits per second (Mbps).

Note

Note that I said kilobits and megabits, not kilobytes and megabytes. Because modems and other network-related devices deal with data a bit at a time as opposed to a byte (which is eight times bigger), they have always used the smaller measure. This can get very confusing because to compare modem transfer rates to other common data transfer measurements you need to divide them by eight. A 56K modem, for example, theoretically offers speeds up to 56 kilobits/second, which is the same as 7KB/second. You may notice these much smaller numbers when using your Web browser to go to different Web sites or to download a file because browsers typically report transfer rates in bytes per second.

Another important point to be aware of with regard to modem speeds is that the speed of data coming into your modem is not necessarily the same as the speed going from your modem. In fact, in most cases, the two are different. The transfer rate coming into your modem is typically called the *downstream* or *downloading rate* and the rate going from your modem is commonly referred to as the *upstream* or *uploading rate*. These types of unequal rates are often called an *asymmetric connection*.

With Internet connections, the downstream rate is much more important because your Web browser primarily receives data from the Internet while outgoing messages are usually nothing more than a simple Web address. As a result, you'll find that many types of modems offer faster downstream rates than upstream rates.

In all cases, what a modem does is acts as an intermediary between your computer and another computer that's attached to a similar type of modem at the other end of the connection. The important point here is that it needs to be two modems of the same basic type. If you try to connect two different types of modems, such as a 56K modem to an ISDN or cable modem, the connections won't work because the two modems won't be able to understand each other. Occasionally, you can also run into problems when you're trying to connect between modems that run at different speeds.

**Cross-
Reference**

See Chapter 18, "Solving Common PC Problems," for tips on how to solve modem-related issues.

As a result, one of the most important decisions in choosing between modems is figuring out the type and speed of the modem you want. But as important as those features may be, in many cases, the choices are already made for you. The reason is that certain types of high-speed modems require special types of lines that will need to be installed into your home or place of business, and not all types of lines are available in all areas of the country. The availability of those lines is typically dependent on the local telephone and cable companies, although sometimes high-speed lines are available directly from Internet Service Providers.

So, before you begin your modem shopping, you'll want to find out what types of services are available in your area. Table 5-1 lists some of the most common types of high-speed Internet access, along with the transfer rates they're capable of supporting and the type of lines they require.

Table 5-1   High Speed Access

Modem Type	Maximum Downstream Transfer Rate	Maximum Upstream Transfer Rate	Type of Line Required
Analog 56Kbps	53Kbps	33Kbps	Standard phone line
ISDN	128Kbps	128Kbps	ISDN line
Cable	Up to 38Mbps	Up to 1Mbps	Two-way cable line
DSL	Up to 1.5Mbps for Universal ADSL, up to 8Mbps for ADSL	Varies, though 384Kbps for Universal DSL	DSL-enabled phone line (ADSL also requires a splitter in your home or business)

Analog modems

The most popular type of modem by far is the traditional analog modem, which can connect to any standard phone line. As with virtually all modem types, you can find analog modems both in external forms, which typically connect to your computer's serial or USB ports, or internal versions, which take the form of plug-in cards that attach to one of your computer's ISA or PCI slots.

Note

One benefit that analog modems still have over higher-speed types is that they support fax software features, which the other types do not.

Some lower cost computers and handheld computers actually have software modems, where all the basic data sending and receiving chores are handled by the computer's processor. Like software-based music synthesis (described earlier in the chapter), software modems are made possible through special programs that take advantage of the excellent processing power available in today's PCs. Of course, running a software version of a modem slows down a computer's overall performance while it's in operation, but it offers the benefit of being easily upgraded. As with software-based synthesis, a computer with a software modem still needs a certain amount of hardware (in this case, phone connectors) to be capable of connecting to the outside world.

On notebook computers, modems typically come in PC card format, which is the credit card–sized expansion format that most notebook peripherals come in, though some notebooks offer special built-in modems that are attached to the motherboard. Like computers with software-based modems, built-in modems provide a standard telephone jack connector to which you can connect.

Most modems offer a pass-through port that you connect a telephone to, in addition to the connector for your modem's phone jack connection. This pass-through port is important if you want to share single phone line with a modem and a standard phone. When a phone is connected to this port, and you aren't using the modem, phone calls will ring on the phone as normal.

For desktop PC users, external modems are generally a bit more expensive than their internal counterparts, but some people prefer them because they like being able to see the status lights that flash on and off while a modem is use. Status lights show things such as data being sent and received. Internal modems offer this capability through the operating system software, but it's not as obvious as it is on an external modem.

56K modems

Most new analog modems run at the rate of 56Kbps and conform to the V.90 specification, which ensures that any two 56K modems can speak to each other. (See the sidebar "Modem standards" for more.)

Modem standards

Like people, different types of modems often speak in different languages. As a result, not all modems are inherently able to communicate with all other types of modems. To make communication possible, there need to be universally accepted standards that ensure that two modems from different manufacturers can speak this same language and properly communicate with each other.

In the world of modems, these standards or protocols, are created by the International Telecommunications Union, or ITU. ITU protocols are typically designated as V.xx, where xx represents a specific two-digit number. If your modem supports the official standards, you can be sure it will be able to operate with other modems that also support those standards.

The V.90 standard is the official 56K modem standard, while V.80 defines standards for videophone communications if you want to do direct videoconferencing over standard phone lines. Other protocols you might see are V.42, which is a standard for error correction on higher-speed modems, and V.34, which is the 28.8Kbps/33.6Kbps modem standard.

Another related, but different, set of protocols involve different modem compression schemes. In order to offer the best possible data throughput rates, modem manufacturers realized they could compress the signal before it was sent and then decompress it on the receiving modem. By using compression, older 19.2 and 28.8 modems, for example, could offer throughput rates that were nearly twice as fast on certain types of files.

In order for this to work, however, both the sending and receiving modems need to be able to understand the same compression methods — hence the need for standards. The most well known modem compression protocol is the V.42bis standard.

If you work with older computers, you may come across modems that run at 33.6Kbps, 28.8Kbps, 19.2Kbps, or even 14.4Kbps. These ratings refer to the maximum possible data transfer rate that each type of modems support. As you would expect, lower numbers mean slower transfer rates.

There's a good chance that you'll also come across some older 56K modems that haven't been upgraded to the V.90 specification and still work with one of the two original competing 56K standards: x2 or K56Flex. (See the sidebar "The 56K battle" for more on older 56K modem standards.)

Secret

Unfortunately, some companies offered upgrades to the preliminary V.90 spec but those upgrades don't necessarily ensure compatibility with the final version of the specification. You may need to do a second upgrade to ensure that your modem supports the official standard.

The important thing to realize when it comes to working with modems of different speeds is that the slower of the two modems connecting to one another determines the speed of the connection. So, for example, if you attempt to connect a 56K modem to a computer equipped with a 28.8 modem, the fastest the connection can go is 28.8Kbps.

The 56K battle

Several years ago, it was widely believed that the fastest that traditional analog modems would ever be able to transfer data was 33.6Kbps because of limitations in the quality of analog phone lines; however, several different companies discovered ways to offer higher-speed connections over analog lines. Unfortunately, the methods that they discovered were not compatible with each other. As a result, modems built around the various technologies could not communicate with each other at the highest rates. (They could still connect at slower speeds, however, because they supported the existing modem standards.)

Two of the three companies who made these discoveries decided to combine their efforts and make their products and technologies work together. Lucent and Rockwell created the K56Flex standard, which was used in modems from a wide range of manufacturers. USRobotics (now a division of 3Com) stuck with their own x2 standard, but made the technology available to other companies. Any modem that supported the K56Flex standard could work with any other K56Flex-based modem from any other company at rates above 33.6. Similarly, any x2-based modem could talk to any other x2 modem at rates up to 53Kbps. (This is the technical data transfer limit for all 56K modems, regardless of who makes it, because of limitations in analog phone lines.) However — and this is where the problem lies — K56Flex modems and x2 modems could not communicate directly with each at these higher rates.

Though each standard tried to outdo the other, the resulting confusion in the marketplace over which type of modem to buy, K56Flex or x2, actually slowed the acceptance of 56K modems. With the development and official approval of the V.90 standard, which incorporates elements of both K56Flex and x2 technology, the problems of trying to connect between the two competing standards have started to disappear.

Not everyone has upgraded their older modems to the new standard, however, so it's still possible to run into problems when connecting between your 56K modem and the 56K modems available at your ISP.

Note though, the modem upgrade process typically involves running a small utility that will update a chip inside your modem. This chip holds the modem's firmware (which is software stored in hardware — hence the compromise name). Some older 56K modems are not software upgradeable, however, which means the firmware chip needs to be physically replaced.

The best way to avoid problems is to make sure both your modem and the modem you're connecting to supports the official V.90 specification. If it doesn't, you'll need to make sure that you select an ISP that supports the specific type of 56K modem that you have.

Note

By the way, all faster modem transfer standards are backwards compatible with the earlier, slower versions. So, a 56K modem can connect with any modem standard used in slower modems.

Also, just because you use two modems that are rated at the same speed doesn't mean you will necessarily connect at that speed. In fact, most times you'll connect at lower speeds, such as 45Kbps on a 56K modem or 31Kbps on a 33.6 modem. The reason for this is that high-speed modem transfers are dependent on high-quality phone connections and not all phone connections are always as clear as they need to be.

We've all experienced this when making voice calls — sometimes the connection is bad. When a modem gets a bad connection, or one that isn't clear enough for to operate at its maximum speed, the modem automatically drops down to a slightly slower speed and then, if necessary, to the next slower speed, until it finds the speed it determines it can maintain over the course of a call. The higher the speed you connect at, the more sensitive the modem is to the quality of the phone line. This explains, for example, why 28.8 modems often can connect at 28.8, whereas 56K modems rarely connect above 50Kbps.

Cross-Reference

For more on modem connection speed issues, see Chapter 18, "Solving Common PC Problems."

Voice modems

Since modems deal with phone lines, it only makes sense to incorporate some telephony features into modems. The problem is, standard modems don't have the special circuitry they need to be able to digitize and playback your voice, which is obviously a critical part of any telephone-like application. So, manufacturers added some basic digital audio capabilities to modems so that they could do things such as function as a speakerphone or an answering machine.

Note

The circuitry required to make a modem voice-enabled is identical to what's use in sound cards, which is one of the reasons why you can now buy a combination sound card/modem in a single plug-in card. It's just one more example of the types of logical consolidations that keep reducing the number of different parts needed for PCs.

Voice-enabled modems, *voice-capable modems*, enable you to turn your PC into a complete communications center that functions in place of a standalone answering machine or phone. Just plug a microphone into the back of a voice enabled modem and plug speakers into the modem's outputs, and you have the equivalent of a speakerphone.

Well, actually, you may not want to plug speakers into the modem's output, because then you won't be able to hear your sound card (unless you have two sets of speakers, which would be an unnecessary waste). Instead, if you have both a voice modem and a sound card, you want to plug the modem's line output into the sound card's line input, and then control the volume of the modem's audio signal (typically the volume level of the person calling you) through the sound card's mixer application. (Some internal modems can connect to sound cards via an internal ribbon cable, which can clean up a bit of the clutter behind your PC. Check to see if your sound card has a connector for a voice modem.) Figure 5-5 shows the appropriate connections.

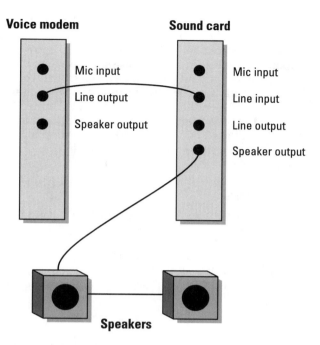

Figure 5-5: Connecting voice modems and sound cards
Sound cards and voice modems duplicate certain bits of circuitry, which can lead to confusing options about what you should connect your speakers to. The most straight-forward solution is to connect the modem's line output to the sound card's line input, and then connect the sound card's output to your speakers. In this type of setup, the voice modem's speaker output does not connect to anything (because the sound is routed through the sound card).

To use the modem as a phone, you need to connect a microphone to the modem. But if you only have one microphone and you also want to use it to record sounds on your sound card, you will need to switch the microphone over to the sound card (which will get old — fast); you may want to get a separate microphone for each. Many sound cards and voice modems come with their own mics, anyway — but you'll have to remember which one is which. If you do get a voice modem, make sure it supports full-duplex audio, which, as described in the earlier part of the chapter, lets both you and the person you're calling speak at the same time.

Secret

You don't necessarily need a voice-enabled modem to place phone calls with your PC. In fact, most Internet-based phone calls — where you initiate a phone call after connecting to the Internet — can occur over any type of Internet connection. The audio is just handled by your sound card in those situations.

In order to use a voice modem both to speak and send data at the same time, you either need to use an Internet-based conferencing program, such as the NetMeeting application Microsoft bundles with Internet Explorer, or get a DSVD (Digital Simultaneous Voice and Data)-capable modem. DSVD modems, which were big a few years ago, but have since fallen from favor, can compress spoken audio into the data stream and send it simultaneously with data. The problem with DSVD is that it requires a direct connection to another person with a DSVD modem, which is why DVSD is rarely talked about any more. Internet-based conferences, on the other hand, can occur between any two individuals with connections to the Internet. The hardware they use to connect does not need to be the same.

Wireless modems

Notebook computer users who don't always have easy access to phone lines can consider another option: wireless modems. Wireless modems come in two basic types: those that work in conjunction with cellular phones and those that work entirely on their own. (Satellite dishes that offer data connections are another wireless option for desktop users. Figure 5-6 shows a typical satellite-dish-based setup. See the sidebar "Satellite connections" for more.)

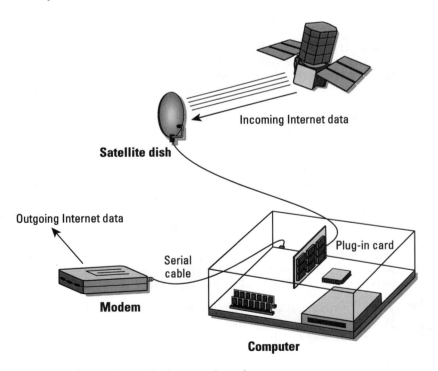

Figure 5-6: Connecting to the Internet through space
Satellite-based systems connect to your PC through a plug-in card that goes into one of your computer's expansion slots. You send data through a connected modem and then receive data from the satellite dish.

Satellite connections

If you happen to live in a very rural area, or if you're just fascinated by the notion of having your own satellite dish, you may also want to look into a product such as Hughes Network Systems' DirecPC. DirecPC, which looks and essentially works like the various TV-based satellite dish products, offers a wireless satellite link that's capable of receiving data at rates up to 400Kbps. However, all current satellite systems are one way—that is, they can only receive data. So, in order to use a satellite system (and be able to send data as well as receive it) you would also need to buy a standard analog modem and have a separate Internet account for it—in addition to the account you'll need for the satellite.

Many, though not all, PC Card modems designed for notebooks offer support for cellular phones. If they do, you'll find a special connector on the modem card that connects to a special cable used to link the modem and the cell phone. Then, when you go to use the modem, it dials up the number through the cell phone and then uses its wireless connection to send and receive data. Some cell phone connections use CDPD (Cellular Digital Packet Data) technology to transfer data wirelessly, although there are other connection technologies.

Secret

Not all cellular phones support data connections, and of those that do, some only work with certain cellular-capable modems. So, the only way to guarantee that you'll get a cellular modem connection to work is to ensure that your particular phone works with your particular modem.

Another option for mobile computer users are self-contained wireless modems that include their own antenna for sending and receiving data. These devices, such as the Ricochet Wireless modem from Metricom, typically attach to your notebook's serial ports (although some wireless modems come in PC Card format) and work just like an external modem. They usually aren't as fast as wired modems, and you need to live or be traveling in an area where the service is available for it to work. Right now, this is very limited, but self-contained wireless modems can be a very convenient solution for people who need the flexibility of a wireless data connection.

ISDN modems

If your local phone company offers ISDN, or Integrated Services Digital Network, at a reasonable price, and you're interested in higher-speed Internet access, you may want to investigate an ISDN modem, or terminal adapter.

ISDN modems require a special ISDN line to function—they won't work without one. This means you have to have a line installed (which costs you money) and pay a separate monthly charge for this line (which costs you more money), in addition to the monthly fee you'll pay for Internet access from your ISP (which costs you even more money, especially because rates for higher-speed access technologies are always more expensive than the normal rates for telephone dial-up lines). In some places, there are even special ISDN line access charges. I'm not saying this to discourage you; in fact, I had an ISDN line at home (until DSL became available) and found it well worth the money, but I do want to make you aware of the costs involved.

In this regard, ISDN is no different from most other high-speed access technologies. They all have a variety of different costs associated with them that you need to be aware of before you make the plunge.

With an ISDN connection, and in return for your higher outlay of cash, you receive data at a faster rate, which translates into waiting less time for pages to appear and files to download. Most recent ISDN modems offers support for two BRI, or Basic Rate Interface, channels, each of which can run at either 56 or 64Kbps. You can use those lines individually or, if your modem supports a feature called *bonding*, combine the two into a single 112 or 128Kbps data line.

Note

It's also possible to bond two analog modems into a single data line if you own two modems, but you'll need some software to do it. Several commercial products include this capability, but you can also get a basic version of this capability bundled as part of Dial-Up Networking 1.2 or greater for Windows 95, or any version of Dial-Up Networking incorporated into Windows 98. Once you've set this type of software up, and properly configured two modems, your computer and software essentially see it as a single line that works at the combined rate of the two modems.

One of the nice improvements that ISDN modems offer over traditional analog modems is that they can connect in less than three seconds. While that may not sound like a big deal at first, it turns out to be a big a benefit versus the 20-second or longer time frame it takes for analog modems to connect. This is especially true when you make a lot of connections to check your e-mail or visit a Web site, as most people do.

AO/DI

One important feature to look for with ISDN modems (and service providers you connect to) is support for Always On/Dynamic ISDN (AO/DI) technology, which uses the ISDN D-Channel to maintain a constant 9.6Kbit connection to your ISP. Older ISDN modems that don't support this feature are like dial-up analog modems in that they only make a connection when requested. One of the benefits of cable modems and DSL technology, however, is that they always have an open connection so that, for example, you'll instantly receive notification of e-mail, or you'll be able to receive content that's pushed to you over the Internet without having to actually dial in.

AO/DI provides a similar capability to ISDN by enabling a low-speed connection to be constant and then jumping up to the faster connection speeds as your needs demand (such as when you start to use your browser to visit a Web site). To make this work you'll need to check with your phone company to ensure that your ISDN line is equipped to handle this feature, as well as your ISP and your ISDN modem.

Multiple phone lines

ISDN lines actually consist of two different phone numbers, and most ISDN modems have pass-through connectors for at least one, if not both of these lines. These connector are often called *POTS* connectors, which, believe it or not, actually stands for Plain Old Telephone Service. (I'm not kidding.) This makes ISDN a tremendous solution for home offices and other small businesses because you can use one ISDN line and have a phone line, a separate fax line, and a high-speed Internet connection all in one. Figure 5-7 shows a typical setup.

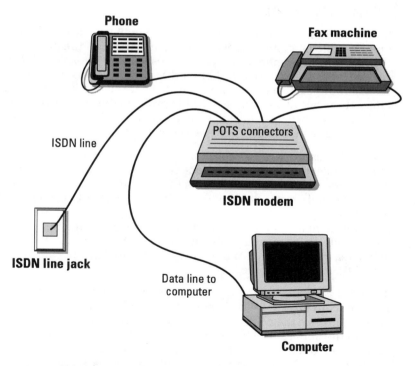

Figure 5-7: The ISDN home office
If your ISDN modem offers two POTS connectors, you can connect a phone and a fax machine to the connectors separately and be able to use data, voice, and fax in any combination of two at once.

Secret

If you ask your phone company to enable the Additional Call Option, or ACO, on your ISDN line, you can have incoming phone calls or faxes cut in and ring your phone or fax machine while you're connected to the net.

To do this, the modem transparently drops one of its two lines, dropping the data rate down to 64Kbps, and routes the incoming call to either of the two analog phone passthrough switches, which will then ring your phone or connect with your fax machine. Once the conversation or fax is done, the modem will automatically reconnect the second data line, pushing the data rate back up to 128Kbps. (As long as your ISDN modem supports ACO — make sure you check before you buy.)

ACO, which is often a free service, also offers the equivalent of Call Waiting if you receive an incoming voice call while using one of the two lines to make another call. All in all, it's a great service, but to get it to work properly you need support for it in your ISDN modem as well as from the phone company.

Cable modems

If you live in the right area of the country, you'll have access to an even faster option: cable modems. Widely hyped as the savior of the Internet because of their very fast potential download speeds (up to 38Mbps) and relatively low service costs (often around $40/month), cable modems have been very slow to take root because cable companies have taken a long time to make cable Internet service available. That's a big problem, because if you do not have a two-way, data-capable cable line installed in your home, cable modems are useless (because there's nothing to connect them to).

In most instances, if your cable company does offer Internet cable service, you won't need to buy a cable modem because most cable companies lease cable modems to the public. Part of the reason for this is that although there is a cable modem standard called DOCSIS (Data Over Cable Service Interface Specification), not all cable systems were designed with these types of modems in mind. As a result, there are still a variety of different proprietary cable modem systems currently in existence. So, to ensure that their service will work, cable companies buy the types of modems they need, and then install them in your home.

To install a cable modem on your own, you must purchase an Ethernet network card in your PC and connect the external cable modem to it. In most cases, however, the cable company provides the Ethernet card, including its cost, in the initial setup fee. Then they install the Ethernet card in your PC (you'll need to have an open slot and to find out if they use ISA or PCI format cards) and simply connect it to the cable modem box which, in turn, is connected to the cable line.

Secret

Cable modems are actually more like little network devices because they essentially connect your PC to the network of other cable modem customers. In other words, it's very much like how your PC at work is connected to your company's network. This has several important ramifications, some of which are good and some of which, well, aren't.

First, on the positive side, because you're connected to a network, you're essentially always connected, which means you don't have to worry about making a dial-up connection. You just launch your browser and go immediately to wherever you want to go.

On the other hand, like any network or other shared connection, the performance of a cable modem can vary tremendously, depending on how many people are using the network at one time. If there are too many people on the network, its performance will degrade, or slow down. So, if your cable company doesn't maintain a sufficiently robust network, the speedy connections you used to enjoy when you first signed up may slowly tumble to much slower speeds as more and more people sign up for the service and start to use the network. If this happens, the only thing you can do is complain to the company about the need to beef up their networks.

The other potential problem is that in some rare instances, other users on the network may be able to access any files you have inadvertently shared through Windows 95 or Windows 98's built-in file sharing. This issue raised its ugly head in some of the earliest cable modem installations, when some cable modem customers discovered they could get full access to the hard drives or folders of other customers who also used the service. (They could have been mounted as network drives, in case you're wondering how this was possible.) Needless to say, this was a big problem. In most cases, this situation has been remedied, but it doesn't hurt to ask your cable company about file sharing and privacy problems.

One other limitation of cable modems is that they typically don't offer traditional telephony functions (because they don't use a phone line). As more and more phone calls and other telephony-related functions are being placed over the Internet, however, this limitation will disappear. This is because a cable modem (or any other type of Internet connection device, for that matter) can send and receive the digital data used to make and receive Internet-based phone calls. In other words, with a high-speed data connection, you don't need a voice line to make phone calls. You can simply make them with a data connection.

DSL modems

The most recent entry into the world of high-speed Internet access products is called *Digital Subscriber Line*, or DSL, modems. DSL is a technology that was originally developed by the phone companies in the mid-1980s to deliver interactive video over standard phone lines. This never came to pass, but the companies later realized they could use it to deliver high-speed connections over standard analog (sometimes also called copper, in reference to the metal used inside the phone wires) phone lines.

DSL technology works by taking advantage of the fact that voice communications over phones are limited to frequencies up to 4kHz. By using frequencies above 4kHz, DSL enables data communications to occur on a normal phone line and at the same time as a voice call is being made. In other words, you can use a single phone line both to make and receive phone calls and simultaneously access the Internet.

DSL can get confusing because there are several different variations on the DSL standard. In fact, the acronym xDSL is often used to signify one of any number of DSL variants.

The most popular DSL alternative is sometimes called Universal ADSL (UADSL) or DSL Lite. Universal ADSL offers download transfer speeds of up to 1.5Mbps and upload speeds of up to 384Kbps. While this isn't as fast as other implementations of DSL, such as ADSL (Asymmetrical Digital Subscriber Line), which offers download rates of up to 8Mbps per second, UADSL has one important advantage: it doesn't require that an extra piece of phone line equipment (called a *splitter*) is installed. Modems that support this service conform to the G.lite standard or G.992.2.

With ADSL, SDSL (Symmetrical DSL, which has identical upload and download speeds), HDSL (High data rate DSL, which offers even higher theoretical transfer rates than ADSL), and VDSL (Very high data rate DSL, which supports up to 52Mbps over short connections), the receiving end of the connection (in other words, your house or business), needs to have a splitter installed. It takes the incoming signal over the phone line and splits it into voice calls, which are routed to your phone, and data calls, which are routed to your DSL modem.

The technology used to implement Universal ADSL, on the other hand, doesn't require a splitter to separate different types of calls, but that convenience comes at the cost of a lower potential transfer date. (Although, even at 1.5Mbps, that's as fast as T-1 lines which, until recently, were very expensive data lines that were typically shared by an entire company.)

External DSL modems are similar to cable modems in that they connect to your PC via an Ethernet card and maintain a constant connection to the Internet. Also, in many cases, the phone companies will provide a DSL modem (and Ethernet card) as part of the standard installation cost (although you can buy them separately as well, if you know what kind of DSL your phone company supports).

One of the benefits that DSL has over cable modems is that the connection is dedicated, meaning performance won't necessarily degrade as more people start to use DSL.

Secret

The one exception is that if the phone company's switches — which are what your DSL modem connects to — become overwhelmed by too much data traffic, then your DSL connection can slow down. Again, the only solution to this problem is to complain to the phone company.

Unlike cable, DSL connections are sensitive to distance. As a result, the further your home or business is away from a phone company's central office, (CO) which is where the DSL switching equipment resides, the slower it will be. In fact, if your home is further than about three miles from a CO, you may not be able to get DSL service at all.

Recommendations

One of the biggest bottlenecks in today's PCs is the relatively slow speeds of traditional analog modems. The horsepower sitting inside your computer's case often goes to waste when you're surfing the Internet or doing other communications-based applications because data is essentially just trickling into your computer.

The best and only way to really improve the speed of your Internet connection is to get a faster connection (sometimes referred to as a faster or bigger *pipe*) between your computer and your Internet Service Provider or favorite online service. Unfortunately, the availability of a faster pipe is often out of your immediate control (unless you're willing to move to get faster services) because it usually depends on where you live and what services are available. ISDN, cable modems, and various types of DSL are all becoming more widely available as time goes on, but they are far from universal.

Even 56K modems, which can be used on any phone line anywhere in the country, only achieve their maximum potential in areas with high-quality phone lines. Older neighborhoods or older homes are sometimes unable to get transfer rates at much higher than 33.6 because the quality of the phone line won't support the higher speed connection.

If you happen to live in an area where cable modem service or DSL is available for a reasonable rate, I would highly recommend you investigate one of these options. Both of them offer extremely fast access, the convenience of immediate connectivity, and usually don't require the installation of a new type of line into your house. If you have the luxury of choosing between the two, I think DSL is the better choice (even though it's theoretically not as fast) because DSL service doesn't share bandwidth between users. And if you live in a rural area, your best choice is probably a satellite connection.

If those high-speed services aren't available, your next best bet is ISDN. Don't forget, however, that you'll have to pay to have a special line installed, and you'll pay both a monthly fee for the phone line, as well as a monthly fee for the Internet access. (DSL installations have separate phone line and ISP charges as well.) If possible, take advantage of the Always On/Dynamic ISDN (AO/DI) feature.

Finally, if you're stuck with analog phone lines, don't settle for anything less than a 56Kbps modem. Now that the V.90 has been standardized, there's no reason to force your computer to sit around and wait because of a slow

Internet connection. If you plan to use some telephony applications, you'll want to be sure either that your sound card can work together with your modem to handle telephony or that your modem is voice-enabled.

Summary

In this chapter, I described the important characteristics of sound cards, speakers, and modems.

▶ The two types of sound that sound cards create are digital audio, which is an exact replica of a piece of music or audio, and synthesized sound, which is generated dynamically from a series of MIDI commands.

▶ There are several different methods for synthesizing sound, including FM synthesis, wavetable synthesis, and physical modeling synthesis, each of which work and sound differently.

▶ Most sound cards offer several types of audio processing effects, including some that can generate 3D audio.

▶ Sound cards can offer several different types of connections, including multiple speaker outputs, digital audio outputs, and MIDI /joystick ports.

▶ Computer speaker systems commonly use a subwoofer to increase the range of sounds they can produce and many now include four or more speakers to create a home-theater-like experience for computer games and DVD movies.

▶ USB speakers connect digitally to your PC and enable it produce audio without a sound card.

▶ Modem speeds are generally determined by the type of line they are connected to.

▶ Analog modems with voice support can function as full-featured telephones and answering machines.

▶ ISDN modems require the installation of a dedicated ISDN digital phone line, but offer the benefit of two phone lines and a data connection in one.

▶ Cable modems and DSL modems offer extremely fast, always-on connections, which are ideal for the Internet. Unfortunately, you can only use them where the service is available.

▶ Cable modem bandwidth can decrease as more people start to use the service.

▶ DSL modems support simultaneous voice and data calls on a single, standard phone line.

Chapter 6

Printers, Scanners, and Digital Cameras

In This Chapter

▶ You will learn what distinguishes one printer from another.

▶ You will learn what types of features impact print quality.

▶ You will learn how various types of printers, including photo printers, work.

▶ You will learn what distinguishes scanners from one another.

▶ You will learn the factors that affect a scanner's quality.

▶ You will learn what features to look for in digital still cameras and digital video cameras.

▶ You will receive recommendations on printers, scanners, and digital cameras.

Computers are great at working with information in digital form, but last time I checked, people weren't. We're much better at working with tangible objects. So, it's probably not terribly surprising that computer printers, which crank out information-rich paper (a fancy name for printouts), are the most important of all computer peripherals.

In fact, despite the much-anticipated promise of a paper-less office, today's computer-equipped homes and offices are generating more paper than ever, which makes a printer even more essential to your computer system. You may find that due to specialization among printers, you'll end up owning several different kinds.

Along with this growing use of paper, there's an increasing desire to copy existing materials, such as photographs and other paper-based information, onto the computer, where it can be manipulated, processed, and stored. The best way to do this is through a device that converts the tangible piece of information into the digital form that computers are capable of working with. The device that does this conversion is called a *scanner*. Scanners essentially take digital pictures of papers, photographs, or other objects and transfer this information into the computer.

Many people use scanners to digitize photographs and, in fact, there's a growing interest in having digital versions of photos. In response to this, many companies have developed digital cameras, which are essentially a specialized type of scanner. Digital cameras save the user the hassle of shooting pictures with traditional film, processing photos, and scanning them into the computer. With digital cameras you simply shoot a photograph and transfer the digital image straight to your computer. This convenience has made digital cameras one of the fastest-growing computer peripherals ever. In addition, many people are interested in adding small video cameras to their PC systems for applications such as videophones.

Printers

Computer printers come in a wide variety of shapes, sizes, speeds, and capabilities (and colors they support, for that matter). They all share the capability to generate printed output from your PC — typically onto regular paper, though today's printers also work with labels, iron-ons, banners, cloth, and more.

In most cases you'll be able to find a single printer that can match all your needs, but you may also want to consider multiple printers for specific needs.

The most important features to look for in printers are:

- The type of technology it uses to print
- The resolution
- The printing speed
- The number of simultaneous colors it supports
- The type of connection it provides

Inkjet versus laser versus other options

The most important distinguishing factor between printers is the manner in which they generate text and images on a page. The two most popular types of printing technology are *inkjet printing* and *laser printing*, although you may also come across technologies such as *dye-sublimation, thermal transfer*, and other proprietary schemes.

Inkjet printers work by placing tiny drops of ink at various places on the page. The printer advances the paper forward a bit at a time and moves the inkjet cartridge (which holds liquid inks) laterally across the page. Based on instructions it receives from the printer's driver software, the inkjet cartridge along with the print head drops tiny drops of ink at the appropriate places on the paper.

Figure 6-1 shows an example.

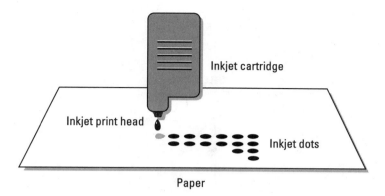

Figure 6-1: How an inkjet printer works
Inkjet printers generate their printouts by placing thousands of tiny dots of ink on a page. The inkjet cartridge holds the ink and connects directly to the print head, which places dots at different places on the page.

On a laser printer, the image on the page (which may consist of text, graphics, or both) is generated by attracting toner particles to a magnetized drum and then fusing those particles onto the paper. Picture those old kids toys where you use a magnet to attract metal particles to a particular area of a screen to create a picture; this is essentially what happens inside a laser printer — although in reverse. A beam of laser light etches out a pattern on a rotating, magnetized drum by moving back and forth across the drum a line at a time, and then toner particles are attracted to the demagnetized section of the drum. The drum and attached toner particles roll over a piece of paper, and a device called a *fuser* essentially irons them onto the paper.

Figure 6-2 illustrates the process.

Because of the way laser printers work, they need to be capable of generating and holding the entire page in memory before they can etch the image onto the drum. As a result, you'll often see laser printers come with several megabytes of memory that serve as a storage area for the page image.

A potential downside of this arrangement is that if you try to print a complex drawing onto a laser printer, it is possible to run out of memory in the printer. If this happens, the printer will only be capable of printing a portion of the page, or it may generate an error message and be unable to print anything at all. This does not occur very often, but it is a possibility if you're working with complex graphics.

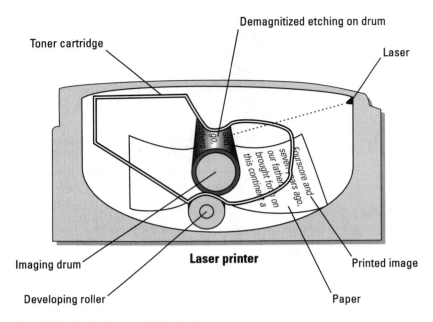

Toner cartridge

Demagnitized etching on drum

Laser

Imaging drum

Laser printer

Printed image

Developing roller

Paper

Figure 6-2: How a laser printer works
Laser printers work by etching a demagnetized image onto a rotating drum, then attracting toner particles to the demagnetized area, and finally ironing this image onto the page.

Inkjet and other types of printers don't have this problem because they don't need to create an image of the whole page before they start printing. Instead, they simply take a chunk of the page image at a time and print that portion, and then they get another chunk and print that portion, and so on, until the process is complete. As a result, inkjets tend to be a bit slower than lasers (particularly when making multiple copies of the same page) although newer inkjets have gotten much faster.

Another printing technology you may come across is dye sublimation, sometimes inncorrectly called thermal transfer. In printers using dye sublimation technology, the inks are made up of a clear cellophane-like material that works kind of like a print cartridge in old typewriters. The page image is created by a specialized print head that melts this material immediately from a solid to a gaseous state (a chemical process that's generically referred to as sublimation) and sprays it onto the paper a line at a time.

As you might expect, dye sublimation printers tend to be slower than inkjets and lasers, but the paper doesn't warp and the ink doesn't run if any liquid falls onto the page. (Many inkjet printers suffer from these problems, although newer ink formulations that dry more quickly and thoroughly have greatly reduced these kinds of issues.) In addition, dye sublimation printers can generate what are called *continuous tone images*, which means there are no visible gaps or drops in the image, even up close. The result is something that looks identical to a traditional photograph from a film-processing lab.

Cross-Reference

For more on continuous tone images, see the section, "Halftones" later in this chapter.

All the various types of printing technologies are capable of generating black-and-white, grayscale (where only black ink is used, but through a process called *halftoning*, numerous shades of gray are created), and color output, although most lower-cost laser printers only support black-and-white and grayscale printouts. Color laser printers are available, but they're still expensive.

Regardless of the type of printing technology, there are several different specifications that you can use to compare different printers including print resolution, speed, cost per page, and more.

Print resolution

Probably the most commonly quoted printer specification is its resolution, which refers to how fine an image it is capable of producing. Resolution is typically measured in dots per inch (dpi). Dots are the smallest element that a printer's print engine (the part that actually makes the images) can generate, so this specification refers to how many of these tiny elements can fit in a given area. The smaller the dots, the more that can fit in one area and hence, the finer (or higher) the resolution. Figure 6-3 shows an example.

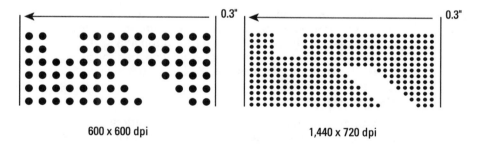

600 x 600 dpi   1,440 x 720 dpi

Figure 6-3: High resolution
Most popular inkjets and lasers can generate at least 3,600 individual dots (600 × 600) in one square inch of paper, and many can generate even more. On inkjets that offer different horizontal and vertical resolutions, the horizontal resolution generally has dots that are finely packed together, but the vertical resolution (the space between the lines) isn't as small.

Many printers provide a single number resolution; that is, their specifications say that they are a 600 or 720 (or any other number) dpi printer. (Most printers, by the way, are capable of printing in a variety of different resolutions, but they always quote their highest possible resolution.) In most cases, this means that both the horizontal and vertical resolution of the printer is that number. In other words, an inch-long line that goes horizontally across a page would be made up of x number of dots (where x is the printer's dpi specification), and similarly an inch-long line that goes vertically down a page would be made up of the same number of dots.

Another way to denote this is to say that the printer offers 720 × 720 (or any other number) resolution.

Secret

On many printers, however, the horizontal and vertical resolution is not the same. Some printer manufacturers are very forthright about this and quote their printers as offering 600 × 300 dpi or 1,440 × 720 dpi, and so on. (In most cases the higher number is the horizontal resolution, and the lower number is the vertical resolution.) Others only quote the highest number (surprise, surprise) and hide the real truth inside their detailed specifications.

Also note that some printers offer higher resolution in black-and-white mode than they do in color, and some can only achieve their highest printout quality on special (read: expensive) paper. So, when you're comparing printers, be on the lookout for the real figures. You want to know the horizontal and vertical resolution on regular paper.

The reason for these differences, by the way, has to do with how printers work. Stepper motors advance the paper forward as the print head moves across the page horizontally. Improvements in print head resolution, which is where all the interest usually is, typically translates into higher horizontal resolutions.

Tossing all this specsmanship aside, the visual difference between output from printers that have equal horizontal and vertical resolution and those with higher horizontal resolutions can actually be quite small. Though intuitively you would think that printers with unequal resolutions would generate strange-looking printouts, the printouts are actually very attractive. In most cases, printers with equal resolution at a particular dpi (such as 720 × 720) create slightly sharper images than those with a related unequal resolution (such as 720 × 360), but not always.

Print quality

As with most computer peripherals, specifications for printers don't tell the whole story. The real acid test for printers is to look at the quality of their printouts. You'll find that even though two printers may have virtually identical specs, their print quality may vary dramatically. One may be much better at printing photographs, while another might generate brighter-looking printouts, and so on.

The reason is that the print quality is actually determined by a combination of all the different elements inside a printer as well as the printer driver (which is the software you install on your computer that talks to your printer). The printer driver, in particular, can have a very large impact on the printout quality. Two identical printers using different versions of a printer driver may generate very different results.

By the way, if you do side-by-side comparisons of print quality, make sure it's an apples-to-apples comparison. For example, don't compare the printouts from one printer on expensive glossy paper with those from another printer on normal paper. For the most part, I'd recommend that you do plain-paper to plain-paper comparisons.

Print speed

Another commonly quoted printer specification is print speed. It refers to how quickly a printer can output a page. Print speed is usually listed as some number of pages per minute (ppm), although some older color printers list it as minutes per page (mpp) — a rather sneaky way of denoting their very slow speed.

A rating of 8 ppm means that a printer can produce up to eight pages in a minute, or about one page every seven seconds. A rating of 2 mpp, on the other hand, means it takes two minutes to generate a single page. Honest manufacturers call this rating 0.5 ppm.

Note that these speed ratings are usually listed for ideal conditions and often are based on using some of the printer's lower resolution settings. I've never seen a printer come close to its published rates in real-world performance, particularly at the printer's highest resolution. Unfortunately, there's no established standard for determining these ratings, which means one manufacturer's 8 ppm printer may only run as fast as another's 5 ppm printer on normal pages. Caveat emptor.

Printers typically have different ratings for black-and-white pages and color pages. Not surprisingly, the rates for color pages are generally much slower because the printer has a lot more work to do when generating color images. (Producing particular colors requires putting multiple dots of different colored inks on or around the same spot, which obviously takes more time.)

Cost per page

One specification you may not see listed by the printer manufacturers but which you will often see in magazine reviews for printers is cost per page. This is actually a very important piece of information to have because it gives you insight into a critical but commonly overlooked aspect of printers: print consumables.

A printer's consumables are those things that enable it to actually generate an image on a page. On inkjet printers these are the ink cartridges, on laser printers it's the toner cartridge and imaging drum. Printers use a certain amount of these consumables every time they print a page. The more that these consumables cost and the more a consumable is used to generate a page, the higher the printer's cost per page.

Eventually, of course, the consumables run out, and you'll have to replace them. This is when the cost-per-page issue really kicks in, because you'll probably find that the print consumables cost is a lot higher than you expected. On some low-cost inkjet printers, for example, it's not unheard of to find that replacement cartridges cost nearly $1/3$ the price of the printer itself.

Tip

To avoid any unpleasant surprises, be sure to check out the cost of replacement consumables for the printer you're interested in before you buy it. Make sure you get the prices of the consumables for the specific printer you're looking at because most printers require their own special replacements — you can't just pick the least expensive inkjet cartridge you find, for example.

Also note that different printers use different size ink or toner cartridges, so find out the typical number of pages that each of the different cartridges can generate. You may find that a more expensive cartridge required by one printer offers a lower cost per page than a less expensive cartridge used by another printer.

Table 6-1 offers a comparison of different printers and their costs per page.

Table 6-1   Printer Costs Per Page

Type of Printer	Consumable Costs Per Page
Laser	$0.02
4-color inkjet	$0.20
6-color photo inkjet	$1.91

Inkjet Cartridges

Inkjet printers, in particular, have surprisingly high consumable costs. In fact, many companies don't make very much money on the printer but instead count on making profits from their consumables. It's very much like the old story of the Norelco chairman who explained that, despite images to the contrary, his company wasn't really in the razor business. Instead, he said, it was in the blades business. Inkjet cartridges are the blades of the computer printing business.

Part of the reason inkjets cartridges are expensive is because some of them have a bit of circuitry on them that communicates with the rest of the printer. Also, the inks used by the cartridges often have special qualities that make them a bit expensive to produce. But, that doesn't mean printer manufacturers don't make a good buck on them; they do.

To save some costs, some people simply refill their cartridges with ink via one of the many refill kits available. While the printer manufacturers recommend against this, I've found that you can refill an inkjet cartridge once or twice with no problem. (Just don't spill it, or you're in for a big mess.) The quality of the ink in a refill kit can vary from that found in real replacement cartridges, so be aware of this, but in many instances it works just fine. I don't recommend using the same cartridge over and over, however, because the print quality does begin to suffer after a few uses.

One common problem that refilling can help with is that many color inkjet printers use color cartridges that consist of the cyan, magenta, and yellow packaged into a single entity. While this can be a simple convenience, in many cases it leads to wasted ink because as soon as any one of those inks run out, you need to get a replacement for all of them. Many color inkjets won't let you replace just the yellow or just the cyan. Instead, you have to pull the whole thing out, regardless of what may be left in the other color containers. (The reasoning behind all this, by the way, is that printing most color images uses an equal amount of each of the different colors. Hypothetically, that principle is true, but the reality is often different.) If the printer also includes black along with the color in a single cartridge, this can be a really big problem because you always use more black than any color.

Some slightly more expensive inkjets do offer individual color cartridges and, if you're planning to do a lot of color printing, it is certainly a feature worth considering. Another thing to look at is the size of the different cartridges. Many color inkjet cartridges have relatively small amounts of ink and need to be replaced fairly frequently (depending on how much color printing you do, of course). So, again, if you're planning on doing a lot of color printing, look for a printer with big cartridges.

Specialty Papers

Another potentially hidden cost with color inkjet printers is the price of specialty papers. Some printers can only generate their highest-quality output on special papers that are specifically designed to work with the inks they use. Also, some printers can only achieve a glossy, photo-like finish by using special high-gloss papers.

It's good to know if your printer can work with a variety of different papers or other media types for special projects such as transparencies, iron-on transfers, and even thin cloth, but be aware that some of these specialty papers can cost $1 per sheet or even more.

Paper size

Another important factor to look at is the maximum paper size that a printer can support. Most printers work with standard $8^1/2$-inch × 11-inch paper, but there are a number of reasonably priced printers that can work with 11-inch × 17-inch paper, which can be ideal for creating newsletters, posters, or other large printing projects.

You may also want to investigate the margin widths supported by the printer. I know this may sound a bit ridiculous, but many people are disturbed to find that their printer can't print as close to the edge of a piece of paper as they would like. If you ever want to print something that has color from edge to edge (called *full bleed*), for example, you'll be out of luck with most printers. A few printers do have the capability to print all the way to the edge of a piece of paper (typically with special oversized paper that has perforations at the normal paper size), but most printers cannot print on borders that vary in size.

Secret

In fact, on some printers, the margin edges are unequal, which means they can print closer to some edges of the paper than others. Depending on the type of project on which you're working, this can be a real pain.

Printer language and OS support

In addition to the points I've described previously, there are a few other considerations to bear in mind when looking at printers. First, you'll want to check the page description language the printer uses to generate its pages. Most PC-based printers use PCL (Printing Control Language), but some can also support the PostScript language. PostScript printers, which are very popular with Macintosh users, are typically used with high-end graphics and page layout programs such as Quark Xpress and Adobe InDesign. Even those programs don't require PostScript, but using them in conjunction with a PostScript can offer higher-quality printing.

One limitation you may want to be aware of is that some lower-cost printers are Windows-only printers, which means they cannot print from DOS applications (such as DOS-based games). For most people this is not a big issue, but if you think you'll ever want or need to print from DOS, it's something you'll want to avoid. (The reason for this limitation, by the way, is that the manufacturer has chosen to save costs by not creating a DOS driver.)

Also, be sure to find out what operating systems the printers support. If you want to use Windows NT, Windows 2000, or Linux, for example, you need to be sure that the printer has drivers available that support those operating systems.

Color printing

While color printers used to be considered somewhat extravagant, they are now the standard for all the various types of printing technologies except lasers; they are still the exception. This does not mean, however, that all color printers handle color the same way. There are several important differences between the way different color printers generate their colors.

First, a bit of background: Traditional printing commonly uses four different color inks in various combinations (hence the phrase "four-color printing") to recreate all the different colors we're used to seeing in printed materials. The four colors are cyan (a light blue), magenta (a dark pink), yellow, and black, and together they're referred to as CMYK. (I know, it should be CMYB, but Black was changed to K a long time ago, as the result of some old printing press standards, I believe.)

Most color printers offer four-color printing, but some low-cost printers "cheat" and only offer three-color (CMY) printing. To create black, these printers combine all three of the colored inks, but instead of a true black the end result is usually a muddy brown. (You can usually tell which printers do this because they let you use either a color cartridge or a black cartridge, but not both simultaneously.)

If at all possible, avoid these types of printers because the results they generate on color photographs or other images are not very good. The lack of a real black often affects the printout's sharpness, or definition.

At the other extreme, some inkjet printers offer six or even seven different inks. As the interest in digital photography and the printing of photographs from computers has increased, there have been increased demands on creating higher-quality photographic printouts. The problem is that by limiting the printer to four basic colors, it's hard to create the wide variety and range of colors found in many photographs — particularly skin tones.

To help improve the range of colors that a printer can produce, several manufacturers have created inkjet printers that offer lighter versions of existing cyan and magenta inks in addition to the four standard colors. The end result is a more continuous, smoother range of colors in the printed output. While the extra inks are commonly found in special photo printers, they are also starting to appear in all-purpose printers as well.

See the section "Specialty printers" later in this chapter for more.

Cross-Reference

Another effect found on some color printers, including some photo printers, is the capability to give the printout a glossy coating, somewhat like those found on traditional photographs. Many printers can only achieve this by using special glossy papers, but some are capable of adding a glossy finish even to images printed on plain, bond, copier-style paper. They achieve this effect by using a clear, glossy coating ink on top of the existing color inks. So, if you want glossy printouts, make sure the printer you're interested in supports this capability.

Finally, in addition to the traditional color inks, some printers also offer neon or metallic inks for special printing projects. If you think you'll want to use these types of inks, again, make sure your printer offers them as an option.

Color Management

Another problem associated with creating accurate skin tones, or accurate color of any sort, is matching the output you see on your screen with what comes out of your printer. This is a job handled by color management software.

Intuitively, you would think that if you take a color picture, scan it into the computer, view it on your screen, and print it, all the colors would stay the same at each separate phase. This is because our eyes see color in one, consistent way.

Different components of computers do not see color in the same way, however, and the result is that there can often be dramatic (and not always pleasant) color changes in an image as it moves through different sections of your PC system. Scanners handle color one way, computer monitors handle it another way, and printers handle it yet another way.

The differences in how your monitor creates different colors by filtering beams of red, green, and blue (RGB) light versus how your printer creates different colors by adding together bits of cyan, magenta, yellow, and black (CMYK) ink, in particular, are enormous. The unfortunate result is that the colors in a printed image often do not match what you see on the screen.

To resolve those problems and overcome these important differences, your computer needs to use software that incorporates features of color matching, which attempts to maintain consistent colors across all the different components of your PC. In some cases, color-matching functions are built into specific applications, but usually the color matching is handled by the operating system. Windows 95, 98, and 2000 all include color matching functions, but not all programs are designed to take advantage of it. So, if you print out some photographs that don't look right, make sure you find out if any color matching tools are available in the program you're using before you start blaming your printer.

Cross-Reference

See Chapter 15, "Working with Pictures and Video" for more on color matching.

Halftones

Halftones, which are small grids of dots used to create the illusion of different colors (or shades of gray), are essential for printing photographs because unlike monitors, most printers cannot produce any of 16 million colors on a single dot. (A printer that can create any color on a single dot is called a continuous tone printer, and they're usually very expensive.)

Instead, to accurately recreate different colors on paper, printers use small halftone grids of different colored dots — typically the four or six main inks used in a printer. (The process of re-creating different colors through a combination of basic colors is called *dithering*.) For example, to create royal purple, the printer might actually use four magenta dots, three blue dots, and two black dots arranged in a 3 × 3-pixel halftone grid. (It would probably actually take a lot more pixels than that in real life, but we'll use it as an example.) The resolution of these halftone grids is often referred to as the printer's lines-per-inch (lpi) resolution, which is different from the dots-per-inch (dpi) resolution. (See the sidebar "Dpi vs. lpi" for more.)

Figure 6-4 shows an example.

Specialty printers

Depending on which type of printing you plan to do, you may find that a traditional printer won't meet your needs. This is okay, because there are several different types of specialty printers that might give you what you're looking for. In some cases, you might realize that you want both a traditional printer and a specialty printer (or a color inkjet and a black-and-white laser).

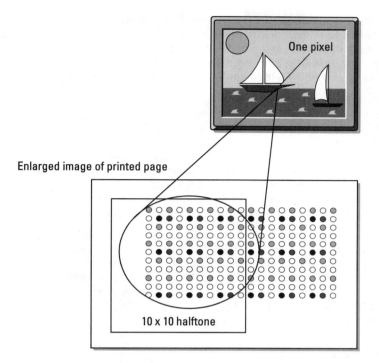

Figure 6-4: Making sense of halftones
Because printers don't have the same level of resolution as monitors, they usually need to use several dots to recreate a color that a monitor can display in a single pixel. To recreate a single purple pixel from your screen, for example, a printer needs to use multiple colored dots arranged in a square grid called a halftone.

If you're tight on space and are also interested in having a copy machine and fax machine, you might want to look into multifunction devices, which typically combine a printer, scanner, copier, and fax machine into a single desktop peripheral. For high-quality photographs, you may want to invest in a dedicated photo printer. For printing labels, you may want to check out label printers.

Multifunction devices

Multifunction products are a great solution for many small businesses or home offices that are working with limited space and on a limited budget. By combining the primary functions into a single device — printing, scanning, copying, and faxing — you can make very efficient use of your space and money.

Most multifunction units essentially consist of a printer and fax machine combined into one. As with all fax machines, the fax part of a multifunction device actually consists of a scanner, which converts any page you insert into the unit into digital format, and a fax modem, which takes the digital image and converts it into an analog audio signal that can be sent over normal phone lines. The built-in printer prints received faxes. Copies are made by scanning the original and then immediately sending that scan to the device's printer.

The convenience does come at a certain cost, however. In most cases, the quality of the printer or scanner built into a multifunction device is not as good as you'll find in dedicated devices. If you're concerned about super high-quality printing or scanning this can be a problem, but the quality is generally good enough so that it's not an issue for most people. Also, unlike standalone copiers and flatbed scanners, multifunction devices can typically only scan or copy single pages — they won't work on things such as books or magazines. In addition, many cannot scan in color. Finally, one other issue to consider is that if the device breaks, all of its capabilities go along with it.

If you are concerned with the quality of a particular element of a multifunction machine, another possibility is to use most of the functions of the device but still add another standalone peripheral for the specific application for which you need higher quality. For example, it's not uncommon to add a standalone flatbed scanner that is capable of higher quality color scans (and has the capability to copy books) to a computer system that also has a multifunction device.

Photo printers

As the interest in digital photography has grown, so has the interest in printing high-quality photographs straight from your PC. Many of today's better color inkjet printers offer remarkably good quality on digital pictures, but very few can generate a print that looks and feels like a traditionally processed photo.

To address this need, several manufacturers have developed photo printers, which are specifically designed to create photograph-like printouts from your PC. While many of these devices can also be used for general printing purposes, they're optimized to work with digital photos.

Most photo printers use inkjet technology, but they improve upon traditional inkjets by offering six or more inks to help maintain smoother transitions between colors. More important, most photo printers also offer the capability to mix multiple inks on a single dot, which both increases the range of colors the printer can generate and improves the quality of halftones that the printer can create.

Given all the effort involved, you probably won't be surprised to hear that photo printers also take their time to ensure that all the dots get put in the right place — it's not uncommon for a photo printer to take six minutes or more to print a 8"-x-10" photo.

Another important factor in recreating the look and feel of traditional photos is to use the right size and type of paper. Most photo printers use 4"-x-6" and 8"-x-10" special, thick, glossy paper to create a photo feel, although they can also work with regular paper.

Dpi vs. lpi

One of the most confusing and little understood issues regarding printer resolution is a unit's dots-per-inch resolution and its lines-per-inch resolution. Dots-per-inch is the widely quoted specification that describes how many basic elements, or dots, can be printed within a span of one inch. It's a number that's essentially fixed in hardware — that is, the hardware capabilities of the printer determine what this can be (although, you can use the printer's driver software to temporarily reduce the resolution for faster printing).

Lines-per-inch, on the other hand, is determined by the halftoning algorithms (which are basically mathematical equations that are used to figure out how to break up images into little chunks) used in application software and printer driver software. There is still a practical limit that any printer is capable of, but the specific lpi is much more fluid and varies depending on different printer driver settings. This is part of the reason you don't see it quoted very often. Just to give you a frame of reference, most professional books and magazines are printed on equipment that supports 133 lpi and many newspapers are printed on equipment that supports 85 lpi.

By the way, these line numbers stem from tiny screens that are used in professional printing. Unless you're doing professional print work you don't have to worry about specific lpi settings, but it can help explain why certain printers generate better looking photographic prints than others.

Lines per inch can also vary depending on the type of material that you're printing. Line art, which is any computer graphic that's essentially made up of a series of lines and black text, for example, is typically printed at very high lpi (commonly one half of the printer's dpi). Grayscale and color photographs usually print at much lower lpi resolution because of the need to use halftones. This explains why you'll often see different settings in your printer driver that are based on the type of material you're planning to

print. For example, you'll probably find different settings for photos, charts/graphics, and general purpose printing. Those different settings are essentially using different halftone algorithms.

Lpi settings are also related to the number of colors (or shades of gray) that a printer is capable of using on a particular page. The higher the lpi resolution, the lower the number of shades or colors that can be printed on a particular page, and the lower the lpi, the more colors that can be printed. The maximum number is determined by the printer's physical capabilities — that is, its dpi resolution — as well as the type of halftoning algorithm the software uses. For example, on a 1,200 dpi black-and-white laser printer, a 10-dot-×-10-dot halftone grid enables the printer to generate up to 100 different shades of gray (plus one for no ink, but reduces the lpi to 120. Here's the math:

$$lpi = dpi/width \text{ (or depth) of halftone grid}$$

So, a 6-dot-×-6-dot grid on the same printer would only for 36 shades of gray, but would enable an lpi of 200.

Things can get more complicated with color printers because of dithering algorithms, but the same basic principle applies: the more colors you want in an image, the lower the resolution will be. Again, the different settings you'll find in your printer driver software essentially adjust the halftone algorithms used to make the page.

The bottom line result of this is that when printing photographs, most color inkjet printers only have a small fraction of their dpi resolution. In other words, a 600 dpi printer may only have a 70 lpi resolution or even less.

Photo printers and inkjets that offer photo-quality printing, on the other hand, are capable of creating smaller halftone grids (because they can produce a wider range of colors in a smaller space), which results in a higher lpi resolution and, ultimately, a better-looking photo print.

Label printers

If you're one of those insanely organized types who likes to keep everything in its place and labeled, or if you regularly organize events where you need to create name tags, you may want to look into a label printer. As its name implies, a label printer is designed to print labels, such as disk labels, name tags, general-purpose labels, and so on.

While you can certainly create labels on other types of printers, label printers can be handy if you need lots of labels on a regular basis. Unlike other types of printers, many label printers are serial devices, which means they attach to your computer's serial port (or a switch box that you connect to your computer's serial port).

Printer connections

Many printers connect to your PC via a parallel port, although many more are now starting to use USB ports. The actual communication occurs via a piece of software called a *printer driver*, that connects through the port to the printer. Figure 6-5 shows a typical example.

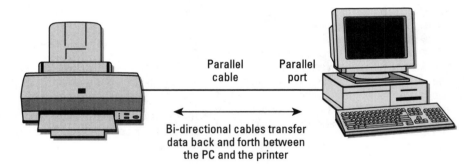

Parallel cable   Parallel port

Bi-directional cables transfer data back and forth between the PC and the printer

Figure 6-5: Making the connection
Printers often connect to PCs via the computer's parallel port, although newer models use the USB port. In either case, a printer driver enables your computer's programs to talk to the printer.

Most of today's printers communicate bidirectionally with your computer's parallel port. This means they both receive messages from the computer regarding what to print and send messages back to the computer regarding their status, such as the page number they're currently printing, the amount of ink or toner left, and so on. To achieve these bidirectional communications over a parallel port, printers need to use cables that support the IEEE 1284 standard — they're commonly referred to as bidirectional printer cables. Some older and/or less expensive cables don't support bidirectional communications (they don't connect or don't use some of the wires inside the cable) and, as a result, may cause problems when you're trying to print.

This is important to know because, for reasons I have never understood, some printers are actually sold without a parallel cable, which means you'll have to buy your own.

Another important issue regarding printer connections has to do with the speed at which data travels between your computer and printer. The standard parallel port (SPP) connection runs at about 80–300KB/second, but virtually all of today's printers and computers support the faster EPP (Enhanced Parallel Port) or ECP (Extended Capabilities Parallel Port) parallel port standard, which both run at rates of up to 3MB/second.

Table 6-2 has a breakdown of the different types of parallel ports.

Table 6-2 A Plethora of Parallel Ports	
Type of Port	*Connection Speed*
Standard Parallel	80-150KB/second
ECP Parallel	300KB - 3MB/second
EPP Parallel	300KB - 3MB/second

Printers typically respond to these faster transfer rates automatically — you don't have to make any adjustments on them. Computer parallel ports, on the other hand, need to be specifically adjusted to work at these faster rates. You make this adjustment in your computer's BIOS (Basic Input/Output System) Setup program, which is only available when you first start up your computer.

See Chapter 8, "How Your Computer Works" for more on your computer's BIOS and the BIOS Setup program.

To ensure compatibility with older devices, most computers are shipped with the parallel port set to run at the slower, standard parallel port rate. By manually adjusting this setting to the faster EPP or ECP parallel port modes (check to ensure which modes your printer supports — some support only one of the two, while others support both), you can often noticeably speed up your printing.

Parallel ports

Parallel ports started out primarily as a means to attach printers to computers. While they still generally provide this function, several other types of devices have been developed which take advantage of the two-way communications (between the computer and the device) that parallel ports offer. Most of these devices include pass-through connectors for your printer, which usually enable you to still use your printer when the device is attached by connecting your printer to the device and the device to the computer. The only limitation is that you can't usually print and use the device at the same time, but this is usually not too hard to work around.

Figure 6-6 shows how the connections work.

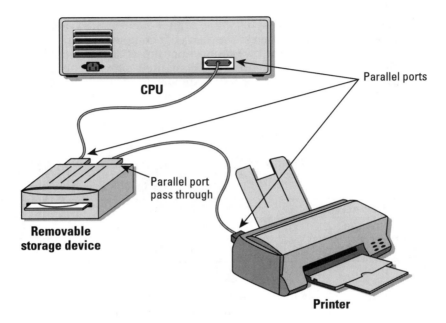

CPU

Parallel ports

Parallel port pass through

Removable storage device

Printer

Figure 6-6: Just passin' through
Most parallel-port-based storage devices include a pass-through port that lets you still use your printer without requiring an extra parallel port.

The one important exception to this is with certain types of printers that use the previously mentioned IEEE 1284 standard (which is different from IEEE 1394) for bidirectional communications. This means the printer has the capability to both receive messages from the computer and send response or status messages back to the computer.

Secret

Parallel port devices that require bidirectional communication, such as most laser and multifunction printers, often do not work with pass-through parallel ports. The reason is that most pass-throughs don't connect all the various pins straight through and some communications between the host computer and the parallel port device break down.

Many removable storage devices are also IEEE 1284-compliant, which means nothing more than that they can take advantage of the faster transfer rates, if your computer's parallel port supports it (and virtually all new machines do). So, if you want to make sure you're getting the full potential out of your parallel port drive (or scanner or any other parallel-port-based device), make sure you've made the necessary changes in your computer's BIOS Setup program.

Switch boxes

If you want to try and connect more than one parallel-port-based printer to your PC, you have several options. One solution is to simply add another parallel port, typically through an add-in card, but this can take up precious computer resources, specifically an IRQ (Interrupt Request Line), that you may be unwilling or unable to share.

Cross-Reference

See Chapter 8, "How Your Computer Works" for more on resources and IRQs.

The more common solution is to add a switch box, which is a small device that connects between your computer and the printers (or any of a number of other peripherals) and routes the messages from the computer to the currently selected (via the switch on the box) printer. Figure 6-7 shows how a switch box works.

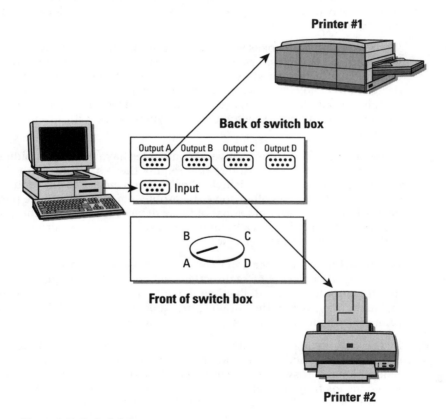

Figure 6-7: Switch box
A switch box lets you share a single port on your computer, such as the parallel port, among several devices, all of which need to be connected to that single port. Only one device can be active at a time when using a switch box, but it saves you from having to unplug and reconnect devices over and over again.

Different types of switch boxes are available for different types of ports. Some only work with parallel ports; some only with serial ports; some offer multiple sets of ports, such as four matching video, parallel, serial, and keyboard ports you can switch between; and so on. Be sure you get the right kind.

Secret

It's not relevant for printers, but another important thing to know about switch boxes is that for some stupid reason (which no one has been able to explain to me), most serial port switch boxes only have male connectors. The problem is, most serial port devices also have male connectors. As a result, to connect serial devices to these types of serial switch boxes, you also have to buy gender-bender adapters with female connectors on each side. This is one of those incredibly dumb design issues that you occasionally run across and that no one warns you about. (And which you'll be thanking me for after saving you a trip back to the computer store to buy the silly adapters!) The one sure way to avoid this problem is to open the box and look at the connectors before you buy.

While simple switch boxes work for some applications, they don't always work with multiple printers. The reason has to do with the bidirectional communications required by many printers. Most switch boxes aren't designed to enable messages to flow from the printer, back through the switch box, and to the computer. Printers that need this type of arrangement won't work with normal switch boxes — typically, they start to print and then just hang.

To get around this problem, several companies have developed bidirectional switches specifically for printers that require these back-and-forth communications. Not surprisingly, they're much more expensive than regular switches, but they can often solve the problem of sharing a single parallel port with multiple printers. Most of these devices are autoswitches, which means they can automatically route your print jobs to the correct printer without you needing to flip a switch.

Unfortunately, even those don't always work — some printers just refuse to print properly unless they're directly connected to the computer. If you run into this problem — as I did — then the only solution is to do things the old-fashioned way: switch the parallel port cable back and forth between the two printers by hand. It's not pretty, but it works.

Tip

By the way, if you're interested in the opposite scenario — multiple computers attached to one printer, you can usually use one of the bidirectional autoswitches I mentioned. Most of them are also reversible, which means they can automatically route print commands from either PC to the printer. The other option is to build a simple network.

Cross-Reference

See Chapter 12, "Setting Up a Small Business or Home Network" for instructions.

USB

Instead of parallel ports, many newer printers connect via USB (Universal Serial Bus). The USB port offers many advantages over parallel ports, including the capability to plug in or unplug devices while the computer is turned on. While technically speaking some parallel port connections can go faster than the 12Mbit (or 1.5MB)/second rate of USB, the reality is that USB printers are at least as fast as parallel-port-based models and, in many cases, are faster. Plus, Version 2.0 of the USB specification promises to raise the data transfer rate of USB by a factor of ten or more. (Unfortunately, it will only work on PCs that have USB version 2.0-compliant ports. You can't upgrade your existing ports to the faster speed.)

In addition, USB ports are much easier to share among multiple devices. If you're using multiple USB-based printers and you've run out of USB ports, you can invest in a USB hub, which is essentially like a digital extension cord for the USB port. You plug one USB cable into it, and it then offers typically four or six more USB ports into which you can plug other devices.

Tip

Some USB hubs also have serial or parallel port connectors on them that you can use to add additional serial or parallel devices to your PC without having to put in an extra plug-in card.

Infrared wireless (IrDA)

In addition to traditional wired connections, some printers also offer an infrared wireless port through which you can beam over your print jobs. This is particularly useful for notebook, handheld computers, and PDA (Personal Digital Assistant) users who don't want to bother with hooking up cables just to make a quick printout of something.

Most wireless ports on printers conform to the IrDA (Infrared Data Association) data standard and offer transfer rates of either 115Kbps, 1.15Mbps or 4Mbps (sometimes called FastIrDA). If your PC has an IrDA port, you can just hold it near the port on the printer, hit print, and you'll be in business (don't walk away until the print job is done, however).

Tip

Fast IrDA ports are backwards compatible with older 115KBps IrDA, although you may have to just the setting that your notebook or PDA uses to send data if you're connecting to a printer that only offers a 115KBps connection. On many notebook computers, you may have to make this change in the computer's BIOS Setup program.

Cross-Reference

See Chapter 18, "Solving Common PC Problems" for more on changing settings in your PC's BIOS Setup program.

Digital camera connections

To ease the process of getting color prints made from digital cameras, some printers also include slots for the various types of storage media used with digital cameras (particularly CompactFlash and SmartMedia). If you have a digital camera and printer that supports this, what you can do is take the media — which functions as digital film — out of the camera, put it straight into the printer, and generate color prints.

You can always achieve the same result by downloading the image into your PC and printing from there, but having these types of slots can save you a step.

Recommendations

A printer is an essential part of any computer system, so you need to have a high-quality device capable of handling all the different projects that you think you'll throw at it. In most situations this means you'll probably need color. Given the prices of today's color printers, frankly, there's no excuse not to get a color-capable unit.

As I pointed out earlier in the chapter, not all color is created equal. I recommend that you go for a true CMYK (four-color) inkjet printer. While there are other color options available, this is the most popular and well-supported choice. Make sure you check the price of replacement cartridges before you buy, or you might feel burned by your purchase a month or two down the road. Also, if you're concerned about print quality, be sure to base your purchase decision on real print samples — not specifications. Given the various ways different companies' printers create their images, it can be misleading to only look at raw specs.

If you're only planning to print text 95 percent of the time, you're better off with a black-and-white laser printer. Lasers are still generally faster than inkjets for printing black text, and they offer lower costs per page. If you want the best of both worlds, you could pop for both a color inkjet and laser (which is what I did).

If you're working on archiving old family photos and/or have lots of images on Photo CDs or Picture CDs that you want to print out, a photo printer is probably something you'll want to consider. Although they're still not quite as good as the real thing yet, photo printers can offer reasonably good facsimiles of real photos. Note that you'll probably also need a general-purpose printer for most of your printing chores.

Finally, while it shouldn't be the deciding factor, you should find out what software is bundled with the printer. Virtually all color printers now come with a variety of different software packages, some of which are better and/or more useful than others. Also, if you can, find a printer that uses USB connectors — they're a lot simpler to install onto your system.

Scanners

To get existing paper documents or photographs into your computer, you need a device called a *scanner*, which can translate those materials into a digital form that your computer and software can use. Like printers, scanners come in a wide variety of formats, but the most popular types are called *flatbed scanners* and *sheet-fed scanners*.

Flatbed scanners look (and function) kind of like a miniature copy machine, although all the controls for a scanner are typically found in software that's used to control the scanner. They have a lid covering a plate of glass, onto which you place the materials you want to be scanned — whether it's papers, photographs, books, or even small objects. Inside the scanner is a moving light and sensor device that essentially analyzes and then digitizes an image of the object(s) placed on the glass.

Flat-bed scanners typically use one of two types of technology for capturing their images: CCD (charge-coupled device) or CIS (contact image sensor). CCD is an older, established technology that's also used in digital cameras, camcorders, and other devices. CIS is a newer technology that reduces the complexity of scanners and makes them much smaller in size. Unfortunately, early implementations of CIS technology offered image quality that couldn't compare to CCD-based scanners. As with most technologies, later versions are bound to be better. Still, if you're primarily interested in image quality, I'd stick with a CCD scanner.

Sheet-fed scanners, such as the popular PaperPort line of products, operate more like printers, but in reverse. You feed a document into them one page at a time (which makes them unsuitable for anything but individual pages, by the way), and the scan head inside them scans the page as rollers pull it through. Like a flatbed scanner, the end result is a digitized image that's sent along to your computer.

The critical features to look at when comparing scanners are:

- The optical resolution and color bit depth
- The interface it uses to connect to the PC
- The software bundled with the scanner

Resolution: Optical versus interpolated

The most important specification to look for in terms of comparing scanner quality is the resolution. The scanner's resolution, like a printer's, determines the degree of detail that it's capable of working with.

Scanner resolutions, which are also quoted in dots per inch (or sometimes pixels per inch, or ppi), refer to how many pieces an image is broken down into in order to convert it into digital format. As you would suspect, the higher the resolution, the smaller the pieces, and the smaller the pieces, the better the quality (usually—though there are several other factors at play, just as there are with printers).

Life isn't always this simple, however, because you'll often find that scanner manufacturers list two different resolutions: the optical resolution and the enhanced or maximum resolution. For example, promotional materials for a scanner might say that it has an optical resolution of 600 or 1,200 dpi, but it offers an enhanced resolution of up to 9,600 dpi. The optical resolution is the real resolution of the scanner—it reflects what the scan head is actually capable of doing.

Enhanced resolutions stem from the fact that most scanners also have the capability to enhance this optical resolution by essentially adding in extra pixels in between the pixels the scan head actually generates (a process referred to as interpolation). So, for example, if the scan head generates two adjacent pixels with slightly different shades of brown, the scanner can use a technique called *pixel doubling* in which it inserts another pixel in between those two with a shade that also fits between the two. In theory, at least, this can enhance the resolution of the scan. In reality, however, it rarely works this well and generally causes more problems than it's worth. So, for most applications, it's pretty much worthless. In other words, ignore a scanner's enhanced resolution spec, and look only for its optical resolution.

As with printers, you'll find that some scanners have matching vertical and horizontal resolutions (such as 600-x-600 dpi), while others offer mismatched sets, such as 1,200-x-600 or 600-x-300. Again, the reason generally has to do with the resolution of the scan head versus the resolution of the motor that drives it down the page. Some manufacturers are straightforward about providing both numbers, and some only tout the higher of the two. Check the official product specs to be sure.

Color depth

The other commonly quoted scanner specification is color depth, and it is measured in bits. The higher the number, the more colors the scanner is capable of capturing. As with video cards and printers, the default setting for most scanners is 24-bit color (or 16.7 million colors). Some sheet-fed scanners designed primarily as text input devices only offer 8-bit grayscale (or 256 levels of gray).

Interestingly, although monitors and printers max out at 24-bit color, many scanners offer 30- or 36-bit color resolution. The reason for this extra resolution (which you can't really see on your monitor or from your printer) is because the scanning process inevitably generates a few imperfections in its color range. By having the extra resolution, you can essentially reduce the errors that occur in the visible range of colors. Instead, the errors occur in the lower bits, which aren't visible on the screen or on the page. (A similar phenomenon has led to the rise of audio cards that digitize audio signals with 20- or 24-bit precision, despite the fact that most audio ends up on CD players, which only deal with 16-bit resolution.)

Interface type

Scanners usually connect to your PC either through a SCSI (Small Computer Systems Interface) connection or a parallel connection, such as the kind found on printers, although some newer devices use the USB port. Also, some sheet-fed scanners connect via your computer's serial port. Scanners create and need to transfer a lot of data, so the higher-performance SCSI and USB connections will enable a scanner and your PC to work more efficiently.

However, while most new PCs do include USB ports, they don't come standard with a SCSI connector, so most SCSI-based scanners also include a simple SCSI interface card (sometimes in ISA format) that you'll need to install and configure in your PC. Depending on how your system is currently configured, this can be either a very easy or a very challenging process. The real question is how many IRQs your system has available and whether or not the bundled SCSI card can work at any of those IRQs.

Cross-Reference

See Chapter 17, "Troubleshooting Techniques" for more on solving IRQ-related problems.

Note

For some reason, most SCSI cards bundled with scanners only work with the scanner. Unlike standalone SCSI adapters, which can support up to seven (or more) devices off of a single card, the SCSI cards bundled with scanners are crippled in such a way that they only work with one device. If you already have a SCSI card, you can simply use it to connect to a SCSI-based scanner and just toss the card that comes with the scanner.

Parallel port scanners can simply plug into your PC's parallel port, though you'll probably find that your printer already uses this port. To address that concern, some parallel port scanners include pass-through ports that enable you to connect your printer to them (and then you connect the scanner to the computer). In some instances these work, but most of the time they do not because they interfere with the bidirectional communications that most new printers need to operate properly.

One solution is to add another card with an additional parallel port (which again, may prove to be easy or extraordinarily difficult), and another is to use a bidirectional switch box, as described in the "Switch boxes" section earlier in this chapter.

Size and speed

Other important features you want to look for in scanners include the maximum size of documents that the scanner is capable of working with. Some work only with $8^1/_2$-inch × 11-inch paper, some can work with $8^1/_2$ × 14-inch legal size, and still others can work with even larger formats.

Somewhat related to this is the scanner's speed. While this usually isn't a critical issue for scanners, it can be important if you plan to use one all the time. Part of it relates to the size of the image being scanned, part of it relates to the scanner's internal electronics, and part of it is controlled by its interface. Most modern scanners are called single-pass scanners, which means they capture all three basic colors (red, green, and blue) at once. Some older scanners were referred to as three-pass scanners because they could only capture one color at a time. These types of scanners are much slower and less accurate than one-pass scanners, so avoid them if at all possible.

Finally, you may want to find out if the scanner you're interested in offers the option of a sheet feeder or a transparency adapter. If you need to scan in many pages of text, for example, a sheet feeder can speed up the process tremendously by automatically feeding a stack of pages one at a time into a scanner — kind of like the automatic feed capability you find on most copiers today. Transparency adapters, which only work with flatbed scanners, are designed to enable the scanner to work with transparencies and photo negatives.

Specialty scanners

As with printers, several types of specialized devices are available for scanning purposes as well. One of the most interesting, in fact, actually converts a printer into a scanner. Canon offers several inexpensive scanner heads that work with some of their BubbleJet line of inkjet printers. Essentially the scanner head replaces the printer head and turns a printer into a scanner. You pull out an inkjet cartridge, which houses the print head, and replace it with a scanner cartridge. Then you feed the printer the already printed documents you want to scan, and the scan head moves across the page, digitizes it, and sends the results back to the computer.

If you're a professional photographer, and you work with a lot of slides or 35mm color negatives, you may to invest in a slide scanner. As the name implies, slide scanners are specifically designed to work with slides. They are generally designed for professional use and typically offer very high resolutions, although they are also usually fairly pricey. Internally, however, they operate and have specifications similar to flatbed scanners.

At the other of the price spectrum, several companies have released photo scanners, which are specifically designed to work with 3-inch × 5-inch and 4-inch × 6-inch color photos. Other than their unusual shape, these too work essentially like flatbed scanners — they're just designed to make it easy to work with color (or black-and-white) prints. Many photo scanners don't offer as high a resolution as flatbeds, but they're often fairly inexpensive.

One other benefit of some photo scanners is that they're small enough to fit inside your PC's case — they essentially look and even function kind of like floppy drives (or photo drives). These internal models fit into one of your computer's drive bays and suck photos in to scan them and then eject them when they're done.

Finally, another category of scanner you may come across are business card scanners. Again, as the name implies, these tiny scanners are specifically intended for scanning in business cards. They work in conjunction with software that comes bundled with them to read the information on the card, convert it to text, and store that information in an address-book program.

Bundled software

Virtually all scanners come bundled with a variety of different software packages. Most include some kind of image editing program for scanning in and editing photographs and an optical character recognition (OCR) program, which can convert the digital image created by a scanner into editable text. What this means is, if you tried to scan this book page, the scanner would actually just create a digital picture of it — it doesn't see the words on the page any different than it would see a graphic or photograph. An OCR program, on the other hand, analyzes a scanned image, converts the letter shapes it recognizes into actual letters, and puts them all together in a text or word processing file.

The quality of the image editing and OCR programs that comes with different scanners can vary tremendously. Not surprisingly, lower-cost scanners tend to come with less powerful programs (or cut-down versions of more powerful programs), and higher-priced scanners tend to come with more full-featured programs, such as Adobe Photoshop.

In addition, some specialized scanners come with programs that are unique to their function. Sheet-fed scanners, for example, often come with document management programs, which essentially help you keep track of and organize all the documents that you've scanned into your computer with the scanner.

You can always upgrade or add to the software that comes with your scanner after the fact, but if you're looking for a specific type of capability, make sure you check to see if the software that comes with your scanner offers it.

Cross-Reference

For more on the types applications you can use with scanners, see Chapter 15, "Working with Pictures and Video."

Recommendations

First of all, if you don't have a scanner of any kind yet for your PC, I'd heartily recommend that you look into one. Now that computers' resources and processing power have reached the level that they have, working with digital images is almost as easy as working with digital words. And besides, it's a lot more fun.

I'd recommend getting a USB or SCSI-based flatbed model with an optical resolution of 600 dpi and a color depth of 30 bits. Sheet-fed scanners can be handy for some applications, but I think flatbeds are better all-purpose scanners. USB connections are the easiest of all, but not all computers are equipped with USB ports. If you don't have USB ports, then I recommend going with SCSI.

Buying a SCSI unit can entail extra expense and make for a more difficult installation, but once you've made that effort, you're done. Plus, if you opt to purchase a true SCSI card (as opposed to the crippled version that often comes bundled with scanners), you'll be able to add other SCSI devices, such as removable hard drives, by simply attaching them to your SCSI chain down the road.

Cross-Reference

See Chapter 3, "Hard Disks and Removable Drives," for more on SCSI.

With easier-to-install and generally less expensive parallel port versions, you may run into hassles getting your printer to work properly on an annoyingly frequent (perhaps even daily) basis because of the problems associated with trying to connect a printer to the scanner's pass-through port. Plus, even if you get it to work with your current printer, if you ever decide to upgrade the printer, you may find that your scanner won't happily coincide with that new device.

As for resolution and color depth, if you're simply planning to post images on the Web, my suggestion may be overkill. For posting on the Web, 300 dpi, and 24-bit color is fine. But, if you ever plan to print out any digital images, you'll be glad you have the extra resolution, particularly as printers start to offer even higher resolutions themselves.

Digital Cameras

Digital cameras are one of the fastest-growing image-related peripherals there are. Of course, this is not really a big surprise because digital cameras are one of the few computer peripherals that are easy to understand. Digital cameras look and function like the good ole film cameras that have been around for over a century. The one important difference is that they can either connect directly to your PC, typically through either a serial port or a USB port, or store images on storage devices (digital film) that you can plug straight into your notebook or desktop PC.

Despite the outward appearance, digital cameras are essentially like special-purpose scanners. They enable you to take a picture of external objects, much as scanners do, and that picture consists of a digital image made up of a whole bunch of individual colored dots, or pixels, which is identical to what scanners generate. Of course, one of the biggest benefits is that digital cameras enable you to move photographs directly into your computer, without having to worry about developing them.

Basically, digital cameras just offer an alternative and, in some cases, a more convenient way of getting images into your computer. The following are the critical features to look for in digital cameras:

- The image resolution
- The type and amount of storage
- The quality of its onboard display
- The regular camera features it offers

Resolution

As with scanners, one of the most important specifications to consider for digital cameras is their resolution. Digital camera image resolutions are quoted in pixels per image. Their color resolution, as with scanners, are typically expressed in bits, such as 24-bit, 30-bit, or 36-bit.

Unlike scanners, which offer a relative image resolution that can vary depending on the size of the photo being scanned, digital cameras have an absolute image resolution per photo. In other words, if you scan an 8-inch x-10-inch original on a scanner at a 200 dpi resolution setting, you would generate a photo that measures 1,600 pixels × 2,000 pixels ([8 × 200] × [10 × 200]), whereas a 3-inch x-5-inch version of the same photo scanned at the same settings would generate a photo that measures 600 pixels × 1,000 pixels. On a digital camera, any picture you take at a particular setting will have the same absolute size in pixels. So, a camera with a resolution of 832 × 608 will generate photos that are 832 pixels high and 604 pixels wide (or vice-versa) every time—that is, as long as it's in its high-quality mode.

Many early, reasonably priced cameras offered relatively low resolutions, such as 640 × 480 pixels, but more recent cameras typically offer much higher resolutions, such as 1,152 × 864. Cameras with resolutions of at least one million square pixels (height in pixels × width in pixels) are often referred to as having megapixel resolution. In general, you'll find that megapixel cameras, as they are sometimes called, offer very good quality.

Just to put this all into perspective, analog film has resolution that is roughly equivalent to several thousand pixels per side (about 13.5 million pixels total), which is ten times higher than even a megapixel camera. So, in other words, if you need the absolute best quality, you're probably still better off with a high-quality traditional picture scanned on a high-resolution scanner. You can find digital cameras with resolutions similar to regular film, but they are generally very expensive. For most people and for most applications, megapixel cameras are plenty good enough.

A camera's resolution is determined by its CCD (or charge-coupled device), which is the sensor that actually captures the image and converts it to digital form. The CCD is the digital camera equivalent of the scan head in a scanner.

The two types of CCDs used in digital cameras have an important impact on the type of applications for which the cameras can be used. Area CCDs can capture an entire image at once, which is critical for motion photography and flash. Linear CCDs, on the other hand, work more like tiny scanners and capture the image a line at a time (although much quicker than normal scanners). As a result, cameras with linear CCDs are more appropriate for still life and well-lit subjects. One other CCD-related issue is that some devices use a single CCD to capture all three basic colors (red, green, and blue), while others use a single CCD for each of the three. As you might suspect, multiple CCDs can provide a better quality image, but they're more expensive.

Compression

The other factor that affects a digital camera's quality is the type and amount of compression it uses. Because digital cameras have to store images before they can be downloaded to a PC, and because images can take up a lot of room, virtually all digital cameras use some form of image compression. Image compression increases the number of pictures a digital camera can store before its memory is full.

If you take a quick look the math, you'll see why: an uncompressed 24-bit color picture with a resolution of approximately one million pixels (such as is possible with a megapixel camera) takes up 3MB of space.

> 1,000 pixels × 1,000 pixels × 3 bytes (24 bits/8 bits per byte) = 3,000,000 bits or approximately 3MB

Some digital cameras only offer 4MB of storage space, which means they can just barely fit a single image inside—not exactly a workable solution for a camera. (Although some cameras do enable you to capture uncompressed images for specific, quality-sensitive applications.) Most cameras automatically compress their images, which means they shrink the files down to smaller sizes using some complex mathematical formulas known as compression algorithms. The image quality is generally affected for the worse by compression, but often times the impact is very minimal. It depends on the nature of the original picture—some photos are more conducive to compression than others—as well as the type and quality of the compression algorithms used. Again, some are better and more effective than others. As you would expect, the more compression that's used, generally the more detrimental the impact on the photo quality—although more compression also means smaller file sizes.

The practical result of compression is that you can fit more pictures into a fixed amount of storage area. So, instead of fitting one image in a camera with 4MB of memory, you might be able to fit 16 or 32 pictures. In fact, many cameras offer several different quality modes with the higher quality modes only allowing for a few pictures to be stored in memory, while the lower quality modes allow you to fit more. What's going on behind the scenes here is usually one of two things (or both at once). First, in some cameras' lower quality modes, they capture lower resolutions than the maximum. So, a camera with a resolution of 1,024 × 768 may only capture these lower-quality mode images at a resolution of 320 × 240 pixels. (A company will never call it a lower-quality mode, by the way. Instead, they'll call it an economy mode or something similar.)

In addition, each of the different modes probably uses a different compression algorithm that throws out more or less of the original image, resulting in more photos or a lesser number of higher-quality photos. It's always a tradeoff between the two: number and quality. You can have one or the other, or most likely, you'll have some compromise in the middle. The bottom line is: if you're shopping for a digital camera, you'll want to be sure to find the different levels and quality of compression found in different models.

Cross-Reference

For more on image compression, see Chapter 15, "Working with Pictures and Video."

Storage

Unlike scanners, which are always attached to your computer, digital cameras are meant to be used away from the computer. As a result, they need some method of temporarily storing the images you take until you can connect the camera to a computer and download the images. The storage is done with the digital equivalent of traditional film, which, if you think about it, essentially stores the photographs you take until they've been processed and printed on paper. On early digital cameras this film usually came in the form of RAM, but later cameras have built-in floppy disks, minuscule micro hard drives, removable RAM memory cards, or some other type of removable storage media. In all cases, they provide a way to store the images taken with the camera until they can be downloaded to your PC. Then, once they've been downloaded, they can be erased (or you may prefer to keep a copy on a floppy disk or other storage medium), and the memory can be used over and over again.

Cross-Reference

See Chapter 3, "Hard Disks and Removable Drives," for more on removable storage devices.

Many cameras use removable flash memory cards, which are special battery-backed cards. The most common kinds are CompactFlash and SmartMedia, although some cameras also use full-size flash memory cards. CompactFlash and SmartMedia are not compatible with each other, so you cannot use one type in place of another.

In order to get the pictures from your camera into your PC, you need some type of adapter. For notebook users, both CompactFlash and SmartMedia can use a simple adapter that slides into one of your computer's PC card slots. In addition, some SmartMedia cards come with a floppy disk adapter that enables you use it with a regular PC floppy drive. Finally, there are also both internal and external memory card readers that you can attach to desktop PCs and have the images appear as if they were on tiny hard drives.

The benefit of using memory cards, tiny micro hard drives, or other small removable storage media is that you can buy additional cards in a variety of different memory sizes. Flash memory and micro hard drives are more expensive than the memory and hard drives used inside your PC, but like PC memory, they are becoming less and less expensive over time. This means the same amount of money buys you more and more memory (translating into the capability to fit more pictures on a single card or drive).

Camera issues

The last thing to remember about digital camera seems obvious, but it bears mentioning anyway: it's a camera. And because of this fact, you also need to think about all the normal camera issues that differentiate regular film cameras. Some are automatic, some are manual; some have built-in flash; some offer multiple aperture; f-stop, and white balance settings; and so on. Other factors to consider include what shutter speeds it supports and whether or not it can handle extra lenses (and if so, will it work with any existing 35mm lenses you already own).

Unlike a scanner, where the lighting and exposure levels are essentially fixed, digital cameras still have to deal with the same issues that traditional cameras do. So, the more flexibility you have in the camera controls, the more control you can get over the final image.

One other issue to consider is the camera's display. Some units offer tiny LCD screens that work both as a viewfinder as well as a display that allows you to view your image as soon as you take it or later when you're deciding whether to keep the photo or not. This can be very handy if you need to adjust the lighting or see exactly what you just shot but, of course, you'll pay extra for nicer quality displays. Other units include a traditional viewfinder as well (or only).

Finally, a feature that's unique to some digital cameras is the capability to store short voice recordings with each photo so that you can remember the circumstances or situation occurring at the time the photo was taken. Similarly, some still image cameras have the capability to store a small amount of motion video.

Other digital imaging devices

Digital cameras aren't the only devices you can use to capture digital images. Another alternative is frame grabbers; these products work with camcorders to capture still images from video or TV signals. In addition, if you're interested in moving digital images, such as for videophone applications, you should consider a video camera for your PC.

Frame grabbers

People use analog camcorders and other video cameras so often these days that many of their favorite images are actually on tape instead of in picture form. Frame grabbers can give you access to individual images on tape, just as if they were taken by a digital camera. Newer DV (Digital Video) digital camcorders are capable of transferring individual frames to a computer by themselves, without the need for a frame grabber.

What a frame grabber does is takes an incoming video signal (from your VCR or DVD player) and digitizes, or converts into digital format, individual frames of the video signal, turning them into still pictures — much like what you would get from a digital camera or a scanner. Frame grabbers typically come in the form of small external devices that attach to your computer's parallel port or USB port.

Specifications for frame grabbers are often similar to scanners or digital cameras — you want to pay particular attention to their true resolution. In addition, because the quality of individual images from a videotape isn't typically as high as those from cameras, you want to check to see if the device includes any special functions that can automatically clean up and sharpen captured images.

Many video capture cards are capable of capturing individual frames, but these tend to be more expensive than frame grabbers, which are optimized to digitize only one or just a few frames of video at a time. Video capture cards, on the other hand, are designed to record an entire video stream and often cannot capture individual frames as cleanly as dedicated frame grabbers.

Cross-Reference

See Chapter 4, "Video Cards and Monitors," for more on video capture cards and video capture features of standard video cards.

Video cameras

Many of today's PCs are now being bundled with simple video cameras that can be used for things such as videophone calls over the Internet and recording brief video segments. The cameras essentially work like miniature camcorders, with your computer screen as your viewfinder. One important difference is that most of the bundled cameras are digital, whereas most common camcorders are still analog. In other words, whereas the signal from a camcorder needs to be turned into a digital form, or digitized, before it can be viewed on your computer's monitor, the output from a digital camcorder can be viewed directly.

Digital motion cameras have specifications that are similar to digital still cameras. So, as with those devices, you'll see video cameras discussed as having certain color resolution, often expressed as 16-bit or 24-bit color, and certain image size resolutions, which are typically expressed in pixels.

Like early scanners, older video cameras only supported black-and-white images, but virtually all recent cameras offer 24-bit, or full color, resolution.

As for image size, a traditional full-screen video image as shot by your camcorder, for example, is often 640 × 480 pixels. Most of these small computer video cameras, however, provide quarter-screen, or 320 × 240-pixel resolution images, which is fine for general communication purposes, such as video phone calls.

Like video capture cards, digital cameras differ in the amount of frames they can record per second. Most lower-cost video systems are incapable of handling the bandwidth required to digitize uncompressed full-motion video. As a result, most resort to lower frame rates (10–15 frames/second is common) and some type of compression, both of which reduce the amount of data being transferred to more acceptable amounts.

The visual effect to your eye of reduced frame rates is a degree of choppiness or jerkiness in the video — it doesn't look as smooth as what you're used to seeing on TV. For many purposes, however, it's fine.

Cross-
Reference

See Chapter 15 for more on the issues involved in capturing video on your PC.

Recommendations

In the world of digital cameras, I recommend you go with at least a one megapixel resolution device that offers removable storage and an LCD screen. Initially, digital cameras with this level of resolution were very expensive, but they've come down dramatically in price and now offer great quality for the money. The removable storage is important because it lets you decide the storage capacity of your digital film and add to it whenever you want to by buying additional, larger-capacity memory cards. Finally, LCD screens enable you to ensure that the photo you're taking (or that you just took) is really what you want.

Your level of photography skills should determine the traditional camera features you want. If all you've ever used is a point-and-shoot film camera, you probably shouldn't get a digital camera that requires manually setting f-stops, apertures, shutter speeds, and so on, whereas if you do know photography, you'll probably want these features.

Summary

In this chapter, I described the important characteristics of printers, scanners, and digital cameras.

▶ The most important differentiating factor between printers is the technology they use to print.

▶ A printer's resolution describes how many dots of ink (or toner) it uses in a given area.

▶ A printer's output quality is affected by more than just the resolution. Another critical factor is the printer's driver software.

▶ When comparing various types of printers you need to consider the costs per page. Many inkjet printers, for example, have expensive replacement ink cartridges.

▶ Not all color printing generates images the same way. Photo printers, for example, often use six inks instead of the standard four found in regular color printers.

▶ The quality of a printer's photographic output is determined by its halftone algorithms, which are directly related to its lines-per-inch (lpi) ratings.

▶ In addition to standard printers, there are other types of specialty printers, such as photo printers, multifunction devices, and label printers.

▶ Different printers use different types of connection methods to attach to your PC. The easiest is USB.

▶ The most important specification for scanners is the optical resolution, which tells you the device's true capabilities.

▶ As with printers, there are scanners available for specific applications, including slide scanners and business card scanners.

▶ Scanners also use a variety of different connection methods. Again USB is a good choice.

▶ Digital cameras are like scanners that can work detached from your PC.

▶ Most of the specifications that are important for digital cameras are the same ones that are important for scanners, although you also need to consider traditional camera features.

▶ Different cameras use different types of digital film. Some of the most common types are CompactFlash and SmartMedia memory cards.

▶ Alternative methods for digitizing pictures include frame grabbers and digital video cameras.

Chapter 7

Input Devices and Power

In This Chapter

▶ You will learn about the different types of keyboards and mice.

▶ You will learn about various alternative input devices, including graphics tablets.

▶ You will learn about various types of game controllers.

▶ You will learn how surge protectors and uninterruptible power supplies work.

▶ You will receive recommendations for keyboards, mice, graphics pads, game controllers, and power accessories.

When most people think of computers, they think about the processor, memory, hard drive, monitor, and printer. But without devices that can input data into your PC and keep it powered on, all the computing power in the world is pretty much useless. Just ask anybody whose keyboard or mouse got lost or stopped working or who lost important data in a power outage, and see how much good their computer did them.

Many people believe that having any keyboard or mouse will do, but it's worth knowing a bit about different options, especially because they'll get more physical use than any other piece in your system. If you plan to do anything other than work with words or numbers, you may want to look into something such as a graphics tablets, which can dramatically improve your ability to work with graphics and certain other types of computer data.

If you start to play any computer games, you'll quickly realize that while mice and keyboards may be fine for word processing, they leave a lot to be desired when it comes to piloting spaceships, driving race cars, or tracking down bad guys.

In addition, without a high-quality, consistent source of power, all that processing capability hidden inside your PC just kind of sits there. It's even easier to take the electricity needed to run your computer for granted than it is your mouse or keyboard, but you do so at your own potential peril. The reason is inconsistent or irregular power leads to nothing but trouble: random crashes, corrupted files, and more can all be caused by power-related problems.

Input Devices

Though it doesn't always appear this way, computers are under our control. They only do what we tell them to (at least, usually). The mechanisms we use to provide these directions are referred to as input devices. The most common input devices are keyboard and mice, but other types are available for different applications. Graphics tablets, for example, are used for various types of creative work, and computer games are typically best experienced through one of many different types of game controllers.

The only really critical features to look for in input devices are:

- How they feel
- What type of connector they use

Keyboards

The most important input device any computer has is the keyboard. As unexciting as they may be, keyboards continue to be the primary mechanism for entering information into PCs and probably will be for a while to come.

A few companies have begun to offer impressive speech recognition programs, which will help you break free of the tyranny of the keyboard, but it's going to be several years before voice replaces the keyboard as the primary input device for your computer. (See sidebar "Keyboard of the future? Your voice" for more.)

Most computer systems come bundled with a keyboard, so you may be stuck with what you get, although several companies offer different options to choose from when you buy your PC. In addition, many companies sell replacement keyboards that offer some additional capabilities beyond the standard fare, such as built-in pointing devices, ergonomic layouts, and more.

PC keyboards used to have a standard 101 keys. This included the normal QWERTY (the name comes from the five letters found on the upper left portion of the keyboard), alphanumeric section of the keyboard; a row of function keys; some navigational keys (Home, PgUp, and so on); cursor keys; and a numeric keypad. With the popularity of Windows 95, 98, and 2000, however, most new keyboards include three special Windows keys. These keys include two Windows logo keys (usually located next to the two Alt keys) and a Context Menu key (usually located between the rightmost Windows logo key and the Ctrl key), which basically duplicates the function of the right mouse button on two-button mice. These extra keys aren't required to run your computer, but they can make certain operations more convenient (although not all applications support them).

The Windows logo key is primarily used to automatically display the Windows Start menu, but the really nice thing about having these extra keys is that they give you more options for keyboard shortcuts, simple mechanisms for automatically starting programs and performing certain functions without having to use the mouse.

Keyboard of the future? Your voice

Keyboards are reasonably effective computer input devices, but to be honest, they aren't always the most intuitive means of getting data into your PC. Plus, a computer's dependence on the keyboard has effectively cut many folks out of the computing loop. People who are unable to type, either because they never really learned or because they're physically incapable of doing so as the result of an injury, handicap, or other disability are at a real disadvantage when it comes to computers.

The technology that many people are looking towards is *voice input*, where you can both control and enter data into your PC simply by speaking to it. While this capability, called *voice recognition*, once was in the realm of science fiction, it is now a very real solution for lots of different people. Products such as Dragon System's Naturally Speaking and IBM's ViaVoice, for example, enable you both to tell your computer what to do (a technique often referred to as *command-and-control*) as well as let you speak in a normal voice and have your words appear on the screen (a technique called *continuous speech recognition*). In the past, command and control software was separate from speech recognition, but most companies are starting to combine the two capabilities into a single product. (However, some products only offer one capability or another, so be sure you check before you purchase something.)

So, for example, you could say, "Launch Word" into a microphone attached to a computer running this type of software, and your computer would automatically start your word-processing software, just as if you double-clicked on it with your mouse or selected it off the Start menu. Then, once the program was open, you could start speaking sentences into the microphone and see those sentences appear as text on your screen. You need to train these systems to work effectively, but they are opening up tremendous new applications both for those with physical limitations (including those who suffer from conditions like carpal tunnel syndrome), as well as those who simply want to operate their computer hands free.

As wonderful as this all sounds, voice recognition is still far from perfect, so you often have to suffer through correcting mistakes that occur in the recognition process. However, programs are becoming better through technological development and, as faster computers become available (voice recognition is one of the more demanding applications you can use). Realistic recognition percentages are in the high ninety-percent range, but that's still a long way from perfect hundred-percent recognition.

Secret

Did you know, for example, that if you hold down the Windows logo key and the *e* key at the same time you can automatically launch Windows Explorer? Try the same thing with the *f* key, and you'll launch the Find File function. Try the same thing with the *d* key, and you'll minimize all open applications and switch to the Desktop. (Pretty nifty, huh?) There are actually several more of them built into both Windows 95, 98, and 2000, but I'll let you find them on your own.

In addition to the Windows keys, some keyboards offer other special keys or different arrangements of existing keys. With the popularity of the Internet and e-mail, some companies have developed keyboards that make it easier to get at the now ubiquitous @ key.

Notebook keyboards

Keyboards on notebook computers are an especially important consideration because they're part of the computer itself. While most notebooks enable you to connect an external keyboard if you want, you'll probably spend most of your time with the keyboard that's built in.

Very few notebook computers offer the full complement of 104 (101 standard plus three Windows-specific) keys — most leave out the numeric keypad — but many newer notebooks do include the Windows keys, giving you an 87-key keyboard. Notebooks that leave out the Windows-specific ones typically offer 84 keys. Because of their small size, notebooks are not only forced to reduce the number of keys, but also the size of each key and the space between keys. The result is that it's often more difficult to type on notebooks (particularly the tiny subnotebook variety) than it is with normal desktop computers.

Of course, the critical issue with notebook keyboards (frankly, for all keyboards) is how it feels. Not all keyboards work and feel the same way. Try a few and you'll quickly notice that some feel kind of mushy and others feel tighter and crisper. Keyboard feel is an entirely subjective matter (different people prefer different feels) but if you're going to do a lot of typing on the computer, it's a good idea to give it a quick test. Again, the problem is particularly acute with notebooks, so if at all possible, try the keyboard before you buy.

Ergonomic keyboards

One of the most interesting developments in computer keyboards has been the appearance and popular acceptance of ergonomic keyboards. Because many people are suffering from repetitive stress injuries (RSIs), such as carpal tunnel syndrome, several companies have developed keyboards that enable your hands to stay in a more natural position while you're typing. Most ergonomic keyboards position the keys on two sides, and let your hands maintain a more natural and comfortable position.

The idea is that if your hands maintain a more comfortable position, you're less likely to develop any repetitive stress problems. Having used keyboards like this, I can tell you that they do take a bit to get used to, but once you are, they definitely are more comfortable than traditional models. If you have any signs whatsoever of an RSI (sore wrists, tingling in your arm while typing, and so on) I highly recommend that you purchase an ergonomic keyboard — before it's too late.

Tip

Another way to help avoid carpal tunnel syndrome is to use a foam wrist pad right in front of your keyboard that your wrists can rest on while they type. They really do make a big difference. And while you're at it, make sure you get one for your mouse hand as well. Many people don't think that using the mouse a lot can cause problems, but it can and definitely does, so be prepared.

You also want to make sure that your keyboard and mouse are at a good, reasonable height. If necessary, adjust the height of your chair and your posture so that your elbows are at roughly the same height as the drawer or other portion of your desk that holds your keyboard.

Mice

In addition to the keyboard, the other critical input device for all PCs is the mouse. Mice were originally developed to meet the unique demands presented by graphical operating systems and applications and have since become one of the most important and popular parts of the typical PC.

Most PC mice offer two buttons and connect via a special connector on the back of the PC called a PS/2 mouse connector, which is named for the line of IBM of computers on which this connector first appeared. Many newer mice (and keyboards) are starting to take advantage of the USB ports. In addition to PS/2 and USB mice, you may also come across serial mice, which look and function identically to PS/2 mice but have a different connector at the end of their cable.

The reason these varieties exist is that some older computers don't have a PS/2 mouse connector and are forced to use a serial port mouse, which, as you would suspect, attaches to your PC's serial port. If you have a dedicated mouse connector, I highly recommend you use a PS/2 mouse instead of a serial one because of the wealth of devices that need access to your serial port. You'll be much better off if you leave the serial port available for these other devices. The best choice of all is a USB mouse because you can plug and unplug it while the computer is on without any problems.

Secret

Unfortunately, even if you use a USB mouse, you typically won't gain back an IRQ from the PS/2 port because on most computers it's hardwired to IRQ 12 and can't be turned off.

Cross-Reference

See Chapter 8, "How Your Computer Works" for more on IRQs and their importance.

Mice features

In addition to all the standard mouse functions, you can find a seemingly unending variety of special mouse features. Many mice offer more than two buttons, for example. By using the special mouse software that comes with these mice, you can program the extra buttons to automatically launch your favorite programs or do any variety of different functions.

One of the most useful additions to a standard mouse that I've experienced is a small wheel located in between the standard buttons. First introduced by Microsoft in their Intellimouse, this feature has been duplicated by many different mouse makers. The way it works is, you move the wheel back and forth with one of your fingers, and your applications (if they support the wheel) will respond. The specific effect varies from program to program, but in most applications it can be used for scrolling through a document (or Web page) without having to first move over to the program's scroll bar. As trivial as that may sound, it actually makes a huge difference in regular use. Now that I use a mouse with a wheel, I can't go back.

Another interesting option you'll find in some mice (and some keyboards) is that they have no cord: they're wireless (or tail-less — if you prefer). Typically, these types of devices either come with a PC that has a built-in infrared receiver (such as the kind you find on your TV or VCR) or they come bundled with a separate receiver that you plug into the PS/2 mouse, keyboard, or serial port connectors on the back of your PC. They operate similarly to wired mice, but they can be more convenient in some situations (that is, as long as there's a good sight line between the mouse and the receiver — otherwise, they're more of a hassle than anything else). The industry-standard specification for wireless devices is called IrDA (Infrared Data Association). (See the sidebar "Make mine wireless" for more.)

Yet another variety you may come across is the 3D mouse, which, in addition to working like a normal mouse, enables you to pick it up off the mouse pad and move the cursor around the screen by moving your hand and wrist in the air. They take a bit of getting used to, but this type of mouse can be handy for kicking back in your chair and surfing around the web or playing one of your favorite games. They work by having a little gyroscope inside them that senses the angle at which you're holding or moving the mouse and then translating that to movements on the screen.

Make mine wireless

To help ease the process of setting up and using computers, more and more companies are starting to offer wireless computer accessories, as well as wireless ways to transfer data between devices. The beauty of these connections, of course, is that they don't require fussing with wires — all you need to do is point one device's infrared, or IR, port towards the direction of another's and you're in business.

Of course, to make everything work properly and to help avoid the complete lack of standards found in wireless remotes for TVs and other entertainment devices, there needs to be a common language for all these devices to use. In the case of computer-related devices, that language or standard is called IrDA (Infrared Data Association), after the computer industry organization that created it.

Devices that conform to the IrDA Control specification (formerly known as IrBus), such as wireless mice, keyboards, and other input devices, can all work with any computer that has an IrDA Control–compliant infrared port. This doesn't necessarily mean all IrDA ports, however — you'll need a driver that specifically supports IrDA Control. By the way, IrDA Control, which runs at a maximum of 75KBps, is related to but different from the IrDA Data transfer protocol found on notebooks and printers.

Trackballs and built-in pointing devices

One of the most popular mouse varieties, called trackballs, is essentially an upside-down mouse. Most mice have a small rubber ball inside them that rolls around your mouse pad as you move the mouse. What's happening inside the mouse is that the ball is used to track the horizontal and vertical movements that you make by moving small rollers. These rollers convert the movement into different positions on your computer's screen.

Tip

If you notice that an older mouse seems to have stopped working or appears to be working erratically, the first thing you should do is take out the little ball from underneath the mouse and clean off the little metal rollers it comes into contact with. Many times, little bits of hair and other dirt can gum up the inside of the mouse and make it appear to be broken. A cotton swab and some rubbing alcohol may save you the (unnecessary) expense of a new mouse.

A trackball gives your hand direct access to the ball normally found underneath a mouse (albeit in a much larger form) and lets you move your cursor around the screen by rolling the ball. Some people prefer the more tactile feedback it provides and believe that trackballs give them more precise control.

Trackballs are available as a standalone mouse alternative and are often found built into keyboards. They are also popular in notebooks, which need to incorporate a pointing device (a fancy name for a mouse alternative commonly used with notebooks) into the computer itself. Like keyboards, the *feel* of notebook pointing devices is very subjective, but they do make a difference in the computer's overall usability, so try one out if you can. For example, many notebook computers incorporate a pencil eraser-like device — generically it's called a *pointing stick*, although most manufacturers have their own unique names — in the middle of the keyboard. Personally, I cannot stand these devices and try to avoid notebooks that include them, but many people find them quite effective.

Another popular pointing device that's built into notebook computers (as well as some keyboards) is called a *trackpad* or a *touchpad*. With a trackpad, the cursor position is determined by your finger's position on a small, touch-sensitive square made of special material. You move the cursor by dragging your finger across the surface of the pad. In some instances you can set the pad to provide absolute positioning such that if you put your finger on the upper left-hand corner of the trackpad, the cursor will move to the upper left-hand corner of your screen. In most cases, however, you'll want to use a relative positioning system so that, as with regular mice, you can simply move your finger, and the cursor will make a corresponding move, regardless of where your finger (or a mouse) starts its movement.

The one problem to be aware of with trackpads is that many of them are ultrasensitive. The tangible result of this is that your cursor may seem to jump around on the screen. Once again, this is a good reason to try any pointing device before you buy.

Graphics tablets

As handy as mice may be, there are certain tasks that they really weren't designed to do. Creating graphics, for example, can be very difficult with a big, bulky mouse. It's kind of like trying to sketch with a 2-inch paintbrush, when you really need a sharp pencil.

To address this need, several companies have developed alternative input devices called graphics tablets, which typically consist of a flat drawing surface and a pen-like stylus. The drawing pad typically connects to your PC's serial or USB port and the pen, if it's wired, attaches to the tablet, although most newer tablets offers cordless pens.

As you draw on the tablet with a stylus, the results are transferred into your PC and displayed on screen. You can use them for drawing graphics, manipulating photos, or even signing your name.

Conceptually, graphics tablets are really no different than mice (actually, they're more like trackpads — but you get the idea). In fact, some people use their graphics tablets completely in place of their mouse for all applications.

Like mice, graphics tablets provide a means to control the cursor on your screen via a pointing device and they have buttons with which you can make various selections. The difference is that the graphics tablets commonly have resolutions of 1,000 dots per inch (many Wacom tablets actually offer 2,540 dots per inch) versus a few hundred for the typical mouse. Even more importantly, it's much more intuitive to draw with a pen-like device than it is with a mouse or any other type of mouse alternative.

Graphics tablets vary in the size of their drawing area. As you might suspect, larger drawing areas cost more than tablets with smaller drawing areas. Also, different tablets support different resolutions, both in terms of their dots-per-inch support and the number of different pressure levels that they can generate. In other words, as with real pens and pencils, the harder you push down with a graphics tablet pen, the darker and/or wider the line you draw becomes (actually, the specific effect is set by the application, but that's usually what happens). Note that only certain applications support this pressure sensitivity — usually graphics programs — so before you make a purchase, be sure that the applications you use are supported by the graphics tablet you're interested in. Most newer graphics tablets support 256 levels of pressure, but some support less.

Another difference between graphics tablets is in the pens they use. Most pens have at least one extra button in addition to the tip (which is generally used as a left mouse-button equivalent), but a few have several. In addition, some tablet pens — notably those from Wacom — have the equivalent of a digital eraser. Again, if the program you happen to be using supports the eraser function, you can turn the pen over and simply erase what you've done, using a pressure-sensitive eraser.

If you want the absolute best (and most expensive) graphics tablet solution, you may want to look into tablets that feature a display built into them. Using one of these devices, you actually draw on the notebook-like LCD screen and immediately see your results. Now that's what I call a digital canvas.

Game controllers

Another place where standard mice and keyboards typically don't cut it is in the area of computer games. As computers have grown more powerful, computer games have grown increasingly realistic. We're not quite to the Star Trek holodeck era yet, but we are getting there. Higher resolution graphics, full-frame video, and better sound have all contributed to a more encompassing experience.

As a result of this, there has been an increased interest in dedicated gaming devices, which enable you to more easily and more effectively play various types of games. Most gaming devices connect to the game or joystick port found on your computer's sound card, but I suspect we'll be seeing more and more USB-based game controllers in the future.

The standard sound card can actually support two simple gaming controllers if you buy a y-cable or splitter, but today's more sophisticated controllers commonly use up all the available resources by themselves.

Feel the force

One of the most important factors in creating an immersive, realistic gaming experience is the sense of touch. Until recently, however, computers haven't really been able to provide any type of tactile feedback. (Slapping the side of a computer that's crashed doesn't count.) With the introduction of force feedback joysticks, however, the computer industry has begun to take a few baby steps in that direction. What force feedback joysticks do, essentially, is push back in coordination with events occurring on the screen. (A computer game has to specifically support these types of joysticks for the effects to occur, and not all games do.)

So, for example, if you're playing a driving game and you accidentally run into the wall, the joystick (under the control of a motor) actually moves and make your hand feel the impact. On flight simulators, the joystick can vibrate like the throttle on a real plane.

The net result of this force feedback is that you feel more involved in the experience, which generally leads to a more satisfying, more entertaining experience. So, if you're thinking about adding a joystick to your sound card's joystick connector, I'd take a serious look into this new category of gaming devices. They cost a lot more than traditional joysticks, but they can be a lot of fun. Note that some devices have much more convincing force feedback than others, so as always, it's best to try out any that you are interested in.

Joysticks and game pads

The most common type of gaming device is a joystick, which, in its most basic form, includes a sticklike device that can move in one of four quadrants (up, down, left, and right) and a few buttons. More sophisticated joysticks feature sculpted, throttlelike handles, multiple groups of programmable buttons, and more. Using a joystick like this, you can create and save custom mappings of the different buttons for different games.

The latest generation force-feedback joysticks make computer games even more realistic by providing tactile feedback. (See the sidebar "Feel the force" for more.)

Another popular type of game controller is the gamepad, which looks and works like the controllers that typically come with Nintendo and Sega-style video game systems. Instead of a joystick, they offer a directional pad for moving things around a game. Functionally, there's no real difference between gamepads and joysticks, but some people simply find one type of device more conducive for playing one type of game than another.

Other gaming accessories

If you're really into gaming, or at least heavily involved with one type of game, you may find that even joysticks or gamepads are not enough. Many people find themselves practically addicted to flight simulator games in which you pilot various aircraft on different types of missions and so on. To maximize their enjoyment, some people opt to purchase dedicated flight controllers, which take the place of a joystick and are intended to provide a more realistic flight experience. Other people who prefer racing-style games opt for steering wheel and pedal controls. Another area that dedicated gamers may want to investigate is head-mounted displays, which create a virtually reality-type environment in which the computer's display is projected onto a set of goggles that you wear. These devices are not for the faint of heart or stomach — literally, it makes some people sick to wear them — and they aren't cheap, but they can offer a rather astounding experience with most any type of game.

Recommendations

Keyboards, mice, and other input devices may not be the most critical piece of your overall system, but they can (and do) have a critical impact on how usable your computer system is. You need to make sure you have peripherals that are functional, well built and most important, that feel good to you.

For keyboards, I recommend a Windows key-enhanced ergonomic keyboard for virtually all users, but particularly those with a history or a concern about stress-related injuries such as carpal tunnel syndrome. You can get away with a non-ergonomic model, but be sure you use it in conjunction with a wrist pad. If at all possible, try the keyboard before you buy, particularly if you're purchasing a laptop. It doesn't matter how much processing power and other capability it has if you find the keyboard unusable or difficult to use.

Mice and mice alternatives are one of the most subjective components in any computer system so it's hard to make a definitive recommendation here, but I prefer the standard two-button mouse with the built-in wheel. I know the wheel-equipped mice cost more, but the amount of time I've saved just in scrolling through documents has long ago made up any difference in price. If you have the option, be sure to get a PS/2 or USB mouse as opposed to a serial one.

As for laptop pointing devices, again it's a very subjective call, but I like touchpads. If you end up buying a notebook with a pointing device you can't stand, you can always plug in a regular mouse, but it's a lot easier if you try your choice out ahead of time and find something you like.

When it comes to game controllers, if you only plan to play occasionally, a simple, low-cost joystick is probably fine. But if you're a game junkie, I'd go for one of the new force-feedback-enhanced joysticks. They really can make a big difference in the quality of your gaming experience. Be aware that some of the early units had relatively loud fans inside them, so if noise is a concern, try to listen to one plugged in before you buy.

Finally, in all cases, try to get USB versions of the devices. They're easier to set up and make better use of your computer's resources.

Secret

The only potential issue with USB keyboards and mice is that you can't use them under DOS (such as if your computer has a boot-up problem) or in your BIOS Setup program unless your computer's BIOS specifically supports them. If necessary, you may need to get a BIOS update, or a USB-to-PS/2 port adapter.

Power

As electrical devices, computers are completely dependent on a steady source of power to operate. Without it, they're reduced to nothing more than worthless hunks of silicon, metal, and plastic. In most cases, the power comes from an electrical outlet in the wall, although with notebook computers it sometimes comes from various types of batteries.

Regardless of the source, the important issue with power is to make sure it's steady and reliable. Many computer components are very sensitive to fluctuations in power. When power is not steady, such as when you notice that your lights quickly dim, the fluctuation can cause all kinds of strange problems, such as corrupted files, random crashes, and more. In general, newer computers are less sensitive than older ones to these types of issues, but that's not always the case.

Logically speaking, it doesn't seem like maintaining steady power would be a very big deal, but there are a number of different factors working against this ideal. The primary problem is that power from the wall is rarely as steady or consistent as most people presume (or just hope) it to be. This is particularly true in older homes or buildings, but it can be a problem in newly built houses as well. Voltage fluctuations from wall outlets are actually the norm, not the exception, and computer equipment can react in strange or unexpected ways to those fluctuations.

In addition, there's no guarantee that the power will always be there when you need it. Modern utility companies are generally reliable, but we've all certainly experienced power outages at seemingly random times. Inevitably they seem to come when we forgot to save our work.

As a result of all these types of issues, there are several kinds of power-related products that can have a positive impact on your PC, including surge protectors, line conditioners, and uninterruptible power supplies (UPSes). But the most important piece of power-related equipment is your computer's power supply.

Because these types of devices are so different, there are no general features to look for.

Power supplies

The power supply is the component in the computer that takes power from the wall and spreads it around to all the pieces inside your PC. As its name suggests, the power supply supplies power to the motherboard, disk drives, all the components that attach to the motherboard, and even some external devices, such as the keyboard and USB- and IEEE 1394-based devices.

On desktop computers, power supplies tend to be large units built into the computer's case, while on many notebooks they are relatively small bricklike devices that attach between your notebook and the wall outlet. Some notebooks actually have tiny power supplies built into them. The great thing about these built-in power supplies is that they get rid of the need to carry around the inevitably heavy, bulky cords and the aforementioned bricks that many notebooks use. With an internal power supply all you need is a simple, lightweight cord.

Of course, often times with notebooks the power supply is actually the computer's batteries. (See "Portable power" for more.)

Power supplies vary in the number of watts they're capable of producing. Some desktop computers use 180-watt power supplies while others use 250-watt supplies or even higher. Generally speaking the higher the wattage the better, although there are reasonable limits and other issues that do play a factor.

Portable power

One of the great benefits of a notebook is the freedom it gives you from having to find an electrical outlet. Notebook batteries enable you to use your computer on the beach, in an airplane, or wherever it is you feel like working (or playing, as the case may be).

Notebook batteries are based on several different metal-based battery technologies, including nickel-cadmium (NiCad), nickel metal hydride (NiMH), lithium ion (Lion), zinc air, and more. In most cases these batteries generate heat through simple chemical mixtures, and this heat is converted to electricity.

Different chemical combinations are more effective at creating electricity than others are (lithium ion batteries are some of the current best performers), so you'll often see that different batteries last for different amounts of time. Of course, two other factors that influence a battery's usable run time are the physical size of the battery — larger batteries tend to run longer than smaller ones — and the overall power efficiency of the notebook itself. Some systems

are optimized to use very little battery power while they run and other systems use a fair amount of power, which reduces their overall battery life.

Factors that typically affect battery usage include the brightness settings on the screen, as well as how often the hard disk is accessed. In general, you want to keep these to a minimum.

The other important factor to think about with regard to notebook batteries is recharging. Most notebook batteries begin recharging as soon as you plug the computer in, but some systems also offer dedicated battery chargers, which enables you to charge multiple batteries at a much faster rate. Also, some older batteries, such as NiCads, don't charge effectively unless they have been completely run down first. If you try to charge them before they've completely run down, they won't last as long as they should. This is due to a phenomenon called a memory effect, where the battery basically remembers that it still has some power left and doesn't completely recharge.

For most people, the capability or wattage of the power supply isn't something they'll ever have to worry about, but if you're building your own machine or need to replace a power supply, there is a general rule of thumb for determining how much power your system uses and, therefore, how big or how beefy a power supply you'll need: You add up all the voltage requirements for the different pieces in your system and then include a fudge factor of 30 to 50 watts. So, for example, your motherboard and CPU might use 50 watts; your hard drive, 10; your built-in modem, 5; and so on. Add those numbers up, throw in the fudge factor, and you'll know the minimum power supply wattage that your computer needs. (You can certainly buy more than the minimum, but a bigger power supply will use more power and typically require a bigger, louder fan to keep cool.)

In many instances the higher wattage (and therefore more expensive) power supplies have other attractive features that may make them worth the investment. For example, some power supplies have built-in line conditioning, which saves you from having to buy an external device.

If you're really paranoid about your computer's system power, such as if you're running an important Web server, you should consider multiple redundant power supplies. In a system with redundant power supplies, as soon as one power supply stops working the backup kicks in and takes over without the system ever stopping. Typically, these types of systems provide a warning to let you know that one of the power supplies is down so that you can pull it out and replace it with another — again, all without having to turn the machine off.

Power management

One of the more annoying parts of working with PCs is the time they take to boot up. Notebook computers solve that problem by using a Sleep feature that gives them the capability to both save battery power and enable you get back to something you were just working on very quickly.

Some desktop computers offer this capability, which is generically referred to as power management, as well. In newer Windows-based PCs, the feature is called OnNow. An OnNow-enabled desktop computer essentially never really gets turned off. Instead the computer and all the components inside it and connected to it go into a Sleep or hibernation state when you hit the Power button while the machine is on. The machine looks like it's turned off, but inside it's actually maintaining a small bit of power so that it can be instantly wakened when you hit the Power button the next time you want to turn it on.

What actually happens is that the operating system copies what you were working on in the computer's RAM, or memory, to the hard disk, and then restores it back to memory when you turn it back on and bring it out of its Sleep or hibernation mode. Again, for those of you who have used notebook computers that offer a Sleep mode, this should sound very familiar.

Another benefit of OnNow, which is called for in the PC98 and PC99 specifications, is that it greatly reduces boot times when you do actually have to reboot your machine.

Cross-Reference

See Chapter 1, "How to Buy a New Computer" for more on the PC98 and PC99 specs.

OnNow is made possible by a technology called ACPI (Advanced Configuration and Power Interface), which needs to be supported in your computer's BIOS, chipset, and power supply, as well as the operating system — Windows 98 and 2000, in order for it to work.

Note

ACPI essentially supersedes the older Advanced Power Management (APM) 1.2 standard that was supported in many older notebook computers. One practical difference is that some APM implementations of save-to-disk features on notebooks didn't work properly with FAT-32 formatted hard drives, but ACPI and OnNow will. Another difference is that APM is primarily a BIOS-based feature, whereas OnNow is controlled by the operating system (specifically, Windows).

Surge protectors

Probably the most common power-related computer accessory is the surge protector. Surge protectors prevent your computer system or any other devices plugged into them from being fried if a large voltage surge comes through your electrical lines. Basically, they work kind of like an electronic insurance policy. Some surge suppressors even include phone line attachments to protect your modem or fax machine from being hurt by power spike sent down a phone line — a rare, though still possible, threat.

In most cases power surges come during storms, such as when lightning hits an electrical line, but it's also possible to get them during periods of heavy electricity usage, such as during a hot summer day when a lot of people are running their air conditioners. In some cases, destructive surges can occur to your computer system even if it isn't turned on. As a result, if there's a raging storm outside, you may want to consider disconnecting your computer from the wall — even if you have it connected to a surge protector. That's the only way to really ensure that your system won't get fried.

Secret

One common misconception about surge protectors is that they protect you from fluctuations in your home's electrical voltage; in general, they do not. In fact, most surge suppressors do absolutely nothing other than act as a simple extension cord until a surge comes in. At that point, they essentially absorb the impact of the surge and prevent it from being passed along to your computer. If you want to continuously monitor and adjust the more common smaller fluctuations in power you need a line conditioner (explained in the next section).

Surge protectors vary in the speed with which they can react to a surge and in the amount of surge (measured in joules) they can withstand. As you undoubtedly suspect, faster reaction times and larger joule ratings translates to higher prices. Another important thing to look for is that the let-through voltage (which is how much voltage escapes through in the event of a power surge) should be low. In addition, you need to have a grounded three-prong socket or a grounding wire for the surge protector, otherwise the electricity has nowhere to go.

Note

By the way, if your surge protector does absorb a surge, you need to replace it right away because most of them are only designed to be used for a single surge.

Line conditioners

To ensure that your system gets a rock solid, consistent 117 volts from the wall outlet, you need to invest in a line conditioner or a device that incorporates true line conditioning. Note that this is different from simple line or noise filtering, which can also clean up the electrical signal coming from a wall outlet, but won't adjust the level of the signal as a line conditioner will.

Like a surge suppressor, a line conditioner plugs into a wall outlet and the computer devices plug into it. Unlike a surge suppressor, however, which essentially is a passive device (until or unless a moment of electrical truth), a line conditioner continuously monitors the level of power coming from the wall and automatically adjusts it slightly upward or downward. In other words, it conditions the level of power to ensure that devices plugged into it receive a steady 117 volts. (See Figure 7-1 for more.)

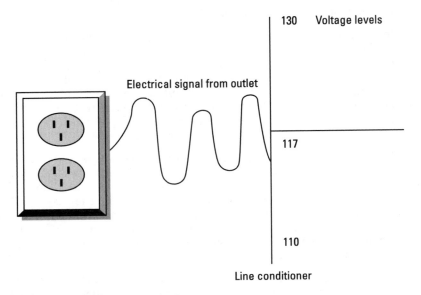

Figure 7-1: Smooth, consistent power
A dedicated line conditioner or a device that does true line conditioning ensures that your computer system gets clean, regulated power on a consistent basis, regardless of the quality at which the electrical signal starts out.

So, for example, even if the voltage from your wall varies between 110 and 130 volts, a line conditioner will output a steady 117 volts. Some dedicated line conditioners actually include display lights to show you both the fluctuating level of the incoming signal as well as the steady outgoing signal.

Line conditioners are great tools for overcoming brownouts, which are fairly common dips in electricity that, while not as devastating as a blackout, can still cause problems for computers that aren't protected.

Secret

One potential problem with line filtering and line conditioning devices is that they can interfere with the operation of powerline-based home networking products.

Cross-Reference

See Chapter 12, "Setting Up a Small Business or Home Network" for more on powerline-based networking products.

UPSes

The final link in the power chain are uninterruptible power supplies (UPSes). UPSes provide backup power via batteries in the event of a power outage. Again, you plug your computer in the UPS and then the UPS into the wall. Some UPSes even have serial or USB ports that you can use in conjunction with monitoring software to check the status of various components in the UPS, particularly the battery level.

The way a UPS works is that it contains a battery to store power as well as a simple pass-through circuit that enables your system to function normally while power is present. When the UPS is plugged into the wall, it passes most of the voltage onto the computer normally, but it also reserves a bit to charge its battery. As soon as it detects that the power has gone out, it immediately switches over to the internal battery (hopefully quickly enough so as not to have caused a power-related glitch in whatever work you were doing) and powers the system for as long as the battery has power. Ideally, you should be able to gracefully save the work you were doing at the time and then quit before the power runs out. In some instances, you may even be able to simply keep working for another thirty minutes or more before you have to shut down. This might just be long enough for the power company to get the electricity restored.

UPSes differ primarily in the amount of battery power that they provide, which in turn, determines how many devices it can support and how long they can run once the power goes off. UPS capacities are typically measured in watts, with larger numbers translating to larger battery capacity and longer run time.

Not surprisingly, there's a direct correlation between the amount of power a device uses and the amount of time it can last. So, for example, a desktop computer with a big 250-watt power supply and a 19-inch monitor may only last for ten minutes on a particular UPS, but a system with a 200-watt supply and a 15-inch monitor may last 20 minutes or more on the exact same UPS.

Again, as with your power supply, you can often determine how long your system will last by adding up the voltage requirements of the devices attached (although in this case, it's simply the wattage level of the power supply, not the internal devices that you count when it comes to the CPU), including computers, monitors, printers, and whatever else is connected.

Another difference to look for between UPSes is whether or not a particular unit also incorporates surge protection and/or line conditioning in addition to battery backup. Some devices do and some do not. So, don't presume that just because you have a UPS you'll be protected from either a power surge or fluctuations in voltage.

Finally, as with any type of rechargeable battery, the batteries inside UPSes will eventually run out, so with most (though not all) units, you just replace the battery without having to buy an entire new unit. Over time, that can prove to be a very handy feature.

Recommendations

Power peripherals may not speed up your computer, but they can definitely make an impact on your system's stability and reliability. In addition, with OnNow, they can have a big impact on your system's overall usability. As a result, they may not be one of the most exciting peripherals you can buy, but they could easily prove to be one of the most important.

At the very least, you should plug your PC into a surge protector to reduce the risk of having it fried by an errant, unpredictable surge of electricity. If at all possible, I'd also try to get a line conditioner. That way you can be assured that your system is getting clean, consistent power (and you can stop worrying about whether random crashes are the result of power problems, or something else).

Depending on what area of the country you live in (or the timeliness of your computer file-saving habits), you may also want to consider a UPS. If you suffer from regular blackouts, it could really save you from a lot of unnecessary hassles and lost work.

The best power solution of all, however, is to have access to all three of these devices — or, even better, a single device that incorporates all three functions. Here's why: you need to be prepared for all types of power conditions and each type of device is necessary for different types of conditions.

For example, line conditioners can handle the minor fluctuations on the line that occur on a regular basis; however, line conditioners cannot adjust for the large fluctuations in voltage caused by a power surge on one end or a blackout on the other. To avoid power surge problems you need a surge protector, and a UPS can help you get through complete blackouts. So, if you can find a UPS that offers line conditioning and surge suppression, you'll have the best of all worlds.

Summary

In this chapter, I described the important characteristics of keyboards, mice, graphics tablets, game controllers, and power-related peripherals.

▶ Many keyboards now include the three special Windows keys.

▶ Ergonomic keyboards can make a big difference, particularly if you have a repetitive-stress-related condition in your arms or wrists.

▶ Mice with built-in roller wheels are much more convenient for things such as Web surfing than standard mice without the wheel.

▶ Trackballs and trackpads provide a convenient alternative to mice, particularly if your PC is in a tight space.

▶ Graphics tablets offer the most natural way to create drawings on your PC.

► Force-feedback joysticks and other game controllers can bring a game to life by providing a tactile sensation while you're playing a game.

► Game controllers come in a wide variety of different packages, including steering wheels, head-mounted displays, and more.

► Power supplies play a critical role in the stability and operation of your computer.

► Power management systems such as OnNow can not only improve battery performance in laptops, they also can enable you to keep your desktop computer in a sleeplike state from which they can be awakened very quickly.

► Surge protectors are essential devices for any PC system, but if they take a surge, they need to be replaced.

► Line conditioners supply a steady voltage to your PC and peripherals, which can help resolve some erratic problems with your computer system.

► A UPS can help save you from losing data during a blackout by providing battery power that keeps your system going.

Part II

Enhancing Your PC

Chapter 8: How Your Computer Works

Chapter 9: Adding, Upgrading, and Removing Software

Chapter 10: Adding and Removing Hardware

Chapter 11: Upgrading Your PC

Chapter 8

How Your Computer Works

In This Chapter

▶ You will learn the basic principles about how computers operate.

▶ You will learn the details of how your PC hardware works.

▶ You will learn what computer resources are.

▶ You will learn how your software works.

▶ You will learn what happens when your computer boots up.

▶ You will learn what happens when you run applications and print.

Though few will really admit it, many people see computers as rather mysterious devices. They somehow think that computers work almost magically. And for this reason, many people either presume that they'll never figure out how computers really work, or they don't really care to find out how they work because they think it doesn't really matter. Well, the truth (at least as I see it) is that computers aren't that hard to figure out, and it really does matter.

Now, I don't mean to say that figuring out all the details of how your computer's processor calculates numbers or how a component moves electrons is straightforward. It's definitely not, and, frankly, knowing this level of detail is not usually that helpful (unless you're an engineer, of course). Understanding the basic principles of how your computer and all its various components operate is useful, however, and can be very helpful when you're trying to figure out why something isn't doing what you think it should be doing.

So, with this idea in mind, let's take a look at the various components of your computer system, how they work together, and what actually happens when you turn your computer on and start doing some work.

The Basics

First things first. It's very helpful to remember that a computer is essentially a very fancy calculator with a pretty display: it performs a number of different calculations based on instructions it receives from software applications and displays the results on a screen. The process involves taking instructions from the application, getting data from either your input or the application itself, and manipulating this data with the given instructions.

To perform those calculations, it uses nothing more than lots and lots of little on/off switches — both to store the stuff it's working on as well as to do the math itself. If you really think about this, it's amazing that computers work at all, let alone as effectively as they (sometimes, hopefully, usually) do.

Another important point to remember is that, although everyone does their best to make a computer appear like a single entity, a computer is actually made up of a whole bunch of components that do specialized tasks. The challenge, whether you're putting together a system of your own or just trying to keep the one you have working properly, is to make sure all these different components communicate with each other properly and efficiently. One piece of hardware has to work with all the other pieces of hardware, one piece of software with all the other pieces of software and, most important, the hardware and software have to work together as a cohesive whole. Many computer-related problems stem from a communication breakdowns between one component and another.

Cross-Reference

See Chapter 17, "Troubleshooting Techniques," for more on dealing with various types of communication breakdowns.

Hardware and software

As lifeless and unemotional as they may first appear, computers are actually based on a number of important relationships. Well, okay, I'm stretching it a bit here, but in reality, there are a number of very important dependencies that enable a computer to function. In fact, there are many layers of dependencies, and each layer has relationships of its own.

The most critical relationship is between the computer's hardware and software. Hardware refers to everything you can physically touch and/or see, whereas software refers to the unseen commands that drive a computer's operation. We often think of computers as merely boxes of one shape or another, but without a set of instructions telling it what and how to do things, a piece of computer hardware is about as useful as an empty box. It's the computer's software — specifically the operating system, but individual applications as well — that provides these instructions and enables a computer to do useful things.

The operating system (such as Windows 98 or Linux) is the most critical software component in a modern computer's overall operation. In fact, without an operating system (OS) a computer is essentially worthless. (If any of your operating system's critical startup files get accidentally erased or otherwise corrupted and you can't start your computer, you'll know what I mean.)

The OS's job is to manage how and where various pieces of software are loaded when you turn your computer on, to store and locate information on your computer, to provide an environment in which application programs can run, and to communicate with all the different components inside a PC. It's a complex, diverse group of tasks, which is why operating systems are such big, elaborate, and sometimes problem-filled pieces of software. Making all of that work properly on a wide range of different computers is not a trivial task.

Figure 8-1 shows the relationship between a computer's hardware and software.

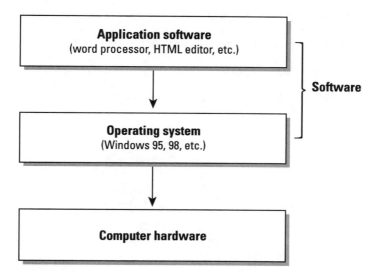

Figure 8-1: The basic relationship
The most fundamental relationship in any computer system is the connection between the computer's hardware and software, specifically the operating system. The operating system acts as an intermediary between the applications we use to get work done (or to play) and the computer's hardware.

Input and output

Another critical relationship at the heart of a computer's operation is the link between the computer's microprocessor — which is the main chip inside your computer that does most of the number-crunching work — and all of the other components. Virtually all operations inside your computer are either controlled by or actually run through the processor. What this means is there's a lot of data traveling around inside your PC. Some of it is heading towards the processor, and the rest is coming from the processor. Most of these *movements* are categorized as data input or data output, respectively. In other words, in a very general sense, data input involves moving the bits and bytes of computer information towards the computer's processor, and data output entails taking the results from the CPU (Central Processing Unit) and distributing them elsewhere. This notion of input and output is a critical part of how all computers work.

At the most basic level, a keyboard and mouse are input devices because they enable you to enter information into your computer, and your monitor and printer are output devices because they take data from the processor. Many output devices convert the data that comes from the processor into another form, such as turning it into dots on a page or pixels on a screen display. At a deeper level, the internal workings of your PC consists of a number of data highways that move information around from one part of the PC to another. Many of those movements occur internally, but some involve attaching to and communicating with external devices. In all cases, they essentially involve data input and output (commonly called I/O).

Figure 8-2 shows an example of typical I/O paths.

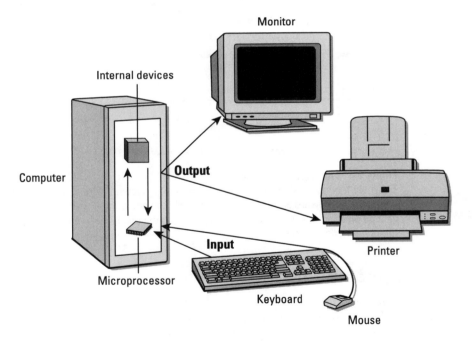

Figure 8-2: Coming and going
At the heart of any computer's operation is the notion of data input and output. Computers perform their magic by moving bits of data around from one place to another in a series of operations that effectively move data into and out of different components that are either part of or connected to the computer itself.

The notion of input and output relates to the connections that exist between a computer's hardware and software as well. Generally speaking, the way it all ties together is that the input and output paths that the data follows are hardware issues, but the contents of the data messages being sent around are controlled by software.

General operation

Today's PCs put these principles into action in the following way:

When a computer starts, it loads the operating system and associated files from the hard disk into memory and displays the results of its efforts on your monitor. It determines what to do next from you via input devices, such as mice and keyboards, attached to your computer. Figure 8-3 shows this process graphically.

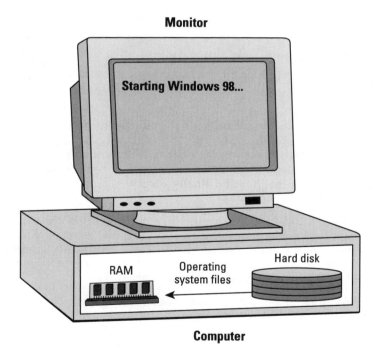

Figure 8-3: Getting started
The first action a computer takes when it's turned on is to load the operating system from the hard disk. While this occurs, the computer displays the results on its monitor. When the loading process is finished, you can control the computer with a keyboard and/or mouse.

When you launch, or *run*, an application, the operating system informs the hard drive where the file is located, starts the program, and then passes control of the computer and its attached devices to this program. Figure 8-4 depicts this action.

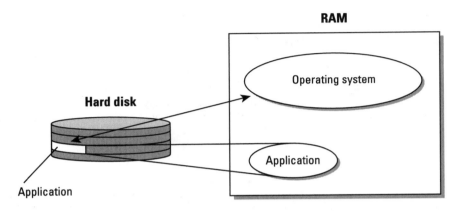

Figure 8-4: Launching
Starting a program on your computer involves communication between the operating system and the hard disk.

As you type on the keyboard or move the mouse, the application converts these actions into specific results (such as calling up a dialog box), and passes the results to the operating system, which communicates with the video card. The video card then converts those communications into a signal that is sent to your monitor and, finally, displayed on the screen. Figure 8-5 shows how this process works.

The application and operating system also put a record of those actions in your computer's memory or RAM (Random Access Memory). When you save the results of your work in a program, the application sends a message along to the operating system which, in turn, talks to the hard drive, and your work is copied from memory into a file on your hard disk.

Figure 8-6 shows an illustration of moving a file from your computer's memory to its hard disk works.

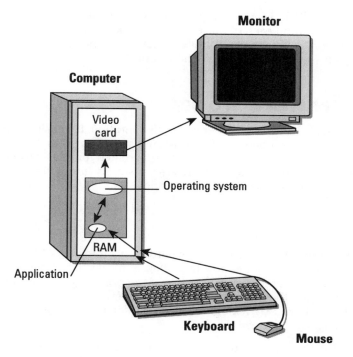

Figure 8-5: On display
As simple as it may seem, the process of turning what you type or click in a particular program into something you can see on the screen actually involves several steps.

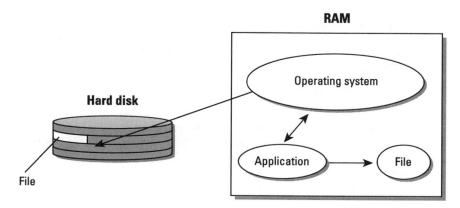

Figure 8-6: Saving to disk
Your computer work takes permanent form when you save it to the hard disk. In the process, several pieces of your computer system are put to work.

This is essentially how your computer works. Of course, there are a few other details buried within each of these different actions, which is what I get into in the rest of the chapter, but if you've understood those concepts, you're well on your way to understanding how your PC works.

How the Hardware Works

To better understand a computer's overall operation, it's easier if we break the operation into sections on hardware and software. I want to be clear that these sections are artificial boundaries created for explanations only, because hardware and software are constantly interacting during a computer's operation, as explained previously.

Structure

When I first think about a computer's hardware, I think about the overall structure of a computer and how the different pieces fit together. At a very basic level, a computer system consists of the primary physical devices that connect together: the main unit (sometimes referred to as the central processing unit or CPU); a monitor, a keyboard, and a mouse. Functionally, however, a computer consists of:

- An input system for entering information into the computer
- A processing system for storing and manipulating information
- An output system for displaying the results of the computer's and your work

On a physical level, a computer consists of motherboard with a whole bunch of things attached or connected to it. There's the processor, memory, chipset, PCI slots, AGP slot, internal connectors for hard drives and CD- or DVD-ROM drives, as well as external connectors for serial ports, parallel ports, USB, IEEE 1394, and other types of devices.

Figure 8-7 shows an example of a motherboard.

Knowing where all these devices are located on a motherboard can be important, particularly when you're building or upgrading a computer. But if you're just trying to make sense of how it all works, this information really isn't very important; instead, you need to know about how it all fits together logically.

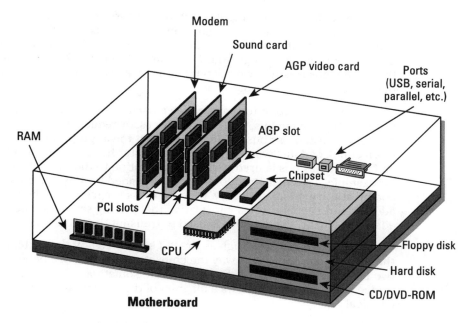

Modem

Sound card

AGP video card

Ports (USB, serial, parallel, etc.)

RAM

AGP slot

Chipset

PCI slots

Floppy disk

Hard disk

CPU

CD/DVD-ROM

Motherboard

Figure 8-7: Motherboards
Virtually all of the critical components that help bring a computer to life are found on or attached to its motherboard — which seems an appropriate name.

Buses

On a logical level, a computer consists of a hierarchy of different devices all organized around the processor. The processor is the computer's central core and either directly performs or coordinates and manages all the important calculations going on behind the scenes as your computer is running.

All the devices are connected together through a series of buses, which are simply pathways connecting the devices to each other. Think of buses as highways connecting one point to another. And, as on the roads you find anywhere you travel, some computer buses are wider and capable of handling more data traffic than others. In addition, many of the buses run at different speeds, which affects how fast your computer operates as well as how fast some peripherals are versus others that may use a different bus.

The largest, most important bus in a computer system is referred to as the *system bus*. It connects the processor to special circuitry, called the *chipset,* and to main memory. A computer's chipset incorporates many specialized functions, but one of the most important is its role as a traffic director. In conjunction with the system bus, the chipset essentially routes the internal data traffic running through your PC to the right places. To make sure of this, the system bus is actually broken up into three components: the control bus, the address bus, and the data bus.

The control bus is used to signify when a particular action is about to occur on the system bus, such as the processor requesting some data from memory. The address bus is used to pinpoint the appropriate location for a given chunk of data. Every device in a computer has a numerical address, and the address bus is used to direct information to the right place so that, for example, a set of instructions or data intended for the sound card doesn't end up at the modem. (Actually, what happens is each device listens for its address and simply ignores information that's being sent to a different address.) Finally, the data bus is used to transmit the actual information.

Other higher-level buses, such as the PCI bus, attach off the system bus through the chipset. In this way the chipset acts as a bridge between these two buses, which explains why chipsets are sometimes also referred to as bridge chips. Figure 8-8 shows a diagram of the logical flow of devices inside a typical PC.

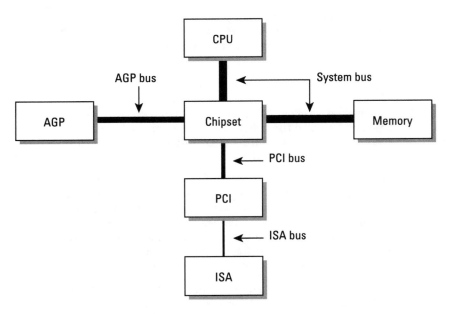

Figure 8-8: Logical connections
To really start to understand how PC hardware works, you need to have a good idea of how the various pieces connect to each other via a computer's buses. As you can see, there are several buses that branch off the main system bus.

By the way, don't bother trying to find a physical equivalent to a bus on your computer's motherboard because you won't find anything. The closest equivalent is all the tiny traces, or metallic lines, spread out all over your motherboard, which move electrical signals from place to place. Buses are more of a logical construct that, as with many elements of computers, you simply have to understand in the abstract.

Bus speeds and bandwidth

As mentioned previously, not all buses inside a PC are created equal. It would be nice if they were, because it would simplify computer design a great deal, but for a variety of reasons including technical, historical, and financial ones, they aren't. As a result, it's important to be aware of the relative speeds of the different pathways inside your PC. It will give you a better understanding of overall computer performance, why certain computers are faster than others, and the value of some recent technological advancements.

All computer buses have two important specifications: the speed at which they run, typically quoted in megahertz (MHz), the same measurement used with processors, and the width of the bus, commonly quoted in bits. (Simply divide any number given in bits, such as bus width, by eight to get the equivalent in bytes).

You'll also hear people discuss the bandwidth of certain buses, which is a measurement of how much data the bus can move at once. To calculate the bandwidth, which is typically measured in megabytes per second (MBps) — although some are measured in megabits per second (Mbps), which is one-eighth as fast as MBps — you simply multiply the bus speed by the bus width (again, bearing in mind the bit-to-byte conversion mentioned previously). So, for example, the PCI bus in most computers runs at 33MHz and is 32 bits (or 4 bytes) wide. The bandwidth of this bus is 33 × 4 or 132MBps. (Later versions of the PCI spec call for systems to include PCI buses that run a speed of 66MHz and a width of 64 bits, which would quadruple the bandwidth to 528MBps, but not many computers support them yet.)

Another important point to remember about computer buses is that the bandwidth of any bus is shared by all the devices that use this bus. Every device doesn't have access to use the entire bandwidth (unless absolutely nothing else needs it at a particular point in time — but this is fairly rare). So, for example, Version 1.0 of the Universal Serial Bus (USB) offers a total bandwidth of 12Mbps (1.5MBps) but this bandwidth is shared by all the devices that are using it. If a USB scanner that uses 6Mbps of bandwidth starts sending the results of a scan over the USB bus, then all the other devices only have 6Mbps left to share amongst themselves. In this example, as soon as the scan has finished sending, then the bandwidth taken by the scanner is freed up for other devices but be aware that some devices (on the USB, PCI, and other buses) take, hold, and regularly use a certain amount of bandwidth.

Processor and memory

The most important transactions that go on inside a computer occur between the processor and various types of memory — specifically the normal memory and a computer's Level 2 (L2) cache (that is, as long as it has an L2 cache — unfortunately, not all computers do). Memory and L2 cache are where the processor gets the instructions and data it needs to perform its calculations. In systems with L2 cache, the instructions and data typically go into L2 cache first and then into the processor.

Cross-Reference

See Chapter 2, "Microprocessors and Memory," for more on L2 cache.

Because of the importance of the connection between the processor and these different types of memory, the fastest bus in most computer systems is between the processor and L2 cache, and the second fastest is between the processor and memory. On computers that have CPUs with onboard L2 cache (such as the second generation and later of Intel's Celeron chips, the AMD K6-3, and others) the processor and L2 cache communicate at the speed of the processor. So, if the processor runs at 400 or 500MHz, then the bus connecting the CPU and the cache also runs at 400 or 500MHz. On most Pentium II- and III-family chips, the L2 cache runs at half the speed of the processor, so a 600MHz processor has a 300MHz connection to its L2 cache. On older Pentiums and Pentium-compatible systems, the CPU and L2 cache are connected via the system bus and communicate at this speed (commonly 66 or 100MHz).

In all cases, the width of the bus connecting the processor and cache is 64 bits. So, a system with a 200MHz path between the processor and L2 cache offers bandwidth of 1.6GBps and a 300MHz path offers bandwidth of 2.4GBps, which is pretty darn fast. Just to put it in perspective, really fast hard drives can transfer data at rates of about 12MBps, which is about 200 times slower than the 2.4GBps transfer rate between the processor and cache found in some systems.

The connection to standard memory typically runs at the speed of the computer's system bus; 66, 100, and 133MHz are common now, but even faster speeds are just around the corner. In most all cases, the width of that bus is also 64 bits. So, the bandwidth of the processor-to-memory connection on a computer with a 66MHz bus is 528MBps. On a computer with a 100MHz system bus, it's 800MBps, and a computer with a 133MHz bus, it's 1.06GBps (66 × 8, 100 × 8, and 133 × 8, respectively).

Figure 8-9 summarizes these results by graphically displaying the bandwidth of different connections.

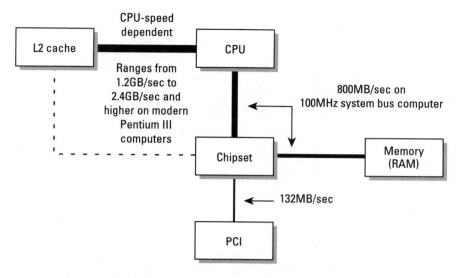

Figure 8-9: Relative speeds
The fastest buses, or *fastest pipes,* in your computer are between the processor and L2 cache and the processor and memory. These pathways are critical because it is through them that the vast majority of real computing work occurs. On older computers, the L2 cache connects via the chipset, as shown by the dotted line.

One notable exception to the previously described system design is for RAMBus DRAM (sometimes called RDRAM). RDRAM uses only a 16-bit path between the processor and memory, but does so at much faster speeds than the system bus. Initial RDRAM computers, which commonly have Pentium III or later processors, have buses that run at 800MHz, which offers memory bandwidth of 1.6GBps (800 × 2). If you add multiple memory controllers, the devices that coordinate the communication between the processor and memory, you could have multiple *channels* at this rate, meaning systems with 3.2, 4.8, or even 6.4GBps transfer rates between the processor and memory.

Even with this speed, however, RDRAM can still run into delays in accessing the first chunk of data that the processor needs.

Cross-Reference

See Chapter 2, "Microprocessors and Memory," for more on memory access speed issues.

Figure 8-10 shows how an RDRAM system can work.

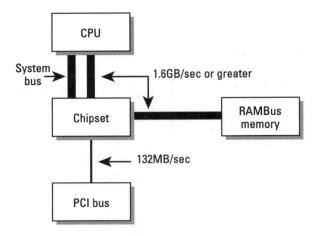

Figure 8-10: RAMBus changes everything
Systems that take advantage of RAMBus have a dedicated, high-speed connection between the processor and memory and don't need to go via the system bus.

Peripheral buses

Of course, there's a lot more to a computer than just the processor and memory. To use your video card, hard drive, plug-in cards, and other peripherals, the computer also has pathways that communicate between the system bus and these appropriately named peripheral buses, including the AGP (Accelerated Graphics Port) bus, PCI (Peripheral Component Interconnect) bus, and ISA (Industry Standard Architecture) bus.

Probably the most important of these is the connection to the video card. In order to keep your screen updated, a tremendous amount of data needs to be communicated between the processor and video card (and eventually on to your monitor, of course — but this is a simple connection and doesn't have an impact on your computer's overall performance).

Video: PCI to AGP

Over the years, the processor to video card connection has seen a great deal of interest and development. Originally, all video cards sat on, or were connected to, the ISA bus. As performance demands increased, however, computer system designers realized that the slow speed (8MHz) and low bandwidth (16MBps) of the ISA bus was a real bottleneck for overall computer performance.

As a result, they developed the VESA local bus, also called VL-Bus, which ran at 33MHz and provided a dedicated 32-bit-wide pathway between the processor and cards that sat on this bus (typically video cards, although a few other types of cards that worked on it were developed). In addition to giving the video card a faster connection to the processor, by moving the bandwidth-intensive video card off of the ISA bus, it also cleared more room for other devices to use the available resources. As a result, overall system performance was improved as well.

The PCI bus evolved from the VL-Bus, but included other refinements that made it better suited for more than just video cards. Like VL-Bus, the original implementations of the PCI bus are 32 bits wide and run at 33MHz, which translates into bandwidth of 132MBps.

For many years, PCs came with video cards on the PCI bus (in fact, some still do), but history repeated itself, and after a while, system designers found that video cards were hogging much of the PCI buses' bandwidth, as well as occasionally running into bandwidth bottlenecks.

To address the problem again, Intel and other members of the computer industry developed the Accelerated Graphics Port (AGP) bus. (Technically, AGP is a port instead of a bus because it is a dedicated connection between two points — in this case, the chipset and the video card — and it has no provisions for adding other devices to it, as the PCI bus or any other bus does.) AGP offers two important benefits: first, it adds a higher speed connection between the processor and the video card, and second, it removes the bandwidth-intensive video card from the PCI bus, freeing up bandwidth for other devices. In this way, AGP is very much like an updated version of the VL-Bus.

The AGP bus is 32 bits wide and runs at 66MHz, regardless of the computer's system bus speed. So, standard AGP has 264MBps of bandwidth; however, most AGP video cards take advantage of a technology called AGP 2X in which the throughput is doubled to 528MBps by sending or receiving data twice every clock cycle. (In case you're wondering, this is achieved by using the rising and falling edges of every clock cycle. Frankly, it's something only engineers have to worry about.) The new AGP 4X mode is twice as fast as the AGP 2X bus.

Logically, AGP sits directly opposite of memory, on the other side of the chipset. Figure 8-11 shows how AGP fits in.

Designers of AGP took advantage of the high-speed connection between AGP and the chipset as well as its logical proximity to memory by giving AGP video cards direct access to a certain chunk of memory for storing certain bits of video information. As explained in Chapter 4, "Video Cards and Monitors," video cards all have a certain amount of dedicated memory for storing graphics before they appear on your monitor. Many complex 3D graphics, such as those found in computer games, have large texture maps that are too big to fit into a video card's typically limited dedicated memory, however. So, in systems with AGP, if the video card supports AGP texturing (not all do), those large textures can be temporarily stored and processed in a special area of regular memory set aside for the video card and then passed to the video card's dedicated memory.

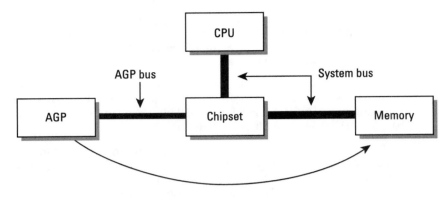

Figure 8-11: The AGP connection
AGP video cards connect directly to the chipset through their own high-speed port, just as memory does. In addition, certain AGP cards have the capability to directly access memory to do things such as store textures for 3D images and more.

Cross-Reference

See Chapter 4, "Video Cards and Monitors," for more on how 3D graphics accelerators work.

In theory, this enables computers to handle more complex 3D graphics and, even more important, reduces the need for video cards to have large amounts of expensive video memory, which should reduce their cost. In practice this is also true, although as long as video memory prices stay low, cards can come with large amounts of their own memory, which is still faster than using regular memory over AGP. Even cards with large amounts of base memory, however, can take advantage of AGP for very complex graphics.

Older PCI video cards can't compete with this because any transfers between the card and the system memory holding the texture have to pass over the slower PCI bus. The end result is that when playing computer games these cards typically have to use smaller texture maps, which results in less complex graphics, or work at lower frame rates (which means the game feels and plays slower).

Drive interfaces

Two other critical components of your PC system are your hard drive and CD- or DVD-ROM drive. If you recall from Chapter 3, "Hard Disks and Removable Drives," these devices commonly attach to your PC via IDE, SCSI, or IEEE 1394 interfaces. So, you might be asking, where are those attachments and where are those buses?

There aren't any because IDE, SCSI, and IEEE 1394 aren't buses in the same sense as PCI or ISA, but interfaces, which means they provide a means (and basically a language) with which to communicate to and from the drives. They do not, however, involve themselves with communicating back with the rest of the computer. Instead, a device called a *controller*, which sits as an intermediary between the computer's buses and hard drives, handles these chores and controls the information being sent back and forth.

Most IDE, SCSI, and IEEE 1394 controllers now sit on the PCI bus. This means they are either hardwired to the bus, as in the case of most IDE and some IEEE 1394 controllers, or they plug into one your computer's PCI slots, as in the case of most SCSI and some other IEEE 1394 controllers. These controllers serve as translators between the computer's buses and the devices attached to them. So, for example, if the processor requests more data from an IDE hard drive, what happens is the message gets sent through the chipset to the PCI bus and then finds its way to the PCI/IDE controller. From there, the controller converts the request into a language the drive can understand and passes it along to the drive itself, which ultimately executes the request.

Figure 8-12 illustrates the various connections.

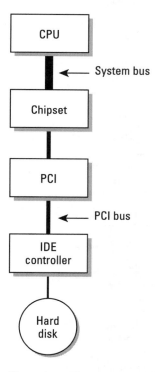

Figure 8-12: Talking to the hard disk
Like many devices on a computer, the hard disk is actually several steps and several devices removed from the main system bus. Sending a request from the processor to the disk involves going over the system bus to the chipset and from there to the PCI bus, then on to the IDE controller, and finally to the disk itself.

I/O buses

Hard drives and CD- or DVD-ROM drives aren't the only devices that use controllers to serve as intermediaries. Universal Serial Bus– (USB-) based peripherals and other IEEE 1394–based devices also connect, via the PC's USB and IEEE 1394 ports, to controllers that logically attach to a computer's PCI bus. The USB controller, which is actually built into many current chipsets, and the IEEE 1394 controller, which can be found either as a plug-in card, or built into chipsets or other chips on the PC's motherboard, each receive information and/or requests over the PCI bus, execute the appropriate translation, and forward it onto the devices attached to these input/output (I/O) buses.

Figure 8-13 shows the connections.

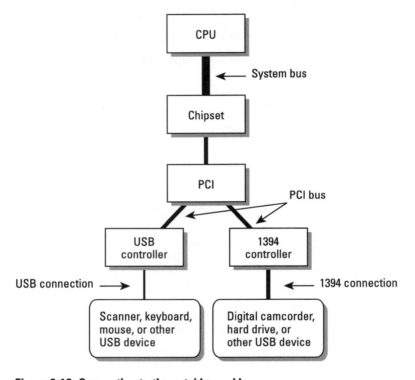

Figure 8-13: Connecting to the outside world
By taking advantage of input/output buses such as USB and IEEE 1394, external devices become extensions of the computer. Messages and data from the processor can be sent to the PCI bus and from there to the USB or IEEE 1394 controller and then on to the devices themselves. Similarly, data or information from those devices makes its way into the computer system and into the processor through these connections.

Computer peripherals that attach to the Device Bay connector on new machines do essentially the same thing because the Device Bay connects to both the USB and IEEE 1394 buses (peripherals typically use one or the other, depending on their bandwidth requirements). In this case, the connection just happens to be an internal one, but the concept is still the same. These buses can be used to bring data into and out of the computer.

SCSI and IDE are also I/O buses in this regard because they can be used to attach peripherals to a computer and make them a part of the overall system.

IDE only works with up to four internal devices, but SCSI can work with any combination of seven (or fifteen, in some instances) internal and external devices. Again, the controllers for each of these devices — whether they exist in the form of plug-in cards or are simply built into a computer system's motherboard — handle the communications between the rest of the computer and the individual devices to which they're connected.

ISA bus and X bus

Not everything in your computer connects via the PCI bus or I/O buses, particularly on older computers. Sound cards, modems, SCSI controllers, extra serial or parallel port cards, network adapters, and more often use the old, slow, but still reliable ISA bus to connect to the rest of your PC.

ISA cards, which are commonly called *legacy devices*, (see sidebar "Legacy devices" for more) work similarly to PCI versions in that they send and receive data to the rest of your computer through a bus that attaches to your system bus — they just do so a lot more slowly. As mentioned previously, most ISA buses are 16 bits wide and run at speeds of 16MHz, which gives them an effective bandwidth of 32MBps. (The original ISA bus was only 8 bits wide and ran at 8MHz.) Also, they are a step removed from the system bus because information and requests destined for the ISA bus must first pass through the PCI bus and then through the PCI/ISA bridge chip that's part of the chipset.

Legacy Devices

In one of the sadder twists of the English language, the word legacy — which in all other respects is an ennobling word with very positive connotations — has come to mean the old baggage we're stuck with when used in conjunction with computers. Legacy devices are sometimes seen as a burden that computer system designers have grown tired of having to support.

Recently the ISA bus has been a source of some controversy because many computer system designers feel that its limitations are holding back the development of faster, better computers. Because they are forced to maintain backwards compatibility with the ISA bus and computer peripherals that attach to it, they claim that they're forced to make compromises that they don't really want to make.

As a result, the PC 98 and PC 99 specifications (see Chapter 1, "How to Buy a New Computer," for more) call for the eventual elimination of the ISA bus. For computers to be qualified to meet those specs and earn the "Designed for Windows" logo, they must not include any ISA devices for PC 98 and no ISA slots for PC 99.

The problem is, a lot of people — big companies, in particular — have a fairly large investment in older ISA cards, which continue to work just fine. Many sound and network cards, for example, don't need anything more than the bandwidth available to them via ISA and so don't gain as many tangible benefits from moving to PCI as other types of cards do. Consequently, many companies are not happy about having to throw out their investment in these older cards in order to be able to purchase and use new computers.

So, will the ISA bus go away anytime soon? Personally, I think it will, but not without a bit of a fight.

Figure 8-14 shows how the connections work.

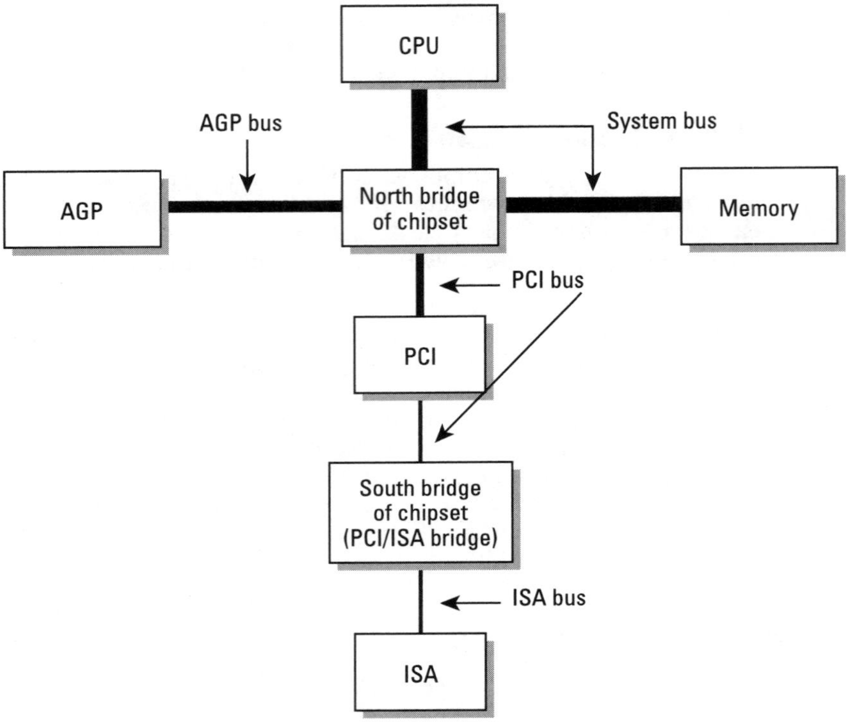

Figure 8-14: Last link in the chain
The ISA bus is the final link in the chain of devices that starts with your processor and works your way down to the slowest elements in your computer system.

In addition to the main ISA slots, there are several important PC components, such as the floppy drive, that sit on a special section of the ISA bus sometimes referred to as the X bus. As mysterious as it may first sound, it's actually quite mundane. The X bus refers to a group of devices that have been a part of PCs since the first IBM PC and have basically remained unchanged for a long time. Because the ISA bus was the first (and only) bus found on these early computers, these devices have remained there ever since. In a way, they are kind of similar to devices that are attached to the PCI bus, such as the IDE hard disk controller, USB controller, and so on. You typically don't see them if you open up your PC's case, but they are there, contributing to the computer's overall operation.

With the computer industry moving away from the ISA bus (see the sidebar "Legacy devices" for more), Intel has announced plans for a new connection and bus specifically for these devices that they call LPC or Low Pin Count (the name refers to the fact that chips with lower pin counts often have lower bandwidth.) LPC connects directly to the chipset and from there to the system bus, which eliminates the need to maintain an ISA bus just for these older devices. Eventually, all of these devices are expected to connect straight to the PCI bus.

Pulling it all together

You are completely excused if you've read through the last few sections scratching your head and wondering, "What the heck is he talking about?" and/or "How does this all fit together?" Some of this stuff is not easy, but once it clicks, you'll really be able to get a handle on how a computer does some of its magic.

To get a better idea of how everything fits together, take a look at Figure 8-15, which shows a complete layout of all the different components I've been describing, including a visual indication of the speed and bandwidth of the different connections.

Here are a couple other points to bear in mind when you're looking at how a PC works:

First, just as individual buses share their available bandwidth among all the devices attached to them, so too does the system bus share its bandwidth among all the other buses that attach to it. So, if you do a quick bit of math, you'll notice that the combined bandwidths of the memory bus, the AGP bus, and the PCI bus are much higher than the system bus. What this means is, they can't all possibly be running at their fastest rate at the same time. They have to share the system buses' bandwidth. Because this can be allocated dynamically, however, at any given moment one of the buses attached to the system bus might be running near its maximum rate while the others are running at much slower rates.

Second, these are all theoretical maximum rates. The real-world rates for all of these buses are much lower. In fact, the bus utilization, which is just a fancy word for saying how busy a bus is and how much traffic it's carrying, is typically less than 70 percent.

Finally, you can begin to get an idea of why it is that computer hardware seems to be constantly evolving and getting new features, capabilities, and technologies. Often times the "new technologies" are really fixes to existing system design problems or enhancements that help take better advantage of changes that were made in previous rounds of technological improvements. Yes, new technologies can and do make computers run faster, but it's often because they've removed old roadblocks that have been sitting there for a while.

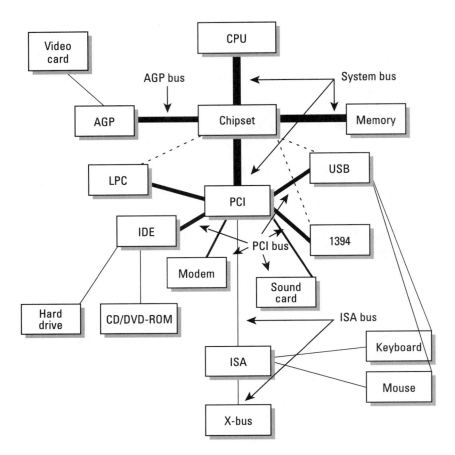

Figure 8-15: The big picture
You can understand your PC's hardware by thinking of your computer as a set of connected roads that are designed to carry data back and forth to different places — primarily to and from the processor. As you move further away from the processor, the roads get narrower and slower. The dashed lines from the USB, IEEE 1394, and LPC controllers are used to indicate that in many (though not all) systems these devices are actually built into the chipset.

If you think about it this way, you realize that computer system design is kind of like a game of technological leapfrog where new jumps forward in one area simply leave a different area of the computer in need of updating. Eventually this area gets updated, but then another bottleneck shows up somewhere else, waiting for the next technological advancement to improve upon it. Depending on your perspective, it's either a never-ending challenge or a source of never-ending frustration in which you'll eventually end up with a computer that starts to fall behind.

Resources

Resources are another issue you need to think about when it comes to computer hardware. By resources I mean a commodity used by your computer to function and carry out the activities the computer was designed to do. And like resources of the natural variety, resources on your computer are generally limited.

There are actually two levels of resources when it comes to hardware. On the most basic level, the resources of any computer are its identifying characteristics — the amount of memory it has, the size of the hard drive, the number and type of plug-in slots, the number and types of external connectors, and so on. These resources affect how quickly your computer can work as well as the machine's overall capabilities — the types of things it can or cannot do.

A second level of resources buried within the deep recesses of your computer's operation — well, ok, they're not *that* hard to find — refer to various types of communications channels and specific memory locations that are reserved for certain types of devices. In most cases, the word device refers to a piece of hardware or some hardware component inside your PC, but pieces of software that perform certain types of functions (which I'll explain later) are also considered devices and also make use of certain resources. These resources have to be allocated, or shared, amongst the various components inside your PC — remember that your computer actually consists of a whole bunch of different devices working together — to ensure that all the different pieces can talk to one another.

Most of a computer's resources are hardware-based and are independent of the operating system your PC is running. Some, however, are specific to various versions of DOS and Windows, as I'll explain shortly.

If you're running most any type of Windows, the easiest way to see any computer's resources is through the Device Manager, which is included as part of the System Control Panel. Figure 8-16 shows an example of a screen from the Device Manager.

The four main types of computer resources listed in Device Manager are Interrupt Requests (IRQs), DMA channels, I/O Addresses, and Memory Ranges. While it's possible for a single device to use all four types of resources, most devices inside your computer only use one or two of the resources. There are also some devices that don't use any. The amount and/or types of resources that any device uses depend on the needs of the device — it's not anything you can control (other than buying a different type of device that uses different resources). What you can control, however, is the specific resource number that the device uses.

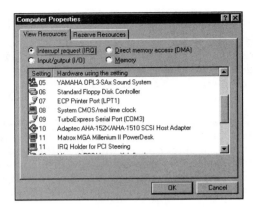

Figure 8-16: Computer resources
You can view the resources used in any computer running Windows 95 or 98 by opening the System Control Panel, selecting the Device Manager tab, and double clicking the computer icon at the top of the list.

Cross-Reference

See Chapter 10, "Adding and Removing Hardware," for more on what types of devices use various types of resources and what devices don't.

IRQs and DMA channels

The most common type of hardware resource is called an *Interrupt Request* (IRQ). Most PCs are limited to 16 IRQs (numbered 0–15). Another hardware-related resource you'll hear discussed is DMA, or Direct Memory Access, channels. The limit for DMA channels on most PCs is 8 (numbered 0–7). Both IRQs and DMA channels are internal mechanisms that the computer uses to keep track of and communicate with the various pieces of hardware inside your computer.

IRQs, for example, are used to send a signal to the processor asking it to literally interrupt, or stop, what's it's doing temporarily to handle data or requests from the device sending the interrupt. In other words, it's basically a way for the particular system component to get some attention from the processor when the device needs to do something. Without hardware interrupts, the processor would have to constantly poll all the attached devices to see if they needed attention, which is not a very efficient use of its time and processing power.

The problem with IRQs is that most devices in your computer require a separate interrupt. (One important exception is devices that attach to I/O buses, such as individual IDE hard drives, USB devices, and others. In these cases, only the various controllers to which those devices attach require an interrupt, not the actual devices.) As computers have grown more sophisticated and stocked with more and more components that need their own interrupts, the 16 IRQ limit has become a big problem. The PCI bus alleviates this somewhat by offering a set of four shareable interrupts (labeled A–D to avoid confusion with IRQs) designated specifically for PCI plug-in cards, but in many cases PCI cards also use standard interrupts as well, which basically defeats the purpose.

Cross-Reference

See Chapter 17, "Troubleshooting Techniques," for more on dealing with IRQ problems.

DMA channels, typically only used by older ISA cards or ISA/X bus components, that sit on the computer's motherboard, provide a specific *route* through which the devices that require them can send and/or receive information directly to and from memory (hence the name Direct Memory Access) without having to go through the processor. As with IRQs, devices that specifically require a DMA channel each need their own. In other words, you can't typically share computer resources. In fact, some will only work if they are using the specific channel—or IRQ number, in the case of IRQs—that they are assigned to work with. (The specific channel, or IRQ, is determined by the maker of the device.)

I/O Addresses and Memory Ranges

The other main two types of resources are I/O Addresses and Memory Ranges. I/O Addresses are specific locations for all the different devices inside your computer. They are used by your computer's processor to send and receive messages and/or data to and from a particular device (hence the name input/output) along the various buses that connect the pieces of your PC together. So, for example, by sticking an address at the beginning of a message, the processor can be sure that a message intended for the USB controller gets there instead of, say, the hard disk controller or some other device attached to the PCI bus.

Memory Ranges refer to specific places in memory where software associated with a particular piece of hardware has to be loaded. (I realize that I've jumped into software here but, as I said at the beginning of the chapter, it's hard to separate hardware and software. In fact, to explain this, it's downright impossible!) Memory Ranges are the one type of resource that are specific to DOS and Windows. Actually they only impact DOS, Windows 3.1, Windows 95, and Windows 98. Windows NT and 2000, as well as Linux, OS/2, BeOS, and other alternative operating systems don't have this issue.

To really make sense of Memory Ranges, you need to understand a bit how PCs running DOS, Windows 3.1, Windows 95, and Windows 98 view memory. If you recall from Chapter 2, your computer's memory is divided up into addresses or locations where different bits of information can be stored. (Note that while similar in concept, this is different than the I/O addresses described previously. I/O addresses essentially describe where in the overall computer system a particular device is, whereas memory addresses refer to specific locations within RAM.)

The basic issue is this: when it comes to memory, not all addresses are created equal if you're using DOS, Windows 3.1, Windows 95, or Windows 98.

The first 1MB of memory is treated much differently than the rest of the memory in your PC (see sidebar "The famous first megabyte" for more). The reason for this is because of the history of the PC and the old DOS operating system, which is still a part of both Windows 95 and Windows 98.

Under DOS (and Windows 3.1, 95, and 98), the first megabyte, or 1,024KB of memory, is divided into 640KB of what's called *conventional* memory and 384KB of upper memory. This upper memory is commonly divided into 64KB chunks that are referred to as Upper Memory Blocks (UMBs).

The lower 640KB is designated as the area where DOS and DOS programs reside (hence the infamous 640KB DOS limit), and the upper 384KB is reserved for certain core pieces of software and certain settings. This includes the BIOS (which will be explained later in this chapter) and special settings for video cards, network cards, and other types of plug-in devices. Figure 8-17 shows this breakdown.

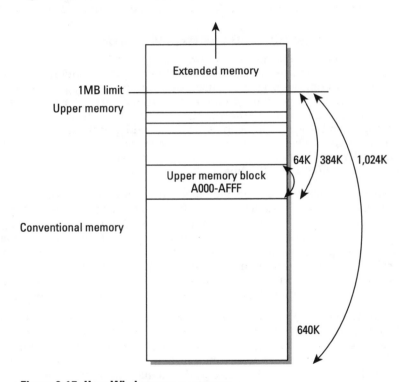

Figure 8-17: How Windows sees memory
The first megabyte of RAM in any PC running a Windows operating system has special significance and is broken up into several distinct sections. Conventional memory is the infamous 640K DOS limit and the next 384K are upper memory. Upper memory is divided into 64K chunks called Upper Memory Blocks (UMBs), which are commonly referred to by their actual hexadecimal (base-16) addresses.

The Famous First Megabyte

DOS treated the first megabyte of memory differently because, originally, this is all it had to work with. This is because the 8088 processor found in the original IBM PC—which was what DOS was designed to run on—could only address, or see, one megabyte of memory. Later processors could work with larger amounts of memory, but to retain backwards compatibility, this one megabyte software divider stuck.

Software that works within this one megabyte limitation is often referred to as real-mode software. Another way to think of this is that any real-mode software, such as drivers (explained in the "Software" section), is essentially DOS software and is designed to work with DOS and DOS applications. You'll also see references to protected-mode software, which means the software isn't bound by the old DOS-based one megabyte limit.

These modes refer to operational modes inside the computer's processor. In order to maintain backwards compatibility with software written for the old 8088 and 8086 chips, later processors offered different methods of operation that could basically fool the software running on it into thinking it was working with one of the older chips. This enabled the older programs to run on the newer processors without having to be rewritten, but it didn't take full advantage of the processor's capabilities. Protected-mode software, including all versions of Windows from 3.0 onwards (as well as other operating systems, such as NT, Linux, and Windows 2000), takes advantage of later processors' capability to see more memory and work with larger chunks of data at once.

Even to this day, however, many computers (including all those using Windows 95 and Windows 98) still run a small amount of real-mode software to maintain compatibility with older hardware and software (or new software still written to the old DOS standard).

Now, very few people are still running DOS on a regular basis (although the occasional DOS application—particularly some older games—do see a fair bit of use), but certain parts of Windows and certain core components of your computer still maintain these memory distinctions. As a result, the tiny 384KB chunk of RAM known as upper memory still maintains a special place of honor in the world of Windows-based PCs (except, again, for those running Windows NT or Windows 2000). In fact, it is the individual UMBs that the Memory Range resource in the Device Manager refers to. Certain devices require a chunk of upper memory or a range of memory addresses—hence the name Memory Range—in order to function properly. As with IRQs, however, the number of memory ranges is limited and so sometimes computers—well, actually, the computer's users—run into a situation that's generally known as a resource conflict.

Resource conflicts

As you might guess, problems arise if (and when) devices try to use the same IRQ numbers, DMA Channels, or Memory Ranges. What happens is messages or data being sent from or to devices using the same resources basically step on top of each other, causing a big confusing mess internally. The end result for you as a user is that your computer lock ups (or may not even start up) and stops working until the conflict is resolved.

A seemingly easy answer to the problem would be to simply increase the number of resources so that these types of issues wouldn't arise. Unfortunately, because these system resource limits are embedded at such a low level—theoretically speaking—of the computer's operation, adjusting them could end up confusing lots of software and hardware. Basically, they wouldn't work. This is particularly true of older or legacy hardware and software.

Most resource conflicts are a result of dealing with older ISA cards or other ISA/X bus components on the motherboard. In fact, this is one of the primary reasons why the computer industry is working towards eliminating the ISA bus from future generations of computers (see information about the PC 98 and PC 99 specifications in Chapter 1 for more). By moving away from ISA, the industry is trying to shed one of its most troublesome bits of heritage.

For the foreseeable future, however, resource conflicts will continue to be an unfortunate reality for lots of computer users.

Cross-Reference

See Chapter 17, "Troubleshooting Techniques," for more on dealing with resource conflicts.

Plug and Play

Thankfully, the situation is much better than it used to be, thanks primarily to the Plug and Play (or Plug-n-Pray, if you find it doesn't work as it's supposed to) feature found in Windows 95, 98, and 2000. What Plug and Play does is it attempts to automatically resolve resource conflicts so that you don't have to worry about adjusting resources on your own.

Before Plug and Play, DOS and Windows 3.1 users, for example, used to have to manually keep track of and adjust all the different computer resources, which could prove to be a real pain. Adding new plug-in cards often meant configuring little connectors called *jumpers* and moving incredibly tiny DIP switches on the card and/or running software configuration utilities to set the appropriate resource settings for the device. If you didn't have a thorough record of what was already being used, however, you may have had to do this multiple times on multiple cards (including cards that previously worked fine) just to get all the different pieces of your computer working together. Frankly, it was a ridiculous mess.

Plug and Play automates this process by essentially asking devices what resources they need and then automatically shuffling them around to make them fit within the PC's resource limitations. In general it does a pretty good job, but it is not foolproof. There are still situations where you may have to go in and manually adjust some settings or take some other actions to get all of the pieces inside your computer working harmoniously together. And of course, this is one of the reasons there's an entire troubleshooting section at the end of this book.

How the Software Works

The job of your computer's software is to bring the PC hardware to life and give it something useful to do. Software provides the directions that help different devices inside your computer talk to each other, as well as providing an interface that you use to put your computer to work or play.

As with computer hardware, there are many different layers of software and various types of interconnections between those layers. In fact, software is much more layered — and consequently, more complicated — than hardware. Some layers of software talk directly to your computer's hardware, other layers are completely removed from the hardware and serve only as a portal through which you can view and edit your data, and still others work as messengers in between various layers of software. Together, all these various layers combine to form a complete software system, just as all the different hardware components work together as a unified whole — at least, ideally.

Basic connections

As described previously, the most basic layers of software are provided by the operating system (for example, Windows 98 or Linux) and application programs. In this regard, the operating system provides an environment where the programs that we actually use on our computers can run. The operating system also handles communications between the programs and the computer's hardware so that the individual programs don't have to worry about these details and can concentrate on doing the work they were created to do. (Old DOS programs, on the other hand, often had to both worry about talking with the hardware as well as performing the specific functions they were created for, such as word processing, number crunching, or what have you.)

Figure 8-18 shows the relationships between different software layers.

This notion of providing an intermediary layer, sometimes called *abstracting*, is common throughout all types and levels of software. The basic concept behind it is to provide more specialization and dedicated focus to different pieces of software so that each one can focus on a specific task or capability. It also encourages the breaking up of large pieces of software into smaller, more manageable chunks. The Windows operating system (in all its varieties), for example, consists not of one or two large pieces of software, but hundreds of smaller pieces that each focus on some specific tasks or capabilities.

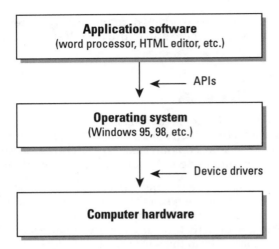

Figure 8-18: Layers of software
Computer software works through a series of layers. On the most basic level, application programs, such as word processors and photo editing programs sit on top of the operating system (for example, Windows 98 or Linux), and the operating system, in turn, talks to the hardware. By maintaining this separation, or level of abstraction, application programs are shielded from having to work directly with the hardware and can concentrate on doing the functions they were designed to do.

The benefit is that this makes it easier to concentrate on specific features one piece at a time. But, as you can probably guess, making all the different pieces work together seamlessly as a cohesive whole isn't easy. In fact, one of the reasons computers run into problems on such an annoyingly frequent basis is because it only takes a problem with one piece of software buried somewhere in the complex puzzle of today's computer systems to cause big headaches for you and me.

Software layers

In addition to the large-scale layers between the OS and applications, the operating system and applications themselves each consist of multiple layers. The operating system, in particular, is a very complex group of files that has multiple levels of abstractions going on inside of it. Only programmers really need to worry about this (usually), but it's good to be aware of when you're trying to figure out how all this stuff fits together.

It's also important to remember that the levels I'm describing refer to the overall structure and organization of the software as a whole. In day-to-day use when you sit down at your computer you typically don't see these levels — in fact, everything looks to be (and in a certain sense is) on the same level. For example, Windows 95/98 may handle saving a file to disk, but as far as you're concerned, you saved the file in your word processor and it took care of saving the file.

Or, at an even more basic level, it's Windows 95/98 that actually takes care of creating and moving around the window in which your spreadsheet may be running, but as far as you're concerned, it's all just the spreadsheet software at work. And as an end-user, this is the way it's supposed to be. You're not supposed to have to have to worry about what element in your overall software system performed what function—unless, of course, it doesn't work, in which case it is helpful to find the specific root of the problem.

The one exception is that in a Linux environment, where you can pick and choose the different components that go into the operating system (such as the window manager), you may actually be aware of what component is performing a particular function.

Cross-Reference

See Chapter 9, "Adding, Upgrading, and Removing Software," for more on Linux.

Inside Windows

As mentioned previously, the Windows operating system performs many different functions and is made up of a lot of files. Many of these files and functions are too esoteric and confusing to really worry about, but there are several critical capabilities that everyone needs to understand.

The easiest way to think about this is if you break Windows into three layers. At the top are capabilities, or services that the operating system provides to applications; in the middle are the core functions of the operating system itself; and at the bottom are the components necessary to communicate with your computer's hardware. I want to be clear that this isn't exactly how Windows is structured, but it does give you a good overview of the elements with which you'll typically need to be concerned.

Figure 8-19 shows these levels graphically.

Services

At the top level of services are the capabilities that enable your applications to do things such as print, save files to disk, open windows, and so on. Often times you'll hear that some of these services are made available to software through an Application Programming Interface (API). APIs are what programmers use to connect their applications with the operating system so that everything can work together invisibly in the background. You won't ever have to worry about APIs as an end user, but I think it's important to understand the concepts behind how different layers of software work together. (Besides, you'll probably hear or see the phrase API in computer magazines or other resources and I didn't want you to feel left out . . . .)

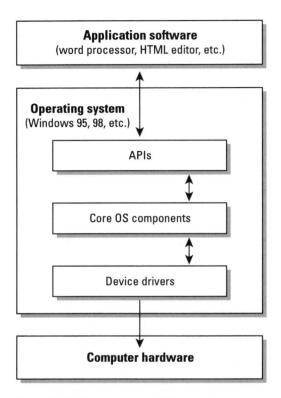

Figure 8-19: Three layers of Windows
From a logical point of view you can break Windows into three basic sections: the parts that communicate with applications, the core internal components that manage your computer's overall operation, and the parts that communicate with the hardware.

DirectX, for example, is a whole series of APIs that Microsoft has created to enable better quality games and other multimedia under Windows 95/98/2000. So, if you see an ad for a computer game that touts support for DirectX, that means the games' programmers have taken advantage of the DirectX services that Microsoft added to the operating system. The hope is that, by doing so, the game's programmers will be able to create a better experience.

To actually play a game that supports DirectX on your computer, you need to have the DirectX service, which provides the API hooks that the game needs, installed on your PC. This is why games that use DirectX typically install it along with the game when you install the program. What they're doing is adding the DirectX files to your operating system so that those services will be available when the game runs. If you accidentally delete these files, when you run the game, it wouldn't work because it would ask Windows for the DirectX services and Windows would basically have to say, "Sorry, I don't have what you need."

The files that provide the DirectX service and give programs access to the DirectX APIs come in the form of Dynamic Link Libraries, or DLLs. As mentioned previously, the Windows 95, 98, NT, and 2000 operating systems are actually made up of hundreds of files, many of which perform specific tasks. This open-ended nature enables you to easily add additional capabilities to the operating system simply by installing new files, such as the DirectX DLLs, in the right place on your hard drive. (Typically those files go inside the Windows folder.)

DLLs, which are a critical part of today's operating systems and applications, perform a specific function or set of functions. In the case of DirectX, the different DLLs that make up DirectX each provide mechanisms that enable programs to better coordinate and synchronize all the different multimedia elements, including audio and video, as well as providing a better means of interfacing with devices such as joysticks. Other DLLs do things such as handle Internet connections, perform spell checks, and draw the buttons in dialog boxes.

If everything is working properly on your computer, you'll never have to worry about DLLs. They are automatically installed in the right place by an application's installation program and should just do their magic in the background whenever they are called upon. Sometimes, however, two or more DLLs conflict with each other because they are unable to communicate or they step on each other's toes (that's a, uh, technical phrase, by the way) in the computer's memory. The result in those cases is that one of your programs, or even your entire computer, will crash.

Cross-Reference

See Chapter 17, "Troubleshooting Techniques," for more on dealing with DLL conflicts.

Registry

Another critical part of the Windows 95, 98, NT, and 2000 operating systems is the Registry. The Registry is essentially a large database that stores user preferences and other important settings that applications need to keep track of. So, for example, the Registry remembers any settings you've made in a program's options or preferences menus, as well as things such as what windows were left open and their location on the screen the last time you quit the program, and so on. (And if you haven't made any settings, it stores the program's default settings.)

Interestingly, the Registry also stores settings and preferences for your computer's hardware and, in that way, actually spans across all three of the layers I've broken Windows into.

The Registry is a daunting, complex beast. In fact, many several hundred-page books have been written on the Registry and all its components. I have no intention of going into those details here — I just want you to be aware that it also a part of the upper level of the OS that works with applications. (See the sidebar "Making sense of the Registry" later in this chapter for more.)

Core OS

The core components of the operating system do things such as draw images on your screen and allocate your computer's available memory amongst all the different pieces of software that are running on it at one time. They are the critical pieces that manage your computer's overall operation.

Like all the different layers of software, the Core OS components also communicate upward with layers of software above them and downward, with the layers of software below them. The three main Windows files are Kernel, User, and GDI (Graphics Device Interface — it's used to draw graphics on the screen), and they're each available in two forms, as .exe files and as .DLL files.

Cross-Reference

See Chapter 14, "Working with Documents and Files," for more on file extensions and types.

Unless (or until) your Windows machine crashes, you'll rarely have any interaction with core OS components.

Drivers

The final capability of the operating system is, in a sense, the most important because it enables your computer's hardware and software to work together as a team. What it basically does is translate the requests or instructions provided by the software into real-world messages that your hardware carries out. It does this through special pieces of software called *device drivers* or just *drivers* for short.

A driver is the last link in the long software chain that stretches down from a particular application program, through the operating system and to the hardware itself. Drivers handle the direct communication between the operating system and the various pieces of hardware inside your computer. Each component in your PC has a driver associated with it — some, in fact, have several because they may actually perform several functions. In those instances, there's typically a driver for each function that a particular component does.

In addition to drivers, another critical piece of software that communicates between your operating system and your computer's hardware is the BIOS, or Basic Input/Output System. The BIOS comes in a special form of hardware called firmware, which is basically software permanently stored in hardware. The software is stored in a type of circuit called Read Only Memory, or ROM, which enables it to remain available even when the computer is turned off. For this reason, it's sometimes referred to as the ROM BIOS. (On most newer computers, the BIOS is actually stored on an EPROM, which can be upgraded, but otherwise functions like a pure ROM-based BIOS.)

In older computers — and whenever you run the DOS operating system on newer computers — the BIOS functions as another layer of software, sitting between the operating system and the hardware and coordinating communications between the two. In this type of environment, software drivers almost act as extensions to the BIOS, adding support for new plug-in cards or other devices in your computer that the BIOS may not support.

Figure 8-20 illustrates the connections between the BIOS and other drivers.

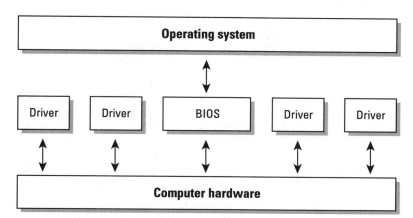

Figure 8-20: Drivers extend the BIOS
Under DOS, driver software extends the BIOS so that the operating system can communicate with pieces of hardware that may have been created after the BIOS was created.

Under Windows 95, 98, NT, and 2000, however, the BIOS doesn't serve this same type of intermediary role. Instead, Windows 95, 98, NT, and 2000 drivers generally talk directly to the hardware themselves, bypassing the software layer provided by the BIOS.

This doesn't mean the BIOS is unimportant, however, because it still plays a critical role in starting up your computer, loading the operating system, and passing along configuration information about the computer hardware to the operating system. For example, the Plug and Play feature in Windows 95, 98, and 2000 requires a Plug and Play BIOS that can recognize a new Plug and Play card and then pass along this new information to the operating system.

In Action

Knowing the principles is one thing, seeing how they really work is another. In the next few sections, I'm going to describe what really happens when you perform certain actions with a Windows-based PC, putting some of the concepts I described in early sections into a practical perspective. In most cases, I will just be hitting the main points because detailing all the steps involved would be incredibly tedious.

Along the way I'm also going to describe some other important concepts that you need to be aware of if you want to figure out how all this stuff really works — which is really important to know when (not if) you run into problems. The first process, logically enough, is what happens when you first turn on, or boot up, your computer.

Booting

As mundane as it may first appear, turning on your computer and having it boot to the Windows Desktop is actually a long, complicated process. Along the way it involves your computer's processor, BIOS, hard drive, operating system, and a group of special files called *startup files*.

The word *boot* actually comes from the phrase pull yourself up by your bootstraps, which is basically what the computer's BIOS does when you turn it on the processor kicks on and starts looking for instructions it can process. Thanks to a hardwired connection to the BIOS, it finds and loads the BIOS software into memory and starts to work. The first thing the BIOS does is perform some diagnostic tests called the Power-On Self Test (POST). These tests look at the various components plugged into your computer's motherboard and check to see that they're functioning properly.

On older computers POST was very important, but on newer computers with more reliable components it doesn't do a whole lot of good. As a result, newer systems go through a very brief POST, and most all systems enable you to turn POST tests on and off via the BIOS Setup program, which I'll explain shortly.

From there, this main BIOS, or system BIOS, looks for a BIOS on your video card and loads it into one of the Upper Memory Blocks (see above for more) specifically designated for this purpose.

Once it's successfully loaded the video card's BIOS, the video card can begin to function, and the computer is able to put its first message on your monitor. Not surprisingly, it's a line about the video card BIOS' version number, which is an indication that the loading was successful. It also commonly displays a message with the system BIOS manufacturer and version number at the same time. Next comes a memory check, which you'll see as a series of numbers counting in place.

Around this time the computer will often display a line that says something such as Hold Esc key to launch Setup, although instead of Esc it might say F2 or some other key or combination of keys.

Tip

Some computers hide these messages with a graphical startup screen that has the company's logo or something similar. If this happens with your computer, you can typically hit the Esc key to get rid of this display and view these messages.

If you don't do anything, the boot process pauses for a few seconds and then continues on with messages about finding an attached keyboard and mouse. If you do hold down the appropriate key, however, you'll launch another important piece of software called the BIOS Setup.

BIOS setup

The BIOS setup is where you can make a variety of settings that impact how your BIOS communicates with your PC hardware. The results of those settings are saved in special type of battery-backed-up memory called the

CMOS (Complementary Metal Oxide Semiconductor), which actually is a description of materials used to make PC components. When PCs were first designed, CMOS materials were generally only used for this special battery-backed memory—hence the name—but the materials are now used in most all modern computer components.

Many people confuse the BIOS and CMOS or refer to the program as CMOS Setup, but the connection is this: the settings that you make in the Setup program are stored in the CMOS and used by the BIOS to determine how it operates.

The available parameters in your BIOS Setup program vary from computer to computer and depend on the manufacturer of the BIOS used in your computer. They range from really practical to very esoteric, but it's important to remember that they can have an impact on how your computer operates. It's also important to remember that you can only get to them through the Setup program, which is usually only available when your computer first boots. Except for a few rare instances in older computers, you can't get to the BIOS Setup program once your computer has started except by restarting.

One group of settings that all BIOS Setup programs have is for the drives inside your computer, which are typically attached to your IDE controllers. This includes any internal hard drives, CD-/DVD-ROM drives, and other removable storage devices. You'll be able to tell which drives the BIOS recognizes and is communicating with by the listing of drives on your monitor—this usually occurs very quickly—right after the message regarding Setup.

After the drive messages are displayed, the system BIOS will look for and load any BIOSes on other plug-in cards, such as SCSI controllers and some network cards. Finally, when that process is done (you'll see messages on your display regarding those BIOSes if you have those types of cards installed) the BIOS looks to the main boot device—usually the hard drive—and starts to load the operating system. Right before it does this, the BIOS signals the computer to create a single beep sound, which signifies that everything is working properly. If you hear multiple beeps or no beep at all, that probably indicates a problem with your computer's hardware or the settings you've made in the BIOS Setup program. You'll need to track down a reference of BIOS beep codes if you do run into a problem (yes, a reference really does exist.)

Up until this point, the computer hasn't used any software on your computer other than the BIOS that's built into it. You can easily tell this because the hard drive indicator light on the front of your computer—which turns on and off whenever the hard drive is reading or writing data—will not have come on yet.

Master Boot Record

Just as the processor has a predefined route to find the BIOS when the computer boots, so the BIOS has a predefined route to find the operating system on the main boot device. The location it looks for is the first sector on the drive and the file it looks for when it gets there is the *Master Boot Record* (MBR).

Boot Viruses

Because the Master Boot Record plays such an important role, it has, unfortunately, also become the target of many computer viruses. So-called *boot viruses* are virus programs that change, corrupt, or overwrite the Master Boot Record. If the Master Boot Record is corrupted or missing, either because of a virus or for some other reason, then the boot process will stop and an error message will be displayed. The only way to

fix those problems is to start your computer with a floppy disk that has the necessary system files on it and use an antivirus utility to erase the virus or to repartition and/or reformat your hard drive and create a new Master Boot Record in the process. (See Chapter 18, "Solving Common PC Problems," for more on how to repartition and reformat your drive.)

The Master Boot Record is a critical file that stores both information on how your hard disk is divided up (if at all), as well as the master boot program. The master boot program is started by the BIOS, takes over control of the PC from the BIOS, and continues the boot process. (If you have a problem at this point in the boot-up process, it may be due to a boot virus. See the sidebar "Boot viruses" for more.)

The Master Boot Record holds disk information called a *partition table*; it describes how your hard drive is divided up into logical structures called *partitions*. (See the sidebar "The point of partitions" for more).

The Point of Partitions

Life used to be easy. All computer hard drives were viewed and treated as a single entity, and if you wanted to have multiple volumes on your computer you had to buy and install another hard drive. As hard drive sizes increased, however, users began to run into software-based limitations in the maximum size of hard disk volumes. In addition, people's computing needs have become more sophisticated. As a result, this simple structure proved too limiting. So, the notion of dividing hard drive into several logical chunks, or partitions, was developed.

Partitioning a drive means nothing more than dividing a single physical hard drive into several logical units that operating systems and applications see as distinct. So, for example, you could partition a 16GB drive into one 8GB and two 4GB chunks. You don't change any physical

characteristics of the hard drive in the process, just how the hard drive is viewed by the software that interacts with it. You create partitions by using the DOS FDISK utility or with third-party partitioning programs such as PowerQuest's PartitionMagic.

There are many reasons for partitioning a hard drive, but the primary ones have to do with organization and using multiple operating systems. (For example, some people use partitioning to organize all their applications on one partition and all their data on the other, and some do it in order to run two or more different operating systems on their computer, such as Windows 95 and Windows NT, or Windows 98 and Linux.) See Chapter 9, "Adding, Upgrading, and Removing Software," for more on installing multiple operation systems.

PC hard drives can be divided into a maximum of four main partitions, using one of two different partition types: primary and extended. You can have either up to four primary partitions or up to three primary partitions and one extended partition. This one extended partition, in turn, can be broken up into multiple logical partitions, which is how you get around the four partition limit. The extended partition, in fact, is not a real partition in that it doesn't hold any data. Instead, it is a logical container that incorporates any number of logical partitions.

The following figure shows a typical example of a partitioned hard drive.

Hard drive

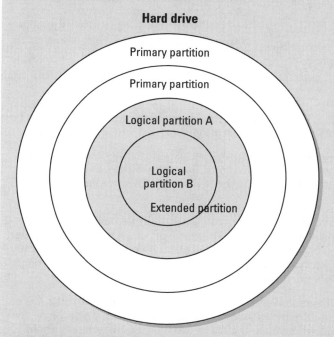

Making sense of partitions
You can divide a hard drive into logical pieces by using partitioning. In this example, the hard drive has two primary partitions and one extended partition that incorporates two logical partitions.

Primary partitions are typically used to hold operating systems and logical partitions are typically used to organize data, although you can do the reverse in a few limited situations. If you only have a single operating system on your computer, but a few hard drive partitions, you probably have one primary partition and one extended partition with several logical partitions inside it.

Each partition can have its own file system, which is a mechanism used by the operating system to keep track of files on the hard disk.

DOS and older versions of Windows use the File Allocation Table (FAT) file system, while later versions of Windows 95 and all versions of Windows 98 can read and understand both FAT and FAT32, an enhanced version of the file system. Windows NT uses NTFS (New Technology File System), but can also read FAT volumes. Unfortunately Windows 95 and 98 can't read NTFS and NT 4.0 can't natively read FAT32 (although Windows 2000 can read FAT32 volumes).

Continued

(continued)

If you do have multiple primary partitions, only one can be active at a time, otherwise multiple operating systems might try to boot at once, which could lead to total chaos. Special utilities referred to as boot loaders get around this by first loading themselves onto your computer's Master Boot Record and then, after they've started, they enable you to pick your OS of choice for a particular session. Once you do, the boot loaders automatically activate the appropriate primary partition and then find and launch the boot files for the operating system on this partition.

By the way, if you use multiple operating systems and multiple primary partitions, be aware that when you boot to one OS, you will not be able to see the other primary partitions if they use a file system that your boot OS doesn't understand. For example, if you boot into Linux, it won't necessarily be able to see a FAT32, Windows 95, or Windows 98 partition and vice versa. So, if there's data or applications you need to be able to see and run in both environments, you'll probably need to put it on a logical partition using a file system that each OS understands, such as the original FAT.

Cross-Reference

See Chapter 9, "Adding, Upgrading and Removing Software," for more on the partition requirements of different operating systems.

On many computer systems there's only one partition, but other systems break a single drive into several partitions. Sometimes the computer user does this and sometimes it's done at the factory by the company that has made your PC.

Note

Under Windows, the easy way to tell if you have multiple partitions is to look at your computer's drive letters (for example, C: drive, D: drive, E: drive, and so on). Each partition is assigned a drive letter, so if you know that you only have one hard drive and yet you see three different hard drive letters, you probably have multiple partitions.

The one important caveat is that removable drives, including Zip, Jaz, CD or DVD-ROM, and recordable drives also take a drive letter. So, if you have one or more of these types of devices, the extra drive letters may be for them. Once you've determined what drive letters are used by your removable drives, then you'll know whether or not your main hard drive is broken up into partitions.

The active partition on a hard drive is the one that has the primary operating system files needed to start your computer. It is these files that the master boot program looks for once it has been started, and it is these files that then take control of your PC in the ongoing torch-passing of PC control.

Startup files

If you're using Windows 3.1, 95, or 98, the first real operating system file to load on your computer is called Io.sys, which is basically DOS. DOS, or MS-DOS, simply short for Microsoft Disk Operating System (to distinguish it from DOSes made by a few other companies, such as IBM or Digital Research), was the first operating system for IBM PCs and compatibles. It remains part of both Windows 95 and Windows 98 (although it's not part of Windows NT or Windows 2000). It's still included to provide backwards compatibility with the thousands and thousands of programs that were built to run on top of it and because older versions of Windows were built around DOS as a foundation. Windows 95 and Windows 98 don't really use their old DOS underpinnings for very much, but it is undeniably part of these more modern operating systems.

When Io.sys is loaded from the hard drive into your computer's memory, it initializes the memory, divides it into predefined sections (see the sidebar "The DOS memory mess" for more), and begins the process of loading a series of startup files. These startup files configure your computer and set a number of parameters that determine how your computer will function once it finishes the boot process.

The first file that Io.sys loads is called Msdos.sys. It is a small hidden System file that includes things such as what paths, or directories, to look for Windows in, whether or not to launch into the Windows 95/98 desktop or DOS command prompt, whether to display the Windows 95/98 launch screen, and so on.

On a normal Windows 95/98 boot-up the next step is for Io.sys to process, or load, the Windows Registry files, which consist of System.dat. and User.dat. Specifically, the boot-up process needs the sections of the Registry that include 32-bit, or protected mode, device drivers for all the hardware components in your PC. These drivers are required in order for the operating system to talk to the hardware. To get your computer started, the BIOS includes basic drivers for your floppy disk, hard drive, and video card — just enough to get your computer up and going. To talk to anything more than this — and to talk to these components in a more full-featured way — you need driver software.

The next file to load on some computers is Config.sys, one of two startup files that you commonly hear about (the other — Autoexec.bat — comes a bit later in the startup process). I said some computers because neither Windows 95 nor Windows 98 require a Config.sys file — it only appears in systems that need it to maintain compatibility with older software that's installed on that particular machine. The reason for this is that Config.sys' purpose, which was/is to set up the system environment and load DOS/Windows 3.1 real-mode device drivers, has largely been taken over by the Windows Registry.

Next comes a series of a small real-mode drivers needed to set the system up. Himem.sys enables the computer to work with memory about 1MB (see the sidebar "The DOS memory mess" for more), and Ifshlp.sys (Installable File System Helper), is required for Windows to be able to use long file names (and yet still remain compatible with DOS' eight character file name limit).

The DOS Memory Mess

One of the unfortunate parts of retaining compatibility with older applications, and using DOS as the first operating system that loads when your computer starts, is that DOS requires a convoluted memory structure to function properly. Once again, it's the dreaded legacy problem.

Actually, in its original versions, DOS used a fairly straightforward memory organization, with 640KB of conventional memory used for loading applications and drivers and another 384KB of upper memory blocks for storing the system and video card BIOSes and a few other special things. As computer memory capacities increased beyond one megabyte and DOS applications began to require more and more conventional memory,

however, several techniques and programs were developed to work around these limitations. And the confusing mess it created is, unfortunately, the environment in which today's versions of DOS (and even Windows, to a degree) now operate.

Under DOS or any version of Windows except NT or 2000 (including 3.1, 95, and 98), memory is divided into conventional memory, upper memory (the same thing as Upper Memory Blocks, or UMBs), and extended memory (sometimes called XMS for eXtended Memory Specification), which is all the memory beyond 1MB. In addition, the first 64KB of extended memory is called the High Memory Area (HMA). The figure below displays the memory map graphically.

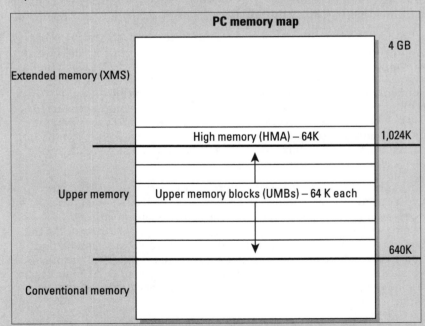

The DOS/Windows memory map
Under DOS and Windows, your PC's memory is broken up into three main chunks: conventional memory, upper memory, and extended memory. In addition, the first 64KB of extended memory is referred to as high memory and, through the use of an expanded memory manager, you can convert some of the upper memory and extended memory into expanded memory.

In order for DOS or Windows (again, all versions except NT and 2000) to get access to and make use of any memory beyond 1MB, a special program called Himem.sys must be loaded. Himem.sys is one of two memory manager programs (the other being Emm386.exe, which is explained below) included with DOS — and Windows — to help structure your computer's memory so that the operating system(s) can work properly. You can think of Himem.sys as a memory extender that enables your operating system(s) to break through the one megabyte barrier imposed by working in real mode (which itself is a barrier required to maintain compatibility with older software — see how complicated and messy this is?). In addition to providing access to extended memory, Himem.sys also sets aside the special high memory area.

Under Windows 3.1 and DOS, you specifically had to load Himem.sys via one of your computer's startup files to get access to extended memory. If you didn't, your computer would be unable to work with anything more than one megabyte of memory — even if you had 16MB, 32MB, 64MB, or more. Windows 95 and Windows 98 take care of this by putting a command in the Io.sys file to automatically load Himem.sys as soon as it starts, but if Himem.sys ever gets deleted or corrupted, Windows won't be able to load.

But just having access to more memory in general isn't always enough. If you need to run DOS applications (including many games), the problem is that there needs to be as much conventional memory as possible for the game to load and run. Normally, DOS itself, certain real-mode drivers, and occasionally some other utility programs (commonly referred to as Terminate and Stay Resident programs, or TSRs, which basically means they load into memory and stay there whenever the computer is running) take up a portion of conventional memory. And whatever memory they take up is memory that's not available to DOS applications. So, the trick is to figure out how to move some of those elements out of conventional memory into other areas of memory, because this frees up more conventional memory in which applications can run.

By the way, if you don't ever run any DOS applications, then you probably won't have to worry about this type of memory management. Unlike extended memory, which affects Windows and Windows applications, freeing up extra conventional memory generally only affects DOS applications, although there are some older Windows applications that also require larger amounts of conventional memory to run properly.

There are two basic ways to free up conventional memory. One is to take advantage of the special high memory area created via the Himem.sys program and load portions of DOS there instead of into conventional memory. You do this by telling DOS to Load High in your Config.sys startup file (which is explained a bit later in this chapter). The other is to take advantage of another memory manager program called Emm386.exe, which is referred to as an expanded memory program.

Though the names are confusingly similar, expanded memory (EMS) is different from extended memory (XMS). Think of expanded memory as a type of memory that can expand how much conventional memory your computer has — jumping from 640KB to, say, 740KB or more — within the larger confines of how much total memory your computer has. Extended memory, on the other hand, extends the total amount of memory that DOS and Windows can see.

Emm386.exe, as well as popular competitors such as QuarterDeck Expanded Memory Manager (QEMM), offers the opportunity to load some real-mode device drivers (the kind required for DOS, not Windows 95/98) and other DOS software that normally loads into conventional memory into available spaces in upper memory

Continued

(continued)

(UMB). In addition, it can convert a portion of your computer's extended memory into expanded memory, either for loading other device drivers that don't fit into upper memory or for DOS applications that specifically require access to expanded memory. Emm386 depends on extended memory to work, so it can only be loaded after Himem.sys, which first provides access to extended memory. Expanded memory managers like Emm386 can't work on their own.

Nowadays it seems ridiculous to have to worry about freeing up an extra few kilobytes of memory to run applications, but such is the nature of DOS. Of course, this also partially explains why hardly any new applications are written for DOS — it's just too much of a pain for the average person to deal with.

Io.sys then loads Command.com, which is a critical DOS file that provides the environment in which you can interact with DOS (when and if you do this). In a certain sense, Command.com provides the user interface for DOS and enables it to interpret DOS commands (hence the file's name) and convert them into actions that the computer can take. In the early days of computers, some companies provided alternatives to Command.com that provided a slightly different set of commands that you could use and, consequently were considered alternative interfaces for DOS (although they all still used the familiar command prompt, such as C:\>, as the sole user interface).

With the capability to execute DOS commands now available (through Command.com), Io.sys runs the Setver.exe command, which is used for backwards compatibility with some old DOS programs. What it does is simply fools those applications into thinking that they're running an older version of DOS (which those applications need in order to run properly).

Next comes the Autoexec.bat file, which is essentially a list of commands to be carried out by Command.com every time the computer is started. Again, like Config.sys, Windows 95 and 98 do not require an Autoexec.bat file and many newer computers do not have one. If you do have one, it's typically used to load certain driver-related files that are mentioned in the Config.sys file as well as telling DOS where to look for application programs and other folders. (See the sidebar "Making sense of Autoexec.bat" for more.)

The final command in the Io.sys is to load Windows, which starts the process of reading the Windows files from your hard disk.

Note

If you ever want to see what files are being loaded when your computer starts, you can have Windows load each file one at a time by using the Step-by-Step Confirmation option from the Windows 95/98 Startup menu. You get to this by holding down the F8 key when your computer starts to boot.

Making Sense of Autoexec.bat

Computers earned a reputation for being confusing and hard to understand early in their history, and they've been fighting it ever since. If you've ever looked at the contents of an Autoexec.bat file (or Config.sys, for that matter), you'll probably understand why. What you'll see, if you do, is a bunch of individual lines with characters and numbers on them that seemingly have very little to do with the English language. What they are is a series of commands or simple instructions that the computer is supposed to automatically execute — hence the name — whenever it starts up.

The file extension .bat is short for batch file, which means it's a file that includes a group of commands that are to be processed as a group. (A file extension is the three characters following a period in a computer file's name. To view them in Windows 95/98, you need to make sure that you have turned on the Show All Files option and turned off the Hide File Extensions for Known File Types option in Windows Explorer.) If you're familiar with macros in other computer applications, a batch file is kind of like a macro. See Chapter 14, "Working with Documents and Files," for more on file extensions.

The contents of the Autoexec.bat file, which is nothing more than a simple text file — meaning it only contains words and can be viewed and/or edited in any program that can read text files — can contain a wide variety of different things. I'm not going to try to explain what all the terms mean, but I will explain a few to give you an idea of what's involved.

- The Load command simply means to load the program following the command.

- If you see Path=, it's telling the computer where to look for executable application programs — this simply saves you from having to type in the full directory name at a DOS prompt to run an application.

- The Set= statement provides instructions on where to look for other folders that the operating system may need.

- The letters `rem` or a semi-colon (;) at the beginning of a line signify that the instructions or words on that line are to be ignored. These are often used during troubleshooting to test for problems with individual lines in the Autoexec.bat file as well as to provide remarks — hence the rem — that explain what some of the lines are for.

In addition to the main commands, you may see additional characters (such as slashes and letters) following them. These characters are usually switches, which are common in the world of DOS software. Switches are essentially additional parameters that can affect how a particular command is done or what mode a particular program will run in when it starts.

To find out what switches are available for a particular DOS command, type the command's name followed by a /?. In most cases, you'll see the available switches and a brief summary of what they do. In addition, if you have Windows 98, you'll find lots of great tips in the Config.txt that should be in the root directory of your hard drive.

Windows Startup

Even though we've made it to Windows, the boot process isn't finished yet. Windows has a few startup files of its own that it runs through when it starts. Most of these files end with a .ini extension, which means they are initialization files (sometimes they're called configuration files).

The most important Windows initialization files are System.ini, Win.ini, and Protocol.ini. They provide information about your overall system setup, your specific Windows setup, and any networking protocols your computer may be using. Even if your computer isn't on a regular network, it's probably using network protocols in order to get on the Internet.

Cross-Reference

See Chapter 12, "Setting Up a Small Business or Home Network," for more.

Secret

Under Windows 95 or 98, you can see and edit all these files, as well as your Config.sys and Autoexec.bat, by using a utility bundled with Windows 95 and 98 called the System Configuration Editor (Sysedit.exe). To run it, simply click your Windows Start button, select the Run option, type in **Sysedit** (capitalization does not matter), and click OK. Under Windows 98, you can use the more powerful System Configuration Utility by typing in **Msconfig**.

Cross-Reference

See Chapter 18, "Solving Common PC Problems," for more on fixing startup problems.

As their name suggests, the purpose of initialization files is to initialize your software settings and to set up your preferences for your computer, such as what background pattern to display, what screen saver to use, and more. If you ever search for all the .ini files in your computer, you'll find that you probably have a lot of them — this is because many individual applications use them to store their own preference settings.

Ideally, all of these settings could (and should) be stored in the Windows 95/98 Registry. In fact, the Registry was specifically created to store and organize all the information that used to be scattered across all kinds of different .ini files inside your computer. And the reality is, most of the settings found in .ini files are also in the Registry and are loaded via the Registry. But again, for backwards compatibility with older Windows programs that look for certain settings in these initialization files — especially System.ini and Win.ini — Windows 95 and 98 include copies of them and uses them as needed. (To find out more about .ini files and the Registry, see the sidebar "Making sense of the Registry.")

As part of its initialization process, Windows can also load programs that are associated with specific Run commands inside the Registry. When the Registry is processed, these programs will be automatically started.

Finally, after any initialization files have been loaded and gone through, Windows has basically finished the boot process. However, your computer may continue working, and your hard-disk light may continue to flash because Windows also includes another mechanism for automatically loading software as soon as the OS boots: the Startup folder.

Making Sense of the Registry

The Windows Registry has developed a well-deserved reputation for being difficult to decipher, but the basic purpose for and organization of the Registry is relatively straightforward. The idea behind the Registry was to create a central repository that could hold all the configuration information that your computer needs to operate, including references to drivers and system and application preferences.

Previously, many of these settings were scattered all over the place, including the Config.sys file (and Autoexec.bat to some extent) and in many, many different .ini files, such as System.ini and Win.ini. In fact, it was the overwhelming mess of different .ini files that apparently pushed Microsoft to create a single place where all the different pieces of information could be con-solidated. Unfortunately, to maintain backwards compatibility and because of programmers who continue to ignore the Registry, that goal hasn't quite been reached. Right now, we have both the old places for storing this configuration

information and the new ones, but there's still hope that some day, everything will simply go inside the Registry.

The Registry, which is actually made up of two different files (User.dat and System.dat) that are merged into one entity when Windows starts, is organized into a group of six main sections (or keys). The idea was to structure it similarly to .ini files, which are commonly broken into different sections with bracketed headings. Unlike .ini files, however, the Registry can take advantage of subheadings (or subkeys) to organize the information in a more logical, more structured fashion. In this way, the Registry is organized and looks like the directory structure on your hard drive.

In most cases you'll never to worry about digging into the Registry in its native form, but if you do ever need to (or if you're just curious), the accompanying figure shows what you'll find.

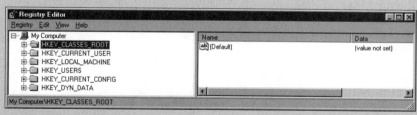

Inside the Registry
The Windows Registry, which you can view and edit via the free Regedit.exe utility included with Windows, is broken up into six main keys (or branches). Three of the keys, however, are just shortcuts to information that can be found buried within the other branches.

The Registry's six top-level keys are actually made up of three main keys and three keys that are exact duplicates of sections found within other keys. They're available at the top level simply as a matter of convenience—any changes or additions made to these copies are immediately reflected in the original settings and vice versa.

Be very careful! You don't want to make any changes to the Registry unless you know exactly what you're doing. Even one improper change can really screw up your PC and prevent it from booting. Simply viewing it is fine, however, and won't cause any problems. Just be aware that it's easy to make inadvertent changes to the

Continued

(continued)

Registry because the Regedit utility records changes *as you make them*.

The three main branches of the Registry are the HKEY_ USERS key, which stores information about user-specific settings; HKEY_LOCAL_ MACHINE, which stores information about all the hardware and software stored on your machine; and HKEY_DYN_DATA, which keeps track of performance data that Windows 95/98 creates dynamically as it operates. As you might guess, the real meat of the Registry is in the HKEY_ LOCAL_MACHINE branch.

Of the other main keys, both the HKEY_ CLASSES_ROOT and the HKEY_CURRENT_ CONFIG can be found a few levels down in the HKEY_LOCAL_MACHINE branch, and the HKEY_CURRENT_USER key can be found in the HKEY_ USERS branch. In fact, unless you've defined more than one user via distinct logons and other settings within Windows — which most people don't do — these last two branches will be the same (except for one folder called Default at the top level of HKEY_USERS).

As I said previously, you generally don't want to change settings at the Registry level, but this doesn't mean you won't ever change the settings that make up your Registry. In fact, you're probably doing it quite a bit; it's just that you don't realize it. The reason is, Windows actually provide numerous tools for changing Registry settings on your computer, but it hides the fact that you're actually changing a portion of the Registry. All the Control Panels you can find off the Start menu, for example, are actually just friendly little user interfaces for changing settings within the Registry.

If you really wanted to, for example, you could change the screen saver on your computer by finding and changing the appropriate subkey within your Registry. However, I think it's a heck of a lot easier to just double-click your Display Control Panel and change it there. Either way the same thing is accomplished — you change some settings in your Registry that affect how your computer operates. In this way, you can think of Control Panels as easy, little Registry editors.

As its name suggests (believe it or not, many computer files actually have logical names — once you figure out what is the logic is), the Startup folder is a place where you can store software that you want to automatically load when Windows starts up. Actually, you don't even need to store the real software there — just a Windows shortcut file, which is basically a small file that points to where the real program is inside your computer's directory structure. (In other words, what folder it's in.)

What happens is, as soon as Windows finishes loading, it looks to see if there are any programs or shortcuts inside the Startup folder, and if there is, it launches them automatically. Many utility programs that run in the background start this way. It's also a handy way to launch your favorite programs if you happen to use the same thing(s) every time your start your PC.

Once the programs inside the Startup folder have run, then your computer has finally finished booting, and you can get on to doing some work. Thankfully, it all happens a lot faster than it takes to read about it.

Table 8-1 offers a summary of all the Startup files that are used in the process of booting your computer to a Windows 95 or Windows 98 desktop.

Table 8-1   Windows Startup Files

Name of File	Required or Optional for Windows 95/98 to Boot	Basic Purpose
BIOS*	Required	Starts boot process, looks for master boot record on hard drive, provides basic drivers
Io.sys*	Required	Initializes memory, starts loading other startup files
Msdos.sys*	Required	Sets a variety of boot parameters, such as what mode to start Windows in
System.dat	Required	One half of Windows Registry, stores 32-bit Windows drivers, hardware and software settings
User.dat	Required	Other half of Windows Registry, includes user-specific Windows settings
Himem.sys	Required	Real-mode memory manager required to access memory above 1MB
Ifshlp.sys	Required	Real-mode driver used to read and understand long file-names
Config.sys	Optional	Used to load any other real-mode drivers and other settings necessary for backwards compatibility
Command.com*	Required	Provides interface for DOS and includes capability to interpret DOS commands
Setver.exe	Optional	Used for backwards compatibility with some older DOS programs
Autoexec.bat	Optional	Stores a variety of DOS commands that can be run whenever the computer is started; also used for backwards compatibility
Windows core files	Required	The core Windows operating system files
System.ini	Optional	Sometimes used to load some drivers and set up system-wide preferences
Windows.ini	Optional	Used to set up Windows-specific preferences

Continued

Table 8-1   *(continued)*

Name of File	Required or Optional for Windows 95/98 to Boot	Basic Purpose
Protocol.ini	Optional	Provides basic networking protocol settings
Other .ini files	Optional	May be used with certain utilities or other applications
Windows Registry Run entries	Optional	Automatically starts certain programs or background processes when Windows boots
Windows Startup Folder	Optional	Used to automatically start applications after Windows boots

*Files required to boot to a DOS prompt

Running an application

After your computer starts and you sit there staring at the Windows desktop, you can start doing something useful by launching (also called starting or running) an application, such as a word processor, Web browser, and so on.

You can launch an application by either double clicking it, selecting it off the Start menu, or typing in the exact location of the program (including the directory and subdirectories) in the Run command window. Regardless of how you start the process, the operating system looks through the file allocation table on the hard disk (which is a very important file that keeps track of where all the other files on your disk are stored), finds the program you selected, and begins to load the application into memory. If the application requires more memory than you have available, then the computer starts to use something called *virtual memory* (see the sidebar "Making memory virtual" for more).

Secret

Application programs usually consist not of a single file, as you might suspect, but instead of a small umbrella application and many DLLs (Dynamic Link Libraries — also called shared libraries or application extensions) and other small components that are controlled and organized by the main application.

When you start an application, what typically happens is the main application and a portion of the DLLs are loaded into memory. The remainder of the DLLs included with an application sit dormant on the hard drive unless or until you use a portion of the program that requires their use — such as the graphics editing tools within your word processor. In the event you do use them, they're also loaded into memory and put to use by the program.

Making Memory Virtual

Unless you've got a lot of memory and are running a very clean system with few (or no) extra utilities loaded, there's a good chance that you may not have enough physical memory (that is, RAM) to load all the software you want to run at once. If this is the case, then your computer will start to use what's called virtual memory.

Virtual memory is a feature offered by Windows (as well as most other operating systems) that enables you to use a portion of your hard disk as pseudo-RAM. What happens is, when your computer runs out of space in physical memory, it stores some of what it has in memory (but isn't using at the time) onto an area of the hard drive that's specifically set aside for virtual memory. The process is often called *paging* because the memory is broken up into chunks called *pages*.

If you switch back to an application that was running in the background and the computer needs to get access to the information it stored in virtual memory on the hard disk, Windows reads the data it had previously paged to the disk back into memory and stores a different chunk of memory onto the disk. This process happens as often as the operating system needs to.

The amount of memory specifically set aside for virtual memory is usually handled by Windows 95/98 (unlike Windows 3.1, which forced you to pick the amount yourself), but you also have the option of manually setting this amount.

The benefit of virtual memory is that it enables you to run more things at once than your computer would otherwise be capable of doing. The downside, however, is that constantly reading and writing data from and to the hard disk slows your computer's overall operation down because hard drives are an order of magnitude slower than RAM. This is one of the main reasons why many computers seem to run faster when you add more memory to them because what you're doing is reducing the number of times the computer has to use virtual memory—and slow itself down in the process.

In order to run properly, most applications also take advantage of certain capabilities provided by DLLs that are included as part of the operating system. For example, instead of building their own tools for creating and displaying dialog boxes within their programs, many application programmers use the services made available by Windows and simply provide the specific settings that their application requires. This enables them to have Windows standard dialog boxes and buttons that include the choices they need, without having to build them themselves.

The shared DLLs that provide these services are available to any application that wants them, including multiple applications running at the same time.

Figure 8-21 shows how all the different pieces involved in running an application program interact.

By taking advantage of the shared DLLs, programs can take up less space on the hard disk and less space in memory because they don't have to include every bit of functionality they require to run. Plus, they won't duplicate functions that other applications also need and that the operating system has to supply for itself anyway. In addition, by taking advantage of shared DLLs, programs can operate more efficiently, which translates into better performance.

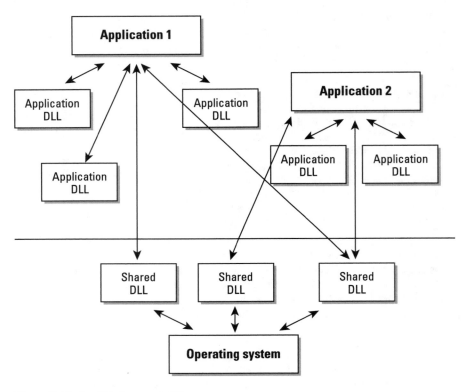

Figure 8-21: Applications and DLLs
Most application programs actually consist of an umbrella application and many DLLs that provide specific functions within a program. In addition, most applications depend on certain services provided by shared DLLs that Windows provides.

As nice as that all sounds in theory, however, the sometimes ugly reality is that some applications can only work with certain versions of the shared DLL files. As a result, if another application updates some of those files when it's installed, an application that used to work just fine with a previous version of the shared DLL may no longer work. (The fact that Windows enables applications to easily update shared files is real sore point with some people.) In addition, some DLLs conflict with each other, so just adding a new DLL file into an existing mix can also cause a lot of software-related problems.

Cross-Reference

See Chapter 17 "Troubleshooting Techniques," for more on DLL conflicts.

Once these problems get worked through — that is, if you even run into them, because not everyone does — your application and Windows work hand in hand to store your working files in memory. If you create a document or some kind of file, the application also works with Windows and the appropriate device drivers when you want to save this work to your hard disk.

Printing

If you decide you want to print the file, here's what happens. When you choose the Print command in your program, it sends a message to Windows saying that it wants access to the printer driver software. When this connection is made, the program passes the data off to the printer driver, which converts the file into a format that the printer can understand. Then the printer driver passes the printer data to the parallel port or USB driver, which takes care of sending the data out your computer's appropriate port and onto the printer.

Once the printer receives the data, the printer translates it into specific messages that control how the device's printing mechanism turns those messages into dots on the page. If you have problems printing, it could be because any one of those steps or hand offs between different pieces of software didn't work. If everything does work properly, as it hopefully should, then you end up with a printed page.

Cross-Reference

For more on solving printer problems, see Chapter 18 "Solving Common PC Problems."

Summary

In this chapter, I described how your computer works, both on a basic, operational level and on a more detailed, technical level.

▶ Computers basically work by loading software applications and data into memory from the hard disk and performing calculations on this data based on instructions included in the software.

▶ Internally, your computer's hardware consists of a number of specialized components that all connect together through the motherboard.

▶ Your computer's hardware is structured as a set of data paths, or buses, that all revolve around the microprocessor, which is the heart and brain of your computer. Different buses work at different speeds.

▶ A computer's resources must be properly set up and distributed in order for the machine to work properly.

▶ Your computer's software is organized into a series of layers where applications interact with the operating system, the operating system connects with device drivers, and the device drivers communicate directly with your computer's hardware.

▶ Starting up, or booting, your computer is a long, complicated process that involves ongoing interaction with your computer's hardware and software and the loading and processing of many separate startup files.

▶ Application programs actually consist of many separate pieces of software, and these pieces work in conjunction with different pieces of operating system software in order to create the familiar environment we're used to seeing on our screens.

▶ Behind the scenes, printing a file actually involves several different layers of software.

Chapter 9

Adding, Upgrading, and Removing Software

In This Chapter

▶ You will learn how to install applications, including ones you've downloaded off the Internet.

▶ You will learn what really happens when you install these different types of software.

▶ You will learn how to upgrade your existing applications.

▶ You will learn how to install and/or upgrade Windows 95 and Windows 98.

▶ You will learn how to install other operating systems, including Linux.

▶ You will learn how to set up your PC to dual boot with multiple operating systems.

▶ You will learn different techniques for removing software.

Once you have your computer set up and working, the one activity you'll probably return to more often than any other—other than simply using the computer, of course—is installing software. After all, it's the software that enables your computer to do things. Plus, different combinations of software give each computer a different personality. (We are all unique individuals, after all, so our computers should reflect that, right?)

Most computers sold today come bundled with a variety of applications already preinstalled, but rarely do these applications meet all of your needs, particularly after you've been using the computer for a while. More than likely you'll add new applications, upgrade some of the software that came with your machine and, inevitably, find some nifty new stuff out on the Internet that you've just got to have.

In addition, you'll probably be forced to deal with driver upgrades, software incompatibilities, and other hassles that are part and parcel of the PC user experience. After a while, you'll undoubtedly also want to remove some of the software that is cluttering up your computer's hard disk.

The end result is that your computer's hard drive will soon have a constantly revolving door where new pieces of software come in, get upgraded, or are removed on a regular basis.

Installing New Programs

On the one hand, installing new programs on your computer is incredibly easy: you insert the CD/DVD or floppy disk into your computer's appropriate drive, start the installation program, answer a few questions, and sit back and let the process run its course.

Note

On CDs/DVDs that take advantage of the AutoPlay feature in Windows 95 and Windows 98, starting the installation program may be as simple as clicking a single button that appears on your screen after the disk has been inserted. For some CDs and all floppy disks, you may have to go to the Run command off the Start Menu, type in either **setup** or **install,** and hit OK. Another easy way to do it with any type of media (such as CD, DVD, or floppy disk) is via the Install button in the Add/Remove Programs Control Panel, which can be found via the Settings command off the Start Menu (see Figure 9-1).

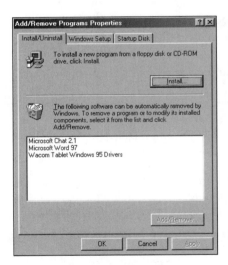

Figure 9-1: Installing applications the easy way
Under Windows 95 and Windows 98, one easy way to install software is to open the Add/Remove Programs control panel and click the Install button.

On the other hand, there's a lot going on behind the scenes. During the procedure, the installation program will put different pieces of the program in different places on your hard disk. (See the sidebar "Making sense of folders and directories" for more on how files are organized on your PC.)

Some files will be placed in the application's own folder, some will be placed in various folders inside the main Windows folder, and some may even be placed in other folders. In addition, the installation program will make entries and/or changes to the Windows Registry and may also make additions or edits to other startup files. Finally, the installation program will also add the program's name or a folder name (sometimes called a Program Group) to the Programs menu off the Start menu.

Cross-Reference

See the "Installation example: Publisher 2000" section later in this chapter for more.

In addition, it's important to remember that most of the software on your computer works together — or at least, simultaneously — during normal operation. Any time you make changes to the pieces in your particular software puzzle, or configuration, problems can arise. They shouldn't, and generally don't, but they are not at all uncommon.

Cross-Reference

See Chapter 8, "How Your Computer Works," for more on how software works.

A real-world example of this principle is the common advice to quit all currently running applications when you install another program. The reasoning behind the advice is that some application installations make updates to shared files that may be in use by another application. If this happens and the currently running application tries to access a now-updated shared file, the application can crash (stop working). This usually doesn't happen; most people install applications with other things running and find that they don't have any problems. But it is possible, so, consider yourself forewarned.

Cross-Reference

See Chapter 17, "Troubleshooting Techniques," for more on software conflicts.

Making sense of folders and directories

How files are organized on the computer's hard disk is a concept that confuses many computer beginners and even intermediate level users. Here's the basic idea: just as you use folders in a storage cabinet to organize all your papers, you use folders (or directories, as they are sometimes called) to organize the different files on your computer.

When application programs are installed they often create their own folders, although you will always have the ability to reorganize, edit, rearrange, and create any of the folders on your

hard disk. This said, it is not a good idea to move around the folders that installation programs create because it can confuse the programs. In fact, if you move around these original folders, the next time you try to run those programs you might get error messages that say that the computer is unable to find certain files. One important point to know about folders and directories on your computer is that you can have folders within folders to any degree. You can set up these *nested folders* — as they are sometimes called — as deep as you want.

Continued

(continued)

Also, it's important to be able to read and understand a directory structure listing (sometimes called a *path*). If you read that something is located in the C:\ directory (sometimes called the root directory) that means the file (or folder) is at the first level of your main hard drive. (You may also have a D:\ or other letter drive if you have multiple hard drives, multiple drive partitions, and either a CD-ROM or DVD-ROM drive.) The basic DOS startup files Autoexec.bat and Config.sys, for example, are in the root directory. (See Chapter 8, "How Your Computer Works" for more on these DOS startup files.)

If you see that a file is located in C:\Windows\System, it means the file is inside the System folder, which is inside the Windows folder, which is located in the root directory (C:\). Or, another way to look at it is you find the Windows folder on the main level of the hard drive and open that, then find the System folder inside the Windows folder and open that and that's where you'll find the file. The accompanying figure gives an example of how folders can be organized.

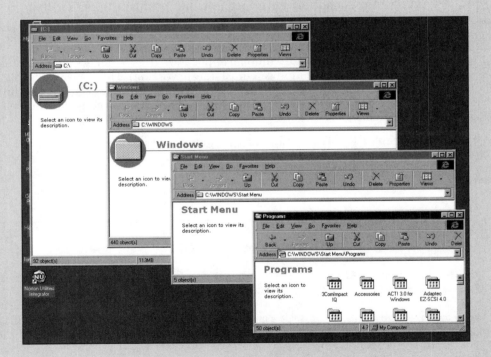

Folders within folders
To find files that are buried within your computer's directory structure, just follow the path of folders included in the listing and know that each \ (backslash) indicates a new folder. So, for example, a file in the C:\Windows\Start Menu\Programs folder can be found inside the Programs folder, which is inside the Start Menu folder, which is inside the Windows folder, which is located at the root directory of your main hard drive (typically, C:\).

Downloading programs off the Internet

An increasingly common way to add new software to your computer is via the Internet. Most companies offer application upgrades, driver updates, bug fixes, and add-ons to their existing applications via their Web sites. Best of all, much of this software is free for the taking.

In addition, many businesses have been set up to sell commercial applications over the World Wide Web. In these cases, what you're doing is buying the exact same software you would normally get in a box from a computer store, minus the box and all the goodies that may go in it, such as printed documentation.

The benefit of buying online is that you can get immediate access to software, even if it's two o'clock in the morning. Some companies will even send you printed documentation once you've filled out and sent in a registration form or something similar.

Not all companies offer the documentation, however, which is obviously one of the big pitfalls with buying online. As more and more companies move to electronic manuals — that is, onscreen versions of their Help files — this may become less of an issue, but it's still a problem now. The other bigger downside of buying online is that you don't have a ready backup of the program that a CD/DVD (or floppy) provides you with in the event your hard drive goes bad or you need to reinstall the program.

In addition to commercial applications, there's also an untold amount of freeware, shareware, and demoware available on the Internet. (See the "What's the deal with freeware and shareware?" sidebar for more.) With the enormous popularity of the Internet and the growing usage of personal computers, it has gotten to the point where software is available for just about any subject or task you can think of — just as there are Web sites on nearly every subject imaginable (as well as a few that are unimaginable). To start your search for freeware or shareware on the Internet, you might try heading over to the www.shareware.com or www.download.com Web sites — two giant repositories for downloading files off the Internet — and start browsing around.

CD

On the CD that accompanies this book you'll find freeware, shareware, and demoware that you can install and try on your PC.

How it works

Whether it's commercial software or free software, the way to download software is to copy a file or group of files off a server and onto your hard drive. On the Internet, the copying or downloading of the file is done via something called the File Transfer Protocol (FTP), and the file transfer occurs via your Internet connection (which is typically through your modem). Figure 9-2 shows how everything works.

What's the deal with freeware and shareware?

Many people who write computer programs do it purely for the satisfaction of tackling a problem they have with their own computers or a problem that they see others have. When they're done with their software, they make it available for free to anyone else who wants to use it—hence, *freeware*. (Sometimes the people who write these programs ask for a small token of recognition from those who use their software as a courtesy; it may be something like a postcard from the user's home town, but it's never required.) You'll find an enormous amount of software available for free on the Internet—everything from full-blown application programs to document templates to utilities with very specific functions.

It used to be with freeware that you got what you paid for, and in some cases, you still do. But that generally isn't the case today. In fact, some of the most important pieces of software that drive the successful operation of the Internet and Web sites are actually freeware. In addition, the growth of the free software movement called open source software, which the Linux operating system is the best example of, has added yet another wrinkle to the notion of free software. With open source software, not only are the program, operating system or other support files free, so is the source code, or programming instructions that went into making the software. Unless you're a programmer, the files won't do you any good, but the fact that they're available means potentially thousands or tens of thousands of programmers could be working to make it better. Again, the growth and rapid advances in the Linux operating system are probably the best example of this concept in action.

Because of the enormous effort involved in writing most computer programs, some programmers who make their work available on the Internet ask for a small payment if you decide to use their software. Software that falls into this category is called shareware.

Many of these individuals work on their own and depend on these payments as their sole (or an important supplementary) source of income. You can download, install, and try shareware for free, but if you continue to use it, you're asked to send a payment to the program's creator. Shareware payments range from about $5 to $75, but most are in the $20 to $30 range.

There are actually several different types of shareware. Some just use the trust system and depend on the honesty of the individual users to send in a payment. Others combine the notion of freeware and shareware by offering a limited set of functions for free, but provide a more complete set to those who register their software and pay the shareware fee. Another variation on shareware enables you to use the complete feature set for a limited amount of time, but after that time is up, reminders pop up, telling you that if you're continuing to use the software, you should pay for it. This type is sometimes referred to as nagware because it nags you about paying the shareware fee.

Recognizing the enormous popularity of freeware and shareware and the value in enabling people to try before they buy, many commercial software vendors started offering demo versions of their applications. This demoware works kind of like shareware in that it often enables you to use all the features of a program for a limited amount of time or it enables you to use everything except a few critical features (typically save, print, and copy) for as long as you'd like.

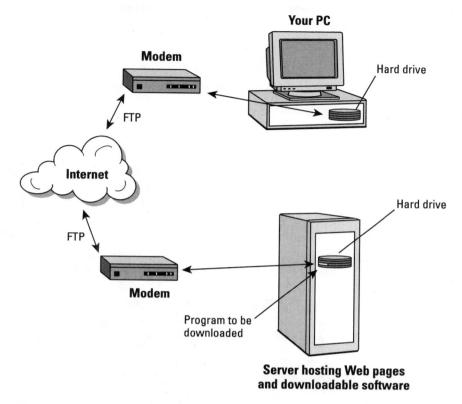

Figure 9-2: Downloading files
The process of downloading software off the Internet involves copying the file(s) from the server onto your computer's hard drive.

Today's Internet browsers all include the capability to copy files via FTP, but in the past you actually had to run a separate application, called an FTP client, which set up the connection between your computer and the server and monitored the downloading process. Some people still use separate FTP programs, such as the shareware WS_FTP, for this purpose, although most people only use FTP programs for uploading files from their computer onto a server on the Internet when they're doing things such as working on a Web site.

You'll find a copy of WS_FTP LE (a limited edition version of the program with only a basic set of features) on the CD-ROM accompanying this book.

STEPS:

Downloading Files Off the Internet

Step 1.   Launch your Internet browser and find the Web site and Web page that has the software you want to download.

Step 2.   If required, fill out the registration form. (Many sites require you to provide some amount of personal information, such as name and e-mail address, before they'll enable you to download a file.)

Step 3.   If necessary, make sure you pick the appropriate platform and/or operating system that you are running. You don't want to download a Macintosh or Windows 3.1 version if you're running Windows 98 (although virtually all software that says Windows 95 will also work with Windows 98).

Step 4.   Click on the specific file you want.

Step 5.   If you're using Internet Explorer, confirm in the File Download dialog box that the File is set to be saved to disk (see Figure 9-3).

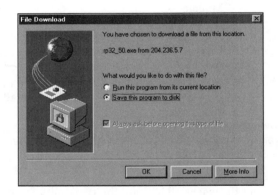

Figure 9-3: File download dialog box
In Internet Explorer, this dialog box enables you to save a file to disk or, if it's an application or file that can be opened directly, to open it.

Step 6.   In the Save As . . . dialog box, select the folder you want the downloaded file(s) to be stored in. You have the option to rename the file, but I don't recommend it because some installation programs may not work properly if you change the name. You need to be particularly careful not to change the file's three-character extension, which determines the file type.

See Chapter 14, "Working with Documents and Files," for more on file extensions and types.

Cross-Reference

People who are new to downloading files may forget to notice where the file is being saved to. The Save As dialog typically defaults to whatever folder it was previously used for, and this may or may not be where you want to store the downloaded file.

Tip

The easiest way to organize your downloaded files is to create a Downloads folder in the root directory of hard drive (C:\) and store all the files there. Inside this folder, create separate new folders with descriptive names for every download you copy onto your machine. In addition, the Save As dialog enables you to create a new folder before you save the file (just click the Folder icon with the little starlike symbol on it). If you don't, you'll end up with a folder full of confusingly named files and not know what is where. (Trust me, I've already made this mistake.) Figure 9-4 shows how to create a new folder.

Figure 9-4: Remember where you're saving
Believe it or not, the most important step in downloading a file is picking the location to save it in. You pick the location in the Save As dialog box. You can create a new folder for your download by clicking the Create New Folder Icon.

You can also create a Downloads folder on your Windows 95/98 desktop, which makes it very easy to find files after they've been downloaded. In fact, by default, Windows 98 creates a Downloads folder on your Desktop for you. The only problem is the contents of the Windows Desktop is actually a folder that's buried within your Windows Folder (C:\Windows\Desktop is the full path), which makes it a little bit harder to find when you're inside the Save As dialog box.

After you select a location, the file will be downloaded, and you'll be able to watch the progress in the Download dialog box as shown in Figure 9-5.

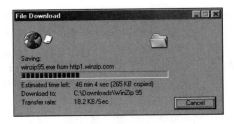

Figure 9-5: Watching the download progress
The Download dialog shows you the percentage of the file downloaded, the estimated time left until the download is complete, and the actual data transfer rate (in KBps). To make sense of the data transfer rate you'll probably need to multiply the number by eight to get kilobits per second (kbps), since most modems are rated that way. In this screen the download rate is 18.2KBps × 8 bits/byte or 145.6kbps.

Finding and installing the files

Once the file has been downloaded, use Windows Explorer to open the folder the file was downloaded to. If you ignored my advice on where to save your file and now can't find it (shame, shame), you'll need to use Windows 95's or Window 98's built-in Find utility, which is available off the Start menu. Just be aware that the file name you're looking for probably has very little semblance to the application you downloaded because many files on Web servers are limited to eight-character names. In addition, many companies need to use those characters to distinguish between different platforms and versions, so the file names end up looking very strange. (Yet another reason to follow the advice I gave previously on how to organize your downloads.)

If you can't recall the original file name, which you would have seen in the Save As and File Download dialogs, you might also be able to find it by doing a search for all files created on the day you downloaded the file.

STEPS:

Finding Files by Date

Step 1. Open the Find utility by going to the Start menu, selecting Find, and then selecting Files and Folders off the submenu. Alternatively, hold down the Windows logo key on your keyboard and hit the F key.

Step 2. Click the Date tab.

Step 3. Click the Find All Files radio button, and select Created from the drop-down menu.

Step 4. Either select a date range during which you downloaded the file by choosing the Between radio button or, if it was today, select the during the previous day button (see Figure 9-6).

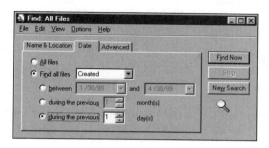

Figure 9-6: Finding by date
If you forgot to check what folder you downloaded a file to, you can search by date to try and track it down.

Step 5. Click the Find Now button, and the results will be displayed in the window at the bottom of the dialog box. If you see the file you want, you can either double-click it directly or look in the In Folder column to find out what folder it got stored in.

Compressed files

Most files that you download off the Internet are in compressed form and must be decompressed before they can be used. (Some files automatically decompress and install themselves after they've been downloaded, but most do not.) The benefit of compression is that it reduces the size of the files, which also reduces the amount of time it takes to download a file. In addition, companies who distribute software commonly use compression to package a whole number of files into a single download, which makes it much easier to deal with.

Secret

Most programs come in self-extracting format. This means that when you double-click the downloaded file, you launch a little application (often a DOS program) whose sole purpose in life is to separate and uncompress the files bundled into the downloaded file. With some downloaded files this little decompression program quits automatically, but with others it doesn't. When you see the word *Finished* in the upper right hand corner of a DOS Prompt window that doesn't close automatically, you'll know the program is done with its work and it's safe to close that DOS session. You can do this by clicking the X box in the upper right hand corner of the window or by typing **exit** at the command prompt (such as C:\).

After the decompression is done, you'll end up with a bunch of individual files that will install the program on your computer. Again, in the vast majority of cases, simply decompressing a program does not install it on your computer. You generally have to download it, decompress it, and install it in three separate steps before you can use your new software on your PC.

To install the program, look for a Setup.exe or Install.exe file and double-click it. Doing that typically brings you to an installation program that is similar to the kind you use to install software from a CD.

Secret

In some cases — such as with small utilities — you might find that the program doesn't come with a full-blown installation program. Instead, the program may simply come with an Information file that ends with the file extension .inf and bears a similar name to the application itself. If you right-click the .inf file, you'll have the option to install the program. Just let go on the Install menu choice available there and you're done. (Note that this technique works on any .inf file, but if an application comes with its own Setup program, you should always use that instead.) See Figure 9-7.

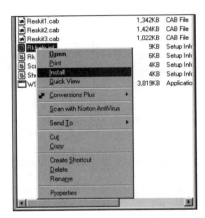

Figure 9-7: The mini-installer
Some applications, such as utility programs, can be installed by right-clicking the .inf associated with the application and choosing Install off the list of available actions.

If you downloaded an application that is not self-extracting, or if you download a document, you may still have to decompress the files before you can use them. Many PC files on the Internet are stored in Zip format, which is a popular compression format. (Note that this has nothing whatsoever to do with Iomega's popular Zip drives.) If the file names you've downloaded end with the extension .zip, then the files must be unzipped before they can be used. (To see file extensions you may have to go to Windows Explorer, select Folder Options from the View Menu, select the View Tab, and deselect the Hide file extensions for known file types checkbox.)

To decompress, or *unzip*, these compressed files, you'll need to download or otherwise procure a copy of a decompression utility that supports .zip files. There are many excellent freeware and shareware choices available on the Internet, including WinZip and PKZip. Again, try either www.download.com or www.shareware.com for the latest versions of these popular programs.

CD

You'll find a copy of WinZip 7.0 on the CD that accompanies this book.

Once you have one installed, the process of unzipping a file is simply a matter of opening WinZip and choosing where you want the decompressed file to be stored (see Figure 9-8).

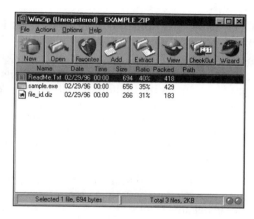

Figure 9-8: Unzipping
To decompress, or unzip, a compressed file you've downloaded off the Internet, simply open it with a utility such as WinZip and extract the results onto your hard drive.

Installation example: Publisher 2000

As I mentioned previously in this chapter, the process of installing a program on your computer actually involves putting a lot of different files in a lot of different places on your computer's hard drive. To give you a better idea of what's involved, here's roughly what happens when you install Microsoft's Publisher 2000 desktop publishing program, part of the company's Office 2000 suite, onto a computer running Windows 95 or 98. (The specifics vary on whether or not you choose a typical or custom install, what files you already have on your computer, and so on. Note that all numbers are approximate.)

■ The Setup program checks for previous installations of Publisher or other Microsoft Office applications and if necessary, creates the appropriate folders to hold the files it's going to install, including a Program Files\Office directory and a Program Files\Common Files\Microsoft Shared directory among others. (Several subdirectories inside these folders are also created.)

- The Setup program copies the various application and support files to those folders, including about 365 application-related files into the Program Files\Office directory (this is where the main Publisher files and templates go), about 100 application-related files inside the Program Files\Common Files\Microsoft Shared directory, about 1,000 clip art files in the Program Files\Common Files\Microsoft Shared\Clipart folder, and a little over 200 fonts inside the Windows\Fonts folder.

- In addition, about 25 files are installed in the Windows folder, another 65 or so go into the Windows\System folder, and another 15 go into a variety of different places. Many of these 100+ files are DLLs and other types of shared system files.

- Like other Office 2000 applications, Publisher includes Internet Explorer 5.0, so it installs about 90 files associated with it as well.

- In addition to all these files, the Setup program adds a little over 400 entries into the Windows Registry. Among the things these Registry keys do are *register* important file extensions, including .pub. It tells Windows that any files that end with .pub should be associated with Publisher so that whenever you double-click one of those files, Publisher will open automatically. It also makes several entries regarding user preferences; basically, it just enters in the program's default settings. You can change these later through the program's Options dialog boxes.

- One of the final steps in the process is to add an entry to the Programs listing off the Start menu by putting a shortcut to Mspub.exe inside the C:\Windows\Start Menu\Programs folder.

- In total, there are almost 1,850 files copied over from the installation CD onto your hard drive, plus about 400 new entries into your Windows Registry.

Table 9-1 summarizes the approximate number of files involved in the installation.

Table 9-1   Installing Publisher 2000

Folder into Which Files Are Installed	Approximate Number of Files or Entries	Types of Files
Program Files\Office	365	Main program files, templates, wizards, and so on
Program Files\Common Files\Microsoft Shared	100	Shared files, such as proofing tools
Program Files\Common Files\Microsoft Shared\Clipart	1,000	Clip art and backgrounds

Folder into Which Files Are Installed	Approximate Number of Files or Entries	Types of Files
Windows\Fonts	200	Different typefaces
Windows	25	Support files, such as DLLs
Windows\System	65	Support files, such as DLLs
IE 5.0	90	Internet Explorer 5.0 and support files
Miscellaneous	15	Various
Registry	400	New Registry Keys

Like most any other application you install on your computer, Publisher installs several shared DLLs that essentially become an extension to the operating system. This means that other applications can and will use some of those shared DLLs (that's why they're called *shared*). The problem is, other applications you install at a later date, which also happen to use those shared DLLs, may install a later (or even earlier) version of the DLLs that Publisher may or may not be able to work with.

In addition, it's possible that the versions that Publisher 2000 installs may be slightly different than the versions already installed by another application. If that happens, Publisher or the other application could stop working because of a DLL conflict. Again, this doesn't always happen, but it can and it does. Publisher 2000 and other Office 2000 applications are actually better than most others in this regard because they include a built-in repair feature that can automatically reinstall any DLLs that get overwritten and keep the program from functioning.

The Version Conflict Manager bundled with Windows 98 can also help with this problem, but it isn't foolproof. There's no equivalent built into Windows 95, so Windows 95 users will probably run into these types of problems more frequently than those running Windows 98.

Cross-Reference

See Chapter 17, "Troubleshooting Techniques," for more on dealing with DLL problems.

Unfortunately, troubleshooting DLL problems is probably the single hardest task there is to do with personal computers. But if you want to learn more about it, the first step is finding out what DLLs are associated with what programs. Thankfully, there are several tools available to do that (see the sidebar "Finding the links" for more).

Finding the links

Okay, we're going to get a little geeky here — I'm warning you ahead of time. The way many software programs really work on your computer is pretty complicated. Many programs actually consist of a main umbrella application — sometimes it's fairly big, but for some programs it's actually quite small — and a bunch of application extensions called DLLs (because they have the file extension .dll). In some cases the main application contains the software routines that handle the program's basic operation and farms out only a few specific functions to DLLs. In other cases the main application does little more than coordinate all the DLLs that do the program's real work. In either case, both types of programs also rely on operating system DLLs to provide certain low-level functions, such as drawing dialog boxes on the screen, providing scroll bars, and so on.

To figure out the web of connections that tie together a software program and all the DLLs that it uses, you can make use of one of several commercial and shareware utilities that provide this type of information. The full Windows 98 Resource Kit (not the smaller version that comes on the Windows 98 CD) comes with a utility called

Dependency Walker (Depends.exe) that enables you to do this on any application. Simply open the utility and find the application, then Dependency Walker will build a link of all the different DLLs used by the main application. Various versions of Symantec's Norton Utilities for Windows 95 and Windows 98 add a tab to all applications' File Properties dialog boxes that shows Dependencies. To take advantage of it to find dependencies, simply use Windows Explorer to find the main application you're interested in, right-click the file, and select Properties from the context menu. Select the Dependencies tab and you'll see the connections to DLLs and other pieces of software.

Finally, on the CD accompanying this book, you'll find a handy utility that can help find these dependencies: SANDRA. If you run SANDRA and double-click the Processes icon, you'll get a list of all the things that are currently running inside your PC. If you open the particular program you're interested in investigating, you can see a list of all the DLLs it is using by selecting the application from the Processes menu and scrolling down. The figure below shows an example from SANDRA.

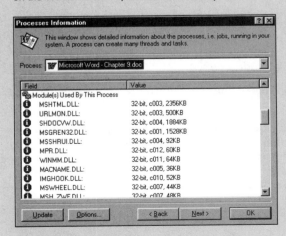

Making the connections
Among its many useful capabilities, the SANDRA utility included on the CD accompanying this book enables you to find what DLLs are being used by any particular application currently running on your PC. SANDRA uses the official technical term *Process* to describe an application in use.

Upgrading applications

Once you've installed a set of applications on your computer, you'll have to face the next, inevitable step: upgrades. Whether you're besieged with mail from the companies whose products you bought and/or registered for, or if you just read or hear about a new version of one your products through a computer magazine, television show, or radio program, you're going to have to face the question of whether or not you should upgrade.

The first thing you have to do is decide for yourself whether you really need the upgrade. (Then ask yourself if you really still want it anyway.) Look at the features the upgrade contains, the costs, and anything else you consider relevant to make that decision.

For some applications, you'll probably realize that it's fine to keep the version you have, but for your workhorse applications — those that you use all the time — it often is a good idea to upgrade to the latest version. You're bound to find some additional goodies or features you can use. Note, however, that some upgrades bring with them changes in file formats. If you send files in these new formats to people who still have older versions of the applications, they won't be able to open them. Not all new applications have this problem, but it's definitely something you need to consider in the upgrade process.

Cross-Reference

See Chapter 14, "Working with Documents and Files," for more on file compatibility problems.

Also, if you start getting in the habit of trying to keep all your software up to date, you're going to find yourself spending a lot of money, so take a critical look at the need and cost involved.

Patches

If the upgrade is nothing more than a free bug fix or patch (sometimes also called a service pack) to an existing application, then I generally recommend that you get it and install it. These patches are sometimes referred to as updates as opposed to upgrades, but there's no hard and fast rule. The two words — updates and upgrades — are commonly used interchangeably.

Some people strongly believe in leaving things as they are (under the general principle, if it ain't broke, don't fix it), and there certainly is something to be said for this, particularly if you have a stable environment and don't plan on adding a bunch of new software. If you do plan to add new programs or upgrade some existing ones, however, there's a good chance that even if you aren't having problems with a particular application now, you may run into problems down the road. For example, a new application could conflict with the un-upgraded version of one of your existing programs. So again, to prepare for those possibilities I generally recommend that you install any application updates that you come across. At the very least, download the update so that, if necessary, you can quickly apply it.

Automatic upgrades

With a number of newer applications you may not have much choice in the matter. More and more programs are starting to incorporate features that automatically scan the company's Web site for upgrades every month or so and download and install whatever patches they find. In virtually all cases it's possible to turn this feature off, but generally, the default setting is to have these types of automatic upgrade features enabled.

One of the big features of Windows 98 (and Windows 2000), for example, is Windows Update. What Windows Update does (only if you're running Windows 98 or later) is check the Microsoft Web site for updates to any core Windows files as well as drivers for devices you have installed on your computer. (The drivers only get upgraded if the manufacturer has chosen to give Microsoft their updates — if the company hasn't or they're a bit slow about it, then you won't necessarily get the latest drivers this way.) If Windows Update finds anything, it gives you the option to download and install the upgrades on your computer. Figure 9-9 shows what this looks like.

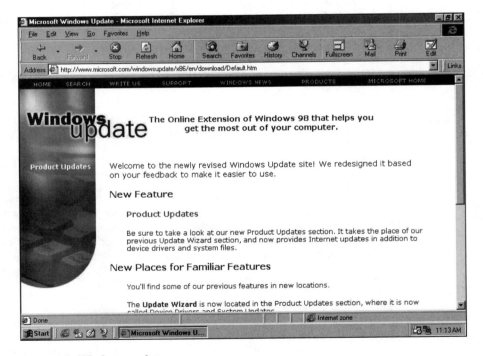

Figure 9-9: Windows update
The Windows Update feature built into Windows 98 will automatically upgrade your computer's core operating system files.

In addition, several companies sell utility programs that are designed to scour the World Wide Web looking for updates for all your computer's software and drivers, whether the applications include automatic updating or not. (In fact, they kind of step on the toes of applications that do have automatic updates of their own.) What applications such as Oil Change really do, however, is check a special Web site that the software company who makes the utility creates, maintains, and updates. In general, the better and more up-to-date the database of software updates on that Web site is, the better the utility works. At the same time, if that data is out-of-date, the utility won't do much good at all.

Secret

In fact, in some cases you can be more effective by manually checking the Web sites of companies whose products you use on a regular basis. Most companies (at least, the smart ones!) now have links straight from their home pages to their software updates or driver updates pages. If you make a point to check the sites that are relevant to your computer on a monthly basis, you'll be as up-to-date as you ever want to be.

Caution

In theory, all the various types of automatic upgrades are a great idea because they can keep your computer up-to-date. They are somewhat of a two-edged sword, however, because it's possible to have an automatically installed update conflict with another piece of software on your computer. So, instead of making things better, they could actually make things worse by breaking something that used to work fine. Plus, it might be very difficult to figure out why something stopped working properly on your PC if an update occurred without your really knowing about it.

Cross-Reference

See Chapter 17, "Troubleshooting Techniques," for more on solving software conflict problems.

Thankfully, most of these features — including Windows 98's Windows Update — enable you to know what upgrades they plan to install and give you the option of not installing a particular one. Not surprisingly, however, the default option — that is, the one that will occur unless you choose otherwise — is to install the update(s). So, be conscious of what you plan to update.

Removing upgrades

In addition, most — though not all — applications that have this automatic upgrading capability offer the option of removing an update if downloading and installing it creates a problem on your computer. (And given the complex web of software that makes up the typical PC these days, it's not that unusual for problems to arise this way.) In the case of Windows Update, any updates it makes can be removed later through the Windows Update Feature itself. Figure 9-10 shows an example.

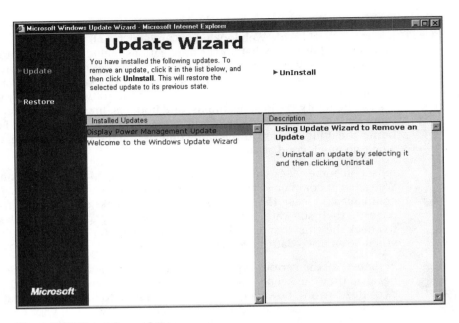

Figure 9-10: Removing updates
Automatic updates made by Windows 98's Windows Update feature can be removed by going back to the Windows 98 Update Web site and using the Web Update wizard to uninstall what you had previously installed.

If you download actual program additions, you can remove them through the Add/Remove Programs Control Panel. Unfortunately, not all individual applications take advantage of this Control Panel, which means there's no single repository for all the changes and updates you've made to your computer. On top of that, the control panel doesn't necessarily remove everything.

See the "Removing Software" section later in this chapter for more.

Cross-Reference

The tangible result is that you'll probably have to have look in a lot of different places if you're trying to figure out all the different updates that have been installed on your computer. Of course, if you're incredibly organized, you could keep a list of every update you've ever manually installed or that's been installed automatically, but I don't think too many people are really going to do that.

Reinstalling

Reinstalling is running the installation procedure for a program you've already installed on your computer a second (or third or fourth) time. If you buy a new hard drive, are forced to reformat your existing drive, or need to reinstall an application to try and solve a problem, you'll need to think a bit about the implications and issues regarding reinstalling a particular program.

Backing up your applications

If God had delivered a set of ten Computer Commandments to Moses, I have no doubt that this would have been the first one: Thou shalt backup thy computer data on a regular basis. (Scriptural exegesis would have then focused on what exactly was meant by regular.) Backing up your data is, in fact, an absolutely critical part of using a computer. You really shouldn't do one without the other.

But backing up your data used to mean just the files you had created. With the way software works these days and the number of updates that we're typically forced to download and install, it's equally important to make backups of any software you've downloaded off the Internet. Otherwise you'll have to go through the often long and tedious process of redownloading software, including application upgrades, that you've already installed. And with the proliferation of multimegabyte upgrade files, that's not something you're going to want to do very often.

The first thing to remember is that reinstalling a program from the original disc means that you end up with the original version of the program. If you've made any updates to the program (or if any automatic updates have occurred since you first installed), you'll need to go through the process of reinstalling all the updates as well. (See the sidebar "Backing up your applications" for more.)

Unfortunately, automatic software updates can make this process difficult because they don't often leave a backup of the patches they've downloaded. In these cases you'll probably have to go through the process of automatically upgrading again.

Tip

Regardless of how you go about upgrading your applications, remember that unless the latest upgrade incorporates all the previous fixes, you may have to go through several upgrades — from the first to the most recent — to bring your application(s) up to date.

You'll also need to find out how your particular application handles reinstallation. Some programs indiscriminately copy over all the files that come with the application, even if a newer version of one or more of them exists on your computer, some only copy over files that have changed (including files that may have been updated), and some verify whether the existing files are okay or not. In addition, some will ask you whether they should copy over files that have changed, and others won't.

Tip

If you're reinstalling a particular piece of software to try and solve a problem, what you might want to do is first try to uninstall the application and then do a clean reinstall. Often times this is the only way to overcome difficult software conflicts because some reinstalls just leave existing files there and don't give you a fresh copy of everything.

Unfortunately, depending on the way you uninstalled an existing application, sometimes even this doesn't work. In many cases, however, it does the trick.

Cross-Reference

See the "Removing Software" section later in this chapter for more on how to uninstall applications.

Installing Operating Systems

The most important piece of software you can install on your computer is the operating system (OS). The operating system is what gives your PC its identity and determines what applications you can run on your system and how it will work. Most computers come with an operating system preinstalled on the hard drive. This means you usually don't have to worry about installing an operating system, but if you add a new hard drive to your system, build a computer from scratch, decide to clean out your system and start over again, or if you want to try working with a different operating system, you may need to install an OS.

While the prospect of doing so may seem daunting, the automated features of today's OS installation programs usually make it a straightforward process that requires little interaction on your part.

General issues

The operating system is always the first piece of software you need to install on a new computer system or hard disk (again, unless it's already been preinstalled at the factory). Without an OS, your computer doesn't have any instructions to tell it how to operate — this is one of the primary functions of the operating system.

In most cases, the operating system comes on a CD (or two). You can't always just insert them into your CD- or DVD-ROM drive and expect them to work, however, because without an operating system already in place, the computer doesn't know what to do with the disc. Consequently, most new operating systems also come with a boot floppy disk that you use to start the computer, have it recognize your CD or DVD-ROM drive, and then begin the installation process. (Operating system upgrades, on the other hand, typically do not come with this boot floppy because they can be installed over your existing OS.)

Some computers support the capability to boot directly from a CD with an operating system on it, which can ease the process somewhat, but many don't. Even if yours has this capability, you'll typically need to enable this function in your computer's BIOS because most have it turned off by default. To enable the function, turn on your PC and hit the key that's required to enter the computer's BIOS or CMOS Setup program. Once you're in there, look for boot settings and set the system to boot from the CD. Save your changes, exit the Setup program, and insert the OS CD into your computer's CD- or DVD-ROM drive.

Secret

Even with this feature turned on, the system will only boot if the CD itself is bootable, meaning it has the necessary startup files located in the root directory of the disc. Windows 95 CDs, for example, are not bootable, but most Windows 98 CDs are.

Using multiple operating systems

Most people will only use a single operating system on their PC, and more than likely, it will be some version of Windows. Those are not the only operating systems available for your PC, however, and it's certainly possible to install a different OS either in place of Windows or in addition to Windows. (It's also possible to install and use more than one different type of Windows.) A number of people are now interested in Linux, for example, which is a version of the UNIX operating system that runs on PC hardware. BeOS is another OS for people interested in multimedia-related work. In addition, some PC users prefer IBM's OS/2.

Regardless of what type of OS you plan to use, there are a few critical issues you need to understand before replacing Windows or adding another OS to your system. First of all, if you plan to use an alternative operating system in place of Windows, then you cannot use any existing Windows applications or drivers you have under that operating system. (The one exception would be if you installed a Windows emulation program, but they don't represent a complete solution — not everything will work with them.)

Applications and drivers are dependent on the operating system to function, and you need to buy and use applications and drivers that are specifically designed for or are compatible with the operating system you choose to load onto your system. In addition, many of your existing documents may not be easily usable or even directly accessible under the new OS. In most cases it will be like starting over with a completely clean slate.

Additionally, don't expect to be able to use your Windows knowledge or skills on the new OS. While general computing principles are the same across platforms — you still work with applications and documents under any OS, for example — the terminology and techniques for doing so can vary tremendously. Now, for some people, half the fun of working with a new OS is learning how it does things and what terminology it uses, but others may get frustrated at having to learn many computer skills all over again.

Finally, if you plan to install multiple operating systems on your system, which is typically referred to as the capability to dual boot, be aware that you can only use one at a time. In most situations, you choose the operating system you want to use for a particular *session* when you turn your computer on. When you want to use another operating system, you need to restart your computer. On doing so, you'll find that not only is the operating system new, the files you use from within the other operating system may appear to be gone. In some situations you are able to access the files designed for one OS under a different one, but again, most of the time it will seem like you're working with an entirely different PC, complete with different user interfaces, different applications, and different documents.

In addition to these general issues, there are some other technical issues you need to consider if you want to install and use multiples OSes on your PC.

Partitions

Operating systems differ from each other in many different ways, including how they're structured, how they function, how they interact with applications, and more. Probably the most practical difference, however, is that they also use different methods for storing and organizing data on your PC's hard drive. Specifically, different operating systems use different types of partitions, and only certain operating systems can read certain types of partitions. Even the different versions of Windows use different partition types.

Cross-Reference

For more on partitions, see Chapter 3, "Hard Disks and Removable Drives."

Windows 3.1 and early versions of Windows 95, for example, use the FAT-16 (commonly shortened just to FAT) partition format, whereas Windows 98 and later versions of Windows 95 use FAT-32 as their primary partition. Windows 2000 can read both FAT-16 and FAT-32 formats, but its primary format is based on (but still different from) the NTFS format used by Windows NT 4.0. IBM's OS/2 uses HPFS, and Linux uses both Ext2 (for its main format) and LinuxSwap (for its required swap file partition). Sound confusing? Well, it certainly can be.

To help make a bit more sense of it, Table 9-2 lists operating systems, their preferred partition type, and other types they can also read.

Table 9-2 Operating Systems and Partition Types

Operating System	Preferred Partition Types	Other Partition Types it Supports
Windows 3.1	FAT-16	None
Windows 95 and Windows 95 A	FAT-16	None
Windows 95 B and C	FAT-32	FAT-16
Windows 98	FAT-32	FAT-16
Windows NT 4.0	NTFS 4.0	FAT-16
Windows 2000	NTFS 5.0	NTFS 4.0, FAT-32, FAT-16
Linux	Ext2, LinuxSwap	FAT-16
BeOS	Be	FAT-32, FAT-16, HFS, HFS+ (Macintosh)
OS/2	HPFS	FAT-16

The information in Table 9-2 is valuable because you have to divide your hard drive (or drives) into the appropriate type of partitions if you want to be able to install the various operating systems. In fact, you have to partition the drive first, otherwise you can't install the OS. (Some operating system installations will do the partitioning for you as the first part of the install, but others require you to do it first as a separate step.)

Another reason this information is important is if you want to be able to access certain files from more than one operating system, you need to choose a partition format that's compatible with both of them. As you can see, the most commonly supported format — in fact, the only one that's universally supported — is the older FAT-16 format, so that's generally the best bet for a partition that you need to share across multiples OSes.

In some cases you might decide that you want to keep all the files from each operating system separate and distinct. If that's the case, then you can just create partitions in the preferred format for each OS.

Partition Types

In addition to thinking about the format of the different partitions, you also need to concern yourself with the partition type. In order to boot a PC, an operating system's startup files must be loaded onto a primary partition (of which you can only create four), but applications, documents, and other files can be stored on extended partitions. Practically speaking, this generally means you're limited to installing, at most, four operating systems per hard drive.

Creating Partitions

The method for creating partitions varies slightly depending on whether you're starting with a new or recently reformatted drive or if you want to turn some existing free space on one of your hard drives into new partitions. In either case, you'll need a disk partitioning tool, but in the latter you'll also need one that can resize existing partitions, which not all partitioning programs can do.

My personal favorite is PowerQuest's Partition Magic, which enables you to easily create, edit, and resize existing partitions for numerous different operating systems. The main program is primarily designed to run under Windows 95/98, but it also enables you to create a DOS-based boot floppy that includes a text-only version of the program that you can use to create, delete, and edit partitions.

CD

A demo version of PartitionMagic 4.0 that enables you to visually lay out a set of partitions (but which doesn't actually create them) is included on the CD accompanying this book.

On a new drive, you can simply create the new partitions in the type and format that you need and then move onto installing the OS. On an existing drive, you'll first need to free up available space by either shrinking the size of an existing partition or deleting a partition. (Note that deleting a partition will destroy any data that's stored on it, so backup anything you have on it, or even better, only delete partitions that are empty.)

Once you've created the unused, unpartitioned space, you can move onto creating the number, size, and format of the partitions you need in that space and then install the new OS into that (those) partition(s).

Boot loader

Once you've organized your disk with all the different types of partitions you need and you've successfully installed the various operating systems, you also need a way to tell your PC which OS you want to use for a particular session. This task is handled by a small program that's generically referred to as a boot loader. Some operating systems come with their own boot loader (Linux comes with LILO, for example), but you can also find one included with some disk partitioning tools, such as the previously mentioned PartitionMagic.

Boot loaders are typically installed in your hard drive's master boot record, which is the first part of the drive that gets read after your computer's BIOS finishes working. After you turn on your PC, the BIOS runs, and the final command in the BIOS is to go to the first sector of the first hard drive it finds (which is where the master boot record is located) and follow whatever instructions it finds there. If you only have one operating system installed, then that OS's main boot files are typically located there, so the instructions are to load that operating system. With a boot loader, however, the instructions are to load the boot loader. Once it loads, you choose what OS you want to run, the boot loader points to where that OS's boot files have been moved, and the boot process continues on as normal. In other words, the boot loader inserts itself into the beginning of the boot process.

Secret

If your hard drive's master boot record ever gets corrupted or infected by a virus, your system may not boot or the boot loader may not run, which means you won't be able to get to your choice of operating system. If that happens, you'll need to clear out your master boot record and reinstall your boot loader.

If you have a basic Windows boot disk with the FDISK partitioning program on it, you can overwrite your master boot record by booting to a DOS prompt and then typing **fdisk /mbr**. After that you'll need to either reinstall the boot loader or any single OS's startup files that you want to boot into.

Installing Windows 95 or 98

If you plan to install either Windows 95 or 98 onto a new PC or new hard disk, the process is very easy. As long as the disk is formatted to have a FAT-16 or FAT-32 partition (FAT-32 will not work with early versions of Windows 95), and you have at least 200MB of free hard-disk space (you can actually get away with a bit less if space is really tight), then you simply follow the prompts to complete the installation.

New installation

A brand new Windows 95 or 98 install requires nothing more than a startup floppy disk with a CD or DVD-ROM driver (in some cases), the Windows CD, and a little time. All you have to do is answer a few basic questions, supply a product key number, and watch as the installation program does its work.

If you're installing Windows 98 onto a system that supports booting from the CD or DVD-ROM, then you can use that option to boot your computer from the Windows 98 CD and run the setup process from there. To install Windows 95 on any system or Windows 98 on a system that doesn't support booting from the CD or DVD, however, you'll need a boot floppy disk that includes a CD or DVD-ROM driver on it in order to be able to see the CD on your system.

**Cross-
Reference**

If you don't have access to a boot floppy disk, the "Troubleshooting Tools" section of Chapter 17 contains step-by-step directions on how to make one.

If you boot from that type of floppy, all you have to do is switch over to your CD or DVD-ROM drive at a DOS prompt and then type in **Setup**. You can do it all in one fell swoop by typing in **D:\Setup [Enter]** after your computer finishes booting from the floppy. (If you have multiple hard drives, CD- or DVD-ROM drives, or use the Windows 98 boot disk, you may have to change the drive letter in that previous line from D: to something else, such as E: or even F:.) This launches the main setup program and starts the installation process.

Standard vs. custom

The only real question you need to answer when installing Windows 95 or 98 is whether you want to go with one of the Standard installs or choose a Custom install, which enables you to select the individual components you want to install. Even if you only want a standard install, you can go ahead and choose the custom option because its default choices are the same as those for a Standard install. So, if you don't change anything, you'll get the same thing, but you'll have the benefit of seeing what the actual components are.

If, later on, you decide you wish you would have installed or not installed a particular component, it's no problem. You can always change your Windows 95 or Windows 98 installation at a later point by selecting the Windows Setup tab in the Add/Remove Programs Control Panel. See Figure 9-11.

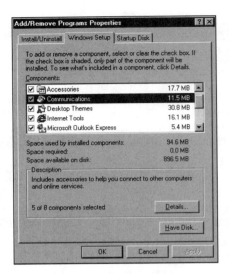

Figure 9-11: Changing your Windows setup
You can add or remove individual components (or even several at once) of your Windows 95 or Windows 98 setup at any time by selecting the middle tab in the Add/Remove Programs control panel. Simply click an empty box to add a component or click a check marked box to remove the check mark and, therefore, the component.

Upgrading

Upgrading your existing Windows installation to a new version is very similar to creating a new installation, but you don't have to worry about booting from a startup disk. Just insert the Windows 95, 98, or 2000 CD into your system and run the Setup program. Windows Setup will walk you through the process and make the appropriate changes and additions to your computer's operating system files.

Most upgrades work just fine, but occasionally problems do arise. One of the most common has to do with drivers for your PC's hardware. If the version of Windows you're installing doesn't have an up-to-date driver for a piece of hardware that is built into or connected to your system, you may run into a situation where that particular device or sometimes even your entire system doesn't work properly. If that's the case, you'll need to try and figure out which device is causing the problem, locate an updated driver for it, and install that updated version.

Cross-Reference

For more on solving driver-related problems, see Chapter 17, "Trouble-shooting Techniques."

Reinstalling Windows 95 or 98

In many ways, the operating system (whether it's Windows 95 or 98) is no different from applications when it comes to reinstalling. At certain critical junctures during a troubleshooting session with your computer, you might decide (or be told) to reinstall Windows, just as you may need to reinstall certain applications to get them to work. Similarly, the reinstallation process is usually very similar to the basic install. Because the operating system has such a dramatic impact on your computer's overall operation, however, there are some special issues to consider.

First, on a practical level, if you run the Windows 95 or 98 Setup programs on a machine that has the same version of the operating system already installed, you should get the option to Verify your setup — though, in some cases, you may not. (If the versions are different, you'll get other options and/or messages. See the section "Upgrading the Operating System" in this chapter for more.) In other words, instead of doing a blanket reinstall of the entire operating system, Verify verifies that everything that's supposed to be there really is.

Secret

What Verify does is looks at a file on your computer called Setuplog.txt — created by the Setup program when Setup is first run — to see what files were installed where. It then goes through and confirms that all of those files are where they should be and haven't been somehow changed or corrupted (it does this by looking at file size, version number, and date of creation). If it finds any file(s) that is/are either missing or corrupted, it simply replaces that/those file(s) on your hard drive with the original files off the installation CD or floppies. Unfortunately, it doesn't tell you what files are being replaced, which would be handy to know for certain troubleshooting problems. Instead it just silently makes its changes and then finishes up.

Note

If you're curious, you can look at Setuplog.txt with any text editor, including NotePad or WordPad. You should find the file in your root C:\ directory. To be honest, though, it's really hard to make much sense of it. If you do open it, be careful not to make any changes to it, or you could cause problems down the line if you try to reinstall the OS. (See Figure 9-12.)

Secret

The one exception to this rule is if the Verify option doesn't show up when you rerun Setup, it may be because there's a bracketed heading somewhere in the Setuplog.txt file that's more than 32 characters long. If that's the case, simply add a semicolon at the beginning of the line with the long heading, save the Setuplog.txt file, and try rerunning Setup again.

If you can use it, Verify is a handy option because it saves you a lot of time and hassles. Verify doesn't go through the time-intensive process of detecting your computer's hardware, and it doesn't attempt to completely reinstall all the operating systems files, as a complete reinstall of either Windows 95 or Windows 98 will do.

```
"Character Map"=0
"Quick View"=0
"Multimedia Sound Schemes"=0
"Sample Sounds"=0
"CD Player"=1
"Microsoft NetMeeting"=1

[System]
"Display"="Standard PCI Graphics Adapter (XGA)"
"Keyboard"="Standard 101/102-Key or Microsoft Natural Keyboard"
"SelectedKeyboard"="KEYBOARD_00000409"
"MultiLanguage"="ENGLISH"
"Machine"="MS_CHICAGO"
"Monitor"="Plug and Play Monitor"
"Mouse"="PS/2 Compatible Mouse Port"
"Power"="APM"
"Locale"="L0409"
"UI_Choice"="Win95UI"

[NameAndOrg]

[Destination]

[]

Drive=:A:, Host=::, Flags=:0x107:
Drive=:C:, Host=::, Flags=:0xd:
Drive=:D:, Host=::, Flags=:0xf:
Drive=:E:, Host=::, Flags=:0xf:
Drive=:F:, Host=::, Flags=:0x205:
vfs.boot=:C:, vfs.boothost=::
FSLog: BIOS Heads=:255:, BootPart Heads=:255:
batch settings:
[Setup]
```

Figure 9-12: Seeing what's installed
If you can figure it out, the Setuplog.txt file created when either Windows 95 or 98 is installed on your computer will tell you what components of the operating system were actually copied to your hard drive.

Note

I've found that many times the Verify option does not appear, which means you need to go through the entire installation process when you reinstall. Should that happen, and if you're using a Windows 98 upgrade CD, you need to be prepared to provide proof of a previous Microsoft OS by having your Windows 95 CD or Windows 3.1 Disk 1 floppy ready. As with a standard upgrade, during the installation process the Setup program verifies a previous installation (this is a different type of verification). Also, you should prepared with driver disks for any hardware you have in your system; in many cases you'll need to copy them onto floppies *before* you begin the reinstallation process.

Windows 98 users can also take advantage of the System File Checker utility, which offers similar capabilities to the Setup program's Verify option and has a more straightforward interface.

Cross-Reference

See the "Troubleshooting Tools" section of Chapter 17 for more on System File Checker.

Windows installation files

After you've successfully installed Windows 95 or Windows 98, you may want to copy the operating system files over from the CD onto your hard disk. This takes up a bit of space, but it saves you from having to hunt for the CD if and when you're asked to insert your Windows CD. (You may be asked to insert your Windows CD after you've installed a new piece of hardware, are reinstalling certain portions of the operating system, or in a variety of other situations). It's also handy if you upgraded from a floppy disk version of Windows 95 to a CD-based version.

STEPS:

Copying the Windows CD Files onto your Hard Disk

Step 1. Insert the Windows 95 or Windows 98 CD into your hard drive and open Windows Explorer.

Step 2. Copy the folder holding the operating system files from the CD onto the root level of your hard drive. The folder should be called Win95 or Win98 — it contains the compressed .CAB, or cabinet, files that hold the operating system files, as well as other files needed to install the OS.

Caution

Before you copy it over, make sure the folder name on the CD isn't the same as the standard Windows directory on your C: drive. In most cases your hard drive's Windows folder is simply called Windows, but if you used Win95 or Win98 instead, then create a new folder with a different name and copy the contents of the CD's Win95 or Win98 folder into that new folder on your hard disk.

Step 3. After you've finished copying over the files, you'll also want to inform the Windows Registry to look for those files in that new location. To do that, you need to edit one key in the Registry. Start the process by going to the Start menu, selecting Run and typing in RegEdit, which launches the Registry editing application bundled with both Windows 95 and Windows 98.

Caution

Always be extra cautious whenever you're making changes to the Registry because it's possible to make changes that will make your computer inoperable. In fact, you should make a backup copy of the Registry files System.dat and User.dat (they're hidden files in the Windows directory) before you do anything.

Step 4. Go to the Edit menu in RegEdit and browse through the Registry by clicking the appropriate folders until you reach the following folder:

```
HKEY_LOCAL_MACHINE\Software\Microsoft\Windows\CurrentVersion\Setup
```

Once you've found that folder, click Setup and look for the key that says SourcePath. See Figure 9-13.

Continued

Copying the Windows CD Files onto your Hard Disk *(continued)*

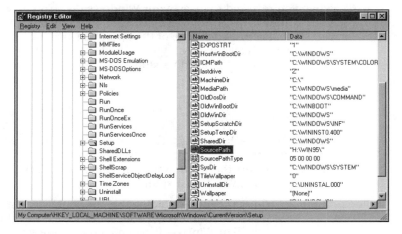

Figure 9-13: Changing the Windows source path
Once you've copied the Windows 95 or Windows 98 system files onto your hard disk, you can change one key in the Registry to tell Windows to look to that location instead of asking for the CD whenever it needs access to another file.

Step 5. Select the SourcePath key on the right side of the Registry Window, and select Modify from the Edit menu. In the Edit String dialog that comes up, type in the complete path where you stored the Windows files from the CD. It'll probably be C:\Win95 or C:\Win98.

Step 6. Hit OK in the dialog, exit RegEdit, and you're done.

Upgrading the operating system

If you're a longtime Windows 95 or even Windows 3.1 user who's decided to make the plunge into Windows 98, then you'll need to upgrade to Windows 98. If you're starting in Windows 95, the process couldn't be much easier. You insert the Windows 98 CD into your computer, run the Setup program, answer a few simple questions, sit back and watch (or just walk away and come back) for about 30–60 minutes, and you'll be done.

If you're upgrading from Windows 3.1 or are installing it onto a new hard drive, you'll need to run the Windows 98 Setup from MS-DOS. To do that you'll need a startup disk that includes a real-mode CD-ROM driver.

The "Troubleshooting Tools" section of Chapter 17 includes step-by-step directions on how to create this disk.

Just boot from that floppy, switch to the CD, run the Setup program, and you're in business. You'll have to answer a few more questions this way, but it's still easier and more straightforward than installing Windows 95.

If you're unsure of whether or not all your applications and hardware will work, you can install Windows 95 or 98 into a new Windows directory, but I think it's much more hassle than it is worth. If you're going to make the plunge, I say just go for it. You can always save your previous operating system settings — which I do recommend — and then uninstall either Windows 95 or Windows 98 and return to your previous operating system if you have big problems. (You uninstall Windows 95 or 98 via the Add/Remove Programs Control Panel.)

If you do run across a Windows 3.1 application that won't work under either new OS, you can take advantage of the little-known Make Compatible program to trick the application into thinking it's still running under Windows 3.1 and get it to work. Open the Run command window and type in **Mkcompat**. In the resulting window, select the program you want to trick and then make any adjustments to the various options that are available. See Figure 9-14.

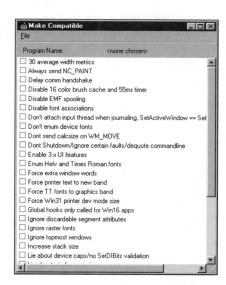

Figure 9-14: Making Windows 3.1 applications compatible
If you select Advanced Options from the Make Compatible utility's File menu, you can try a wide variety of different setting options to get a recalcitrant 16-bit Windows 3.1 application to work under Windows 95 or 98.

Updating Windows 95

If you have an older version of Windows 95, it's also possible to update certain parts of your OS without actually upgrading to Windows 98. To be honest, though, the easiest and most complete way to upgrade your machine is to go for Windows 98 because it incorporates all the fixes and updates from previous versions of Windows 95, plus more. But if you're a stubborn (or stingy) type and don't want to feed the Microsoft monopoly, you can upgrade your computer's version of Windows 95 by downloading and installing a variety of different patches, service packs, and other upgrades that Microsoft has released.

Before you do anything, however, you need to find out which version of Windows 95 you're currently running. To do that, right-click the My Computer icon on your desktop, and select Properties from the bottom of the context menu that appears. In the dialog box that appears, look for a number on the right-hand side under the System heading that starts out 4.00.950. If you just see this number, then you have the original version of Windows 95. If you see this number with an A at the end (4.00.950 A), you have Windows 95 A, which means you have the original version of Windows 95 with Service Pack 1 installed. This is sometimes referred to as OSR 1 (OSR stands for OEM Service Release). If you see this number and then see a B at the end, you have Windows 95 B, or OSR2 as it is often called. Finally, if you see this number and then a C at the end, you have Windows 95 C, which is also called OSR 2.5. (For a history of what features were added in each version, see the sidebar "Windows 95 version history" for more.) Figure 9-15 shows an example.

Figure 9-15: Windows 95 version numbers
To see which version of Windows 95 you have installed on your PC, right-click My Computer, select Properties, and look for the letter after 4.00.950. The letter B shown here signifies that this computer is running Windows 95B or OSR2.

Windows 95 version history

Microsoft released several different versions of Windows 95 to computer manufacturers (or OEMs — Original Equipment Manufacturers) over the years. As a result, if you have it installed on your computer, the version of Windows 95 is dependent on when the PC was purchased and what version of the OS happened to be available at the time.

Table 9-3 lists the various versions of the OS and the most important files that were changed and/or added in subsequent versions.

The only difference between the original Windows 95 and Window 95A is the addition of the Service Pack 1 Bug fixes (which you can download from Microsoft's Web site). The biggest jump, in terms of changes, occurred between OSR1 and OSR2. In addition to FAT32 support, OSR2 adds many other minor tweaks and improvements, such as an updated version of Dial-Up Networking, enhanced PC Card drivers, Advanced Power Management features for notebooks, PCI IDE bus mastering support, and more.

Between OSR2 and OSR2.1, the only real difference is support for USB. Because both of these versions show up as Windows 95B, the way to tell if you have OSR2 or OSR2.1 is to see if you have the USB Supplement to Windows 95 installed on your computer. You can check by opening your Add/Remove Programs Control Panel and looking for the file. The figure in this sidebar is an example.

Windows 95 OSR2.1

If you have the USB supplement to Windows 95 in your Add/Remove Programs Control panel, then you have OSR 2.1 (or 2.5).

Table 9-3   Windows 95 Versions

	Windows 95	Windows 95 A (OSR 1)	Windows 95 B (OSR 2)	Windows 95 B (OSR 2.1)	Windows 95 C(OSR 2.5)
Original Windows 95 Release	X	x	x	x	x
Service Pack 1 Bug Fixes		x	x	x	x
FAT32 File System and Supporting Utilities			x	x	x
Internet Explorer 3.01			x	x	
Support for USB				x	x
Internet Explorer 4.01					x

Each of the later versions of Windows 95 has all the changes from the previous version already incorporated into it. This is important to know because it affects which files you may want to download and install on your computer. For example, you wouldn't want to download and install Windows 95's Service Pack 1 on a system with Windows 95 B or C because the Service Pack 1 changes were first incorporated into Windows 95 A (and therefore are already included in Windows 95 B or C).

Now, you would think that Microsoft would have, therefore, prevented Service Pack 1 from even being installed on newer systems with later versions of the OS. Unfortunately, that's not the case. It is possible to inadvertently install Service Pack 1 and various patches to versions that already incorporate the changes or even have later versions of certain files. Even worse, doing so can screw up your PC because you'll end up with earlier versions of certain Windows system files, that can cause any number of strange, nasty problems. (How something like this is allowed to happen is beyond me.)

Caution

Microsoft's Web site is pretty good about informing you of which upgrade files are intended for which OS version, but it's still very possible to make a mistake, so be careful.

Another important point: you can't upgrade an earlier version of Windows 95 to a later one by simply downloading updates. Critical bug fixes and a few minor upgrades can be downloaded but they won't take you all the way from one version to the next. Microsoft specifically chose not to offer downloadable versions of certain features they added to later versions of Windows 95, such as the FAT32 file system. (Instead, they make you buy Windows 98 to get all the upgrades and bug fixes in a single release. Not a very nice move in my opinion.)

Windows 95 CD upgrades

It is technically possible to upgrade an earlier version of Windows 95 to a later one and get all the upgrades and enhancements included in those later versions, but the process is not straightforward and there are several caveats. First of all, you have to have a CD version of, say, OSR 2.1 or OSR 2.5, which isn't necessarily easy to get because it was typically only bundled with new computer systems.

Note

Microsoft did not sell later versions of Windows 95 in stores, but you could get a copy of OSR2, OSR2.1, and OSR2.5 when you bought a new hard drive or motherboard. (Some smaller computer dealers apparently sold copies under the table as well.) Also families and/or businesses that bought multiple computers at different times might have multiple versions of Windows 95 bundled with each of their different machines.

If you try to run Windows 95 Setup off a later version CD on a computer with a previous version installed, it won't work. Similarly, if you try to run an older version of Windows 95 Setup on a machine with a newer version of the OS, you'll get an error message saying that you can't continue because a newer version is already installed. (As strange as this sounds, it's very possible to mistakenly try to install an older version because the Windows 95 CDs are not marked with easy identification of the version they include. As a result, it's easy to mix them up.) Figure 9-16 shows an error messages you'll see if this happens to you.

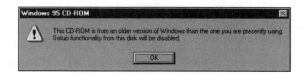

Figure 9-16: You can't go backwards . . .
Windows 95's Setup program is smart enough to prevent you from going backwards and trying to reinstall a previous version of Windows onto a more current version.

Caution

As I alluded to earlier, there are some important caveats to be aware of. First, OSR 2 and 2.1 will install Internet Explorer 3.01 over whatever version you already have installed. If you have IE 4.01 or later, this will definitely cause some big problems. If you want, you can uninstall your current version of Internet Explorer, perform the Windows 95 upgrade, and reinstall your current version (as long as you have a copy of the installation files). OSR 2.5 installs IE 4.01, so you could run into a similar problem if you have Internet Explorer 5.0 or later and you're updating to OSR 2.5

In addition, you need to be sure you install all the same components of Windows 95 in the upgrade that you had in the original version, otherwise they'll be removed from your computer. So, for example, if you have the original version of Dial-Up Networking installed on your computer and you specifically choose not to install Dial-Up Networking with the upgrade version, the upgrade treats your decision as if you want to uninstall the Dial-Up Networking that exists and removes it.

The trick to making the upgrade work is as follows:

STEPS:

Upgrading to a Later Version of Windows 95

Step 1. Boot your computer using a CD-ROM driver-equipped version of a Windows 95 boot disk.

Cross-Reference

See the "Troubleshooting Tools" section of Chapter 17 for instructions on how to create this disk.

Step 2. After the computer boots to an A:\> prompt, switch over to Windows directory on your hard drive by typing the following:

```
cd C:\Windows [Enter]
```

Step 3. Rename the Win.com file in your C:\Windows directory to Win.xxx. (The installation process looks to this file to see whether or not it should proceed, so you need to rename it to trick the installation into performing the upgrade.) To do this, type in the following at the C:\Windows prompt:

```
Rename win.com win.xxx [Enter]
```

Step 4. Confirm the renaming worked by listing the files in the Windows directory and looking for Win.xxx. (You should see it right near the bottom of the list.) Type in the following:

```
dir /w [Enter]
```

If it didn't work and you still see Win.com, go back to Step 3.

Step 5. Insert the Windows 95 CD into your CD-ROM drive and switch over to the drive and start the Windows 95 Setup program by typing the following:

`D:\setup.exe [Enter]` (or whatever letter your CD-ROM drive happens to be)

Step 6. The default installation folder will not be set correctly when you upgrade this way, so when you get to the dialog box that asks where you want Windows installed, be sure to change it to C:\Windows (or wherever your current Windows 95 installation is).

Upgrading Windows 95 in this manner will update various components of your operating system, including the Registry, but it will not force you to reinstall applications, as a complete reinstall of Windows 95 may, in some situations, do. Everything should look and work as it did before (with the exception of things that have been updated).

Updating Windows 98

Since the original release of Windows 98, Microsoft has also made some new additions and/or updates that are available. Windows 98 Second Edition is an upgraded version (sometimes also called OSR 1) of Windows 98 that includes both bus fixes and some new features, notably Internet Connection Sharing (ICS).

Windows 95 users who haven't upgraded to Windows 98 can simply jump straight to Windows 98 Second Edition. Windows 98 users, however, have two options. They can either purchase the Windows 98 Second Edition Updates CD, which will bring them up to complete Second Edition, or they can use the Windows 98 Update feature to get the free Service Pack 1 for Windows 98. The Service Pack incorporates all the latest bus fixes, but does not include any new features, such as ICS.

Installation problems

If you run into problems while installing Windows 95 or 98, the first thing you should do is simply restart your computer. Both versions of Windows offer a Safe Recovery option that will kick in if, for some reason, the installation does not complete itself successfully. In some rare instances, you may have to use Safe Recovery more than once to finish the installation.

There are log files that are created when you install Windows 95 or 98 that you can look at in any word processor or text editing program to try and find out what may have caused the problem. All of these files are located in the root directory of your hard disk and most are normally hidden, so you may have to turn on the capability to view hidden files, if you haven't already done so. To do this, open Windows Explorer via the Start menu, select Folder Options from the View menu, choose the View tab, and make sure the Show all files radio button is selected. Figure 9-17 shows what the Folder Options dialog box looks like.

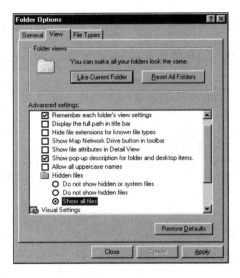

Figure 9-17: Seeing everything
In order to see all the hidden files on your computer, you have to tell Windows that's what you want by going into Windows Explorer's Folder Options settings off the View Menu.

- The Setuplog.txt file tracks what occurs during the setup process, including listing which Windows components were installed and which weren't (a 1 next to the component means yes, it was installed, and a 0 means no, it wasn't installed.)

- The Netlog.txt offers similar information on network-related hardware and software.

- The Detlog.txt contains information about the hardware detection process that both Windows 95 and 98 go through when they're installed on any PC.

- If the installation process stops during the hardware detection phase — a not uncommon scenario — you may also see a Detcrash.log file, which keeps track of which hardware detection already occurred and what step caused the problem. The Setup program needs this information so that the Safe Recovery mechanism built into Setup can skip over that step and attempt to complete installation the next time you restart. Unlike the other log files, Detcrash.log is in binary format and can only be read by the Setup program. In practical terms this means if you try to open it with a text editor or word processor, you'll see nothing but a bunch of gibberish.

I'll warn you now that all of these log files can be very difficult to decipher, but they may help provide a clue to your problem. If you can find some clues, use that information and additional troubleshooting tips in Chapter 17 "Troubleshooting Techniques," and Chapter 18, "Solving Common PC Problems," to help you work through it. With some hardware-based problems, the best solution sometimes is to simply remove or detach the problematic device (as long as it's not one of your PC's critical components — such as the hard drive or video card) and then try to install it separately later.

Installing Windows 2000

The first thing you need to know when considering Windows 2000 for your PC is that Windows 2000 Professional is an upgrade to Windows NT 4.0 — not Windows 95 or 98 — and consequently it's designed to be used in a networked, business environment. You can certainly use it on a home PC if you want to, but that is not its intended audience (as confusing as the name may be).

The retail price and system requirements for Windows 2000 are quite high — you need at least 64MB of RAM and a 300MHz processor on desktops, for example (though I've run it on slightly slower machines as well) — because of the audience for whom it is intended. In addition, because of the security features it includes and how the system is designed, you also need to worry about logging in every time you start your PC. Finally, and most importantly, it's important to note that not all Windows 95/98 applications will necessarily work under Windows 2000 — those that say they'll work under Windows NT 4.0 generally will, but don't presume the same for other Windows applications that don't support NT.

Still, Windows 2000 is the most recent version of Windows and includes support for the most recent hardware and software advancements, And if all of those issues aren't enough to deter you, then feel free to put it on your home PC. You can upgrade existing Windows 95, 98, or NT 4.0-based computers to Windows 2000 in the same way that you can upgrade Windows 95 machines to Windows 98 — just insert the installation CD and run the Setup program.

As with other operating systems, you may want to create partitions that conform to the Windows 2000's preferred format — NTFS 5.0, in this case — before you install it (see the section on partitions earlier in this chapter for more), but you can also do that after the fact via various disk partitioning utilities. If you want to dual-boot between Windows 98 and Windows 2000, you can do so on single disk that conforms to the FAT-32 format courtesy of the boot loader that's bundled with Windows 2000. Be sure to install Windows 98 first if you're installing both OSes onto a new hard drive.

Windows 2000 shares many similarities with Windows 98 (and Windows 95), so you'll find the operation to be similar to previous versions of Windows. Figure 9-18 shows an example of how it looks.

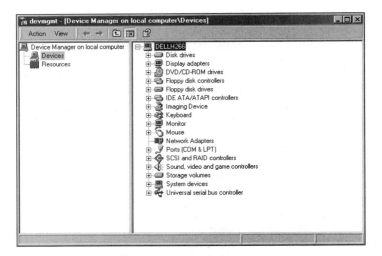

Figure 9-18: Windows 2000 look and feel
Much of the Windows 2000 interface is similar to Windows 98 (or 95, for that matter), but there have been changes and enhancements made in a variety of different areas, such as the new version of the Device Manager.

In some instances certain settings are found in different places or are somewhat redesigned, but the basic concepts are the same. The installation-related procedures are also similar. For example, you'll be able to find a Setuplog.txt file at the root directory of the Windows 2000 boot drive that's conceptually similar to the file you'll find under Windows 98 or 95. It provides a great deal of detailed information about what files were installed and what hardware was recognized during the installation process.

Installing Linux

Probably the fastest-growing operating system being installed on computers today is Linux, which is a version of the UNIX operating system that's designed for PCs. UNIX is a complex, multiuser operating systems designed over thirty years ago for use by engineers on networked computer workstations, mainframes and minicomputers. While great strides have been made to make Linux more user-friendly than other flavors of UNIX, its technical heritage still shows through on a very regular basis. In other words, Linux can be very confusing, particularly if you're not very knowledgeable about your PC and how computer software works in general.

Like other alternative operating systems, you cannot use your existing Windows applications with Linux. (For more on another Windows OS alternative, see the sidebar "The Be option.") Instead you'll have to either download or purchase Linux applications. Partially because of this, and because of its relatively complex nature, many people believe Linux is best suited for computer tinkerers — the type of people who like to mess around with their PC to see what it can and cannot do. Recently, however, there have been several improvements that have helped make it a reasonable mainstream choice for adventurous PC users, particularly those who are willing to live with two (or more) operating systems on their computers.

One of the main reasons Linux is so popular is because it's free. (Another reason, frankly, is because it provides a viable alternative to the various types of Windows and Microsoft in general. Many people are frustrated with the software giant and will support almost anything that *doesn't* come from them.) In fact, not only is the completed product available for free, but the source code for the software — which is the actual lines of computer code written by the programmers to generate the finished product — is also freely available. This type of arrangement is referred to as open source software, and while Linux wasn't the first and isn't the only example of open source, it is by far the most well known. In addition, most applications that are written for Linux are also open source.

One of the many benefits of this arrangement is that any programmer who cares to spend the time can contribute to improving the code base, or software, that makes up Linux. Often times this means any problems released in new versions of the OS or applications are quickly found and fixed, because there is a whole community of developers and users that are available to do the work.

Basic concepts

Before getting into any details on how to install Linux, there are some important concepts you need to understand. First of all, while the core Linux files are free, many companies (such as Red Hat, Caldera, and others) charge for what they call a distribution of Linux. A distribution is the main Linux kernel, which are the core operating system files, along with additional operating system files, plus other applications, accessories and documentation that the company putting together the distribution feels add value to the mix. It's functionally equivalent to what you get when you install Windows.

Having multiple distributions available is great because you have choices within the category of Linux. On the other hand, it can be a real problem because some Linux applications are designed to work under certain distributions due to their dependence on certain files that may be included in one distribution but not another.

For example, as with most aspects of Linux, you have multiple choices available for virtually all aspects of the OS — even its graphical user interface and windowing system. (For Windows users that are used to having the graphical interface as an integral part of the OS this may seem a bit strange, but this is typical of how Linux is and works.) The problem is, if the window manager that comes with your distribution of Linux is different from the window manager used by an application you want to try, this application may not work on your system in its current form. For example, an application designed for KDE (Kool Desktop Environment), one of several possible graphical interfaces for Linux, may have problems if you're using the GNOME (GNU Network Object Model Environment) user interface and vice versa.

The Be option

If you're attracted to the notion of a Windows alternative, but you're turned off by the complexity of Linux, you may want to consider the BeOS, particularly if you're interested in doing multimedia-related work on your PC. Like Version 2.2 and later of the Linux kernel, the BeOS offers a powerful Windows alternative that takes advantage of the latest hardware developments, including support for symmetric multiprocessing (where the computer can use two or more processors simultaneously to accomplish its tasks).

Unlike some types of Linux, the user interface of BeOS is much more like Windows — or even Macintosh. The following figure shows a screen from the BeOS:

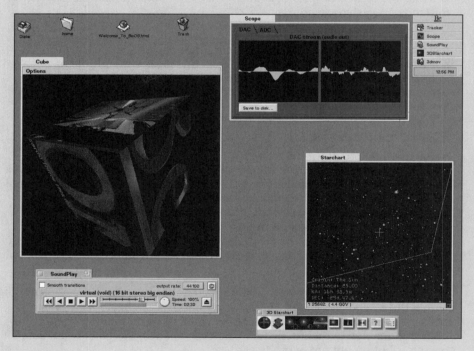

The BeOS

The media-rich BeOS offers a very simple, graphical environment, but also offers extensive support for real-time media such as audio and video. In addition, it supports advanced technologies such as symmetric multiprocessing.

BeOS comes with its own boot loader, so you can install it on its own partition and use it whenever you choose. In addition, it supports multiple Windows and Macintosh partition formats, including FAT-16, FAT-32, HFS, and HFS+, which makes it easy to get access to your existing Windows or Mac files.

One of the hallmarks of Linux is its flexibility, however, so if you run into this type of situation you can try several different solutions. The easiest is to simply install the window manager that the application requires. Linux supports the capability to have multiple versions of different operating system components, including graphical user interfaces; so by installing the one the application requires, you won't overwrite the window manager that came with your distribution. Another possible, but much more complicated solution is to take advantage of the free source code available along with most applications and recompile, or rebuild, the application to make it work with the components you have installed. While you don't have to be a software programmer to do this, it's certainly not a viable option for anyone but the most advanced users.

Along those lines, there are times when you may have to rebuild your Linux kernel, such as when you add new hardware to your PC. This process tends to be more common and, as a result, it's a bit more straightforward, but it's something you should be aware of. (Note that not all hardware installations require this, but some might.)

Finally, because of its command line-driven interface and its fundamental differences from Windows, Linux takes a fair amount of effort to learn. Thankfully, there are a growing number of Linux resources available, particularly on the Web but also in book form, and many Linux users are happy to share their knowledge and experience with others. Before you install Linux, I highly recommend you check out some Linux Web sites and newsgroups online and purchase a Linux book (or two) so that you're prepared for the differences.

Installation issues

Most Linux distributions come on a bootable CD that you can use to start your system and install the operating system. If your system doesn't support booting from a CD, you may find that the Linux distribution comes with its own boot floppy. At worst, you'll find that the Linux CD has a DOS or Windows-readable folder or two that includes a utility that will create a Linux startup disk for you (although you usually have to create it at a DOS command-line prompt).

Partitions

Depending on the distribution type and version you're trying to install, you may find that the installation will take care of creating the necessary Linux partitions for you from available hard disk space you have. If not, you'll have to manually create several different partitions before you can install Linux. At the very least, you'll need at least one Ext2 format partition for installing the Linux OS and application files and another LinuxSwap format partition for storing Linux' virtual memory-based swap files.

Tip

The size of the LinuxSwap partition should be roughly equal to the amount of RAM you have in your system, up to 128MB. Any more than that and you're just wasting space.

Ideally, many Linux installations create several Ext2-format partitions for storing different components of the OS. While there is no hard-and-fast rule here, it's common to create a root partition (recognized as /under Linux) of around 100MB for storing the main Linux kernel files, a /usr partition of around 750MB for storing other operating system and application files, and a /home partition for all other files. You can even create more if you want, but these three plus the swap partition will typically do.

One potentially confusing part about creating partitions with Linux is that it uses a completely different naming system for hard drives and partitions. So, instead of the familiar C: and D: drives, you'll see things like hda1 or sdb5. The first two letters refer to the type of drive (hd is typically an IDE hard drive and sd is typically a SCSI drive); the next letter refers to the physical number of the drive (a is the first physical drive for that type, b is the second); and the number refers to the partition on that drive (numbers 1-4 are the primary partitions and 5-up are the extended partitions). So, for example, hda1 is the first primary partition on the first IDE drive and sdb5 is the first extended partition on the second SCSI drive (not the second drive overall, but the second SCSI drive in particular).

Hardware Recognition

Most recent Linux distributions include Plug and Play-type features that can automatically find out what type of hardware you have in your system and install the right drivers for you, but the hardware recognition is not always as robust as what you find in the various types of Windows. As a result, it's generally a good idea to have a written list of not only the main components you have installed in your system (such as the brand and model of the video card, sound card, and modem), but also the capabilities of those cards. For example, you may need to know what type of chipset is used on your video card (such as S3, nVidia, and so on), how much dedicated video memory it has on it, what refresh frequencies it and your monitor support, and more.

Cross-Reference

For more details on video card and monitor specifications, see Chapter 4, "Video Cards and Monitors."

If the installation process can't figure out what hardware you have or what its capabilities are, you'll need to enter that kind of information into dialog boxes at certain stages during the install.

Tip

Windows users can open the Device Manager in the System control panel and either write down the details about their PC's hardware or print out a report. To print the report, hit the Print button and then choose the All devices and system summary option. Be forewarned that it's a big one, but it should provide most of the information you'll need to complete a Linux install.

Logging in

Once all the files are installed, there are still a few steps you need to complete before you can start using Linux. First of all, as part of the installation process you'll be asked for a password to gain access to the computer as root. Linux, like all versions of Unix, is based around the notion of users logging into a computer to get access. In addition, Linux uses a multitiered model where there are different levels of users with different rights to that computer. Root is the lowest level, giving you access to everything on the system and enabling you to perform whatever administrative tasks are necessary.

One of the most important of these administrative tasks is creating other user accounts. In fact, that's generally the first thing you need to do when you first boot a new Linux installation. Most of the time you're using Linux, you're going to want to sign in with a regular user account and not the root account. While this may seem like a bit of a hassle, it's designed to help prevent accidental changes to your system that may cause it to break.

To PC users who are only familiar with Windows 95 or Windows 98, this may seem very foreign, because anyone who uses the computer has complete access to all levels of the PC and can basically get to and do anything they want. Imagine, however, having different settings in Windows where only people who typed in a special password could get access to the computer's Windows folder, for example. Windows NT 4.0 and Windows 2000 Professional, in fact, have this type of security structure and this type of limitation.

One point to remember is that in all of these cases, one person can have multiple accounts. In other words, you can both have control of the root account and your own user account (or even multiple user accounts).

STEPS:

Creating New Linux User Accounts

Step 1. Log in as root by typing in **root** at the username prompt you receive when you first start Linux, and then typing in the root password.

Step 2. At a command prompt, type in **useradd <account name>** where <account name> is whatever name you decide to use. (You don't need to use the <> characters.) Case generally does not matter in user names, by the way, but it does matter for passwords, which are covered in the next step. Generally speaking, most Linux and Unix usernames and passwords are lower case.

Continued

Step 3.   Type in **passwd <account name>** where <account name> is whatever name you chose in Step 2. You'll be prompted to type in a password and then type it in again to confirm it.

Step 4.   Check that your account works by typing in **logout** at a command prompt to log out of the root account, and then type in your newly created username and password to log in with that account.

Once you've got the login process covered, you may have one last issue to deal with before you can enjoy a graphical Linux environment. Depending on the distribution you install and the components you install from it, your PC may not automatically boot into a graphical desktop environment that you might expect. Instead, you may need to first configure your windowing system (such as X-Windows) to automatically launch when you boot Linux. To get it started in the first place, you commonly type **startx** (which means to start X-Windows) at the command prompt. Check your distribution's documentation for details on how to have the graphical user-interface launch automatically. Once that's done, you can start using Linux in a familiar, graphical environment. See Figure 9-19.

Removing Software

After you spend a great deal of time and energy installing a variety of applications, you may soon want to get rid of some of them. This is either because you're running out of room on your hard drive, you've determined that one application is conflicting with another, or because you've stopped using something.

Regardless of the reason, there are several different ways to go about removing software from your PC. Before I explain what will work, however, it's equally important to know what won't. Specifically, just deleting the folder an application is stored in will not remove all remnants of the application from your computer. Even if most of the application's files are stored inside that folder, there will always at least be a few entries in the Registry. Plus, more than likely, there are probably a few other shared files strewn across other portions of your hard disk (as they were strewn when the applications were installed in the first place).

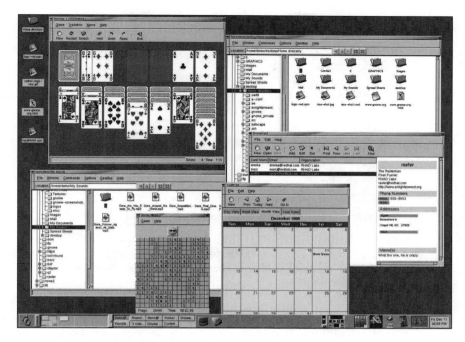

Figure 9-19: What Linux looks like
If your distribution of Linux uses the new GNOME user interface, then you may see a
graphical user interface that looks and operates similarly to Windows.

Standard techniques

The easiest way to remove a piece of software under Windows is via the
Add/Remove Programs Control Panel. Simply open the Control Panel,
highlight the software you want to remove, and click the Add/Remove button.
Doing so kicks off an uninstallation process that should remove the
program's main files and folders, any shared files and folders, and any
Registry entries unique to the program. See Figure 9-20.

Unfortunately, in some instances the process ends with the frustrating
message that some elements couldn't be deleted because they may be in use
by another application. Even worse, the Uninstall Shield program that
performs this work doesn't tell you which components (or Registry entries)
couldn't be removed, leaving you to wonder exactly what kind of junk was
left.

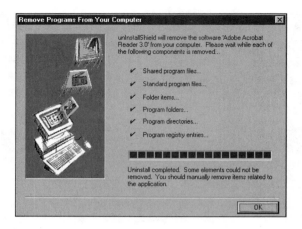

Figure 9-20: Uninstalling
If you use Windows 95/98's Add/Remove Programs control panel to delete a program from your PC, the Uninstall Shield application will automatically launch and (quickly) give you a listing of what it's doing.

Another way to remove some programs is to use the application's own uninstall utility — that is, if one is available. Some applications come bundled with a separate uninstall program that's specifically designed to remove all of an application's program's installed files when it's run (including deleting itself when it's done). Generally speaking, these dedicated uninstall utilities do a more thorough job of removing all of an application's pieces then the Add/Remove Programs Control Panel so if you have a choice, use the program's own uninstaller first.

The final option for removing software from your PC is with the help of a dedicated uninstaller program, such as Uninstaller, CleanSweep, or Remove It! What these products do is make informed decisions (or educated guesses, in some situations) about what files can be removed safely from your computer's hard disk.

Tip

Uninstallers work best with programs that have been installed after the uninstaller has — in fact, if you buy a new computer or new hard disk and need to reinstall your applications, make sure you install the uninstaller first (as strange as that may sound).

Uninstallers monitor the process of installation programs and keep track of where every little piece of software goes on your hard disk, as well as what entries are made to the Registry and any other startup files. That way, if you later decide to remove an application with your uninstaller utility, the uninstaller can simply look up in its records what was installed where and do the reverse, taking out all the pieces associated with an application.

For programs that are already installed before you add an uninstaller to your computer the process is more difficult. Some uninstallers have records of where popular applications store their files in standard installations and can use that to try and remove a popular application, and others use various techniques for determining what .DLL and other file dependencies a particular program has and try to uninstall an application that way. (See the "Finding the links" sidebar earlier in this chapter for more information on these dependencies.)

Unfortunately, uninstallers typically have mixed records when it comes to using these techniques — sometimes they work well and sometimes they don't — so you may need to use a combination of the various software removal techniques I've described here to get rid of software that's already on your machine.

Tip

In general, if you have the choice, I suggest using a program's own uninstaller first, then the Add/Remove Programs control panel, and finally an uninstaller utility — in that order.

Additional steps

Regardless of what method you used to remove your software, you may find that certain elements of a program still remain. As an example, you may discover that your Registry or other startup files (such as .ini files) may still have references to the application you thought you had already removed. (Of course, unless you're mucking around with your Registry, you may never see those entries, but it's possible they would still be there.)

To do a last bit of cleanup, you may want to do a search for any .ini files (search for *.ini to get all files that end in that extension) and look through those files to see if they have any references to programs you've removed. If they do, simply remove the offending line, save the changed file, and exit whatever editing application you used to open the file. (NotePad and WordPad work well for this.)

Some programs still use dedicated .ini files for storing their preferences, so if you come across one of those for a program that you've already deleted, you can drag it to the Recycle Bin as well.

Caution

Only throw something into the Recycle Bin that you're absolutely sure you don't need. If you're not sure, just save it. A few extra files and even a few hundred bytes of wasted storage space isn't going to hurt anyone. If you accidentally drag something to the Recycle Bin, don't worry. Neither Windows 95 nor Windows 98 actually deletes any files in the Recycle Bin until you specifically tell it to Empty the Recycle Bin. Until you do that, you can open the Recycle Bin, drag out any file(s) you may have accidentally put there, and store those files somewhere else on your hard drive.

The other thing you'll want to do occasionally is run a Registry cleaning utility that will go through your Registry files and delete any obsolete or empty keys. Microsoft offers a free utility called RegClean that you can get from the company's support Web site at support.microsoft.com (the site is a tremendous resource for lots of other useful and cool stuff as well.) What RegClean does is to look for various types of Registry junk and cleans it out. (See Figure 9-21.)

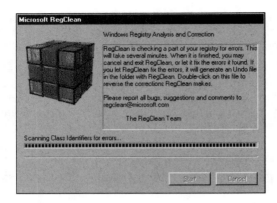

Figure 9-21: Cleaning the Registry
Microsoft's free RegClean utility offers a spartan interface but does a great job in cleaning up your Windows Registry files.

Tip

The trick with RegClean is to get a completely clean run, which means that it reports that it found no problems. That usually means you need to run it at least twice in a row because it will more than likely find and fix some problems the first time you run it.

Windows 98 users can also use the ScanReg utility, which is bundled with Windows 98 only, to help take care of other Registry-related problems.

Cross-Reference

See the "Troubleshooting Tools" section of Chapter 17 for more on ScanReg and other Windows 98 troubleshooting tools.

Summary

In this chapter, I described how to add, update, and remove software from your computer.

▶ Adding or installing new software on your computer can be done in several, easy ways, including the useful Add/Remove Programs control panel.

▶ Downloading programs off the Internet, including freeware and shareware, involves copying the files from another computer onto yours. The act of downloading doesn't necessarily install the software, however, because in many situations you need to download the software, decompress it, and then install it — three separate steps.

▶ Most programs that are installed on your computer put files in many different places all over your hard drive. Many go in the application's own folder, but some go into the Windows folder and other locations. In addition, almost all Windows applications make additions to the Windows Registry.

▶ Upgrading your applications is generally a good idea, although it's often overkill to update all of them. More and more programs, including Windows 98, are starting to do upgrades automatically.

▶ Reinstalling an application to try and fix a problem often means reinstalling updates as well.

▶ Installing an operating system is the most important task you can do on your PC. With the advancement of hardware recognition systems, such as Windows' Plug and Play, that process has gotten much easier.

▶ If you want to install an operating system other than Windows on your PC, you first need to create the right kind of partitions on your hard drive.

▶ To run multiple operating systems on a single computer you also need to install a boot loader, which enables you to choose from the available OSes when you first turn your computer on.

▶ Reinstalling Windows 95 or Windows 98 requires some special considerations, but it can be invaluable in helping to fix a sick computer. To do it, you need to have a floppy boot disk that includes a CD-ROM driver.

▶ You can upgrade an early version of Windows 95 to a later version of Windows 95, to Windows 98, or to Windows 2000.

▶ Installing Linux usually has some special requirements, including creating user accounts and configuring the graphical interface.

▶ You can remove software from your computer via an application's own uninstall program, the Add/Remove Programs control panel, or a dedicated uninstall utility.

Chapter 10

Adding and Removing Hardware

In This Chapter

▶ You will learn how to attach external peripherals to your PC, including those that use serial, parallel, USB, SCSI, and IEEE 1394 connections.

▶ You will learn how to install expansion cards inside your computer.

▶ You will learn how to use PC cards with notebook computers.

▶ You will learn how to add, upgrade, and remove driver software.

▶ You will learn how to remove hardware from your computer system.

Adding software to your PC is a great way to get access to some nice new capabilities, but software can only go so far. If you want to explore entirely new vistas, then adding hardware is where all the really interesting action is.

New hardware can extend the reach of your computer, enabling it to do things that it simply wasn't capable of doing before, as well as greatly improving the speed and efficiency of some of the things it may be able to do now.

For some reason, the thought of plugging in new hardware often strikes fear in the hearts of even those people who have no problems configuring their software down dark paths of detail that only the bravest digital daredevil dare tread. I guess there's just something more substantial about adding to or changing the paths through which your computer's data can travel. After all, this is what adding a new piece of hardware to your computer essentially does. (Come to think of it, I guess PC hardware really *is* more substantial than software.)

The goal of this chapter is to break through those fears and to show you that with just a bit of forethought and a little common sense, adding new hardware to your computer — whether it's an external device or an internal add-in card — can be as easy as installing new software.

If you want to find out more about adding RAM, a new hard drive, a processor upgrade, or a new motherboard to your PC, go to Chapter 11, "Upgrading Your PC." For anything else, just keep reading . . .

Connectors and Resources

Unlike software, which can basically be added to your system without much thought or consideration (other than making sure you have the room on your hard disk to store it, of course), there are several issues you need to consider when planning to add hardware to your computer.

The most obvious question is, do you have the right kind of connections on your PC? And more important, are those ports supported by your operating system (or OS)? For example, you can only attach a USB-based device to a computer with USB ports and the appropriate USB drivers. Similarly, hardware intended for the Device Bay can only be attached to computers that feature Device Bays and support for those Device Bays in the OS. The original version of Windows 98, for example, doesn't include basic Device Bay drivers. Also, some really new computers may lack support for the old serial and parallel ports that used to be standard on virtually all PCs.

In some instances, the lack of a particular port can be overcome by simply adding another piece of hardware. So, for example, if you have an older PC or notebook that lacks USB or a newer (or older) PC without IEEE 1394 — sometimes called *FireWire* or *i.Link* — ports, you can buy an add-in card that will plug into one of your computer's expansion card slots (or into a PC card slot in the case of notebooks) and will enable you to attach USB or IEEE 1394 devices to it. These types of add-in devices that enable you to attach other devices are typically called *controllers* because they control the communications between your PC and the devices attached to the controller. Figure 10-1 shows how the process works.

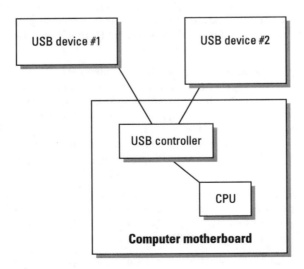

Figure 10-1: Taking control
A controller, such as a USB controller, acts as an intermediary between the rest of your computer and the devices attached to the controller. In some cases, a controller takes the form of a plug-in card, while in other cases, it's built right into the computer's motherboard.

As another example, very few PCs ship with built-in support for the SCSI interface, so if a particular scanner or other device you want to use comes standard with a SCSI connection, you'll need to first add a SCSI controller to your PC in order to have a SCSI connection. A SCSI controller (as well as USB and IEEE 1394 controllers) enables your computer to communicate with other devices that use a particular type of interface, or language — in this case, SCSI.

Cross-Reference

See Chapter 3, "Hard Disks and Removable Drives," for more on SCSI.

Worrying about what type of connectors your computer has — and therefore what types of devices it's capable of supporting — is becoming less and less of an issue because many computer peripheral manufacturers are starting to offer several versions of their products with different types of connectors. For example, you can find similar model scanners that are essentially identical except for the fact that one comes with a parallel port, another a SCSI port, and a third a USB port.

The one important difference between these three (or any group of connectors) is their performance, or the speed at which they can transfer data back and forth between the computer and the device. On some peripherals, such as scanners, this really isn't very important, but on things such as removable hard drives, this can be enormously important. So, before you make a purchase, you need to know which of the various buses and interface schemes offer the best performance and then determine what you're willing to pay for (devices with faster connections typically cost more money). Table 10-1 lists the throughput rates of different peripheral buses.

Table 10-1   Connection Speeds

Connection Type	Maximum Throughput
Serial	115Kbps
Parallel	300KB – 3MBps
USB	1.5MBps (12Mbps)
SCSI-2	10MBps
Ultra2 SCSI	40MBps
IEEE 1394	50MBps (400Mbps)

In addition, some devices, such as digital cameras, include multiple connectors on them enabling you to select whatever connection method you prefer to use. Again, if you're concerned with the performance of a particular piece of hardware (and who isn't), then you'll want to ensure that you can use the fastest connection type possible. Sometimes this means tacking on the added expense of a controller for the type of connection you want, which may be more than you're willing to spend. For example, if you're interested in a piece of hardware that offers an IEEE 1394 port and a SCSI or USB port, but your computer doesn't have an IEEE 1394 connector, then you'll have to decide if the added cost of a IEEE 1394 controller is worth the performance boost it would provide. In some cases it probably will be, but in many others it clearly won't.

Be aware also that many devices do not offer the flexibility of multiple connection options, so make sure you check for the type of connectors your computer has and the type of connectors required by a particular piece of hardware *before* you make your purchase.

Tip

Another option to consider is adapters that enable you to switch between various types of interface schemes. For example, several companies make adapter cables that enable you to connect older serial or parallel port devices to your computer's USB ports. Iomega also makes an adapter device for the original Jaz removable storage drive called the Jaz Traveller that converts the device's standard SCSI port into a parallel port that can be attached to computers that lack a SCSI connection.

If you're installing an internal card, make sure your computer has the right kind of slots as well as an open slot for your new card. Most current plug-in cards come in the PCI (Peripheral Component Interconnect) format — as opposed to the older ISA (Industry Standard Architecture) format — but there can be differences in the type of PCI bus they support. Most plug-in cards are 32-bit PCI cards and are designed to run on a 33MHz PCI bus, but there are also 64-bit PCI cards and cards designed for a 66MHz PCI bus. (You need a system and a chipset that specifically supports these types of cards to use them and right now, they're primarily only found in servers.) In addition, most newer video cards use the related but still different AGP (Advanced Graphics Port) connector.

On notebook computers, most PC cards use the nearly universal PCMCIA Type II form factor, but some cards require support for Zoomed Video (see Chapter 4, "Video Cards and Monitors," for more). In addition, a few hard-disk-based PC cards use the fatter Type III format, which is basically equivalent to two stacked Type II cards. So, if you have space for two Type II cards — as most notebooks do — then you should have no problems working with a Type III card.

Resources

In addition to physical concerns, you may also need to check your computer's resources, because many hardware peripherals require certain resources from your PC in order to function properly. As explained in Chapter 8, "How Your Computer Works," a computer's resources are a set of physical and logical entities required in order for all the various pieces that make up your computer to communicate with each another. The most commonly discussed type of resources are called interrupt requests (IRQs), but other types of resources include Direct Memory Access (DMA) channels, input/output (or I/O) addresses, and Upper Memory Ranges. Table 10-2 summarizes computer resources and the limits for each type.

Table 10-2   Resource Limits

Resources	Limit
IRQs	16 (numbered 0–15)
DMA Channels	8 (numbered 0–7)
I/O Addresses	Unlimited
Upper Memory Range	384KB (commonly divided into six 64KB segments labeled A000-FFFF)

Under Windows, you can quickly find out what resources your computer is using by opening the System Control Panel and selecting the Device Manager tab. Double-click the little computer icon you'll see at the top of the list, and you'll be presented with a dialog box that shows you what resources you're computer is using. Figure 10-2 shows what it looks like.

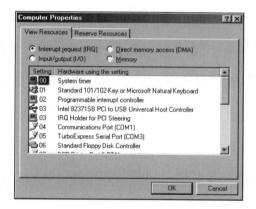

Figure 10-2: Using resources wisely
The specific resources used by all the different devices inside of or attached to your computer can be seen via the Windows Device Manager, which is part of the System Control Panel. This screen shows which of the 16 available IRQs (numbered 0–15) are in use.

You can switch between viewing IRQs and other resources by simply selecting the different radio buttons available in the dialog box.

Before you can install a piece of hardware, you need to find out what resources (if any) it requires and what resources your computer has available. Be aware that with some hardware, simply determining the resources isn't always good enough because some devices have very specific requirements. For example, some cards that require an IRQ can only work with specific numbered IRQs, such as numbers 9–11. So, just because your computer has an available IRQ doesn't always mean it will work with any device that requires an IRQ. If at all possible — and finding this out isn't always easy — try to determine specifically what resources a hardware device needs.

If you try to install a piece of hardware that requires computer resources you don't have — for example, if all of your computer's IRQs are in use and you try to install a piece of hardware that requires a dedicated IRQ — you will run into a nasty resource conflict: either the device you plugged in won't work or it will work but something else on your computer will stop working. Unfortunately, if the latter scenario occurs, you may not discover that something else has stopped working until you go to use it. Some PCs, on the other hand, notify you of an IRQ conflict at startup.

Tip

Generally speaking, it's a good idea to make sure your computer's existing hardware works after you've successfully installed a new piece of hardware.

You can also manually look for resource conflicts by using the Microsoft System Information Utility under Windows 98 (it's available off the Start menu at the Programs menu item under Accessories and then System Tools). See Figure 10-3.

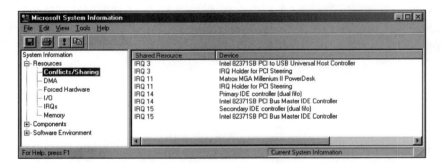

Figure 10-3: System Information utility
One of the many useful features of the System Information utility bundled with Windows 98 is its capability to enable you to easily see any conflict your computer might have.

Windows 95 enables you to use the Device Manager to determine conflicts. (You can also use this method under Windows 98.) If you have a hardware conflict or another hardware-related problem, one of the branches under the device listing will be open, and you will see either a yellow exclamation point or a red international no symbol (you know, the circle with the slash through it) next to one or more of your computer's components. See Figure 10-4.

Cross-Reference

If you don't see those symbols, you're fine. If you do see these symbols, head over to Chapter 17, "Troubleshooting Techniques," where I give you advice on how to work through this.

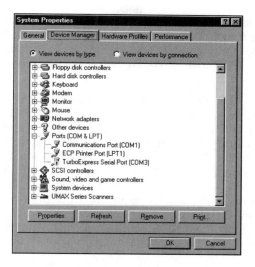

Figure 10-4: Resource conflict
The little yellow exclamation point on a piece of hardware listed in the Device Manager tells you that the device is suffering from some kind of hardware problem that often has to do with a resource conflict.

What uses resources?

Not all hardware devices require use of your computer's resources. In fact, most external hardware peripherals do not. Instead, the ports or controllers to which external devices connect use resources — such as IRQs — but the individual devices do not. So, for example, individual USB, IEEE 1394, or SCSI devices don't require IRQs, but a USB controller, IEEE 1394 controller, and SCSI controller do. This is not to stay there aren't any limitations on individual devices, because there are, although they aren't usually that constraining. Most SCSI controllers support a maximum of seven connected devices (advanced UltraSCSI models support up to 15), IEEE 1394 controllers support up to 63 daisy-chained peripherals, and USB's theoretical limit is a comfortable 127 devices.

What this means is, in the case of a SCSI controller, a single IRQ supports up to 7 peripherals and, in the case of a USB controller, a single IRQ supports up to 127 devices.

Older serial and parallel port standards work similarly. Printers and modems that attach to parallel and serial ports don't use IRQs, but the parallel and serial ports generally do. Unless you have switch boxes that enable you to connect multiple devices to a single port and switch between them, these ports are particularly limiting because they basically only support one device per port. In other words, one IRQ per device.

If you add an extra parallel or serial port card to your PC in order to connect an additional device, the ports on those cards will each take up an IRQ (as well as other resources). This resource limitation is one of the main reasons the computer industry is moving away from these older connection schemes and towards the multiperipheral chains offered by USB and IEEE 1394.

Tip

One way to get around this problem is to invest in a USB hub with serial and/or parallel ports built in. (A USB hub is a device that works like an outlet strip, turning one of your PC's USB ports into, say, four or more additional ports.) Another option is to buy one of the previously mentioned USB-to-parallel or USB-to-serial cables. Either way, you can add additional serial or parallel port devices without worrying about IRQs because the hub or adapter cable basically fools the PC into thinking the device is just another USB peripheral. This is a great way to keep using older peripherals after you upgrade to a newer machine. Note, however, that not all serial or parallel devices will work through these types of connections. In some cases, you have to have a dedicated port.

Unlike external devices, most internal hardware does require the use of computer resources. In addition to the standard plug-in cards, this includes components built into your computer's motherboard, such as the system timer, memory controller, and more. You can see references to these components and the resources they use under the System Devices branch of the Device Manager.

Secret

In fact, some devices can still use IRQs if they're not being used or not even there! The PS/2 mouse port, for example, virtually always takes IRQ 12 and the keyboard typically uses IRQ 1, even if your system comes with a USB mouse and keyboard and doesn't use those older connections.

There are some internal devices that don't use system resources. Hard drives, CD/DVD-ROM drives, and other removable storage devices, for example — because they typically attach to IDE controllers (or in some cases, SCSI or IEEE 1394 controllers) — do not take up resources. Again, however, the controller generally does use an IRQ. In fact, the IDE controller built into most computers actually uses two because it needs one for each of its two channels.

Cross-Reference

See Chapter 3, "Hard Disks and Removable Drives," for more on IDE.

Table 10-3 lists different connection mechanisms and the number of devices they can support per IRQ.

Like controller cards, video cards, TV tuner cards, sound cards, and virtually all of the other devices that plug into your PC's expansion slots also use IRQs. Memory you add to your computer's motherboard, or to a video card, is not included in this category, however. Thankfully, memory does not use or require any resources.

Table 10-3   Devices per IRQ

Port/Controller Connection	Number of Devices per IRQ
Keyboard	1
PS/2 Mouse	1
Serial	1
Parallel	1
IDE	2
SCSI	7 (15 for some UltraSCSI controllers)
IEEE 1394	63
USB	127

Cross-Reference

See Chapter 11, "Upgrading Your PC," for more on installing memory.

As with plug-in cards, most all PC cards that plug into a notebook computer also use IRQs and other resources — although only while they're actually plugged into the computer. If and when you take them out, the resources they use are freed up. So, for example, even if you have multiple PC cards with similar resource requirements, you can use them all interchangeably on a notebook computer — although you could run into a problem if you tried to use two of them simultaneously because they would then be fighting for the same resources.

Table 10-4 summarizes what types of devices need the most problematic type of computer resource (IRQs) and which ones don't.

The basic issue surrounding computer resources and hardware is that you need to find out whether your computer has the resources available to support new hardware. Again, I must emphasize that resources are only an issue with internal plug-in cards — you don't have to worry about this if you just want to attach a USB-based digital camera to your PC or plug in a printer to your computer's parallel port.

If you are planning on adding a new 3D accelerator or some other new plug-in card inside your PC, however, it's very possible, for example, to find that your computer may have open expansion slots, but no available IRQs. Unfortunately, there's nothing that can solve this problem other than taking out or somehow disabling another device that's currently using an IRQ.

Table 10-4   IRQ Users

Typical Devices	Does it Use an IRQ?
Keyboard	Yes, via dedicated keyboard port (No if the keyboard attaches via USB)*
PS/2 Mouse	Yes, via dedicated PS/2 mouse port (No if the mouse attaches via USB)*
Printer	No
Parallel Port	Yes
External Modem	No
Internal Modem	Yes, usually (because it adds its own serial port)
Serial Port	Yes
SCSI-Based Scanner	No
SCSI Controller Card	Yes
USB Camera	No
USB Controller (either built-in or added to PC)	Yes
IEEE 1394–based Digital Camcorder	No
IEEE 1394 Controller (either built-in or added to PC)	Yes
Video Card	Yes
Sound Card	Yes (sometimes two)
Hard Drive or CD/ DVD-ROM Drive	No
IDE Controller	Yes (two)

*Sometimes the IRQs for these devices cannot be turned off, even if your PC comes with a USB mouse and keyboard.

Tip

In theory, you should be able to install PCI-based plug-in cards into computers that have all their IRQs in use, and the PCI devices should be able to share IRQs up to a maximum of four PCI devices. (The PCI bus has its own set of four interrupts, sometimes referred to as PCI A-D to avoid confusion with numbered IRQs.) In practice, however, I have found that this is not always the case. Depending on the type and version number of the BIOS inside your computer, as well as the version of Windows you're running, and the drivers that come with the PCI card, PCI–IRQ sharing sometimes works and sometimes doesn't. In some cases, one or two PCI-based cards in your system may be capable of sharing IRQs, while others may not. The problem is, many PCI cards use their own regular IRQs (in addition to one of the PCI interrupts), which means if you try to install one into a machine that's already using all its IRQs you may run into an unresolvable resource conflict problem. Caveat emptor.

Cross-Reference

See Chapter 17, "Troubleshooting Techniques," for more on PCI–IRQ sharing problems.

Adding External Hardware

Okay, now that we've covered the intellectual issues, it's time for the fun part: plugging everything in. Plugging external peripherals into your PC is usually just as simple as it sounds, although there are a few issues you may need to think about.

Getting ready

First of all, depending on the type of device you're attaching, the computer may need to be turned off. Only USB, IEEE 1394, and Device Bay (which actually uses USB and/or IEEE 1394) support *hot plugging,* which means you can plug a device into the computer (or a chain of devices that's attached to the computer) while the PC is still on. Other devices, such as parallel-port-based printers, serial-port-based modems, cable modems that attach to Ethernet cards, or SCSI-based scanners, or removable drives can only be attached to their respective connectors when the computer is off. (One exception is that some UltraSCSI 2 peripherals and controllers also support hot plugging.)

In most cases, if you accidentally try to plug in one of these types of devices when your PC is on, it won't cause problems — although it sometimes can with chains of SCSI devices — but in virtually all cases, the device won't work.

Tip

Before you plug anything into the computer, make sure you look at the connectors on both ends of the cable. This is particularly important for parallel cables, SCSI cables, and other types of connectors with lots of tiny pins. I've run into several situations where bent pins — which theoretically should prevent you from plugging a cable in, but in reality don't — caused hours and hours of wasted time as I struggled to figure out why something wouldn't work. Note, however, that while bent pins are a bad thing, missing pins aren't necessarily bad. In many cases, cables are supposed to be this way.

Be sure to plug the cables in snugly and, if you can, tighten any screws that may be part of the cable connector. I know they're a pain to deal with, but they guarantee that you've got a good snug connection, and this can prevent problems caused by intermittent connections.

Special considerations

Many types of devices connect easily and don't have any extenuating circumstances you need to worry about. Others, however, do require special attention or may be subject to certain limitations or problems. The next few sections describe these special issues.

Parallel ports

In an effort to make themselves more resource friendly, certain parallel-port-based devices, such as scanners and removable drives, include pass-through connectors that enable you to attach another parallel port device — typically a printer — to them. The idea is that you can share your computer's parallel port by taking advantage of this pass-through connector (although you can't use both devices at the same time).

Unfortunately, as nice as this sounds in theory, it doesn't always work in reality. Sometimes it does, however, so it's certainly worth trying if you have the opportunity. But if it doesn't, it probably has to do with the fact that most of the recent parallel-port-equipped peripherals require bidirectional communications with your computer. In other words, they need to both be able to send and receives messages from your PC simultaneously. For reasons that are unknown to me, some of these pass-through connectors apparently don't connect all of the pins between themselves and the parallel-port input. The end result is that often times devices attached to the pass-through connector can't communicate properly with the PC and don't work.

Tip

You can sometimes get around this problem with a device called a reversible, bidirectional autoswitch. This little device creates a T-connection that enables two parallel port devices to share a single parallel port and automatically routes the communications to the appropriate device as necessary. (It's called reversible because it can also be used to enable two computers to share a single printer or other parallel-port-based device.) Figure 10-5 shows how the reversible, bidirectional autoswitch works.

This won't work with everything — I've come across some printers that simply must have a direction connection to your PC's parallel port in order to function properly — but it can help out in many situations.

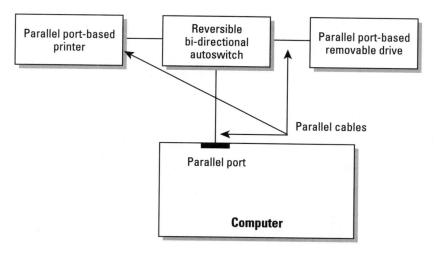

Figure 10-5: Sharing parallel ports
One possible solution for sharing a single parallel port among two devices is to use a device called a reversible, bi-directional autoswitch which sits at the heart of the T-connection between your PC and the two peripherals.

SCSI

Devices that connect via the Small Computer Systems Interface (SCSI) have two special requirements: ID numbers and termination. First of all, each device in a SCSI chain needs to be given a unique number — typically between one and seven — which you select via small dip switches or some other mechanism on the back of the drive. The ID numbers are used to distinguish between devices so that messages are sent to the right place.

In addition, a chain of SCSI devices needs to be terminated at each end so that signals going across the bus don't interfere with one another and cause errors. If you're only using external SCSI devices (or only internal, for that matter), termination is taken care of on one end by the SCSI controller (sometimes also called a *host adapter*) but it also needs to be terminated on the other end of the chain. If you only have one SCSI device attached to the controller, this means the one device needs to be terminated (although a SCSI chain with one device will often work without termination). If you have two devices attached, the one in the middle of the chain must not be terminated, but again, the one on the end must be terminated. Figure 10-6 shows an example of a SCSI chain.

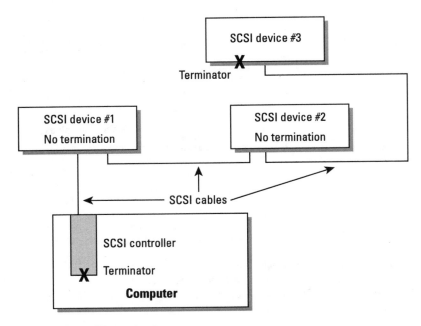

Figure 10-6: SCSI termination
The last device in a chain of SCSI-equipped products must be terminated. All the devices in the middle, however, must not be terminated and/or must have their internal termination turned off.

Tip

If you mix both internal and external SCSI devices, you'll probably have to turn off termination on the controller itself because it will sit in the middle of the SCSI chain, in between the internal and external devices attached to it.

Thankfully, terminating SCSI devices does not require the services of Arnold Schwarzenegger, but instead can be achieved in a couple of different ways, depending on the device(s) you have. Some newer SCSI devices have automatic termination which enables them to determine if they are in the middle or at the end of a chain and automatically turn their built-in termination either on or off, as appropriate.

Many other devices have termination switches that you can turn on and off manually. (Note that even devices with automatic termination typically have switches you can use to override the automatic settings.) Finally, some SCSI peripherals come with hardware terminators, which commonly come in the form of cable plugs that you simply attach to one of a device's two SCSI ports.

Most SCSI devices include two SCSI ports so that you can daisy-chain one device to another, but there are some SCSI peripherals that only come with one port. If you have one with only one port, you'll need to make sure that it's at the end of your SCSI chain and that it has its termination enabled.

USB

Despite its all-encompassing name, the Universal Serial Bus (USB) isn't quite as universal as everyone hoped it would be. Part of the problem is that Microsoft's USB drivers for Windows 95 (available only with OSR 2.1 and OSR 2.5) have some limitations.

Cross-Reference

See Chapter 9, "Adding, Upgrading, and Removing Software," for more on different versions of Windows 95.

As a result, USB device manufacturers need to write drivers to specifically work with the Windows 95 Version of USB. Many of them have chosen not to do so, however, instead focusing their efforts on Windows 98 and 2000 drivers. This means if you really want to take advantage of your PC's USB ports, and if you want to run Windows, you're probably going to have to upgrade to Windows 98 or 2000. If you want to use another operating system, you'll just need to make sure that the version you're using supports USB.

In addition, some of the earliest implementations of USB ports were apparently not exactly done to the letter of the USB specification. As a result, the USB ports on some older (circa early 1997) machines may not ever work right, even with Windows 98.

Another issue is that there are two main types of USB controllers built into PCs (Universal Host Controller and Open Host Controller), and some drivers for early USB peripherals only work properly with one type or the other. If your computer has one type, but your peripheral needs another, you're going to have to convince the device's manufacturer to create an updated driver to work with the other type of controller. You can usually determine what type of controller your computer has by looking for the Universal Serial Bus controller branch in your Device Manager and seeing what type of controller is listed (universal or open).

Tip

If it turns out that either your USB ports aren't functional or won't work with a particular USB peripheral, you don't have to run out and get a new PC. You can simply purchase a separate USB controller card and plug it into one of your PC's expansion slots. (Of course, this also works if your PC predates USB entirely.) If you do, you may have to disable the existing USB ports in your computer's BIOS Setup program.

Cross-Reference

See Chapter 8, "How Your Computer Works," for more on what the BIOS Setup program is.

Secret

By the way, if the first time you try your USB ports you discover that they don't work, it may be because they're turned off in your BIOS Setup program. To test this out, restart your computer, enter the BIOS Setup, and look for the USB port settings (they may be in a section that says Peripherals or Advanced). Many machines bundled with Windows 95 were shipped from the factory with these ports disabled. If this is true in your case, enable the ports, exit the BIOS Setup program (saving changes), and restart your machine.

As Windows 95 or 98 launches, the Add New Hardware Wizard should automatically recognize that the ports are now enabled and install the necessary driver software. You might have to reinstall the drivers for any devices you were trying to connect.

Some of the most critical issues have to do with powering USB devices. One of the more attractive aspects of the USB specification is that it's supposed to be able to provide power to connected devices so that you don't have to mess with clunky power adapters and lots of extra cables. The problem is, it only provides a limited amount of power, and if you exceed those levels — either because you've attached multiple low-power devices, one really high-power device, or some combination of the two — you're going to have to use a separate power supply on one or more of your USB peripherals, which is a real disappointment.

Unfortunately, determining when you've exceeded those levels isn't always easy either, but if a new USB device you've tried to attach doesn't work, insufficient power could be the problem.

Cross-Reference

See Chapter 18, "Solving Common PC Problems," for more on solving USB power-related problems.

Finally, the last issue to consider is that because USB devices are not daisy-chainable, meaning you cannot simply connect one USB to another, you may run out of ports. For example, if you attach a digital camera with a single USB connector to your notebook's sole USB port, and then want to try to attach another USB device to the chain, you might be stuck without a connector. Thankfully, USB's capability to hot plug means you can simply unplug the digital camera while your computer is still on and then plug in the other device. But, if you want to be able to use both devices at once, you'd have to use a USB hub, which is essentially like an outlet expander. You plug the hub into your computer's USB port, and it provides an additional two, four, or more USB ports for attaching other devices. Figure 10-7 shows how a USB hub increases the number of available USB ports.

USB hubs are available in powered and unpowered varieties. Unfortunately, the nonpowered varieties are often referred to as *bus-powered*, which can be very confusing. Powered hubs provide additional power at their USB ports, and unpowered, or bus-powered, hubs do not (see what I mean). In fact, as its name suggests, bus-powered hubs actually use some of the USB line's power in order to function.

Tip

As a result of the possible power problems and limitations in USB ports, I think a powered USB hub will be a required piece of equipment for many computers. Many new monitors feature a powered USB hub built into the base of the display, which can be a very handy, space-saving solution.

Secret

Unfortunately, some monitors only feature an unpowered, or bus-powered, USB hub, which may not be that useful in the long run. Be sure to check before you buy.

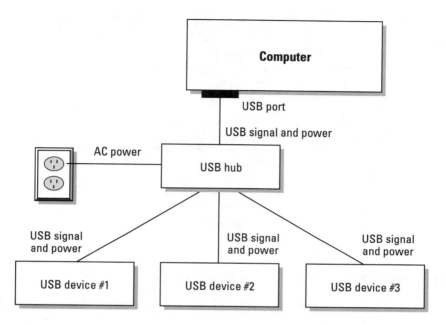

Figure 10-7: USB hubs
To get all of your USB devices attached to your PC, you may need to invest in a powered USB hub. It connects to one of your computer's USB ports and provides additional ports (and power — if it's a powered hub) for your other USB peripherals.

One handy option that some USB hubs offer is the capability to attach older serial- or parallel-port-based devices. In these cases, the hub is functioning as a serial- or parallel-to-USB converter.

Device Bay

The Device Bay specification, which defines a new type of connector and mechanism for installing internal PC peripherals, was specifically designed to make installing new hardware on your PC as easy as inserting a floppy disk or CD/DVD-ROM. PCs that support Device Bay have slots of various sizes that you can plug Device Bay-compliant devices into. Nevertheless there are still a few things to consider.

Primarily, you must be aware of the size of the device and the size of the bay you're inserting the devices into. There are three different Device Bay sizes, and not all devices can fit into all bays. The DB32 size, which is the largest one available and is found primarily in desktop computers, supports devices that are 32mm (millimeters) high. In addition, a DB32-sized bay can accept DB20- and DB13-sized devices through the use of an adapter (the same adapter works for either size device).

Logically enough, the 20mm DB20 size bay, which is found primarily in notebook computers, accepts DB20-sized devices, but cannot fit DB32 devices. It can, however, fit DB13 devices without an adapter. And yes, a DB13-sized bay can only accept DB13-sized devices (but you figured this out already, didn't you). Table 10-5 summarizes the different device and bay sizes and notes with an *x* what fits where.

Table 10-5	Device Bay Sizes		
Device Size	*DB32 Bay*	*DB20 Bay*	*DB13 Bay*
DB32	x		
DB20	x (w/adapter)	x	
DB13	x (w/adapter)	x	x

Adding Internal Hardware

The first thing to think about when it comes to internal hardware is getting past any concerns you may have about cracking open the case of your PC. It's really not that big of a deal. Most computers made these days are specifically designed so that they are easy to get into, because the manufacturers know that many people need to get into their PCs to add new plug-in cards or upgrade their RAM or hard drive.

As you would expect, opening notebooks is generally a lot more involved than trying to get into a PC. But many notebooks are starting to offer relatively easy access to their innards — that is, on machines for which this feature would have a useful purpose (some notebooks just aren't user-upgradeable).

General precautions

Of course, with any type of computer, there are a few general precautions that you want to take when installing internal hardware. First of all, the computer needs to be completely turned off (not just put into a Sleep mode).

The way to get in to a computer's case varies from machine to machine, but it usually involves unscrewing a few screws — many of which are designed to be done with your fingers and not a screwdriver — and sliding off the cover.

Before you touch anything inside the computer, you want to make sure you release any static electricity you may have built up on your hand and ground yourself to avoid possible shocks. As even young children know, rubbing your stocking feet on a carpeted floor can build up a pretty good charge that will be released as soon as you touch anything metal. If the first thing you happen to touch is a circuit board inside your PC, your finger may quickly become The Terminator because many PC components are very sensitive to static electricity and can be fried by a single zap of it.

To help avoid those kinds of problems, many plug-in cards include a grounding strap inside the box, which is a long, skinny strip of paper-like material with a metal (usually copper) band along the inside of it. What you do is wrap one end of it around one of your wrists and then attach the other end to a large metal device inside your computer — typically the PC's power supply. As silly as it may feel (and look), doing so can help you avoid static and grounding problems. See Figure 10-8 for an example of how it attaches to your wrist.

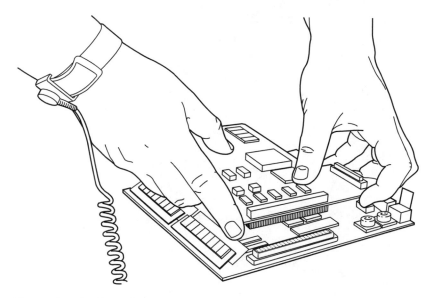

Figure 10-8: Getting grounded
A grounding strap wraps around your wrist and then typically attaches to your PC's power supply via some sticky tape or a special cable. Using one of these while installing new hardware helps prevent accidental static discharges that can quickly fry your new add-in card or even your PC's motherboard.

Tip

If you didn't get a grounding strap inside your plug-in card box, you can always buy one separately at an electronics store, such as Radio Shack. If you can't be bothered, you can at least avoid static problems by touching your computer's power supply after you open the box and right before you touch anything else inside your PC. In fact, even if you have a grounding strap on, I still suggest you touch the power supply with your hand to release any potential static electricity you have built up.

Making the connection

Once you're in and grounded, you need to figure out where the device you'll be connecting goes. Different motherboards are laid out in different ways so you'll need to check your computer's documentation to determine where the type of slot you're looking for is actually located. Figure 10-9 shows a typical motherboard with a variety of different possible slots.

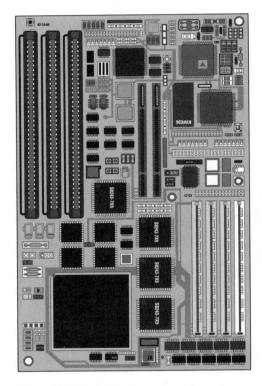

Figure 10-9: Installing an expansion card
The first step in installing a new piece of hardware inside your PC is figuring out which empty slot you plan to plug it into.

Most newer computers provide relatively easy access to expansion slots, but it's not unheard of to have to remove some existing pieces inside your PC to get to where you need to go. This is typically only an issue with memory or hard drive upgrades, but it can happen with upgrade cards as well.

Secret

Not only do you need to know where the slots for a particular type of card are, you may have to look for a specific slot number. For example, on some computers only a few of the PCI slots are capable of accepting cards that make use of a technology called PCI Bus Mastering (see Chapter 3, "Hard Disk Drives and Removable Drives," for more details). Examples of cards like this include SCSI controllers, some video capture cards, and more. So, if you're installing a card that requires PCI bus mastering capability, you'll need to confirm that the slot you're going to plug it into can support it. If it can't, you may need to rearrange your existing cards to get everything to peacefully coexist.

In addition, on some computers, the different PCI slots are hardwired to the four PCI interrupts (A-D). As a result, there are some situations where you may need to move a PCI card from one slot to another in order to make it work.

There is another issue to consider if you're installing a card that's supposed to work in conjunction with and connect to one of your existing cards: you may have to make room for the new card. For example, some 3D accelerator cards work in conjunction with your existing video card and come with a short cable that connects between the two cards' video feature connectors. In most instances those two cards must be located next to each other in order to make the connection.

Once you've determined where the card will go, you'll need to prepare the PC for installation by removing the slot cover that aligns with the particular expansion slot into which you'll be installing the card; this slot cover is found on the back of the computer. Figure 10-10 shows an example of removing a slot cover.

Tip

Now that you have your PC open, it is a good time to clean up all the dust that's inevitably connected inside. To do this, you can either use a can of compressed air or purchase a special little vacuum that's specifically designed to suck dust out of electronic equipment. I don't recommend using a larger general-purpose vacuum hose attachment because you could easily knock into and damage some of the components inside the case. If you do vacuum, make sure you do a thorough job and don't just move the dust around.

Before you install the card you may also need to rearrange some of the cables inside your PC's case. Some companies are very good about neatly tying these cables to give you easy access to your PC's guts, and others, well, let's just say they're a bit on the messy side.

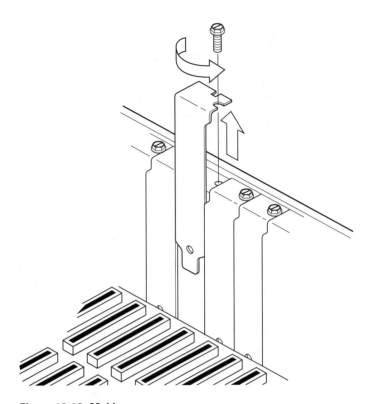

Figure 10-10: Making way
Before you can install a card inside your PC, you need to remove the slot cover. You may also need to temporarily move some of the cables inside your PC out of the way.

Caution

If you really want to, you can tie together some of the cables yourself, but I don't think it's a very good idea because many of the cables are relatively weak. And if you accidentally cut or rip a portion of a cable — which you could easily do without even realizing it — then you'll have a bear of a time down the road trying to figure out why, all of a sudden, your hard drive only seems to work intermittently or why any number of other really strange things start happening.

Once the slot is clear, the back cover is removed, your hand is grounded by touching the power supply, and you've got the card in place, all you have to do is maneuver the card's connector panel into the open hole, align the card's connector with the motherboard, and push it in. The trick is to make sure you get the card all the way seated into the slot: you'll hear a good solid thud when you hit the bottom of the connector. Don't be afraid to give it a hard push because often times this is what it takes to get the card all the way in.

In fact, one of the most common problems in installing hardware into PCs is that the card doesn't get fully seated into the connector. If you have any doubt, pull the card out and reseat it. Also, if after installing the card and restarting your computer it appears the card isn't working, it may be because the card isn't fully seated. So, before you bring it back to get a new one or call the company's tech support, try to pull it out and push it back in (after you've turned off your computer, of course).

Notebook PC Cards

Most PC Cards that plug into notebook computer PC Card slots (sometimes also called *PCMCIA* — an acronym for Personal Computer Memory Card International Association — slots) are designed to provide the equivalent of an internal expansion card in an external, credit card-sized form factor. In addition to the convenient size, this arrangement enables you to plug in any card, while your computer is running, which is similar to how Device Bay components and external USB and IEEE 1394 peripherals work.

The first time you insert a new PC Card you'll probably be asked to install the driver software (which I'll get to in just a bit), but on subsequent occasions you can plug in and remove the card at will. The computer should automatically recognize that you've installed (or removed) the card and will automatically load (or unload) drivers and any other software necessary to enable you to use the card.

Most PC Cards work without too many hitches, but there are a few points to think about. Worrying about which PC slot to a plug a card into shouldn't be one of them, however. The most common types of PC Cards are those that conform to the 5mm-thick Type II PC Card format. Any standard Type II format card will work in either the upper or lower slot on a notebook that provides two slots (as most do). You may have to check on the type of connections between your notebook's PC Card slots and the rest of the system, though.

Some PC Cards require a notebook with CardBus support. CardBus is a faster, wider version of the original PC Card bus specification. The original specification was only 16-bits wide and supported transfers up to 20Mbps, whereas the CardBus spec is 32-bits wide and supports transfers up to 132Mbps. CardBus was designed to complement PCI buses in notebooks and to enable PC Cards to have closer ties to the PCI bus. Virtually all newer notebooks support CardBus, but if you're trying to add hardware to an older notebook, you could run into some trouble if the card requires a CardBus-compatible PC Card slot (man, that's a mouthful).

Installing Drivers

The final step in completing a hardware installation—regardless of whether you add external or internal hardware to your computer—is to install the driver software, sometimes called device drivers or just drivers. All new computer hardware (except for memory and processors) needs a driver in order to communicate with the rest of your PC's components and in order for your software to be able to use it. In other words, without a driver, new hardware won't work.

As I explained in Chapter 8, "How Your Computer Works," drivers are small pieces of software that handle communications between your computer's hardware and the operating system. They handle all the dirty work of translating any application software or operating system requests—such as "draw this picture here"—into instructions your hardware can understand in order to complete the request.

When you install some pieces of hardware, such as Device Bay drives and some USB and IEEE 1394 peripherals, the process of installing the driver is done automatically, so you may not even be aware that it's happening. But don't think that means those devices don't need drivers because they definitely do—it's just that the operating system and the device are taking care of some of the work for you.

To ease the process of hardware installation and make it truly Plug and Play (where you literally attach the device and then start using it), Microsoft and many other companies have been trying to develop ways to hide certain steps from the user. As far as I'm concerned, this is a great development—anything that makes computers easier to use and upgrade is good news in my book—but it's still good to know what's really going on.

With some USB and IEEE 1394 devices, Microsoft preinstalls the drivers when you install or upgrade to Windows 98 or Windows 98 Second Edition so that the drivers are actually already on your hard disk. When you attach a device that has a driver already installed, the process simply activates the driver and enables you to start using the peripheral immediately.

With many devices, however, including some USB and IEEE 1394 peripherals, you'll be asked to install the drivers as soon as you attach the component or the first time you start up your computer after the new piece of hardware has been installed. In most cases you'll see the Add New Hardware Wizard dialog, which walks you through the process of installing the drivers from a floppy, CD, or DVD you inserted into your machine. Figure 10-11 shows Add New Hardware Wizard.

Figure 10-11: Add New Hardware Wizard
The first dialog you'll typically see once you've attached a new hardware peripheral or restarted your computer after plugging in a new hardware card is the Add New Hardware Wizard. It walks you through the simple task of inserting a disk or CD and copying the driver files from there into the appropriate location on your computer's hard disk.

Upgrading drivers

As important as drivers are for your PC, they're also notorious for causing problems. If you've spent any time trying to troubleshoot computer problems, probably the most common piece of advice you'll hear is to upgrade the drivers for this piece of hardware or that (or heck, upgrade *all* the drivers on your machine). And the truth is, upgrading your drivers can make a big difference in your computer's overall reliability and operation.

So, the question is, how do you do it? Well, the first step is to find out what driver versions you have and then find out what's available. To find out what you have, if you're running Windows, turn to your trusty friend, the Device Manager. You can open the Device Manager either by double-clicking the System Control Panel (inside the Control Panels folder) or by right-clicking the My Computer icon on your desktop and selecting Properties from the context menu that appears. (Another shortcut is to hold down the Windows Logo — if your keyboard has one — and hit the Pause/Break key.) In any case you'll be presented with a tabbed dialog box that offers information on what version of Windows 95 or 98 you have installed. The second tab at the top of the dialog box is called Device Manager. Simply click this, and you're there. Figure 10-12 shows the Device Manager.

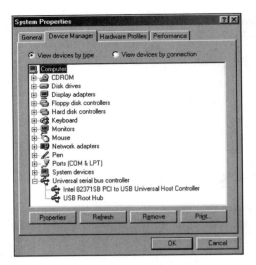

Figure 10-12: The Device Manager is your friend
The Device Manager lists all the different internal and external components attached to your computer, organized into categories, or branches. To find out more about a specific device, you simply click the plus sign next to the branch you're interested in, and all the devices in a branch will then be visible. As with Windows Explorer, you close a branch by clicking the minus sign next to an open branch.

To find out information about what driver versions you have for the various components inside of or attached to your PC, open the Device Manager, select a device category by clicking the plus sign next to the area in which you're interested, and then find the specific device you want to check on. Select it and click the Properties button, and you'll get a multitabbed dialog that offers various types of settings for the device you highlighted. One of the tabs for each device should say Driver.

Under Windows 95, the Driver tab does not provide much information. In fact, in many cases it will say "No driver files are required or have been loaded for this device" even when drivers are needed. If the Driver File Details button is not grayed out (as it often is), you can click it to find out which driver version a particular device happens to be using.

One of the many minor improvements under Windows 98 is that both the main Driver tab and the Driver File Details button include more information than is available under Windows 95. With Windows 98, you'll find things such as the driver version and a graphical map that shows where the driver files are located and shows the relation between multiple drivers if a device uses multiple device drivers (as some hardware components do). Figure 10-13 shows the Driver tab.

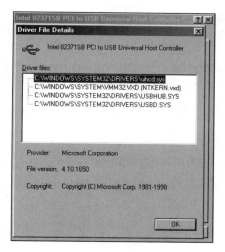

Figure 10-13: Windows 98 Driver Tab
Under Windows 98, the Driver tabs available through the Device Manager provide you with more detailed information about the driver files used by specific hardware devices.

Once you know the version numbers of the drivers for your devices, you need to find out what's available. You can do this by either visiting the Web site of the company who made your computer or — if you know the manufacturer of a specific peripheral whose driver you want to upgrade — by visiting a specific vendor's site. Many hardware vendors make the process of finding driver updates easy by providing a link from their home pages, but not all companies do, so you may have to search around a bit to find where they're hiding their latest drivers.

Secret

If you don't know who manufactured a particular component in your PC and, therefore, don't even really know what you're looking for, all is not lost. Every computer-related device available for purchase in the United States has to have a FCC (Federal Communications Commission) ID number located somewhere on the device. Conveniently, the FCC offers an online database located at www.fcc.gov/oet/fccid/ where you can enter this number and find out what company manufactured the product. It may not give you the specific model number you need, but it should give you a company name and contact information which can help you in your investigation.

If you can't find what you need at either the computer vendor or device vendor's Web site, there are also several repositories of drivers available for free download on the Internet. These Web sites can be particularly helpful for older pieces of hardware, but they're certainly worth a look for newer stuff as well. Check out WinFiles at www.winfiles.com, the Driver Zone at www.driverzone.com, WinDrivers at www.windrivers.com, and Frank Condron's World of Windows at www.conitech.com/windows.

If you find that you have the latest driver versions, then you're all set. But if it turns out a more recent version than what you have is available, you'll need to first download the file and then install it.

As described in Chapter 9, "Adding, Upgrading, and Removing Software," the act of downloading a new driver doesn't automatically install it (although sometimes it does). Typically, you'll download and then decompress the file into a particular folder and then use the Device Manager to upgrade the driver.

Cross-Reference

See Chapter 9, "Adding, Upgrading, and Removing Software," for more on downloading and decompressing files off the Internet.

Once you've got the driver file ready for use, here's how the upgrade process goes:

STEPS:

Upgrading a Driver with the Device Manager

Step 1. Open the Device Manager by double-clicking the System Control Panel and then selecting the Device Manager tab.

Step 2. Select the branch of the Device Manager that you want by clicking the plus sign next to the name of the branch.

Step 3. Click the particular device you want to upgrade from the list of devices now shown.

Step 4. Select the Properties button and then click the tab labeled Driver.

Step 5. Click the Update Driver button. The Update Device Driver Wizard will then appear to walk you through the rest of the process. Figure 10-14 shows the Update Device Driver Wizard.

Figure 10-14: Update Device Driver Wizard
Windows 95 and 98 help you through the process of finding and updating your new driver files via the Update Device Driver Wizard.

Step 6. Click *Yes* in the Update Device Driver Wizard's first dialog and you should be all set. If for some reason the Update Device Driver Wizard can't find the downloaded file, you may need to specifically tell Windows where it is. (You do remember where you stored it, don't you?)

Using the Device Manager in this fashion isn't the only way to install a driver. Some drivers come with their own installation programs that will automatically update the drivers for you, although they are relatively rare. Other files come bundled with Information (.inf) files that enable you to install the drivers by right-clicking the .inf file and selecting Install from the context menu that appears.

Cross-Reference

See Chapter 9, "Adding, Upgrading, and Removing Software" for more on installing software.

In addition, some driver downloads require you to make installation floppies before you can use them. In other words, they provide instructions on how to copy the files onto blank diskettes, which you can then use to upgrade your drivers. (In cases I've seen it involves more than just copying the files over, but it's still usually pretty easy.) These can be a bit of a pain at first because you need to find some extra blank floppies and go through the process of creating the disks. Once you're done, however, it's nice to have a backup of your drivers in a readily accessible format.

If the new drivers you download don't require you to make a floppy to install (and again, most will not), make sure you make backups of them. I recommend you back them up along with any application updates you may download. You'll need them if your hard disk ever crashes, if you upgrade to a new hard disk, or if you decide to reinstall everything from scratch.

Tip

Of course, if you have Windows 98 you may be able to avoid this whole process by simply taking advantage of the Windows Update feature off of the Start Menu. In addition to checking for fixes and other additions to Windows 98, the service is supposed to automatically download and install drivers for any devices you have on your computer. Now, the reality is that this service will only work if your computer is relatively new and if the companies who made the hardware components inside of or attached to your computer keep Microsoft up-to-date with the latest versions of their drivers. If they don't, then you'll still have to look for, download, and install updates manually as I've described previously.

Removing drivers

There are many occasions where you might want to remove drivers from your system. You may be installing a new driver update that doesn't seem to be taking, you may need to troubleshoot, or you may plan to remove and stop using a particular component in your PC (such as when you're upgrading to a better, newer version of something you already have).

Tip

One common and very effective troubleshooting technique, for example, involves removing a device's driver software, restarting the computer, and enabling Windows' Plug and Play feature to find the device again and step you through the process of reinstalling the drivers for the device. For a variety of different reasons, driver software and/or Windows Registry entries for the device can get corrupted or get into strange conflicts with other software, and clearing the slate and starting over this way often solves difficult problems.

**Cross-
Reference**

See Chapter 17, "Troubleshooting Techniques," for more on solving driver problems.

Regardless of why you want to remove the driver, the steps for doing so are very simple. Once again, most of the action takes place in the Device Manager.

STEPS:

Removing Driver Software

Step 1. Open the Device Manager by double-clicking the System Control Panel (located inside the Control Panels folder).

Step 2. Click the tab that says Device Manager (the second one over).

Step 3. Find the branch that holds the device whose driver you want to remove and, if necessary, click the plus sign next to the branch heading.

Step 4. Select the specific device you want to remove the driver for by clicking it, and then click the Remove button.

Step 5. Click OK (or hit Enter) in the Confirm Device Removal dialog that appears, and you're done. See Figure 10-15 to see the Confirm Device Removal dialog box.

Figure 10-15: Removing a device
When you choose to remove a piece of hardware via the Device Manager — a process called *logically* removing the device — you delete both the driver software for the device, as well as any Registry entries associated with it.

The process of removing driver software in this way is often called *logically* removing a device because even though it may still physically exist inside your computer, the operating system doesn't know that it's there and can't communicate with it; hence, it has been logically removed from the system. This process removes both the driver software and any references to the device in the Windows Registry, which also keeps track of all the hardware connected to your computer.

Secret

In fact, it's the Registry entries that determine what devices are displayed in the Device Manager. In other words, like most of the Windows 95 and 98 control panels, the Device Manager is essentially a user-friendly Registry editor that enables you to adjust certain portions of the Windows Registry.

This can be important to know if you come across a situation where a device you've previously installed suddenly isn't showing up inside the Device Manager or you find that the information about a particular device isn't correct. This could mean that there's a problem with the portion of the Registry that maintains that data.

Although I don't generally recommend it, you can also remove driver software directly by finding the driver files inside the Windows folder — which is where they usually reside — and deleting them. (See the sidebar "Where do all the drivers go," for more on where drivers are stored on your PC.) In some extreme situations, where deleting drivers in the normal fashion doesn't work, this may be necessary. Be aware, however, that deleting drivers in this way will not delete the Registry entries for the device as removing a device via the Device Manager does.

Where do all the drivers go?

Most drivers reside in various places inside the Windows folder. Some of them live in the main Windows directory, but many of them reside inside the Windows/System folder or in some of the subdirectories inside this folder, such as *Iosubsys* or *VMM32*.

Iosubsys is short for Input/Output subsystem and it holds drivers that are involved with bringing data into or out of your computer. This includes things such as drivers for hard drives; removable drives; SCSI, USB, and IEEE 1394 controllers; network cards; and more.

VMM32 stands for Virtual Machine Manager 32-bit, and it refers to Window's capability to run multiple applications at once — a technique known as multitasking — and treat each one as if they were running separately on their own virtual computer or virtual machine. In other words, Windows essentially tricks each application into thinking that they have complete access to the entire computer and all its resources, even though those resources are really being shared among all the applications.

Continued

(continued)

In order to do this, Windows needs to use virtual device drivers (vxds) so that each application can think that it's having a separate conversation with each of the different components inside the virtual machine. So, for example, a virtual display driver (vdd) that controls your video card acts as if multiple copies of itself were running at once and each one was communicating individually with each application. In reality, only a single copy of the driver is active, but the fact that the driver is virtual enables it to virtualize itself and act as if it were multiple copies. Figure 10-16 shows how the Virtual Machine Manager works.

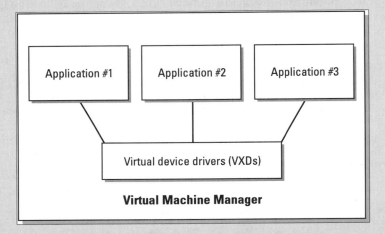

Virtual machines

Windows 95's and 98's capability to run multiple applications at once is enabled, in part, by the 32-bit Virtual Machine Manager (VMM32) that's part of the operating system. The VMM32, in turn, controls all the various virtual device drivers (vxds) that communicate with the individual pieces of hardware inside of or attached to your computer.

The VMM32 file — which itself is a virtual device driver — acts as a master driver and initializes and loads as a group all the individual drivers that are stored inside the VMM32 folder and in other places inside the Windows/System folder. The only problem is if one of the drivers inside the group is corrupted and/or missing, then VMM32 can't start up properly. And if VMM32 doesn't work, your computer won't boot, because the Virtual Machine Manager is at the core of how Windows operates.

**Cross-
Reference**

If you come across VMM32-related problems, see Chapter 18, "Solving Common PC Problems," for more.

Removing Hardware

As with many things in life, taking hardware out of or detaching it from your computer is a lot easier than installing it. If it's an external peripheral, just detach it from your system and remove references to the device in the Device Manager by following the steps listed previously in the section "Removing Driver Software".

Tip

Don't forget to do this last step because if you don't remove a device's drivers and Registry entries via the Device Manager, it can cause software conflicts and other types of problems down the road.

If the device attaches via your USB or IEEE 1394 ports or installs via your Device Bay (if your computer has one), you can do this all while the system is still on and plugged in. If it's a serial, parallel, SCSI, or other type of device, then you'll need to turn your computer off first. (In most cases, an OnNow-enabled Sleep mode is not good enough—you need to make sure the computer is completely off.)

**Cross-
Reference**

See Chapter 7, "Input Devices and Power," for more on OnNow and power management.

Also note that if you're disconnecting a SCSI device you may need to adjust your termination on the SCSI chain. If the device you're removing is in the middle of a chain of SCSI devices, then there should be no problem; however, if it's at the end, then you will have to make sure that whatever device is now at the end of the chain is properly terminated. To terminate this device, you either turn on its own built-in termination, add a terminator to it, or verify that its automatic termination is working properly.

The process for removing internal hardware is conceptually similar to that for external hardware, but it's a bit more involved because of the need to get into your PC's case. First, remove the device's drivers and Registry entries by removing it from the Device Manager (see the section "Removing drivers" earlier in this chapter for step-by-step instructions.) Then you can move on to the physical removal of the device.

As when you install internal hardware, you need to completely shut down the machine and open the case to find what you intend to remove. If possible, use a grounding strap to remove any static electricity from your hand and to avoid possible shock problems (see the section "Adding Internal Hardware" earlier in the chapter for more). At the very least, make sure you touch the computer's power supply to release any static electricity you may have built up before you touch any of the computer's internal components.

If the card is attached to the back plane of the computer via a screw, make sure you take the screw out first. Once you've done this, pull the card out, being careful not to bang into any other cards in the process. Sometimes getting cards out takes a good bit of force, by the way, so don't be afraid to give it a good tug.

When the card is successfully removed, replace the back plate on the computer's case if you're not planning to put another card into the same slot. (You did keep it, didn't you?) If you don't have a back plate, you can either buy one from a computer parts store, or just use some tape to block up the hole. I wouldn't leave it open because it's a great way for a lot of dust to get inside and potentially mess up the rest of your PC.

Once the slot is closed, you should turn your machine back on and make sure everything still works right. If it doesn't, you may have accidentally damaged a cable or other component inside your PC during the hardware removal process, so open the machine back up and look for damage. Unfortunately, not all damage is visible so if you suddenly have a machine that won't work, you may need to take it to a shop to have various components tested.

If everything does work, then your mission is accomplished. Congratulations!

Summary

In this chapter, I described how to add internal and external hardware to and remove internal and external hardware from your computer.

▶ Before you can install any hardware on your system, you need to make sure the computer has the appropriate connectors and any resources that may be necessary for the device to work.

▶ If you don't have the right kind of connector, you can often add it to your system via a controller or via special adapter hardware or cables.

▶ Adding external hardware often involves simply attaching the device to the appropriate connector on your PC, although there are some special considerations for certain types of connections.

▶ Adding internal hardware to your computer isn't very hard, but you do need to take extra precautions to avoid potential problems.

▶ If at all possible, you should use a grounding strap when you're adding (or removing) internal components to (or from) your computer.

▶ No hardware installation is complete without installing device driver software, which enables your new peripheral to communicate with the operating system and through that to other components inside your PC.

▶ One common way to solve problems on your computer is to upgrade the driver software for a particular device (or devices). Under Windows, you can upgrade, as well as remove, drivers via the Device Manager.

▶ Removing hardware from your computer requires you to physically disconnect and/or remove the peripheral from your PC and logically remove its driver software and Registry entries via Window's Device Manager.

Chapter 11

Upgrading Your PC

In This Chapter

▶ You will learn whether a computer is worth upgrading or not.

▶ You will learn how to install RAM into your computer.

▶ You will learn how to add a new or upgrade your existing hard drive.

▶ You will learn how to upgrade your CD or DVD drive.

▶ You will learn how to upgrade your computer's BIOS.

▶ You will learn how to upgrade expansion cards and other peripherals.

▶ You will learn how to upgrade your computer's processor.

▶ You will learn how to replace your entire motherboard.

Once you've had a computer for a while, you're bound to get itchy to make it better. Just a little more performance here, a little more room there, you keep telling yourself, and all will be well in your computing world. And the truth is, sometimes a few technical nips and tucks can make a real difference.

You may also find yourself running into real barriers that keep you from using some new software or hardware you've just purchased or from completing a project on which you've started. In those cases, upgrading your computer isn't elective surgery, it's more like a lifesaving operation.

Regardless of the reason, most computer users eventually find themselves entering the world of computer upgrades, where they try to stretch their computer's capabilities as far as they can. The great thing about upgrades is that they can bring new life to your existing computer — whether it's several years or only several months old.

Inevitably, though, a certain group of people approach the idea of messing with their computer's guts with as much trepidation as facing a major medical procedure. But the reality is, armed with the right information, it's more like simple first aid. The content of this chapter will give you the instructions you need to upgrade several different components inside your PC, including the motherboard.

Before you get your hands dirty, however, you first need to decide if upgrading is the right thing to do.

To Upgrade or Not to Upgrade, That Is the Question

Well, okay, it may not carry the weight of Shakespearean drama, but deciding whether you should upgrade your computer or simply get a new one is still a tough question. The problem is made even more difficult by the fact that there are so many good computers available for such low prices. In the recent past, upgrade decisions were much easier. New systems tended to cost much more than individual pieces, and you could make a good argument for upgrading several pieces of an existing PC.

With the phenomenal growth of sub-$1,000 and even sub-$500 computers, and the general lowering of computer system prices in general, it's getting much easier to justify simply purchasing a new computer. Then you can hand the second one over to the kids, another family member, a school, or a church or any other charitable organization. A new computer not only gives you better performance and/or capabilities in the particular area you were thinking about upgrading, it also usually provides better performance in many of different areas. In addition, you'll usually also get support for the latest technologies, such as IEEE 1394 and Device Bay, for example.

Cross-Reference

If you decide you want a new computer, the seven chapters found in Part I of this book — called "Buying a New PC" — have everything you need to know and more.

In fact, from a purely economic perspective, it's getting harder and harder to justify anything but simple upgrades (such as RAM, a hard drive, a CD-ROM or DVD-ROM drive, or a 3D video card for playing games) for most computers. Ultimately, you'll have to decide for yourself if you want to invest in something such as a processor upgrade, or several new plug-in cards. There's no hard and fast rule or simple equation that says you should only spend x number of dollars on upgrading your existing computer. But given today's computer prices, I don't think spending much more than $400–$500 to upgrade your existing machine makes very much economic sense.

Of course, there are many good reasons besides economic ones to upgrade your computer. First of all, some upgrades are necessary in order for your computer to be able to use new peripherals that you may purchase. For example, BIOS upgrades are often required in order to use large hard drives and USB-based keyboards and mice with your PC. In addition, many computers need BIOS upgrades into order to get around the Year 2000 (Y2K) problem.

Cross-Reference

See the "Upgrading Your BIOS" section later in this chapter for more on the issues and benefits involved with BIOS updates.

Second, it's kind of fun to add some new capabilities to your existing machine. PC hobbyists, in particular, get a real kick out of enhancing existing machines or even building new ones from pieces.

Finally, if you're interested in learning more about how your computer works, there's nothing like cracking open your computer's case and making some changes. Admittedly, this can lead to big problems if you're not sure what you're doing, but as long as you've got some basic information and are careful, it's really not that big of a deal.

There's no reason we should view computers as mysterious, unfathomable devices. In fact, I think falling into the trap of believing that computers are too hard to figure out is dangerous. As computers continue to become more embedded into everyone's lives, it's going to be increasingly important to know at least a little about how they work; otherwise, it will be easy to be fooled or misled by people who can take advantage of people's lack of knowledge. (I'll get off my soapbox now.)

Adding Memory

The most common, most often recommended and most useful upgrade you can make to nearly any computer is adding more memory. Adding RAM is a straightforward process that increases your computer's working area, letting it do more things more efficiently.

The only trick with memory upgrades is to find out the speed, type, and size of the memory your system uses. You should be able to find this information in your computer's manual or from the computer vendor's web site or tech support (that is, if you, ahem, accidentally threw away or lost the manual.)

As an example, many computers use 100MHz SDRAM in DIMM format — in other words, the memory type is Synchronous DRAM (SDRAM), it works in systems with 100MHz system buses, and the physical format is a 168-pin Dual Inline Memory Module (DIMM).

On older systems, you might find that you need 72-pin, 60 nanosecond (ns), EDO RAM SIMMs (sometimes the specs are listed in a different order). This means you need Extended Data Out (EDO) RAM, rated at a speed of 60ns in 72-pin SIMM format. Newer machines, on the other hand, may use RDRAM (Rambus DRAM) RIMMs.

Some notebook computers use proprietary memory types which you can only get from a limited number of memory manufacturers or from the computer vendor itself, but many others use the standard SO DIMM (Small Outline DIMM) format.

**Cross-
Reference**

For more on various memory types and memory specifications, see Chapter 2, "Microprocessors and Memory."

Once you've determined what you need, you also need to find out how many slots your computer system has available. Many computers that use SIMMs have four SIMM slots on their motherboards, organized into two banks of two. Many system with DIMMs and RIMMs have three slots, each of which is addressed and used individually.

In general, SIMMs must be installed in matching pairs (such as two 16MB SIMMs or two 32MB SIMMs, and so on), which is why they're organized into banks of two — typically labeled Bank A and Bank B or 0 and 1. The only exception is 486-based systems or earlier, which can support one SIMM at a time. DIMMs and the newer RIMMs (used on computers that support Direct RAMBus), on the other hand, can be added individually. In other words, three DIMM slots are actually more flexible than four SIMM slots (and if you've got four or more DIMM slots, well, hey, that's even better).

Most new computers are shipped with at least one bank of SIMMs or one DIMM or RIMM slot available, so if you've never upgraded a new machine, then you can generally feel confident that there's room to upgrade. (If and when you buy a new computer, make sure the vendor uses a smaller number of higher capacity memory modules — such as two 32MB modules instead of four 16MB modules — so that you can easily upgrade in the future.) The only way to really tell what kind of memory expansion room your system has, however, is to open the computer and see what's already installed.

Secret

One way you may be able to tell whether or not you have open RAM slots available without having to open the case is by running your BIOS Setup program the next time your computer starts. Many Setup programs have screens that display what type of memory (if any) is installed in a particular bank, DIMM, or RIMM slot.

Opening the case

Before you can actually install memory or perform most other upgrades, you need to open your computer's case. For most desktop systems, it's simply a matter of removing a screw or two and then sliding off the case's cover. Some notebooks have special panels that provide easy access to slots where memory can be added, but others don't. In some instances, you may even need to have an authorized service center install memory into notebooks because the manufacturer didn't provide any easy access to their innards. (Of course, you'll remember to avoid this problem in your *next* notebook.) Note that with some notebooks, opening the case may void the warranty.

Caution

Before you touch anything inside your computer's case, you should ground yourself to avoid static problems. The best solution is to use a grounding strap, but another easy way to do it is to simply touch your PC's power supply or any other metal part of the PC's case. If you don't perform either of these options, you can accidentally fry a particular component inside your PC or even the entire motherboard with a zap of static electricity. So, be careful. At the same time, don't get paranoid. Touching or moving any of the various cables filling up the inside of your computer's case, for example, will generally not cause any problems. Just use good judgement, and you should be fine.

Cross-Reference

See Chapter 10, "Adding and Removing Hardware," for more on grounding issues.

The first step in the installation process is to find the memory slots and see how many are empty. The location of memory varies from computer to computer and motherboard to motherboard, but your computer's documentation should have a graphic that shows you where to look. Figure 11-1 displays a typical system with DIMM slots.

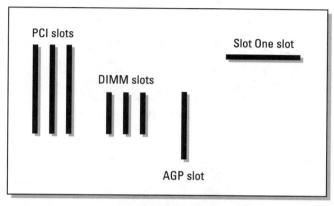

PCI slots

Slot One slot

DIMM slots

AGP slot

Motherboard

Figure 11-1: Finding the slots
Before you can install your new memory, you need to find out where your computer's SIMM, DIMM, or RIMM slots are. On this system, the three DIMM slots are located towards the middle of the motherboard.

On some systems, the RAM slots are actually hidden underneath hard drives or other components. If your computer fits into this category, you've got your work cut out for you because you'll first have to remove those components — or at least partially disconnect them — before you can do anything. If you do end up removing any cables or other devices, add a simple masking tape label to each one with matching numbers or letters on them, so you know where to return them when you put your system back together. The extra two minutes this takes is well worth the effort, so don't forget!

Thankfully, very few systems have this type of user-hostile design, but be aware that some do, so if you can't easily find the location of memory modules, it may be because they're hidden behind something else inside your PC.

Each of the different types of memory is physically different so the installation procedures for each type varies slightly. Figure 11-2 shows the three main types of desktop memory (SIMMs, DIMMs, and RIMMs) and their different connectors.

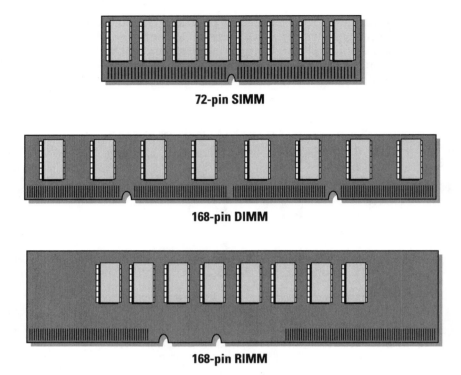

72-pin SIMM

168-pin DIMM

168-pin RIMM

Figure 11-2: Memory types
You can tell which type of memory your computer uses by simply looking at the different connectors. Some systems include two different types of connectors, but they generally only enable you to use one type of memory at a time. You'll typically need to make this choice in the computer's BIOS Setup program.

Installing

Regardless of the type of memory you're installing, they all have some kind of notch on the memory module that helps you put them in the right way. With SIMMs, you need to bring the module in on an angle, line up the notch with the corresponding slot on the motherboard, put the module into the connector, and move it upwards into position. See Figure 11-3 for suggestions on installing SIMMs.

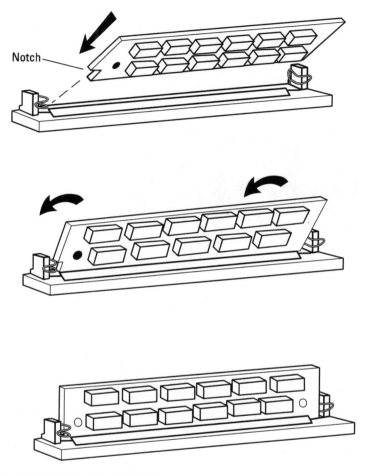

Figure 11-3: Installing SIMMs
The trick with SIMMs is to come in at about a 45-degree angle, make the initial connection, and pop them into position.

SIMMs are held in place by little metal tabs on either side of the module, and if you perform the installation properly, those little tabs will connect into matching holes on the side of the memory module. In addition, you should feel a good solid thunk when you lift the module into position. If the tabs and holes don't line up, then the memory isn't seated properly into the connector, and you'll need to remove it and try again. To remove a SIMM, you need to slightly pry apart those little metal tabs with your fingers — I can tell you from experience this it isn't always easy — and then pull the module out. DIMMs and RIMMs are easier to install because they have simple latches on either side of the connector that you lift into place once you've lined the memory up and pushed it straight down into its slot. Figure 11-4 shows an example of installing DIMMs and RIMMs.

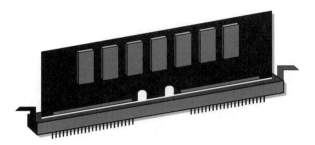

Figure 11-4: Installing DIMMs and RIMMs
With DIMMs and RIMMs, you simply put the memory module into place — being careful to align the notch on the module with the connector on the motherboard — and then lift the little latches on either side of the memory connector.

To remove DIMMs and RIMMs, simply release the latches and pull the module out.

Secret

One difference between DIMMS and RIMMs is that RIMM-based systems cannot have any empty slots — instead they include devices called continuity modules that need to be placed in slots that are not filled by RIMMs.

Reconfiguring

If you open your computer to upgrade its memory and you find that all the memory slots are full, all is not lost. You'll simply need to pull out the smallest existing SIMMs, DIMMs, or RIMMs to make room for your new ones. Unfortunately, determining which ones are the smallest is not very easy (unless you specifically know what size the memory modules are in each slot).

To determine the size of the memory modules, there are some markings on each memory chip that may give you a hint of their capacity, but generally they don't. You can use the BIOS Update tip I mentioned earlier to see how much memory is in each bank, DIMM, or RIMM slot; however, for this to work, you'll need to know which bank or slot is which. Again, you can use the documentation or decipher some small letters on the motherboard itself that are used to label each of the banks or slots.

If this still doesn't work, you can simply remove the memory a bank or module at a time, restart your computer (you can do it with the case off) and watch your startup screen to see how much memory the system has after your removal. (Be careful not to touch anything inside the PC when it's turned on.) Eventually you'll figure out which memory to leave in and which to take out.

Testing the memory

To confirm that you've installed the memory successfully, restart your computer and watch the memory counter that generally appears right after the first BIOS message. You should see the counter go up to the correct number of bytes (remembering that 1MB equals 1,024 Kbytes — so, for example, 64MB shows up as 65,536 Kbytes, and so on) and then continue on with the boot-up process.

Once it boots, shut the computer down, put the case back on (that is, unless you'll also be performing other upgrades), and you're done. Congratulations!

If the memory counter doesn't match what you expect, some of the modules may not be properly seated or they may be in the wrong bank. On most computer systems you add the memory to the slots in order, but some machines use memory slot 1 and 3 for Bank A, for example, and memory slot 2 and 4 for Bank B. In this case, you may have to rearrange the different SIMMs. Again, check your computer or motherboard's documentation to be verify what memory slots should be used in what order.

Also remember that if you are installing SIMMs on a Pentium-level machine or better, they need to be installed in matching pairs. You can't typically add an 8 and a 16MB module when you perform an upgrade with SIMMs. Another common problem is mismatching access speeds. You might run into problems if you try to install a 60ns and 70ns module into a single bank or if you try to install 70ns modules into a computer that requires 60ns. You can also run into problems matching parity or ECC (Error Correcting Code) memory with nonparity or non-ECC memory. In some cases you can override this in the BIOS, but in other cases you cannot.

Cross-Reference

See Chapter 2, "Microprocessors and Memory," for more on parity and ECC memory.

Finally, if you're still having problems and you've double- and triple-checked the type of memory you have (and need), as well as tried moving both the existing and new memory around into different slots to see if it's a connection problem, you could just have bad or incompatible memory. Some computers are very finicky about what type of memory is used inside them and, in addition, it's not unheard of to come across memory that just doesn't work.

Adding a New Hard Drive

Another common upgrade for many computer users is to buy and install a bigger, faster hard drive — either to use in place of or in conjunction with their existing drive. In addition, many computer users are adding removable storage drives, such as Iomega Jaz or recordable CD or DVD drives, which install in a similar manner to regular, fixed hard drives.

Adding a new hard drive is typically more complicated than adding RAM because not only do you have to do the physical installation, you often need to some simple configurations, re-install your operating system and applications, and copy over the files from your existing drive. But it's not as hard as it sounds and it's a great do-it-yourself project.

The first step in this process is to decide on what type of interface, or connection type, you plan to use for your upgraded drives. The most popular choice is IDE, sometimes also called EIDE, drives, but some users prefer SCSI for some applications. In addition, hard drives that attach to IEEE 1394 controllers are becoming available, so now there are three choices.

Cross-Reference

See Chapter 3, "Hard Disks and Removable Drives," for more on these different interfaces.

More than likely the type of controllers you have built into your PC will determine the choice of interface. This is because you need a controller for your hard disk or removable drive to communicate with the rest of your computer. Because most all computers come with built-in IDE controllers, most users opt for IDE drives, but some machines incorporate SCSI controllers, and a few newer machines even have built-in IEEE 1394 controllers on the motherboard. If you want, you can also add separate SCSI or IEEE 1394 controllers to your system and then attach your new drive to this controller.

In addition to interface type, you may have to decide on the dimensions of your drive. Most desktop systems can fit either 3 ½-inch or 5 ¼-inch drives (measured across the front of the drive), but some can only fit the smaller 3 ½-inch size, so check your computer's documentation.

If your notebook's drive can be upgraded, then you'll need a 2-inch or smaller drive. Note that not all notebooks have user-upgradeable hard drives — you may have to send it to the vendor or bring it to a service technician. Also, some notebooks come with removable hard drives that fit into proprietary drive bays, so the only way to get a new hard drive in those types of systems is typically through the manufacturer.

Along similar lines, removable drives for both notebooks and desktops are starting to become available in the standard Device Bay format, which makes adding a new drive to your system as easy as loading a floppy. You may pay a bit for the privilege and ease of use, but in many situations it'll probably be worth it. Remember that there are three different Device Bay sizes, so if you have a notebook you'll need to make sure the device comes in DB20 or DB13 format.

See Chapter 10, "Adding and Removing Hardware," for more on Device Bay.

Configuring drive settings

Depending on the type of interface you use with your hard drive, you may also have to deal with a few other factors. For IDE/EIDE drives, you'll have to determine whether you want the drive to be a master or slave device on the primary or secondary IDE channel. If the new drive will become your primary hard drive, it needs to be the master device on your primary channel.

Most new hard drives come preconfigured to be master, but if you're installing a removable drive, you may want it to be a slave. If you're keeping your original hard drive, you can either switch it over to be a slave on the first IDE channel or make it a master on the secondary channel. To move it to the second channel, you'll need to disconnect the cable it's currently attached to and switch to the other IDE cable.

With some computer systems, the speed of each IDE channel is actually determined by the slowest device on the channel, while in others each device is handled independently. Some computers enable you to turn this feature — which is sometimes called independent device timing — on and off in the BIOS Setup program. If your computer fits into the former category and your old drive is relatively slow, you may want to disconnect it and move it onto the secondary IDE channel with your CD-ROM or DVD-ROM drive where the performance doesn't matter as much.

Changing from master to slave typically involves removing or adding a few tiny plastic pieces called jumpers that make or break certain connections inside the drive's electronics. Check the drive's documentation or the manufacturer's web site for specifics on how to do this. On some drives you adjust tiny DIP switches instead. Remember also that computers with IDE controllers can only support a maximum of four IDE/EIDE devices.

If you're installing a SCSI drive, you need to deal with termination and device ID issues. Essentially, each SCSI device needs to have its own unique ID number and both ends of a SCSI chain need to be terminated (but everything in the middle needs to be unterminated). Both of those settings are typically made with jumpers or other small switches on the back of SCSI devices.

See Chapter 3, "Hard Disks and Removable Drives," for more on SCSI.

IEEE 1394–based drives typically don't require any configuration whatsoever, other than installing a driver, which is yet another benefit of this newer interface.

Connecting the cables

Once you've decided on the drive type and other specifications, it's time to install. Unless it's a Device Bay drive (you have an open, externally accessible drive bay, which is different), you'll have to open your case and find a place for the drive. As explained in the previous section on adding RAM, be careful to avoid static electricity problems.

Most computers come with specific drive bays that are designed to hold additional hard drives and removable drives. One important difference between the two, of course, is that removable drives have to be located so that you can get access to the drive's opening, whereas fixed hard drives can be buried in other locations inside your PC's case. However, most PCs are designed so that even fixed drives should go into these bays, which include removable panels on the case's front panel or bezel. See Figure 11-5 for a look at how drive bays fit into a typical PC.

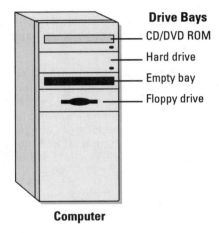

Figure 11-5: Drive bays
Most PCs enable you to easily add both fixed and removable drives via front accessible drive bays. You'll need to remove the panel — often times from the inside — in order to get the drive in.

If you're just replacing your old hard drive, I would recommend you put the new drive into the same position the old one occupied — just make sure you get the same-sized drive. If your old drive is really tiny or really slow, however, you might as well keep the original for backup and/or additional storage space.

In the case of removable drives, you'll obviously need to remove the panel on the PC's case in order to be able to get to the drive. With fixed hard drives, you'll commonly keep the panel on after the installation is complete. Some drives come with alternate case plates that include an indicator light that shows you when the hard drive is being accessed.

Tip

If your new drive doesn't come with an indicator or activity light, and you plan on keeping both drives, you may want to put the new drive where the old one is currently located and move the old one into one of the drive bays. The reason for this is it's very important to have an indicator light on your primary drive in case you ever need to troubleshoot any drive-related problems, and virtually all computers come with an indicator light for this primary drive.

If one of the drive's locations doesn't have an indicator light and you're really ambitious, you could check to see if your drive has an indicator light connector (most do) and go to a computer parts or supply store and buy a separate front panel plate with an indicator light. The problem here may be getting it to match your case's color and style.

Once you've determined where the drive will go, you need to connect it to a power connector and the appropriate data cable. Most computers come with several extra power cables inside the case. As Figure 11-6 shows, the power connector is usually a *D*-shaped, 4-pin plug.

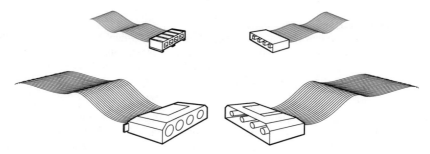

Figure 11-6: Give me juice
The power connectors inside most desktops are *D*-shaped. In most cases they are covered with little plastic covers that you'll need to remove before use.

If you can't find any available power connectors, you can purchase a Y-cable that splits the power line from another connector into two. Simply disconnect the power connector from your original hard drive or other internal component, plug in the Y-cable, and then plug one of the Y-cable connectors back into the device from which you took the power cable and the other Y-cable connector into the new drive.

Once the power's connected, you'll need to connect the appropriate data cable from your controller — which, in many cases, is built into the motherboard itself. Figure 11-7 shows what the different connectors look like.

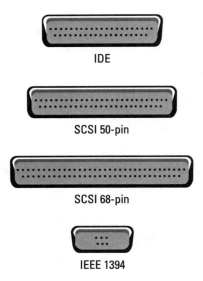

IDE

SCSI 50-pin

SCSI 68-pin

IEEE 1394

Figure 11-7: Hard drive connections
Different interfaces use different types of connectors. IDE/EIDE connectors typically feature 40 pins (although ATA/66 drives can also have 80 pins), most SCSI connectors have either 50 or 68 pins (although some Ultra2 SCSI devices use a different 80-pin connector), and the new IEEE 1394 controllers use only 6 pins.

You'll connect the drive to the controller via a ribbon cable, which is a thin, wide, typically gray connector. On machines with IDE controllers built-in, you'll find the cables and unused connectors — which are often located in the middle of the cable — inside the computer's case. (You may find a similar situation on machines that feature IEEE 1394 controllers built into the motherboard.) Simply connect any matching open connector to the back of the drive, being careful to line up the drive's Pin 1 to the appropriate side of the cable.

Many IDE cables feature a red or pink stripe along the cable where Pin 1 should be attached, and most drives put Pin 1 closest to the power connector on the drive. Plug the side of the cable with colored stripe near where the power connector is — that is, unless Pin 1 is clearly labeled on the other side. If you accidentally plug it in the wrong way, the drive just won't work. So, if you restart and the drive doesn't show up (after making any necessary BIOS settings — as explained in the next section), you may need to turn the cable around and connect the drive again.

If you added a SCSI or IEEE 1394 controller to your machine, or they were preinstalled in the form of plug-in cards, you'll generally need to attach a separate cable from the controller to the drive. If you already have other SCSI or IEEE 1394 devices attached to the controllers, you can attach the new drive to the other device's pass-through connector.

Note

In some cases, drives will come with the appropriate cables, but in others they won't, so try and find out *before* you come home from the store. Otherwise you'll have to go back and buy one.

The last step in the physical installation is to screw the drive into position so that it doesn't slide around. As you would expect, the drive's label should go up when positioning it inside the case — unless the drive is mounted vertically inside the case, in which case it doesn't really matter which way it faces. Most drives come with standard screw holes and tiny screws that you can use for mounting purposes. If not, you can add them to the list of things you need to go back to the computer store for.

If you're trying to install a 3½-inch drive into a 5¼-inch drive bay, you'll also have to deal with drive brackets, which act as adapters. You attach the drive to the brackets and the brackets to the PC's case. Again, if you know you're going to need brackets, check to see if the drive comes with some (many do) or add them to your shopping list.

BIOS settings

If you're adding an IDE/EIDE drive, the next step in the process is to change your computer's BIOS settings in the BIOS Setup program so that it can recognize the new drive you've installed. Some newer BIOSes can do this automatically, without you having to do anything, but most still require you to make a few adjustments.

To make the changes, restart your computer, hit the key your computer display tells you to, in order to enter your computer's Setup — or sometimes BIOS or CMOS Setup — program. The specific key varies from computer to computer — in some cases it's F2, in others Delete, and so on.

Tip

On some PCs that show a graphic logo when you turn them on, you'll first need to hit the Esc key before you can see any messages about how to enter the Setup program.

Once you're in the BIOS Setup program you may need to look for a hard drive parameters page, although you might find what you need in the program's first screen. The basic issue here is that you need to enable the devices you've attached, which tells the computer they're there, and you have to set (or at least confirm) certain parameters to ensure that communications between the drive and the rest of the computer function properly.

On most computers and with most IDE devices, all you need to do is enable the particular port (master or slave on the primary or secondary channel) and set it to be auto configured. What happens in this case is the IDE controller basically asks who's connected and the attached device responds with what it is and what its parameters are. In 99.9 percent of all cases, this should work fine. If you're dealing with a really old computer or IDE device, however, you may have to manually set the number of Cylinders, Heads, and Sectors (CHS) the drive has in order to ensure proper communications (and avoid corrupted data). To get this CHS information, you'll need to check the device's documentation or contact the manufacturer of the drive.

Testing the connection

If everything's configured properly, the next time you start your computer you should see a listing of attached IDE devices that includes the new device you installed. (Unfortunately, most but not quite all BIOSes display attached IDE devices during the boot process, so if you don't see anything listed it may be because of a limitation in the BIOS and not a problem with the installation. In this event, you'll probably need to reenter Setup to confirm that everything is working properly.) If the drive you just installed is not listed, you should turn off the computer, double- and triple-check the power and data cable connections, and recheck the settings in the BIOS Setup program. This should fix it. If it doesn't, I would suspect a problem with the drive itself, and I would bring it back to where you purchased it.

If you're adding a SCSI or IEEE 1394-based drive, you generally don't need to do any configuration after the physical installation — although you'll need to partition and format it before you can use it or boot from it, as explained in the next section, "Partitioning, formatting, and copying software." With SCSI drives, you'll know the connection is working properly if right after the message about your SCSI adapter you see the new drive and its ID number listed along with all of the other SCSI devices attached to your SCSI controller.

Tip

If you don't see your new device show up, then there's a problem somewhere on the SCSI chain. Turn the computer off, unplug and replug the drive's power and data connections, double-check for SCSI ID conflicts or termination problems, and try it again. I temporarily solved one particularly troublesome SCSI recognition problem by wiggling the cable connection a bit and restarting a few times. It wasn't exactly a scientifically rigorous troubleshooting technique, but hey, it worked. (The final solution was a better SCSI cable.) In some cases, simply reordering the devices in the chain can solve other types of SCSI problems.

In a few rare instances with SCSI drives you may need to enter the SCSI BIOS's setup program to make a few minor alterations to the SCSI controller's basic parameters. As with the computer's main BIOS, you'll need to hold down a set of keys at a certain point in the computer's boot process to get into the SCSI BIOS Setup program (popular SCSI controller manufacturer Adaptec calls their BIOS settings program SCSI Select). After the initial computer BIOS message you should see a message about your SCSI BIOS (as long as you have a SCSI controller, of course) and a set of keys you need to hold down to enter it. In many cases, it's Ctrl-A, which means to hold down both Control and A simultaneously.

Secret

Some newer SCSI drives that support the SCSI Plug and Play or SCAM (SCSI Configuration Automatically) standard will automatically configure their SCSI ID if you enable the SCAM setting in the SCSI adapter's BIOS. In addition, controllers and drives that support the new Ultra2 SCSI standard can even be hot-plugged — which means they can be plugged into the SCSI chain while the computer is on. Unless you're sure your SCSI controller and drive support the SCAM standard, however, I wouldn't recommend that you try this because it could (theoretically, at least) cause a problem with some SCSI devices.

Partitioning, formatting, and copying software

Once the drive is properly installed, you may need to prepare it for use by partitioning and formatting the new disk. Many new drives come already partitioned and formatted. In some cases, however, and almost always if you're using an alternative operating systems (such as Linux), you'll have to partition and format the drive yourself. If you are using something other than Windows, you'll need a program that can create the right kinds of partitions for the operating system you plan to install.

Cross-Reference

See the "Using Multiple Operating Systems" section in Chapter 9, "Adding, Upgrading, and Removing Software," for more on the partition requirements of different operating systems.

To partition a disk for use under Windows 95 or 98, you use the DOS-based FDISK program bundled with Windows or any utilities that may have come with the drive. Formatting is done via either the DOS Format program or the Windows Format command (found under Windows Explorer). Formatting differs from partitioning because partitioning organizes the drive into one or more usable sections and formatting prepares each of those sections for use.

Cross-Reference

See Chapter 3, "Hard Disks and Removable Drives," for more on partitioning.

If you're installing a removable storage drive, all you have to do is format (and possibly partition) an individual piece of media, such as a Jaz cartridge.

STEPS:

Preparing a New Hard Drive For Use

Step 1. Physically install the new drive as explained previously and, if it's an IDE drive, confirm that it is the master drive on the primary IDE channel.

Step 2. Restart the computer with a boot floppy disk that includes a CD-ROM driver. (If you're using Windows 95, see the "Troubleshooting Tools" section of Chapter 17 for instructions on how to create this disk. If you're using Windows 98, the standard Windows 98 boot floppy disk should work.)

Step 3. Once you reach the A:> prompt, type

```
FDISK [Enter]
```

This starts the DOS FDISK utility and lets you set the number and type of partitions (FAT 16 or FAT 32) that you want.

Step 4. On the screen that appears with text describing support for large format disks, answer Y if you want FAT32 or N if you want to use the older FAT16 format.

STEPS

Preparing a New Hard Drive For Use *(continued)*

Step 5. If you want the drive to be a standard single volume disk, choose option 1: Create DOS Partition. See Figure 11-8 for an example of this screen.

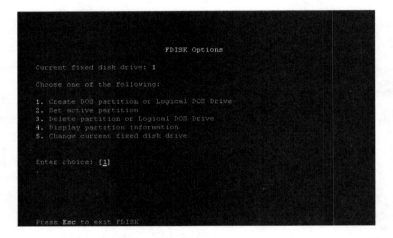

```
                            FDISK Options

Current fixed disk drive: 1

Choose one of the following:

1. Create DOS partition or Logical DOS Drive
2. Set active partition
3. Delete partition or Logical DOS Drive
4. Display partition information
5. Change current fixed disk drive

Enter choice: [1]



Press Esc to exit FDISK
```

Figure 11-8: Creating the partition
You tell FDISK that you want to create a partition on this screen.

Step 6. In most cases you'll want the partition to be a primary one, unless you plan to divide the disk into multiple logical partitions, in which case it should be an extended partition. On the following screen, select option 1 again to create a primary partition. When this is complete hit Esc.

Step 7. Confirm that the C: drive is set to be the active partition by selecting option 2 and choosing the drive from the list. Unless you make a partition active, the computer won't try to boot from it.

Step 8. Hit Esc twice to exit the FDISK utility. Enter the formatting utility by typing

`Format C: [Enter]`

Step 9. Answer Y to the confirmation that you're going to wipe any existing data on the drive.

By the way, if you're not comfortable using FDISK for creating partitions, there are several powerful third-party utilities available for partitioning your drive, such as PowerQuest's popular PartitionMagic.

You'll find a demo copy of PowerQuest's PartitionMagic 4.0 on the CD-ROM that accompanies this book.

If you are installing a new hard drive that you want to function as the boot drive (from which the computer will start up), you have to set a partition as active and install the operating system's boot files. If you don't, the computer will stop the boot process shortly after it starts because it will be looking for boot files and won't be able to find any. In plain English, your computer won't work. After partitioning and formatting a drive, it has nothing installed in its master boot record, so when the BIOS finishes its portion of the boot process and tries to hand it over to the hard drive (where the operating system's boot files should be stored), the boot process stops.

**Cross-
Reference**

See Chapter 8, "How Your Computer Works," for more on how the boot process works.

There are two ways around this problem. The first is to install your new hard drive as a slave first, do the necessary disk preparation, and configure the new hard drive to be the master when you're done. To do this, you:

- Set up your new drive as a slave
- Partition the drive
- Set it as the active partition
- Format it
- Install the operating system on the new drive
- Copy your existing files over
- Shut down
- Reset the new drive as a master (and the old drive as a slave)
- Restart

Unfortunately, this won't work very well because all your applications commonly install files into the Windows folder, and they all make additions to the Windows Registry. So, if you copy over your applications and files from the old drive to the new, or even simply try to run them off the old drive, they won't be able to find all the files they need in your freshly installed Windows folder.

Tip

A similar problem is that if you try to move an older hard drive into a newer computer and set it to be your boot drive, it probably won't work because the version of Windows installed on the hard drive includes the drivers for your old machine. It needs to have the new drivers installed for it to work, but to do this you have to be able to boot to Windows first. As a result of this vicious circle you'll find yourself in, you'll probably have to either install it as a second drive or wipe it clean and start over.

If you're thinking that you could just copy over your existing Windows folder (or, for that matter, everything on your existing drive) onto the new drive instead of reinstalling everything—it's not that easy. Among other things, a straight copy won't work because Windows 95 and 98 can't copy files in use (and some have to be in use for the OS to be running. As a result, you'll end up with about 95 to 98 percent of the files you need, which is actually worse than having none of what you need because there's no easy way to find exactly what's missing.

You can only use this copying trick if you have a program that can create a byte-for-byte image of one hard drive onto another or if you use a utility that's specifically designed for disk copying. PowerQuest's DriveCopy, for example, is specifically intended for this purpose.

In fact, once you've physically installed your new drive, DriveCopy can take care of partitioning, formatting, and copying all the files over from one drive to another. Version 2.0 and later generally needs to be installed and run from your original drive, so you'll want to keep it as the master and your new drive as the slave until you've used the software. Then, you'll need to switch the two (between master and slave or to different IDE channels) before you can use your new drive as the main boot drive for your system. Many people find that the hassles programs such as DriveCopy save are well worth their relatively minimal cost.

Another alternative to the problem takes a bit longer, but it's more thorough and will cause you less problems in the long run. Essentially what you're going to do is to start over on the new drive by installing Windows 98 (or Windows 95) onto the drive, reinstalling your applications onto the new drive, and copying over your files from the old one to the new one. When you're done, you can repartition and reformat the old drive and use it for additional storage.

STEPS:

Doing a Fresh Install of Windows

Step 1. Follow the steps on partitioning and formatting a drive earlier in this chapter.

Step 2. Boot your PC with a floppy disk that includes a CD-ROM or DVD-ROM driver. The standard Windows 98 boot floppy disk will generally work, but if it doesn't, or if you're using Windows 95, you'll need to create one.

Cross-Reference

See the Troubleshooting Tools section of Chapter 17, "Troubleshooting Techniques," for step-by-step instructions on how to create a boot floppy disk with a CD-ROM driver.

Step 3. Insert your Windows 95 or 98 CD into your computer's CD-ROM or DVD-ROM drive, and switch to that drive by typing in the appropriate drive letter. In many cases, this may be E:, but you may also have to try D:, F:, or even G:.

Step 4. Confirm that you're looking at the proper drive letter by typing in DIR at the command prompt to get a directory of the drive's contents. You should see a few directories listed and a file called Setup.exe.

Step 5. Once you're sure you're looking at the correct drive, type

`Setup [Enter]`

at the prompt to start the process of installing either Windows 95 or 98.

Once the OS installation is complete, you can reinstall all your applications (you did keep copies of any application updates on your original hard drive, didn't you?) and copy over any files you need from the old disk onto the new one.

Cross-Reference

Chapter 9, "Adding, Upgrading, and Removing Software," has many tips on reinstalling applications, so look there for more detailed advice.

Depending on what you want to do with the old drive, you can then repartition and/or reformat the drive to erase everything off of it and use it for additional storage. Because it's not the active partition, you can simply format it using the Windows format command in the Windows Explorer, or you can open a DOS Prompt window and use FDISK and the DOS Format command from there. Just be careful not to accidentally partition or format your new drive!

Large drive problems

One problem that can occur, regardless of the type of interface that you connect a drive to, is that if you install a large hard drive (over 8GB), your BIOS may be unable to properly recognize the drive's full size. On some older computers, the BIOSes could only recognize drives up to 2GB in size (or only 504MB on *really* old computers). In many instances the drive will install and work just fine, but Windows may report that it only has 2 or 8GB of total storage, even if it's a 16GB or larger drive. So, after you've installed your drive, make sure you check the total storage capacity of the drive in Windows Explorer, by right-clicking the drive, selecting Properties, and checking the total capacity. If you've divided the drive into multiple partitions, don't forget to add up all the partitions that exist on the one physical drive.

If it turns out that the computer is reporting an inaccurate size, there are two ways to fix the problem. The first method — which is also the preferred one — is to upgrade the computer's (or SCSI adapter's) BIOS, as explained in the "Upgrading Your BIOS" section later in this chapter. The second option is to use drive overlay software, such as OnTrack Disk Manager, which basically fools your computer into working with the larger drive.

Many large drives are bundled with these types of utilities in case your BIOS isn't or can't be updated to ensure that you can use your new drive on your computer, regardless of the type of BIOS you have. The problem is, they slow down your system's overall performance, occasionally cause compatibility problems, and are potentially subject to the same kind of corruption that any software faces. In general, they provide a reasonable interim solution, but I would only use one until I got a BIOS upgrade (or if a BIOS upgrade for my system was not available).

Adding or Upgrading Your CD or DVD-ROM Drive

The process of adding a new CD-ROM or DVD-ROM drive to your PC — for example, if you want to replace your older CD-ROM drive with a DVD-ROM or if you want to add any variety of rewritable or recordable CD or DVD drives — is very similar to adding a hard drive, but even easier. In fact, it's virtually identical except that you don't have to worry about partitioning, formatting, and installing an operating system on the drive.

IDE interfaces

You have to determine the type of interface you'll be connecting to, and you need to physically install the drive, as explained in the previous section on installing hard drives. If the CD/DVD drive you plan to install uses the IDE/EIDE interface, then you'll probably want to make it either the slave on the primary IDE channel or the master on the secondary IDE channel (or the slave on the secondary IDE channel if you already have several IDE devices installed).

IDE drives also typically need to be enabled via the computer's BIOS setup program, as explained in the previous section. One problem that may crop up is that some older BIOSes are incapable of recognizing certain rewritable CD and/or DVD drives, so you may also need to upgrade your BIOS to get the drive to be recognized by your system.

Cross-Reference

For more information on this, see the "Upgrading Your BIOS" section later in this chapter.

SCSI interfaces

You may run across a related problem if you try attaching a SCSI-based CD- or DVD-ROM drive to an older SCSI controller. In this case, you may need to update the BIOS on the SCSI controller, sometimes called host adapter. See the next section on doing BIOS upgrades for more details.

If you're adding an external CD or DVD-ROM drive to a notebook that lacks an internal drive, you may need a PC Card adapter/controller (such as a SCSI card) that will plug into one of your notebook's PC Card slots and then into the drive itself. Be sure to check if the drive you're buying comes with the necessary controller and cables — most do, but some do not. Also note that some of the controllers that come with external drives offer dedicated connections to the drive only, while others are general-purpose SCSI cards that can be used to attach several different SCSI devices. If you plan on attaching more than just the drive, make sure the drive you want comes with (or you separately purchase) the right kind of controller. Finally, some drives are also available that use the parallel or USB ports on notebooks. Attaching one of them is no different than adding any other external peripheral.

Cross-Reference

See Chapter 10, "Adding and Removing Hardware," for more.

DVD-ROM

If you're installing a DVD-ROM drive to a desktop system, you may also need to install a plug-in card that goes with the drive in order to watch DVD titles on your computer. All DVD movies use compressed video and audio formats, and the files must be decompressed before they can be seen or heard. Some DVD drives come with a card that handles the MPEG-2 video and Dolby Digital (sometimes also called AC-3) audio decoding in hardware, while others come with software-based decoders that take advantage of the fast processors available in today's newer computers. If your drive comes with a card, you'll also need to make connections between the drive and the plug-in card.

Installing drivers

Once all the appropriate physical connections and BIOS-level changes have been made, you can simply restart your computer. If you're using Windows 95, 98, or 2000, in most cases, as the operating system starts up, it will recognize that new hardware has been attached to the system, and it will automatically start the Add New Hardware Wizard.

Typically, you'll be prompted to insert a driver diskette or CD/DVD disc in order to install the driver software necessary for the computer to communicate with the drive. In some cases, you'll be prompted to insert either the Windows 95 or 98 CD, and the driver will be installed from there. If you're really lucky, such as with some DVD-ROM drives under Windows 98, the driver may already be installed and will simply be activated when the computer starts.

Once the driver's installed, you may have to restart your computer for it to work properly, but once you do, it should be ready to go.

Upgrading Your BIOS

One of the more obscure but potentially critical upgrades that computer users have to make is to their system's BIOS (Basic Input/Output System). As explained in Chapter 8, "How Your Computer Works," the BIOS is the very first piece of software that loads when your computer turns on. As a result, it controls or is involved with a number of very important steps in the computer's boot process, as well as its overall operation, including recognition of new hardware, the computer's time and date, and reading and writing files to and from your hard disk.

There are several reasons why you may want to upgrade your BIOS, including adding support for new hardware, improving support for existing hardware, and fixing one possible source of the Y2K problem. (See sidebar, "Dealing with Y2K" for more.)

Dealing with Y2K

The most infamous problem to face computers and computer users yet is the Year 2000 problem, also commonly called the Y2K problem or the millennium bug. The basic issue behind Y2K is that computers are very dependent on dates and times in order to function properly, and many computer systems and computer software programs were designed with only two digit dates in mind. As a result, when the clock rolls over to January 1, 2000, some computer systems will think it's actually the year 1900 (or 1980 or some other incorrect date). And, as a result of this, applications that don't know how to handle this date may crash, generate error messages, or do any number of other strange things.

Some people are concerned that it will lead to power outages, bank failures, and other mishaps, causing a major negative impact on the world's economy—all because of modern society's dependence on computers for so many aspects of our lives. Most of these claims are overly melodramatic and play on peoples' fears of the coming millennium in general, but I also think we're bound to see certain types of problems (though nothing this dramatic) cropping up as a result of the date problem.

Fortunately (or unfortunately, depending on your point of view), mostly older mainframe-type systems will be affected by the Y2K problem. Most personal computers and most software that people run on their PCs will not be seriously impacted. There are exceptions, of course, so the prudent thing to do is confirm, with all the makers of the software you use, that the version of the software you're using is Y2K-compatible; if it isn't, find out if there's a patch that you can download and install. (It is important to get the proper patch for your software. Microsoft, for example, offers separate ones for Windows 3.1, 95, and 98 and NT users.) Most computer hardware and software companies have prominently positioned statements on their Web sites regarding Y2K compatibility.

The only area that will probably affect a large group of PCs is the real-time date and clock maintained by their BIOS (and used by other software to date- and time-stamp the files they're using). Even computers built and sold as late as early 1998 could run into the Y2K date problem. Several utility programs are available to determine if your system's BIOS is Y2K-compatible, but again, you can also contact your computer's manufacturer if you want to be sure. If it turns out your computer does need a BIOS update to be Y2K-compliant, the process is quite easy, as explained in the rest of this section.

Also, if for some reason you can't get a BIOS update for your computer or you just forget to do it, there's an exceedingly easy way to fix it. The first time you turn on your PC after the new millennium arrives, just reset your clock to the new date. On most systems, this is all you need to do. In some cases this won't work, though, so you might want to pick up one of several utilities that have been written that basically fool your computer into working with dates past 2000.

A copy of Symantec's Y2K BIOS fix, which can either adjust your BIOS or, if necessary, take control of your system clock and ensure that it accurately rolls over into the year 2000 without a problem, is available on the CD accompanying this book.

For example, if you want to be able to boot a computer with a USB-based keyboard and mouse, you need to have a BIOS that recognizes the USB ports on startup. If you don't, you could get error messages about not being able to find a keyboard and/or mouse when you start your computer. In addition, you won't be able to use either of them in your BIOS Setup program or under DOS (because the drivers for the devices don't load until Windows does). Many computers that include USB ports do not have this capability, so they need to have their BIOS upgraded in order for this to work.

In addition, many BIOSes are unable to see hard drives bigger than 8GB (or in some cases only 2GB). If you try to install a hard drive larger than that in a computer that hasn't had a BIOS upgrade, you may face a situation where the computer only reports seeing, for example, 8GB of your 16GB drive. Even worse, it's possible in some situations to actually lose data on the areas of the drive beyond where the BIOS can see.

Other capabilities added by some BIOS upgrades include support for power management features such as OnNow and ACPI, as well as support for new types of hardware, such as DVD drives.

The BIOS is stored in a chip on your computer's motherboard so that it is always available when you turn your computer on, regardless of problems you may have with your hard drive, operating systems files, or other things. On older computers, to upgrade the BIOS you had to physically remove the chip and replace it with another that had a more recent update of the BIOS software burned into it. Most computers made over the last few years, however, have a Flash BIOS that takes advantage of a technology called flash EPROMs (Erasable Programmable Read Only Memory). With a Flash BIOS, you can essentially reprogram the chip by using a special updater utility that erases the old BIOS code and stores a new version of it into the chip's onboard memory.

STEPS:

BIOS Upgrade

The upgrade procedure for Flash BIOSes can vary from computer manufacturer to manufacturer, but here's how most work.

Step 1. Download a BIOS updater from the company's Web site onto your hard drive.

Step 2. Run the utility by double-clicking it (or if it automatically decompresses and creates a Setup file, you can run after it downloads instead).

Step 3. In most cases the utility will prompt you to insert a floppy disk. What it then does is creates a bootable floppy disk that includes the necessary updating program. If double-clicking it doesn't seem to work, it may be because the file you've downloaded is the actual flash updater. In this case, you'll need to create a bootable diskette (type in **format A: /s** at a DOS prompt), and copy this file onto it.

Step 4. Restart your computer with the floppy disk you just created. In some instances the updater will automatically load and begin the process of updating your BIOS, while in others you may need to type in the name of the updater at the A:> DOS prompt and hit Enter. (If you don't know the name, use the DIR command to list all the files on the disk.)

Step 5. Once the update is done, remove the floppy disk from the drive and restart your computer. You may notice new startup messages as soon as your system turns on or a few changes in the BIOS Setup program if you choose to enter that (although you don't have to).

Another updating procedure that people associate with their computer's BIOS involves replacing the CMOS (Complementary Metal Oxide Semiconductor) battery. The CMOS is a small amount of nonvolatile — which means it doesn't disappear when you turn the power off — memory that stores settings associated with the BIOS and the BIOS Setup program. The CMOS stores the settings made in the BIOS Setup program, and those settings, in turn, are used by the BIOS when the computer first boots. A small battery typically located on the computer's motherboard is used to maintain those settings when the power is off. Like all batteries, the CMOS batteries on your computer will eventually run out of juice.

Tip

The average life expectancy on most CMOS batteries is five years or more, so this isn't something you'll probably have to worry about more than once during the life of a computer (if ever). But, if you notice that your computer continuously loses track of the date and time, or if you get a specific message about the CMOS battery being low, then you'll need to open your computer up and replace it.

As with any procedure inside your computer, you need to follow the appropriate safety precautions and common sense guidelines outlined in Chapter 10, "Adding and Removing Hardware." Finding the CMOS battery shouldn't be too hard because it's located on the motherboard and it's the only battery your computer has. On some systems it's buried underneath cables and/or other peripherals, however, so you may have to search a bit.

Unfortunately, on some computers the batteries are soldered onto the motherboard or otherwise attached in such a way as to be difficult to remove them, but on most machines they're relatively easy to replace. If you have a system that makes the battery replacement difficult if not downright impossible, you're going to have to start thinking about replacing your motherboard (see the section, "Replacing Your Computer's Motherboard," later in this chapter for more). Another option is to bring it to a service center to see if they'll de-solder the battery. Finally, if this doesn't work, you have a darn good excuse for buying a new computer!

You probably won't find the type of battery you need at your local drug store, by the way, so be prepared to head over to a computer or electronics store to buy a replacement.

Tip

If you ever do replace the CMOS battery—or even if you're just starting to get low CMOS battery messages—be sure you write down the parameters on the various pages of your BIOS setup program. Some BIOSes even support printing them out. After you've replaced the new battery you'll have to reenter those settings in order to get your system working the same way it was before.

Other Hardware Upgrades

Depending on the type of components that came with the computer system you're now using, as well as the type of applications you find yourself using it for, you may decide to upgrade another existing piece of your system. Many people who get into computer games, for example, decide that all they need is a better video card that accelerates all the new 3D graphics standards or has more onboard memory for storing textures. Other people decide to upgrade only the modem that came with their computer or perhaps the SCSI controller if they move into bandwidth-intensive applications, such as digital video editing.

In most all cases, the process of upgrading an existing component inside your PC simply involves removing the old hardware — both physically and logically — from the system and installing the new hardware.

Chapter 10, "Adding and Removing Hardware," has plenty of advice on how to do this, including explaining how to remove an older device's drivers.

Certain components of some proprietary computer systems from big name manufacturers (including Compaq, HP, Packard Bell, and more) are built into the computer's motherboard and cannot be physically removed. For example, some computers feature built-in modems, sound cards, and/or video circuitry that are an integrated part of the computer. In some situations, this might mean you're unable to upgrade a certain component of this computer.

In many cases however, all you need to do is disable the built-in hardware in the computer's BIOS Setup program. You may have to look around a bit for the settings, but most systems enable you to do this specifically so that you can upgrade a built-in component at a later date. You still probably need to logically remove the device by deleting its drivers through the Device Manager (see Chapter 10, "Adding and Removing Hardware," for more details), but turning off these settings in the BIOS Setup essentially removes the component from your computer.

Firmware updates

Another option you may have is to upgrade the existing hardware inside your computer. For example, some video cards enable you to attach additional video memory, which can enable the card to support higher resolutions on bigger monitors and/or store more 3D textures for graphics-intensive games. In addition, some sound cards enable you to add additional sounds either via a wavetable ROM upgrade or via adding RAM for storing your own custom sounds.

In virtually all cases, individual card upgrades require you to remove the card from your system, perform the upgrade, and reinstall the newly upgraded card. In fact, in most instances, even if the instructions suggest that you can try it without removing the card, I wouldn't recommend it. The only exception is if there's an easily accessible daughterboard connector at or near the top of the card.

If you plan on doing this, be sure to follow the same safety procedures (explained in Chapter 10, "Adding and Removing Hardware") you would when installing a new add-in card. Also, be sure to firmly reseat the card into the same slot from which you removed it.

In addition to computers, some peripherals also support upgrades. Many modems, for example, can be upgraded to newer communication standards — such as V.90 for analog modems AO/DI for ISDN modems, or G.lite for DSL modems — in a process that's conceptually very similar to upgrading your computer's BIOS. Again, in some cases, you need to physically replace a chip inside the modem, while in most other cases you simply run a one-time software updating utility that will upgrade the EPROM inside the modem. These types of updates are generically referred to as firmware updates, because the chip holding the software instructions that you're updating is called the device's firmware (it's software burned into hardware, hence the compromise name).

Other devices, including things such as recordable CD or DVD drives, also have firmware updates that can fix bugs or add new features to the device's basic operation. These upgrades operate in a manner somewhat similar to BIOS updates, where you run an updater program from a boot floppy disk or simply from your hard disk, as with standard applications.

Printer memory

Certain printers — notably lasers — can also be upgraded by adding more memory to them. In some cases this increases the resolution the printer supports, while in virtually all cases it increases the speed at which it operates and the types and sizes of files the printer can handle. Most printers use proprietary types of memory, so the upgrade process typically entails contacting the manufacturer for the memory upgrade and following the instructions provided with the printer. As with installing memory inside your computer, you want to handle the memory carefully and be careful to avoid problems with static electricity. (It's yet another application that calls for a grounding strap!)

Upgrading Your Processor

Sitting at the very heart of your PC is the processor, the number-crunching component that drives your computer's overall operation. Logically, it would seem that upgrading the processor could have the most dramatic impact on your computer's overall performance.

In reality, however, while the processor does play the primary role in a computer's operation, it's only part of an overall computing system, and there are many other components that affect a computer's overall performance. In other words, simply upgrading the processor doesn't always make as big a difference as many people expect (or hope).

For this reason, as well some other technical issues I'll explain in a bit, upgrading processors has started to fall out of favor. In fact, Intel has even gotten out of the processor upgrade business. Still, there are some situations where it can make sense to replace your existing processor with another.

Determining processor types

The first issue you have to determine is the type of processor socket you have on your motherboard. Most 486es and 486-compatibles, such as the AMD K5 and Cyrix 5x86 used what is called Socket 5. All Pentiums and most Pentium compatibles from AMD, Cyrix, Centaur/IDT, and Rise fit into the

Socket 7 slot on your computer, while most of Intel's Pentium II and III processors as well as its Celerons fit into a 242-pin connector commonly known as Slot One.

Older Pentium Pros use Socket 8, some AMD's K7 chips use Slot A, and a few recent Celerons have a 370-pin connector that's somewhat similar (but not compatible with) the old Socket 8. If you're dealing with a server or some workstations, the Intel Pentium Xeon chips fit into the larger Slot Two architecture, which features a 330-pin connector.

Cross-Reference

See Chapter 2, "Microprocessors and Memory," for more on processor types and connectors.

Table 11-1 summarizes different processors and their types of connectors.

Table 11-1   Processor Connections

Processor Family Type	Connection
Most 486s and compatibles	Socket 5
Intel Pentium and Pentium MMX	Socket 7
AMD K6	Socket 7
AMD K7	Slot A
Cyrix 6x86 and MII	Socket 7
Centaur/IDT WinChip	Socket 7
Rise MP6	Socket 7
Intel Pentium Pro	Socket 8
Intel Pentium II and III	Slot One
Intel Celeron	Slot One and Socket 370
Intel Pentium Xeon	Slot Two

And this is just for desktop computers. Most notebook computers use special processors and connectors specifically designed for mobile machines. Intel, for example, originally offered standard Pentiums and now Pentium IIs and IIIs in the Mobile Module format (of which there are several variations), which is a reduced size design specifically intended for the cramped quarters of a notebook. Even with this mobile design, however, in general, trying to upgrade the processor in a notebook is very difficult. It's technically possible in certain situations, but it's something that only an authorized service center or even the original manufacturer can do (and not all of them are willing to do so).

Unfortunately, none of these various connection standards are compatible with one another, which means you can't upgrade from one to another. So, for example, you can't upgrade to a Pentium III if you have a Pentium or other Socket 7-based processor. The only way to do this is to get a new motherboard with the right kind of connector, but at this point you're probably better off just buying a new computer.

In addition, it's not always possible to upgrade within the same family of connectors. For example, you can't upgrade a 233MHz Pentium II to, say, a 450MHz or 500MHz Pentium III because those faster chips require a faster system bus, and support for a faster system bus comes from the chipset, which cannot be upgraded (again, unless you buy a new motherboard). In fact, in the case of Pentium IIs with 66MHz systems buses — which includes all systems up to and including the 333MHz Pentium II — the fastest you can upgrade those systems to is a 333MHz processor.

Note

There are some hardware hacks available that, in some cases, can overcome this type of limitation, but I don't recommend them because they involve modifying your computer's hardware and could lead you to destroying your CPU.

So, for example, you could upgrade a 233MHz Pentium II to a 333MHz version — although the performance boost would not be that great — but a 333MHz version cannot be upgraded at all. (If you wanted to get support for the Streaming SIMD Extensions added to the Pentium III, you could install one in place of your existing PII, but you wouldn't get any significant performance increase because your processor will automatically be clocked down to 333MHz or less.) If you try to install, say, a 450MHz processor into a system with a 66MHz system bus, the faster processor will automatically revert down to a clock speed of around 266MHz or 300MHz. And, on a related note, if you try to install one of the earlier Pentium IIs into a system with a 100MHz or greater system bus, the computer will recognize the chip and will automatically slow down the system bus to 66MHz. In other words, you won't get any benefit from a faster system bus.

Some similar problems face faster Socket 7-based processors, such as 350MHz versions of the AMD K6. Many of these chips are designed to work with motherboards and chipsets that feature 100MHz or faster system buses — these are often called Super 7 boards. If you install one of these faster processors in an older system with a 66MHz system bus, you will get some benefit, but not the kind of speed improvements that they provide in new systems with 100MHz or faster system buses. Older Socket 7 processors, however, such as some of the early Pentiums are good potential candidates for processor upgrades.

Installing the processor

Once you determine the type of processor connector you have, as well as the new processor you want to install, you need to make sure the two are compatible. For example, some of the very first Pentiums — which ran at 60MHz and 66MHz — used slightly different-sized connectors than later Pentiums, so if you have one of those systems, make sure you check to see whether any upgrade you're interested in will work with the type of computer you have. In fact, this is sound advice for any type of processor upgrades because certain systems and certain upgrade processors can be notoriously finicky about working with each other.

Secret

In some situations, you can buy a replacement processor for your computer, while in others you may need to buy a processor specifically designed for upgrades. The primary difference between these two types has to do with voltage settings for the processor. Processor upgrades commonly have a tiny bit of additional circuitry that takes care of matching or adjusting any voltage differences between what the processor requires and what power level the motherboard provides. Raw processors, on the other hand, lack this circuitry and must have the appropriate voltage settings made on the motherboard or they can be easily fried (in other words, destroyed).

In order to install the upgrade, you usually need to make some changes to your motherboard's settings, including the internal and external processor voltages, as well as the system bus speed and the multiplier that runs your processor at a specific multiple of the system bus speed (such as 3x or 4.5x). Internal and external voltages are different, so make sure they are set according to the requirements of the processor. (Even minute differences can cause problems.) The bus speed and the multiplier settings should also match the suggestions of the processor vendor. Setting them higher than suggested is referred to as overclocking (see the sidebar "Getting overclocked").

If your computer supports changing these types of settings (not all do) you typically make these changes via tiny DIP switches on the motherboard. The specific technique varies from motherboard to motherboard, so you'll need to check the documentation that came with it. By the way, even if the board supports alternate settings, it may not support the specific setting your new processor needs, so be sure to check before you buy.

Getting overclocked

In an attempt to get slightly better performance from their PC, some people ignore the CPU manufacturer's recommendations on bus speed and multiplier settings and turn them up. This technique, which is called overclocking, can help eke out a bit more performance from a processor, but it can also fry the processor and cause other types of system stability problems. As a result, I (and virtually all CPU makers) don't recommend it.

To perform the upgrade, you'll need to get into your computer's case, locate the old processor, remove it, make any DIP switch changes as necessary, and install the new processor. Again, be sure to follow the safety measures explained in Chapter 10, "Adding and Removing Hardware." One other thing to be aware of is that processors can get quite hot, so if you were just using your system prior to the upgrade, make sure you let it cool off a bit.

The actual removal and insertion of the processor is usually very easy. Many Socket 7–based systems use what's called a ZIF (zero insertion force) socket that features a tiny lever on one side that you simply lift up. Once you do, you're able to remove the processor with ease. Some CPUs include fans or heatsinks mounted on top of the processor which also need to be removed (and which can slightly complicate the removal process.)

To install the new processor, make sure you line up the notch in one corner of the processor and in the ZIF socket. Be careful not to bend any of the processor's many pins in the process. See the Socket 7–based system in Figure 11-9.

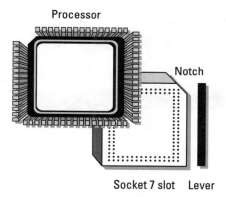

Figure 11-9: Processor upgrades
On a Socket 7–based system, just align the processor notch with the socket's notch, put the processor's pins in line with the socket's, and pull down the lever. This is all there is to it.

The new processor should slide right into the socket's existing holes — if you need to push it, something isn't lined up right. Once it's in place, just pull down the ZIF socket's lever, and you're done.

If you're trying to upgrade an older system that doesn't have a ZIF socket, look to see if there's an empty processor upgrade slot right next to your existing processor. On some 486es, this is where the upgraded processors are supposed to go. Unfortunately, some systems have no easy way to remove the existing processor — in those cases, you're just out of luck.

If you decide to upgrade a Slot One system, just unlatch the connectors on either side of the processor and pull the old processor card out. Insert the new one into its place, being sure to align the notches on the processor card and the Slot One connector, reconnect the latches, and you're done.

Secret

There are actually at least two slightly different types of Slot One, or 242-pin, connectors that feature different types of connecting posts. Most Pentium II, Pentium III, and socket-format Celerons will fit into either type (sometimes called SECC 1 and 2) of connector, but some provide a snugger fit than others. As a result, you may want to find out which type your system has before you upgrade.

Figure 11-10 shows an example of the installation process.

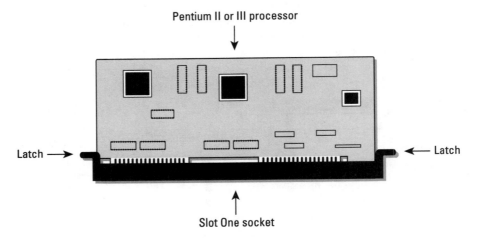

Pentium II or III processor

Latch → ← Latch

Slot One socket

Figure 11-10: Slot one
Upgrading the processor on a Slot One–based system is as easy as adding memory. Just unlatch and pull up the old processor, push the new one in, and reconnect the latches.

As mentioned previously, many processors can get very hot and will overheat if there isn't adequate cooling inside the computer. To compensate for this problem, many processors have metal heat sinks of various types attached to them to help release the heat they generate. If you're upgrading a processor that has a heat sink attached, it's probably a good idea to make sure the new one also has a heat sink. Another option is to add a small fan to the top of the processor — several companies sell little CPU fans specifically for this purpose.

One final note on processor upgrades is that some systems also require a BIOS upgrade in order to be able to recognize the new CPU. Without it, the system may not be able to boot. This is particularly true if you're installing an x86-compatible processor from companies such as AMD, Cyrix, Centaur/IDT, or Rise into a system that used to include an Intel processor. Make sure you find this out before you proceed with the processor upgrade. If a BIOS upgrade is necessary, do it first.

Replacing Your Computer's Motherboard

The mutha of all computer upgrades is, appropriately enough, replacing your computer's motherboard. Doing a motherboard replacement is as close to getting a new computer without actually buying a new machine as you can get. And I will warn you now, it's not for the fainthearted. So, if you're not the type who likes to get your hands inside your system, I wouldn't recommend it.

At the same time, if you've successfully made a few upgrades and are eager to try more, it's not that terribly difficult. You just need to take your time, be well organized, and be prepared to tackle things that don't always work the first time (oh, and being patient helps too).

Technically, you're ready for a motherboard upgrade if you want to jump from one processor type to another (Socket 7 to Slot One, for example) and/or you want to get access to the features enabled via a new chipset, such as a faster system bus, new onboard peripheral controllers, or other things. In most cases, those kinds of upgrades cannot be made to existing systems — the only way to achieve them is with a new motherboard (and the new chipset that accompanies it).

Now, I have to admit that with the rapid decline in PC prices it's getting harder to economically justify a new motherboard versus buying a new computer, but as long as you know this is the case and you still want to proceed for the fun of it, fine. (Just don't say I didn't tell you so.)

Getting organized

Before you begin the process of upgrading your PC's motherboard, you need to take stock of what you have. Make a list of the following items:

- The number and type of plug-in boards you have (and plan to continue using)
- The amount and type of memory
- The types of peripherals and the ports to which they attach (including any internal drives)
- The wattage of your power supply
- The dimensions of your current case and the motherboard itself.

You'll use this information to help determine what features to look for in a new motherboard. For example, if you want to use your existing memory, you'll need to make sure that the new motherboard supports the type of memory you have.

Of particular importance are the dimensions of the existing motherboard, as well as your current case. Computer motherboards come in several different form factors, including ATX, MicroATX, and NLX, and not all cases can fit all motherboard types. In particular, the NLX form factor, which puts the expansion cards into a plug-in cartridge that makes them run parallel to the motherboard, can generally only go into systems specifically designed for that form factor.

In general, it's good to look for a motherboard with the same dimensions or same form factor as your current one, but in some instances it's possible to fit one of the smaller new motherboards into larger, existing cases. The critical issue is checking to see if the new motherboard can somehow be securely attached to the old case. Many motherboards and cases have holes and/or connectors in a variety of places to compensate for different types of combinations, but not all motherboards fit into all cases.

For example, some systems from larger manufacturers use nonstandard sized motherboards in proprietary cases, and the case for this system may not be able to accept any standard motherboard sizes. Of course, you could always solve this problem by simply buying a new case and essentially building a new computer from scratch.

If you're planning on filling this upgraded machine full of nifty stuff, such as extra add-in cards, new hard drives, CD-ROM or DVD-ROM drives, and other things, you may also want to consider purchasing a larger power supply.

Cross-Reference

See Chapter 7, "Input Devices and Power," for more on power supplies

Once you've done your homework in these areas, it's time to start preparing for the upgrade. Give yourself plenty of room and uninterrupted time to do the work. You don't want to do this in cramped quarters or in a time-crunched situation.

Caution

Before you start disconnecting anything, back everything up! There's a good chance that you're going to need to repartition and reformat your hard drive (which wipes out *all* the data on it) as part of this process, so you need to have a complete backup of whatever files, programs, and updates you want.

Cross-Reference

See Chapter 14, "Working with Documents and Files," for more on backup advice.

Once you've made your backups (and not before!) you can start on the replacement process. Disconnect all external peripherals and remove the computer's cover. Once you're inside, the first thing to do is to label all the existing cables inside your machine. Use masking tape and some kind of pen or marker to note what all the various cables are connected to.

Removing the old motherboard

After the labeling process is complete, you can begin disconnecting cables from your computer's motherboard, being careful to follow the safety precautions explained in Chapter 10. Take your time and notice how the connectors fit into your current motherboard. Note that on some older systems, the serial and parallel ports (and sometimes even the hard drives) actually attach to plug-in cards instead of the motherboard. On the new motherboard, however, these will all attach directly to the motherboard itself.

Once the connectors have been removed, you can start to remove the components on the motherboard, such as the plug-in cards and memory. If possible, store them in their original antistatic bags — that is, if you still have them — or put them onto a clean cloth, such as a dish towel.

Next it's time to remove the motherboard itself. This is usually the hardest part. In some instances the board may be attached to your computer's case via small screws and in others there might be some small plastic connectors or standoffs that are keeping it in place. You may need to use needle-nose pliers or tweezers to get some of these plastic connectors out. Figure 11-11 shows how to use needle-nose pliers or tweezers to remove a motherboard.

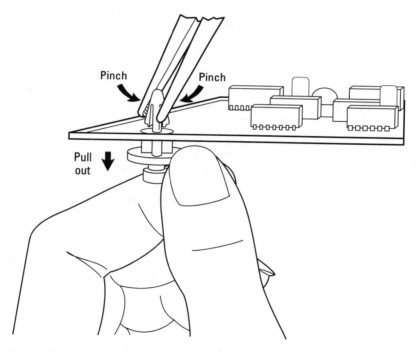

Figure 11-11: Breaking free
To remove your existing motherboard from the computer's case, you may need to squeeze one side of these type of expanding plastic connectors with a small pair of pliers.

Depending on how the computer is laid out, you may also need to remove the power supply and internal drives before you can get the motherboard out of the system. If you do, make sure you label and keep track of any connections you had to remove to get these pieces out.

Installing the new motherboard

Once you've successfully removed the old board, it's time to reverse the process and put the new one in. Before you do, you should install any memory from the old motherboard that you plan to continue using in your new system — it's easier to plug them in while the motherboard is outside the case.

If the new motherboard has connector holes for the case in different places, you may need to put the screws or connectors you originally removed into new spots. If necessary, you should also reconnect any other components — such as the power supply or internal drives — that you had to remove to get the original motherboard out.

With the new motherboard successfully in place, you can reconnect any expansion cards that you plan to use with the new system. Remember to reseat them firmly to enable good, solid connections. Many motherboard replacements require multiple attempts to get everything working, so save yourself some time down the road by double- and triple-checking all your connections now.

Next, it's time to reconnect all the cables you neatly labeled and pulled aside at the beginning of this process. Take your time and be sure, again, to make good solid connections. Don't put the case back on yet, you'll want to try everything out before you put the computer back together.

Plug any external peripherals back in and turn the system on. Watch the BIOS messages that appear, carefully noting if the proper amount of memory appears. In many cases, you'll need to enter the computer's BIOS Setup program right away and tell it to automatically search for any IDE drives you have attached. Make and save those changes in the BIOS Setup program and see if it boots and recognizes all the drives you have connected. If it doesn't, go through and check all your connections again. Very few motherboard surgeries work perfectly the first time, so be prepared to make some fixes.

In many cases, any existing hard drive will not be able to boot to Windows (or any other operating system) because it contains drivers for your old system and old motherboard; however, it's certainly worth a try. You may get lucky and, in the case of Windows, have Plug and Play and the Add New Hardware Wizard kick in to install new drivers for all the new hardware the OS has found on your new motherboard. If it doesn't work, be prepared to follow the directions in the section "Partitioning, formatting, and copying software" in this chapter on how to repartition and reformat your drive, and reinstall Windows (or whatever OS you're using) and your applications and files.

If the boot process does work, however, and you make it all the way to the Windows desktop, you still need to make sure that Windows recognized everything in your system. Open the Device Manager by right-clicking the My Computer icon, selecting Properties from the bottom of the context menu that appears, and selecting the second tab over in the dialog box that appears. If you have a problem with a piece of hardware, you'll see a yellow exclamation point or red internal no sign (circle with the slash) over the particular piece (or pieces) that aren't working right.

One easy way to try and fix those problems is to click the device, click the Remove button, and restart the computer. As long as the physical connections with the device are okay, this will force Windows to re-recognize the device and install the appropriate drivers for it. In many cases, this solves the problem.

Cross-Reference

If it doesn't, go to Chapter 17, "Troubleshooting Techniques," for more troubleshooting advice.

While you're in the Device Manager, you should also confirm that everything that's supposed to be there is (and that everything that's *not* supposed to be *isn't*). In some instances, if you forget to reconnect one of the cables or the hardware connection between the motherboard and a particular device is really bad, it may not show up in the Device Manager at all. If this is the case, recheck your connections and restart yet again. Similarly, you may need to move any driver references from older hardware that you didn't bring over to the new system.

Once everything properly starts up and is recognized, try printing a document and using any other peripherals you have attached. If you have problems here, you may want to logically remove the devices and/or reinstall their drivers.

Cross-Reference

See Chapter 10, "Adding and Removing Hardware," for more details on how to reinstall drivers.

Once you're sure everything works, crack open a can or bottle of your favorite beverage and enjoy—your work is complete.

Summary

In this chapter, I described how to extend the useful life of your computer by performing a variety of different upgrades.

▶ One of the easiest and most useful upgrades is to add more memory to your PC.

▶ The real trick with memory upgrades is to make sure you get the right kind of memory for your PC.

▶ Adding a hard drive to your computer involves selecting the right kind of interface, adjusting your BIOS settings, partitioning and formatting the drive, and, in most cases, reinstalling the operating system.

▶ Adding a new removable drive, CD-ROM, or DVD-ROM drive is virtually identical to installing a new hard drive, but it's even easier because you don't have to worry about operating system issues.

▶ BIOS upgrades can help your computer work with new types of hardware, including big hard drives, as well as fix the Y2K problem for your PC.

▶ You can add new life to some of your existing peripherals by doing things such as adding more memory to your video card or upgrading your modem.

▶ Processor upgrades are relatively easy to perform, but they don't often provide the kind of boost many people expect them to.

▶ Replacing your computer's motherboard is almost like getting a new computer. The process takes some time, requires good organization, and doesn't always work the first time, but it's actually very straightforward.

Part III

Connecting Your PC

Chapter 12: Setting Up a Small Business or Home Network

Chapter 13: Connecting to and Using the Internet

Chapter 12

Setting Up a Small Business or Home Network

In This Chapter

▶ You will learn what networking is.

▶ You will learn how connecting two or more computers works.

▶ You will learn what type of hardware and software is required to put together a network.

▶ You will learn how to combine PCs and Macs on a single network.

▶ You will learn about some of the new technologies and products being developed specifically for home-based networks.

▶ You will learn how you can share files, printers, scanners, modems, and Internet access accounts with a simple network.

In today's connected world, no computer is an island. In fact, it's getting harder and harder to find computers that are completely isolated. The reason for this is because virtually all new computers and most existing ones are equipped with at least one device that enables them to connect to and communicate with the rest of the world. In many cases, that device is some type of modem, but in others it's a network card, and in others, it may be one or more of each.

Regardless, by having and using a piece of hardware that offers some type of link to the outside world, virtually every computer now in use is part of at least one network. In most cases, that network is the Internet (which I explain in more detail in Chapter 13, "Connecting to and Using the Internet"), but it's a network still the same. And this means that almost everybody needs to know at least a little bit about how a network works and what's involved in making and using network-type connections.

Another factor driving the importance of networks is the number of households with more than one computer. One study I read said that more than half the homes in the United States that have computers actually have more than one PC. And where there's more than one computer, there's a good reason to start thinking about a network.

Most home computer users don't even consider putting together and using networks — after all, isn't this complicated stuff that only businesses need to worry about? But there are a lot of good, practical, and cost-saving reasons why a home-based network is a good idea. In fact, all the reasons that make sense for small and even big businesses are equally valid for today's home users — sharing printers and other peripherals, using a single Internet connection, and offering easy access to your files. Plus, some applications are particularly well suited to home use, such as multiplayer games.

Even better, the hardest part of setting up a network in a typical home — the wiring — is now taken care of by a variety of different companies that create products and technologies that you can use to put together home networks very easily. In some cases you can put together a network with no new wires, and in others, you can do so without any wires at all.

But before we jump into the fun stuff, I need to give you a little background on what this networking stuff is all about.

Basic Networking Concepts

Networking means nothing more than connecting two or more computers so that they can communicate. That's really it. Of course, a fair amount of effort can be involved in getting these conversations to occur if you're talking about hooking together hundreds, thousands, or even millions of computers, but the concepts behind those big networks are no different from what happens between two computers. A network simply provides a means for shuttling bits of digital data back and forth between computer devices.

By itself, in other words, networking doesn't do anything that exciting. It's what a network connection enables you to do that makes networking so interesting and so important. E-mail and Web browsing, for example, are possible only because computers can connect to each other via a network and pass information back and forth. Transferring files, making Internet-based phone calls, participating in a live chat, and sharing a single printer among two or more computers, too, are all made possible by a link between your computer and others in either your house, your business, or somewhere else in the rest of the world.

To make the communications between two or more computers work, several things need to be in place. First, some type of physical connection mechanism has to exist between the computers involved. Typically, this mechanism is a wire or cable of some kind, but with the growth of wireless devices and wireless networking schemes, it may simply be some kind of transceiver (which is a device that can both transmit and receive information) attached to or built into your computer.

On some computers, you also need to add a component, such as a network card or modem, to which the appropriate type of cable can attach. If multiple computers and/or related peripherals are being attached, you may also need a central device to which several devices can connect.

In addition, you need a set of predefined rules and some software that enables these digital conversations to occur in the same "language." These rules and the accompanying software affect the way the messages are sent, as well as the content of the messages.

Network data

For a variety of reasons, primarily involving data integrity and reliability, computers can't just spit out raw digital data in a continuous stream over a network connection, as one might logically presume that they could. Instead, the data needs to be chopped up, encoded, packaged, and sent in particular ways so that all the various devices that are attached to the network can reliably receive and understand the data being sent.

Figure 12-1 offers a graphical overview of these basic networking concepts.

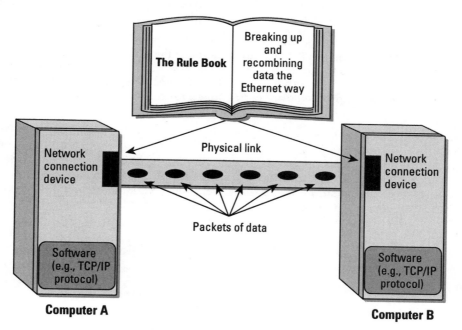

Figure 12-1: What's needed to make a network
In order for a network to exist there needs to be some kind of physical communications link, an agreed upon set of rules for sending and receiving data, and software that can understand the chosen network's language.

Each of these different requirements can be met in several ways, which is what leads to the morass of choices and terminology that surrounds networking. For example, the manner in which connected devices are organized, which is sometimes referred to as the *network structure* or *topology*, can be done via a star network, bus network, ring network, or some hybrid combination of all three.

Even the method for physically connecting can be different. In a traditional *local area network*, or LAN, most computers use *network interface cards*, or NICs, to connect to the network, but in a home environment, you may just use a modem, a terminal adapter, or a simple external device that attaches to one of your computer's existing ports.

Most people don't think of a modem as a networking device, but when you dial up your Internet account, or perhaps dial in to your company remotely, you're connecting to another computer and setting up a (typically) temporary network connection. While you're connected, your computer is part of the network, and your modem is acting as your network interface card. In fact, the only differences between a dial-up connection and a direct network connection are the rules used to break up, send, and receive messages, which are called *protocols*.

So, for example, whether you try to send a file through a direct network connection or via a dial-up modem connection, the end result is the same. The file is transferred. The manner in which it is sent, however, is different because each method uses different types of protocols. The reason is that different protocols are better suited for the different types of physical connections. See Figure 12-2.

The *point-to-point protocol*, or PPP, for example, is optimized to work on serial connections over phone lines, whereas Ethernet is great for direct wire connections (as well as lots of other applications). In all of these various instances, the same basic principles apply. It's just a matter of how the communications occur that differs. Once you understand this, you're well on your way to making sense of the various ways in which networks work.

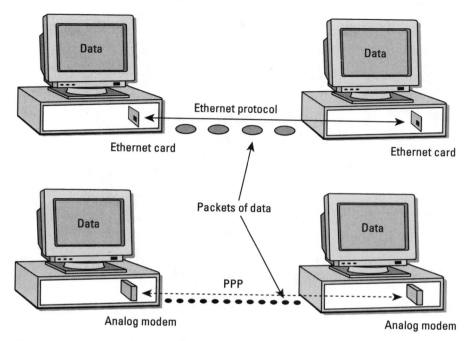

Figure 12-2: It's only the middle that's different
Different types of network connections and different types of network protocols may break up a file or bit of data you send from your computer to another in different ways, but the end result is always the same.

Network structures

The most primitive level of the network is the structure or layout used to physically connect the different computers and other devices. As mentioned previously, the three basic type of network structures are bus, ring, and star networks. Figure 12-3 shows them graphically.

A bus network consists of a series of computers attached together in a line, a ring network is a bunch of computers hooked together in a circle, and a star network is group of computers that typically connect through a central device called a *hub*.

Of course, as nice as these pictures look in theory, the reality of how networks are actually connected is usually a lot messier, and a lot harder to decipher. In offices, for example, most computers, much like phones, simply connect to a jack in the wall. What happens from there is unknown to anyone but the people who put together and manage the network. (Most users don't know and don't need to know.)

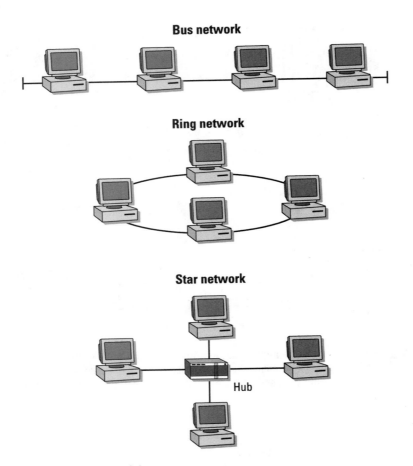

Figure 12-3: Network layouts
There are several different ways to connect computers together, and each method has a name that corresponds with its physical shape.

If you did look behind the wall, you'd find that there is a structure to the overall network layout, and it conforms to one of these types, or a combination of them. The reason it's important to know this layout, just in case you were wondering, is because it determines what type of equipment you use to connect the computers.

For example, if you use a star network, which is the most popular and most flexible type, you need a device called a hub to sit at the center of the star and connect to all the various components on the network. In addition, you need network cards designed to work with a hub and star-shaped network layout. A bus network, on the other hand, needs a different type of network card (although many cards can support both bus and star-type networks).

The type of network layout also determines how reliable a network can be in the event of a problem. With a bus network, for example, any network-related problem with a single cable or interface card on any computer connected to the network causes the entire network to fail. See Figure 12-4.

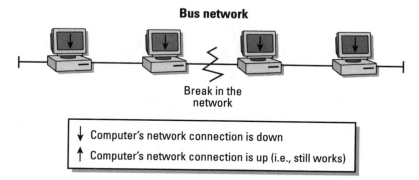

Bus network

Break in the network

↓ Computer's network connection is down

↑ Computer's network connection is up (i.e., still works)

Figure 12-4: Bus failure
A bus network depends on the entire chain of computers, the "bus," to function. If a breakdown occurs at any point in the chain, then the entire network is affected.

Similarly, on some ring networks, data is passed in only one direction around the ring, so a problem with one computer can affect several other computer users' ability to use the network. See Figure 12-5.

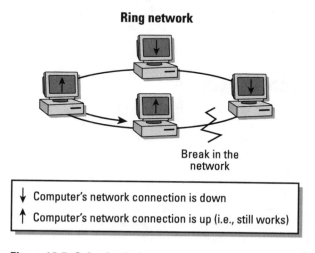

Ring network

Break in the network

↓ Computer's network connection is down

↑ Computer's network connection is up (i.e., still works)

Figure 12-5: Going in circles
A ring network sends data around the circular chain of computers in a single direction. If a failure occurs at a certain point, all the computers before the break are still able to function, but those after the break cannot.

On a star network, however, any problems with a particular device are isolated to the connection between that one device and the hub, and no other users are affected. This is one of the main reasons that, despite the additional cost of a centralized hub, virtually all networks today are built using some type of star arrangement. See Figure 12-6.

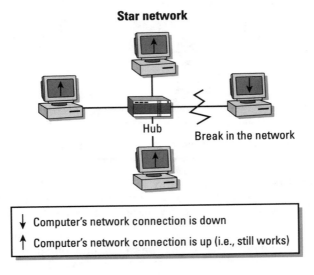

Star network

Hub

Break in the network

↓ Computer's network connection is down

↑ Computer's network connection is up (i.e., still works)

Figure 12-6: Centralization
By forcing all the computers and other peripherals attached to the network to connect a single, central point, a star network topology avoids many of the problems that occur with other types of networks. If a problem occurs in this type of network, only the broken machine is affected.

Network architectures

In addition to the physical layout of the network, another critical factor is the architecture of the network, which is the baseline protocol used to route and send information from computer to computer. The most popular network architecture is Ethernet, of which there are several variations, including standard or 10Mbps Ethernet, Fast or 100Mbps Ethernet, and Gigabit or 1Gbps Ethernet. As their names imply, each of these different versions of Ethernet runs at different speeds, with the faster versions offering higher bandwidth. In practical terms, the higher the bandwidth, the quicker things get done. (In addition to different speeds, some different types of Ethernet vary according to the connectors they use. See the sidebar "Ethernet connections" for more.)

Ethernet connections

As if there weren't already enough different kinds of Ethernet based on speed alone, you may also come across different types of standard Ethernet cards and connectors. The most popular type of Ethernet is called *10Base-T*, which is a form of standard 10Mbps Ethernet that uses unshielded twisted pair cables; the same kind used for phone cords and RJ-45 connectors. These RJ-45 connectors essentially look like wider versions of standard phone jacks, which use RJ-11 connectors.

The other kind of Ethernet you may hear about is *10Base-2*, which is also sometimes called *thinnet*. 10Base-2, which also runs at the standard 10Mbps rate, uses coaxial cable; the same kind used for cable TV connections and BNC connectors. *10Base-5* Ethernet, which is relatively rare, uses a thicker type of coaxial cable. The figure below shows a comparison of the different type of connectors.

10Base-2 Ethernet is typically used on bus networks, but as that network topology has fallen out of favor, so has this type of Ethernet connection. Most modern Ethernet networks, including the faster 100Base-T and some implementations of Gigabit Ethernet, use the RJ-45 connectors and unshielded twisted pair cable.

As a convenience, some Ethernet adapter cards include jacks for both 10Base-2 and 10Base-T, but not all do, so make sure you get cards with the right types of connectors.

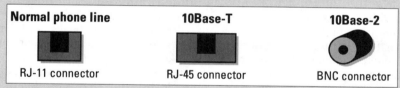

| Normal phone line | 10Base-T | 10Base-2 |
| RJ-11 connector | RJ-45 connector | BNC connector |

It's all in the jacks
You can easily tell the difference between 10Base-T Ethernet and 10Base-2 Ethernet by looking at the connectors. 10Base-T uses RJ-45 jacks, which are similar to the RJ-11 jacks used for phones, and 10Base-2 uses BNC connectors.

Other networking architectures you may hear about are Token Ring, ArcNet, ATM (Asynchronous Transfer Mode), FDDI (Fiber Distributed Data Interface), and Apple's LocalTalk (sometimes also called "AppleTalk"). Each of these different architectures is capable of running at different speeds and offers different ways of sending the data from one point on a network to another.

The way a network works is that it breaks data being sent from one computer to another into small chunks called *packets*. The network architecture determines how these different data chunks are bundled into packets and how they are sent from place to place. Logically enough, all the devices attached to a particular network need to use the same baseline protocol in order for communications between the devices to occur. In other words, Ethernet-based devices can talk to other Ethernet devices, but not to Token Ring or AppleTalk devices (that is, not without the assistance of a special piece of hardware called a *bridge*).

Like the network layout, the type of architecture chosen for a particular network also determines the type of hardware used in a network. So, for example, if you choose to build an Ethernet network — the most widely supported choice — you need to use Ethernet-based network cards, whereas if you were to build a Token Ring network, you would need Token Ring–based cards.

Ethernet has become such a *de facto* standard, however, that virtually all generically named "network" cards are, in fact, Ethernet cards. Not all Ethernet cards support the different types of Ethernet, however; unless a card is specifically designed for 100 Mbps, for example, it won't be able to run at that fast speed.

Network protocols

Sitting one layer above the baseline network architecture protocols are a network's messaging protocols, which determine the content of each of the packets sent around a network. This is different than the manner in which the packets are broken up and sent around the network, which is what the Ethernet protocol does.

Think of Ethernet as the "unspoken" rules of communication that enable two people to at least attempt a conversation — first one person speaks, and then waits for the other to speak, and so on. The network protocols, on the other hand, are like the language used by each speaker. Two people who speak different languages can attempt to have a conversation with each other, using the universally understood "rules" of communication, but they'll be able to have a meaningful conversation only if they both speak the same language.

Common network protocols include:

- *TCP/IP*, or *Transmission Control Protocol/Internet Protocol*, which is the language of the Internet

- *IPX/SPX*, or *Internetwork Packet Exchange/Sequenced Packet Exchange*, which is a popular protocol used by Novell for their NetWare operating system, as well as by other companies for other applications

- *NetBEUI*, short for *NetBIOS Extend User Interface*, a protocol used by Windows 95/98 for simple peer-to-peer networks (explained in a bit)

- *AppleTalk*, which is also the name of the protocol used on some older Mac-based networks

Unlike network architectures, which must be the same for an entire network, it's possible (and sometimes necessary) to use multiple network protocols on a single network. For example, many small business and home networks use the NetBEUI protocol to communicate between computers with file and print sharing, use TCP/IP to make Internet connections, and may even use IPX/SPX to play multiplayer games over a network. It's also possible to use different protocols for the same thing (although not at the same time — you just have the option of choosing among them). So, for example, you can also use TCP/IP or IPX/SPX for simple file and print sharing on Windows-based networks.

Part of the reason this is possible is because *protocol stacks*, which is what a complete set of protocol services is often called, are implemented in software and can be easily added to an existing system. The network architecture, on the other hand, is determined by hardware, which is obviously much harder to change.

Network protocols are generally independent of the network's architecture so it's possible, for example, to run TCP/IP on an Ethernet network or a Token Ring network. One doesn't determine the other (except in the case of simple Macintosh-based networks).

The way this works is that protocols get wrapped around other protocols in a multilayer fashion. In a typical network connection, for example, one of several different TCP/IP protocols, such as *http*, which stands for hypertext transfer protocol and is the mechanism used to access Web pages, is wrapped by a generic TCP/IP protocol which, in turn, is wrapped by the Ethernet protocol. (The reality is actually more complicated, but at least this description gives you an idea of what's going on.) See Figure 12-7.

Data Packet

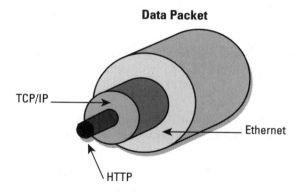

TCP/IP

Ethernet

HTTP

Figure 12-7: Protocol wrapping
Most packets of data sent across a network connection are actually a fairly complicated "sandwich" of different protocols wrapped around each other.

Network types

In addition to a network's structure, architecture, and protocols, which together control how information is sent across a network, there are two basic network types, peer-to-peer networks and client-server networks. The network types determine how the network functions, how it's constructed, the equipment involved, and the number of users that a particular type of network can support.

A peer-to-peer network is designed for small networks, which makes it perfect for both home and small business networks. In a peer-to-peer network, all computers are treated equally. All the networks resources and peripherals are connected to individual computers, but they're made available to other users on the network. See Figure 12-8.

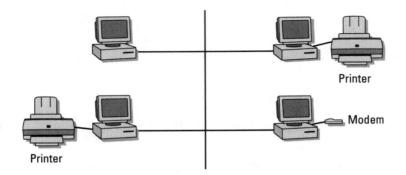

Figure 12-8: Peer-to-peer
A peer-to-peer network is ideally suited for small business and home networks because it doesn't require the purchase of a special computer called a *server*. Instead, all the individual computers and any peripherals attached to them are made available to everyone attached to the network.

A client-server network, which is used with larger business networks, consists of one or more centralized computers called *servers*, and all the individual user computers, called *clients*, connect to the server (or servers). See Figure 12-9.

Note

Note that while the role of a server is similar in concept to what a hub does in a star network, a server doesn't necessarily sit in the middle of a network. In fact, in many instances a server connects to a hub in a star-based network, just as any other client computer does, or connects to any point in the line on a bus network, again, just as the clients do. However, special "client" software enables all the client computers to communicate with the central server.

Peer-to-peer networks are much easier to set up and maintain than client-server networks — yet another reason why they're favored for small business and home networks — but they don't always provide the flexibility and power of a client-server network. For example, while both types of networks enable you to share a printer, on a peer-to-peer network, the computer with the printer attached to it usually slows down when someone else on the network tries to print to it. On a client-server network, with print server software, print requests are handled by the server, and no computer's performance is affected.

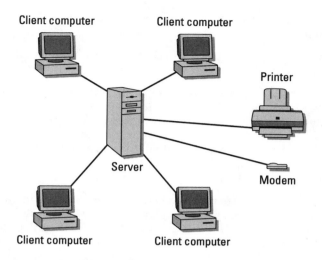

Figure 12-9: Client-server
In a client-server network, a centralized computer called a server acts as the focus point for the network, and all standalone computers, called clients, attach to it.

Note

You can avoid this slowdown on a peer-to-peer network as well, but it requires the addition of an extra piece of hardware called a *print server*. A print server connects directly to a printer and then to the rest of the network. The print server's task is to accept print jobs sent over the network without tying up another computer.

In addition, peer-to-peer networks are really only practical on networks of about ten computers or less. If you try to go much beyond that, the performance of all the computers on the network are slowed down too much because of the overhead, or extra work, required to handle the network data. Client-server networks, on the other hand, can easily handle hundreds or even thousands of individual users (as long as you have powerful enough servers, that is).

Note

By the way, network structures, architectures, and protocols are independent of the network type, so you could have an Ethernet-based, star network using TCP/IP with a peer-to-peer network or a client-server network. Similarly, just because you're running a Token Ring on a ring network doesn't necessarily mean that you have a client-server network (although, in this example, you probably would).

Network operating systems

The type of network you can create is often determined by the network operating system you use. Like a regular operating system for your PC, a network operating system coordinates how all the individual software applications on a network work and how the network interacts with the hardware attached to it.

Cross-Reference

See Chapter 8, "How Your Computer Works" for more on how a computer's operating system works.

Windows 95, 98, and 2000 (as well as Windows NT Workstation and the older Windows for Workgroups, for that matter) function as simple network operating systems, in addition to being regular operating systems for your PC. In other words, you can create simple networks using only Windows 95, 98, 2000, or NT Workstation (in any combination) on any PCs attached to that network. However, Windows 95/98/2000/NT Workstation enables you to create only peer-to-peer networks.

If you want to build a client-server based network, you have to install a dedicated network operating system, such as Windows NT or 2000 Server, or Novell's NetWare or IntranetWare, on the server, and then install special network client software on each of the PCs attached to the network. (You also have to install client software on each PC for a peer-to-peer network, but I'm getting ahead of myself.)

As mentioned previously, dedicated server software offers much more capability than what you'll find on a peer-to-peer network, including sophisticated security features, full-featured file and printer sharing, built-in backup tools, and a lot more. It's also a lot more complicated than a peer-to-peer network. In fact, many people find that they need a full- or part-time network administrator to handle all the software and configuration issues involved with putting together and maintaining a client-server network.

Another option that won't require a network administrator is to install software such as Mango Software's Medley onto a peer-to-peer network. Medley brings some of the capabilities and benefits of a client-server network, such as backup, to a peer-to-peer environment.

The OSI network model

If you really want to know more about how networking works, you need to understand something known as the *Open Systems Interconnection*, or OSI, *model*. The OSI model, which forms the basis of virtually all modern networking connections, details seven different layers. These layers provide a framework that enables computers on different platforms to communicate.

For example, imagine you're using a PC running Windows 98 and you want to get access to information stored on a Linux-based Web server that's located somewhere on the other side of the world. Or what about just trying to connect to your spouse's Macintosh in another room? How could you do it?

Well, without some set of predefined and well-accepted standards you couldn't. And when computer networks were first being developed, that's exactly what happened. Different companies were using a variety of proprietary or semiproprietary ways to exchange information, and a lot of stuff just didn't work together.

To fix this problem, the *International Standardization Organization*, or ISO, got together to describe a model of how information should be transferred from one computing device to another. What they created is called the *OSI*, or Open Systems Interconnection, *model*, which describes all the tasks required to move information across a network. Note that they didn't try to describe *how* to do any of these tasks (that was a job for other standards committees); they simply outlined what needed to happen at each step in order to enable consistent, reliable communications.

As it turns out, the OSI model contains seven layers, each of which handles a different aspect of the communications process. The seven layers are the Application Layer, Presentation Layer, Session Layer, Transport Layer, Network Layer, Data Link Layer, and Physical Layer.

Companies involved in the networking and computer industries embraced the OSI model soon after it was released in the mid-1980s, and it now serves as the basic foundation or framework for virtually all networking hardware and software. The OSI model enables computers with different operating systems and different networking hardware to successfully communicate with one another.

Here's how the OSI model basically works. To send data across a network, you start out with the raw data that is to be transferred and then pass it down through the seven layers from the Application Layer on top to the Physical Layer on the bottom. Each layer adds information to the original raw data being sent, so that by the time the information is sent off across the network, it contains more bits — or just stuff, if you prefer — than it started with. Then, on the receiving end, the opposite occurs. The incoming data starts out at the bottom of the seven-layer model and moves back up to top. In the process, each layer removes the additional information that its matching layer on the sending end had added. Ultimately, the receiving computer ends up with simply the raw data that the first computer originally sent. Figure 12-10 illustrates the process.

What can be confusing is figuring out how the seven layers of the OSI model correspond to the practical network technologies and concepts that many people are used to dealing with, such as Ethernet, TCP/IP, and what have you. As it turns out, there is a correlation between these seven OSI layers and standard network technologies, but it is typically not one to one. In many cases, for example, the seven layers are handled by four components:

- The operating system
- The network protocol
- The network architecture
- The physical network connection

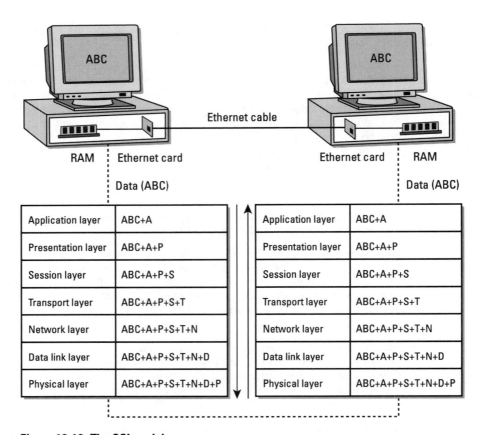

Figure 12-10: The OSI model
In a typical network transfer, data travels through the seven different OSI layers before it hits the actual network, and then the process is reversed on the receiving end.

The correspondence varies from situation to situation and product to product because certain pieces of hardware or software often handle different layers. In addition, there's often some overlap between some of the layers and some of the products because some products handle more than one layer.

Table 12-1 provides a typical match between the seven OSI layers and real-world counterparts in the example of accessing the Internet via an Ethernet-based connection, such as a cable or ADSL modem.

You don't need to worry about all the different OSI layers and exactly how they work when it comes to putting together your own network — you just need to worry about the four or so practical items I listed in Table 12-1. However, if you ever get more involved with networking, you have to know more about the OSI model. If you're interested, many, many good books cover the subject, and some good reference material is available on the Internet.

Table 12-1	**Matching OSI Layers with Real-World Technologies**	
OSI Layer	*Purpose*	*Handled by*
Application	Passes information from application to protocol stack used on network	Windows operating system (specifically, the Winsock .DLL)
Presentation	Formats data for transfer	Windows operating system (specifically, the Winsock .DLL)
Session	Establishes connections between devices	TCP/IP protocol stack
Transport	Corrects transmission errors	TCP/IP protocol stack
Network	Identifies target computer or other device	TCP/IP protocol stack
Data Link	Breaks data into chunks	Ethernet protocol
Physical	Defines physical connections	10Base-T Ethernet card

Putting Together a Simple Network

Okay, enough theory. Time to map out a typical small network and describe both the pieces involved and what type of setup and software configuration needs to be done. For purposes of this example, I'm going to describe the process of building a 10Base-T Ethernet-based, peer-to-peer network using a star topology with PCs running Windows. This is by far the most popular and most flexible type of network for most small business and some home applications, so it's the kind I recommend that you use. Later in this chapter, I describe some even easier setups that are specifically designed for home networks.

The pieces

Here's what you need to put together this type of network:

- Two or more PCs (notebooks or desktops in any combination)
- 10Base-T Ethernet network adapters for each computer (typically plug-in cards, preferably PCI-based, for desktops, and PC cards, preferably Card Bus-based, for notebooks), unless the computers already have built-in 10Base-T Ethernet ports

- An Ethernet hub with enough 10Base-T ports to connect all the individual computers, as well as room for later expansion

- Category 5 (sometimes called "Cat 5") 10Base-T Ethernet cables with RJ-45 connectors (the ones that look like "fat" phone cords)

- Windows 95/98/2000 installed on each computer and the Windows 95/98/2000 CD

You can either purchase these pieces individually or find several of them bundled together in network starter kits from different companies, including Linksys and Netgear.

The "category" reference I listed for the wiring refers to the quality of the cable and the MHz frequency (and therefore bandwidth rate) it is capable of maintaining. Unshielded twisted pair networking cables — the kind used in 10/100Mbps and even some 1Gbps Ethernet networks — are rated according to their capability of handling different data rates, with the higher rated numbers (Category 5 is the most common now) offering support for higher bandwidth. If you were really on a budget you could probably get away with lower-grade Category 3 wiring, which is rated at a minimum frequency of at least 16MHz versus 100MHz for Category 5. However, if you ever want to upgrade your network, I promise you'll be thankful that you invested a little bit more in higher-quality wiring in the first place. Otherwise, you may have to rewire your entire network, which is not a pleasant process.

Tip

If you want to plan for the future, make sure you invest in 10/100Base-T Ethernet cards, which are sometimes also called *Ethernet adapters*. The slash in the name indicates the products can work at either the standard 10Mbps Ethernet rate or the faster 100Mbps Fast Ethernet rate. In most cases these types of adapters can switch automatically between the two rates depending on the speed of the signal they receive from the hub (which is what determines how fast the network can run). You could start out with an inexpensive 10Mbps hub and later on, when your network needs higher bandwidth, invest in a more expensive 100Mbps hub. With these types of autoswitching Ethernet cards, all you would have to do is change out the hub, whereas if you purchase only standard 10Mbps cards to start with, you would have to change both the hub and the network cards to get the faster transfer rates.

STEPS:

The Physical Installation

The process of installing the network is very straightforward — at least, conceptually — and involves four steps:

Step 1.   Install the Ethernet adapters into each PC.

Step 2.   Attach cables from each PC's Ethernet adapter to the hub.

Step 3. Install client and protocol software (or confirm that it's already there).

Step 4. Configure the software to provide the services, or features, you want for your network.

The first two steps involve the physical installation of the network and are explained here, while the last two steps involve the necessary software and are explained in the following sections.

Installing the Ethernet cards is typically easy. Most modern network cards support Plug and Play and install fairly automatically.

Cross-Reference

See Chapter 10, "Adding and Removing Hardware," for detailed information on installing add-in cards in your PC.

Tip

It's also possible to get Ethernet adapters that connect to a PC's USB port, which means you don't even need to install a card (although USB-based Ethernet adapters are typically limited to a maximum throughput of about 8Mbps, instead of the normal 10).

The hardest part of the installation is actually Step 2 because even though making the connections to the hub and the adapter card is child's play (you can plug any PC into almost any port on the hub), the implied part of this task is running the wire. If all the PCs you plan to hook together are in close proximity, then it won't be a big deal. But in most cases they aren't — or even if they are, there may be a wall or two separating them — which means you have to deal with fishing cables through walls, drilling holes, installing connector plates, and a lot of other hassles.

In fact, for this reason (and the fact that most homeowners or apartment dwellers are unwilling or unable to run these cables, no matter how much they love their computers and want them networked) several companies and industry consortiums have been working on standards for creating home networks. These products/technologies work either with some of the existing wiring in your home, such as the power or phone lines, or without any wires at all. I explain some of them in detail later in the chapter, but if you're one of the many people who fall into this category, know for now that there are options that can help with Step 2 (and Step 1 in some cases as well).

If you can and/or are willing to make the effort to run the necessary cable, you may want to think about installing it into most of the rooms in your home, not just the ones that currently have computers. As we move towards a world of more and more computer-like, Internet access/information terminal products for the home, most of which will probably be networkable, it's better to be prepared than to have to face yet another wiring job. Similarly, if you're setting up a small business network, make sure you run network cables and put network jacks in just about every room in your office. You may find that you need them sooner than you think.

Finally, make sure you find a good, centrally located place for your hub. Once it's set up and connected, you shouldn't need to have access to it very often, but you don't want to make it impossible to get to either.

Secret

By the way, if you need to hook only two computers together, you can get away with not using a hub. What you'll need instead is a special cross-over Ethernet cable (a regular cable won't work) that switches certain wires from one end to the other. This cable is the same type that's sometimes used to connect one hub to another if you need to expand your network. Just plug one end into one computer's RJ-45 Ethernet jack, and plug the other into the second computer's Ethernet adapter. This isn't an ideal long-term solution, but it can work in certain situations.

Direct cable connection

If you want to hook together only two Windows-based computers to transfer files, you have a simpler option than a full-blown network. It's called *Direct Cable Connection*, or DCC. DCC is bundled with Windows, although it isn't always installed with the default installation. If you don't see it, go to your Add/Remove Programs control panel, the Windows Setup tab, and then double-click on the Communications folder. Once you find DCC, you can click the box next to it and then hit OK twice to make it available on your system. (You may be requested to insert your Windows CD for the installation, so be prepared.)

Once DCC is installed and running, you can use a variety of different cables that are specifically designed for direct data transfers. On most machines you can use a special serial or parallel cable (the normal types of cables usually don't work), or you can find USB cables that are designed for this purpose.

You can also do these transfers wirelessly if both computers offer an IrDA (InfraRed Data Association) compatible infrared port. This technique is fairly popular for working with one desktop computer and one laptop, for example. Note that you still need to have a network client and at least one (shared) network protocol installed on both machines for DCC to work (these are explained in the next section).

To use DCC, open the Direct Cable Connection software by going to the Start menu, selecting Programs and then Accessories. Select Direct Cable Connection, and simply follow the step-by-step wizard that walks you through the process. See Figure 12-11.

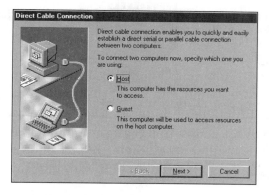

Figure 12-11: Direct Cable Connection
One easy to transfer files between two computers is to use the Direct Cable Connection feature built into Windows 95/98. It isn't as fast or as flexible as a real network, but it's easy to set up and it works.

Installing the network software

Once the physical connections are in place, it's time to move onto the software. Most of the action here centers around the Windows Network control panel, which you can find in the Control Panel folder listed off the Start menu's Settings option.

The specific pieces of software you need to install are called *network clients* and *network protocols*. (When you installed the network card, you also installed a driver for the network adapter, but this is part of the hardware installation process.) As explained in the previous sections, network client software enables one computer to connect to another computer that's running a network operating system. In the case of Windows 95/98/2000/NT Workstation and the older Windows for Workgroups, the networking support is built into the base operating system. (Specifically, these products include built-in peer server software.) However, you still have to install network client software on each computer attached to the network in order to "connect" to the other PCs.

A network protocol is the specific language used by computers on the network to communicate with one another. You need to install at least one protocol (the same one on each machine) for the network to operate. But it's also very common to install two or more protocols in order to enable all the features you may be interested in (such as sharing an Internet account and playing multiplayer network games). In general you want to try to use as few protocols as possible, because each one adds a bit of overhead to the amount of traffic on the network. However, in some situations having several protocols is unavoidable.

Here's how you install the network client under Windows 95 or 98 for a typical peer-to-peer Windows network.

STEPS:

Installing a Peer-to-peer Network Client

Step 1. Open the Network control panel by going to the Start menu, selecting Settings, and then selecting Control Panel from the submenu that appears. Find the Network control panel, and double click it. See Figure 12-12.

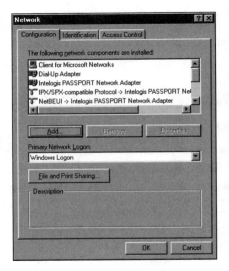

Figure 12-12: The Network control panel
The heart of all your computer's network settings can be found in the Network control panel. From here you can add, remove, and modify network clients, network protocols, drivers for network adapters, and network services, such as file and print sharing.

Step 2. At the top of the control panel window, look for the Client for Microsoft Networks, which is the client software you need in order to create a peer-to-peer network. In many cases, you may find that it's already installed, in which case you're done with this process. You can skip to the section on installing network protocols.

Step 3. If it's not installed, click the Add button, select Client from the subsequent dialog box that appears, and then click Add.

Step 4. From the list of manufacturer names that appears on the left, select Microsoft, and then in the list of clients listed on the right side of the dialog, highlight the Client for Microsoft Networks and click OK. See Figure 12-13.

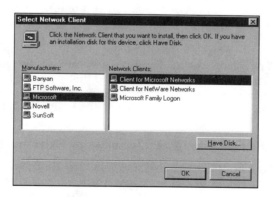

Figure 12-13: Client for Microsoft Networks
The software you need to install for a peer-to-peer network is the Client for Microsoft Networks.

Step 5. Once the software's copied over, your computer may need to restart in order for the network software to be available. However, before you do that, you need to move onto the next process — installing network protocols. So, if you get a dialog asking if you want to restart, click No for now, and then move onto the next set of step-by-step instructions.

Protocols

Once the network client is in place, you also need to install the network protocol you plan to use. Figuring out which protocol (or protocols) to use on your network isn't always easy because tradeoffs are often involved with using one protocol or another. In some instances you may have no choice, however, because certain applications work only with certain protocols. If you know ahead of time what type of applications you want to run on the network, make sure you find out what protocols they use or are capable of using. In general, you want to keep the number of protocols that you use on a network to as few as possible, but it isn't always easy.

For simple file and printer sharing, the most common choice is Microsoft's NetBEUI (pronounced *netbooey*), although you can also choose either TCP/IP or even IPX/SPX. NetBEUI is easy because it doesn't require assigning numeric addresses to each computer on the network, as TCP/IP does.

Instead, NetBEUI uses the friendly NetBIOS name that you assign to a computer (which I explain a bit later in this chapter).

However, if you plan to use a shared connection to the Internet or want to set up a simple intranet (which is a network that uses Internet standards but stays inside the walls of your company or home), you'll have to install the TCP/IP protocol anyway because TCP/IP is the *language* of the Internet (and of intranets). In this case, you'll have to decide if you want the convenience that having two protocols, NetBEUI and TCP/IP, may provide, but it is at the expense of network overhead and the potential confusion of installing and using multiple protocols. If you later find that you also need to install IPX/SPX for, say, playing a multiplayer game, the decision can become even more difficult. The other option is to just bite the bullet, and set up a TCP/IP-only network.

Cross-Reference

See the section "Setting up a TCP/IP network," later in this chapter for more.

In some instances you may not have to worry about installing protocols because the process of installing a network adapter card or Client for Microsoft Networks often installs some protocols as well. However, if you're having networking problems, or just for your overall piece of mind, it's always better to double-check.

STEPS:

Installing Network Protocols

Step 1. Open the Network control panel (in case you closed it after the last process).

Step 2. As before, check for the Microsoft TCP/IP (or NetBEUI) protocol in the list of network-related software already installed on your computer in the top half of the control panel. Again, if the protocol you want is already there, you're done with this step, but you'll want to keep reading to find out how to install other protocols (which you may need to do in order to enable certain applications).

Step 3. If TCP/IP or any other protocol that you need to install is not listed in the top half of the control panel, click the Add button, then highlight Protocol in the next dialog box, and hit the Add button.

Step 4. In most instances you'll want to select Microsoft on the left side of this dialog box and then choose from the available choices that appear on the right side. If you're installing computers onto another type of network, you may need to choose different protocols from different manufacturers. See Figure 12-14.

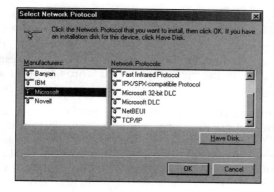

Figure 12-14: Network protocols
Most of the protocols you'll need to use on simple peer-to-peer Windows-based networks are available under the Microsoft listing.

Step 5. After you've selected the protocol you need to install (in this example, TCP/IP), simply hit OK. Once again, you can save yourself a bit of time and a few extra restarts if you hold off on closing the Network control panel and restarting your computer until you've finished checking the protocol bindings (explained in the next section) and naming your computer (which is explained in the section after that).

Tip

If you decide to use only TCP/IP for your network but see that NetBEUI or some other protocol that you aren't using is also installed, you can remove it from your system. You'll have to remove the protocol separately for each computer on the network. You can do so by selecting it in the Network control panel and clicking the Remove button. Removing unnecessary protocols can improve the speed of your network connection and eliminate possible problems down the road.

Bindings

In most cases, simply installing network protocols is all you need to do to make them work. What actually happens behind the scenes, however, is that the protocols you've installed are "bound" to your networking adapter and to any networking service that's been enabled (which I'll actually get to a bit later in this chapter).

In networking parlance, *binding* means to link together a particular network adapter (or network service) with a particular network protocol. (Technically speaking, it's linking the network protocol to the transport protocol.) So, for example, if a network adapter is "bound to" a particular protocol, that means it can use that protocol. If the two are not bound together, then the networking adapter can't use the protocol. Now, if you have only one protocol installed and for some reason it's not bound to the computer's network adapter, then that computer won't be able to connect to or communicate with the network. In other words, it won't work (on the network, that is).

You can bind a particular protocol to several devices and/or network services without creating any problems. It simply means the protocol is used for several purposes. Conversely, you can also have a network adapter or service bound to several different protocols. In this instance you'll be using several protocols on the network, which may or may not be necessary, depending on what you're attempting to do on the network.

To check on a particular device or service's bindings, highlight it in the list of installed network software listed at the top of the Network control panel, select Properties, and then click the Bindings tab, which may be one among several different choices. The boxes listed in that particular dialog are the available binding choices (the specifics vary depending on whether you're looking at a network adapter, protocol, or service Properties sheet), and the ones with the check marks next to them are the options that are "bound." See Figure 12-15.

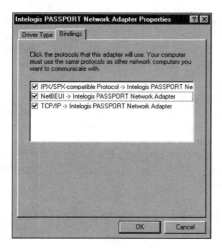

Figure 12-15: Network bindings
In order to ensure that a network functions properly, you need to double-check that network adapters and services are bound to the proper network protocols.

Network names

The final step in your network installation is to identify each computer on the network by giving it a name. Once again, you do so in the Network control panel.

Simply click the Identification tab, type a name for each computer, pick a workgroup name that all the attached computers share, and then type a description of the computer (if you'd like it's optional). The computer and workgroup names are limited to 15 characters and cannot include spaces. In most cases, in order for your network to work, each computer has to have the exact same workgroup name, but they each have to have unique computer names. It doesn't matter what the workgroup name is, as long as all the attached computers use the same one. See Figure 12-16.

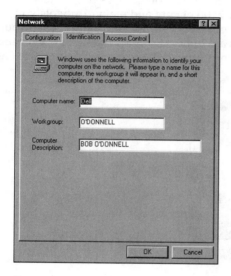

Figure 12-16: It's all in a name
Each PC on a peer-to-peer network must have a unique name, but in most situations, all the computers must use the same workgroup name in order to be "seen" by the other computers on the network.

These computer and workgroup names are used by NetBIOS (short for *Network Basic Input/Output Software*). NetBIOS is software built into Windows 95/98/2000 (as well as Windows for Workgroups and Windows NT) that's involved with basic network communications, much as a regular BIOS is involved with basic communications inside your computer. In particular, this NetBIOS name is used by network services, such as file and printer sharing, to make it easy to find and connect to other computers on your network.

Cross-Reference

See Chapter 8, "How Your Computer Works" for more on how a BIOS works.

Once you've finished naming your computer and workgroup, you can finally close the Network control panel. Be prepared to insert your Windows 95/98/2000 CD into your computer's CD- or DVD-ROM drive when you do because the computer will probably request it. Once the software's been copied over, you have to restart your computer in order for the new network software to be loaded and available for use.

When you restart your computer, you may be asked to provide a username and password for Windows, if you don't already have them. You can choose to not have a password by simply hitting Tab to move out of the password box, but you will have to do this every time Windows starts. In other words, you gnerally can't avoid this logon box once you've installed any networking software, because Windows requires a logon to get access to any network.

After the computer restarts, you should check all your network settings to make sure everything is correct. When you go back to the Network control panel, you should see not only the clients and main protocols you've installed, but also additional protocol listings that are bound to your network card or adapter. These items are indicated by the name of the protocol, a right-facing arrow, and then the name of the network adapter. See Figure 12-17.

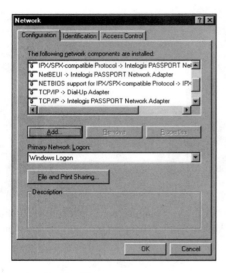

Figure 12-17: The ties that bind
Binding a network protocol to a network adapter card ensures that the adapter uses the particular protocol.

If you've followed along up to this point, you've installed the client and protocol software necessary for all the connected computers to be able to communicate with one another. In other words, the basic network is in place, so congratulations.

Unfortunately, you haven't allowed the network to do anything. That's where network services come in, which I explain in the section "Taking Advantage of Your Network," later in this chapter.

Other network considerations

Before I get to network services, however, I want to address some additional issues regarding creating specific types of networks, connecting different types of computers to the network, as well as using different mechanisms for making home network connections.

Setting up a TCP/IP network

With all the great press that TCP/IP gets as being a fast, efficient protocol and the *language* of the Internet, the obvious question running through your mind probably is: why not just go with a straight TCP/IP network? After all, you can use it for virtually any network application, right?

Well, the problem is that setting up a TCP/IP network is no picnic. The reason is that for TCP/IP to work on a network, each computer has to be assigned its own, unique TCP/IP address, which comes in nonfriendly, numeric form, such as 123.45.67.89. (If you've ever set up an Internet account, these types of numbers may be somewhat familiar to you. To find out about TCP/IP addresses, see Chapter 13.) Specifically, TCP/IP addresses consist of four numbers between 0 and 255; each separated by a period.

Every computer on the Internet, for example, has its own TCP/IP (commonly shortened to just IP) address. If it didn't, you wouldn't be able to find and connect to a particular Web site (which may be hosted on a computer in some remote part of the world). Of course, we don't typically use IP addresses to reach Web sites; instead we type in names such as www.infoworld.com. What really happens, however, is that a computer called a *domain name server*, or DNS, running special software converts the *friendly* name we type in our browser into the numeric name. The DNS server looks up the name in a master database of all Web site domain names. A domain name is the first part of a typical Web address (in this case, infoworld). By looking up the name in the master database, the server finds out what IP address that domain name has been assigned to. It then uses that number to transfer your requests to the appropriate Web site.

The problems in setting up a small TCP/IP network are similar to the issues involved with connecting to computers on the Internet. First, you have to figure out which IP addresses to assign to the computers on the network, which can get a bit complicated if you also want these computers to also be able to access the Internet. Second, you have to figure out a way to convert the numeric IP addresses into friendly names.

With regard to assigning numbers, you could theoretically use any numbers you want if you plan to never connect those computers to the Internet. If you do plan to connect them to the Internet, however, and you choose a number that's already taken, you can create big headaches. To solve this problem, the organization that controls the assigning of IP addresses, called *InterNIC*, or Internet Network Information Center (www.internic.net), has set aside several groups of IP addresses that will never be sold to companies or

Internet Service Providers and that are specifically intended for private networks. The most commonly used ones are called "Class C addresses," and they begin at 192.168.0.0 and run up to 192.168.0.255, giving you 256 different addresses (although individual numbering typically starts with 1 instead of 0). Anyone is free to use these IP addresses on their own networks.

So to create a TCP/IP network, you give each computer a unique IP address, starting at 192.168.0.1 and going up as high as you need. To do so, open the TCP/IP protocol settings page that's been bound to your network adapter (not the generic TCP/IP setting or the one bound to your dial-up adapter) by opening up the Network control panel, selecting the appropriate TCP/IP entry, and choosing Properties. You can tell which one is bound by looking for the name of the protocol, a right-pointing arrow, and the name of the network adapter.

In the IP address tab of the dialog box that appears, choose Specify an IP address and type in the address, starting with 192.168.0.1 for the first machine on your network and counting up from there. So the second machine would be 192.168.0.2. In the Subnet Mask area, which is used to distinguish different groups of computers in large networks, type 255.255.255.0 for each computer. See Figure 12-18.

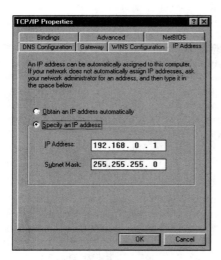

Figure 12-18: Specifying an IP address
To set up a TCP/IP network, you need to assign each computer a unique IP address, which you do via the TCP/IP Properties page in the Network control panel.

Secret

Windows 98 added a feature called *Automatic Private IP Addressing*, which can automatically assign IP addresses to computers running in a small TCP/IP network. The feature, which is on by default, uses addresses that start at

169.254.x.x. To use it, you actually have to *not* specify an IP address (the OS does it for you).

Once all the IP numbers have been assigned, you also need a way to convert those numbers into friendly names. Otherwise, anytime you want to connect to a computer on the network, you have to use the IP address. You can install a simple DNS server to convert the numbers or use another software package, such as WinGate (described later in this chapter), that includes simple DNS services. Probably an easier way, however, is to create a Hosts file, which acts kind of like a mini-DNS server for your network. A Hosts file consists of the IP address of each computer on the network followed by the *friendly name* you want assigned to the computer.

To create a Hosts file, open a text document, and type in the IP address of the first computer on your network, followed by one space, and then the computer's "friendly name." Note that this name doesn't have to be the same as the NetBIOS name that you assign a PC in the Network control panel's Identification tab, but it can be. At the end of the line, hit Enter. Continue this process until you've included all the computers on the network, and then save the file as Hosts with no file extension. See Figure 12-19.

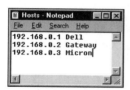

Figure 12-19: The mini-DNS
A Hosts file functions like a mini-DNS on a TCP/IP network, enabling you to match each computer's IP address with a user-friendly name.

This last step is important and easy to overlook because most programs automatically add a file extension to any document you save. One way to force Notepad to save without adding an extension is to type in the name "Hosts" in quotation marks in the Save As dialog box. The other option is to simply rename the file in Windows Explorer. When you do, it should give you a generic Windows icon. (By they way, you must have File Extensions turned on in order to do this. To turn File Extensions on, open Windows Explorer, go to the View menu, choose Folder Options, select the View tab, then deselect the Hide file extensions for known file types check box. You may also have to turn on the Show all files option under the Hidden Files folder.)

Cross-Reference

See Chapter 14, "Working with Documents and Files" for more on file extensions and types.

The Hosts file has to be saved into or copied in the /Windows directory on each computer's hard drive in order for the mini-DNS to work properly. (By the way, if you add a computer to a TCP/IP network, don't forget to add it to the Hosts file on each computer.)

Once that's done and you restart your machine, your TCP/IP network should be all set. To confirm that everything's working properly, use the PING utility to check the connections between computers on the network. PING, which stands for Packet Internet Groper, sends a quick message to a particular IP address and then times how long it takes to get a reply back. It's commonly used to check that connections are set up properly. The version of PING bundled with Windows 95 and Windows 98 is a DOS utility, so to use it you need to open an MS-DOS window and type in **ping** followed by the IP address of a computer on the network. So, for example, on your network you could type in **ping 192.168.0.2** to test your connection with the second computer you set up.

Secret

The other way to do this is to open up the Run command window of the Windows Start menu and enter the ping command and IP address there.

Once you've done that and received a successful reply, try typing **ping** and then the friendly name you've given to one of the computers. If that works, you're all set. Any application you use on the network, such as file sharing, should enable you to use the friendly name you assigned to a computer in the Hosts file. If it doesn't, double-check the contents of your Hosts file and your TCP/IP settings.

Adding a Macintosh to your network

One of the great things about networks is that it enables computers of different types to communicate with one another. And for small businesses or homes that have a mix of Apple Macintoshes and Windows-based PCs, this feature can be a godsend, enabling Mac and PC users to easily share files and even peripherals, such as printers, modems, and more.

As difficult as it may first appear, making Macs and PCs work together on a network really isn't very difficult. You need to follow the same basic rules as you would if you were to network multiple PCs. Each computer needs a common network connection (for example, 10-BaseT Ethernet), the same network protocols, and the same kind of network services installed. The real issue is that getting the right protocols and network services requires the installation of some third-party software because neither Microsoft nor Apple provides everything you need to ensure proper communications between Windows and MacOS-based machines over a network. In other words, it's gonna cost ya.

The actual procedure and software you need depends on whether you want to add Macs to a PC-based network or PCs to a Mac-based network. If you're connecting only one or a few of each, then either method works. (The difference simply boils down to whether you use the protocols that are more common to PCs or those that are more common to Macs.) Because this book is called "Personal Computer Secrets," I presume that you want to attach a Mac or two to a PC-based network.

Lost in the translation

Many people mistakenly presume that just because you can access Mac or PC files over a network that you can automatically use them. In some situations this is true, but in many cases, unfortunately, it's not. Many Mac and PC programs use different file formats (which refers to how the data in, say, a word processing or graphics file, is organized), and not all PC and Macintosh applications can read each other's formats.

So in order to read certain files on either computer, you may also have to install and use file conversion utilities, such as DataViz Mac-Opener (www.dataviz.com), Conversions Plus for the PC, or MacLinkPlus for the Mac. See the following figure.

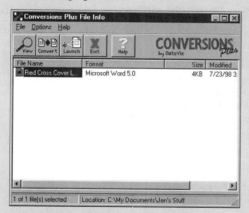

Crossing platforms

In order to read and use Mac-created files on a Windows-based PC, you may need to use a file conversion program such as DataViz Conversions Plus.

What Conversions Plus, MacOpener, and similar products do is take a file that's stored in one format and convert it into another format that an application you have can open and use. Then when you're done using and/or changing the file, these utilities generally can also convert it back.

Over the last few years the file format situation between Mac and PCs has gotten much better. Microsoft Office file formats from Office 97 and Office 2000 on the PC and Office 98 on the Mac, for example, are directly compatible and can be opened on either a Mac or a PC, regardless of which machine created the file. But it's still not perfect. Many programs are also starting to incorporate more full-featured file translation capabilities within the program itself. Another help has been the growth of universal file formats, such as HTML, JPEG, and GIF, which are commonly found in Web-based documents. These types of documents or files can be easily opened on either Macs or PCs.

The only problem you may come across has to do with matching file types on the Mac with file extensions on the PC. The situation is essentially this: each type of computer uses different mechanisms to distinguish between, say, a word processing file and a GIF graphic. The Mac uses an internal file marking called a *Creator code* to tell the Mac what application was used to create this application and a *File Type* to tell it what kind of file it is. On the PC, both of these mechanisms are handled by file extensions, the three-characters that come after the period in a filename. In a file called "letter.doc", for example, the "doc" file extension tells the Windows-based computer that it's a word processing file that's been created in Microsoft Word.

Continued

(continued)

To get cross-platform files to open in the proper application (or to open at all, in some cases), you need to match the Mac File Type with the PC file extension. Apple provides software with the MacOS called "PC File Exchange" that can handle this on the Mac side. On the PC side, DataViz Conversions Plus can also take care of this issue. However, many times on the PC all you have to do is rename a Mac file and add the appropriate file extension to the name. So for example, to open a Mac-created HTML file called

"Site Map" on a PC, you may need to rename it on the PC to "Site Map.htm." Note that even with the proper translation, it's not uncommon to lose certain formatting elements and other minor document characteristics. (See Chapter 14, "Working with Documents and Files" for more on file types and file translations.)

You'll find a demo copy of JASC Software's QuickView Plus file viewing software, which also handles file translations, on the CD accompanying this book.

Many Macs now come standard with 10-BaseT Ethernet (or even 100-BaseTX) ports (and plenty of Mac-based Ethernet cards are available for those machines that don't), so the physical connections between Macs and PCs are simple. You plug the Macs into any port on an Ethernet hub, just as you would if you were adding more PCs to a network.

To get the communications working, you also need to add the proper networking protocols and network services. The best solution for Macs attaching to PC networks is a product called Dave from Thursby Systems (www.thursby.com). Dave installs on the Mac (or Macs) and requires no changes whatsoever on the PC. (Miramar System's PC MacLAN Connect at www.miramarsys.com, on the other hand, is a better choice for attaching a PC to a Mac network. It installs on the PC and requires no changes on the Mac.)

Dave includes the TCP/IP protocol for Macs and supports NetBIOS that, as explained previously, is used on Windows-based PCs whenever you enable File and Print Sharing for Microsoft Networks. Dave also includes the necessary file sharing software that enables Macs to look and work just like PCs in a PC-only network. With Dave installed on a Mac, you can see and view shared Mac resources, including files and printers, from any PC attached to the network. Similarly, with Version 2.0 or later of Dave, Mac users have access to any shared PC files or printers. Unfortunately, as experienced Mac-to-PC computer folks know, just because you have access to each other's files doesn't necessarily mean you can always use them (see sidebar, "Lost in the translation").

Expanding your network

Once you've got a simple network put together in either a small business or a home, adding additional computers (or other peripherals) to it is straightforward. Just connect any new PCs to the existing hub, install the necessary network drivers, clients, protocols, and services, and you should be all set. With the proper settings enabled, each new computer should have complete access to the same network features that all the existing computers have, and other network users can take advantage of whatever new data and/or capabilities that the new machine may add (such as a new printer attached to it).

If your network really starts to grow, then you'll probably want to switch to a client-server type of network, and you may also need to investigate some additional network hardware. Large network setups are beyond the scope of this book (IDG offers plenty of other great networking titles), but I want to give you at least a brief overview of some of the issues and terminology you may hear about.

First, if you run out of ports on your original hub, you may be able to simply attach another hub to it and keep expanding. Many hubs come with an *uplink* or similarly named port that enables you to daisy-chain one hub to another and attach more computers to your network. Not all inexpensive hubs do, however, so if you want to prepare for the future, buy a hub that offers this feature.

If you find that your network is really slow because lots of people are using it all the time, you may want to investigate an Ethernet switch, or a hybrid device called a *switching hub*. Standard hubs divide the Ethernet bandwidth among all the connected computers whereas switches or switching hubs provide a full-bandwidth connection to each port. So, for example, if you have a 10Mbps 10Base-T network with three computers attached to a typical hub, then that 10Mbps is shared among all three computers. With a switching hub, however, each device connected to the hub has its own dedicated 10Mbps (or faster, depending on the type of hub you have) connection to the hub. Not surprisingly, switches and switching hubs are a lot more expensive than regular hubs. Figure 12-20 shows an example.

If you need to connect two different networks, such as a Mac network on one side of the building with a Windows network on the other side, or even two Windows networks on different floors of a building, you'll want to investigate a *bridge*. Most bridges can "translate" between two different types of network protocols and can handle "routing" the network messages that cross the network boundaries. Devices that perform protocol translations are also called *gateways*.

An even more sophisticated (and typically a more expensive) solution for routing network data across different types of networks or over long distance connections is, logically enough, called a *router*. Routers typically include some "intelligence" that helps them figure out the best and most efficient way to send a packet of data to its final destination. For this reason, as well as many others, routers play a critical role in transferring information over the Internet.

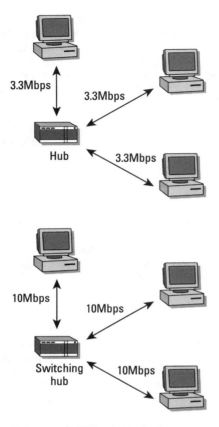

Figure 12-20: Hubs vs. switches
With a hub, all users on a network share the available bandwidth, while a switch or switching hub gives each user a full bandwidth connection.

Creating a Home Network

Even though I've done my best to explain networking as simply as possible, the fact is, it's still pretty complicated. Not only are the concepts and terminology difficult to understand, it's hard to physically connect and configure everything on a network to get it working properly. It's not impossible, but it does take make more work than some people are willing to expend.

Luckily, several companies have recognized this fact and have developed complete solutions for home networks. These products not only solve the problems associated with running network wiring all over and through your house, they also simplify the setup and configuration process. However, even though they make it easier than doing it from scratch, it still helps tremendously to understand what's going on. In fact, in some situations, you'll still have to do some of the manual configuration I explained in previous sections.

Each home networking product has its own specific method for overcoming network configuration difficulties, but they're all using the principles I've described early in this chapter. They all offer some type of network adapter and means of connection between computers, and they all install and set up network clients, protocols, and services. They just do it behind the façade of a single software installation and some simple, add-on hardware. Figure 12-21 shows a typical example.

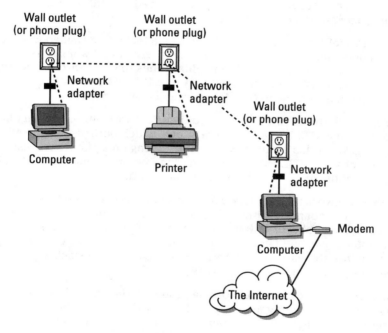

Figure 12-21: Easy home networks
Most home networking products make the process of creating a simple network easy. You attach adapters to each of the computers in your home (and sometimes each printer), run a cable to an available phone jack or power line, run an installation program, and you're done. Some systems even avoid the cables by making wireless connections between your PCs.

The primary differences between these various systems are the types of network adapters they use and the means for connecting the various computers. As I explained earlier in the chapter, most homeowners are unable and/or unwilling to run network wiring throughout the house. This is why each of these different home networking products either take advantage of a home's existing wiring (a feature touted as using *no new wires*) or do their magic without the aid of any wires whatsoever.

One caveat I want to warn you of is that early versions of some of these products had reliability problems, but as with many computer-related products, later versions are more robust.

Phone lines

Most people don't realize it, but if their home features multiple phone jacks (not necessarily extra phone lines — just extra jacks), then they actually have simple network wiring already in place. Members of the Home Phoneline Networking Alliance, or HomePNA, a consortium of computer networking companies, recognized that fact and decided to built their home networking products around this network.

The HomePNA agreed to standardize on a technology called *HomeRUN* that was developed by Tut Systems. HomeRUN offers a 1Mbps Ethernet connection over standard home phone lines that run throughout any home. A faster version that offers speeds of up to 10Mbps but is still backward compatible with the initial 1Mbps products is also available.

Best of all, the technology does not interfere with either normal phone calls or high-speed DSL Internet connections, which both also use regular home wiring. What this means is you can be talking on a phone, accessing the Internet via an DSL modem, and sharing files on a home network, all with a single phone line. Now that's what I call multitasking.

Home networking products that conform to the HomePNA's standard consist of network adapters, either plug-in cards or external boxes that attach to your PC's parallel or USB ports, and software that takes care of the necessary adapter drivers and network protocols. You attach the adapters to your PC, install the software, plug the adapters into any phone jack in your house, and you've got a simple home network.

Like most of the home networking products, the phone line–based networks do not require any type of hub (although they function like a star topology network because a broken connection between one PC and the network does not bring the entire network down).

In the future, the HomePNA is hoping to build computers, printers, and other peripherals with network adapters already built in so that all you have to do is plug a phone line from the device to any phone jack in the wall to add it to your home network.

Power lines

Phone lines aren't the only wiring that already exists in virtually all homes. The other type is power lines, which can be accessed via any electrical outlet in the house. In fact, because there are more electrical outlets in homes than there are phone jacks, power line–based networking products, such as the

Passport Plug-In Network from Intelogis, can be a bit more flexible when you first set them up.

As with phone line–based home networking products, power line–based networking products consist of network adapters that you plug into one of your PC's or printer's ports and software that handles setting up network clients, protocols, and services, such as file sharing. Simply plug the network adapters into the wall and install the software, and your home network is complete.

Initial versions of Intelogis Passport, the first of this kind to ship, offered transfer rates of 350Kbps. This isn't as fast as some of the phone line–based networks but it is adequate for most purposes, even sharing a moderate speed Internet connection such as ISDN (Integrated Services Digital Network), which offers a transfer rate of 128Kbps. As with phone line–based networks, faster versions are also available.

Secret

One potential issue with power line–based networking products, such as Passport, is that the electrical wiring extends your network outside the confines of your home to the nearest power transformer. Because most transformers are shared by several homes, if one of your neighbors also sets up a Passport Plug-In Network, they could conceivably tap into your network (and vice versa). Intelogis takes care of this problem by offering built-in security features that keep your PCs from showing up on any nearby Passport network, but it is something you should be aware of.

Wireless

The final type of home networking product uses no wires whatsoever — it's wireless. The only difference between wireless home networks and the other varieties is that on some wireless networks the required adapters connect only to your PC. The other part of the transfer is handled by the adapter's built-in radio transmitter, which sends data across a relatively short distance (long enough to get from one end of most houses to another, but not long enough to send it into all your neighbors' homes). The transmissions occur using any one of a number of different wireless technologies, including spread spectrum.

Maximum transfer rates across wireless networks vary (some of the initial products promised 500Kbps), but they usually tend to be slower than what's available for wired networks. Unlike most of the "no new wires" products, some wireless networking systems do use a centralized hub, which functions just as it would in a normal wired network.

As with some of the power line–based products, data security can be an issue if multiple neighboring houses are each using wireless networks, so most also include built-in security features to keep your network's data private.

Wireless networks, like any of the other home networking schemes, provide all the capabilities that you expect from a traditional "wired" network, including file and printer sharing, sharing a single Internet connection, and the capability of playing multiplayer games.

Speaking of which, it's time now to move on to what you can do with your network.

Taking Advantage of Your Network

Getting computers connected and speaking the same language may be somewhat interesting for some people, but it's really just a necessary evil to get to the good stuff: putting your new network to use. In order to take advantage of your network, you need to configure network services, such as file and printer sharing, which I've already mentioned several times throughout this chapter. Network services are features or capabilities that the network enables and which don't exist (or which exist in a different form) on standalone PCs.

By far the most popular and most useful network services of peer-to-peer networks are file and printer sharing. With these services enabled you can quickly and easily copy files to and from your computer to any other computer on the network that also has sharing enabled, as well as print from one computer to any printer on the network that's being shared.

To make file and print sharing available, it has to be installed. Many computers already have file and print sharing installed and turned on (in some cases, much to your surprise), but the only way to tell for sure is to check. You do that by opening your now old friend the Network control panel and looking for File and Printer sharing for Microsoft Networks. If it's not there, simply click Add, select Service, click Add again, select Microsoft from the list of available manufacturers on the left, and then choose File and Printer sharing for Microsoft Networks on the right, and hit OK.

Even if it's installed, you may need to make sure that it's turned on. To do this, click the File and Print Sharing button in the opening screen of the Network control panel, and put check marks next to the two service descriptions in the dialog box that appears. See Figure 12-22.

Figure 12-22: File and print sharing
This simple dialog box, available from the Network control panel, lets you turn File and Print Sharing on and off individually on a peer-to-peer network.

If file and print sharing doesn't seem to work and you can't "see" any other computer resources available on your network, make sure that it's bound to the proper protocol. Open the Network control panel, select File and Printer Sharing for Microsoft Networks, hit Properties, find the Bindings tab, and check to see which, if any, protocols are selected. If necessary, install and then bind the required protocols (that is, whatever the other computers on the network are using), using the procedures listed earlier in this chapter.

Sharing files

Once the file and print sharing service is installed and turned on, you need to decide which files, drives, and/or printers you want to share with other computers on your network. Simply turning on file sharing won't automatically make everything on your computer available to other users, which is a common misconception; you need to explicitly make it available to others. If you don't and nothing on the network is shared, then you won't be able to see anything, and it looks as if your network isn't working. In fact, if you're just setting up a new network and it doesn't appear to work, this is one of the first things to check.

Here's how you share files.

STEPS:
Sharing files on a Peer-to-peer Network

Step 1. Open Windows Explorer (available off the Start Menu under Programs), and select either the individual file, folder, or drive you wish to make available. Even though you can make multiple selections in Explorer, you can share only one at a time, so select only one item.

Step 2. Right-click the item, and choose Sharing from the context menu.

Step 3. In the dialog box that appears, click the Share As button, and if you want, type in a different name for the item. The name you type here is the name that other computers on the network see when they browse the network. Any comment you type in is visible to others who are browsing the network with the Detail View turned on. See Figure 12-23.

Step 4. If you want only certain people to have access to certain files or folders that you're going to share, you can use the password sections of this dialog. (See the sidebar, "File security," for more.) If you want everyone to see the file you're sharing, simply leave these sections blank.

Continued

STEPS

Sharing files on a Peer-to-peer Network *(continued)*

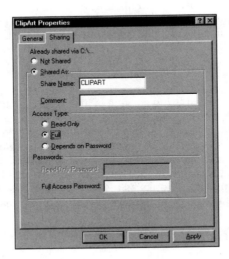

Figure 12-23: Sharing files
To share a file, folder, or volume, right-click the item in Windows Explorer, choose Sharing, and make the item available by clicking the Share As button in this dialog box.

Step 5.   Hit OK and you're done. After a moment or two the icon of the item you shared has a cupped hand underneath it to remind you that it has been shared on the network. See Figure 12-24.

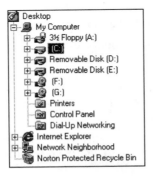

Figure 12-24: Shared icon
Any item that's being shared on Windows peer-to-peer network has a hand icon underneath it in Windows Explorer.

File security

As useful as networks can be, they sometimes create problems of their own. One of the main issues that can arise is the availability of potentially sensitive information. On most home networks, this issue isn't a concern, but if you're putting together a small business network or if you want to avoid having your kids accidentally delete your Quicken file or other important data, you may have to deal with file security.

Of course, you can avoid the problem entirely by simply not sharing any files or folders that you don't want to be seen, changed, and/or deleted, but there are situations where you might want a few people on a network to have access to a file, but not everyone. If that is your situation, the file sharing in Windows offers some fairly flexible options.

First of all, you can decide if you want a file to be marked as read-only, which means that anyone can open it but only you (or whoever uses the machine on which the file was first shared) can edit or delete it. The other option is to give people full access to the file, which means anyone can open it, edit it, or even delete it.

You can also password-protect a file by typing in a required password in the Sharing dialog box. You can require a password for read-only access, require one for full access (which still enables anyone to view the file, even without a password), or specify a different password for each type of access.

If you do use a password, it applies to everyone, including you, so if you forget a password, you won't be able to get access to a password-protected file.

None of these security methods are foolproof. The capability of anyone who uses a computer that first shared a file to have full access to it, even if it's a read-only file, is a particularly bad security hole so don't rely on these security measures for super-sensitive information. However, in most situations, they work just fine.

To view any files that have been shared on a network, you use Windows' Network Neighborhood, which should be available on your desktop if you've installed any network software, such as network clients or protocols. Network Neighborhood looks and works like Windows Explorer. See Figure 12-25.

Figure 12-25: The Network Neighborhood
In order to see any files or folder that are shared on a network, you use Network Neighborhood, which works like Windows Explorer, although it only offers one pane to view the data.

One important difference from Windows Explorer is that the initial screen of Network Neighborhood shows you computers on the network and an icon for the Entire Network. But once you double-click one of those and then any workgroups you've created, which essentially "connects" you to a computer, you'll see files and folders that are shared on that PC. You can open, copy, and depending on the permissions that have been assigned to a file (see the sidebar "File security"), even delete those items, just as you can the files and folders you see on your computer.

Secret

If you prefer, you can even use Internet Explorer to look for files and folders on a network by typing in the "address" of the computer and information you're looking for. Just type in the file's location in the form of //*computername* (filling in the appropriate name, of course) where you would normally type in a Web site address. This trick also works on your own computer's hard drive(s). Simply substitute My Computer, or whatever drive letter you're trying to get to, in place of //*computername* at the beginning of the address, and you're in business. If you don't know the exact location of the information you want, you can also browse through the drive by simply starting out with the computer's name or the drive letter for your own PC.

The difference between Internet Explorer, Network Neighborhood, and Windows Explorer is that Internet Explorer and Network Neighborhood show you only one window pane, whereas Windows Explorer shows you two, which makes it easier to copy files from one place to another.

Sharing drives

In addition to making individual files or folders available to other users on your network, you can also share entire drives. In some cases, such as with home networks, sharing drives is the easiest way to make sure that any computer on the network can get to any files stored on any computer.

Tip

Another really practical benefit of sharing drives is that it lets you do things such as enable a computer that lacks a CD- or DVD-ROM drive to have access to one in order to install and or run software applications that the computer couldn't otherwise have access to. So, for example, imagine you have a desktop machine with a CD- or DVD-ROM and a notebook computer that doesn't. If you want to install a new CD-based program onto the notebook, you can share the desktop's CD drive, and any disc you put into that drive is made available to any computer on the network, including your notebook (presuming you have network connections set up for both, of course). The notebook user simply "connects" to that drive via its own Network Neighborhood and then runs the installation program, just as if it had a CD or DVD drive of its own. Because the program is running over the network connection, the process may take a bit longer, but the installation will still work.

Tip

You can also share removable drives that are attached to a single computer with all the computers on the network, which can be very handy for backup purposes. Instead of having to detach and reconnect a drive (a process that's nearly impossible if the removable drive is an internal one) to each computer on your network, you can simply share the drive on the network, and let others copy their important files onto the drive.

One problem you may run into with sharing drives is different file systems. For example, if you have a network that combines one PC running an early version of Windows 95 with another running a later version of Windows 95 or 98, you can run into a problem if the Windows 98 machine is using the FAT32 file system (see Chapter 8 for more). Versions of Windows 95 prior to OSR2, or Windows 95 B, cannot recognize or work with FAT32-formatted drives and so is unable to connect to a FAT32 drive (or any files or folders from a FAT32 drive).

Cross-Reference

See Chapter 3, "Hard Disks and Removable Drives" for more on partitioning, FAT32, and file systems.

Similarly, Windows 95 and Windows 98 cannot "read" disks formatted with NTFS, (short for NT File System), which is the default disk format of computers running any version of Windows NT and Windows 2000. So again, if you created a peer-to-peer network with a computer running Windows NT or Windows 2000 and Windows 98, you may not be able to share files, depending on the format of the drives being shared.

There are two ways around this problem. You can make sure that all Windows 95/98/2000 computers standardize on FAT32 support, which may mean updating the version of Windows used on the computer and converting the disk to FAT32 (which are two *different* steps). Or if you're using Windows NT as well, fall back to the old FAT16 format (usually just called FAT). *FAT*, which stands for File Allocation Table, is a relatively universal format that can be read by Windows 95/98/2000/NT and Windows for Workgroups. The problem is, it isn't as efficient or as robust as either FAT32 or NT's NTFS.

Mapping drives

One thing you can do to make sharing drives across a network easier, particularly if you want to access data across the network from within an application, is to "map" a shared drive onto one of your own computer's driver letters. What mapping does is simply assign a drive letter on your PC to another drive being shared on a network. For example, if you have a simple two-computer network with your PC and one in your kids' room, you can map the C: drive on your kids' PC to the M: drive on your computer. See Figure 12-26.

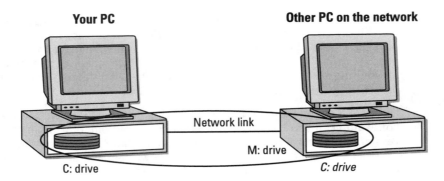

Your PC **Other PC on the network**

Network link

M: drive

C: drive *C: drive*

Figure 12-26: Making a drive your own
The process of mapping a shared drive available on the network turns that drive into a local resource on your computer by assigning it a drive letter on your PC. The drive letter you assign a mapped drive is completely independent of the letter it uses on its native PC.

To map a network drive onto your PC, you can either right-click the Network Neighborhood icon and choose Map Network Drive from the context menu that appears, or open Windows Explorer, and choose Map Network Drive from the Tools menu. In either case you'll be presented with a dialog box where you choose the letter you want the network drive assigned to (this dialog box can be different for each PC on the network) and then type in the name of the drive using the universal naming convention (UNC). See Figure 12-27.

Figure 12-27: Mapping network drives
You can assign a network drive to any unused letter on your PC, although it's generally better to choose something other than the first available letter in the event you add another hard drive or removable drive to your PC.

The UNC syntax for Windows-based machines is *computername**sharename* where *computername* is the name of the computer you're connecting to and *sharename* is the name of the drive or folder being shared. (Linux and other versions of UNIX turn the slashes the other way //.) So, for example, a UNC name might be \\Bob's_Computer\Main_Drive. (You can't use spaces in computer names or shared file names so some people use the underscore character instead.) Note that if a different name was assigned to the drive or folder when it was shared, you have to use that shared name, not necessarily what it's called on the other computer. Also be aware that if you want access to a folder that's buried a few levels deep, the UNC name might be something such as \\Bob's_Computer\Main_Drive\Work\Word_Files.

Tip

One final note on mapping. You don't have to map network drives to get access to them, but it can make the process of getting to data on the network much easier. For example, if you're working in your word processor and you want to open a file on a shared network drive that's been mapped to drive M: you simply go to M: in the Open dialog box of your application. This is really handy if you've mapped M: to a folder that's buried somewhere on the shared drive. If that folder hasn't been mapped, you have to go through the Network Neighborhood icon, which is visible when you go to the My Computer icon in an Open or Save dialog, and then browse your way down to the folder you want.

Sharing printers

Sharing printers on a peer-to-peer network is as easy as sharing files. Simply open the Printers folder on the computer connected to the printer you want to share by going to the Start Menu, up to Settings, and then over to Printers. Select the printer you want to share, right-click it, and select the Sharing option from the context menu that appears. In the dialog box that appears, select Share As, and give the printer a name and, if you want, a password, which other users on the network are required to enter before they can use the printer. See Figure 12-28.

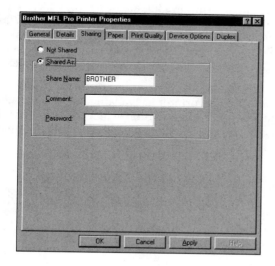

Figure 12-28: Sharing printers
Sharing printers is as easy as sharing files. Fill out this dialog box, hit OK, and your printer is available to anyone else on the network.

In order for others on the network to use a shared printer, they'll have to install the printer's drivers by using the Add Printer Wizard, which is also available from the Printers folder. Just double-click Add Printer, and follow the directions, and be sure to choose Network printer in the second step of the process. See Figure 12-29.

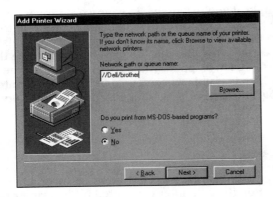

Figure 12-29: Connecting to a network printer
The Add Printer Wizard in Windows 95/98/2000 walks you through the process of making a shared network printer available for you to use. To select the printer, you can either type in its UNC name or use the Browse button to find it on the network.

When Windows 95/98/2000 completes the wizard, it attempts to install the printer's drivers from the main Windows installation files, which may be located on your hard disk or which may require you to insert the Windows 95, 98, or 2000 CD. If you know that you have more recent versions of the printer's drivers on a floppy or other CD, have those disks ready before you start the process and choose the Have Disk option when it becomes available.

Once the drivers are installed, the printer is available for your use. Just open a file in any application, choose Print, and then select the network printer from the drop-down list of choices that are available from within the Print dialog box. See Figure 12-30.

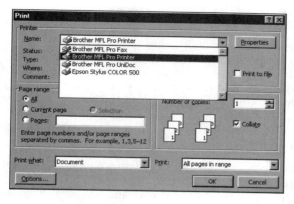

Figure 12-30: Printing over the network
Printing to a network printer is as easy as printing to a locally attached printer. Because the printing process occurs over the network, however, it generally takes a longer time. Also, the machine to which the printer you're using is attached may slow down a bit when other users on the network print to it.

Sharing scanners

In addition to printers, some scanners come with software that enables you to share them over a simple peer-to-peer network. By installing this software on each computer on the network, you merely launch the scanning application, and it attempts to *connect* to the scanner over the network. Once the connection is made, you can use the scanner with the software in the same way you would if the scanner was connected locally. Again, the process typically is a bit slower over a network connection, but it works the same.

Of course, if you need to scan in a photo, you're going to have to walk over to where the scanner is located anyway to put the photo onto the scanner's glass (or into a sheet-fed scanner). But once the document or photo you want scanned is there, you can try out different scan settings from the remote machine.

Tip

Be aware that some network scanning software works only with certain network protocols, so you may have to install some other protocols to make it work. (In fact, this is true of different types of network-aware software in general. Some applications work with multiple protocols, and some work with only one or two specific kinds.) Also, not all scanners can be networked, so if networking a scanner is important, be sure you check on the capabilities of the software bundled with the scanner before you buy it.

Sharing an Internet connection

Another really useful application for home and small business networks — in fact, some people consider it the "killer application" for home networks — is to share a single Internet access account. Rather than having to bother with setting up and paying for multiple accounts, you can use your network to give every computer connected to it access to the Net. In fact, you can set it up so that multiple computers are connected (or can be connected) simultaneously, which is particularly helpful if you have a high-speed connection, such as through a cable or DSL modem.

Note

If you do have an external DSL or cable modem, you'll need two network cards (or adapters) in the PC attached to the modem through which you share the connection. One is for the network and one for the modem.

To set up a shared Internet connection, you can either use hardware, which is the more expensive route, or use software only. If you want to use hardware, you need a device called a *router*, and if you go with software, you'll need something called a *proxy server*. The proxy server is installed on just one PC on the network — the one that's attached to the modem through which you make the Internet connection. In either case, you'll need an already established Internet account. (Several of the home networking products described earlier in the chapter come bundled with the software you need.)

**Cross-
Reference**

See Chapter 13, "Connecting to and Using the Internet" for more on setting up an Internet account.

A router or proxy server takes requests from computers on the network and funnels them through the single Internet connection. It then receives data back from the Internet and passes it back to the specific machine(s) on the network that requested it. So, for example, if the person on computer A requests www.idgbooks.com (by typing the address into their Web browser) and the person on computer B types www.everythingcomputers.com into their browser, then those requests are sent to the router or proxy server and onto the Internet. When both those pages are received, the router or proxy server makes sure that the IDG Books home page goes to computer A and the Everything Computers home page goes to computer B. The router or proxy server do so by using the TCP/IP addresses assigned to each computer on the network. (Remember that the TCP/IP protocol is required for Internet access.)

The most useful option for most home networks is a proxy server. Figure 12-31 shows an example.

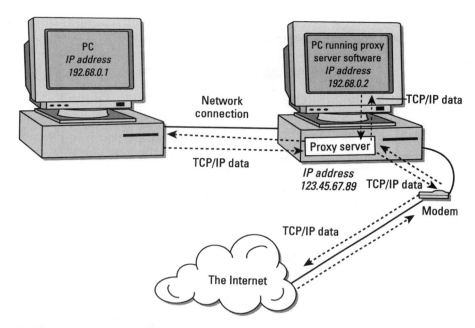

Figure 12-31: How a proxy server works
With proxy server software, such as WinGate, installed on your network, you can share a single Internet connection with multiple computers. The proxy server acts as a gateway, receiving requests from individual PCs and then sending them out to the Internet. It uses the network's TCP/IP addresses to direct the incoming data from the Internet to the right computer.

A trial version of Deerfield Software's WinGate proxy server that supports up to six different PCs is included on the CD accompanying this book.

An even easier option if you have Windows 98 Second Edition is to take advantage of the new Internet Connection Sharing feature built into the OS. To get to it, open the Add/Remove Programs Control Panel, click on the Windows Setup tab, and select Internet Connection Sharing. Once you've installed it, follow the Wizard it uses to set up a shared Internet connection. Note that using ICS takes care of assisting IP addresses automatically, so you don't need to do that separately.

If you do set up a proxy server for your network, you may have to deal with a few software configuration issues. Basically, any software that accesses the Internet, including your Web browser, e-mail package, and even certain browser plug-ins, such as the RealAudio player, has to be set up to work with a proxy server. The default settings for most of these programs is to work with a direct Internet connection, so they cannot work properly with your shared Internet connection unless you change them.

Figure 12-32 shows an example of setting a browser, in this case, Netscape Communicator 4.5, to work with a proxy server.

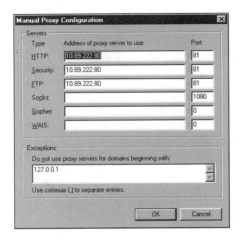

Figure 12-32: Configuring a proxy
The only downside of using a proxy server is that you may have to configure all your Internet applications, including browsers, e-mail, and plug-ins to use a specific proxy server and then supply the IP address for that server.

Thankfully, some proxy servers (including WinGate) come with a utility that makes many of these changes for you, although it may not work on all your Web-based software. In the event that it doesn't, the basic issues are that you have to set the Internet connection to be via a proxy server, and you have to provide the IP address of that proxy server. In most cases that address is the same IP address that you gave to the network adapter attached to the computer running the proxy server software. You'll find it inside the TCP/IP Properties page of the Network control panel.

Note

If you have a dial-up Internet connection through a regular modem, make sure you check under the network adapter's TCP/IP settings and not the dial-up adapter's TCP/IP settings if you need to look this up again. This is because the proxy server uses the dial-up adapter's TCP/IP settings to connect to the Internet. If you have two network cards — one attached to your home network and the other to your cable or DSL modem — make sure you get the IP address assigned to the network card attached to your high-speed modem.

A few other issues you need to consider with regard to proxy servers is whether or not they provide any Web caching. In other words, whether or not they maintain a separate set of files that your browser can access to possibly speed up your web access, and whether or not they support any security features. Some proxy servers, but not all, incorporate basic firewall features, which can prevent hackers from breaking into your home network and getting access to your PC's data.

Tip

In order for any computer on the network to get out to the Internet, the computer running the proxy server software has to be on with the proxy server running. In addition, the proxy server software can have a minor impact on the performance of the computer running it. As a result of these two issues, some people prefer to dedicate an older computer to the job of being the proxy server and then attach it to the network along with any other PCs available. Even an old 486 can typically do the job, although you'll need to be sure that the operating system and proxy server software can be installed on the machine. (If you are willing to be a bit adventurous, you may want to consider the Linux operating system for the proxy server because most distributions of Linux include all the software you need.)

Cross-Reference

See Chapter 9, "Adding, Upgrading, and Removing Software" for more on installing Linux.

You can also share a modem over a network for non-Internet purposes, such as if you want to attach to a bulletin board system. However, as with sharing an Internet account, the software you need is not included in either Windows 95 or 98, so you'll need to obtain it and install it separately.

Playing games

There's more to life than work and there's more to computers than being productive. Sometimes it's important to just have fun. And one of the best ways to have fun with a home network or a small business one (uh, after work hours, of course, ahem) is to play multiplayer computer games over a network.

Setting up multiplayer games is usually simple (as long as the rest of the network is set up and running). In most cases you just need to be sure that you've installed the correct network protocols on each of the computers on the network that you plan to use for playing games. Many games use the IPX/SPX protocol, some use TCP/IP, and some offer the choice of either.

Once you've installed and, in the case of TCP/IP, configured the protocols, then all you generally have to do is tell the game that you want to play over a network. Many games provide this choice on an opening screen, and others require you to enter this choice in an options or preferences dialog box, or another settings page. See Figure 12-33.

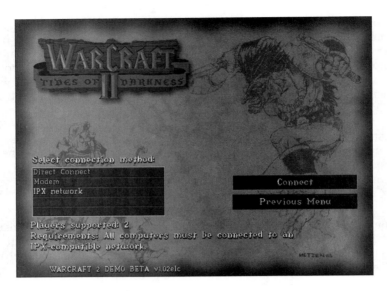

Figure 12-33: Network games
Most games that offer network support (not all do, of course) make it easy to play over a network, though the specifics of how to set them up for network play vary from game to game.

Building an intranet

The hot buzzword in business networks over the last few years has been *intranets*. More and more companies are building intranets to provide information-based resources to their employees and their customers. If you run a small business, don't feel left out. You can have one too.

An intranet is simply a network that uses Internet standards, such as the TCP/IP protocol and internal Web servers. In fact, if you've put together a peer-to-peer network with TCP/IP, as I've described in this chapter, you practically have an intranet already. All you really need to do is to build an internal Web site and post it on that intranet, and you'll be on equal footing with all the big boys (and girls).

Cross-Reference

For more information on how to build a Web site, see the section "Building Your Own Web Site" in Chapter 13.

In order to post a Web site and make it available for others to see, you need to upload or "publish" a site onto a computer running Web server software. The Web server is what takes requests from users who want to view a Web page in their browser software and then sends that page out. When you create a Web site for the Internet, you typically post it to your Internet Service Provider's Web server, and other Internet users can get to the pages on your site through that Web server. If you're creating an intranet, however, you need Web server software of your own in order for other computers connected on your intranet to be able to see the Web site you create.

Thankfully, Microsoft includes a personal Web server in Windows 95 and 98 for free. Under Windows 95 (OSR2 or later), you can install Version 1.0 of the Personal Web Server as a network service. Just go to the Network control panel, click Add, select Service, and select Add again, and then in the dialog that appears, choose Microsoft on the left, and then choose Personal Web Server on the right and hit OK.

Under Windows 98, you have to install Personal Web Server separately. Insert the Windows 98 CD into your computer's CD/DVD-ROM, select the Run command on the Start menu, and type in **x:\add-ons\pws\setup.exe**, where x is the letter of your CD/DVD drive. If you're successful, you should see a dialog such as the one shown in Figure 12-34.

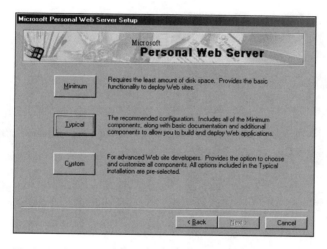

Figure 12-34: Windows 98 Personal Web Server
Under Windows 98, the Personal Web Server has to be installed separately from the operating system.

In either case, the next time you restart your computer, the Web server will be up and running. You can tell because an icon is added to your System Tray at the bottom right corner of your PC (or wherever your Taskbar happens to be located). If you're not sure which one it is, just hold your mouse over the icons for a second or two, and the name of each icon appears in a little yellow text box.

The Personal Web Server bundled with Windows 95 includes the capability of handling both http (hypertext transport protocol) requests, which are used to serve Web pages, as well as FTP (File Transfer Protocol), which is used to copy files back and forth. So, if you install and use the Personal Web Server, you can use it both to serve Web pages and as an alternative method of file sharing for sending and receiving certain files.

Version 4.0 of the Personal Web Server, which is the one bundled with Windows 98 (but which works and can be installed under Windows 95), does not support FTP, but it does offer a much simpler interface and includes tools for building and organizing a Web site.

To get access to the features of the Personal Web Server bundled with Windows 95, just double-click its icon in the Taskbar or open the Personal Web Server control panel (which is installed along with the Personal Web Server under Windows 95 only). The resulting dialog enables you to set whether the Personal Web Server should start every time your computer starts, turn the http and FTP services on and off independently, get access to help files, and open the server's administration software. See Figure 12-35.

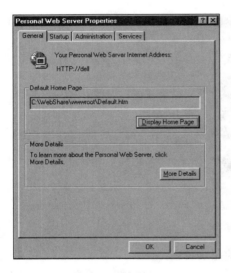

Figure 12-35: Personal Web Server
You can set a variety of options for the Web server bundled with Windows 95/98 in the Personal Web Server control panel.

If you decide to use the Personal Web Server for a simple intranet application, you may not ever need to worry about using the administration software, but it's still good to know a little bit about it. Like many Internet/intranet tools, the Internet Services Administrator is not actually a separate application, but a set of Web pages that contain settings you can use to configure the Web server. The types of settings you can change include setting passwords for accessing certain portions of the Web site, changing the directories where the site's files are stored, turning logging (which keeps track of things such as what pages were "served" at what time) on and off, and so on. See Figure 12-36.

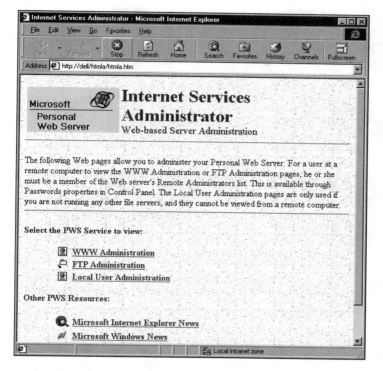

Figure 12-36: Configuring the server
If you want to, you can configure the Personal Web Server bundled with Windows 95 through a series of Web pages that act as a server administration program.

To get access to the Personal Web Server under Windows 98, go to the Start Menu, select Programs, Internet Explorer, Personal Web Server, and then select Personal Web Manager, which is the software that provides the interface to Personal Web Server 4.0. Personal Web Manager combines most (though not all) of the features of the Personal Web Server 1.0 control panel and separate Administration applications into one, and adds features for building a simple Web page. See Figure 12-37.

Tip

In addition to providing information for employees in a small business, building a simple intranet is also a great way to test a Web site while you're developing it and/or upgrading it. Not only can you test your efforts on your own machine before the rest of the world sees it, by connecting to it from other computers on the intranet, you can see what the site looks like from other browsers and at different screen resolutions. (Of course, you'll have to make sure you have the other browsers and different screen resolutions set on the various computers connected to your intranet for this to work.) If you have Macs attached to your network, you can even check your site from multiple platforms.

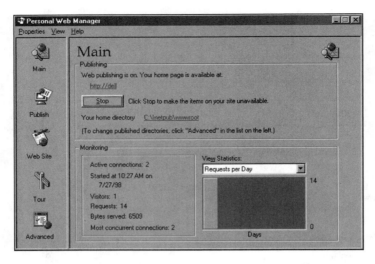

Figure 12-37: Personal Web Manager
Under Windows 98 (or Windows 95 with version 4.0 of the Personal Web Server software installed), you get access to the Personal Web Server's features through the Personal Web Manager application.

Remote access

Another great application for networks is to create what's called a *remote access server* (RAS). (Actually, you can even create this with just a single PC, but it's even more useful if you have a simple network.) With a remote access server you can dial into and connect to your network from a remote location so that, for example, if you forget to bring a file you need with you on a business trip, you can retrieve it from the network via a phone call from your hotel room. The way it works is you set up a dial-up connection on your notebook computer that dials up and connects to a modem attached to your small business network (or even just a single PC at home). At least one computer on the network, most likely the one attached to the modem you're dialing into, has to be running remote access server software.

Note

Creating a remote access server won't work if your home system has only a DSL or cable modem because those devices are incapable of receiving data calls or dialing out to make data calls. They're really just dedicated network connection devices, not really modems.

On the notebook end, you are asked to enter a username and password (which you create when you set up the remote-access server), and once the connection was made, you have access to all the resources on your network, just as if you were connected directly. In essence, the notebook becomes a temporary part of the network. See Figure 12-38 for an overview of how the process works.

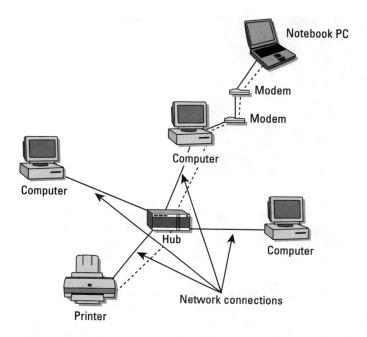

Figure 12-38: Remote access
If you set up a remote access server on one of your PCs, you can dial into your network from anywhere in the world. Once you're connected, your notebook computer can have access to anything that's available on the network, including files and printers.

Like the Personal Web Server, Microsoft bundles a simple remote access server (they actually call it a *Dial-Up Server*) that you can use on a peer-to-peer network with Windows computers, although it comes only with Windows 98. To install it, you go to the Dial-Up Networking folder, which can be found off the Start menu, via Programs, Accessories, and Communications under Windows 98. Once inside that folder, select Dial-Up Server off the Connections menu choice (if you can't see Connections, make the window larger). See Figure 12-39.

If you don't see the Dial-Up Server option on the menu, it's because the software hasn't been installed. Go to the Add/Remove Programs control panel, click Windows Setup, highlight Communications, click Details, and then select the Dial-Up Server check box, and hit OK to install it.

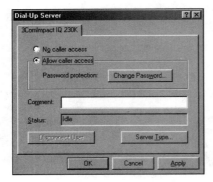

Figure 12-39: Dial-Up Server
You can set up a computer on your network (or even a single PC) to answer an incoming call
and give a remote user access to the network with the Remote Access Server software
bundled with Windows 98. Once you've set it up, it will run in the background and always be
available (as long as the computer running it remains on, that is).

In order for the Dial-Up Server to work, the calling machine (or client) needs
to be running the same network protocols as the machine running the server.
In most instances you can use either NetBEUI or TCP/IP. Whichever protocol
you do choose, make sure it's been enabled in the dial-up connection you
create on the client (in other words, your notebook). To check for that, right-
click the connection icon, choose Properties, click the Server Types tab, and
check to make sure that the appropriate check marks are made in the
Allowed network protocols section of the dialog (at the bottom). See Figure
12-40.

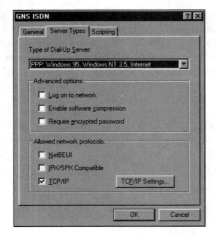

Figure 12-40: Enabling communications
In order for a dial-up connection to work, you need to make sure you enable the appropriate
network protocols in the Dial-up Networking connection's Properties settings.

Caution

If you do install a remote access server, be aware that you've opened up a potential security hole for your network. If you can dial in and connect to your network, that means someone else can as well, including someone who could conceivably cause damage to your network data. If you develop and use some basic security procedures, such as using and regularly changing the passwords required to gain access to the network, then you can help avoid problems. Just be aware that the convenience of a remote access server does come with a certain price.

Other network applications

Once you've got a network up and running, you can add lots of applications to your network to give it even more capabilities, including network backup, network faxing, videoconferencing, and e-mail. Going into detail on these items is beyond the scope of this book, but plenty of other great resources are available, including other networking books and Web sites.

Two additional applications I want to tell you about are handy little utilities bundled with Windows 95/98 that provide simple network messaging and network monitoring.

Network messaging

The WinPopup utility enables you to send a simple text message to all the users connected to your network. So, for example, if you need to announce that the birthday party in the conference room is about to begin or if you want to remind your teenage son or daughter that's currently immersed in a computer game or Web browsing session that dinner is ready, WinPopup works great. (Of course, you can use it for more important tasks as well.)

WinPopup isn't always installed as part of a default Windows installation, so you may have to add it. As with the Dial-Up Server software, go to the Add/Remove Programs control panel, select Windows Setup, then choose Accessories, click Details, and put a check mark next to WinPopup. After you hit OK, you may be asked to insert your Windows 95/98 CD, so be prepared.

Once it's installed you can use WinPopup by going to the Run command off the Start menu and typing in **winpopup**. Once the WinPopup window opens, you can send a message by going to the Messages menu and selecting Send. See Figure 12-41.

Unfortunately, WinPopup has to be running in order to receive messages. So to make it really useful, you'll need to copy it to the Startup folder of each computer on the network so that it starts (and runs in the background) each time any PC on the network starts up.

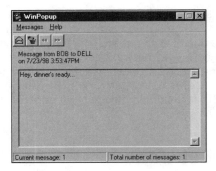

Figure 12-41: Network chat
A quick way to get everyone's attention on your network is to send them a quick message
with the little-known WinPopup utility that's bundled with Windows 95 and 98.

Network monitoring

After you've used your network for a while, you may also become interested
in monitoring its performance. Many sophisticated programs are available for
this purpose, but Microsoft bundles a utility called NetWatcher with Windows
95/98 that's usually more than sufficient for most peer-to-peer networks.
Again, you may have to install NetWatcher before you can find it. Under
Windows 95, it's available in the Accessories folder, and under Windows 98,
you can find it in the System Tools folder.

Once it's installed, NetWatcher appears on the Programs ➪ Accessories ➪
System Tools menu off the Start menu. NetWatcher is designed to monitor a
single server, so if you have a network with multiple peer servers (that is,
multiple computers set up to share their files), then you can run NetWatcher
on each one of them.

In order for NetWatcher to work efficiently, you need to enable remote
administration of the other computers connected to the network. Doing so
enables you, as the self-proclaimed administrator, to adjust settings on other
computers. To do so, you need to open the Passwords control panel on the
other computers on the network, select the Remote Administration tab, and
then put a check mark in the Enable Remote Administration of this server
check box. If you want, you can set a password for each computer, which can
help prevent others from making unwanted (or unintended) changes. See
Figure 12-42.

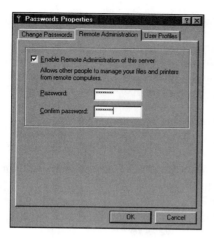

Figure 12-42: Offering access
In order for you to be able to use NetWatcher (or any other network monitoring software), the computers on the network must be set up to permit remote administration, which you do through the Passwords control panel.

With remote administration enabled, NetWatcher enables you to do a variety of things, including watching who's connected to the server and disconnecting them, if necessary; viewing and changing what resources are being shared; and closing open files on the server. See Figure 12-43.

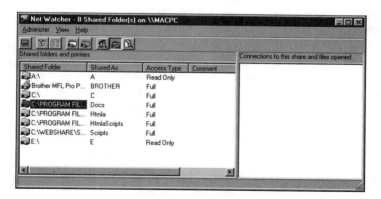

Figure 12-43: Watching the network
The bundled NetWatcher utility gives you a great deal of control over the computers attached to a peer-to-peer network, including changing which files or folders are available to be shared on a peer server.

The capabilities that NetWatcher provides can be extremely handy, particularly if a computer on the network locks up because of a network-related problem. For example, by closing a file that's stuck open on a network server, you may prevent a computer attached to that server from having to be restarted and potentially losing data. NetWatcher also provides information that can be useful for other networking troubleshooting sessions.

Summary

In this chapter I described the basic principles of networking and explained how to use them to set up a small business or home network. I also explained how to take advantage of that network once it was set up.

▶ Networking involves sending data from one computer to another. The problem is, there are lots of different ways to do that, and lots of issues that can make it a fairly complicated procedure.

▶ To put a network together, you need some type of connection between machines, a shared "language" that all the pieces attached to the network understand, and software that can take advantage of those connections.

▶ Physical networks are organized around network layouts, or topologies, such as a star network; network architectures, such as Ethernet; and network protocols, such as TCP/IP, which are the "language" of the network.

▶ Each computer that attaches to a network needs a network adapter and also requires several pieces of software installed, including a driver for the network adapter, network client software, and network protocols. In addition, to take advantage of the network, you need to install network services, such as file and printer sharing.

▶ The two main types of networks are peer-to-peer networks and client-server networks. The most appropriate kind for homes and small businesses is peer-to-peer networks, in which all the resources attached to any computer that's part of the network can be shared with other computers on the network.

▶ Networks that combine PCs and Macs are easy to set up, but they usually require the purchase of additional software.

▶ Products specifically designed for home networks make the process of putting together and configuring a network much easier.

▶ Once a network is set up, it's easy to selectively share files, folders, and entire drives with other users on the network. It's equally easy to share a printer on the network.

▶ Setting up a shared Internet connection over a network requires the use of proxy server software, which is bundled with some networking products.

▶ You can also use a network to play multiplayer games, build an intranet, provide remote access to your files, and more.

Chapter 13

Connecting to and Using the Internet

In This Chapter

▶ You will learn how the Internet works.

▶ You will learn how to connect to the Internet.

▶ You will learn how to customize and optimize your Web-browsing experience.

▶ You will learn how to find information on the Internet.

▶ You will learn how to set up and use an e-mail account.

▶ You will learn about the various ways you can communicate with others on the Internet, including voice calls, videoconferencing, live chat, and newsgroups.

▶ You will learn how to create and publish your own Web site.

To say that the Internet has changed personal computing is so obvious that it borders on the absurd. At this point, I believe it's safe to say that the Internet has had, and continues to have a major impact on the entire world. You can't look at a magazine, watch television, or even talk to anyone without reading or hearing about a Web site or e-mail address. In fact, the Internet is dramatically changing how we communicate with people — friends, relatives, business associates, and even complete strangers.

In addition, the Internet is enabling the information-based economy that so many people predicted. It's setting the groundwork for how we will work and play in the twenty-first century. The fact is, finding and using information is becoming an increasingly important part of everyone's lives, and the Internet is playing an absolutely critical role at the very heart of this new Information Revolution.

OK, fine, you already know all this. What you may not know, however, is what's involved with connecting to and using the Internet. After all, to take advantage of all this wonderful new information infrastructure (or information superhighway or whatever buzz phrase you want to apply to it), you need to be a part of it. Thankfully, making a connection to the Internet is a very straightforward process, although a few tricks can help along the way.

The content of this chapter is organized to provide information on how to connect to the Internet and then how to take advantage of all the opportunities that that connection provides. After all, just because you're connected doesn't necessarily mean you're aware of all the cool things that you can do. Before we get into the specifics of how to connect your PC to the Internet, though, it helps to know a little bit about how the Internet works.

How the Internet Works

The Internet is nothing more, and nothing less, than a vast network of millions of computers connected to each other. The computers, or hosts, on the network all speak the same "language" to communicate with each other (the TCP/IP protocol), and each host has a particular address (the IP address) to distinguish it from all the others.

Cross-Reference

For more on network protocols, such as TCP/IP, see Chapter 12, "Setting Up a Small Business or Home Network."

In addition, each computer attached to the network holds a tiny piece of the information that creates the overall fabric of the Internet (or simply the Net for short). This information consists of whatever companies, organizations, and most importantly, individuals decide is important or interesting enough to share with other people who connect to the Net.

By itself, each piece may or may not be that important (at least, according to your interests), but taken as a whole, they provide an enormous, fascinating slice of human knowledge and experience. And eventually, I imagine, this ever-expanding patchwork quilt will exceed the boundaries of libraries and other traditional sources of information and provide access to most all of mankind's accumulated knowledge (or at least, a helluva lot of information).

The Internet actually started out in 1969 as a project of the U.S. Department of Defense, which wanted to put together a network that would survive a nuclear war. The main issue was to create a communications infrastructure — originally called *ARPAnet* — that provided multiple redundant paths for data to follow in the event that certain points along the network were destroyed. The resulting spiderweb-like network that was built is the basic model on which today's Internet is based.

In the early days of the Internet, several types of capabilities and services were available, including:

- Telnet, which enables you to connect to a computer and run applications available on that computer from wherever you are located.

- Gopher, which serves as a mechanism for presenting information available on Internet-based computers as a directory of files.

- FTP, which is used to transfer files, such as programs and application updates, across the Internet.

By far the most common use of the Internet today, however, is the World Wide Web, or just the Web for short. In fact, many people consider the Web and the Internet to be synonymous, which is not entirely true. Browsing through, or "surfing," the information available on the Web and electronic mail, or e-mail, are by far the most prevalent uses of the Internet, but the other services are still available and are used on a regular basis (though most are being adapted to fit within the context of the Web).

Connecting with a Web site

To understand how the Internet works, let's walk through the process of connecting to a source of information available on the Internet. Generically speaking, this information source is referred to as a *Web site*, and it has a particular location or address, such as `www.everythingcomputers.com`. To get to this information, you need to be connected to the Internet (which I explain how to do a bit later), and you need to use a program called a *Web browser*, or simply a *browser*.

CD

You can find a copy of both Netscape Navigator/Communicator 4.5 and Microsoft's Internet Explorer 5.0 on the CD accompanying this book.

After you open the browser application on your PC, you need to type the address shown in Figure 13-1 into the program's address or location line.

Figure 13-1: An Internet address
To get to a particular location, or Web site, on the Internet, you enter its address into a Web browser's address line.

Technically, this address is called a *uniform resource locator*, or URL, which refers to a standardized mechanism for finding particular files and other resources available from the Internet. Each section of the URL has a particular significance.

Anatomy of an URL

Web site addresses, or URLs, that we commonly enter into Web browsers actually consist of several different parts, each of which is separated by slashes or periods. Each of the different parts provides a clue about the location of the specific files pointed to by the address, as well as the mechanism used to obtain those files from the computer on which they reside.

So, for example, an URL such as `http://www.everythingcomputers.book.htm` tells you:

- The Web browser uses http (hypertext transport protocol) to request the information.

- The name of the computer host on which the information can be found is `www.everythingcomputers.com`.

- The specific file you are requesting is called "book.htm", and it is an HTML (HyperText Markup Language) format file, which is the kind typically used to create Web pages.

In addition, we can learn a bit more about the computer hosting the information, `www.everythingcomputers.com`, by taking apart the different components of its name. The `www` signifies that this document is part of the World Wide Web portion of the Internet, and the `everythingcomputers.com` section is the actual name of the Internet domain on which the various files that make up this site are located. In addition, the `.com`, short for "commercial," end to the address identifies the top level domain, or TLD, to which this site belongs.

Table 13-1 summarizes the Web address breakdown.

When you hit Return or Enter on your keyboard, your Web browser sends a request to the computer located at that particular Web address, or URL. The request asks the computer to send a copy of the particular document you want back to your computer. When your browser software receives that copy, it displays the document in its main browser window. This process is sometimes referred to as "connecting" to or visiting a particular Web site.

Table 13-1   Breaking Down a Web Address
(`http://www.everythingcomputers.com/book.htm`)

Portion of Address	Function
`http://`	Identifies protocol used to request information from the server; slashes are used to separate this prefix from the rest of the address. In this example, `http://` means to use the hypertext transport protocol but other possible protocols include FTP (`ftp://`) and Telnet (`telnet://`).

Portion of Address	Function
www	Identifies type of information requested. In this example, the type of information requested is a Web document, but other options include FTP. (Not all Web addresses include this part because it's considered optional.)
everythingcomputers	Identifies the domain name of the host computer where the requested information is located.
com	Identifies the top level domain, or TLD, of the Web site. In this example, .com means a commercial business, but other common TLDs are .net, .org, and .edu.
/book	Identifies the particular file within a directory that's been requested. In URLs that lack a particular filename, such as www.yahoo.com, a special designated index file is used instead.
htm	Identifies the format of the file being requested. In this example, .htm refers to HyperText Markup Language (HTML files created on a Macintosh or under Unix commonly end in .html), which is the format commonly used to create Web pages.

IP addresses and DNS

Behind the scenes, several important things are happening. First of all, computers on the Internet don't actually use names to locate one another; instead, they use a series of numbers called *IP* (Internet Protocol) *addresses*. So when your browser requests www.everythingcomputers.com, that request is first sent to a special computer called a *DNS* (Domain Name Services) *server*, which translates the name into an address such as 207.20.37.115 and then routes your request onto the computer that matches that numeric address.

Secret

If you want to, you can even get to a Web site by simply typing its IP address directly into your Web browser's address line. So, for example, to get to my Everything Computers Web site, you can simply type in http://207.20 .37.115 and hit Return, and you'll be taken to the site's home page. In fact, if your connection with a DNS server is broken — or the DNS server(s) your Internet connection normally uses are down — entering the IP address is the only way to get to Web sites. What happens is you simply bypass the DNS server and connect straight to the site itself.

The second thing to be aware of is that those requests don't follow a straight line between your computer and the computer from which you've requested data. Instead, the request is broken up into a number of small chunks called *packets*, and those packets travel along an often contorted path that may take them to nearly all parts of the world. Amazingly, not all the packets even follow the same path, so you might find that a portion of your request got to where it was going via one route, another portion via another route, and on and on. Specialized devices called *routers* determine how to break up the messages and what paths each chunk should take.

When all the packets reach the final destination, they're reassembled into your original request by another router and then passed on to the particular computer to which it was addressed. Along the way, some packets may run into dead ends or get stuck in the equivalent of heavy traffic at certain points on the Internet. As a result, some packets may have to be retransmitted several times before all the pieces reach their final destination. This is just one of the reasons why finding information from certain sites at certain times of the day can be so slow. Figure 13-2 shows a graphical overview of the path that your requests take.

Your Internet connection

As mentioned previously, the other critical part of this overall process is connecting your computer to the Internet. There are two basic types of Internet connections: dial-up and network. A dial-up connection is one where you use a standard phone line or ISDN line and have your computer's modem call, or dial up, a phone number to make the connection. In a network connection, your PC is attached to a network, which in turn, is attached to the Internet. As a result, this type of connection—which is available with cable modems and DSL (Digital Subscriber Line) modems—does not require a dial-up and is sometimes referred to as an "always on" connection.

Both types of connections require that you establish an account with an *Internet Service Provider*, or ISP, which is a company that maintains computers that have constant, 24-hour-a-day, 7-day-a-week direct connections to the Internet. (In so doing, these computers become part of the Internet itself.) Even computers with always-on connections provided by cable or DSL modems don't connect directly to the Internet, but do so via their ISP.

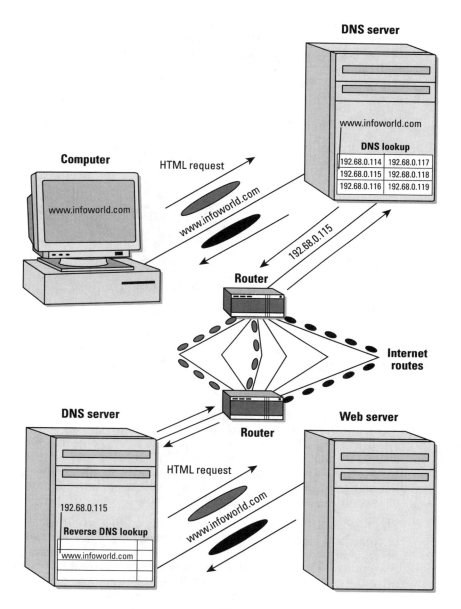

Figure 13-2: Getting information from a Web site
Sending and receiving information over the Web is actually a multistep process that involves several different computers. First, the Web address has to be converted to a numeric IP address, then the request has to be broken into chunks, and then those chunks follow different paths to the final destination. The chunks are reassembled at the final destination, the request is forwarded on, and then the requested data is sent back to your PC, almost always following a different route.

When you create and use an account with an Internet provider, you connect your computer to one of their constantly connected PCs, and through those computers, you have access to the entire fabric of the Internet (see Figure 13-3).

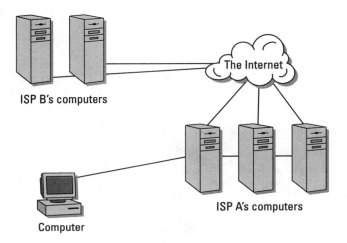

Figure 13-3: The online ramp
Your computer gains access to the Internet through your ISP's computers' connections to the Net. These computers, in turn, are connected to the computers of other ISPs, and so on, and so on.

Eventually, most Internet traffic reaches one of several Internet backbones, which are large data lines that crisscross the United States and the world. These fast and wide backbones are typically run by large telecommunications companies, such as Sprint, MCI, and AT&T. However, none of these companies "own" the Internet. In fact, amazingly enough, no one owns the Internet. In many ways it's the world's largest cooperative (or anarchy, depending on your political point of view).

This lack of centralized control occasionally causes problems, including how to create and assign top-level domain names, how to assign IP addresses, and determining what technical standards to use to deliver different types of content over the Internet. However, a number of different international organizations have taken on these critical duties in order to ensure that the basic structures of the Internet remain constant (or, at least, evolve according to unanimous consent).

Setting up your connection

Now that you understand the principles involved, let's move onto creating your own connection. What basically has to happen is that you have to set up your machine to connect to one of your ISP's computers and, once it's connected, to communicate with other computers available through the Internet. To do so you obviously need to have a modem, or some type of network connection, and the right software installed.

Specifically, if you're going to create a traditional, modem-based dial-up connection you need:

- Dial-Up Networking (which is part of the default Windows 95/98 installation and can be added, if necessary, via the Windows Setup tab in the Add/Remove Programs control panel)

- Dial-Up adapter (which can be added via the Network control panel)

- TCP/IP protocol (also via the Network control panel)

If you have a direct network connection via a cable or DSL modem or through a company LAN, all you need is:

- Ethernet adapter (typically an internal card)

- IP address (supplied by your ISP)

- TCP/IP protocol

Cross-Reference

See Chapter 12, "Setting Up a Small Business and Home Network" for more on installing adapters and other network software.

You also should double-check that the TCP/IP protocol is "bound" to the dial-up adapter for an analog modem connection or to the network card for a cable modem, DSL modem, or other network connection. You can do this by looking for an entry in the Network control panel that looks like this: TCP/IP ➪ Dial-Up Adapter or TCP/IP ➪ Ethernet Adapter (actually, you'll see the specific name and type of your adapter). Again, see Chapter 12 for more on binding network protocols, as well as other fun networking topics.

Depending on the type of accounts your ISP offers, as well as the types of services you want (Web access, an e-mail account, the ability to access an electronic bulletin board–type forums called *newsgroups*, and so on), you'll have to provide either a fair amount of configuration information or very little. In most situations and for most types of accounts, the setup process is simple.

Note

Although some ISPs may try to tell you otherwise, absolutely every piece of software you need to connect to and use the Internet is included as part of Windows 95 and Windows 98 (or came with your modem or network card). In most situations, in fact, all you need to do is to set up a simple Dial-Up Networking connection document — also called a *connectoid*, which you can do either manually or by following the Internet Connection Wizard that Microsoft incorporates into both Windows 95 and Windows 98. If you have a direct Internet connection, such as through a cable modem, you only need to adjust your computer's TCP/IP settings via the Network control panel.

The software provided by ISPs can sometimes simplify the process (and may include a few other goodies, such as a Web browser and other Internet software), but the ISP-provided software is not required to make an Internet connection.

Tip

The only exception to this rule is that some of the big online services, such as America Online and CompuServe, use some tricks to get your PC to both connect to their online service and offer access to the Internet. As a result, if you set up an account with them, you should use their software to do so. Also, once the software is installed, don't mess with the settings they create for Dial-Up Networking and within your Network control panel. If you need to make changes to your connection setup, do it from within their software (they typically have some type of Connection settings dialog).

Regardless of which method you use, you'll need to plug in some information that describes your account and sets up your computer to communicate with your ISP. Your ISP can provide all this information for you. Specifically, you'll need:

- Your ISP's phone number that your computer needs in order to connect (commonly called the *access* or *dial-in number*) if you're using a dial-up connection. If you have a cable modem, DSL modem, or other type of "permanent" connection to your ISP, then getting a phone number is not necessary.

- A username (which you typically pick, although some companies provide you with an initial one that you later change). This username is usually required only with a dial-up connection.

- A password (again, you choose it, but you may be provided with an initial one to first sign up for your account). This, too, is usually required only with a dial-up connection.

- If you're setting up an e-mail account, you also need your e-mail address (which is typically *username@ISPname.com*), as well as a login name (which may or may not be the same as your username for your dial-in connection), and a separate password for it.

- The name of the e-mail server on which outgoing messages are stored (sometimes called the *SMTP server*) and incoming messages are received (sometimes called the *POP3* or *IMAP server*). In some situations, these servers are one and the same. The names often take the format of *mail.ISPName.com*, *SMTP.ISPName.com*, or something similar.

- If you want to access Internet newsgroups, you also need the name of the news server. It may have a name such as *news.ISPName.com*.

In many situations, that's all you need. However, depending on the type of account you set up and/or what your ISP offers, you may also need several IP numeric addresses (which all have four numbers between 0 and 255 separated by periods), including:

- An IP address for your computer (for example, 100.0.0.1)

- A subnet mask setting (oftentimes it's 255.255.255.0), which is used in large networks to separate groups of computers

- A name and IP address for two DNS servers (a primary and a secondary, in case the primary is down); the names may take the form of *dns1.ISPName.com* and *dns2.ISPName.com*

- An IP address for a gateway, which is a computer housed at your ISP through which your computer connects to the Internet

- An IP address for your mail server

Again, depending on how your ISP operates, you may need only one or two of these numbers, or you may need them all (or you may not need any). Many ISPs have computers in place called *DHCP* (Dynamic Host Configuration Protocol) *servers* to automatically assign these numbers as soon as you connect to one of their computers. That way, you don't have to worry about assigning them yourself. If that's the case, these numbers are assigned dynamically every time you sign on (which means they'll be different every time you connect).

Secret

If you ever want to find out what the IP addresses of your computer and the computers you're connecting to via a dial-up connection at your ISP are, you can. Both Windows 95 and Windows 98 include a Windows IP Configuration utility (or Winipcfg for short) that you can run by opening the Run dialog box off the Start menu and typing in **winipcfg**. Note that this utility works only *after* you've connected to your ISP (and had the IP addresses assigned). Figure 13-4 shows an example.

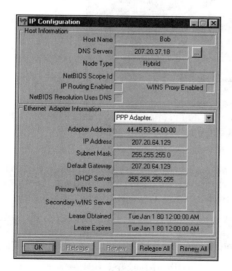

Figure 13-4: IP address sleuthing
The Winipcfg utility bundled with Windows 95/98 enables you to find out what IP address(es) your computer is using, as well as the ones you're connecting to at your ISP.

Dial-up networking

If you use the Internet Connection Wizard, you walk your way through the process of entering this information in a simple step-by-step process. When you're done, you end up with a dial-up networking connectoid that incorporates all the connection information, as well as a properly configured e-mail program (which you choose during the wizard process). If you prefer, you can also enter all this information yourself by creating a new dial-up networking connection or by editing an existing connection.

STEPS:

Creating a dial-up connection for the Internet

Step 1.   Open the Dial-Up Networking folder by choosing Start ⇨ Programs ⇨ Communications (under Windows 95, you need to choose Accessories) and selecting Dial-Up Networking. Once you're there, double-click Make New Connection (see Figure 13-5).

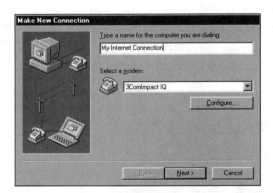

Figure 13-5: Getting connected
The first step in connecting to the Internet is to create a dial-up networking account that uses your computer's modem to connect to your ISP.

Step 2.   Walk through the Make New Connection Wizard by providing a name, confirming the modem you'll use to make the connection, and typing in the number to dial.

Step 3.   Once it's complete, you can adjust the Internet-specific settings by right-clicking the new connection icon you just created and selecting Properties. Next, click the Server Types tab (see Figure 13-6).

Step 4.   If you were given specific IP addresses, either for your computer or the DNS servers that your ISP uses, then click the TCP/IP Settings button, and enter them in the dialog that appears. If you weren't, you can still click this button to confirm that your computer's IP address and that of the DNS servers will be assigned by the DHCP server when you connect, as shown in Figure 13-7.

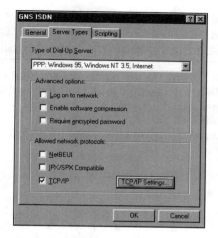

Figure 13-6: Making adjustments
Once you've created a dial-up networking connection, you can make a few specific adjustments to your connections here. In most cases you need to have a check mark in the TCP/IP check box. TCP/IP is the network protocol or "language" used on the Internet.

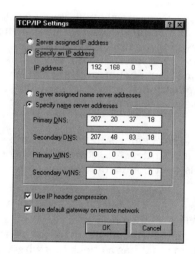

Figure 13-7: Setting your address
If you need to specify a unique IP address for your computer's dial-up connection, you enter that information here. You also use this dialog to specify any DNS servers used by your ISP.

Continued

STEPS

Creating a dial-up connection for the Internet *(continued)*

Step 5.   Once you are finished adjusting the settings, hit OK twice, and your connection is complete. Test it out by double-clicking the connection icon, filling out your name and password, and then hitting Connect. You should connect with your ISP, and then be able to launch your Web browser and navigate to any site on the Web you wish to explore.

Once you've set up this connection, most applications designed for Internet use can automatically open it and start the connection process for you whenever they need to connect. So, in other words, as soon as you open your browser, or type a Web address into an address line, or request that your e-mail package send and receive mail, those processes automatically launch this connectoid, which saves you the step of having to make the connection first.

Tip

If you're using a modem to connect, and you want to turn this feature off, go to the Internet control panel (presuming you've installed Internet Explorer 4.0 or later under Windows 95 or are running Windows 98), and select the Connection tab. Choose the Connect to the Internet using a local area network radio button (even if you don't have a network), and hit OK or Apply. Now, before you can access the Internet, you have to manually connect by running the Dial-Up Connection document first and then your browser or other Internet-based application. If you decide you don't like this and want to change back, simply reselect the Connect to the Internet using a modem radio button (see Figure 13-8).

If you're still running Internet Explorer 3.0 under Windows 95, you must right-click the Internet icon on your desktop, choose Properties, and then uncheck the button that autodials your connection whenever you open Internet Explorer.

Tip

If you have Dial-Up Networking 1.2 or later, another trick that you can use with either version of Windows Explorer is to double-click your connection document and then hit Cancel when it starts to dial. At that point you are presented with a dialog box that has a check box where you can choose to automatically connect (see Figure 13-9).

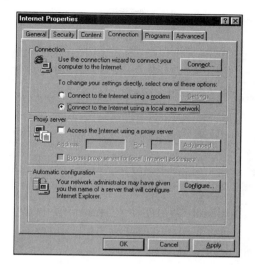

Figure 13-8: Forcing manual connections
If you don't want your modem to automatically dial up your ISP whenever you start your Web browser, you can "trick" Windows into not launching it by telling it that you plan to connect via a local network connection. Depending on which version of Internet Explorer you have installed, your screen may look somewhat different from this one.

Figure 13-9: Turning automatic Dial-up on and off
If you hit the Cancel button when your modem starts to connect to the Internet, you are presented with a dialog box where you can turn the automatic dialing function on or off.

Direct network connection

Cable modems and various types of DSL modems provide a direct, always-on connection to your ISP and, through them, to the Internet. Not only is it a speedy, convenient connection, it's also easier to set up and deal with than an analog connection. One of the main reasons is that you don't have to worry about dial-up networking and the foibles of analog modems and phone lines.

For more on cable modems and various types of DSL modems, see Chapter 5, "Sound Cards, Speakers and Modems."

Typically, the only important setup involved for these types of connections (other than getting the required Ethernet adapter installed) is to enter your specific IP address into the TCP/IP settings that are bound to your Ethernet-based network adapter. As with analog dial-up connections, you do this in the Network control panel.

In addition, you need to configure a default gateway and DNS servers and provide the domain name (your ISP's domain) in the DNS Configuration tab, but you don't have to worry about creating dial-up networking connectoids.

Tip

If you switch from a dial-up connection to an always-on network connection such as that provided by a cable modem or some type of DSL modem, you need to remember to change your Internet connection settings in the Internet control panel from dial-up to LAN. Doing so ensures that your browser doesn't try to initiate a dial-up connection when it starts up. In addition, many e-mail programs and other Web-based software have their own connection settings that you may need to adjust within the program's preferences. Microsoft's Outlook e-mail package, for example, enables you to store different connection settings for each e-mail account you have. To change them, go to the Connection tab of the Account's Properties dialog box.

Tip

If you're fortunate to live in an area where cable modem or some flavor of DSL service is available, then I highly recommend you sign up for it. In many cases there's only a slight premium over traditional analog dial-up lines. If you use the Internet regularly, it's well worth the cost. Plus, the convenience of an always-on connection is something you learn to get used to very quickly.

Customizing Your Web Browsing Experience

Once your Internet connection is set up and working properly, you can dive headlong into the endless sea of information commonly known as the World Wide Web. As you do, you'll discover that most of the Web sites you visit and most of the pages on those Web sites appear properly in a standard Web browser, whether you're using Microsoft's Internet Explorer, Netscape's Navigator/Communicator, or any of a number of other Web browsers that are available.

Occasionally, however, you're bound to run across Web sites that don't seem to work right or don't look right on your computer's display. In some situations it may simply be due to mistakes made in the creation of the pages you're trying to view (or just bad design), but in others it may be because you need an updated version of your browser or some additional software to fully experience what the site's creators had in mind. Some Web sites, for example, may take advantage of features that are available only in Version 5.0 of Internet Explorer or Netscape Navigator. So if you go to one of these sites using, say, 4.0 or even an earlier version of those browsers, the pages may not work properly. (FYI: Good site designers create pages that still work in older browsers but may offer extra bells and whistles to those who visit with newer versions of the browsers.)

Note

By the way, if you don't know what version of a browser (or almost any other software package, for that matter) you're using, you can find out by opening the program and looking for a menu item that's usually called "About *Program Name.*" So, for example, the menu item might read, "About Communicator" or "About Internet Explorer." The About page is usually the last item under the Help menu, which is typically the last menu choice on the right.

Another possibility is that some sites use extensions that are proprietary to a specific browser, which means you have to visit using that browser. (Again, good site design should cover both types of browsers.) In those instances, if you really want to see the content included on a page, you have to download and install the latest version of the particular browser software you need. As with any software available on the Web, that means going to the Web site of the company who makes the software, finding what you want, and going through the upgrade process. Unfortunately, because the Web is changing so rapidly and standards are evolving so quickly, this experience is relatively common.

Cross-Reference

See Chapter 9, "Adding, Upgrading, and Removing Software" for more on downloading and installing software.

Caution

While I generally don't believe in the notion of upgrading your software just for the sake of upgrading, Web browsers and most Internet-related software are one category where it does make sense to stay as up to date as possible. Not only does this keep you up with the rapidly evolving standards of the Internet, it helps you keep your computer and your data safe. One of the unfortunate aspects of the Internet's rapid growth is that it is being used as a mechanism to spread computer viruses and other nasty stuff that can cause big problems. Nearly every other week, it seems, there are new reports about security holes in Web browsers or other Internet-related software. If you don't keep your Web and e-mail software up to date, you could leave yourself vulnerable to a potentially damaging security flaw. Thankfully, most Web-related software is free, so all it takes to stay current is a bit of time and effort on your part.

Plug-ins

In some situations, you need more than just an updated browser to view certain pages or certain types of documents. Many sites with music or audio, for example, have a notice about needing the RealNetworks RealPlayer application (sometimes just called *RealAudio* or *RealVideo*); others with animation require Macromedia's Shockwave or Flash, and still others with highly formatted documents use Adobe's Acrobat (PDF) format, which requires the Acrobat Viewer to display it. All four of these applications are referred to as helper applications or plug-ins.

CD

Two of these plug-ins — RealPlayer G2, and Adobe's Acrobat Viewer — are on the CD accompanying this book.

A *plug-in* is an application that works along with your browser to enable you to open and/or view certain types of documents. If you try to access certain pages and/or documents without the appropriate plug-in, you typically get an error message about not being able to open a particular type of file. The reason for this is that browsers essentially function as HTML document viewers. They do more than just that, but their primary function is to open and display Web pages created and saved in HTML. Because most documents on the Web are in HTML format, this is generally a good arrangement.

However, as useful as HTML may be, it can't present certain types of information, particularly active media such as audio, video, animation, and the like. So, in order to provide access to as wide a range of media types as possible on the Web, many companies developed special software (in other words, plug-ins) that gives you access to these file types on the Web.

To take advantage of any plug-in, all you have to do is install it. (If you don't have it available on a disk or CD-ROM, you probably have to download from the Web first.) Once you do, the next time you try to access a Web page or document that uses that format, the browser "passes" the data along to the plug-in, and the plug-in application launches and gives you access to whatever you were trying to get to. For example, if you want to listen to music or any other type of audio (such as my *O'Donnell on Computers* radio program — plug, plug) over the Internet, you can install the RealNetworks RealPlayer, surf to a Web site that uses the technology (such as www.everythingcomputers.com), and then click the RealAudio or RealVideo link that you wanted to hear. See Figure 13-10 for an example.

Figure 13-10: Audio over the Internet
To listen to radio programs or music over the Internet, make sure you have the right plug-in application installed. With the RealPlayer, for example, you can simply click a link, and the player launches and begins to play whatever audio you choose to listen to.

The RealPlayer even enables you to play video over the Net, but unless you have a really fast connection (such as with a cable or DSL modem), most Internet-based video looks pretty awful.

As handy as plug-ins are, they can cause some problems of their own. For one thing, they are constantly being upgraded, and as with browsers, you often need to have the latest version to work with certain documents. In addition, there are hundreds of different plug-ins, and going through the process of downloading and installing lots of them gets to be a real hassle. Thankfully, many browser upgrades and installations (as well as the software provided by certain ISPs) now include many of the most popular plug-ins as part of the installation, which saves you from having to download and install them on your own.

Another problem is that several incompatible file types are often within one class of media, which may require you to have several overlapping plug-ins. For example, while a lot of audio available on the Internet is available in RealAudio format, not all of it is. So it's possible to run into certain types of audio files that won't work, even if you have the latest version of RealPlayer. In those situations you may have to download yet another audio program. Again, this situation is improving. Microsoft's Windows Media Player, for example, can play back quite a few different audio and video formats. But it's not unheard of to have several audio, several video, several animation, and yet a few more types of plug-ins.

Internet file types

In many ways, all the file types on the Internet are like a macrocosm of what you have available on your computer's hard drive. Just as you probably have word processing documents, spreadsheets, digital pictures, page layout files, personal finance data, and more on your hard drive and need different applications to open each one of them, so on the Internet you encounter a wide variety of different file types and often need different applications to open each of them.

Most documents on the Web are in HTML format, which is what Web browsers are ideally designed to read and display. As mentioned in the main text, other file types are often handled by additional plug-in or helper applications. When you install these applications, they register themselves with your operating system and basically tell Windows, "whenever you run across a filename with the extension .xyz, then pass the file along to me."

In this regard, these applications are no different than any other you install. For example, if you install Microsoft Word, it registers itself and says, "All files that end in .doc are mine." As a result, whenever you click a file that has a file extension of .doc, Word launches and opens the file. Similarly, if you install the RealNetworks player, it registers itself and says, "Whenever you come across a file that ends in .ram, .ra, or .rm, open me." (Of course, things aren't really *that* chummy, but you get the idea.)

One difference between most Internet file types and many standard desktop file types is that most all Internet files are also associated with a MIME (Multi-purpose Internet Mail Extension) type, whereas only a few desktop applications use MIME. MIME types are general categories of files and are used by Internet-based applications (including, but not limited to, e-mail, despite the name) to distinguish different types of files, such as graphics and audio. MIME is also used to

encode certain types of files, such as audio and video, into a generic format so that they can be transferred across different platforms, such as Windows, MacOS, and various types of UNIX. RealAudio files, for example, have the MIME type of audio/x-pn-realaudio. (Note that the x in this and any other MIME name means that it's not an officially sanctioned Internet Engineering Task Force (IETF) MIME type.)

You can find out the file associations for all your Internet plug-ins, as well as your standard applications, by opening the Folder Options dialog. If you're running Windows 98 or Windows 95 with Internet Explorer 4.0 or later, go to the Start menu, select Settings, and then Folder Options. If you're running Windows 95 with a different browser (or an earlier version of Internet Explorer), open Windows Explorer, go to the View menu, and then select Folder Options. Once you're there, click the File Types tag (see accompanying figure).

If you come across a situation where a particular file type is being opened by a different application than used to open it or by one that you don't want to open it, you may find that it's because the file extension association was changed in the Folder Options dialog box. For example, if you install certain plug-ins, you may find that they "take over" certain file types, sometimes without providing any warning that they're doing so.

Web browsers themselves are rather notorious for trying to "take control" and often ask you if they should be considered the "default" browser. This question really means should they be registered as the main application for opening and viewing HTML files. To find out how to switch your default browser between Internet Explorer and Netscape Navigator/Communicator, see the sidebar "Capturing extensions" in Chapter 14, "Working with Documents and Files."

(continued)

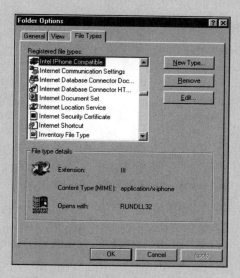

Matching file types with applications

If you want to see, edit, or add to the list of file types that your PC can handle, go to the Folder Options dialog box. From here you can do things such as determine which application opens which type of file and, if you want, change the selected application.

You can usually fix the problem of plug-ins taking over certain file extensions either by reinstalling your preferred plug-in, which will then reregister itself on top of what had taken its place, or by editing the file association here in the Folder Options dialog. Unfortunately, finding the file extension you want to edit can be a bit difficult because files are organized by the file type name, not by the file extension. So you often need to know which application is using a particular file type and search under that application's name. (For more details on how to edit file types, see Chapter 14, "Working with Documents and Files.")

If you're using Netscape Navigator or the Netscape Communicator suite, you can also edit Internet-specific file types in its Preferences dialog box. Select Preferences from the Edit menu, and then under the Navigator category, choose Applications. (You may have to expand the Navigator category by clicking the plus sign next to it.) See the following figure.

As with the regular Windows associations, the files are categorized by file type name, not file extension. The procedure for changing which program opens which file type is similar to the regular Windows associations, although less options are available in the Netscape Preferences dialog.

(Continued)

(Continued)

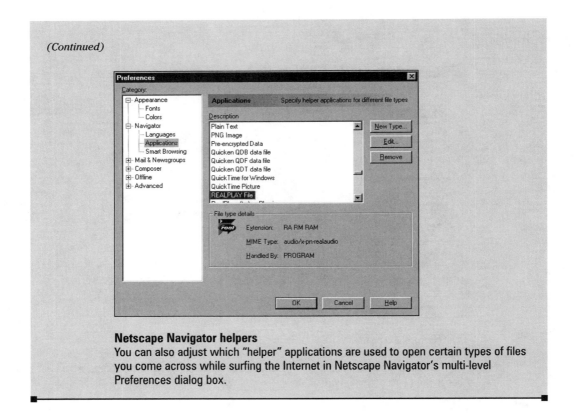

Netscape Navigator helpers
You can also adjust which "helper" applications are used to open certain types of files you come across while surfing the Internet in Netscape Navigator's multi-level Preferences dialog box.

Bookmarks and favorites

To make sense of your various Web-surfing adventures, all browsers enable you to store *bookmarks* (or *favorites*, as they're called in Internet Explorer) of your favorite Web sites. Saving a bookmark or favorite is as simple as visiting a site you're interested in and selecting either Bookmarks ⇨ Add Bookmark off the Communicator menu (for Netscape Navigator/Communicator) or Add to Favorites off the Favorites menu (for Internet Explorer). Each program also has a handy History feature, which keeps track of all the sites you've recently visited in case you want to go back to a site but forgot to bookmark it.

Tip

If, for privacy reasons, you ever want to cover your tracks with regard to the Web sites you've visited, you need to clear the browser's history file. To do so under Internet Explorer, open the Internet control panel, and click the Clear History button. In addition, you need to right-click the taskbar, select Properties from the context menu that appears, select the Start menu Programs tab, and then hit the Clear button (which clears the drop-down list under the Internet Explorer address bar). Under Navigator/Communicator, go to Edit ⇨ Preferences, and select Clear History. You also need to select the Clear Location Bar button if it's available.

Both Internet Explorer and Netscape Navigator/Communicator come with a preset group of bookmarks/favorites that you can add to or remove at will, and both include the capability of editing and organizing your own additions.

Navigator/Communicator keeps all its bookmarks in a single file called Bookmark.htm. (You'll find it in your username folder, which is typically at C:\Program Files\Netscape\Users*yourname*.) If you ever want to upgrade to a new version of Communicator or move your bookmarks to a different machine, you must copy this file. Internet Explorer, on the other hand, keeps a separate file for each favorite and stores them in the Favorites folder (which you'll find inside the Windows folder). Again, you want to backup and/or copy this file if you switch to a different machine.

Tip

Because each program stores the lists of bookmarks/favorites in different ways, you're going to need some type of conversion utility if you want to have the same set available in both programs. Internet Explorer 5.0 and later includes a built-in Import/Export Wizard that enables you to easily move your bookmarks into your favorites and vice versa. See Figure 13-11.

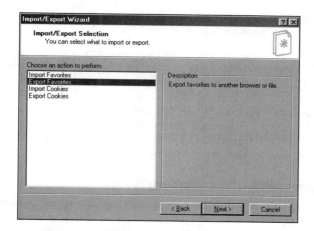

Figure 13-11: Transferring bookmarks and favorites
The Import/Export Wizard built into Internet Explorer 5.0 and later makes it easy to move your bookmarks and/or favorites between IE and other browsers, such as Netscape Navigator/Communicator.

If you don't have (or don't want) IE 5.0, some browser utilities enable you to easily share your bookmarks/favorites between multiple browsers.

Using applications on the Web

With an up-to-date browser, a reasonable selection of plug-ins and a good set of bookmarks/favorites, you can maneuver your way around the Internet and open most documents that you come across. But the Web has quickly expanded beyond the world of documents and now often contains applications that are built into Web pages. In fact, probably the most significant development on the Internet (and on companies' internal intranets) over the last few years is the growth of increasingly sophisticated Web-based applications.

When most people think of applications they think of standalone products, such as a word processor or database. On the Web, however, applications may consist of very simple programs (such as a fill-in-the-blanks registration form, something that enables you to rearrange the view of different columns of data, or even just animated pictures) that are embedded within an otherwise typical HTML page. Many of these little programs are called *applets*, as in "baby application." Applets are primarily little Java programs that require the use of a Java Virtual Machine (which is built into most browsers) in order to run.

In addition, some companies have begun to offer more sophisticated applications, such as full-blown tax software or employee evaluation software, that you can use in place of a traditional application. With tax software, you pay a fee to the company providing the software and then go to a particular Web site and begin using the software (which primarily consists of filling in forms), just as you would if you were using a traditional version of the program on your computer's hard drive.

Other companies offer programs such as backup applications that work over the Internet, enabling you to store your files on a server located somewhere on the Internet. (In case you are wondering, these types of systems encrypt the files so that no one else can get to or open them.) Unless you have a really fast connection, however, it could take a very long time to transfer your data files over the Internet. Finally, in the case of certain online games and some other products, you download and run a traditional application on your PC that's designed to be used along with others over the Internet.

Java, JavaScript, and ActiveX

In most instances, both tiny applets and these larger types of applications do not require anything more than an up-to-date browser that supports one or both of two important programming languages: Java and ActiveX. Another technology that's used to provide some very simple programs, such as animated images, is called JavaScript. (Despite the name, JavaScript is actually quite different than Java.)

Java, which was created by Sun, and ActiveX, which was created by Microsoft, are two critically important technologies that are enabling the Internet to expand beyond its previous role as a document storehouse. JavaScript, which was actually created by Netscape, also plays an important, though less critical, role in this regard. One of the main reasons for the importance of these languages is that applications that are written in Java and, in some cases, ActiveX can run across multiple platforms. In other words, the same application can run on a PC running Windows 98, on a PC running Linux, on a Macintosh, or on a UNIX workstation.

Usually, that is. Unfortunately, Microsoft's ActiveX was originally designed to run under Windows and has only minimal support on other platforms. In addition, Microsoft has made efforts to extend Sun's Java language in proprietary ways that make certain Java applications work, or work best, only under various flavors of Windows. As a result, some applications that were created with these languages are not truly cross-platform.

Note

By the way, Internet-based applications are probably the only ones where you might — and I want to emphasize *might* — need to know what computer programming language was used to create them. In all other cases, you do not need to know, nor would it even do you any good if you did know.

Today's browsers include the capability of opening and "running" applications created in Java by virtue of software technology called a *virtual machine*. A Java Virtual Machine, or JVM, which is directly built into most Web browsers, runs as if it were a computer within a computer, letting a Java application work the same way on a PC as it does on a Mac. This capability is spawning a huge industry of programs that are created solely for the Internet (or company intranets). See Figure 13-12.

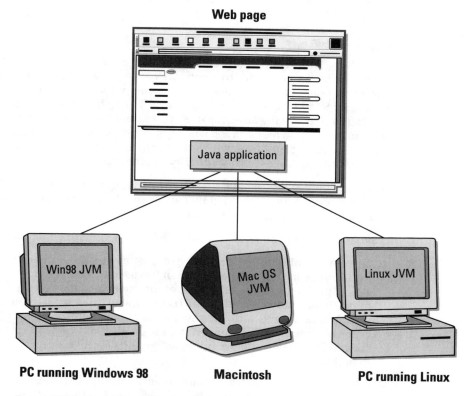

Figure 13-12: Java Virtual Machines
Your browser's built-in Java Virtual Machine (JVM) enables you to run Web-based Java applications on your PC, almost like a computer within a computer. Because most popular platforms have their own JVMs, you can run the same Java application on many different types of computers.

You don't need to know anything about Java, JavaScript, or ActiveX other than whether or not your browser supports them in order to use applications that were created with them. In fact, in many cases you may be running Java, JavaScript, or ActiveX applications without even knowing it. Simply visiting a particular Web page can initiate the process of loading and running certain types of applications. (In most instances, however, Java applications create a message about starting Java in the browser's status bar down near the bottom of its window.)

Because of this "stealth" capability, some people have grown wary of Java, JavaScript, and ActiveX, fearing that a rogue script, applet, or application could wipe out their data or cause other problems. While most of these fears are unfounded, several cases of security holes have been found in these systems that could (theoretically, at least) be exploited by hackers and lead to security problems. In reality, very little (if any) damage has occurred due to these types of security-related issues, but when it comes to the Wild West–like atmosphere of the still relatively immature Internet, it's a good idea to tread cautiously.

Safe surfing

By and large, surfing the Internet is a safe, fun activity. However, whenever you connect your computer to a network of others, as you do when you make an Internet connection, you open up your computer's data to the possibility of being infected by a virus, destroyed by a Trojan horse (a "hidden" application that usually attaches itself to a seemingly innocuous file or program and then wreaks havoc when you least expect it — similar to the infamous historical gift from which these types of programs derive their name), or any number of other security-related issues.

If you have only an occasional dial-up connection, as opposed to an "always on" type of connection provided by a cable or ADSL modem, then the threat is less severe, but it exists all the same.

To avoid possible problems, you can follow a few general guidelines:

- Be cautious about the sites you visit. Just as you're more likely to run into trouble in the "seedier" parts of town, so too do you increase your risk of problems if you visit some of the "seamier" sites on the Internet. In particular, stay clear of *warez* (pronounced "wares") sites, where you are often tantalized with "free" versions of commercial software. These types of sites are run by unscrupulous people who trade in stolen or "pirated" software and are breeding grounds for all the worst types of digital filth.

- Install, use, and regularly update an anti-virus application. These products can prevent lots of horrific problems, although they're really effective only when you make sure the virus definition files are up to date. Many programs now check these files automatically, but some still require you to manually update their virus definition files, so be sure to find out what, if anything, you need to do. (Note that updating the virus definitions is not the same thing as having to upgrade to the latest version of the program. You really need to keep only the virus definition files current.)

- Be careful of the applications you run over the Net. ActiveX, JavaScript, and Java applications could conceivably do things such as wipe out your data, send the contents of your hard drive to another person, or any of a host of other unpleasant problems. Of the three, ActiveX is more potentially harmful because applications that use it can have full access to your system, whereas most Java and JavaScript applications run in a "sandbox," which is essentially a separate, enclosed area of memory that can't access certain critical resources. However, this certainly doesn't mean that ActiveX applications are bad (nor that all Java or JavaScript applications are good, for that matter). Most (if not all) ActiveX-based applications are completely safe, and because they have more access to certain aspects of your system, they potentially can be more powerful.

- If you're buying something over the Web and need to provide credit card information, be sure the page you're connecting to offers a secure SSL (Secure Sockets Layer) connection. Most online stores offer this capability, but not all do, so be careful. You can verify an SSL connection by looking for a closed lock icon in the lower-left corner of the Netscape Navigator/Communicator window or for a similar closed lock along the bottom of the Internet Explorer window. If the page on which you're filling out a purchase form isn't secure, then any information you include could be viewed by individuals on the Internet who are specifically scanning for that type of information. A page that offers SSL security, on the other hand, provides a dedicated link directly between your computer and the server you're connected to and prevents others from electronically "snooping."

- If you're concerned about blocking potentially offensive Web sites (such as those featuring pornographic or violent content) for yourself or your children, you can either use your browser's built in ratings functions (which can prevent certain sites from being loaded if they have been self-rated beyond a level that you determine) or invest in a separate blocking program, such as SurfWatch. The built-in ratings functions, which are available in both Internet Explorer and Netscape Navigator/Communicator, are fine in theory, but not all sites rate themselves, or do so accurately. These ratings functions depend on the site's own rating. As a result, some people prefer the more thorough, though still not infallible, protection of a dedicated filtering or blocking program. A demo copy of SurfWatch is available on the CD accompanying this book.

- Finally, although this issue really isn't Web specific, be cautious of any attachments you receive in e-mail messages from people you don't know. While they may be perfectly harmless, they might also be problematic, so be wary. If you have any doubts, just delete the entire message before you open or detach the attached file.

To deal with the potential security problems, ActiveX applications (as well as Java and JavaScript programs, in certain instances) use the concepts of digitally signing applications and security certificates, which verifies who created the ActiveX control (another name for ActiveX applications) you are about to run.

Depending on the security levels you set in your browser, you can, for example, be presented with a dialog box whenever you load a page or click a link that contains an ActiveX control. The dialog essentially asks whether you trust the organization or individual who created the control and whether you want to run it (see Figure 13-13).

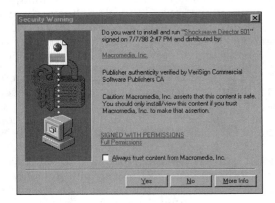

Figure 13-13: Digital certificates
To help control potential security problems with ActiveX programs, you can set your browser to warn you whenever you come across a Web page that contains and/or uses an ActiveX control.

To be honest, this solution is not ideal because you simply may not know the organization that has created a site with a useful ActiveX control, and therefore, you may choose not to run it. Also, although less likely, it's possible that even a trusted organization may have inadvertently uploaded an ActiveX control that actually causes problems.

If you're using Microsoft's Internet Explorer and you want to make changes in your browser's security settings, double-click the Internet control panel, and choose the Security tab. From there you can choose from a number of predefined security settings, most of which affect ActiveX controls and Java programs, or you can create your own by choosing the Custom button (see Figure 13-14).

Netscape Navigator/Communicator doesn't support ActiveX, but it offers security settings for JavaScript and other Java applications, available via the Security button on the program's main toolbar. Like Internet Explorer, Navigator uses the concept of signed certificates and enables you to control what digital certificates you want to accept or reject, as well as what levels of control the applications may have access to.

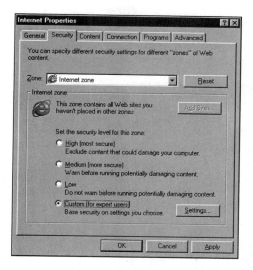

Figure 13-14: Explorer security
The Security page of the Internet control panel enables you to choose from a variety of different security scenarios, or you can create your own security by selecting Custom. Note that if you have a version of Internet Explorer other than 4.0, your screen may look different.

Partially as a result of these concerns, most browsers enable you to turn off individual support for Java, JavaScript, or ActiveX. Note that if you do, and you visit a Web page or site that uses them, you may not be able to take advantage of some of the capabilities that the site might offer. Another possibility is that you may not get the full visual impact of what the site designers intended. In some situations, you might even get error messages or come across other types of glitches.

Nevertheless, here's how to toggle your Java, JavaScript, and ActiveX settings under Microsoft's Internet Explorer 4.0 or later.

STEPS:

Turning Off Java/ActiveX (Internet Explorer)

Step 1. Go to the Internet Explorer Preferences dialog either by launching Internet Explorer and choosing Internet Options from the View or Tools menu (depending on which version of Internet Explorer you have installed), or by double-clicking the Internet control panel (available via Start ➪ Settings ➪ Control Panel).

Step 2. Choose the Zone for which you want to adjust the settings (probably the Internet Zone), and then select Custom and click Settings (see Figure 13-15).

Continued

STEPS

Turning Off Java/ActiveX (Internet Explorer) *(continued)*

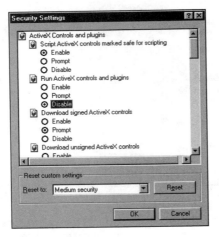

Figure 13-15: Denying access
If you want to turn off ActiveX controls, Java applications, or JavaScript for all Web sites, or only certain sites, you make those adjustments in this dialog box. Anything you turn off will not be available the next time you visit a site that uses one of those technologies.

Step 3. Select the various radio button settings you want in order to enable or disable or to prompt you for permission to use ActiveX, Java, and JavaScript. When you're finished, click OK and then OK again, and your settings will be in effect.

Here's how to disable Java and/or JavaScript under Netscape's Navigator/-Communicator 4.0 or later.

STEPS:

Turning Off Java/JavaScript Support (Navigator/Communicator)

Step 1. Launch Navigator/Communicator, and select Preferences from the Edit menu. Click Advanced in the frame on the left side (see Figure 13-16).

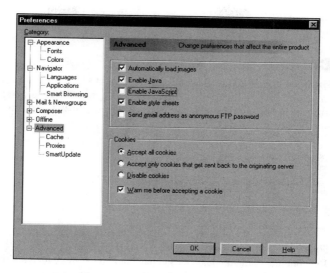

Figure 13-16: Security control
If you want to turn off (or turn back on) support for Java and/or JavaScript with Netscape Navigator 4.0 or later, just go to the Preferences dialog, and choose Advanced.

Step 2.   Deselect the Enable Java and/or Enable JavaScript check boxes, and hit OK.

Despite these issues, many people are perfectly happy running Java, JavaScript, and ActiveX applications over the Internet. In fact, most people find that they can greatly enhance their overall browsing experience. Having access to applications via the Internet is dramatically changing how many people use their computers, as well as their view and usage of the Internet.

Secret

With that thought in mind, here's a little trick for keeping your ActiveX controls up to date. Most ActiveX programs are stored in the Downloaded Program Files folder inside your Windows folder. (By the way, this folder is *not* where you find applications that you have manually downloaded via the Internet. Those are found in whatever folder you chose to store them in when you first downloaded them, as described in Chapter 9, "Adding, Upgrading, and Removing Software.") If you right-click any ActiveX control listed in that folder, you see the option to Update at the top of the context menu that appears. Just select Update, and the control automatically starts up a dial-up connection (if you're not already connected to the Internet) or uses an existing network connection and begins to download the latest version available. You don't have to worry about where the file originally came from or what version you currently have. The update process just happens automatically.

Cookies

Probably one of the most misunderstand elements of Web surfing are *cookie files*. Originally dubbed "magic cookies," cookie files are nothing more than simple text files that are sent to your computer via some, but not all, Web sites that you visit (see Figure 13-17).

Figure 13-17: Cookie ingredients
The contents of most cookie files consist of nothing more than a string of text and numbers and are usually used to identify you the next time you visit the site that "sent" you the cookie.

Despite their generally innocuous nature, cookie files gained notoriety in the early days of the Web and have retained their pejorative reputation over subsequent years. The main problem people have with cookies is that, like some JavaScript, Java, and ActiveX applications, cookies often work completely unbeknownst to you.

In fact, the default setting for most browsers is to "accept" any cookie file sent to your computer, without even letting you know. In other words, when you visit Web sites that use cookie files, the servers that host those Web sites quietly send a cookie file to your computer along with the Web page data that you've requested. If you're using Internet Explorer, this cookie file is typically stored on your computer's hard drive in a directory called "Cookies" and/or another called "Temporary Internet Files," both of which are found inside the Windows folder. Netscape's Navigator/Communicator keeps all cookies in a single file Cookies.txt, which can be found in a subfolder with your username inside the Netscape folder (which is usually inside the Program Files folder).

In most cases, cookie files are used to identify you on subsequent visits to a site so that, for example, if you customize a particular site's preferences or if you enter a username and password to get access to certain areas of a site, the site knows who you are the next time you visit. Then, if you drop by that site again, it checks to see if you have a cookie file on your hard drive. If it finds one, it looks up your record and provides the same settings you selected on your last visit. In some situations, this can save you time and/or make your browsing session on that site more pleasant. In other situations, however, it's merely used to keep track of what pages you visit on a site to get an idea of what types of things you might be interested in.

Not surprisingly, that capability is a problem for people who are increasingly concerned with online privacy issues (as most of us are) even though in the vast majority of cases, the data is collected to help the site's creators provide a better "fit" for your interests. Still, some people prefer not to intentionally or indirectly disclose any personal preferences for fear of privacy invasions.

Note

By the way, despite rumors to the contrary, cookie files and the file records they may be associated with can incorporate only the information about you that you choose to provide or that they collect from the pages you actually visit. They cannot automatically gleam your name, address, or any other personal information simply by your visiting a site. One possible exception is that some systems can automatically retrieve your e-mail address from your browser's preferences if you've entered it in an e-mail preferences page.

Thankfully, if you are concerned about cookie files, all the popular browsers include preference settings (shown earlier in Figures 13-15 and 13-16) where you can disable cookies completely. This means your computer won't accept any cookie files from Web sites you visit or choose to be notified every time a server tries to send you a cookie. Completely turning off cookies generally doesn't cause any problems; it just means the site treats you as a new visitor every time you visit it. As a result, turning off cookies can force you to reenter certain preferences and/or passwords every time you go there.

If you choose the less drastic option of being notified when a server tries to send you a cookie and then visit a site that uses cookies, you'll be presented with a dialog box for each cookie file the server tries to send you. Within the dialog you can either choose to accept the cookie (OK) or reject it (Cancel). Figure 13-18 shows an example.

Figure 13-18: Got milk for those cookie files?
If you choose to be notified before accepting any cookie files, you'll receive a dialog similar to this one where you can enable individual cookies to set and store certain preferences or you can choose not to accept cookies. Because many sites use multiple cookies, replying to several of these types of dialogs can get tedious.

If you want more comprehensive control over cookie files, a variety of shareware utilities enable you either to completely block all cookies (which you can also do by simply changing one setting in your browser) or to more intelligently manage your cookie files. Some of the more comprehensive options are the NSClean and IEClean products for Netscape

Navigator/Communicator and Microsoft's Internet Explorer, respectively, from Privacy Software Corporation (www.privsoft.com).

Optimizing your Web connection

As great as the Internet and World Wide Web are, one of the most frustrating parts of connecting to the Internet is the speed at which things are loaded onto your PC — or more precisely, the lack thereof. (Cynics don't call it the "World Wide Wait" for nothing.)

Unfortunately, other than adjusting the size of the "pipe" connecting your computer to the Net (which you do by selecting the speed and/or type of modem that's connected to your PC — see Chapter 5, "Sound Cards, Speakers and Modems" for more information), there isn't a whole lot you can typically do. Most factors affecting Internet performance, including how fast and/or busy the server you're connecting to is, the route your request and the returning data take over the Internet, the amount of people using that route at the same time, and so on, are simply out of your control.

That doesn't mean you should throw up your hands in frustration, however, because there are some things and some software applications that can help. But first, a bit about how your browser works. When you connect to a Web site, all the elements that are included on a typical Web page, such as the text and individual graphics, are copied to your computer's hard drive and stored in temporary folders that are collectively referred to as your browser's *cache*. If you have multiple browsers, such as Netscape Communicator and Internet Explorer, each browser has its own cache.

As with other elements inside your PC, a cache stores recently used data so that if you need access to that data again, you can get to it quickly. In the case of a Web browser, the cache stores the contents of recently visited pages and enables you to quickly reload pages that you've just been to, such as when you use your browser's Back button. If the browser had no cache to turn to, it would have to rerequest every element on every page you'd been to, which would significantly slow down your browsing. Similarly, without cache files, you wouldn't be able to view any Web pages offline (that is, while you're not connected). See Figure 13-19.

Tip

One way to improve your browser performance is to allocate more space to the cache. That way, if you visit a few sites on a regular basis, there's a good chance that your browser can find some of the files it needs in its cache and won't have to download everything, which always slows down the browsing process.

If you're using Internet Explorer, go to the View or Tools menu, select Internet Options, and in the dialog that appears, click Settings. Once you're inside the Settings dialog box, you can adjust the slider to allocate however much space you're willing to set aside (see Figure 13-20).

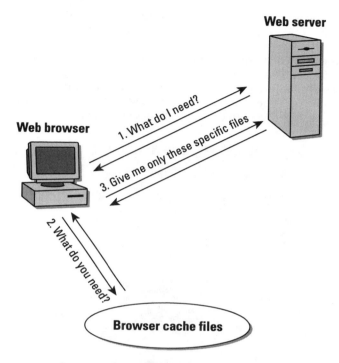

Figure 13-19: How your browser works

Your browser tries to use the most efficient method possible to display different elements of a Web page as you surf the Internet. After it requests a page from a Web server and determines what elements are supposed to be on that page, it searches its local cache to see if any of those elements are already stored on your hard drive. If so, it uses the quickly accessible local copies for whatever it can and then requests and waits only for the pieces of the Web page that it doesn't have over the much slower Internet connection.

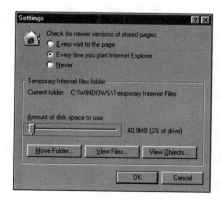

Figure 13-20: Explorer cache

To adjust the size of your local cache in Internet Explorer, move the slider over. You can allocate as much as you want, but don't go overboard because you'll quickly reach a point of diminishing returns.

Under Netscape Navigator 4.0 or later, you can adjust both the disk cache and a separate RAM cache, which is memory set aside and used only during a specific browsing session. As soon as you quit Navigator, the RAM cache goes away, but the disk cache remains for later sessions (which is true of Internet Explorer's disk cache as well). To make the adjustments in Communicator/-Navigator, select Preferences from the Edit menu, click the Advanced options, and choose Cache. Type in the amounts you want to use (in kilobytes — divide by 1,024 to get megabytes), and hit OK (see Figure 13-21).

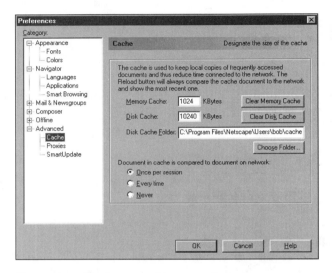

Figure 13-21: Navigator cache
In addition to the standard disk cache, Netscape's browser also enables you to adjust a RAM cache, which is a smaller, but even faster form of cache that uses local memory instead of hard disk space.

After the user-specified limit is hit in either program, the cache starts writing over the oldest files with newer files (using the first-in, first-out principle) so that the cache doesn't continue to grow. At least, that's what's supposed to happen. In some situations, however, the Internet disk cache goes well beyond the defined limits and takes up lots of wasted space. If you find this to be the case on your machine, simply clear the disk cache by clicking the appropriate button in your browser's preferences dialog.

Secret

Occasionally, files in the cache become corrupted. If that's the case, you may find that certain Web sites appear to have strange problems or appear not to work or display properly. To find out if the problem is with you or the Web site, simply clear your disk cache, and then try to visit the site again. Another trick that you can use to check for problems with a particular page is to hold down the Shift key and then hit the Reload button (this works with both Internet Explorer and Netscape Communicator/Navigator). Doing so tells the browser to ignore any files in the cache and re-download everything on the page. If you just hit Reload without holding down Shift, the browser still uses files from its cache.

Cache utilities

A number of companies make utilities that are designed to make more efficient use of your browser cache in an effort to speed up your Web-browsing sessions. Some programs keep the cache better organized, others use tricks such as automatically preloading pages into your cache, and still others offer combinations of these types of methods. In general, these products are typically only moderately effective, but depending on how you use the Internet and the speed of your connection (they're specifically intended for slower connections), you might find them helpful.

Connection utilities

Another group of Web-related programs I refer to as *connection-based utilities* because they enable you to adjust and/or monitor your connection to the Internet. For example, several companies offer shareware or freeware versions of a product whose sole purpose is to adjust the size of packets that your computer sends and receives while it's connected to the Internet. It turns out that the default setting of the Maximum Transmission Unit, or MTU, in both Windows 95 and Windows 98 is optimized for a network connection. If you use a dial-up connection with a modem, however, your performance could suffer as a result.

Products such as MTUSpeed enable you to automatically adjust this setting so that it's optimized for dial-up connections. MTUSpeed performs its magic by making two tiny changes to some settings buried inside the Windows Registry. While results vary widely, some people have found that running this utility has offered fairly dramatic performance improvements (although others find no improvement whatsoever).

Another utility, NetMedic, from INSoft, offers detailed status information about your connection. Running NetMedic enables you to determine if the slowdowns you experience while surfing the Web are due to the Web site itself, the overall traffic on the Internet, slowdowns at your ISP, or configuration problems with your PC. If it finds configuration problems, it can automatically make adjustments to improve your connection speed. If, on the other hand, it finds that the problems are outside your machine, NetMedic can provide the information you need to make decisions on whether to perhaps switch to a different ISP or to try visiting the site at a different time.

You can find a demo copy of NetMedic on the CD accompanying this book.

CD

In addition, both Windows 95 and 98 come with a few basic DOS-based utilities for checking your connection including Ping (Packet InterNet Groper — see Chapter 12, "Setting Up a Small Business or Home Network" for more information) and Tracert (Trace Route). Tracert, in particular, can be handy in tracking down how your PC is connecting to Web sites. As its name suggests, Tracert traces the route that your PC takes when connecting to a particular Web site. It shows you each "hop" that it goes through and the amount of delay that occurs at each one.

To use Tracert, open an MS-DOS Prompt window or the Run... command off the Start Menu, and type in **tracert <*website address*>**, and hit Return. So, for example, to see what route your PC takes in connecting to Yahoo, type **tracert www.yahoo.com**. You'll see a list of all the computers that your request passed through, including their IP addresses and the time taken to get from one to the next. Unfortunately, unless you know, or can figure out, where each particular computer is, this information may not be that helpful, but it's interesting nonetheless.

Finding information on the Web

With a fast, trouble-free connection to the Internet, you can enjoy all that the World Wide Web has to offer. But if you're like most people, you'll soon become frustrated with trying to find the information that you really want. So much information is available that it's often like trying to find a needle in an enormous digital haystack.

For this reason, search engines such as Yahoo, AltaVista, InfoSeek, Excite, and Lycos are some of the most popular destinations on the Internet. These Web sites offer a variety of different methods for finding exactly the information for which you're looking. Even despite some of these differences, however, you should know a few general tricks to help you get the most from any Internet search engine.

The most important point to remember when trying to find something on the Internet is to make your search as specific as possible. If you just type in and do a search for *computers*, for example, you will be completely overwhelmed with all the choices that are returned. To narrow your search, you need to use several search keywords and combine them in a way that will give you what you want.

For example, if what you really want is information on troubleshooting a specific model of Compaq Presario computers, then you need to use all those words in your search. Depending on how the different search engines work, however, just typing in *troubleshooting compaq presario computers* may get you all the pages that have *troubleshooting* or *compaq* or *presario* or *computers*, which may be even more than what you would get when just typing in *computers*.

The problem is that most search engines use something called *Boolean logic* (which actually forms the basis for how microprocessors work, but that's a different topic). Boolean logic uses a combination of ANDs and ORs to figure out what you really want. So, to continue the example, what you really want is a page that has *troubleshooting* AND *compaq* AND *presario* AND *computers* (instead of all ORs). The way to create Boolean ANDs can vary from search engine to search engine, but most accept a plus sign (+) in front of words you want combined. So you enter **troubleshooting +compaq +presario +computers** to get a group of choices that's closer to what you really want.

Another trick to be aware of comes into play if you specifically want to search for an entire phrase, such as *Compaq Presario*. Again, there can be some differences between search engines, but most accept the phrase in quotation marks (""). Thus, typing in *"compaq presario"* finds pages that include only the complete phrase, but not those that have one word or the other.

Finally, you can combine all these techniques to narrow your search as tightly as possible. So, to complete our example, if you type in **troubleshooting +"compaq presario" +computers**, you'll probably get the most accurate returns of all. In addition, by adding the specific model number or some other unique identifier, you'll probably do even better.

Now, having said all this, sometimes even all these techniques don't work. If your keywords are too generic or the combination of words is too specific, you might discover that you find either way too much or just a small portion of what's really available. If that's the case, just keep experimenting until you get something close to what you want. Also, be aware that even the best search engines have only a relatively small percentage of all Web sites that are actually available, and most sites have different collections, so you should try the same search on multiple search engines to get different results.

Setting Up an E-mail Account

Of course, there's more to the Internet than just the World Wide Web. In fact, for many people, the most important part of the Internet is *electronic mail*, or *e-mail*. To get access to e-mail, you need to be connected to the Internet, you need an e-mail software program, and you need to have an e-mail account with an associated e-mail address. I've already covered how to connect to the Net, and several popular e-mail packages are free for the asking, including Outlook Express, which is bundled with Microsoft's Internet Explorer 4.0 or later (and included as part of Windows 98); Netscape Messenger, which is bundled with Netscape's Communicator 4.0 or later; and the standalone Eudora Lite program from Qualcomm. So, all that's left is to set up an e-mail account.

If you want to use Outlook Express or the more full-featured Outlook (which is also bundled as part of the Microsoft Office suite of software programs), you'll end up using the Internet Connection Wizard to set up an e-mail account. Other programs require you to walk through a series of similar dialog boxes. Either way, there are few pieces of information you're going to need before you can get started. Specifically, you'll want to know:

- The name of your outgoing (or SMTP — Simple Mail Transfer Protocol) mail server.

- The name of your incoming (typically POP3 — Post Office Protocol, version 3 — or IMAP — Internet Messaging Access Protocol) mail server.

- Your e-mail address.

- Your e-mail account login name and password. (In some cases the login name is the same as your e-mail address, in others it may be the same as the username and password you use to make your Internet connection, and in still others it's completely unique.)

- The IP addresses of mail servers, which are required only in some situations.

Your ISP should provide this information when you set up an account. Once you have the necessary info, you can either walk through the Internet Connection Wizard or enter the information manually in your e-mail program. By the way, if you've already used the Internet Connection Wizard to set up your Internet account, you can use it again to make changes or additions to an existing account. (Just be careful not to change anything you don't need to change.)

I can't possibly cover all e-mail systems, but here's how to enter the information in Netscape Communicator's Messenger, which is bundled with Netscape Communicator 4.0 and later.

STEPS:

Creating an E-mail Account Under Netscape Messenger

Step 1.   From any application within the Communicator suite, go to the Edit menu, and select Preferences. Once inside the Preferences dialog, click the plus sign next to Mail & Newsgroups, and then click the subheading Identity (see Figure 13-22).

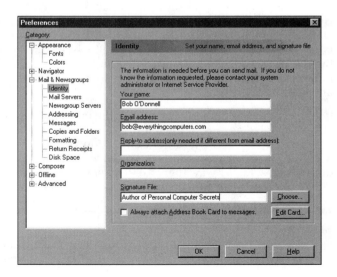

Figure 13-22: Netscape mail
You enter basic e-mail account information such as the account name and your e-mail address inside this Netscape Communicator Preferences dialog.

Step 2.   After you finish entering the basic information there, click the Mail Servers subcategory on the left side of the dialog box, and enter the appropriate incoming and outgoing mail addresses (see Figure 13-23).

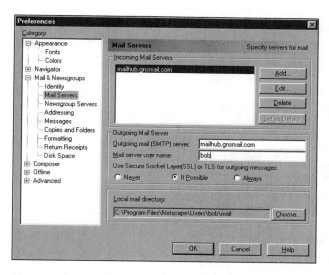

Figure 13-23: Setting the servers
The most important part of creating any e-mail account is specifying the correct type and name for the different servers that handle your outgoing and incoming mail. In some instances, those two functions are handled by the same server.

Step 3.   If you want to, you can make other changes and adjustments to your e-mail account preferences, but you've entered all the required information to make it work. So hit OK, and you're done.

Editing an existing e-mail account

If you ever need to edit your existing account under Netscape Messenger, just follow the same procedures listed previously, and make your changes. If you want to make changes to either an Outlook Express or Outlook account, you can go to the Tools menu in either program, and choose Accounts (it appears in slightly different places in each of the two programs, but it's near the bottom of the window in both instances).

From the list of available Accounts, select your e-mail account, and hit Properties. The dialog box that's displayed is similar in both programs and enables quick access to the critical parameters that are listed in the previous section (see Figure 13-24).

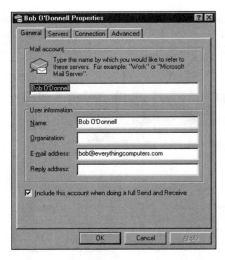

Figure 13-24: Editing Outlook e-mail accounts
If you change your e-mail address or ISP, you need to make changes to your e-mail account configuration in this Accounts Properties dialog box. To change server information, just click the Servers tab.

Tip

If you ever want to use a single computer for multiple e-mail accounts, which you may want to do if you share a computer with a spouse, child, or other housemate, Outlook and Outlook Express make it easy to do so. Just add a new mail account from the main Accounts dialog, and fill in the appropriate information. (Of course, you also have to make sure you set it up with your ISP as well. Most support more than one e-mail address per Internet account, but some may charge for the privilege.) Once you've done so, you can choose to send and receive your mail either individually per account or globally. You can also choose to send any e-mail message through any of the accounts you've created by taking advantage of the Send Using (or Send Message Using) command off the File menu.

Perhaps you access your e-mail from more than one computer, which is the case if you have a main computer at home and a laptop you occasionally use for work (or any of a number of other scenarios). Here's a tip that can help you keep your mail organized. When you retrieve your mail in your e-mail program, you usually copy it from the e-mail server onto your machine, and the message is deleted off the server.

However, both POP3 and IMAP4 servers offer the option to keep messages stored on the server. Now, I wouldn't suggest you leave all your messages there. In fact, many ISPs won't let you, or they severely limit how much space you can use for messages (and if you run out, you might not be able to accept any more incoming messages until you clear some others out). If you want to just check your messages from the road and make sure you can download and store a copy on your main machine, however, this is a great solution.

Here's what you do. On your secondary machine (such as the laptop), set up an e-mail account that's identical to the one on your primary machine except for one critical difference: set the e-mail program to keep a copy of the messages on the server. That way, when you read your messages on that machine, you won't remove them from the server, and you'll still be able to store and organize all your messages on a single machine. (Believe me, it's much easier than trying to synchronize messages between two machines.)

Under Outlook and Outlook Express, you'll find the option to save a copy of messages on the server in the Account Properties dialog box. Go to the Accounts dialog off the Tools menu, select the account name, hit Properties, and then choose the Advanced tab. Once you're in there, select the Leave a copy of messages on server check box, and you're done (see Figure 13-25).

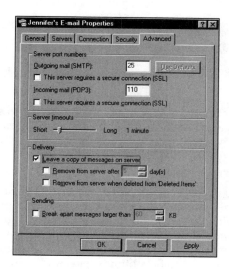

Figure 13-25: Leaving copies with Outlook
Selecting the Leave a copy check box on your secondary machine enables you to read messages from that computer without worrying about trying to keep your messages organized and complete on your main machine.

Under Netscape Communicator's suite of programs, select Preferences under the Edit menu, and choose the Mail Servers subcategory (under the Mail & Newsgroups heading). Select your outgoing POP3 or IMAP server, and choose the Edit button. Select the appropriate tab in that dialog box, and then mark the appropriate check box (see Figure 13-26).

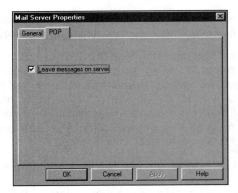

Figure 13-26: Multiple copies with Messenger
If you have a POP3 incoming e-mail server, the setting for leaving copies of the messages on the server couldn't be much easier in Netscape Messenger's e-mail program.

Making the most of e-mail

Once your e-mail account is set up, you can start sending and receiving messages to your heart's content. Once you do, however, you'll realize that you need to figure out some important issues, such as how to find e-mail addresses for people you want to write to, what type of message to send them, how to sign your messages, and how to send and receive files along with your e-mails. The next few sections cover these issues.

Finding e-mail addresses

Just as with regular mail, you usually need to know someone's e-mail address before you can send him or her something. One important exception is that many Web sites include e-mail addresses you can send messages to by simply clicking them. In most instances, though, you'll probably get the e-mail address directly from someone with whom you intend to correspond. Because e-mail addresses often tend to be a bit unwieldy and hard to remember, most e-mail packages also include an address book feature, where you can store e-mail addresses for your friends, family, business associates, and other acquaintances.

But what about trying to write to people whose e-mail address you don't know? Well, thankfully, the Internet has an online equivalent to a phonebook: it's called *directory services*. By taking advantage of one of several companies that provide this type of service, you can look up e-mail addresses directly from within your e-mail program. In addition, most e-mail packages enable you to easily add names you find this way to your own address book.

Here's how directory services work. When you compose a message in your e-mail package, you can choose who to send it to. When you do, you can type in the name of the person whose e-mail address you're looking for, and then choose from one of several directory service companies. When you select Search or Find, the e-mail package connects to the Web site of the company whose directory service you chose and then takes advantage of LDAP (Lightweight Directory Access Protocol) technology to search for the name you requested. If it finds a match, you can select that e-mail address to send the message to and/or add it to your address book.

If you're using Outlook or Outlook Express, you do this by selecting the To button in the message composition window and then Find in the Address Book dialog that pops up next. Another alternative if you have Internet Explorer 4.0 or later installed under Windows 95, or if you're using Windows 98, is to take advantage of the Find People option off the Start menu (under Find, appropriately enough). See Figure 13-27.

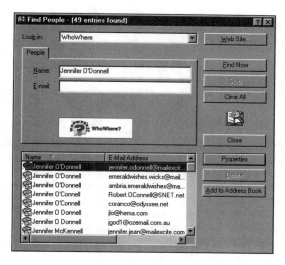

Figure 13-27: Finding people
You can search for the e-mail addresses of long-lost friends or anyone else you'd like to correspond with by taking advantage of the directory services features built into Outlook and Outlook Express.

Under Netscape Messenger, just open a new message window, and click the Address Book icon. Select the directory service you want to use on the left, type a name into the dialog box at the top, and you'll be all set (see Figure 13-28).

Not all e-mail programs support this type of capability, by the way. But even if yours doesn't, you can sometimes get around it by going to a Web site that hosts directory services and doing lookups there. Then you can simply paste the address into your e-mail program's To line.

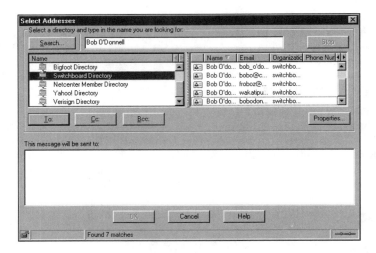

Figure 13-28: Using Netscape's directory services
Like other e-mail packages that support LDAP, the Netscape Messenger e-mail client enables you to search for e-mail addresses using any one of several different directory services.

As great as the idea of directory services is (and as important as it will be in the future when nearly everyone has an e-mail account), the practical usefulness of the current providers is somewhat limited. In other words, you'll be lucky if you find the address for which you're searching. The reason for this is all the current services require you to register with them in order to make your address available. So, unless the person you're looking for has gone through the effort of registering (that is, if they even know about registering at all), then you'll be out of luck. (By the way, this also means that if you want others to be able to find you, you should register with a few of the services by visiting some of their Web sites.)

At this point, not that many people have registered, so the list of available e-mail addresses is relatively limited. As with search engines, different directory services have different lists, so it pays to try the same name on several different services.

Types of messages

Once you have the right address to send a message to, the next task is to determine the format of your message. Most e-mail messages are just plain text, meaning they have no graphics or other type of formatting, which is primarily because older e-mail packages didn't support anything but plain text. Most new e-mail packages, however, provide support for formatted messages. Typically the format they use is HTML, which, as you probably know by now, is the same format used to create Web pages. Some programs also offer the option of Rich Text Format (RTF), which enables you to pick fonts, sizes, colors and more but doesn't include support for graphics. With HTML, however, you can send e-mail messages that look more like published documents, including graphics, photos, background colors, and most any other type of formatting you could possibly want.

Secret

If you want to send hyperlinks to Web sites in your e-mail messages, you'll typically want to send them in HTML (or RTF) format because HTML is well suited for handling them. However, it's also possible to send hyperlinks in plain text messages if you use Microsoft's Outlook or Outlook Express. Both those programs automatically turn a typed-in Web address into a live hyperlink that the recipient can simply click if you use the complete (or "fully documented," as Microsoft calls it) address. So, for example, you need to type in an address such as `http://www.idgbooks.com` in order for this to work in plain text mode, whereas simply typing in `www.idgbooks.com` works in either HTML or RTF mode.

To send HTML-based e-mails, you probably need to specifically tell the e-mail program that you want to send an HTML message because most default to plain text. (If you want, most programs also enable you to set the default to HTML or RTF if it's available). The easiest way to set defaults in Microsoft's Outlook or Outlook Express is to take advantage of the Stationery feature, which automatically creates an HTML message. In Outlook, go to the Actions menu, select New Mail Message Using, and then select from the stationery options that are available. (You may have to choose the More Stationery option the first time you use it.) In Outlook Express, under the Compose menu, the option is New Message Using, but after that, the choices should be the same. Figure 13-29 shows you an example of what you can do.

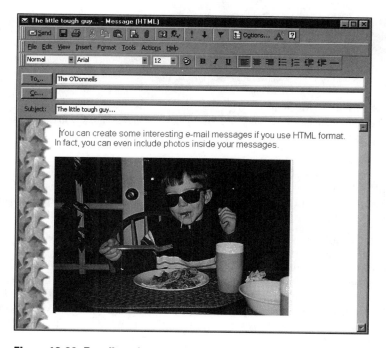

Figure 13-29: E-mail stationery
Using the stationery feature built into Microsoft's Outlook or Outlook Express, you can easily create HTML-based e-mail messages that include background graphics, colored text, and photos.

To create your own HTML message in Outlook Express without Stationery, just select New Message, and make sure the HTML option is selected under the Format menu. In Microsoft Outlook, you have to set the default editor to be HTML if you want to create your own HTML message. To do so, go to the Tools menu in the main Outlook program window, and select Options. (This may not work if you select Options from the Tools menu in the window that appears when you start to create a new message, which can be very confusing.) In the dialog that appears, select the Mail Format tab, and choose HTML from the list of available message format options (see Figure 13-30).

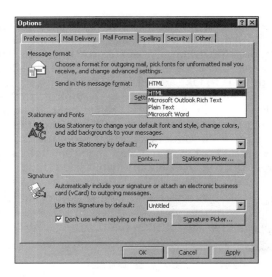

Figure 13-30: HTML mail
If you want to include colors and images in your e-mail messages, you need to send them in HTML format, which Outlook enables you to set as its default format in this dialog box.

Tip

Once you've set HTML to be the default format of your e-mail messages in Outlook, you can quickly change a particular message to be just plain text by choosing it from the Format menu, as you can in Outlook Express. Because of this flexibility, I suggest you make HTML your default for Outlook.

Like Outlook, Netscape Messenger forces you to choose HTML as your default format if you want to send e-mail messages with embedded graphics. Luckily, making that change is easy. Just go to the Edit menu, select Preferences, make sure the Mail & Newsgroups branch of options is expanded, and then click the Formatting subcategory. In the right side of the dialog, select either HTML or plain text as the format of choice. By the way, depending on which option you choose here, the menu items that are available when you create a new message in Messenger change. See Figure 13-31.

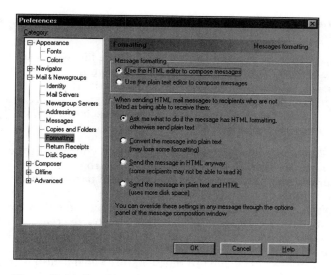

Figure 13-31: Graphical Netscape mail
To use HTML as your default format in Messenger, you have to choose it in the Preferences dialog box.

Note

In order to see one of these fancy messages, the recipient must have an e-mail program that supports HTML (or RTF) mail. If they don't, they'll get a lot of extra text junk in the body of the message. (You can always try sending a message this way and then, if it doesn't work, try resending it in plain text format.) Also, because of the formatting, these types of e-mail messages are larger than plain text messages, which means they take slightly longer to download and slightly more space to store, which some recipients may not care for. However, if you want to communicate your message more effectively, these messages are a lot more interesting than plain text.

Signing your messages

Just as no traditional letter is complete without some sort of mark from the sender, so no e-mail is truly complete without some type of signature. Of course, most people just type in their name at the end of a message, but if you want to add a little snazz to it (or if you're just sick of having to retype the same thing over and over), you might take advantage of the signature features that almost all e-mail packages offer.

By using an electronic signature, you can do such things as automatically include a link to your Web site at the end of all your messages, or include a favorite quote, or include whatever you feel is appropriate. Best of all, once you set up the signature, it is automatically added to the end of all messages that you send. If you really get into this, you can even create several different signatures and then choose the appropriate one for each message. You can also temporarily turn off the signature if you don't want to use it for a particular message.

In most cases you need to create a simple signature file, which contains the text that you want to be included at the bottom of your e-mail messages. If you're using HTML mail, you can also use HTML formatting, such as Web links or even graphics in your signature, but don't go overboard. As much as you may want to include it, no one is going to appreciate a photo of you at the bottom of every e-mail message you send.

Once you've created and saved the signature file in your word processor or HTML editor, all you need to do is tell your e-mail program where it is. In Outlook Express, you can associate signatures with particular stationery files by selecting Stationery from the Tools menu and selecting the Signature button from there. In the subsequent dialog box, you can either type in a simple text signature or choose the signature file you've created. In Netscape Messenger, head over to the Preferences dialog box again (via the Edit menu), choose the Identity setting under the Mail & Newsgroups category, and click the Choose button next to the Signature File line at the bottom of the dialog.

In Outlook, you actually create the signature file via the Mail Format tab of the Options dialog box, which you get to by choosing Options at the bottom of the Tools menu. Follow the steps there under the Signature section to create (or edit) a signature in the same format as your default message type. If you want to, you can also create a signature file as you would with the other programs and then copy it into the proper folder. The default choice is C:\Windows\Application Data\Microsoft\Shared\Signatures.

Tip

In addition to a signature file, all of these programs enable you to attach a *vCard* (or Virtual Card), which is like an electronic business card that includes whatever contact information you choose to include. I wouldn't attach one of these cards to every e-mail message you send, but it is a handy way to pass along contact information that can be easily incorporated into someone else's address book program.

Sending and receiving attachments

Beyond sending simple messages, one of the most useful applications of e-mail is to send files back and forth between your computer and that of someone with whom you're corresponding. For example, if you're collaborating with a business associate on a project, or just want to send the latest pictures of the kids to other family members, you can use e-mail attachments. As the name suggests, attachments are files that are, well, attached to your e-mail message.

In most situations, you simply select the file or files you want to send to the person you've addressed a message to and hit Send. When they receive the message, they should be able to simply double-click the attached files and, as long as they have an application that can open the types of files you sent, can start using them.

Unfortunately, for one of several reasons, this doesn't always work. The most common problem, which is being unable to open the attached messages, is due to what happens behind the scenes when you send an attachment. Because of the wide variety of computer types and operating systems used on computers that make up the Internet, most communications between systems have had to default to the lowest common denominator, which is typically ASCII (American Standard Code for Information Exchange) or plain text. As a result, in order to send more complex binary files (which are used for anything more complex than plain text, including various types of documents and applications themselves), those files have to be converted into ASCII text before they can be sent.

And, in typical computer industry fashion, there are several different ways to do that conversion (sometimes also called *encoding*). The most popular encoding mechanisms in the PC world are MIME (Multipurpose Internet Mail Extensions) and Uuencode (UNIX-to-UNIX encoding is what it stands for, although it's now used on operating systems other than UNIX). Files sent from Macintoshes are frequently encoded with BinHex (short for binary hexadecimal, a type of "shorthand" for binary files) or MacBinary.

Most mail programs automatically encode file attachments when you send the message and decode attachments as messages with attachments are received. In order for everything to work perfectly, this transparent encoding and decoding has to be done with the same mechanism, or you can end up with a garbled mess of strange text characters.

Increasingly, mail programs on a variety of different platforms are moving toward MIME as the default format, which greatly improves the capability to send files over the Internet and receive them in the correct format — even if they're using a different operating system.

Not everything supports MIME yet, however, so most e-mail programs also give you the option to Uuencode file attachments. Programs that provide this option also typically can recognize and decode any Uuencoded files. If your e-mail program can't decode a Uuencoded file or if you receive a BinHex file from a Macintosh user, all is not lost. With the appropriate decoding utility, such as WinZip or QuickView Plus you can decode the attached file.

CD

You'll find demo versions of WinZip and QuickView Plus on the CD accompanying this book.

Secret

If you're not sure whether an e-mail message you've received has a MIME-encoded attachment, you can find out by looking at the message's header. The message header is a small bit of text that's added to the top of every e-mail that's sent across the Internet. Most e-mail packages default to showing you only a small portion of the header (typically the sender, subject matter, and date sent), but if you view the entire header, you can find information such as what servers the message traveled to in between the sender's computer and yours, the format of the message, the e-mail program that generated the message, and much more.

To verify the existence and type of MIME attachments, look for a few lines in the middle of the header that refer to:

- The MIME version, which is self-explanatory.

- The content type, which refers to the generic type and then specific file format of the file, such as image/jpeg, which means it's an image file and is stored in JPEG format.

- The Content Transfer Encoding Method, which is the specific encoding method within the MIME standard used to translate the file to ASCII. This often is Base 64.

- Sometimes the MIME area may also include Content ID and Content Description fields, which provide a specific ID number associated with an attachment to distinguish it from any others, and a textual description of what the content might be.

To view the full message header in Netscape Messenger, select Headers from the View menu, and choose the All option. In Outlook, you need to open the message and then choose Options off the View menu, not Headers (which seems incredibly nonintuitive, but oh well . . .). In Outlook Express, you open the message you're interested in, then select Properties from the File menu, and click the Details tab. Whichever program you use, you end up seeing something similar to the text shown in Figure 13-32.

```
Received: from [205.180.60.87] by mailhub.adwaves.com (NTMail 3.02.07) with
ESMTP id bob for <bob@everythingcomputers.com>; Sat, 8 Aug 1998 11:48:25 -
0700
Message-ID: <19980808185752.12981.rocketmail@send101.yahoomail.com>
Received: from [205.199.198.199] by send101.yahoomail.com; Sat, 08 Aug 1998
11:57:52 PDT
Date: Sat, 8 Aug 1998 11:57:52 -0700 (PDT)
From: rob ricci <rricci94402@yahoo.com>
Subject: Real Audio help
To: bob@everythingcomputers.com
MIME-Version: 1.0
Content-Type: multipart/mixed; boundary="0-434248626-902602672=:11117"
```

Figure 13-32: E-mail message headers
If you view the entire message header at the top of any of your e-mail messages you can find out a wealth of information about the content of the message, where it has been, and where it came from. The MIME attachment information is typically found in the middle of the header.

Note

Note that even if your e-mail package or an extra conversion utility decodes the file into the proper format, you still may not be able to open it if you have don't have the right kind of application. In that case, you may also need to use a file conversion utility to convert the file into a format that one of your applications can handle. For example, if someone using WordPerfect on the Macintosh sends you a file and you don't have a word processor that can read that type of file format, even if you properly receive or separately decode the attached file, you'll need another program to convert it to a format that your word processor can open. Ah yes, aren't computers grand?

See Chapter 14, "Working with Documents and Files" for more on file conversion issues.

Cross-Reference

E-mail security

The final issue to consider when using e-mail is security. While the vast majority of people don't bother with any type of e-mail security and don't run into problems with people reading their e-mails — none that they're aware of, that is — there are situations where it is appropriate and necessary. In fact, as more and more important communications occur through e-mail, e-mail security issues will become increasingly important.

So, here's the basic deal. Most up-to-date e-mail packages include the capability to use encryption technology to scramble messages and/or attachments you send, as well as the capability to decrypt any encrypted messages you receive. The actual encryption techniques can vary, but most e-mail packages have begun to use the S/MIME (Secure Multipurpose Internet Mail Extensions) standard.

With the messages encrypted, it's much harder for hackers and other unscrupulous characters to spy on your e-mail message while they're in transit (which is where any unauthorized access typically occurs). In order to use encryption, however, you often need to obtain a digital ID and learn a bit about how encryption and digital signatures work.

Most e-mail security methods using digital signatures are based on the public key/private key security model, where both you and the receiving party need to have a special file called a *digital ID*, which is kind of like a high-tech version of a driver's license. Digital IDs are issued by companies that are specifically set up for this purpose. VeriSign (www.verisign.com) is the only real big player in this field. Digital IDs consist of two mathematically related parts referred to as a *public key* and a *private key*. In order for you to be able to send or receive encrypted messages or to digitally sign your e-mails, which verifies that they came from you and were not tampered with during transit, you need to have both the sender/recipient's public key and your own private key. In addition, the sender/recipient has to have your public key.

The way the process works is you associate your public key with your e-mail package, and then every time you want to digitally sign and/or encrypt a message, your public key is encoded into the message. In addition, you need to obtain a copy of the recipient's public key and use that to encrypt the message. (And yes, you need to get the public keys for every person with whom you want to correspond with in a secure fashion.) When that person receives the message, the presence of your public key can verify that it came from you, and they can use their private key to actually decrypt the content.

In actual practice the recipient simply has to type in a password they've associated with their private key to get the message. If you're on the receiving end of an encrypted message, all the same requirements apply, but your e-mail package will prompt you to enter a password to use your private key and decrypt the content of the secure message.

The hardest part of the process is obtaining the public key of the recipient/sender with whom you're corresponding. There are two ways to obtain it. The first one is by receiving an encrypted message from the party you are writing to and replying to that message (most e-mail programs automatically store the individual's public key along with their e-mail address if you choose to add them to your address book). The second way is by looking up the public key in one of the directory services described earlier in this chapter. (You need to make sure that the service supports public keys — not many do). Again, however, not everyone has registered with these types of directory services, although you'll probably have better luck finding someone who has registered for a digital ID than you will with just a standard e-mail address because most people who bother to get a key want to make sure others can find it.

Figure 13-33 shows a graphical example of how the process works.

If it all sounds like a hassle, you're right, it is. Couple it with the fact that you have to pay for a digital ID (they cost $9.95/year for a limited Class 1 ID and $19.95/year for a more complete Class 2 ID), and you can probably guess why the concept hasn't exactly taken off yet. (By the way, if the person to whom you want to send a secure message doesn't have a digital ID, and doesn't want to get one, then you cannot send him or her a secure message.) I'm certain this process will be made simpler in the future, but it's still doable now if you really need to have secure communication.

A related option that's free is to just send e-mails that are encrypted with other security programs, such as PGP (Pretty Good Privacy). In this case, what you lose is the capability to verify someone's identity. However, if you know the recipient (or sender), then that isn't a problem.

Other Ways to Communicate via the Internet

As great as the Web and e-mail are for communicating over the Internet, they aren't the only options. You can find lots of useful information from Internet newsgroups and by participating in live chats online. In addition, the Internet is starting to be used for other more familiar collaborative purposes, such as making phone calls and hosting videoconferences, complete with whiteboard-type shared applications, where multiple people can simultaneously collaborate on a single document. For most of these applications you'll use a program other than your Web browser or e-mail package, although most e-mail packages now include the capability to read and participate in newsgroups. In each of these instances communication is made possible by extensions and additions to the core set of Internet protocols.

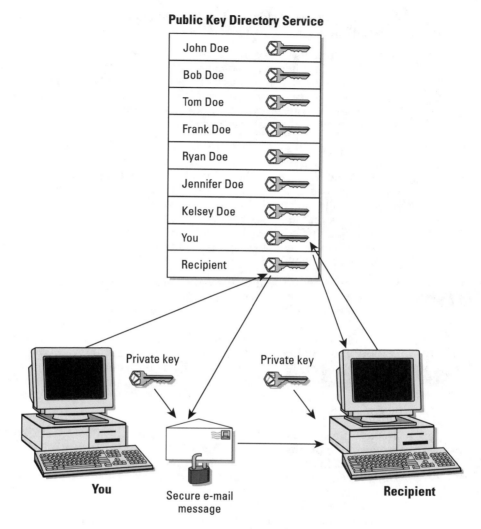

Figure 13-33: Public key/private key e-mail encryption
In order to send or receive secure e-mail messages, you need to have your own digital ID, as well as the public key half of the recipient/sender's digital ID. You typically obtain these public keys from directory services and then store them along with the recipient's e-mail address in your e-mail program's address book.

Newsgroups

Probably the most widely used capability after Web sites and e-mail are newsgroups, which are bulletin board–style discussions of virtually any topic you can imagine. The most well-known newsgroups are Usenet newsgroups, which are a loose conglomeration of computers that host discussions on a variety of subjects, but many companies also host their own newsgroups.

In all the different types of newsgroups, discussions take the form of original messages and replies to those messages. A single message and any replies to that message are referred to as a *thread*, which is why newsgroups are often called *threaded discussions*. (Note that some Web sites have also started to incorporate newsgroup-type sections. While similar in concept, this is different than "traditional" newsgroups.)

Newsgroups are organized into topics based on their names, such as comp.sys.ibm.hardware.misc, which covers nearly any PC hardware-related topic. While a good portion of the Usenet newsgroups are computer-related, thousands and thousands of others cover such subjects as pets, hobbies, philosophy, religion, and current news. As with Web sites, many cover topics that are inappropriate for children and that even most adults would probably find offensive. (Software designed to screen sexually explicit or other types of Web sites that parents want blocked often works on newsgroups as well.)

Note

Because there are so many different newsgroups and the turnover on certain topics is so rapid, it can be difficult to get access to every available topic. One of the main reasons is because the storage requirements for having access to them all are so high. As a result, some ISPs provide access only to a subset of all the available newsgroups. If this is a concern for you, make sure you ask your ISP first. Another option is to take advantage of the DejaNews Web site (www.dejanews.com), which has both current postings and a complete archive of the last few years of Usenet postings. An additional benefit is that this site can be accessed and used to create newsgroup postings with any Web browser.

To read the contents of newsgroup *articles*, as individual "posts" to different groups are typically called, you need a news reader (again, unless you use DejaNews). In the recent past, a news reader was typically a separate piece of software (and some people still prefer using a standalone news reader), but for convenience sake, most e-mail packages now incorporate the capability to view newsgroups. In addition, your ISP needs to provide a name for a news server, such as *news.ISPName.com*. A news server is typically a separate computer or set of computers at your ISP whose function is to keep current copies of the Usenet newsgroups available to all subscribers and to replicate, or copy, any posts that you or any other of the ISP's customers make to all the other newsgroup servers located on the Internet. Individual newsgroup servers, on the other hand, are maintained by the companies or individuals who start them.

You may have entered your news server information when you first created an Internet account, but if not, you can simply enter that information when you set up your standalone news reader or within your e-mail package. In Outlook Express, for example, you create a Newsgroup account in the Accounts dialog box off the Tools menu, and then specify the name of the server you're going to connect to in the Internet Connection Wizard that pops up. You can edit that information later by opening the Accounts dialog box again, clicking the account you want to change, and then hitting the Properties button (see Figure 13-34).

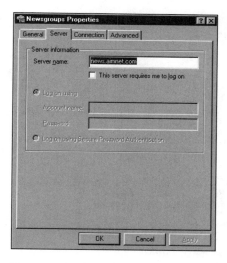

Figure 13-34: Outlook Express news servers
You specify which server to connect to for a particular newsgroup account by selecting the Account, choosing Properties, and then clicking the Server tab.

If you want to connect to other newsgroups, such as Microsoft's public newsgroups, you can create separate News accounts that connect to Microsoft's news servers (msnews.microsoft.com). If you find that you access the newsgroups only occasionally and do so only after you've already connected to the Internet, you can specify in the Connections tab of the Properties dialog box for the particular account (now that's a mouthful . . .) to connect using a local area network. Even if you're using a dial-up connection, you can still get to the news servers you want to connect to, but only after you've already made your Internet connection.

To make newsgroups available in Netscape Messenger, choose Preferences from the Edit menu, expand the Mail & Newsgroups category (if it isn't already expanded) by clicking the plus sign next to it, and then choose the Newsgroup Servers setting. On the right side of the dialog box, you can add or edit any servers to which you want to have access (see Figure 13-35).

The first time you connect to a news server, you are prompted to download a list of all the available newsgroups on that server. If you haven't visited that server in a while, you can also choose to refresh your list. After the list has been downloaded, which may take a few minutes, you can search through the various choices until you find something you're interested in (see Figure 13-36).

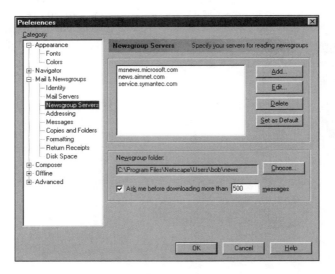

Figure-13-35: Netscape Messenger news servers
To configure newsgroup servers in Netscape's Messenger, you use the Preferences dialog box.

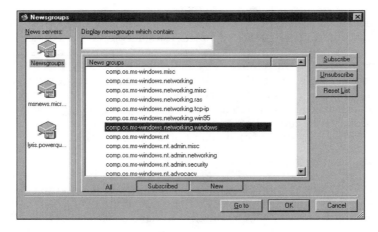

Figure 13-36: Newsgroup topics
Newsgroups are available on almost any subject you can imagine. Once you've downloaded the list of available choices from your ISP, you can choose to visit a particular group and read the messages posted there, or subscribe to a group. Subscribing to a newsgroup helps you follow along in the discussion by automatically downloading any new messages that you haven't read yet.

If you find a newsgroup that you like and whose discussion you want to follow, you can subscribe to it in your news reader program. Subscribing automatically downloads any new messages to the discussion that you haven't read since your last visit. Subscribing doesn't put any requirements upon you; it's merely a convenience you can choose to use or not.

Note

If you're using Netscape Messenger you have to, at least temporarily, subscribe to a newsgroup in order to be able to read its messages. Microsoft's Outlook Express, on the other hand, enables you to quickly and easily visit any newsgroup you want to investigate by using its Go to button (shown earlier in Figure 13-36).

Once you enter a newsgroup discussion, you typically see the headings of messages and replies in a top window and the actual text of each message in the bottom. Figure 13-37 shows a typical example from Outlook Express.

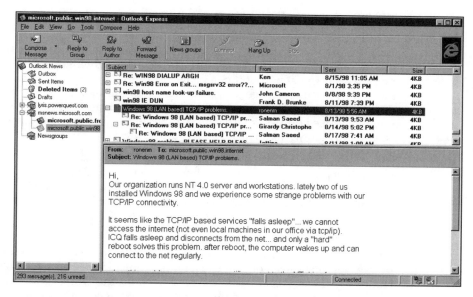

Figure 13-37: Reading newsgroup messages
With most news reader programs, such as Microsoft's Outlook Express, you can view the message titles in one pane of the program and the actual contents of a message in another.

Most people who investigate newsgroups typically just read the messages for a while before they join in the discussion. This is often referred to as *lurking*, and people who do it are called *lurkers*. If you'd like to join in a discussion, which anyone is welcome to do, you can either post a question of your own or reply to an existing message. In some instances you may want to reply directly to the author of a message without creating a public reply that the entire newsgroup sees. In this case, you can use your program's private reply or reply to author feature, which generates an e-mail message to the author.

(For reasons I'm about to explain, this method doesn't always work, however.)

Caution

As handy as newsgroups can be, you need to be aware of a few cautions whenever you participate or read in a discussion.

- Always take what you read online with a grain of salt. Newsgroups are notorious for outrageous claims made by self-proclaimed experts, so set your personal BS filter on high.

- Newsgroups tend to be home to some of the more sordid aspects of and questionable characters on the Internet, so tread with caution (and be careful to watch what your children may be viewing — yet another reason for a filtering utility of some type).

- Be prepared for vicious verbal attacks. Newsgroups are also notorious for flames, which are nasty, mean-spirited replies to what are often innocent questions. Unfortunately, beginners' questions on basic concepts, in particular, can lead to these types of attacks.

Each message you post in a newsgroup has your e-mail address attached to it. The purpose is so people can privately reply to any question or message you may have posted, but it can be used for less noble purposes as well. In fact, many companies use programs that scan through newsgroup postings to automatically collect all the e-mail addresses attached to messages and then compile those addresses into lists that are used to generate junk e-mail (commonly known as *spam*).

As a direct result of this last problem, many people use fake e-mail addresses when they post their messages. Thus, if you want to directly reply to one of their messages, you may need to verify what the real e-mail address should be. (Most people who use fake addresses put a legitimate one in the body of their message or in a signature file at the bottom of each post that they make.)

If you want to try to reduce the amount of spam you receive as a result of newsgroup postings, you can use a phony reply address as well. To do this in Outlook Express, select the newsgroup account that you want to use a phony address with (you can use a phony address per account) by opening the Accounts dialog box off the Tools menu. Click the appropriate account, select Properties, and type a different address into the Reply address textbox (see Figure 13-38).

In Netscape's Messenger, you set a separate reply to address in the Identity section of the Preferences dialog (shown earlier in Fig. 13-22), but unfortunately this address can only be set globally for all of your e-mail and newsgroup messages. This means anyone who attempts to reply to one of your e-mails has to change your e-mail address in order for it to reach you, which is time consuming and burdensome enough that many people simply won't do it.

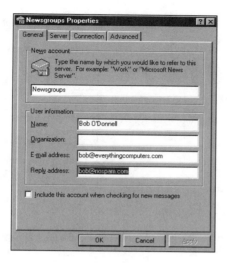

Figure 13-38: Avoid spam with a phony reply address
One way to cut down on junk e-mail is to use a phony reply address for the messages you post to newsgroups.

Live chat

In addition to newsgroups, one of the more popular ways to communicate on the Internet is via live chats, where multiple people engage in a real-time conversation (although participants type their comments as opposed to speaking them — at least, for now). Most chats conform to the IRC (Internet Relay Chat) standard and require the use of an IRC client program, such as mIRC.

CD

You'll find a copy of mIRC on the CD accompanying this book.

Another popular type of chat is referred to as instant messaging, in which two individuals essentially create a private chat channel that enables them to talk to each other (or type at each other, to be more precise) online. Popular examples of this type are the programs ICQ and Instant Messenger, the latter from AOL and Netscape.

Like other Internet-oriented programs, IRC clients rely on some established protocols to communicate with servers used to host live chats on the Internet. The way the process works is you connect an IRC client to a particular server where the chat is being hosted (much as you set your Web browser to visit a particular Web site), and then once you've connected to that server, you choose from or type in one of the many available channels. These channels are analogous to separate radio programs available across the radio dial that you tune into. Figure 13-39 shows a graphical overview of the process.

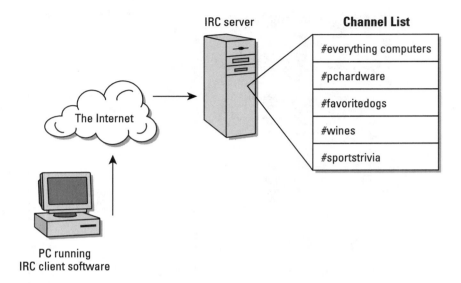

Figure 13-39: How IRC chats work
To participate in an IRC chat, you use an IRC client to connect to a server hosting the chat. Once you've connected, you then choose one of the various channels that are available on that server.

Many IRC programs include a prebuilt list of IRC chat servers so that all you have to do is select one from the list, hit Connect, and you're in. Once you're there, you select a channel by using the program's Join command and then type in the channel, or chat room, name. Most IRC chats have a number sign (#) at the beginning of the name, such as #everythingcomputers. You also have to choose a username, which is your "identity" in the chat room.

Some chat rooms, by the way, are open all the time while others are populated only during specific times. Once you're inside, you type your contributions in an input window and read what others have to say in the main window. A list of current participants is typically listed on the right side of the window (see Figure 13-40).

Most chats are text based, although like all elements of online computing, there are movements to make them graphical. For example, some chats are starting to use *avatars*, which are typically animated characters that you can "inhabit" and control during a chat.

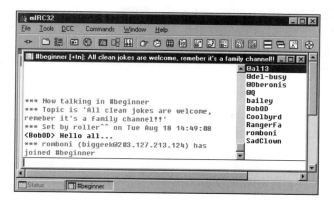

Figure 13-40: Participating in a chat
Chat software such as mIRC, shown here, enables you to type your contributions in a window at the bottom of the screen and read the main text of the chat in the main window. A list of chat participants is in a window on the right.

Internet phone calls

One of the more intriguing uses of the network that forms the backbone of the Internet is making and/or receiving traditional voice calls, particularly long distance calls. The Internet is a global network, and yet most people attach to it via a local phone call or, even better, a direct network connection. So some smart folks realized that with the appropriate software, you could take advantage of that global reach and contact almost anyone, anywhere in the world, for the price of a local call to your ISP or just the cost of maintaining your cable or DSL modem connection.

Here's how the process typically works. You connect your computer onto the Internet with a normal connection and then launch special telephone-like software. When you speak into a microphone attached to your PC, the program (in conjunction with your computer's sound circuitry) digitizes your voice, compresses it, chops it into tiny chunks, and then sends those chunks across the Internet as packets of data. At the receiving party's computer (in other words, the person you are calling), the process is reversed, and the packets of data are recombined into a complete digital signal. That signal is then converted back into normal analog audio so that the person you are speaking with can hear it through the speakers attached to their computer (see Figure 13-41).

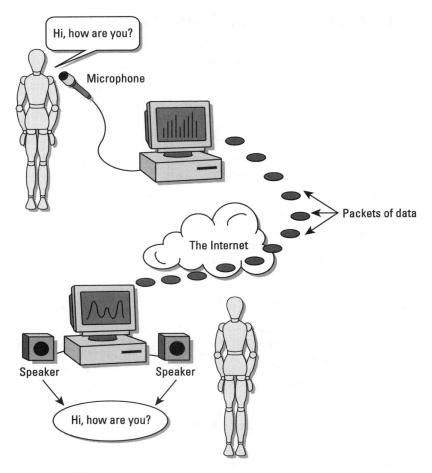

Figure 13-41: Calling on the Internet
To make Internet-based phone calls, a program on your computer converts your voice into digital data, then chops that data into packets, and sends them over the Internet to another person's computer. On the receiving end, the process is reversed.

The tricky part of this process is determining what format the packets should take when they're sent over the Internet. Initially, there were no standards for *voice over IP* (as this application is sometimes called because it sends voice data using the Internet's IP protocol), which meant that both the calling and receiving party had to use the exact same kind of Internet telephony software. In recent years, however, the industry has developed the H.323 videoconferencing standard, which enables any telephony programs that conform to the standard (whether or not they support video calls) to communicate with one another — even if they're on different platforms.

So to give you the most amount of flexibility, if you want to try Internet-based calls, make sure you use an H.323-compliant program, such as Intel's Internet Phone.

Tip

Another problem with voice calls over the Internet is that the sound quality is poor. In fact, the service is often downright unusable (although things have gotten better recently). In some cases, the poor sound quality may be because you have improperly configured your phone software to work at only half-duplex or because your computer's sound circuitry isn't capable of working at full-duplex. If either is true, you'll have a "walkie-talkie"-like connection where only one person can speak at a time. To fix this problem, make sure your hardware and software are set to work at full-duplex.

Cross-Reference

See Chapter 5, "Sound Cards, Speakers, and Modems" for more on duplex issues.

TCP/IP vs. UDP

The TCP/IP protocol was developed to be ultra reliable because its original purpose was to maintain network connections in the event of a war, but it's not always very speedy as a result. To maintain a good-sounding, consistent phone (or any other audio) connection, however, all the packets sent on the Internet have to arrive quickly, in a continuous stream-like fashion. In fact, for audio, video, or any other real-time data, it's actually better to lose, or drop, a packet of data to maintain a constant signal than it is to wait for every single packet to arrive. (A single dropped packet of audio data may sound like just a tiny click in an ongoing audio signal, which really isn't that noticeable or problematic.)

The nature of TCP/IP, however, ensures that every packet will arrive, even if takes a few minutes or even a few hours to work its way over the Internet. While this arrangement generally works fine for static data, such as HTML-based Web pages, graphics, and other data files, it's completely unacceptable for audio, video, or any other real-time signal.

To resolve this apparent contradiction, most audio- or video-related Internet software doesn't use regular TCP/IP to send and/or receive data but instead uses either UDP (User Datagram Protocol) or RTP (Real-Time Transport Protocol). Both of these are fancy names for what are generically referred to as "unreliable" protocols. (Getting back to the OSI model mentioned in Chapter 12, "Setting Up and Using a Small Business or Home Network," UDP and RTP are alternate transport layers.) They're considered unreliable because they place more emphasis on maintaining a relatively continuous stream of real-time data than on the integrity of every packet. So, if a program that uses UDP doesn't "see" the next packet that's supposed to arrive, it simply skips over that one and jumps to the next. If a whole bunch of packets don't arrive, which definitely happens sometimes, then you can get a very noticeable glitch or pause in the audio or video signal. Overall, however, UDP is still a good solution for audio and video, but it's completely unacceptable for static data, such as binary files, Web pages, and so on, where a single dropped packet can make a file unusable.

Ideally, of course, it would be great to maintain a stable, reliable connection for all types of data, but until the Internet's overall bandwidth increases significantly, this is a compromise with which we just have to live.

The main cause of poor audio problems, however, has to do with the way information is sent over the Internet via the TCP/IP protocol, which is the primary mechanism for transferring data on the Net.

Despite some of these problems, Internet-based telephony is growing rapidly, and many believe it will be an increasingly important part of the Internet in the years to come. In fact, many of the large phone companies plan to use the Internet for routing regular calls so that some calls made with traditional phones may actually take advantage of the Internet.

Secret

By the way, most Internet-based phone calls go from computer to computer, but it is possible to call from your computer directly to a regular phone. To do so you need to take advantage of a service called an *H.323 gateway*. It simultaneously takes care of converting the digital signals you send into analog form so that the person you're calling can hear you, as well as converting their voice to digital and then sending the packets across the Internet to your computer. Some businesses and ISPs offer this service to their employees and/or customers, but you can also find companies on the Internet that provide this service for a fee.

Videoconferencing and application sharing

In addition to regular phone calls, the Internet is also enabling the use of video phone calls and videoconferencing. In fact, most of the mechanisms (including the H.323 protocol) and programs used for regular phone calls can also be used for video phone calls — as long as you and the person you're calling have video cameras attached to your PCs. (You don't need a video camera to receive a video signal from someone else, but you do need one to send a signal.)

Note

By the way, if you don't want to use the Internet to place a video phone call or host a videoconference, you don't have to. If you have a modem that supports the V.80 standard (this is different than the V.90 56K standard) and software that supports the H.324 standard (again, different from H.323), you can place a direct phone call to someone else who has a similar arrangement and host a video call over a normal phone connection.

Microsoft's NetMeeting program enables you to place audio and/or video calls over the Internet (or a direction connection). Netscape's Conference program, which is part of the Communicator suite of products, supports audio calls only. In both programs you first need to find the "number" or address of the computer with which you want to connect. While several mechanisms are available to do this, in many cases the process isn't very easy. In fact, sometimes you have to resort to having the person you want to connect to look up their current IP address and send that to you. (You can use the Winipcfg program I referred to earlier in this chapter for this purpose.)

In some cases you can look up the address via a directory service or use the person's e-mail address if they are logged into (that is, connected to) a particular directory server. On an internal company intranet, you can also use the computer's NetBIOS name (see Chapter 12, "Setting Up a Small Business or Home Network" for more information). Once you have the address, just enter it, and hit Dial or Connect. On the receiving end, the person you're calling has to be running an H.323-compliant program that supports similar audio compression methods (this last point can prevent users of, say, NetMeeting and Conference to properly connect and communicate with one another) and then has to "accept" the call. Once they do, you can initiate a conversation.

Both of these programs can be used to do a variety of different types of collaboration, above and beyond regular phone calls, all over an Internet (or an intranet) connection. In particular, NetMeeting supports application sharing (with other Windows users), shared electronic whiteboard, and text chat, while Netscape Conference offers shared electronic whiteboard, synchronized browsing (where you can direct the receiving person's computer to particular Web sites you want them to see), and text chat. And unlike audio and video phone calls, which are typically limited to two parties, you can use these collaboration features with several different people at once if you want to host a "virtual meeting."

Sharing an application with NetMeeting enables you to open any program or file on your PC and then share what you see on your screen with the people you've called. So, for example, if you want to show someone else a slide presentation you've created, you could share your presentation program, and the other person could view in a window on their screen the contents of the application's window on your screen. You could even let the other person remotely control the application (or your entire PC, for that matter, if you share Windows Explorer, which is a potential security issue you need to think about) and make changes to the document.

If you'd rather do some more general brainstorming, you may want to consider using a whiteboard-like function built into these applications. With the whiteboard window open, each of the "meeting" participants can write or sketch ideas on the whiteboard using the program's built-in tools (see Figure 13-42).

Finally, once you've opened a connection with other users via a conferencing-style application, you can also use it to send files to other meeting participants. This can be handy if you want to share the final results of your brainstorming session or just as an alternative method to sending file attachments over e-mail.

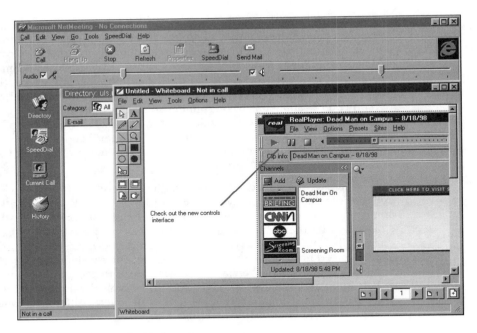

Figure 13-42: A virtual whiteboard
If you use NetMeeting's whiteboard feature, you can have an online brainstorming session where all the participants in the meeting/phone call can interact with each other.

Building Your Own Web Site

Many would argue (and rightly so, I believe) that you're not really taking advantage of all the Internet has to offer unless you contribute to it as well. You can do that, of course, by building your own Web site. The basic process is actually simple and essentially boils down to three steps:

- You create a series of documents or "pages" in HTML, which is the file format used with most Web sites.

- You obtain an address where those files will be located (such as www.mywebsite.com).

- You transfer the HTML pages you've created to a server connected to the Internet that will "host" your pages.

In most cases, each of those main steps also has a few substeps (which I will explain in just a bit), but even still, the whole process from start to finish can easily be completed in a few hours. That is, as long as you keep your site simple. If you have more grandiose plans, you can take weeks, months, and even years to complete a big site, but the essential steps are quite easy.

Site strategy and structure

Before you dive into creating any type of Web site, you first need to plan what you want to do. Many people who decide they want to have a Web site immediately jump into creating the HTML pages that will make up their site; but without some kind of overall strategy in place, that effort may turn out to be wasted. You need to sit down and figure out what kind of Web site you want to have, what kind of information or other material it will contain, and what (if anything) you're trying to achieve with the site.

A site designed to support a small business, for example, has different requirements than a personal site that includes information about yourself, your family, or hobbies you passionately care about. If you want to create a small Web-based business online, such as a mail-order business, you have still different requirements. The capability to take credit card–based orders, for example, requires much more effort than simply providing contact and general purpose information about a business.

While you're in the planning stages, feel free to think big. In fact, it's best to start with a list of all the things you'd eventually like to include on your site because it can help you plan the overall design and structure of the site. Few (if any) Web sites include everything the site owner wants when they're first launched, and even if they do, people inevitably come up with other things they'd like to add. The Web is a dynamic medium, and as a result, Web sites are constantly being added to and redesigned.

Tip

To make the process of planning your site more tangible, draw a visual map of what you want the site to include and how you want the different pages to be related. Not only does this map give you a better idea of how everything fits together (or doesn't), it also helps you as you design your site's navigational structure — that is, how you get from page to page. Some Web-authoring programs include a mode where you can create this visual overview, but if yours doesn't, you can always build one in a basic drawing or flowchart program. (And frankly, none of those methods are as fast as good ole pencil and paper.) See Figure 13-43.

All Web sites start with a main or home page, which is often labeled index.htm or index.html. From there you can branch off in any number of different directions, depending on what type of content you want to include. The "branches" are made via hyperlinks, which are logical connections that point to another Web page or a particular location on the same page. Web sites consist of a number of different HTML pages that are linked together in this fashion.

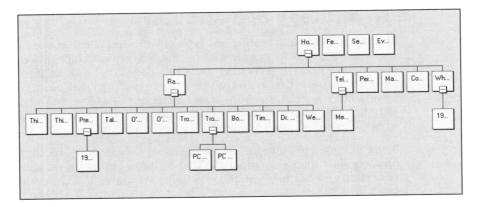

Figure 13-43: Site map
Before you start creating your Web site, you should draw a map of what you want it to
include and how you want the various pages to be related.

Creating Web pages

Once you've figured out an overall map of the site, it's time to start creating
the individual pages. You can create basic HTML Web pages in any word
processor that supports HTML (not all do). You typically just choose Save As
from the File menu and then choose HTML as the file type. Or you can use a
dedicated Web-authoring or HTML-editing program. Some HTML programs
(such as FrontPage Express or Netscape Composer which are bundled for
free with Internet Explorer 4.0 or later and Netscape Communicator 4.0 or
later, respectively) are designed to create individual pages, and some
packages are designed to create entire Web sites.

CD

Demo copies of Adobe's PageMill, Allaire's HomeSite, and Macromedia's
DreamWeaver Web-authoring programs, which offer features to build entire
sites, are included on the CD accompanying this book.

If you're creating a big, sophisticated site that uses a database to build your
pages dynamically, you'll typically just build page templates that leave places
for data to be filled in by the database. The vast majority of sites, though,
feature static HTML pages, which simply means they are complete in and of
themselves. (You can certainly add dynamic elements to static HTML pages,
however, as I explain in the section "Adding Other Elements," later in this
chapter.)

Be aware of these important points when building Web pages. First of all,
each Web page has both a filename, such as books.htm, and a title, such as
"Everything Computers: Personal Computer Secrets." The filename is what
you save the file as in your HTML-editing program, and it's what you use
when creating hyperlinks to the file, such as linking to it from your site's
home page. (As a result, it's also the name that appears in an URL that links

to that page.) The title, or page name, on the other hand, is the name that appears in the title window of your browser when you visit that page, as well as the name that appears in your Bookmarks or Favorites list if you bookmark the page. The two do not have to be the same (typically the filename is much shorter than the title), but you do want to think about both of them when naming a page.

Second, don't let individual Web pages get too large in terms of size (or length, generally). The larger a page and all the elements, such as graphics, it contains, the longer it takes to download and appear on the screens of visitors to your Web site. If the pages are too big, they'll take too long to download, and most people won't bother waiting for them. So, keep your graphics and Web pages as small as you possibly can. One general rule of thumb is to limit all the individual pages to about 60K or less, including graphics. (Of course, this doesn't mean *all* pages should be 60K.) In some cases that's hard to do, but you really should stick to this rule if you don't want to put off potential site visitors.

Cross-Reference

For tips on how to reduce the size of your graphics, see Chapter 15, "Working with Pictures and Video."

Graphic design

As a writer, I would like to be able to say that the quality of the text and other content that you include on your Web site is what keeps people coming back for more. The truth is, however, we are a visual society, and in the vast majority of cases, the appearance of your Web site has as big, if not a bigger, impact on how visitors perceive the site. As a result, you should seriously consider the graphic design of the site, particularly if you want a lot of people to visit.

If you're building a Web site to support a business, for example, you probably want to hire a graphic designer to create visual elements for the site or even design the site's overall look. If you don't have a budget for professional help, take advantage of the graphic templates that most HTML-authoring programs now include. These templates certainly offer a good place to start the design of your site, but unless you want your site to look just like lots of others, I suggest you don't use a style template without adding your own unique touches to it.

Adding photographs and other artwork can make a huge difference in the overall look of your site, but don't just use graphics to provide basic visual imagery. You should also make the graphics on your pages functional by using them to link to other pages or other information on your site. For example, you may want to create a graphical navigation bar that leads to the different sections or individual pages of your site, or use a photograph to link to a particular page.

Tip

By the way, if you use photos or other graphic elements for links, make sure you also provide text-based links in case there's a problem downloading the graphic or the site visitor has graphics turned off. Many sites provide an option for text-only navigation at the bottom of each page.

In addition to graphic issues, think about typography, which refers to how and where you place text on your pages. Simply running a series of paragraphs separated by returns usually doesn't cut it. As with page layout, Web sites need to take advantage of different font sizes, indents, and what have you to make the page more attractive and more readable. Generally speaking, you don't want to use unusual fonts because if visitors to your site don't have the font you use, it is replaced with a generic font (such as Times New Roman) on their screens. The resulting visual impact may not be exactly what you had in mind.

One way to incorporate all these different capabilities into one is to take advantage of Cascading Style Sheets (CSS), which enable you to define typographical and graphics-based styles, which you can then apply to a Web page or an entire site. The benefit of using style sheets (which are supported in versions 4.0 and later of popular browsers) is that you can quickly change an entire site by simply changing the style sheet. In addition, the second-generation CSS specification offers precise control over how elements can be positioned on a page, which is a big improvement over previous mechanisms. The problem is that they're only viewable by people with browser versions of 4.0 or later, which still isn't everyone (although it's now the majority).

HTML basics

Thanks to the rapid development of visually oriented WYSIWYG (What You See Is What You Get) HTML-editing tools, you don't need to know anything about what HTML is or how it works in order to build a Web site. However, it can be helpful to understand some of the basic concepts of how HTML works, both to fix problems with particular pages and to make sense of the pages you do create or otherwise come across.

HTML is basically a text-only format that uses tags to identify different elements on a page and to specify different formatting commands that are to be applied to a particular element on a page. (Some elements denoted by tags don't actually appear on the page but are part of the document.) Specific tags are used to mark the beginning of a particular type of tagging and the ending of that tagging. In all cases, the tags are separated from the text on the page via angle brackets (<>), and all ending tags have a slash character (/) in them. A more complex type of markup is used in XML, or eXtensible Markup Language, which is kind of like a cousin to HTML. (See the sidebar "What is XML?" for more information.)

For example, the HTML tag to start adding bold to a particular word or set of words is , and the tag to "turn off" the bolding is . To create a hyperlink between a particular word or image on the page to another HTML document, you use the "a href" command. The proper syntax, or usage, of the command is as follows:

```
<a href="http://www.everythingcomputers.com/books.htm">Personal
Computer Secrets</a>.
```

What is XML?

As the desire to bring more interactivity and more capability to the Web has grown, so has the recognition that the HTML standard used as the backbone of most Web pages and Web sites has some limitations. In particular, it can work only to display information; it doesn't really offer much in the way of interacting with that information. While it doesn't matter for many small and medium-sized Web sites, that limitation can be a problem for large Web sites whose content is derived from a database. To attempt to address some of these types of concerns, a great deal of interest has been generated by XML, or eXtensible Markup Language. XML is not a replacement for HTML, but rather a companion that's better suited for certain types of applications and certain types of Web sites.

XML is defined as "a common syntax for expressing structure in data." In English, that means it's a mechanism for describing not just what something looks like on a page, but what it is and what it means. For example, in XML you wouldn't define a heading on one of your pages as being only in bold text, you would also say that it's one of several product categories that your business offers, or whatever the information actually is. Like HTML, XML was derived from SGML (Standardized General Markup Language), which is a well-established standard used to describe complex documents. XML can be used not only to describe how a Web page looks, but it can essentially provide a mechanism for building an application with the data on a page (among other things).

One of the primary differences between HTML and XML is that in XML, you can define your own markup tags. In fact, you have to, because XML doesn't have real tag definitions. A Document Type Definition, or DTD, is a document that describes different XML tags and what they mean. (A schema is a similar type of document.) In a very simple way, these definitions can be seen as an agreed-upon set of database fields. One way to understand the difference between HTML and XML is that you can think of the standard set of HTML tags as being equivalent to one DTD. XML, however, enables you to create any number of DTDs for any number of different applications. For example, MathML is a DTD that's been agreed upon by mathematicians to define a set of XML tags that can be used to share complex mathematical information over the Internet.

Different industries can create their own DTDs and then use the agreed-upon standards to share information between sites. In that way, XML can make it much easier to access data that previously existed in a wide variety of different formats. Microsoft offers XML support in their Office 2000 applications, for example, as a means of sharing files complete with all their formatting via the Internet (or company intranets).

In order to view XML documents, you must have a browser that supports it (technically, you need what's called an *XML parser*). While Internet Explorer 4.0 included some XML support, you really need Version 5.0 or later of Explorer or Netscape Communicator/Navigator to view and interact with XML documents.

In this example, the words "Personal Computer Secrets" are linked (which typically means they become underlined and/or appear in a particular color) to the Web page located at `http://www.everythingcomputers.com/books.htm`. So, if you clicked on that phrase, you would access that page.

In some cases, you'll find that the ⟨/⟩ end tags are located near where the tag starts and in others, such as the ⟨HTML⟩ tag that starts off any HTML document and identifies it as such, there isn't an end tag until the very bottom of the page. Some tags are quite long because they include not only a main command, but several *attributes* or *modifiers* that affect the command, such as whether or not to center an item on a page, what font to use, and other settings that are specific to certain types of tags. Again, if you use CSS, you may see all these types of modifiers at the beginning of a page, or in a separate document that's referenced from every page in a Web site, as opposed to next to the individual tags. HTML has lots of different tags, by the way, so it's difficult to remember what they all do or mean, but their essential structure and usage is similar.

- Table 13-2 lists a few of the more common tags, what they mean, and how they're used.

Table 13-2   Common HTML Tags

Tag	Meaning	Example
⟨Body⟩	Used to denote the body, which is the beginning of the main section of the HTML document, as well as general attributes assigned to it, such as the margins, background color, and text color.	`<body leftmargin="0" bgcolor="#FFFFFF" text="#000000">`
⟨a href⟩	Hyperlink, which means the words or images enclosed by the tag create a link to whatever other HTML document is pointed to. If you see a # sign, that points to a particular position or anchor on the page.	`<a href="index.html">`
⟨b⟩	Bold	`<b>O'Donnell on Computers</b>`
⟨I⟩	Italic	`<I>Personal Computer Secrets</I>`
⟨p⟩	New paragraph	`<p align="center">`
⟨Table⟩	Used to denote the beginning of tables, which are used on many Web pages not only to present columns of information, but also for basic page layout.	`<table border="0" cellspacing="6" width="100%">`

Tag	Meaning	Example
`<td>`	Table element is typically used to define the characteristics of a particular table cell, such as its vertical alignment.	`<td valign="top">`
`<tr>`	Table Row is used to define the characteristics of a row in a table, such as its absolute height in pixels, background color, and alignment.	`<tr height="102" bgcolor="#C0C0C0" valign="top">`
` `	Line Break, which is similar, but not identical, to a new paragraph mark. It's often used when you want to wrap text around a graphic.	`<br clear=left>`
`<Img src>`	Image Source is the location of the graphic file that is placed at the point where this tag occurs. You can also assign attributes to the image, such as alternative text, as well as its width and height in pixels.	`<img src="images/ Everything_Computers _Logo.JPG" alt= "Everything Computers" WIDTH="288" HEIGHT ="216">`
`<Script>`	Used to denote the beginning of a script included on the page and the type of language it uses.	`<script language="JavaScript">`
`<hr>`	Horizontal Rule is a line that goes across the page to separate different areas.	`<hr width=50% align=left>`
`<h1>` to `<h6>`	Heading Levels 1–6 are used to signify different sizes of headings with H1 being the largest.	`<h3><font face="Times New Roman">`
`<Style> type="text/css">576`	Used to denote the use of a Cascading Style Sheet within a particular Web page.	`<STYLE`

Continued

Table 13-2   Common HTML Tags *(continued)*

Tag	Meaning	Example
`<Meta>`	Meta tags are a catch-all type of tag used to do things such as assign keywords or descriptions to a page. The words marked by meta tags do not appear on the Web page.	`<meta name="author" content="Bob O'Donnell">`
`<!- -!>`	Comments put in by the Web page's creator (or sometimes the Web-authoring program) that describe something or remind someone about certain aspects of the page. They are ignored by a Web browser or other program that displays the page.	`<!-COLUMN TWO: DO NOT CHANGE ABOVE THIS LINE-!>`

If you want to get a feel for how HTML looks, you can open an HTML page directly in a basic text editor, such as Notepad, or you can view the raw HTML from inside your browser. Under Internet Explorer, select Source from the View menu, and under Netscape Communicator/Navigator, select Page Source from the View menu. See Figure 13-44.

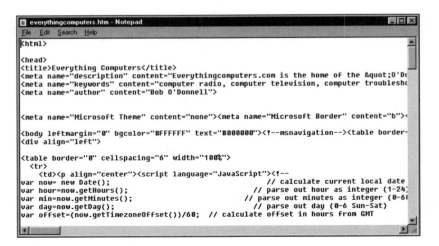

Figure 13-44: Raw HTML
You can view the HTML that goes into most Web site pages by simply selecting the View Source command from your browser's View menu.

On big Web sites whose pages are created dynamically, you may not see very much that's useful, but it's an interesting exercise nonetheless. Web pages that use tables, frames, and other more sophisticated elements, on the other hand, often provide an overwhelming amount of data that can be difficult to decipher.

Tip

If you come across a particular element or design in a Web site that you'd like to incorporate into your own site, you can copy and paste the raw HTML from the Source window that appears in your browser into your own Web pages. While it's not legal to use copyrighted information, it's perfectly legal (and common practice) to "borrow" certain elements or ideas from other sites. Note, however, that because of this potential, some Web sites block the capability to view their raw HTML source.

Adding other elements

Most Web sites consist primarily of text and graphics, but the truth is that it can get a bit boring after a while. If you want to add some dynamic elements to your site, you may want to investigate JavaScript, Java, ActiveX, and other dynamic HTML (DHTML) elements. For example, if you want today's date listed on one of your Web pages and you want it to be automatically updated every day, you'll need to create or find a JavaScript script or some other mechanism that can automatically enter the day's date and paste that script into your page. Similarly, if you want to use creative effects such as having the text on a certain area of one of your pages "fly in" from the left or right side of the screen, you can use one of several different techniques to achieve this effect. (Remember, though, use these types of things only in moderation. They may look cool for the first or second time, but they can get old very quickly.) Many Web-authoring programs, for example, have menu commands that enable you to add these types of dynamic elements to your pages very easily.

You may also want to consider adding audio or video to your pages, though again, moderation is the key here. You can do such things as playing background music as soon as a page loads or including links to small streaming audio or video clips. Video, in particular, can take up large amounts of storage space on the server that hosts your Web site, however, so it may not be practical.

Cross-Reference

For more on adding video to your site, see Chapter 15, "Working with Pictures and Video." For more on adding various types of audio to your site, see Chapter 16, "Working with Audio and Music."

The best way to get lots of returning traffic to your Web site is to provide a reason for visitors to keep coming back. While that sounds rather obvious, doing it isn't always easy. Your best bet is to figure out a way to build a community-like environment that encourages interaction between people who visit your site. One of the best ways to do this is to incorporate a discussion or message board area on your site where people can communicate with each other. Many Web-authoring programs now include the capability of incorporating these types of interactive features to your site relatively easily. Be warned, though, that this technique works only if you're willing to spend the time it takes to keep the interactions moving.

Site navigation

One of the most overlooked, but most important, aspects of any Web site is its navigational structure, which basically means how you move around from page to page. Sites that are difficult to move around in confuse and turn off visitors, much as pages that load too slowly. You should spend some time thinking about what types of different paths people might take to get to different areas of your site and then make sure they can quickly get from one place to another. As a general rule, you should be able to get from any page on your site to any other with two clicks (or less).

One way you can ensure easy movement within your site is to build either a graphical or text-based site map that lists all the pages on your site. Then make sure that each page on your site includes a link to the map. In addition, you should figure out the most popular and/or most important sections of your site, and be sure you include links to them on almost all (if not all) pages of your site as well. You may also want to make sure that any subpages within a particular section are only one click from similar subpages. While you don't want to go overboard in this regard, I've never seen a Web site that was *too* easy to move around.

I recommend you include some basic text-only links at the bottom of each page, in addition to the main navigation links you include on the top or sides of your pages.

Testing your pages

Web site creation is not complete until you've tested your pages in as many different ways as possible. At the very least, you should install both Internet Explorer and Netscape Communicator/Navigator on your PC and try visiting all the pages in both browsers. You may be surprised at what you find.

Secret

If you let the background color of your page stay at the default color, you'll find that it is white in Internet Explorer, but gray in Netscape Navigator. I found this one out the hard way on my own site and had to go back and force all the pages to be white to make sure they looked the same across both browsers.

There are a lot of little problems that can crop up because of differences between the two main browsers, so you really must check. You'll be particularly prone to these types of problems if you've used any tricky (or recent) HTML-based effects, such as text that flies in from the side and what have you. In many cases, these effects work in one browser but not another. You'll have to decide for yourself if that's acceptable, but as a general rule, I suggest you only include elements on your pages that can be viewed similarly across all the different browsers.

If possible, you might even want to check the pages of your Web site with different versions of the same browser. Setting up different versions of a browser on a single computer is nearly impossible because you typically can't have two different versions of the same browser on a single PC. Instead, you'll have to try it from a different computer, which means you'll have to post your pages first and then go to your Web site from that other computer. While you're at it, you might also want to check your site from a Macintosh or a PC running a different operating system.

In addition to different browsers, you need to view your Web pages at different video resolutions. In other words, temporarily switch your video resolution to 640 × 480, 800 × 600, and 1,024 × 768 to see how your Web pages look. (Under Windows, you change your resolution via the Display control panel's Settings tab.) The rule used to be that you should design for a 640 × 480 monitor resolution with 256 colors, but I think it's now safe to bank on an 800 × 600 resolution with 16-bit color. If you've been designing your site at a resolution of 1,280 × 1,024, you may be in for a rude shock. If necessary, resize your graphics and relayout your pages to make sure they work at smaller resolutions.

Finally, after you've posted the pages on the Web server that will host them, make sure you visit them using as many connection speeds as possible. One common mistake that Web site designers with fast Internet connections make is forgetting that most of the world still views the Web via 56K (or even slower) modem connections. Just because something loads quickly via a DSL or cable modem connection doesn't mean it'll be quick on a 28.8 modem. In fact, one short visit from a 28.8 modem should quickly convince you that the huge graphics you've included on your pages are not going to cut it. If your pages consistently load too slowly for you to bear, then they're going to be too slow for most other people too. As a general rule, you don't ever want a page to take much more than about 10–15 seconds too appear. If they take longer, people won't wait for them, and all your efforts will be for naught. So, again, keep your page sizes (and graphics) small.

Obtaining a Web address

While you're in the process of building your site, or sometimes even beforehand, you also have to deal with getting a Web address, which is the location of your Web site in cyberspace and the place that actually holds your files. As part of their regular service, many ISPs include a certain amount of hard disk space (such as 10MB) on one of their servers that you can use to host a Web site. If your ISP doesn't, you'll find no shortage of companies that can host your Web files for a monthly fee and make them available to anyone surfing the Internet. If you can't find a Web site hosting company in the yellow pages, check your local computer magazines (you'll find them for free at most computer retail stores).

In most of these cases, your Web site will end up with an address such as
`www.yourispname.com/~yourname`, or something similar. If that doesn't
work for you and you want to have your own unique Web address (also called
a *domain name*), then you need to purchase one from Network Solutions
(`www.internic.net`), who are currently the owners and maintainers of the
main Web site addresses. (Other companies are expected to compete with
Network Solutions for this service in the near future.)

To purchase a unique address, you visit the `www.internic.net` site, search
through its database of registered domain names to see if what you want is
available, and if so, fill out the online forms. Note that you'll need technical
information about server IP addresses from your ISP or other Web-hosting
company in order to be able to complete the forms, so make sure you talk to
them first.

Posting your pages

Once you have your Web site address and know the location of the Web
server that will actually hold your files and make them available on the
Internet, you can move onto the next step in the Web site creation process,
which is getting the Web site's files from your computer to the Web server.

Transferring files

The process of copying the files from your PC's hard disk, where you first
create your site's files, to the server that will host them is sometimes referred
to as *posting* or *publishing* your files. In essence, however, it's just a matter of
copying them. To copy files from one computer to another over the Internet,
you need to use FTP or File Transfer Protocol. Many Web-authoring programs
include support for FTP so that when you finish creating the files, you simply
hit a Publish or Post button, and the files are transferred. The first time you
do it, you'll need to provide the Web server's IP address so the program
knows where to copy the files. You also have to provide a username and
password that gives you access to the server.

If you aren't using a Web-authoring program that includes this feature, you
can also do it manually via any program that supports FTP. Under Windows,
for example, you can use the popular WS_FTP shareware program, which
makes copying individual files or entire groups of files from your computer to
any other over the Internet very simple. See Figure 13-45.

CD

You'll find a copy of WS_FTP LE on the CD accompanying this book.

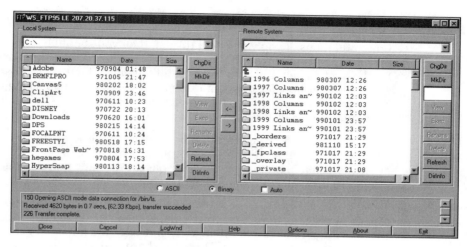

Figure 13-45: Copy via FTP
The shareware program WS_FTP enables you to send, or FTP, files from your computer's
hard disk to the Web server that hosts your Web site.

Web server issues

Depending on the program you use to create your Web site, as well as the
type of content that you include, you may also need to find out what type of
Web server software your ISP or Web-hosting company uses. For example, to
take advantage of certain features in Microsoft's popular FrontPage 98 and
FrontPage 2000 programs, the Web servers have to support specific
FrontPage extensions. If they don't, you may not be able to use certain
features, such as sitewide searches, on your Web site.

In addition, if you want to use streaming media files, you'll need to make sure
that the Web server supports streaming media playback, or adjust your files
accordingly. Also, if you want to upload files or programs that you want other
people to be able to download from your site, make sure the Web server both
supports FTP transfers and has that capability turned on.

One other thing you may want to investigate regarding the Web server
hosting your site is whether or not it offers any site-reporting software you
can get access to. If you want to track how many people visit your site or
certain sections of your site, having access to reports generated by programs
such as WebTrends can be invaluable.

Updating your site

Congratulations. If you've made it this far, then you should have a Web site that's up and running for all the world to see, but don't start thinking you're finished yet. In fact, the hard work is still to come. The truth is, posting a Web site, no matter how big or ambitious, is only the first step in a long process. The most important and most time-consuming task of all is updating and maintaining your Web site.

As I said earlier, the Web is a dynamic medium and if you want to keep people coming back to your site (as well as continue to attract new people), you're going to need to update it on a regular basis. Web sites that don't get updated often turn into the equivalent of online ghost towns with no one but occasional curiosity seekers stopping in to have a look.

The amount of updating that you do depends on the type of site you have, the amount of time you're willing to spend on it, the intended goal of your site, and lots of other factors. There's no hard-and-fast rule about what's "often enough," but I'd suggest you make some updates at least every three months or so to keep things interesting (for you and potential visitors).

If you really want to ensure a high-repeat audience, you should update your site once a week, or even more often, though I warn you that updating this frequently quickly turns into a lot of work.

Publicizing your site

The final step in the Web site creation process is letting the world know that your site exists. Again, depending on the type of Web site you have and the goal of the site, you'll want to spend more or less effort on this task. At the very least, make sure you include your Web address on business cards, stationery, e-mails, letters, and any other type of document you share with others. If you're setting up an electronic commerce site, you'll probably want to consider buying advertisements to promote it, both on other Web sites, as well as in traditional media, such as local newspapers, magazines, and radio and TV shows.

If you're on a limited budget, you can investigate some other options. First of all, you should see if you can get your site listed on some of the more popular search engines, such as AltaVista, Yahoo, Excite, Lycos, HotBot, and so on. To do this, you need to visit the home pages of the search engines and look for a place where you can add a URL or register your site. In most cases you'll be asked to fill out a simple form that asks for information about your site, including its Web address, the type of content, keywords that describe its content, and so on. You should visit each of the search engines individually because each one wants different types of information. After you've filled out these forms, it often takes several weeks (or even months) before your site appears, so get started on this process as soon as you launch your site.

Other alternatives you can consider, particularly if you have a Web site that focuses on a specific subject, is to help create or join a *Web ring*. A Web ring is a group of Web sites, which are usually based on the same subject, that agree to provide links to each other (typically for free) so that people who may be interested in the subject can quickly find other sites like yours (or others in the ring). A related concept is promoted by Link Exchange (`www.linkexchange.com`), which is a free advertising service in which an ad banner that you create for your site appears on other sites in exchange for placing an ad banner on your site.

Finally, if you look around a bit, you'll find other Web sites that are dedicated to or focused on providing links to other sites in a similar category. If you come across a few sites such as this that you think your site fits in with, then send an e-mail to the site's Webmaster or other contact person, and see if they'll add a link to your site.

Summary

In this chapter I've covered how to connect to the Internet, what types of programs you can use with those connections, several different means of communicating over the Internet, and how to build your own Web site.

▶ The Internet is a global network of computers that use a common set of network protocols.

▶ Connecting your PC to the Internet requires that you create either a dial-up or direct connection to your Internet Service Provider (ISP). In order to create this connection, you need a few specific pieces of information from your ISP.

▶ In order to properly view (or hear) certain types of data on Web sites, you may have to download and install plug-in applications that work alongside your Web browser.

▶ In addition to standard Web pages with text and graphics, many sites are now starting to incorporate applications that can be run over the Web. Some of these applications are as simple as animated graphics, and others are equivalent to standalone programs.

▶ E-mail is a great communications tool, but if you want to get the most from your e-mail program, you need to find out how to do such things as leave copies of your messages on the server, look up e-mail addresses with directory services, and format your messages graphically with HTML.

▶ In order to use some e-mail attachments, you may need to decode the files with a separate decoding utility.

▶ You can make your e-mail secure by obtaining a digital ID and taking advantage of the security features built into most e-mail clients.

▶ Other ways you can communicate on the Web include newsgroups, chat, and Internet-based phone calls.

▶ Building your own Web site involves three basic steps: creating the pages, obtaining an address for those pages, and transferring the pages to that address.

▶ Before you start creating a Web site, you need to have a structure in mind.

▶ The graphic design of a Web site is nearly as important as the content it includes.

▶ You can obtain a Web site address or domain name via Networks Solutions at www.internic.net.

▶ The hardest part of building and maintaining a Web site is keeping it up to date.

Part IV

Using Your PC

Chapter 14: Working with Documents and Files

Chapter 15: Working with Pictures and Video

Chapter 16: Working with Audio and Music

Chapter 14

Working with Documents and Files

In This Chapter

▶ You will learn how to create, open, and edit many types of documents.

▶ You will learn how to edit and convert between different file types.

▶ You will learn several different ways to share your documents with others, including printing and electronic document formats.

▶ You will learn a variety of tips on how to better manage and organize your files.

▶ You will learn how to take care of the disks on which your files are stored.

Talking about bits and bytes, hardware and software, big picture issues, and how technology works is all fine and good, but when it really comes down to it, using computers typically means working with individual files, or documents. It's writing a report, creating a spreadsheet, building a Web page, or editing a digital photograph that most people associate with computers. More importantly, it's also what most people spend their time on when using a PC.

So to really get the most out of your computer, you need to know all the ins and outs of creating, opening, editing, converting, managing, organizing, and backing up your files. Now, some of the details on how to do this vary from individual program to individual program, and I can't hope to possibly cover the specifics of how to use individual programs in this chapter. But many general principles apply across the board. In fact, knowing the concepts goes a long way toward solving common problems and making the time you spend on your computer more efficient.

For Windows 95/98/2000 users, one place where it does make sense to provide detail is the Windows Explorer program, where you probably do most of your file management work. From within Windows Explorer, you can create, organize, delete, rename, and do all sorts of operations on your files — many of which you'll need to know about and use on a daily basis.

Before jumping into the specifics about working with your files, though, it helps to understand the relationship between applications and documents.

Applications and Documents

As you undoubtedly know, software is at the very heart of any computer system. It is (to use an already overused analogy) what puts the "ghost" into the machine. And if you think about it, software really comes in only a few specific types:

- The operating system and all its related files
- Application programs and their related files
- Data files created within those applications; in other words, your work

Operating system (OS) files generally work behind the scenes, enabling your computer to start up, perform basic tasks, and most importantly, provide an "environment" in which application programs can run. Ideally, you wouldn't ever have to worry about the OS but the reality, unfortunately, is never that clean (which is why there's a large troubleshooting chapter at the end of this book).

Applications, of course, are programs that enable your computer to do something, such as entertain you (for example, a computer game) or create files (for example, a word processor or other "productivity" application). Most of the unique software characteristics of any computer are determined by the applications that are installed on the system.

But applications, generally speaking, are not an entity unto themselves. Most applications, other than games and reference titles, enable you to create and edit files, which is ultimately what makes your computer a productive tool.

You typically create files, or documents, by using an application and saving a file (a few programs automatically save your files for you, but most do not). In the process, you create an "association" between the file you saved and the application used to produce it. This association links the file to the application so that, for example, if you double-click the file, it automatically launches the appropriate application from the numerous choices available on any computer system.

Note

You can visibly see many file associations on your computer by simply looking at a file's icon on the desktop or in a window, such as the My Computer window or a Windows Explorer window. Documents associated with a particular application generally have an icon that looks similar to the program's icon. If you see an icon that has a generic Windows logo, that means the file is not associated with any program.

You can also see a brief text description of a file association in Windows Explorer by looking under the Type column (see Figure 14-1).

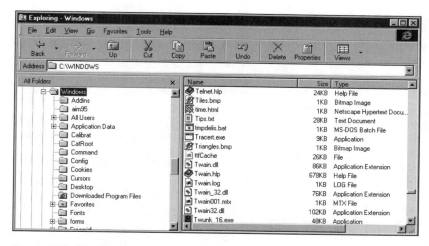

Figure 14-1: File icons and descriptions
You can find out more information about a particular file by looking at its icon and reading the short description of its file type in a Windows Explorer window. The generic Windows icon used on the ttfCache file means that it is not associated with a particular application.

Directly related to a file's association with a particular program is the format in which the file is saved. A file's format refers to both the type of data saved in a file and the manner in which it is saved. So, for example, not only does a word processor save the text you type into a file and any formatting associated with that text, it also stores all that data in a particular manner.

Unfortunately, the manner in which the data is saved usually varies from program to program, which means, for example, not all word processors can read all word processing files created by other applications. Instead, some programs can read only certain types of files and depend on file translators, which are explained in more detail later in this chapter, to read other file types. This scenario is sometimes described as "application-centric computing" because it's the applications you have that determine what type of files you can open and, thus, what type of information you have easy access to.

Thankfully, the rapid growth of the Internet and the standardized file types that it uses (particularly HTML, HyperText Markup Language, and XML, eXtensible Markup Language) are helping make this problem less severe, but it is still an all-too-frequent problem and occurrence.

Cross-Reference

See the section "Building Your Own Web Site" in Chapter 13, "Connecting To and Using the Internet" for more on HTML and XML.

Application-centric versus document-centric computing

In an ideal world, you would never have to worry about whether or not you could open or use a particular file because you would be able to open any document you came across. This would be true regardless of what application was first used to create the file (or even the type of computer and operating system used to create it) or of what applications you have on your computer's hard drive. Instead, in a document-centered computing world, you could focus on a file's content, not its format.

Practically speaking, this would mean that all word processors would store their files in the same standardized format, which would enable anyone with any word processing program to open any file. Similarly, individual graphics files or even complex page layout files could be stored in some type of generic format that would enable any program on any computer to open and even edit them. (The one downside to standardized file formats is that they can impede innovation if a neat new feature is developed but can't be easily incorporated into a standard file type.)

Unfortunately, while the computer industry has taken a few steps in the direction of standardized file formats, we haven't arrived there. This means it's still common to run across files that you simply cannot open without having to go out and buy the program that first created it (that is, if you even know what program that is!). Another common scenario is that you can open a particular file, but it may be in either a more simplistic or an uneditable form.

Interestingly, the Internet is actually helping to solve the file compatibility problem. In fact, you could even argue that the most important development brought on by the Internet is not the variety of information that it has made available, but the move away from proprietary file formats and toward more universal formats. As odd as that may sound, the fact remains that all the information in the world is useless if it's not in a form that people can use and see. The rapid acceptance and development of standardized, Internet-based file types is moving us away from our current application-centric world toward a more logical, more intuitive document-centered environment.

File extensions

Probably the most common way to determine a file's association and its format is by looking at its file extension, which is usually made up of a period and three characters following the file's regular name. By default, Windows 95, 98, and 2000 hide the file extensions of most documents, but you can easily force Windows to show you the file extensions for all files. If you have Windows 98, Windows 2000, or Windows 95 with Internet Explorer 4.0 or later, just go to the Start menu, select Settings ➪ Folder Options, click the View tab, and deselect the Hide file extensions for known file types option under the Files and Folders folder (you may have to double-click the folder to see the options inside it). While you're in there, I also recommend you turn on the Show all files option under the Hidden files folder (again, you may have to open the folder to see the options). See Figure 14-2.

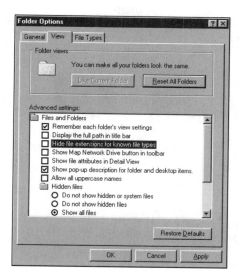

Figure 14-2: Showing file extensions
In order to see all your documents' file extensions, you may have to go into the Folder Options dialog box and tell Windows not to hide them.

If you're running Windows 95 with an earlier version of Internet Explorer or just want an alternative method, you can get to the same dialog box by opening either a My Computer or Windows Explorer window and choosing Folder Options from the View menu.

Note

You get to a My Computer window by double-clicking the My Computer icon on your desktop. You can launch a Windows Explorer window by choosing the program off the Windows Start menu, then Program and then Windows Explorer.

The critical point to remember is that all document files are associated with a particular application and have a particular format and associated file extension, such as .doc, .wp, or what have you. Knowing this can help you work through a variety of different issues. Practically speaking, for example, it means if you have the application associated with a particular document or file, then you can open that document. If you don't, you may not be able to. I hedged from completely saying that you won't be able to because many applications are capable of opening (or "reading") several different file formats. So, for example, Microsoft Word is primarily associated with .doc files, which is referred to as its "native" file type, but it can also open text-only files that end in .txt; HTML files, which end in .htm; and more.

Secret

In fact, in addition to being a good word processor, Microsoft Word is actually a great general-purpose file-opening utility. If you choose the Open command off the File menu in any recent version of Word and then select All Files (*.*) from the drop-down menu at the bottom-left corner of the dialog box, Word enables you to open virtually any file on your computer.

(The asterisk, or star, character functions as a wildcard when performing searches on a PC, so *.* means to look for files with any filename and any file extension.) See Figure 14-3.

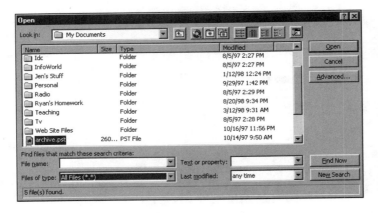

Figure 14-3: Microsoft Word is a file can opener
By selecting All Files (*.*) in the Files of type section of this dialog, you can turn Microsoft Word into a virtual can opener that enables you to open and view almost any file on your computer.

Just because it can open a file doesn't necessarily mean you'll see anything meaningful, however. As with any application, Word can only properly display the contents of files whose format it "understands." Fortunately, Word can work with more file formats, including many graphics file formats, than most applications, which is why it's a good, general-purpose tool.

Tip

If there's a particular bit of data you want to get from within a file, you may be able to open it in Word, scroll through the contents of the file, and then copy and paste whatever you need into a new file in another application, or into another Word file.

If you're primarily interested in converting graphics files, Adobe's Photoshop and JASC's PaintShop Pro have similarly hallowed positions in the graphics world. Both Photoshop and PaintShop Pro can open just about any graphics type available.

CD

A demo copy of PaintShop Pro is on the CD accompanying this book.

Editing file types

To get to the heart of file types and program associations under Windows 95/98/2000, you need to go to the File Types tab of the Folder Options dialog box. To get there, just follow the same procedures mentioned in the previous section, and click the third tab over (see Figure 14-4).

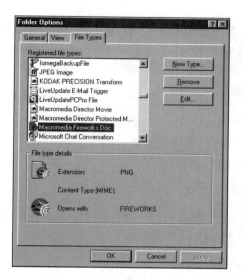

Figure 14-4: Exploring file types and associations
The heart of the relationship between file extensions and applications under Windows can be found here in the File Types tab of the Folder Options dialog.

To find out more information about a particular file type, you click its name in the scrolling list. When you do, its extension (or extensions) and the application it's associated with are listed at the bottom half of the dialog. Windows organizes file types by name, which is fine if you know the name of the application associated with a file, but if you know only the file extension (as is often the case), you have to patiently scroll through the whole list until you find what you need, which is a real pain.

Secret

To see a list of alphabetically organized file extensions and what programs they're associated with, check the following Web site:

http://www2.crosswinds.net/san-marino/~jom/filex/extensio.htm

As the buttons on the right side of the dialog in Figure 14-4 clearly show, you can either create new file types, or remove or edit existing ones. In most situations, the only thing you have to worry about is editing existing file associations (although sometimes removing an old association can be handy for cleaning up your machine or during advanced troubleshooting sessions). If you click the Edit button, you see the dialog box shown in Figure 14-5, where you can make a variety of adjustments to how different file types are handled.

The critical part of this dialog box is the middle Actions section, which is where you set different "actions" that can be performed on these files. These actions, which are nothing more than normal operations that you can do to most files, such as opening, printing, and so on, show up in the context list when you right-click a file in Windows Explorer or simply click the file and go to the File menu in Windows Explorer.

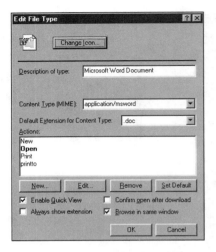

Figure 14-5: Changing how file types work
From this dialog box, you can create, edit, or remove actions that are performed on the files
that have the specified extension, as well as designate what applications are used to perform
those actions.

If you want to change the application that's used to open a file from within this
dialog box (some simpler methods to associate file types with different applications are described later in this chapter), the process takes several steps.

STEPS:

Changing File Associations

Step 1. Select the File Type you want to edit in the File Types tab
of the Folder Options dialog box, and then hit the Edit button.

Step 2. In the Actions area of the subsequent dialog box, select
Open, and then click the Edit button (see Figure 14-6).

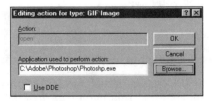

Figure 14-6: Associating programs with files
You select the program you want to use to open a particular file in this dialog
box, which is buried several layers deep inside the Folder Options dialog.

Step 3. Either type in the name of the application you want to use to open the file type (using the exact spelling of the program's main executable file), or simply hit the Browse button and locate the application on your computer's hard drive.

Step 4. Hit OK three times (once each in the three different dialog boxes you run into), and you're done.

If you really want to, you could edit other Actions and have them be performed by different applications or even create new Actions to be performed on the file. In addition, some applications use DDE, or Dynamic Data Exchange, which is a low-level function provided by the Windows operating system to communicate between itself and certain types of applications. I don't recommend messing with anything else, however, because it's generally more trouble than it's worth (and beyond the scope of what I'm trying to do here).

Tip

If you make a mistake while trying to play around with file associations for a particular file type, you can fix the problem by reinstalling the application that is generally associated with that type of file. With certain generic file types, this may entail reinstalling Windows itself. The process of reinstalling generally "recaptures" the extension. In fact, in some situations, installing a new program can cause files that used to be associated with a different application to be opened by the new program. This situation has caused problems for users and fights within the industry for several years now.

Capturing extensions

Over the years numerous problems have been caused by applications essentially taking over certain file types when they are installed — sometimes without even telling the user! This is particularly true with popular Web formats, such as different plug-in types and even HTML files, themselves. The battle for control of your Web-browsing experience between Netscape's Communicator/Navigator browser and Microsoft's Internet Explorer, for example, is essentially a battle over who "owns" the .htm file extension. Generally speaking, whichever application is associated with HTML files (which use the .htm extension) is the default application used to open Web-based HTML documents.

Of course, you can always get around this issue by opening an application (such as your Web browser) first, and then choosing to open the file (or visit a Web site, in this example, and retrieve its files). File associations make no difference in those instances because you're specifically telling your computer to open a file from within a particular program. However, if the file exists in one of your hard drive's folders and you double-click it, then the "associated" application launches and opens that file.

Continued

(continued)

The easy way to switch this association between Communicator and Internet Explorer, if you have them both installed, is usually just to directly open either application. In many cases, doing so gives you the option of setting whichever program you launched to be the default. If it doesn't, you can force this question to be asked in Internet Explorer by going to the Internet control panel, selecting the Programs tab, and making sure the "Internet Explorer should check to see whether it is the default browser" button is checked. If it's not, turn it on.

For Netscape Communicator, the process is a bit more complicated. First, you need to make sure that the Internet control panel button for Internet Explorer is on and that it is currently the default browser. Then you need to find the Prefs.js file inside your specific username folder. Typically, that directory is inside the Program Files\Netscape\Users folder. Open that file (make sure Communicator is not open), and find the following line:

```
user_pref("browser.wfe.ignore
_def_check", false)
```

(Note that yours probably says "true" at the end.) Change "true" to "false", save the file, reboot Communicator, and you should be in business.

I have no doubt that these types of "battles" for file extensions will continue for years to come. At least by understanding the issues, you can figure what actions you need to take to get the kind of computing experience that you want.

Note

As with lots of other procedures for making or adjusting low-level system parameters, all the information about file types and associations is stored in the Windows Registry and can be edited directly there as well. It's easier (and safer), however, to make changes via the File Types dialog box.

Creating new files

The way most people work on computers is to decide what type of document they want to create, open the application program that enables them to create those types of documents, and (if necessary) select New from the File menu. That's not the only way to do it, however.

For example, if you have an idea for a document you want to work on, you can create the document "container" first by right-clicking your Windows desktop or any open area in the right side of a Windows Explorer window.

Secret

By the way, if you're using Windows 98, Windows 2000, or Windows 95 with Internet Explorer 4.0 or later and have a keyboard with a Windows logo key on it, you can quickly get to the desktop by holding down that key and pressing the "D" key at the same time. Using the "E" key instead launches Windows Explorer.

When you select New from the context menu that appears, you see a list of some of the applications on your PC (see Figure 14-7).

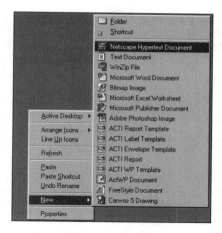

Figure 14-7: Creating new files
A quick way to create certain types of files is to right-click your Windows desktop, select New from the menu that appears, choose an application file type, and then key in the name of the file you want to create.

Choose the file type you want and type in the name, but be sure you maintain the appropriate file extension when you do; otherwise, you lose the file's association. Windows should warn you about renaming files and problems with file extensions before this happens.

If you want to see file extensions at work, you can intentionally either leave out the file extension or type in a different one than the kind you originally chose. In the first instance, you end up with a generic Windows icon on the file, and if you double-click it, the application whose file type you originally opened won't launch. Instead, because you "broke" the file association, you should get a dialog box asking what type of application you want to open this file with. (I go into more detail about this dialog box in the next section.)

In the second instance, if you change the file extension to, say, .wav (which is used for sound files), you see the icon change to a Windows sound icon. And, as you might suspect, if you double-click the file, you launch whatever application is associated with sound files (typically Windows Media Player, although it could be something else).

In many cases this trick does not work because there's more to a particular file's format than just the file extension. So, in this example, even if you change the file to a .wav extension, the audio application associated with .wav files won't be able to open it because the file's internal structure, or format, is not correct.

Secret

The list of file types shown on the New menu is determined by settings in the Windows Registry and the location of files in the ShellNew folder inside the Windows folder. If one of your favorite applications isn't listed there, you can use the following procedure to add one to it. I warn you in advance that this procedure involves editing the Registry, which, if done improperly, can really mess up your system. So before you proceed, make a backup of your Registry (the System.dat and User.dat hidden files inside your Windows folder), and follow along closely.

STEPS:

Creating Your Own New File Templates

Step 1. Open the application for which you want to make a template, and save a blank file inside the ShellNew folder (which is inside the Windows folder — you have to turn on hidden files as described earlier in this chapter in order to even see it). Name the file either with a simplified version of the application name or something such as New. The actual name isn't that important, but make sure the filename has the program's default file extension.

Step 2. Open the Registry Editor by going to the Run command off the Start menu and typing in **regedit**.

Step 3. Open the first key listed there by clicking the + sign next to HKEY_CLASSES_ROOT, and then scroll down until you see a folder with the three-character file extension of the application for which you want to create the new template. The folder name should be the same as the extension of the file you saved in Step 1.

Step 4. Open that folder by clicking it, then right-click the right side of the Registry Editor window, and select New and then Key from the submenu that appears. Type in the name **ShellNew** (with the exact spelling and capitalization), and hit Return (see Figure 14-8).

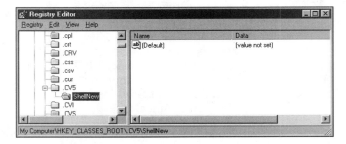

Figure 14-8: Creating a new key
To create a new file template, you need to create a new key called ShellNew in the Windows Registry under the folder of the file extension you plan to use.

Step 5. Make sure that the ShellNew folder is selected on the left side, then right-click the right side of the Registry Editor window again, and select New and then String Value. Type in the name **FileName** (again, with the exact spelling and capitalization), and hit Return.

Step 6. Right-click the FileName string, and select Modify. In the Value data line of the dialog box that appears, type in the filename that you created in Step 1 of this procedure. Make sure you use the exact name and punctuation (see Figure 14-9).

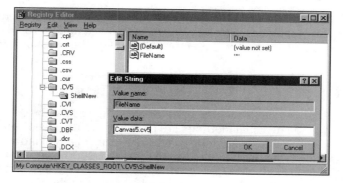

Figure 14-9: Setting the file name
To complete the process, you need to create a String Value and define its value to be the name of the template file you created in Step 1.

Step 7. Close the Registry Editor by selecting Exit from the Registry menu, and then try your new template out by right-clicking the Windows desktop, selecting New, and choosing the template you created. You should see a file appear called something like "New *Application Name* File." At that point you can rename the newly created file (again, remember to maintain the file extension), and then double-click it to open it.

If for some reason the process doesn't work, delete the key you created earlier by reopening the Registry Editor, scrolling down to the folder you were working in, highlighting the key, right-clicking it, and choosing Delete from the menu that appears. (You don't want to leave nonfunctional keys inside the Registry because they might cause problems down the road.) Once you've done that, follow the procedure again, being careful to take your time and to double-check each step.

Tip

Instead of saving a blank file in Step 1 of this procedure, you could create a template file that includes such things as your company logo or anything else you want to have in all files of this type. Similarly, if you want to change some of the existing templates, simply open the files stored in the ShellNew folder inside your Windows folder, make any changes you want, and then save those changes (just be sure not to rename the file or save them with a different file extension).

If you have the TweakUI control panel for Windows 95 or 98, there's a much easier way to do this entire procedure. Just select the New tab in TweakUI, drag a template file into its window of available templates at the bottom of the dialog box, and you're done. TweakUI takes care of creating all the Registry values for you. (Of course, you won't *learn* as much as you can by doing it the hard way.) You can also use TweakUI to remove any templates you no longer need.

Secret

The Windows 98 CD, both the Standard and Upgrade versions, includes a copy of TweakUI along with an extensive help file. You can find it in the Tools \Reskit\PowerToys directory. Right-click the tweakui.inf file to install it.

Opening existing documents

Like creating new files, opening existing files can be done in one of several ways. The usual methods are to either use the Open command off an application's File menu or double-click the file in any Windows Explorer or other folder window. If you use the latter method, the application associated with that file launches first and then opens the file you selected. And, as with creating new files, there are several other methods.

First, by right-clicking a file inside a Windows Explorer or My Computer window, you can usually choose Open from the menu that appears. If you ever want to simply preview the contents of a file without necessarily opening it, you may be able to choose the Quick View option that appears on that menu (see Figure 14-10).

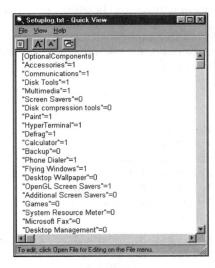

Figure 14-10: A quick preview
By using the Quick View option off the menu that appears when you right-click a file in Windows Explorer, you can preview the file's contents.

Note

The Quick View utilities bundled with Windows 95/98/2000 are not necessarily installed by default, so you have to check your Windows Setup to see if you need to install them. To do this under Windows 95 or 98, open the Add/Remove Programs control panel, click the Windows Setup tab, highlight Accessories, click Details, and then search for Quick View. If you don't see a check mark selected there, it's not installed. To install it, check the box, then hit OK twice, and Windows starts the installation process. You may need to put your Windows 95/98 CD into your computer's CD or DVD-ROM drive, so be prepared. Under Windows 2000, you first need to select the Configure Windows button inside the Add/Remove Programs control panel.

CD

Note also that the simplified version of Quick View bundled with Windows 95/98/2000 supports viewing only certain file types. A demo copy of a more complete collection of file previewers, called Quick View Plus from JASC Software, is on the CD accompanying this book.

Tip

Another way to get a small preview of image- and Web-related files, such as HTML pages or GIF or JPEG images, is to view the folder they reside in as a Web page and simply click the files. To do this, you need to be running either Windows 98, Windows 2000, or Windows 95 with Internet Explorer 4.0 or later. If you meet those simple requirements, just open a Windows Explorer window, and select view as Web Page from the View menu (see Figure 14-11).

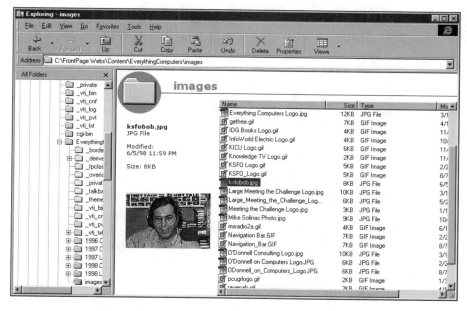

Figure 14-11: Image thumbnails
By viewing folders that include GIF, JPEG, BMP, PCX, WMF, CMG, or TIF images as a Web page in Windows Explorer, you can get a simple thumbnail preview of the image by simply clicking the filename. This trick also works with HTML pages.

Opening with other applications

Most of the time you go to open a file, you want to use the primary application with which the file type has been associated. As I said earlier, that's easy,
just double-click it. Occasionally, however, you may want to open a file with a
different application.

Secret

For example, instead of having your Web browser open a GIF image, you may
want to edit it in a graphics program. To solve this and other types of similar
issues, Windows provides the Open with command. To get Open with to work
on any type of file, simply hold down the Shift key while you're right-clicking
the file inside of a Windows Explorer window, and you get a different drop-
down menu — one that should include Open with.

When you select Open with, you get a dialog box that enables you to choose
from the available applications that have been "registered" with Windows. If
you don't see the application you want there, you can also choose the Other
button to look for it elsewhere on your hard disk or any other connected
disks (see Figure 14-12).

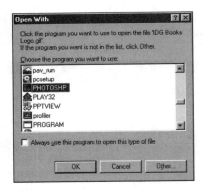

Figure 14-12: Opening with a different application
If you need to open a file in something other than the normal application used to work with a
particular file type, you can use the Open with command by holding down the Shift key while
right-clicking a file. Inside this dialog box, you can choose any program on your hard drive to
open the file.

Remember that each application can work with only certain kinds of files, so
if you try to open, say, a word processing document with an image editor, it
won't work.

If you want to make the association between the type of file you're opening
and the application you choose more permanent, you can choose the Always
use this program to open this type of file check box. Doing so changes the file
association of the file type you're opening so that any time you double-click a
file with the same extension as the type you're opening here, the application
you select here launches and opens that kind of file.

So, for example, if you purchase a new image editing program, you may want all your existing scanned .tif files to be opened with the new program instead of the one you had previously used. By selecting one of them, choosing the Open with command, and then making this selection, you can convert them all to automatically open with the new program.

Note

If you try to open a file type that doesn't have an application associated with it (signified visually by the generic Windows logo icon), the only option you have is the Open with command. In fact, you won't even have to use the Shift key to see it — just double-clicking it brings up the Open with dialog box.

Secret

When you select an application to open the file, the Always use this program to open this type of file check box is checked by default in these situations, so if you don't want to make a permanent association, be sure to uncheck it.

Using Send To

Another powerful, but little-known feature that Windows provides for opening different types of files (as well as performing a variety of different functions) is the Send To command, which you can also find if you right-click a file. Out of the box, Send To provides a convenient way to copy files onto a floppy disk (using the Send To ⇨ 3½ Floppy (A) option), create a shortcut to a file on the desktop, e-mail a file to someone, and more.

Tip

You can also easily customize Send To to enable you to copy files onto a removable drive, send a file to one of several printers, or even have a file be "sent to" and opened by one of several applications. In each case, all you have to do is create a shortcut to the drive, printer, or application you want to add to the menu, and then copy that shortcut into the SendTo folder inside the Windows folder. (Note that you might want to rename the shortcut after you first copy it into the SendTo folder.) See Figure 14-13 for an example.

Using this technique with applications is a nice alternative to the Open With command, particularly if you have only a few applications you regularly use to open different types of files. It's also a convenient way to use multiple printers, although you can print only to the default printer, which may require you to temporarily reassign another printer to be your default. Happily, this process is very simple because a dialog box appears when you try to print to a printer that isn't currently your default, and all you have to do is hit Yes. You can switch back to your normal default printer by just sending it a file to print in this same manner.

Secret

Finally, here's a great tip for getting quick access to either commonly used documents or applications under Windows 95 with Explorer 4.0 or later, Windows 98, or Windows 2000. Just drag a document or application to your Windows Taskbar (typically found along the bottom of your screen), in an area just right of the Start button. A shortcut is automatically created, and you see an icon you can click to launch the application or open the file. If you want to remove it (or any of the default icons you see there), just right-click on one of them, and select Delete from the context menu that appears. (Doing so deletes only the shortcut, not the application or file.) If you run out of room in that area, just move your mouse over the horizontal divider to the right of the icons (until you see arrows pointing in each direction), and then just slide it to the left or right.

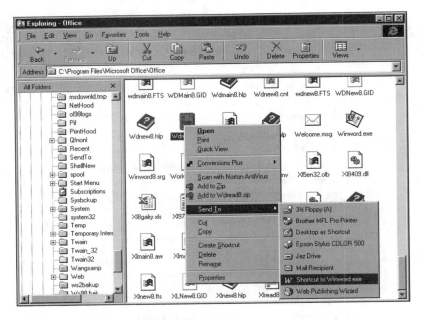

Figure 14-13: Take advantage of Send To
The Send To command built into Windows 95/98/2000 offers many powerful options for manipulating files, including copying them to a floppy, e-mailing them to someone, directly printing them, and even opening them with one of several applications.

Converting Documents

Even though, as I said earlier in the chapter, the popularization of the Internet and common Web-based file formats are making it easier to share files between different computer users, you're still going to run across files that you simply cannot open (at least with the software you have immediately available to you). The unfortunate reality is, until we reach the day when any computer file can be opened by any computer user, regardless of what applications they have available, we're stuck with having to convert between one file format and another.

Thankfully, this situation has improved tremendously over the last few years because many applications are capable of reading and automatically converting a wide variety of different file formats. In many instances, just by launching an application, using a program's Open command, and then choosing from the list of available file formats in a section of the dialog box that usually says something like "Files of type," you can open most of the files you come across.

Cross-Reference

If you want information about converting between Mac and PC formats, see the section "Adding a Macintosh to Your Network" in Chapter 12, "Setting Up a Small Business or Home Network"

If you know who sent you a particular file that you can't open, you might contact them and have them resave the file in a different format. In addition to opening different file formats, most programs can also save files in formats other than their primary one. (Don't presume that just because a program can open a file in a particular format that it can also save it in that same format, however. Opening and saving files in different formats are very different tasks, and most programs offer more flexibility in file formats they can open than in ones they can save.) Most text-related programs, for example, can generate a lowest common–denominator ASCII text file (sometimes referred to as text-only).

In many situations you can find a file format in common between two programs that enables you to transport files back and forth if necessary. Be aware, however, that most conversion processes are imperfect. In many situations you may lose certain types of formatting or even certain advanced elements of a particular file when you use any type of conversion. So, for example, if you settle on a simpler, more generic file format, you may not get the results you expect.

Tip

Another trick you can use is to simply add or change the three-letter file extension at the end of a filename. So, for example, if you download or receive a file that you're fairly sure is primarily made of text, but it either doesn't have a file extension or has one that doesn't match any of the programs available on your computer, you can change the extension to .doc or whatever the file extension of your primary word processing program happens to be. Then when you simply double-click the file, your word processor will attempt to open it.

CD

If the file happens to be a compressed file (such as .zip, .sit, .uue, .arc, .hqx, .bin, .arj, .lzh, .gz, .z, or .tar), this trick does more harm than good. In those cases, you need to use a decompression utility first to convert the file (or files) into their regular formats, and then try to read or convert them. A shareware version of WinZip is provided on the CD accompanying this book to help you in this regard.

Note

In many cases, the standard installation of word processing and/or graphics programs copies only some of the program's available file translation or conversion filters. These filters are small pieces of software that enable a program to read a different file format and then convert it into the program's native file format. If you know that you're going to have to translate a variety of different files or you just want to be prepared in the event you come across some unusual files, you may have to go through some of your applications' Setup programs again. Select the Custom installation option, and then choose whatever other file translators/converters are available.

Finally, if none of these previous options work or give you the results you're looking for, you may want to invest in a dedicated conversion program, such as DataViz' Conversions Plus. Most conversion programs can either work in a standalone mode or can "plug-in" to your existing applications, giving you more robust options in the types of file formats you can open or save from within an application (see Figure 14-14).

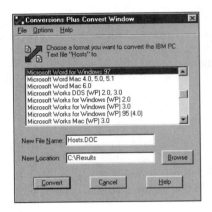

Figure 14-14: Converting files
File conversion utilities such as DataViz' Conversions Plus enable you to translate files in unknown or unregistered formats into a form that you can use.

A demo copy of JASC's QuickView Plus conversion program is available on the CD accompanying this book.

CD

Sharing Your Documents

Sometimes working with a computer is a solitary activity and the documents you create are solely for your own enjoyment or edification. Usually, however, once you've created some files, you'll want or need to share them with others. Several obvious ways to do that including printing the file and handing out the hard copy, copying the file onto a floppy disk or other removable storage device, directly giving or mailing it to someone, or sending the document as a file attachment in an e-mail message.

Tip

As described previously, many of these tasks can be accomplished with the Send To command. In addition, most file extensions/program associations include a predefined Print action, which enables you to right-click a file, either in a Windows Explorer folder or on the desktop, and choose Print from the drop-down menu that appears. This is a handy way to print a quick copy, even if the application that you created the file in isn't open. Using either technique opens the application associated with the file (based on its file extension), opens the file, prints the file from within the application, and then quits the application.

Specialty printing

If you're creating an unusually sized document, such as a banner, poster, envelope, business card, or other nonstandard type, printing may be the only way to share a document with others, but you need to make sure that you have the right-sized paper and/or correct type of media on which to print.

Specialty paper manufacturers now offer glossy format for photographs, long rolls of continuous paper for banners and posters, precut card and label stock for business cards and many types of labels, iron-on transfers for creating your own T-shirts, and even special fabric for creating custom clothes for children's dolls!

In most cases, these specialty paper types work with any inkjet printer (even if the paper you want is made by a different printer manufacturer), but there are a few exceptions, particularly with very thick or unusual (for example, cloth) "paper" types. A more critical issue is determining whether or not your printer's driver software can support a particular type of printing. For example, not all printers can print banners, even if you have both an application that enables you to create them and the right kind of paper. If you run into this problem, you might want to check and see if a more recent version of your printer driver, which is the software that "controls" how your printer works, is available from the printer manufacturer's Web site.

Cross-Reference

See the "Downloading programs off the Internet" section of Chapter 9, "Adding, Upgrading, and Removing Software" for more on upgrading drivers via the Internet.

One other issue is that not all applications can take advantage of specialty inks you may add to your printer, such as photo or metallic inks. Again, the printer driver is usually in charge of converting an application's print commands into a format the printer can use, but if you pop in a metallic ink cartridge and print out an image, you may not get what you expect.

Electronic documents

Another option to consider if you want to send your files electronically is to save them in a popular electronic document format, such as HTML or Adobe's Portable Document Format (PDF). Virtually all computer users now have access to a Web browser or another application that can open HTML files, so it's a relatively good generic format for exchanging files with other people — even if they use different applications or different operating systems (or even different computers, such as the Macintosh).

As useful as HTML can be, however, it doesn't provide a very comprehensive set of layout capabilities, which makes it difficult to maintain the look-and-feel of a particular document. If you want to maintain the exact layout and look of a document, including the size of the page, the particular typeface you use, and lots more, you should investigate Adobe's PDF format. PDF is specifically designed to maintain the graphic look of a document, enabling you to have an exact on-screen representation of what you see in a book or the printed material. (In fact, you'll find a PDF version of this book included on the CD that accompanies it.)

CD

In order to view PDF documents, you need Adobe's Acrobat viewer application, which you can download for free via the Web or simply install from the CD accompanying this book.

To create PDF documents, you need a PDF printer driver, which "prints" a PDF file of any of your documents to disk, or you need to use a more sophisticated product, such as Adobe Acrobat, which does a more thorough job of the same task. In addition, some page layout programs enable you to save files directly in PDF format.

One of the great things about PDF files is that with a PDF printer driver, you can create them from within any application and then "print" them to disk, which essentially means saving a file in PDF format. You don't have to worry about learning a new PDF-specific program. The downside, however, is that the PDF file–creating programs all cost money, and anyone who you want to view the file has to have the Adobe Acrobat viewer. While the viewer doesn't cost any money, it can be a hassle if the person who you want to share the file with has to go through the process of downloading and installing Adobe Acrobat.

Still, if you want an electronic version of a printed document, PDF files are a good way to go. Depending on the manner in which the PDF file is generated, however, and the type of image compression that's used on graphics, it's possible to have problems viewing things, such as screen shots, in certain files. On the other hand, using PDF documents is also a good way to ensure that your document preserves the typeface, or font, you want it to have.

Say, for example, you e-mail a document, such as a newsletter, to someone. When they open it, if they don't have all the fonts that you used in the document, they may not see what you intended. Instead the application substitutes a font that it believes is similar in dimensions to the original font you used. (The font's dimensions are different than its point size. Two fonts with the same point size can take up different amounts of space because of the dimensions of the individual letters.)

If the substituted font is slightly different in size, the text in the document won't fit in the same space, which could lead to such things as text that extends beyond a column or other layout problems. PDF takes care of this issue by incorporating either the actual font or the specific characteristics of the font into the document itself. One downside of PDF, however, is that unless you have a high-end desktop publishing program, such as Adobe PageMaker or InDesign, you can't easily edit PDF files.

Tip

Speaking of fonts, Windows 95/98/2000 offers an easy way to get a visual display of the different fonts on your system. Just open the Fonts folder, which you should find inside your Windows folder, and then double-click an individual font file. You get a visual display of the font in different sizes along with the capability to print a sample of the font for later reference (see Figure 14-15).

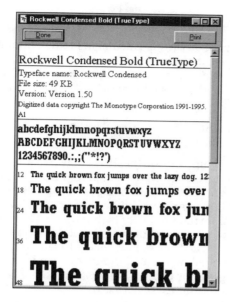

Figure 14-15: Finding fonts
You can get a visual display or printout of the fonts on your system by opening the Fonts folder inside your Windows folder and double-clicking individual font files.

Also, to add or remove fonts under Windows 95/98/2000, just copy font files into or out of the Fonts folder. Be careful of going overboard, however. Too many fonts can slow your system down.

Managing Your Files

As you create all your files, you also need to concern yourself with organizing them. In some cases that may be as simple as creating a hierarchy of folders inside your My Documents folder — or anywhere else on your hard drive. For example, you could create separate top-level folders inside the My Documents folder for letters, photos, graphics, spreadsheets, and other types of files and then create separate subfolders inside those folders for various projects or time periods.

You certainly don't have to do it within the My Documents folder, however. Some people prefer to save their files on a separate hard drive, partition, or removable storage drive. In addition, many programs default to saving their files within the same folder as the program. While that's also a viable way of organizing, it can get very confusing trying to remember where all your own files are. That's why I recommend you pick one central spot for saving files from all your applications. (Although, I recommend you don't just save them in a single folder or you'll create an unwieldy mess. Use subfolders to keep them organized.)

Backing up

Having a central repository, such as the My Documents folder, not only helps you easily track down your files, it also makes it much easier to back up your files, which is an absolutely critical part of using a computer. Backing up simply means to make a copy of the files onto another storage device, such as a removable storage drive.

Cross-Reference

See Chapter 3, "Hard Disks and Removable Drives" for more on removable storage drives.

Many people don't take backing up very seriously (I know because I used to be one of them), but I can't reiterate strongly enough that if you want (or need) some information that's stored on your computer, you have to back it up. Although computers and the components that go into them have gotten more reliable over time, the unfortunate reality is that they will eventually fail. It's not a question of if, but when. And because hard drives are one of the few components with moving parts, they're most likely to fail first, taking with them all the data that's stored on them. If that data hasn't been backed up anywhere, it's most likely gone for good. (One possible savior is a disk recovery utility, such as Norton Utilities' Disk Doctor.)

Disk doctors to the rescue

If you run into a situation where your hard drive suddenly stops working and you don't have a recent backup, all is not necessarily lost. Several companies make disk recovery programs that are specifically designed to resurrect dead drives. In some cases these programs, such as Norton Utilities and Nuts & Bolts, can completely fix the problem and bring your hard drive back to normal operation, and in others, they can provide only a temporary fix. Usually it's long enough that you can make a recent backup and then either try reformatting the drive and starting over, or simply chucking it and installing a new drive. (See Chapter 11, "Upgrading Your PC" for more on installing a new hard drive.)

The way these programs typically work is that they come with a rescue floppy disk that you use to boot your computer and then run the disk recovery utility. You don't want to try to boot your computer from the hard drive or do any additional

work on a drive that seems to be failing because anything you do could cause additional problems. Also, if you're using one of these utilities to try and recover files that you accidentally deleted, which these programs are also capable of doing, then any additional software you run could overwrite the files you're trying to save.

If your efforts at saving your files with these utilities are unsuccessful, you have one last alternative, but it's going to cost you. Specialized companies called "data recovery services" have been known to perform near miracles, retrieving data from hard drives that have simply died and even some that have been utterly destroyed, such as through fire or water damage. Their services typically don't come cheap, but if you absolutely have to have the data stored on a dead drive, they can be life savers. You should be able to find them in your local yellow pages or through a reference from a local computer store.

Also, in addition to your data files, don't forget to backup any program updates or other critical application-related files that you've downloaded from the Internet. While in most cases you could download them again if you had to, you can save yourself a lot of time and hassles by keeping copies of them as part of your backup.

For your really critical files, you should probably make two or even more copies. I realize that this adds yet more time to an already tedious process, but when one of your backup drives or disks goes bad (and they will, too), you'll be glad you did. Many people alternate between various sets of backup disks to protect themselves from this type of problem.

Finally, to maintain the most security for your files, store one of those backups away from your computer. If you ever run into a situation such as a fire or other disaster, all the backups in the world won't do you any good if they're destroyed along with your computer. (I know firsthand about this because I have a friend who religiously backed up his data but stored those backups next to his computer. When his office building burnt to the ground, he lost everything, and his backups did him no good. Needless to say, he now keeps one set of backups off site.)

There are several different ways to back up your files. The easiest is to just copy the files (or folders) you want backed up onto a device such as a Zip, tape drive, recordable CD, or other type of mechanism. Ideally, you should do this on a daily, or at worst, weekly basis. To make sure you have the most recent versions, you can just recopy that same group of files or folders every time you back up, writing over the older versions from the previous backup.

The problem with this system is that, as you create more and more files to back up, it takes a long time to copy things over. Plus, it puts unnecessary wear and tear on your components because you're copying more files than you need to, including those that haven't changed since the last backup.

The most efficient method is to use a dedicated backup program on a regular basis. Most backup programs enable you to perform incremental backups, which copy only the files that changed since the previous backup. Both Windows 95 and Windows 98 come with backup programs, although the one in Windows 95 supports copying only to floppies (which is worthless) and to a limited number of tape drives. The Windows 98 version is a much more robust version and adds support for more types of backup media, including parallel, ATAPI, and SCSI drives, as well as removable drives (see Figure 14-16).

To get to the built-in backup programs in either OS, you can right-click a hard drive icon in Windows Explorer, select Properties, and then choose the Tools tab. From there you can launch the backup utility with a single click. If you don't have the backup utility installed, you are prompted to install it via the Windows Setup tab of the Add/Remove Programs control panel (see Chapter 9, "Adding, Upgrading, and Removing Software" for more).

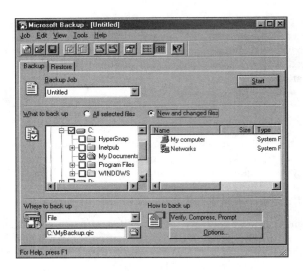

Figure 14-16: Windows 98 Backup
The Backup utility bundled with Windows 98 is based on Seagate's highly regarded BackUp Exec program. It's a huge improvement over the basic tool in Windows 95 and includes support for many different types of backup devices, as well as other sophisticated features.

One other handy feature of the Windows 98 (and Windows 2000) Backup is that it can be automated via the Add Scheduled Tasks Wizard (although not the more widely touted Maintenance Wizard for some reason). Here's how.

STEPS:

Automated Windows 98 Backup

Step 1. Launch the Add Scheduled Tasks Wizard by either selecting it off the Start menu by going to Programs ⇨ Accessories ⇨ System Tools and finding it on the menu there or by opening the Scheduled Tasks folder under My Computer. To do the latter, just double-click the My Computer icon on your desktop, open the Scheduled Tasks folder, and then double-click the Add Scheduled Tasks Wizard (see Figure 14-17).

Step 2. Follow the steps in the Wizard to choose Microsoft Backup as the application you want to automatically launch and set a time and date when you want it to occur. I recommend backing up at least once a week, or even more frequently if you use your computer a lot.

Step 3. In the final step of the Wizard, click the Show Advanced Properties checkbox before you hit Finish. That way you can confirm all your settings (see Figure 14-18).

Figure 14-17: Scheduling tasks under Windows 98
Windows 98's Scheduled Tasks Wizard is an easy, but powerful way to automate a number of tasks on your computer, including backup.

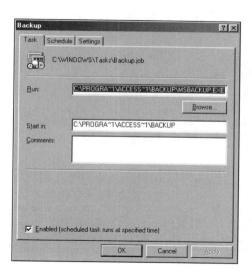

Figure 14-18: Automated backup job
You can confirm and/or adjust the time and settings of your automated backup job in this dialog box.

Freeing up disk space

No matter how big the hard drive on your computer, you will eventually fill it. That's one of the immutable laws of computing — sort of a Murphy's Law for computers, if you will. The only question is how quickly it will occur. When you do reach that inevitable point, you need to start clearing some space on your hard drive. As a general rule, you want to maintain at least 5 percent of your disk's total space free, so when you pass the 95 percent full marker, it's time to start the cleanup.

To find out how much disk space you have used, just open Windows Explorer, right-click your hard drive icon(s), and select Properties. (If you have View As Web Page turned on in Windows Explorer or a My Computer window, you can just click a drive to get similar information.) The dialog box that appears gives you both a graphical and numerical display of how much room is still available on your hard drive (see Figure 14-19).

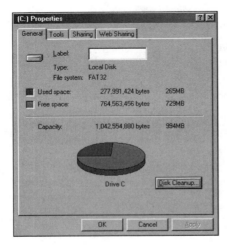

Figure 14-19: Taking stock
You can get a visual display of how much space is left on any of your computer's drives by right-clicking it in Windows Explorer and choosing Properties. Note that this dialog also tells you whether or not your drive is formatted with the more efficient FAT32 file system, as shown here, or the older FAT16 (displayed simply as FAT). The Tools tab gives you quick access to disk maintenance tools included with Windows 95/98/2000, and the Disk Cleanup button, which is only available under Windows 98 and Windows 2000, offers quick access to Windows' Disk Cleanup feature.

Once you know what you're working with, you can make informed decisions on how much stuff you need to get rid of. If you're like most people, finding a few hundred megabytes of stuff you can delete won't really be that hard. Applications or games you tried once and never used again, big files you downloaded off the Internet, and numerous example or tutorial files are all good candidates for deletion. Just remember that if you're going to remove a program, use either the program's own uninstaller, the Windows Add/Remove Programs control panel, or a standalone uninstaller program. Don't just delete the application's directories, or you could cause big problems.

Cross-Reference

See Chapter 9, "Adding, Upgrading, and Removing Software" for more on removing applications.

If you're using Windows 98 or 2000, the Disk Cleanup button shown in Figure 14-19 gives you quick access to a utility that can automatically look for junk that you can easily throw away, such as temporary files (that is, any file that ends with the file extension .tmp), Internet cache files, extra setup files, and more. You can also throw away most of these types of files under Windows 95, but you have to use the Find command off the Start menu to search for them (use *.tmp to find all temporary or "temp" files) and then delete them in groups, which is a rather tedious process.

The Windows 98 and 2000 Disk Cleanup feature also gives you quick access to the Add/Remove Programs control panel for uninstalling applications, as well as the Windows Setup tab (called "Windows Configuration" under Windows 2000) of that control panel for removing Windows components you may not be using.

Moving files

In addition to simply deleting files, you may consider moving certain files that you don't use very often from your hard drive onto another storage device. While a lot of people like to keep everything on their hard drive, it makes sense to copy some types of files onto a removable storage drive or tape backup and then remove them from the main hard drive. Program updates that you downloaded off the Internet and already installed are examples of these types of files.

Tip

Don't try to move installed applications, however, or they may stop working properly (or generate obscure error messages when you try to start them). The problem with trying to move them is that their location is stored in the Windows Registry and if Windows can't find the files where it thinks those files should be, it causes problems. The only way to move applications is with a dedicated application mover utility, such as AppMover, which is bundled with PowerQuest's PartitionMagic.

CD

You'll find a demo copy of PartitionMagic on the CD-ROM accompanying this book.

Compression utilities

One oft-recommended bit of advice to save space that I suggest you *don't* take is to use software compression, such as DriveSpace 3. Although it's available through the Plus pack add-on for Windows 95 or Windows 98 itself, which suggests that it's a safe option, my experience has been that it's more hassle than it's worth.

What DriveSpace 3 or other software compression technologies do is use some special mathematical formulas to squeeze all the files on your hard drive into a smaller amount of space than they normally take, thereby giving you additional room on the drive. Any files that are compressed need to be decompressed before they can be used, however, so software compression programs constantly work in the background decompressing files on the fly whenever you need them. Similarly, whenever you close a program or save a file to disk, the software compression programs then recompress all the files that had been in use.

Tip

In the days when disk storage space was expensive, I think software compression was a reasonable alternative to buying a new hard drive, but now that storage space is so cheap, I don't recommend it. Because of the background work these programs must perform, they slow down your system a bit, and they can cause compatibility problems with other software. Plus, if your hard drive ever crashes, software compression introduces a lot of potential complications that can make it harder to retrieve your data.

Taking care of your disks

Your files are the lifeblood of your computer system so it makes sense to take good care of them. But it's equally important to take good care of the container that holds them: your hard disks. Generally speaking, hard disks in newer computer systems are much more reliable than those found in systems from even just a few years back. Hard drive companies have worked hard to increase the robustness of their products. Technologies such as S.M.A.R.T. (Self-Monitoring, Analysis, and Reporting Technology), included in a recent version of the ATA spec, that are built into some of today's drives do make a big difference.

ScanDisk

Still, you should follow some procedures to keep your drives in top shape. If you decide not to opt for a disk utility, be sure to run the ScanDisk utility bundled with Windows 95/98/2000 on a semi-regular basis to make sure that your drive is in good working shape. ScanDisk does a variety of things, including checking the surface of your hard disk for errors.

Tip

If ScanDisk (or any other disk utility) finds parts of the hard drive that are potentially problematic, it labels those sections as bad blocks and makes them unusable. What this means is it prevents any applications from using them because they could lead to corrupted files or other problems down the road. While it sounds somewhat foreboding, finding a couple of bad blocks on your hard drive isn't necessarily a big problem. In fact, it's a relatively common occurrence. However, if you start to get messages about finding bad blocks on a regular basis, then that's a sure sign that your hard drive is slowly dying. If that's the case, back up your files, and buy a new drive as soon as you can. Otherwise, you risk losing all your data.

Under Windows 95 you have to start and use ScanDisk manually, although Windows 95B, or OSR2, and later versions automatically run ScanDisk on bootup after your system crashes (and given how often that probably occurs, you'll be seeing it on a regular basis!). If the process doesn't occur automatically, it's a good idea to a manually scan a disk after a crash.

Windows 98 and 2000 make this process much easier by automatically running ScanDisk on a regular basis as part of the Maintenance Wizard (Windows 98 only) and Scheduled Tasks features (in addition to running it automatically after a crash). You can either stick with the default settings or increase or decrease the frequency by double-clicking the predefined tasks in the Scheduled Tasks folder (which you can find right under My Computer in Windows Explorer), and clicking the Schedule tab (see Figure 14-20).

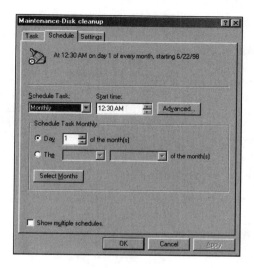

Figure 14-20: Rescheduling tasks
You can adjust the frequency or timing of any scheduled tasks in Windows 98 or 2000 by opening the Scheduled Tasks folder, double-clicking the task, and choosing the Schedule tab of the resulting dialog.

Tip

As handy as Windows 98's Maintenance Wizard and the Windows 98/2000 Scheduled Tasks features may be, they may not work as you expect if you schedule things to occur in the middle of the night, as many of the default settings are designed to do. The problem is, of course, the Scheduled Tasks work only when your computer is turned on in the middle of the night (or whenever you have the tasks scheduled to occur). For many people that means leaving the computer on all the time, which may or may not be a problem.

And even if you schedule the tasks to run at a different time or leave your PC on all the time, you could still run into problems if you have a newer computer that takes advantage of ACPI (Advanced Configuration Power Interface) or any other power management system. The problem in this case is that power management features are designed to put the computer into a sleep state after a certain amount of inactivity or at a certain time, and the scheduled tasks are designed to wait for inactivity or a certain time before they begin. So, if you're not careful, your system could go into a sleep mode, or even shut down, before any of the scheduled tasks are run! In that case you could easily be lulled into a false sense of security, thinking that regular disk maintenance was occurring when, in fact, nothing was happening.

Microsoft obviously thought of this and took it into account when they designed Windows 98 and 2000 because features on the Settings tab of the Scheduled Tasks dialog shown in Figure 14-20 deal with power management. Just to be safe, though, you should check your Scheduled Tasks times and/or settings and compare them with any power settings you have in the Power control panel or in your computer's BIOS setup program.

Disk defragmenting

In addition to checking the disk for errors, it's a good idea to defragment your hard disk on semi-regular (for example, monthly) basis. Defragmenting is the process of taking small pieces of files spread out over your hard drive and bringing them back together as complete entities. While all the files that are installed on your computer's hard drive start out as contiguous chunks of data, over time they often get broken up into pieces (see Figure 14-21).

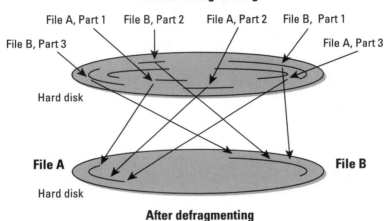

Figure 14-21: Disk defragmentation
As you use your computer, files stored on your hard drive that started out as a contiguous chunk of data end up getting broken up into pieces and spread across the drive. A disk defragmenting utility combines all the pieces into a single chunk again.

Your hard drive's file allocation table keeps track of where all these pieces are, but to use files that are heavily fragmented, the hard drive has to locate and read all the different chunks from different parts of the disk. Ultimately, this leads to more wear and tear on the drive — not to mention the fact that it slows your computer down.

So, by "defragging" your hard drive you can both speed up your computer's operation (although not by a great deal in most cases) and keep the disk working more efficiently. Again, both Windows 95 and 98 come with disk defragmenters, or you can opt for the products bundled with popular disk utilities, such as Norton Utilities or Nuts & Bolts.

The Windows 98 disk defragmenter improves on its very basic Windows 95 predecessor by operating more quickly, working as part of the Maintenance Wizard in Windows 98, and most importantly, improving the launch time of many applications. It achieves this through a special technology originally developed by Intel that keeps track of what specific files an application needs when it launches and then rearranging the files on the hard disk so that those files (or portions of files) can be placed together on the disk.

Again, you can get to the disk defragmenter and other bundled utilities via the Tools tab on any disk drive's Properties sheet under Windows Explorer. Click the Defragment Now button on the Tools tab, and as long as the utility is already installed, the process starts. Depending on how large the drive is, defragging it can take a fair amount of time, so you might want to do it overnight or at some other point when you won't need the computer.

Summary

In this chapter I've covered the role that documents play on your computer, including how they're associated with particular applications. In addition, I described a variety of activities you can do with documents, including opening, printing, converting, sharing, organizing, and backing them up.

▶ Most documents on your computer are associated with particular applications. These associations are determined by a file's three-character extension and internal format.

▶ Under Windows, files that aren't associated with an application have a generic Windows icon.

▶ There are several techniques for creating new files and opening existing files.

▶ You can change some file associations by simply renaming a file with a different extension or can make the change more global by using the File Types tab of the Folder Options dialog box.

▶ You can get a quick preview of many files by either using the QuickView feature of Windows 95/98/2000 or by using the Web View feature of Windows Explorer.

▶ The Send To command in Windows 95/98/2000 is a handy way to open, copy, print, and even convert many types of files on your computer.

▶ Converting files from one format to another can sometimes be done with individual applications but in some cases requires a dedicated conversion utility.

▶ Common electronic file formats, such as HTML or Adobe's PDF, are good ways to share files with computer users on different platforms.

▶ Backing up your files is a critical part of using a computer because all existing storage devices fail at some point in time.

▶ The backup program bundled with Windows 98 is a good tool that can be made even more powerful by making it run automatically

▶ The other automated maintenance tools in Windows 98 and Windows 2000 can help keep your hard drive in good shape, which in turn, should keep your files safe. You can perform similar maintenance under Windows 95, but it takes more work.

Chapter 15

Working with Pictures and Video

In This Chapter

▶ You will learn how to work with digital pictures, including tips on how to get good quality images into your PC from both scanners and digital cameras.

▶ You will learn what image file formats and resolutions you should use with your images.

▶ You will learn how to clean up common problems in digital images and how to apply special effects.

▶ You will learn how to create your own digital movies.

Computers are primarily known for their capability of working with text and numbers and of performing important "productive" tasks. But truth be told, PCs can also be extraordinary creative tools that bring out the artist in nearly anyone. When PCs are used in conjunction with many of today's creativity-oriented software programs, even people with limited artistic skills can produce creative works that they and their friends, family, or other associates find intriguing and satisfying. In fact, many of the applications are now so refined and so easy to use that literally anyone can use them.

Just because you have the right tools doesn't mean you can generate works rivaling great artists anytime soon, however. As with any artistic venture, there are still many tricks of the trade. And even today's most high-powered PC systems have some limitations that keep them from matching the capabilities of real-world media. Still, once you understand a bit of the concepts involved, you may find yourself amazed at all the creative things you can do on a PC.

If your interests are a bit less lofty and more focused on the practical, so much the better. The software and hardware tools aimed at consumers as well as professional artists are all designed to provide practical, real-world benefits. Whether that means removing the annoying red eye effect from your film or digital camera's snapshots, sharpening your pictures, adding a background, or preparing images for a Web site, the available tools are well suited for these pursuits.

And lest we forget, aside from any practical benefits, doing creative activities on a computer is just plain fun. As with the more pragmatic pursuits they're better known for, computers are enablers, artistic ones in this case, making it possible for us to tackle projects that would be difficult or impossible to do without them.

In this chapter, I first look at working with digital pictures, either via scanners or digital cameras. Images are now as important to documents and Web sites as text, but most people aren't as familiar with image-editing techniques as they are with text. In the final part of the chapter, I also look at working with moving images, otherwise known as digital video.

Digital Pictures

Although it used to be a fairly difficult and/or complicated procedure, opening, viewing, editing, and printing photographs on and from your PC is now as easy as typing in a letter or doing any other simple task. In fact, the increased number of consumer-oriented photo-editing programs along with the availability of affordable yet high-quality printers, scanners, and digital cameras have created an absolute explosion in the world of PC imaging (which simply means working with pictures on your computer). Tasks that were accomplished only by highly trained professionals on very expensive equipment as little as five to ten years ago are now commonplace on run-of-the-mill computers.

As with any other type of material you want to work with on your PC, before you can get started with a particular task, you need to have the "information" you're going to work with in digital form. In the case of photographs, that means you either need to scan regular photographs and turn them into digital images, use a digital camera to take a digital picture, or take advantage of photo developing services that do the conversion for you.

Cross-Reference

For more on the hardware used to generate digital images, see Chapter 6 "Printers, Scanners, and Digital Cameras."

In addition, you need a software program that enables you to work with digital photographs or other digital image files. More than likely you've already got at least one somewhere on your hard disk. And even if you don't have a dedicated photo-editing program, you probably have a word processor or other simple graphics program that enables you to do some basic work with digital photos.

CD

If you don't have anything or want to try a different option, a demo copy of Adobe's PhotoDeluxe is on the CD accompanying this book.

To get started with digital photos, you just launch the image application of your choice, open the files you're interested in, and start playing with the images.

What you need

Getting started with digital pictures on your PC is easy. All you really need is:

- A moderately equipped computer (Pentium-class processor, 16MB of RAM, 1GB drive)

- A program that enables you to open and edit digitized photos

- Some images to work with

- Some type of color scanner and/or a digital camera (if you want to use your own photos or custom images)

- Color printer

You get best results from a printer that's specifically designed for photo printing, but almost any four-color inkjet (or other type) printer can work. Three-color printers that can only use either a three-color cartridge or a black cartridge (but not both simultaneously), don't usually work very well with digital photos because the lack of black affects the color accuracy and "crispness" of the printed photo.

The image files you use can be clip art that someone else has created (such as the sample files that come with most programs) or your own digitized photos.

File formats

Digital images are commonly stored in TIFF (Tagged Image File Format), JPEG (Joint Photographic Experts Group), GIF (Graphics Interchange Format), PNG (Portable Network Graphics), Photo CD, or FlashPix formats, although you may run into others as well. If you're not sure what format a photo is in, you can usually tell by looking at its file extension.

Cross-Reference

See Chapter 14, "Working with Documents and Files" for more on file extensions and formats.

Tip

Be aware that depending on the file format of the images you want to work with and the application, you may not automatically see the files you're interested in when you use the Open command off the File menu of whatever application you choose to use. In that case, look for an option in the Open dialog box that enables you to view (and open) files of different types and/or formats. Typically it's a drop-down menu choice.

Table 15-1 summarizes popular image formats and their file extensions. It also describes what type of compression is used to store the images. All graphics files use some type of compression to reduce their size, but some achieve it without losing any data, a technique called "lossless" compression, while others sacrifice parts of the image data to create a smaller size file, called "lossy" compression. The table also lists whether or not the file types are used on the Internet.

Table 15-1	Digital Image File Formats		
File Type	**File Extension**	**Type of Compression**	**Used on the Internet?**
TIFF	.tif	Lossless	No
JPEG	.jpg	Lossy	Yes
GIF	.gif	Lossless	Yes
PNG	.png	Lossless	Yes (although less common)
Photo CD	.pcd	Lossless	No
FlashPix	.fpx	Lossless	Yes (although less common)

Digital picture sources

The easiest way to get photos into your PC is with a scanner or digital camera. If you don't have either one, but still want to use your own photos, several services are available that can take your traditional print film and give you photos back in digitized form that you can use on your computer.

The most well known of these is Kodak's Photo CD format, which can store up to 100 images with five different resolutions each on a single CD. Resolution refers to the number of individual dots that are in a given digital picture. Generally, the higher the resolution, the more dots there are, and the better the image quality is. (I explain resolution in the section "The Details on Resolution," later in this chapter.) The way Photo CD works is it combines all five different resolutions of an image into a single compressed ImagePac file, which is kind of like a set of files within a file. Photo CD is a bit expensive (around $2 to $3 per image), however, so it's primarily used by professional photographers or picky consumers who like the high-quality images it offers.

Caution

One potential problem with Photo CD is that not all graphics programs are capable of reading the proprietary Photo CD (.pcd) format, so make sure you check before you invest in either a graphics program or a Photo CD.

A less expensive, more compatible option is the relatively new Picture CD format, which was codeveloped by Kodak and Intel. Picture CD uses the JPEG file format for all its pictures and stores them at a single resolution (1,536 × 1,024 pixels), which is more than adequate for most purposes. In addition, Picture CDs, which typically hold one roll of film, are also bundled with some simple image-editing programs that are stored on the CD along with the digital images. The cost for most Picture CDs is typically $10 or so over the cost of traditional developing, which makes it a pretty good bargain.

A similar, though increasingly less common, format is the FlashPix CD, which can store up to 400 images at 1,536 × 1,024 pixel resolution in the FlashPix format. The FlashPix format is unique in that it stores the image as a series of small tiles, which generally makes images that use it faster to open. Unlike Picture CDs, but like Photo CDs, FlashPix CDs do not contain any image-editing software on the CD — just the images.

FlashPix files can store information regarding the photo in addition to the digital image itself. This information, which is typically stored in a special area of the file called the *header*, includes things such as the camera settings that were used to create the image, the basic luminance, or light, values, and more that can be useful in the image-editing process. (A header is a section at the beginning of a file that's commonly used to store information about the data in the file, but not the file content itself. Many different file formats use headers.) Some programs automatically take advantage of this extra information to do things such as make adjustments to the image's colors and so on.

Secret

Much of the header information in the FlashPix file format is also incorporated into the special JPEG EXIF (Exchangeable Image File) 2.0 format used in Picture CDs. In addition, many digital cameras use JPEG EXIF 2.0 as their primary method of storage, which means images downloaded from cameras that support it also have this extra information built into the image file.

One other unique characteristic of FlashPix files is that they can be delivered over the Web via a technology called IIP (Internet Imaging Protocol), which enables you to deliver high-resolution images that you can zoom into without requiring enormous download times.

In addition to these CD-based photo delivery systems, many photo labs also offer a service called Picture Disk where you can get copies of your photos on a floppy disk. Picture Disks store up to 28 images at a resolution of 400 × 600 pixels on a single floppy disk, or you can choose to have a single high-resolution FlashPix image stored on a Picture Disk Plus. Obviously the image quality on a standard Picture Disk is lower than what you can get from Photo CD or Picture CD, but for applications such as Web sites or electronic mail, they're usually fine (plus, they're usually even cheaper still).

Table 15-2 compares the different file resolutions offered by Kodak's various digital picture formats.

Table 15-2 Kodak Digital Picture Formats

Format	Disk Type	Maximum Number of Photos	Number of Resolutions per Image File	Resolution of Those Image (in pixels)	File Type (Extension)	Compression
Picture Disk	Floppy	28	1	400 × 600	JPEG (.jpg)	JPEG
Picture Disk Plus	Floppy	1	1	1,024 × 1,536	JPEG (.jpg) or FlashPix (.fpx)	JPEG or Proprietary
Picture CD	CD	36*	1	1,024 × 1,536	JPEG EXIF 2.0 (.jpg)	JPEG
FlashPix CD	CD	400	1	1,024 × 1,536	FlashPix (.fpx)	Proprietary
Photo CD	CD	100	5	128 × 192 (Base/16); 256 × 384 (Base/4); 512 × 768 (Base); 1,024 × 1,536 (4 Base); 2,048 × 3,072 (16 Base)	Photo CD Image Pac (.pcd)	Proprietary Photo CD

*Also includes photo-editing software

Scanning your own images

If you use a scanner or digital camera to get your pictures into a digital form, the first step is to get the digital photos into your PC. Even though that sounds relatively straightforward, it can actually be one of the most confusing parts of the process.

The problem is not transferring the files from either device to your PC (typically, once one of these devices have been set up, they work fine), but figuring out what size and resolution image you should use. In other words, if you have a 1,200 dpi scanner or a multi-megapixel camera, what settings should you use to scan the photo or take the picture?

Tip

Although many newcomers to digital imaging presume that you should use the best quality available, that's not typically the case. The general rule of thumb is that you should always base your scanning or picture-taking resolution on the output device you intend to use. In other words, if you plan to just view the images onscreen, such as for a Web site, use a resolution setting that's typically pretty low (around 70 to 90 dpi) and if you plan to print them, use another that's much higher (such as 200 to 300 dpi).

If you're using a scanner, you make these and other scanning-related settings in your scanning software, which typically works in conjunction with your image-editing program. Oftentimes you see options such as Image Acquire or Image Import off of the program's File menu. In addition, you may see something referring to TWAIN or TWAIN32, which is the standard software interface for connecting between scanners and digital photo-editing programs. (In a rare example of technological humor, TWAIN actually stands for Technology Without An Interesting Name — really.) When you select these type of options, you typically bring up your scanner's dedicated software, which uses the TWAIN interface to communicate with the scanner. Figure 15-1 shows a typical example.

Many consumer-oriented photo-editing programs hide you from this level of detail by offering completely automated operation. In addition, many TWAIN-based scanner programs offer both automatic and manual operation. See Figure 15-2 for an example.

In many cases these automatic settings work quite well, but they're far from perfect. I suggest you try them first if they're available. You also need to understand a bit about the advanced settings for situations where you aren't satisfied with the automatic results. The most important of these is image resolution.

Figure 15-1: TWAIN scanning software
The VistaScan 32 software bundled with Umax and other brand name scanners is typical of the TWAIN software that you can use to adjust scanning parameters, including resolution and more.

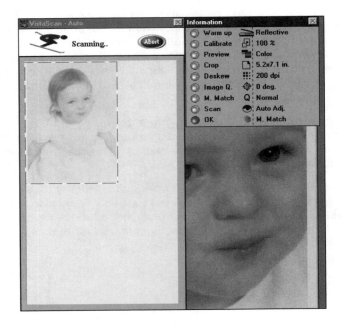

Figure 15-2: Automatic scanning
In addition to the manual settings, many TWAIN software programs offer an automatic mode that adjusts all the important scanner settings for you. Many times these automatic settings work fine but not every time.

The details on resolution

Determining the proper resolution to use for scanning an image or taking a digital photograph is actually a tricky issue. Not only do you need to think about the intended output device, but you also have to understand a bit about how they work because, as I explained in Chapter 6, "Printers, Scanners, and Digital Cameras," scanner resolution, monitor resolution, and printer resolution are not the same thing. Actually, scanners and monitors match up on a one-to-one basis with one scanner dot (or one digital camera pixel) corresponding to one monitor pixel, but printers and their "dot" specifications are a different animal entirely (for the most part). In most cases, it takes several printer dots to recreate a single monitor/scanner dot (some photo printers are a bit of an exception).

The basic problem is that while scanners, digital cameras, and monitors have the capability to generate any one of 16.7 million possible colors (for 24-bit, or true color) at each of the millions of "dots" that together make up a digital photograph, many inkjet printers cannot. In fact, in order to recreate any one of those 16.7 million available colors at a particular point on a piece of paper from a palette of only four (or maybe six) printer cartridges, printers often use a variety of sophisticated dot placement techniques called *halftone screens* and *dithering algorithms*. In most cases, these halftones require several printer dots per image pixel.

Cross-Reference

See Chapter 6, "Printers, Scanners, and Digital Cameras," for more on halftoning techniques.

Scanner resolution versus printer resolution

The practical result of all this is that a 1,200 dpi scanner, for example, actually has much higher resolution than a 1,200 dpi printer. In fact, when it comes to printing color photographs, most printers have only about ⅙ (or even less) of their "claimed" resolution. So, for example, a 1,200 dpi printer may only offer 200 lines-per-inch (lpi) resolution. Printers designed specifically for printing photographs and others that use sophisticated dot-blending techniques often have dpi and lpi specs that are closer together (for example a 300 dpi photo printer may have higher resolution than a 720 dpi nonphoto printer when it comes to printing digital photographs), but they're usually not one-to-one.

Tip

The reason you need to know all this is that if you're planning to scan a photo you will print on a particular printer, you should scan the image not at the printer's dpi resolution, but nearer to the lpi. (Some people recommend scanning at 1.5 or 2 times the printer's lpi to guarantee the best quality image.) Because the lpi specification for a particular printer (and printer driver setting) is hard to find (and can vary), a general rule of thumb is to scan most photographs intended for printing on a color inkjet at around 200 dpi. If you're using a photo printer, you probably want to scan at 300 dpi. You may have to experiment to find what works best for your printer. Also, if your printer manufacturer has a specific recommendation for printing scanned images, or specifically lists the lpi resolution at a particular setting, you should follow that, bearing in mind the 1.5 or 2× suggestion previously mentioned. But as a general rule, the 200 and 300 dpi numbers are good reference points.

What you definitely don't want to do is to scan an image at 600, 1,200, or whatever the maximum dpi resolution your scanner has to offer. (The one exception to this rule is if you're scanning a very small photo or small section of a larger photo and want to enlarge it.) If you do scan at these higher resolutions, you generate an enormous image that wastes space on your hard drive, slows down your computer when trying to open, edit, or print it, and most importantly, absolutely does not give you a better printout. (If you don't believe me, try scanning the same image at, say, 200 dpi and 600 dpi, and then print them both. Take a good look at the two printouts—go ahead and use a magnifying glass to be sure—and you'll see what I'm saying.)

Table 15-3   Common Image Resolutions and File Sizes

Photo Size	Scanning Resolution	Color	File Size
3″ × 5″	75 dpi	Grayscale (8-bit)	82K
3″ × 5″	75 dpi	24-bit	247K
3″ × 5″	150 dpi	Grayscale (8-bit)	330K
3″ × 5″	150 dpi	24-bit	989K
3″ × 5″	300 dpi	24-bit	3.86MB
3″ × 5″	300 dpi	30 or 36-bit	7.72 MB
4″ × 6″	75 dpi	24-bit	396K
4″ × 6″	150 dpi	24-bit	1.54MB
4″ × 6″	300 dpi	24-bit	6.18MB
4″ × 6″	300 dpi	30 or 36-bit	12.36MB
5″ × 7″	200 dpi	Grayscale (8-bit)	1.34MB
5″ × 7″	200 dpi	24-bit	4.01MB
5″ × 7″	200 dpi	30 or 36-bit	8.01MB
8″ × 10″	200 dpi	Grayscale (8-bit)	3.05MB
8″ × 10″	200 dpi	24-bit	9.16MB
8″ × 10″	200 dpi	30 or 36-bit	18.31MB

This is not to say that the extra dpi resolution of your scanner should (or will be) going to waste. The truth of the matter is that a 1,200 dpi scanner creates a better 300 dpi scan than a 300 dpi scanner because of the improved electronics and electronic "headroom" that the higher-resolution scanning head built into a 1,200 dpi scanner offers.

Resolution and image size

As I've said before, computers are mathematical devices, and many issues related to computers and files can be explained with simple mathematical formulas. Such is the case with the relationship between a digital image's resolution and its file size. The higher the resolution of a scanned image, the more dots it has, and the more dots it has, the more space it takes up. Here's the formula:

File size (in bytes) = height of photo (in inches) × scanning resolution (in pixels or dots per inch) × width of photo (in inches) × scanning resolution (in pixels or dots per inch) × 3 (for 24-bit color, which is made up of three 8-bit bytes).

So, for example, a typical 4-inch × 6-inch photograph scanned at 100 dpi with 24-bit color is:

$4 \times 100 \times 6 \times 100 \times 3 = 720,000$ bytes or 703 Kbytes (7,200/1,024 bytes per kilobyte)

If you scan at different sizes, scaling factors (where you essentially enlarge or shrink the image), or color depths, these numbers vary, but the basic principles are the same. One potentially confusing point is that 30-bit and 36-bit scans take up twice as much space as 24-bit scans (not one-and-a-half times or somewhere in between 1× and 2×) because each color (red, green, and blue) requires two bytes to describe the data captured in a 30 (or 36-bit) scan, versus one byte each in a 24-bit scan.

To save you some time, Table 15-3 shows common photo sizes, scanning resolutions, and their resulting file sizes.

Screen resolution versus print resolution

In addition to file size, you have to keep the photo's final destination in mind. The specific resolution you choose to scan a photo at (or which you use to shoot a particular digital picture at) again, depends on the "output" device to which the image is going. If you're simply scanning a photo to make a digital copy of it and aren't sure of the final resolution of some future output device, you can choose higher resolutions than what I've previously suggested, but be warned that you will be creating enormous files.

More than likely, the biggest choice you have to make when capturing a digital image is between screen resolution and printed resolution. If you're planning on adding a photo to a Web site or other electronic document that will be viewed only onscreen, a lower-resolution image that's a closer match to the dpi resolution of the typical computer monitor is appropriate. An image destined for a color printer, on the other hand, requires a higher-resolution scan (or picture setting) in order for it to look good when it's printed.

While it's commonly claimed that screen resolution is 72 or 90 dpi, the truth is that it can be any number of different resolutions, depending on the resolution setting of the video card and the size of the monitor. A 15-inch monitor (remember, they're measured diagonally) and a video card set to work at 800×600 resolution, for example, has an onscreen resolution of about

75 dpi if the viewable image on the monitor is a little over ten inches wide. (The math for this is width of monitor in inches/width resolution in pixels [in this case, 800] = dots per inch of viewable image on the monitor.) If a 17-inch monitor is 12-inch wide and is set to work at a resolution of 1,280 × 1,024, then the screen resolution is nearly 107 dpi (1,280/12 = 106.7).

The important issue to remember here is that the exact same image can be different sizes on different monitors, depending on their resolution setting. Figure 15-3 illustrates this principle.

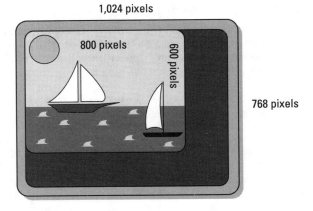

Figure 15-3: Image size vs. screen resolution
Because there's a one-to-one ratio between pixels in an image and pixels onscreen, the size of any image varies according to the resolution of the monitor.

Because you typically have no idea (nor any control over) what size the monitor is on a computer viewing your work (other than your own), this means that when scanning an image for a Web site, you just have to pick something you think looks best on a wide variety of screen sizes. Also, be sure to test it at various resolutions on your own screen to see if it's acceptable.

Secret

When you scan an image or take a digital picture for printing, however, the size of the printed image is not determined by the image resolution, but by the size of the original image you scanned (or took) and any scaling factor (which can magnify or shrink any image you scan) you applied to it. So, for example, if you leave the default scaling factor of 1, scan a 4-inch × 6-inch photo at 100 dpi, and then scan it again at 200 dpi, both images would print out at a 4-inch × 6-inch size, but the second one would look better than the first because it had a higher resolution. Frankly, that's what most people expect when it comes to scanning and resolution. Digital cameras typically provide one printed image size, with the resolution setting you use to take a picture affecting the image's printed resolution. Again, this is what seems logical.

What can be confusing, however, is that if you view both the low- and high-resolution images on your monitor, the high-res one scanned at 200 dpi looks much bigger than the low-res one scanned at 100 dpi. (To see this at work, make sure that both images are being viewed at 100 percent in your scanning or image-editing program. Many programs automatically scale images onscreen to different resolutions so that you can see the whole picture at once.) The reason, again, is because unless you shrink the onscreen image to a smaller size through a process called *resampling* (which basically discards certain pixels in the original scan), the monitor shows all the individual dots of the 200 dpi image and all of the dots of the 100 dpi image at the same size. Because there are more dots in the 200 dpi image, it appears much larger.

Tip

If you want to adjust the printed size of an image you scanned, then you need to adjust the scaling factor when you scan the image or use your image-editing program to adjust the printed size of the image. (In some instances, you probably need to adjust the resolution as well, which typically involves using the resampling function mentioned in the previous paragraph.) Look for the specific settings in your program's Image Size or similarly named command.

Scanning tips

If you have access to a 30- or 36-bit scanner, one common question is whether or not to use these higher "bit" resolutions when you scan images. In theory, of course, they should provide an even higher-resolution image than a normal 24-bit scanner, but the reality is that on most photos, these settings make little difference (but they double the size of your scanned image, anyway). Photos with a lot of details in shadow can often benefit from these higher resolutions, but not all image-editing programs can even work with images at higher than 24-bit resolution.

Even Adobe's high-end Photoshop image-editing program, for example, can't edit images with more than 24-bits (or 8-bits per color channel). In some situations, in fact, the extra bits are simply "tossed out" by the image-editing programs. Depending on your scanner's TWAIN software, you may be able to have the scanner create a 30- or 36-bit scan in hardware and then do its own manipulation of the image to transfer what it considers to be the "best" 24 bits to the image-editing program. In other situations you can perform these same "interpolations" in your image-editing program.

Tip

One adjustment that you can make to most images before you scan is to edit the level of colors that your scanner is capturing. You do this through the fancily named Histogram tool available in most TWAIN software. A Histogram enables you to look at and adjust the overall range of lights and darks that your scanner captures. The basic concept is that a 24-bit scanner (or a scanner working in 24-bit mode) can capture 255 different levels of light and dark, but very few images actually use all 255 levels. So to make the most of your scanner's available capabilities, you can set the lightest and darkest color intensities that you want it to capture, and then it effectively increases its resolution by spreading those 255 levels within the smaller range that you've defined.

Now, while this may sound like a daunting process, the Histogram makes it easy. A Histogram gives you a simple black-and-white graph that shows the levels in the photo you are about to scan. In most cases, the software also enables you to make adjustments to those levels in the Histogram dialog box (although some programs have a separate Levels dialog box to make adjustments). If you want to, you can make individual adjustments to the red, green, and blue channels, but it's easier (and faster) to make one overall adjustment. Here's how.

STEPS:

Adjusting Levels For Betters Scans

Step 1. Place the image you're going to scan on your scanner, launch your photo-editing software, and begin the scanning process. Make a preview scan. (If you don't do this first, you may accidentally make adjustments based on the last image you tried to scan!)

Step 2. Once you've got the Preview, open the Histogram tool (see Figure 15-4).

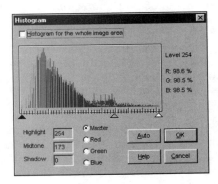

Figure 15-4: An image histogram
A typical image histogram shows you the overall levels of the different colors in the image you're going to scan. Notice the black-and-white triangular markers at the bottom of the histogram. You use those in the next step.

Step 3. Adjust the black triangle so that it lines up with the left end of the histogram. Adjust the white triangle so that it lines up with the right of the histogram. It's okay to go a little inward on either end, particularly if the image levels in the graph are very low (see Figure 15-5).

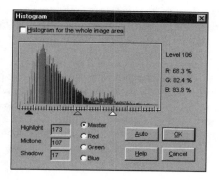

Figure 15-5: Adjusting levels
By moving the "outside" ranges of what the scanner attempts to capture in any given photo inward, you can increase the effective resolution of your scanner.

Step 4. If you want to (and if the program provides it), you can move the middle gray triangle to make an overall adjustment to the lightness and darkness of the scan. Once you've made any adjustments, hit OK, and then scan the image.

If you don't like the results of your scan, go back in, and adjust the settings again (or try the program's automatic settings). If you reduce the levels on either side too much, you may end up with washed-out colors, so experiment until you get what you want.

Cropping and resizing

One other critical step in the scanning process is to make sure you have the right size image. While this may seem obvious, it's important to set the software to scan only the area of the image you want to scan. Of course, in most cases that is the entire photo, but there are exceptions where you want to scan only a portion of the image.

If you aren't sure what you need, you can always scan the entire image and then "crop" the photo in the image-editing program. Cropping refers to cutting out the portions of the image (typically the outside edges) that you don't want. In the process, you simply throw away pixels that you don't need. One additional benefit of cropping is that it reduces the file size of the image, which helps in opening, editing, and saving the file.

Tip

If you need to resize the image to appear larger onscreen or to print at a larger size, you can typically perform these operations in an image-editing program as well. But in most cases, you're better off scanning the image again at the size, resolution, or scaling factor you need. (That is, as long as you still have access to the original.) The reason is that to change the size of an image (other than through the simple cropping technique I just described), the image-editing program has to essentially "make up" some pixels that weren't in the original scanned image. While the calculations required to do that (again, often called "resampling") can do some amazing things, they can't possibly match the original image.

If you don't have the original image and have to use the program's resizing features, I suggest you use the bicubic resizing option, which is typically the default. *Bicubic* refers to the mathematical equations used to generate the extra pixels. If you don't like the results it generates, use the program's undo feature, and experiment with other options that the program offers.

Editing images

Once you've got the proper size and resolution inside your image-editing program, it's time for fun. Most image editors offer an amazing wealth of things you can do with your digital images, including cleaning them up, adjusting the colors, completely distorting the images, or turning them into painting-like works of art. In all cases, it's just a matter of performing some impressive mathematical trickery on the original bits that make up your scanned image.

Regardless of your intended result, the best place to start most photo-editing sessions is with some straightforward adjustments that improve the original image quality. As nice as your original scan may be, almost all digital images can benefit from the following tips.

Sharpening the image

Probably the first place to go in your photo editor once you've scanned in or transferred an image from a digital camera is the image-sharpening options. Most programs provide menu options such as Sharpen and Sharpen More, while some programs also offer the confusingly named Unsharp Mask. (Unsharp Mask is essentially a user-defined sharpening filter that enables you to set a variety of sophisticated parameters in order to create the best possible sharpening of a digital image.) All of these functions increase the perceived sharpness in your digital picture by highlighting and enhancing all the areas of the image where light colors (or light grays) and dark colors (or dark grays) come together. See Figure 15-6 for an example.

As amazingly effective as these features can be in sharpening up an image, they can also be overdone. So don't automatically go for the Sharpen More command three times in a row for every image you scan. You really have to judge it on an image-by-image basis.

Figure15-6: Photo sharpening
By taking advantage of your image-editing program's sharpening features, you can make a dramatic difference in the crispness of your digital photo. Be careful not to go overboard on sharpening, however.

Also, if you used the sharpening features that some TWAIN software provides when you first scanned the image, you may quickly overdo the sharpening if you use your image-editing programs sharpen feature as well. In fact, if you have the opportunity, you may want to experiment and see whether the scanner software or your image-editing program's sharpen feature works more effectively.

In addition to sharpening, another common image adjustment is to the overall brightness and contrast of the image. Many programs provide simple brightness and contrast adjustments for this purpose. Be aware, however, that the brightness and contrast (or even the colors) you see on your monitor may be very different than what someone else sees on their monitor or what you get when you print the image.

The problem has to do with the inconsistency of color across various devices: a lime green color in an original photo may become more chartreuse-like on your PC monitor and look almost forest green coming out of your printer. Color management software is designed to provide a consistent set of colors for scanning, viewing onscreen, and printing, but not all programs support color management. In addition, they don't necessarily support the same color "space," which is essentially a definition of what each color is.

Cross-Reference

See the section "Printing tips," later in this chapter, for more on color management.

Getting the red out

Another common image-editing technique involves fixing the "red-eye" problem that is so prominent on many snapshots. Again, some programs have features that attempt to automatically take the red out, and many of those are quite effective. They aren't perfect, however, and the following manual techniques can help you with lots of problems similar to red eye.

The trick in fixing red eye as well as cleaning up dust, scratches, and other imperfections you often find in older photos is to use the image editor's stamp or cloning tool (most image-editing programs have something that performs this function, even though the specific name may differ). What these types of tools do is copy a small portion, basically a few pixels, of the image around where the problem is (or wherever on the image you click with them) and then enable you to "paint" or stamp (think rubber stamper) over the problem area.

If you have a scanned photo with an annoying scratch across someone's face (or for that matter, you want to "erase" a physical imperfection on someone whose photo you're editing), you select the stamp/cloning tool, click an area of the image near where the problem is, and then patiently fill in or copy over the problem with the "stamp" you created with your first click.

In some cases you just paint with a single color, while in others you may actually use a small pattern of pixels. In either instance, this stamp you're using should look very similar to its surroundings so that when you "paint" over the problem area, it looks like the image blemish has simply gone away. See Figure 15-7 for an example.

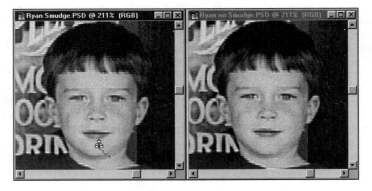

Figure 15-7: The magical stamp
An image editor's stamp or clone tool enables you to perform image-editing miracles by taking a tiny portion of an image and then basically "painting" over any nearby problems with what you've copied.

The trick with using the stamp tool effectively is figuring out where to take your sample from and how large a sample to take. In the case of red eye, zoom into the photo near the eye area, click a portion of the eye that isn't red with the stamp/cloning tool, and then paint or "stamp" over the red portions. To adjust the size of the sample, you need to adjust the brush size you're using. (In fact, the brush size affects many different image-editing tools.) In most instances, you have to look for the brush size setting in a different area of the program.

Photo collages

Another seemingly magical task that image-editing programs can perform is to combine two previously distinct images into a single composite photo and create the illusion of something that never existed. You can also use the same technique to create a simple photo collage. Needless to say, however, the capability to create "unreal" photos is what has gotten the most attention, and not always for the best reasons (can you say, *National Enquirer*?).

So if you ever wondered how they put UFO pictures over New York City, or put two people who weren't together into the same photograph, here's the trick: It's called *masking*. A mask is nothing more than a very exact outline, or selection, of a particular element or area in a digital photograph. If you really wanted to, you could try to make a masked selection of a person in one photograph by just cutting it out with a pair of scissors. The problem is that the mask wouldn't be precise, so when you tried to paste this cutout picture on top of another to create a composite, it wouldn't look realistic, and the effect would be ruined.

With image-editing programs, however, you can quickly and easily create precise selections using tools such as the Magic Wand and Magic Lasso. Unlike traditional selection tools, which usually select a portion of an image based on a particular shape, the Magic Wand, Magic Lasso, and other such tools enable you to create image selections based on colors or levels of lightness and darkness. For example, by using the Magic Wand, you might be able to select all the elements of an image that fall within a range of certain blue hues. Or you might be able to further refine your selection to being all those blue-hued pixels within a certain portion of the image. Figure 15-8 shows an example.

Once you've created a mask, which essentially is like a saving a particular selection within a photo, you can use it to do things such as change the color of a picture element in a digital photo without effecting anything else. For example, you could change the color of a dress from blue to red. Many fancy photo-retouching tips, in fact, are made possible by tools that enable you to quickly grab various portions of an image.

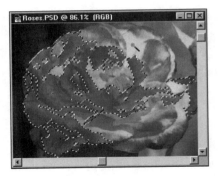

Figure 15-8: The Magic Wand
The secret to making amazing changes to digital photographs is the capability to hone in on a very specific area of an image. And the key to making selections based on color instead of just shape is the Magic Wand tool. In this photo, the Magic Wand has enabled me to select a group of pink shades that are in the rose.

And getting back to our earlier example, not only do these clean selections enable you to neatly copy this image from one photograph and paste it into another (including such details as being able to see "through" locks of hair where the selection area precisely followed the outline of a person's hair), they also enable you to adjust only the selected, or masked, portion of the image to make the composite even more realistic. For example, if the lighting in the image being copied is much brighter than the one it's being pasted into, then with the masked area you pasted in still selected, you can darken just the copied image until it's a better match for the background of the other picture into which it has been pasted.

Special effects

Probably the most fun you can have with image-editing programs is to take advantage of all the special effects features that most programs provide. If you want to distort someone's face into a twirl of color, or turn an ordinary photo into something that looks like an oil painting, or perform any number of other creative twists on a digital image, you'll want to head over to your program's filter-related menu options.

Many of the filtering/special effects are quite simple and with a single click can convert an ordinary image into something extraordinary. Others, however, require adjusting a variety of different parameters to get just the right effect. The great thing is, most programs now have preview options so that you don't really have to know what exactly you're doing with certain of these settings — you can just play around with them until you get something you like. In fact, the same can be said of most of the functions you find in image-editing programs (or for that matter, most of the creative applications you use on a PC). This is one type of program where you can really appreciate the undo feature (or even better, multiple levels of undo).

Tip

One idea to consider in your creative experiments is to adjust only a certain portion of the image with a particular effect. While some effects are meant to change the whole picture, others can be used creatively in conjunction with masks to adjust only a chunk of the photo.

In addition to the special effects settings that come standard, many image-editing programs enable you to add additional effects or other neat, creative features to the base program through the use of plug-ins. Plug-ins are typically small pieces of software that you purchase, or sometimes just download, and install separately. They extend the features or capabilities of the program with which they're designed to work. Some image-editing plug-ins, for example, can do things such as add new menus of effects, create 3-D type inside a digital photo, or any number of other cool things.

The most common plug-in format is Adobe Photoshop plug-ins. In fact, a whole cottage industry of Photoshop plug-in manufacturers now exists. Thankfully, because of their popularity, many applications are capable of working with Photoshop plug-ins, and you don't need the expensive Photoshop application to use them. Be aware, however, that not all image-editing applications do, so make sure you check before you buy one.

Many plug-ins have grown so sophisticated that they are like mini-applications unto themselves. However, in most cases, plug-ins cannot work on their own but rely on other capabilities of the "host" program in order to function, so again, be careful before you buy.

Printing tips

Once you've done all your creative work, you probably want to print your digital masterpiece. In most cases, all you have to do is hit the Print function from inside your image-editing program, but you can do a few things to ensure high-quality output.

Tip

First of all, make sure you're printing with the appropriate printer quality setting. Most printers default to a mode that's best suited for text and graphics, so you may need to make some adjustments to your printer's driver software. If you want to make those adjustments on a global basis, right-click the printer in the Printers folder (from Start ⇨ Settings), and then use whatever tabs are available to the right of the Sharing Tab. (The specific number of tabs and their names vary from printer to printer.) If you want to make the changes on a per-document basis, click the Properties button that's available through the standard Windows 95/98/2000 Print dialog box. Also, if you just want a reasonable looking "proof" copy, you can choose a slightly lower-quality setting, but if you want a final copy, make sure you're using the best setting your printer offers.

In addition, most color inkjet printers offer dramatically better results if you use special glossy paper that's designed for printing photos. This varies from printer to printer, but if your printer manufacturer suggests using the special (read=expensive) paper for best results, I suggest you follow their advice. In some cases you may find that there are even several types of glossy paper with differing prices and quality. If possible, you may want to experiment with different types of paper from different manufacturers until you find something that gives you the results you want (or looks best in side-by-side comparisons).

The final issue of concern is color matching, or making sure that the printer outputs roughly the same colors you see on your monitor. Logically speaking, you would think this would happen automatically, but as explained in Chapter 6, "Printers, Scanners, and Digital Cameras," that isn't necessarily the case. Some printer drivers include color-matching features that you can adjust, but the best way to achieve consistent color is through color profiles handled by the operating system itself. (Professional graphic artists often use a third-party program for color management.)

Color profiles are essentially descriptions of how your monitor and printer "understand" different colors. By comparing your system's monitor and printer profiles, the operating system, or another color management utility, can make any necessary translations between the two and ensure that the colors you see on the screen match the colors that come from your printer. The specific adjustments they make are to the gamma curves, or just the gamma settings, which affect how different devices display color. Some applications enable you to manually adjust gamma curves for your monitor, scanner/digital camera, or printer, but color management essentially takes care of these settings for you.

Secret

Windows 95 has some automatic color management built-in, but Windows 98 and 2000 improve on it by adding user-configurable color profiles. You can get to the choices you have for monitors via the Display control panel's Settings tab, then the Advanced Options, and finally the Color Management tab. For printers, right-click the Printer icon in the Printers folder, select Properties, and then go to the Color Management tab (see Figure 15-9).

Some monitors and printers install their own color profiles inside the Windows/System/Color directory (which is also where they reside under Windows 95), but you can also install, remove, or set as default various ICM (Image Color Management) color profiles from the Display control panel or printer Properties page if you're using Windows 98. To find out more about a particular color profile, click the Add button, and once you're in the standard Open dialog box, right-click the various profiles.

If you don't currently have a profile selected, the default for monitors and printers is the sRGB Color Space Profile.icm. Note that the Windows 98 and Windows 2000 Image Color Management 2.0 profiles you select do not "kick in" unless you specifically tell a program to use them via a Color Management option off the program's File menu. If you don't see that choice in a particular program, then the application does not support color management, and the settings you've made will not have any impact.

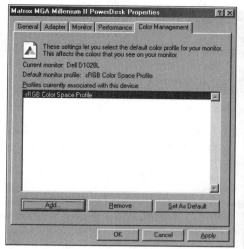 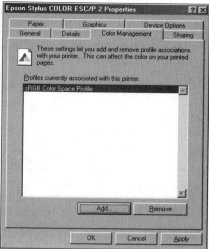

Figure 15-9: Color management control
Under Windows 98 you can set color profiles for your monitors and printers via either the Display control panel or a printer's Properties page.

Using the pictures in other programs

Moving your photos from an image-editing program into another application is usually quite easy. Simply copy the photo, switch to or open the application and/or document into which you want to insert it, and then paste it in. In some situations you may need to first convert the image into a file format that the receiving application can accept. For example, a Photo CD image would probably first have to be saved as or exported to JPEG, or some other popular format, before you could paste it (or insert it) into a word processing document.

Note

By the way, with some applications, the very act of copying a file to the clipboard automatically converts it into a standard format, such as .bmp for graphics files.

Another way to insert images into files is to use a program's import feature. In other words, if you're using a page layout program, for example, and you want to add a picture that you've created and saved in another program, you may find that it works better to import or place your image file into the page layout file in which you are working.

Depending on what you plan to use your image files for, you may want to keep a high-resolution version of them saved in your image-editing program's default format, but also save a compressed JPEG version for things such as attaching to e-mail messages or using in a Web site.

Using images on the Web

One of the most common applications for digital pictures is to use them on Web sites. Good digital images can go a long way toward improving the overall feel and professionalism of a site. To use an image on the Web, you just need to make sure it's saved in one of the formats that Web browsers can see — typically GIF or JPEG, although the PNG format is also starting to be used more. (See the beginning of this chapter for more on image file formats.)

GIF images are limited to 256 colors but use lossless compression techniques, so they usually look best with computer-generated graphics, logos, and things of that sort. JPEG, on the other hand, supports 24-bit color and is the primary format used for digital photos. PNG graphics are a third option, primarily in place of GIF, because the PNG format supports 24-bit color and lossless compression. It also provides the same types of benefits for computer graphics as GIF, but PNG doesn't use any licensed compression technologies (in other words, it's royalty-free for developers who want to use it). The problem with PNG is that only browsers of Version 4.0 and later support it, so it's still relatively rare.

Just selecting the format isn't enough, however, because the real trick with Web-based images is to make them as small (in file size) as possible. To that end you'll find that JPEG files, for example, can typically be saved with one of several different compression ratios. As you might suspect, the higher the compression, the smaller the file size, but also the more negative impact on the image's quality. You have to find a balance between reducing the image size and reducing the image quality. If you're ever in doubt, err on the side of file size because one of the major problems with many Web sites is how slow they are in loading — a factor that's typically directly attributable to the number and size of images on a given Web page.

You can create the image at full resolution and then try different compression until you get something that you can live with and is small enough. Generally speaking, you want to keep your total Web page under 60K, which means all your images and all your text should fit within that tiny size.

See the section "Building Your Own Web Site" in Chapter 13, "Connecting To and Using the Internet," for more.

Cross-Reference

One good trick you can use to shrink the size of image files headed for the Web is to reduce the color palette that's used to create them. The color palette is a section within all computer image files that, like a painter's palette, determines what colors can be used in an image. The larger the palette, the more colors you can have in an image, but the larger the file size. By shrinking the palette, you can dramatically reduce an image's size, but shrinking the palette also reduces the number of possible colors in an image. Many times this can lead to an ugly posterization effect (just as if you turn your computer's monitor setting down to, say, 4 or 16 colors) so, once again, there's a tradeoff. With images that have many similar colors, however, you can reduce the palette of available colors without affecting the image quality much at all.

Tip

The standard 256-color VGA palette is typically reduced to 216 colors when working with Web-based images because Macs and PCs display colors differently. So if you do get into making color palette changes, make sure you use a Web-safe palette that's limited to these 216 colors because you want to be sure that any images you create for the Web look good on any kind of computer system.

CD

Programs such as Adobe's ImageStyler and Macromedia Fireworks, demo versions of which you'll find on the CD accompanying this book, can greatly enhance the process of reducing Web-bound images to their smallest possible size without drastically impacting image quality by automating some of these types of palette tricks.

Digital Video

The next logical step beyond still images is to jump to moving images, which are commonly known as *video*. While PC-based video recording and editing used to be possible only on high-powered expensive computers, today's high-speed, low-cost CPUs and the growth of high-speed connection technologies, particularly IEEE 1394, is making video editing on your PC an increasingly common reality. So, if you're anxious to turn hours of monotonous home video into a polished hour-long program, or if want to add some video clips to your company's Web site, there's hope.

I warn you, however, that depending on what you want to do, a fair amount of powerful equipment is still going to be involved. Digital video editing is one of the most storage- and bandwidth-intensive activities you can engage in on your PC, which means you're going to need a fast, well-equipped machine to do it. In other words, if you've been looking for a motivation to buy a big, new machine, video editing is it. (By the way, it's also why computer manufacturers such as Intel are so hot on the idea.)

Cross-Reference

See Chapter 3, "Hard Disks and Removable Drives" for more information on storage devices.

What you need

Video editing on a PC is an intensive application that places heavy requirements on virtually all the components inside a computer. As a result I suggest:

■ A fast, well-stocked computer (350MHz Pentium II or greater, 128MB or more of RAM, 10GB or more of storage).

■ A large-capacity removable drive for backing up and storing digitized files (1GB or greater).

■ An IEEE 1394 port if you're working with a digital camcorder, or a video capture card with S-video connections for working with an analog video camera. If you want to

Continued

(continued)

record the results of your edits back out to videotape, make sure the card has a video output as well as an input.

■ A high-quality sound card or sound inputs and outputs on the video capture card.

■ A video-editing application in which to do your work. A demo version of Adobe's Premiere 5.0 is included on the CD accompanying this book.

If you really want to get the best possible performance, you may even want to invest in a SCSI or IEEE 1394-based drive array or RAID that's specifically designed for digital audio and video editing. A drive array includes two or more individual drives that work in tandem as a single storage device. Also, because of the high-bandwidth requirements of digital video, SCSI (or IEEE 1394) drives are definitely better suited to this task than IDE drives.

Making the connections

The types of connections you make and the things you can do on your PC depend somewhat on the video equipment you have. For example, if you have a relatively new DV digital camcorder equipped with an IEEE 1394 port, then you want to have a matching connector on your PC. If your PC doesn't come with one, you can add a 1394 port to most PCs with a PCI plug-in card. The 1394 connector takes care of transferring both the video and a stereo digital audio signal straight into your PC without having to worry about digitizing (which I explain in the next section).

If your video footage is coming from an analog camcorder or a VCR, you need a video capture or digitizing card. I recommend one with the higher-quality S-video connectors because they provide better image quality than the standard RCA-type video connector. Again, some PCs come with video capture cards (or video capture circuitry) already installed, but most do not. In those cases you have to purchase a separate plug-in card and install it yourself. If you do, make sure it comes with a video-editing software package you're interested in using.

Cross-Reference

See Chapter 10, "Adding and Removing Hardware" for more on installing a plug-in card into your PC.

The critical thing to investigate with video capture cards is the size and rate of the video signal they capture. Some cards are designed to capture only a small (such as 320 × 240-pixel) size signal at a rate of about 15 frames per second. This is okay for creating small videos intended for CD-ROMs or Web sites, but it is completely unacceptable for creating a video program that you want to record back out to videotape. Standard video resolution is approximately 640 × 480 pixels at 30 frames per second. In addition, some video-oriented products are designed for what's called *online editing* and others for *offline editing*.

Cross-Reference

See Chapter 4, "Video Cards and Monitors" for more on different types of video capture cards.

Online editing versus offline editing

Video signals take up such an enormous amount of space that when people started to look at doing computer-assisted video editing, they realized they were going to have to make some compromises. Specifically, they realized that if they were ever going to be able to offer some low-cost editing options, they were going to have to figure out a way to use the quick, random-access capabilities of a computer without have to record a high-resolution video signal onto a computer's hard disk. Hence the use of offline editing.

In offline editing, which most low-cost video-editing systems offer, you are not editing the actual video program (that's what online editing is), but instead are typically figuring out a series of commands (they're technically called *Edit Decision Lists*, or *EDLs*) that then, in turn, are used to control VCRs. So, for example, you might use these types of systems to capture a low-resolution video signal on your PC and then make some edits on that low-resolution signal. Then,

when you're finished with your editing, you attach your source VCR (or camcorder) and destination VCR (or other camcorder), and the computer will automatically move the source tape to the location you selected in your edit, start it playing and simultaneously start your destination VCR to start recording. When that segment is finished they both stop and move onto the next location, and so on.

The end result is that you've used your computer to help in the editing process, but you haven't actually digitized a storage- and bandwidth-intensive video signal. Most of these types of systems up the ante a bit more by also enabling you to overlay text on the video (called *titles*), add computer-generated graphics, and perform some limited special effects. You achieve these effects on your final, or master, tape by running your source video through a special video-processing box on its way to the destination deck. The following figure shows a typical offline video-editing setup.

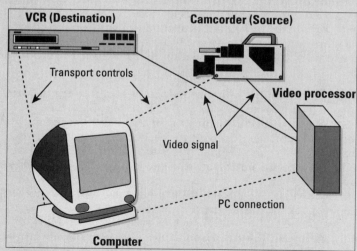

Offline video editing

When creating your master tape with an offline system, the computer and some attached hardware is used to control the transport controls of attached video decks. To create special effects and add titles, the output from the source deck is typically run through a video-processing box (which also attaches to your PC), and then the resulting signal is recorded onto the destination deck as the master tape.

Continued

(continued)

Though these types of systems don't give you the same type of flexibility as a true online editing system, they're much cheaper and can be done with much simpler PCs.

If you want to be able to create more sophisticated video effects, such as true A/B rolls, where one scene fades out while another scene begins to fade in, then you have to use a true online editing system. To do that, however, you need to digitize all your source video, which takes a long time and a lot of space. Once you're done, however, you can cut and paste video segments essentially as you would a word processing file.

Finally, one other piece of equipment you may need to attach to your system is a small television monitor where you can watch the results of your editing work. Many video capture or digitizing cards include a dedicated video output for this purpose.

Capturing the video

As with scanning in photos, getting video into your computer system involves a series of tradeoffs. If you want the highest possible quality, then you're going to take up huge amounts of storage space, and even the speed of the fastest PCs can be dragged down in trying to deal with these enormous files. In fact, if you tried to record uncompressed video at a resolution of 640 × 480 pixels, it would take up to 27MB a second or just over 1.5GB per minute, which is more bandwidth than even today's fastest machines can handle. If you try to work with higher-resolution HDTV signals, the problem gets even worse.

As a result, virtually all video that's digitized, or converted into digital form, on a PC is compressed with some method or other. To play back the compressed video, you also need a decompressor that can reverse the effects of the compression. Taken together, the technologies that perform these operations are called *codecs*. Some codecs are software-based, including Cinepak and Indeo, which means the encoding and decoding can be done in software, while other popular video codecs are usually hardware-based, such as MPEG2, which means you usually need hardware support to both create and play back the files in that format. Some of today's faster processors, however, are enabling things such as software-based MPEG2 playback. In addition, the MPEG4 standard enables video performance to be scaled so that video segments encoded with that standard can be played back with either software or hardware.

Another way to describe the video quality of different compression schemes is in terms of the data transfer rate, usually given in kilobytes or megabytes per second, with higher data rates generally translating to a higher-quality image.

By the way, popular video compression architectures, such as QuickTime and Video for Windows, can incorporate any one of several different codecs.

You inevitably face the tradeoff of image quality versus amount of storage space required, just as you do with scanning images. And once again, there's no right answer. In fact, there's even less agreement when it comes to settings you should use for digitizing video. Still, you can follow the general guideline of setting your scanning resolution (or, in this case, digitization settings) according to the output device(s) on which you intend to use the final result. If you're creating a video for a Web site or CD-ROM, then you can use a codec that's designed for that application (such as Cinepak or Indeo), and if the intended output is DVD (or for recording out to an external tape), you use another (such as MPEG2). Most video programs have guidelines on what specific settings to use for different applications.

Editing

Once you've finally got the video signals onto your PC's hard disk, then the fun begins. As mentioned elsewhere, you can cut and paste video signals to your heart's content, just as you do any other type of digital data. In the case of video, the edit points are often made more visually appealing through the use of wipes and dissolves, which are different types of transition effects, sometimes called *digital video effects* or DVEs, that you can use to segue from one video segment to another.

As with special image-editing effects, effective use of wipes and dissolves can greatly improve the overall look of your video program, but don't overuse them. Most of the time just a straight cut from one video segment to another works best. In fact, most video editors suggest you do a "cuts-only" edit of your video first and then add transitional effects to "sweeten" the final package.

Most video-editing packages now support multiple video and audio tracks, which makes it easy to combine multiple different elements into a montage. This multiple track arrangement is also great for experimenting with such things as briefly using the audio from one segment over the video of another to help create a smoother transition. (In other words, you don't have to cut both the audio and video at the exact same time when joining together two segments.) Figure 15-10 shows an example.

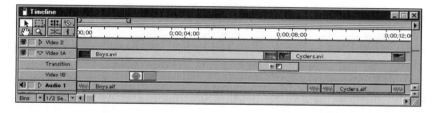

Figure 15-10: Creative edits
One way to create more professional looking and sounding transitions in a video is to edit the video and audio cut points at different times to ease the transition.

Another thing you can do with multiple tracks is to add a musical soundtrack, sound effects, or other ambient noise to the original sound found on your source videotape. Most video-editing programs have a number of audio-mixing features that enable you to adjust the volume levels for different tracks so that you can create the overall effect that you want.

Cross-Reference

See Chapter 16, "Working with Audio and Music," for more on audio-related applications.

Note

Speaking of audio and video, one important point you do have to be aware of is synchronization between the audio signal and the video signal. If you're working on a longer video piece, in particular, you need to make sure that the two different signals stay in sync. In some instances this might even mean cutting out small segments of silence in the audio track to make sure you don't end up with something that looks like a badly dubbed foreign film.

Titles, graphics, and special effects

To really add some professionalism to your videos, you can use your video-editing program's capability to add titles and any other computer-generated graphics either on top of an existing video signal, a technique called *overlay*, or just as visual elements in and of themselves within a certain portion of the overall program.

To give your video a distinctive look, take advantage of one of the many different fonts you probably have installed on your system to create the titles. Again, be careful, when it comes to mixing too many different fonts. In the right hands, a mixture of two different fonts can be very successful, but in the wrong hands, well, just try to remember the days of early desktop publishing and all the horrific-looking flyers that were generated as a result.

In addition to static titles or graphics, most programs enable you to create animated titles by "flying in" words or even individual letters from virtually anywhere on the screen. Similarly, company logos and other graphical elements can follow an interesting path into a particular scene and then fly back out when they're no longer needed. All of these types of motion effects can be powerful when used wisely, but when overused, they get annoying.

When it comes to special effects, most video-editing programs provide a wide variety of different options, including slow-motion, fast-motion, color changes, and more. In addition, the same type of special effects that can be applied to still images can also be applied to moving video, with the additional capability of having the changes occur gradually over time. Many Photoshop plug-ins, for example, work in Adobe's Premiere video-editing package (as well as other video-editing programs) and enable you to do such things as gradually fade a scene into a mosaic-like still image.

Finishing the program

Once you finish making all your edits, adding titles, graphics, and any other special effects, it's time to complete the project. Depending on where the video is going, you either need to send it back out to videotape, or save it in a format that's appropriate for your needs. If it's going back out to videotape, you obviously have to make sure you have all the proper connections, and then check for the proper recording levels on the final recording deck.

If you plan to include the video on a Web site and you want it to be streamed, then you may want to save it in RealVideo format, which is becoming the *de facto* standard for playing video over the Web. (*Streaming* video or audio files means starting to play the file before the whole thing has been downloaded so that you don't have to wait forever for the file to download.) To create a RealVideo file, you may need to download or invest in a RealVideo encoding program if you're video-editing program doesn't natively support that format, or any other format you plan to use. Another option you can consider for video streaming over the Web is Xing StreamWorks, which uses MPEG1 as a codec.

In addition, you have to make sure that the Web site on which you plan to place the file can support video streaming. In other words, you have to find out if it has a streaming video server of some type. If it doesn't, then visitors to the site may have to download the whole video before they can see anything, which most people do not wait for.

Cross-Reference

See the section "Building Your Own Web Site" in Chapter 13, "Connecting To and Using the Internet," for more on Web site issues.

If you plan to use the video in other files, you need to save it in a format that you know is supported by the application you're adding it to, as well as one that the person receiving the document can open and play. Your safest choice in that regard is probably Video for Windows, although QuickTime is also widely supported. To create a Video for Windows or QuickTime file, you'll need to either export it in one of those formats or use the video-editing program's Save As feature to select the proper file type.

Summary

In this chapter I've described how to work with images and video on your PC.

▶ Digital images are stored in several different file formats, most all of which use some type of data compression to save space.

▶ Most scanners come with TWAIN (Technology Without An Interesting Name) software, which you can use to either automatically scan in an image or manually adjust to get just the type of image that you want.

▶ Dot resolutions on scanners, digital cameras, and monitors are very different than dot resolutions on most printers. As a result, you generally shouldn't scan an image at the same resolution as your printer's DPI.

▶ An image's onscreen size and printed size can vary, depending on the scanning resolution and the scaling factor.

▶ Using a Histogram can help you increase the effective resolution of a scanned image.

▶ Virtually all digital images can be improved with some sharpening, but as with many image-editing effects, it's also easy to go overboard.

▶ Stamp and clone tools can help you get rid of blotches and other imperfections in any digital photo.

▶ Magic Wand-type tools enable you to select portions of an image by color instead of by shape. You use this effectively with image masks to make some dramatic retouching effects to digital pictures.

▶ Color management software helps make sure that the colors you see in an original picture are the same colors you see on your monitor and from your color printer.

▶ Online video-editing systems require a fast, well-equipped computer.

▶ The best way to do digital video editing is to make all the cuts between segments first, and then add transitions, titles, graphics, and special effects when you're done.

Chapter 16

Working with Audio and Music

In This Chapter

▶ You will learn how to how to work with digital audio files, such as MP3-format music and how to create your own audio CDs.

▶ You will learn how to record and edit digital audio.

▶ You will learn what MIDI is, how MIDI sequencers and other music programs work, and what accessories you need to make music with your computer.

▶ You will learn how to add digital audio and MIDI files to a Web site.

Space may be the final frontier for *Star Trek* fans, but when it comes to your computer, sound is one of the final barriers that most users cross in their quest to exploit all that their PCs have to offer. Both music and regular audio have been essential parts of the typical computing experience for several years now, thanks to the prominence of sound cards, but few users have done much to explore what's possible with audio on their PCs.

Part of the problem is that many people have presumed that in order to work with sound, they need to have musical skills or somehow be musically inclined. But just as it's possible to do graphics work on your PC with little or no "traditional" art skills, so too, can you work with audio and even create music with no "traditional" music skills. Certainly having musical talents can help, particularly if you're interested in using MIDI (Musical Instrument Digital Interface) software, but they aren't required.

Even if you aren't interested in creating music, many great audio applications work with existing audio files or other audio files you can easily create yourself. More and more Web sites are starting to include audio, for example, and with the popularity of recordable CD drives, it's now easy to create your own CDs with a customized selection of your favorite music.

If you are interested in recording or playing music, a wealth of powerful software tools, including MIDI sequencers and notation programs, as well as applications that enable you to combine MIDI and digital audio are available. In this chapter, I cover all these different types of sound-related applications, and I show you how you can be creative with music and audio.

Getting Started with Sound

Pictures are undeniably fun to look at, but when it comes to really adding life to your PC and/or your Web site, music and audio is really where it's at. (Of course, as a musician, I may be a tad bit biased here.) Seriously, though, music and audio applications are also a great creative outlet that your PC can help you explore. Even if you're not the least bit musically inclined, you can do lots of interesting things with audio on a computer.

What you need

Here are the pieces you need to explore music and audio on your PC. Note that if your primary interest is playing back sounds, some of these requirements are unnecessary.

- A Pentium-class PC with at least 32MB of memory (more if you plan to work extensively with digital audio) and at least a 2GB hard drive (again, more if you want to do a lot of digital audio work).

- Some type of MIDI synthesizer — typically it's available as part of a sound card, although it's possible to have a software-only synthesizer.

- Audio inputs and outputs for recording and playing back digital audio, as well as playing the output of any internal hardware of software synthesizer your system may have — again, audio inputs and outputs are commonly found on sound cards, although some systems have external USB-based devices with the appropriate connections.

- Speakers for hearing both MIDI and digital audio output — most attach straight to the audio outputs on sound cards, but "digital" speakers are also available that use your PC's USB connectors.

- A CD or DVD drive that supports audio CD recording as well as CD recording software if you want to make custom audio CDs.

- Software that enables you to record and playback MIDI files and/or digital audio files — Microsoft's Windows Media Player can play back various types of digital audio and MIDI files, and the basic Sound Recorder program bundled with Windows enables you to record short digital audio files, but to do anything useful, you need a third-party application. On the CD accompanying this book, you will find a demo copy of Cakewalk Home Studio 7 MIDI/Digital Audio Sequencer, and Cakewalk Guitar Studio MIDI/Digital Audio Sequence to get you started.

If you want to work with external MIDI devices, you also need some type of MIDI Interface. Many sound cards enable you to attach a MIDI interface to the joystick/MIDI port found on the card. In most cases, it's simply a cable that has a MIDI input jack, a MIDI output jack (both of which use 5-pin DIN plugs), as well as a pass-through connector for attaching a joystick. In addition, you can buy standalone MIDI interfaces that connect to your PC's USB, parallel, or serial ports, or you can find MIDI ports integrated into external audio multifunction devices that also include audio inputs and outputs.

Playing back sound files

The experience that most computer users have with sound is simply hearing sounds being played back. Whether you're playing a computer game, downloading a piece of music, or listening to a radio show over the Internet, you're somehow involved with getting audio information into your PC and then out to your speakers. You don't have to worry about who created the files or how they were created, you simply need the right mechanism to be able to hear them.

If you're playing a game or using an entertainment title that includes audio, the playback should happen automatically. (If it doesn't, you need to make sure your sound card is properly installed and configured. Under Windows 95 or 98, check the Multimedia control panel as a starting point.) If you want to play a standalone audio file, you need both the right type of "player" application, as well as the appropriate hardware. For example, if you want to download and listen to a piece of music from the Internet that's stored in the popular MP3 format (see the section "File Formats," later in this chapter, for more), you need to have an MP3 audio player, such as the Windows Media Player, WinAmp, or MusicMatch (see Figure 16-1).

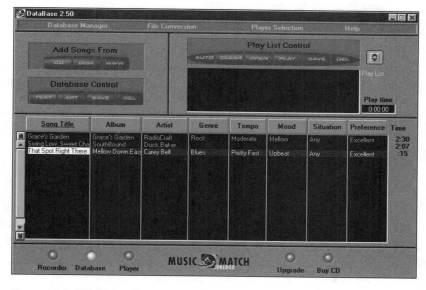

Figure 16-1: MP3 Audio Player
Products such as MusicMatch enable you to play back high-quality MP3 audio files you can download off the Internet on your PC. You can even use it to turn your PC into the equivalent of a digital jukebox.

CD

A copy of the MusicMatch MP3 players, as well as Windows Media Player are included on the CD accompanying this book.

Similarly, if you want to listen to a radio show that's broadcast over the Internet (such as my weekly "O'Donnell on Computers" program, available at `www.everythingcomputers.com`—plug, plug), then you need a program that can handle live audio feeds, such as the popular RealPlayer (see Figure 16-2).

Figure 16-2: RealAudio and RealVideo
The RealPlayer enables you to listen to and/or watch live and recorded audio and video broadcasts over the Internet.

Finally, if you want to play back MIDI files, you need both an application that supports MIDI (such as the standard Windows Media Player) as well as hardware that can generate the sound because MIDI-based audio is actually generated on the fly.

Digital audio basics

In addition to distinguishing between MIDI and digital audio, you also need to be aware of several different digital audio file formats. As with digital pictures, there are several different types of digital audio file formats to choose from, several of which use various types of compression to reduce their size. But before jumping into specific file types, you also need to understand a little about how digital audio works.

Cross-
Reference

For more on file types and extensions, see Chapter 14, "Working with Documents and Files."

Sampling rates and compression

Most sound originates as an audible waveform that we can hear: this is also called an "analog" signal. To get it into a computer or other digital device, this audio waveform must be converted from analog to digital form, a process that's called *sampling*. (Think of digital sampling as the audio equivalent of scanning a picture.) You can perform this sampling process at any number of sample rates and depths. The most common sample rate is 44.1kHz, and the most common sample depth is 16 bits, both of which are used on traditional audio CDs.

It is possible to record at both lower and higher rates, however, which gives you smaller files that don't sound as good or bigger files that, theoretically speaking, at least, sound better, respectively. For example, many basic computer systems sounds, such as beeps and other warnings, are actually 8-bit sounds recorded at 22kHz or even 11kHz. Similarly, some professional audio applications record 24 bits at sampling rates of 96kHz.

The difference between digital audio and MIDI

When it comes to music or sound on a computer, there are two basic types: digital audio and MIDI. Digital audio refers simply to digitized sound. Those sounds could be music, but they could also be sound effects, a human voice, the chirping crickets you might hear on a warm summer evening, or anything else that a microphone can capture. MIDI, or Musical Instrument Digital Interface, on the other hand, is actually not sound at all but a series of events that is typically used to generate music. You can also use MIDI to trigger sound effects, a line of spoken dialog, or any other type of sound, but I'll get to that application a bit later. (See the section "MIDI Basics" later in this chapter for more.)

To use a visual analogy, using MIDI to create music is like creating an illustration with a drawing program, whereas using digital audio is more like scanning a photograph. Either way you can create great music (or great pictures), and in many cases, combining the two gives you the best of both worlds. Most people, however, are more comfortable with simply scanning existing photos, and similarly, most audio applications use existing sound files or easily created sounds (such as your voice).

Virtually all sound cards include a MIDI synthesizer as part of their basic circuitry, but you can also add your own software-based synthesizer to any current system and use it to play back MIDI files instead. To do so, you need to download or purchase the software synthesizer, install it on your system, and then configure the Multimedia control panel to route MIDI files to it. (See the sidebar figure.)

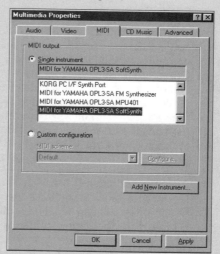

MIDI playback choices
With a software synthesizer installed on your system, you can choose to have that be the "device" that plays back your MIDI files. Inside the Multimedia control panel's MIDI tab, you just have to select it.

For more on synthesis techniques, see Chapter 5, "Sound Cards, Speakers, and Modems."

Lower sample rates have traditionally been used to reduce file sizes (recording CD-quality stereo audio takes about 10MB of disk space per minute), but recently a number of different audio-encoding schemes have been developed to reduce audio file sizes but maintain high quality. (As mentioned previously, recording at lower rates degrades the audio quality.) Some of these techniques use fancy sounding technologies called *perceptual audio coding* or *psychoacoustic modeling*. What these basically do is use information about how the human ear hears (or perceives) audio to be able to figure out what parts of a digital audio signal they can "throw away," and thus, reduce the file size, without drastically affecting the quality.

Probably the most well-known implementation of this technique is MP3 audio files, which reduce audio files by a factor of just over 10:1. "MP3" stands for "MPEG Audio Layer 3," which is an audio compression method originally developed as part of the MPEG (Moving Pictures Experts Group) 1 and MPEG 2 video standards. (Don't confuse the MPEG 1 and 2 with Layer 3. Layer 3 audio is supported in both the MPEG 1 and 2 specs. In fact, a more advanced version called "Structured Audio" is part of the new MPEG 4 spec.) Another relatively common type of audio file that uses this type of compression is *Liquid Audio*.

File formats

The most common types of sound files on PCs are .wav files, which store all the audio data as a single entity in an uncompressed form. Wave files, as they're commonly called, come in a variety of different sample rates and depths. Other similar file types include .au and .aif files. All of these types of files can be played back by standard audio players, including the Windows Media Player, and their sound quality typically depends on the sample rates used to create them. MP3 files, on the other hand, typically start out as 16-bit, 44.1kHz but then are compressed via different audio-coding techniques. One common characteristic that all these file types share is that if you use them or access them via the Internet, they must be downloaded before they can be played.

Another important type of audio files called *streaming audio* do not have this requirement. In fact, the defining characteristic of streaming audio files, which often consist of a live audio signal, are that you can start listening to them before they are completely downloaded. (And many streaming audio files, in fact, cannot be downloaded and saved.) Another important difference is that whereas the fixed types of sound files mentioned in the previous paragraph are used both in desktop applications and on the Internet, streaming audio files are used almost exclusively on the Web.

Virtually any type of existing audio file format can be converted to streaming media, including files with different sample rates and depths. To get the best quality, however, it's best to start out with a high-quality signal, such as a 16-bit, 44.1kHz file, and most streaming files do start out in that form. That doesn't mean all streaming media files are the same, however. The important differentiating factors for streaming audio have to do with the bandwidth they take up.

Bandwidth refers to how much available room there is for transferring data between two points, such as your computer and a particular Web site. The easiest way to understand it is to think of a straw. If you use a coffee stirrer as a straw to try and get a drink from a cup, very little liquid can pass through at any given time, which translates to very little bandwidth. On the other hand, if you used a one-inch hose as a straw, you could transfer a lot more liquid at once, which is the equivalent of a lot of bandwidth. Streaming audio compression systems are designed to squeeze the file into whatever size "straw" or "pipe" you think people use to get access to the file. So, instead of saying you want to use such-and-such a compression ratio, when you create streaming audio (or streaming video) files, you say that you want to take up so much bandwidth. What happens in the background is that the audio-encoding program that converts the files into streaming format adjusts accordingly. For example, to squeeze something into a 28.8Kbps modem connection, which supports at most 28.8Kb, or about 3.5K (28.8 divided by 8 bits per byte) of bandwidth, requires more compression than squeezing the same file through a 128Kbps ISDN (Integrated Services Digital Network) connection.

Cross-Reference

For more on modem types and connection bandwidth, see Chapter 5, "Sound Cards, Speakers, and Modems."

Typical examples of streaming audio include RealAudio (.ra, .rm), QuickTime (.qt), Windows's ASF (.asf) streaming files, and Liquid Audio (.lqt). Unlike other audio files, which have a finite beginning and ending, many streamed audio files are essentially a never-ending flow of data. You listen to them by tapping into the stream for a certain portion of time, just as if you turn on your radio and tune into a certain station for a period of time. Turning your radio off doesn't "end" the station's programming (it continues on regardless of what you do), but it does end your reception of that signal. So, too, when you quit a streaming audio application, the audio stream being broadcast may continue, but you're no longer tapping into it.

Things can get a bit confusing because some streamed files actually consist of prerecorded audio segments (sometimes referred to as *audio archives*) that have a defined ending. In theory, these files could also be saved in something like a .wav format, but most streamed files are heavily compressed to save space, and they have the added advantage of being able to start playing back before the entire file is downloaded, as mentioned previously. In fact, most streaming audio files can start playing after only a tiny portion of the file has been downloaded, which saves a tremendous amount of time.

The only downside to streaming is that it can lead to the audio signal breaking up or momentarily disappearing (sometimes called *dropping out*) while you're playing it. The reason for this is that the streaming player is counting on the capability of getting continuous access to the next chunk of data that it needs to play. If the next chunk doesn't arrive in a timely fashion because Internet traffic between your computer and the site delivering audio suddenly increases, then the player doesn't have anything to play, and you hear a short period of silence in the middle of the signal. Depending on how long it takes for the next chunk to arrive and to refill the streaming media player's buffer, this period of silence may be readily distinguishable, or it may just appear as a brief glitch in the audio. (Unfortunately, if you experience this problem, you can't really do anything about it other than trying it again at a different time when there's less Internet traffic.) In contrast, once a .wav or similar file is loaded onto your system, you shouldn't experience any dropouts when you go to play it because all the necessary information is already there.

The final audio type to discuss is not really a file type at all; they're the audio tracks found on a standard audio CD. Through a process called *audio extraction*, some audio programs can "read" the raw digital audio information on the CD (which is sometimes called *Red Book audio* in honor of the cover of the report that defined the standard) and use it for a number of different applications, including making direct digital copies. In order to be able to use audio extraction, you need to have a CD- or DVD-ROM drive that supports it — not all do.

**Cross-
Reference**

See Chapter 3, "Hard Disks and Removable Drives" for more on CD- and DVD-ROM drives.

Table 16-1 summarizes some common audio file formats and their characteristics.

Table 16-1   Digital Audio Formats

File Extension (Format)	Fixed or Streaming	Compression	Applications
.wav (Wave)	Fixed	None, but variable sample rates and depths	Playing back standard system sounds, audio for games, professional audio recording and editing
.au	Fixed	None, but variable sample rates and sounds	Sounds on Web sites
.aif	Fixed	None, but variable sample rates and depths	Professional audio recording and editing
.pcm or .rbk (raw digital audio from CD)	Fixed	None	CD recording
.mp3	Fixed	Varies between 10:1 and 20:1	High-quality music playback
.lqt (Liquid Audio)	Streaming	Varies between 10:1 and 20:1	High-quality music playback
.ra, .rm, .ram (RealAudio)	Streaming	Varies between 20:1 and 70:1	Broadcasting over the Internet, sound on Web sites
.qt (QuickTime)	Streaming	Varies between 20:1 and 70:1	Broadcasting over the Internet, sound on Web sites
.asf (Windows Media)	Streaming	Varies between 20:1 and 70:1	Broadcasting over the Internet, sound on Web sites

Recording your own CDs

One of the more interesting and straightforward audio applications you can use on your PC is creating your own audio CDs — that is, as along as you have a recordable CD drive or another drive format that supports audio CD recording. You also need an application that supports CD recording, such as Adaptec's Easy CD Creator, and about 650MB of free hard disk space (see Figure 16-3).

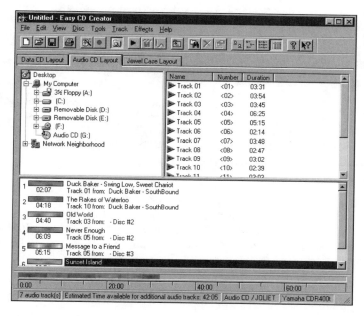

Figure 16-3: Burning CDs
Recording, or "burning," your own CDs involves creating an image, or layout, of the CD on your hard disk and then copying it over to the recordable disc.

With that combination, you can make customized CDs that include your favorite selections from existing audio CDs or your own musical creations. (One concern some people have about doing this is whether or not they're breaking the law.)

In the case of existing audio CDs, many programs use audio extraction to "suck" the audio data straight onto your computer's hard drive — again, if your CD or DVD drive supports it. If it doesn't, many programs can "record" the analog signal from your CD or DVD-ROM drive through your sound card; it's just not as fast. If you have your own music, you typically just need to save it as a .wav file, which is the format most commonly supported by these types of CD mastering programs.

Is this legal?

One question that inevitably comes up (or should come up) whenever you discuss making recordings of existing musical material is about the legality of the practice. Most people know that prerecorded music is copyrighted material, and unauthorized use of copyright material is illegal. However, while making multiple copies of copyrighted material and then selling them is considered unauthorized use, making single copies for your own personal use is not. In other words, putting together your own favorite hits CD from your existing CD collection (which you already bought) is fine.

Where things start to get dicey is if you start using digital audio files you've downloaded off the Internet that you haven't paid for and that were posted without the copyright owner's (typically the record company's) permission. So, for example, if you snag copies of the latest hit from your favorite band's new CD off a Web site that has these "pirated" versions of the songs, then technically speaking, you're breaking the law. While it's doubtful you would ever get caught and punished, the person who posted the file in the first place could get in deep legal trouble.

The music industry has attempted to address this issue with the Secure Digital Music Initiative (SDMI), which provides a type of encryption that ensures that you can download and listen only to files you've paid for.

If you have a bunch of MP3 audio files that you've collected, you first have to convert them into .wav format and then have the CD recording software burn them onto the CD. Traditional audio CD players can not read MP3 files, so you can't just copy them over to a recordable CD and expect to be able to play them.

Digital Audio Recording

In addition to playing back existing audio, it's also easy to create audio files of your own on your PC. Conceptually speaking, using digital audio on a PC is just like making tape recordings on an old cassette recorder. You plug in a microphone or other sound source, hit Record, and you're off. When you're done recording, you hit Play, and whatever sound came in is what you hear back out of your computer's speakers (or whatever speakers you have connected). And, as with stereos, the first thing you have to worry about is getting all the equipment hooked up.

The hookup

Depending on the type of recording you plan to do and how serious you are about it, your computer-based audio setup can be relatively simple or very complex. Figure 16-4 shows a typical setup of equipment used for recording and editing digital audio on your PC.

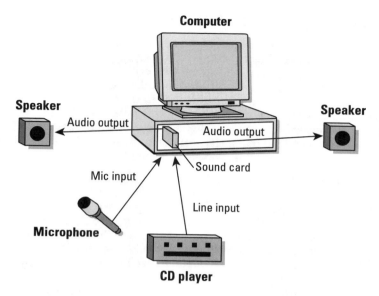

Figure 16-4: Digital audio setup
To record and edit sound on your PC, you need some type of sound input device — typically a microphone and/or a line input. You also need a device to convert the sound from analog to digital format (usually the PC's sound card or other audio-related peripheral) and some type of speakers on which you can hear your results.

If you're working with an audio source that's already in digital form, such as a CD player, DAT (Digital Audio Tape), MiniDisc, or other device with a digital audio output, you need to make sure you have a digital audio input of the right format either built into or somehow connected to your PC. The most common format is S/PDIF (Sony/Philips Digital Interface) on a single RCA plug (the type of connector usually found on stereo equipment and VCRs), but it's not uncommon to see various type of optical connectors and/or the AES/EBU (Audio Engineering Society/European Broadcast Union) signal standard with three-prong XLR connections (the same type used on professional microphones). Another digital connection format that's starting to be used for audio is IEEE 1394.

If you come across any incompatibilities, you may need to invest in a digital audio converter device that takes both the kind of physical connector and the type of audio signal format you have and then convert them into the format and connector type you need. You typically find these types of devices, which are commonly nondescript external black boxes, at music or professional audio stores. They are not a common computer peripheral, although some professional digital audio cards for PCs include multiple connector types and support multiple audio formats to avoid these types of problems.

Recording and editing

Once all the appropriate connections are made, recording and playing back files is just a matter of using standard tape transport controls — record, play, stop, rewind, fast forward, and so on. One critical difference between analog and digital recording is that you need to make sure that the recording levels are set properly and that, in particular, they aren't too high. While analog recorders can be somewhat forgiving in this regard, digital recorders or computer programs that record digitally are not. Sound levels that are recorded too high lead to a nasty form of audio distortion known as *clipping* where the peaks of the audio waveform essentially get "clipped" off.

Unlike tape and CD recorders, audio-editing programs aren't limited to two tracks. You can create dense, multilayered sound collages or complete musical compositions by recording on multiple tracks. The way the multitrack recording process works is you listen to what you've recorded on any or all of the previous tracks while you add a new track. To avoid problems with rerecording signals out of your speakers while using this procedure, which is called *overdubbing*, you generally need to use headphones. Then, when you've got all the tracks you want, you play them all back and adjust their levels, left and right panning and other settings (a process called *mixing down*), and rerecord the output as a traditional two-track stereo file.

Along the way, once you've recorded some files, you can easily cut and paste within the file and between files, as well as perform other simple editing procedures, just as you would with a word processor. The only difference is that you're editing large strings of 1s and 0s that describe an audio waveform instead of words or characters.

One important difference with digital audio editing is the interface you use to see and edit the files. To make it easier to find various points in a file, digital audio-editing programs provide a visual display of the audio waveform that you've recorded. You primarily need to use your ears for audio editing, of course (just as you primarily use your eyes for visual editing), but by looking at the waveform display in an audio-editing program, you can get a visual confirmation of what section you want to cut out or where you want to add a new section to, or whatever editing action it is you want to take.

Figure 16-5 shows a typical example.

Processing

As with editing digital photos, there are a number of things you can and should do with all your digital audio files as soon as you record them (or at some point in the editing process.) The most popular type of audio processing is using *equalization*, commonly shortened to *EQ*. EQ controls enable you to adjust the timbre of the sound, much like a stereo's tone controls, and either accentuate or diminish certain frequencies.

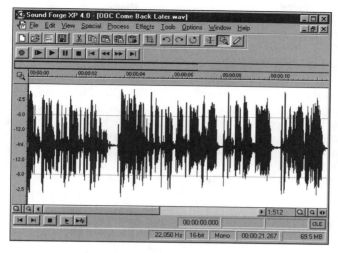

Figure 16-5: Audio waveform display
The primary interface for most audio-editing programs is a visual waveform display, which enables you to see the sound file with which you're working.

Tip

Most people adjust the EQ levels by pushing a particular frequency up, but many times a more effective solution is to bring other frequencies down. This can prevent the sound from getting too "muddy," and it can help avoid clipping problems because adjusting the EQ upward often raises the overall level of the signal.

Speaking of levels, to ensure you're getting the best volume levels, you need to normalize the audio signal. Normalizing finds the loudest point in a file, moves it up to the maximum level that the system can support (before clipping), and then adjusts all the other signals proportionately. If you have a big sound file, this process can take a long time, but the net effect is well worth it, particularly if you were overly cautious and kept your recording levels low. Normalizing files recorded at low levels can really bring them back to life (see Figure 16-6).

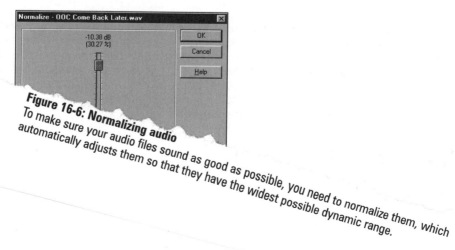

Figure 16-6: Normalizing audio
To make sure your audio files sound as good as possible, you need to normalize them, which automatically adjusts them so that they have the widest possible dynamic range.

Some people normalize their files as soon as they record them, so that they know that they're working with a maximized signal. Others, however, choose to normalize at the end, after they've performed other processing because adjusting an EQ level, for example, can sometimes push a normalized file to the point of clipping.

A related, but different type of processing that can affect a sound's overall levels is called *dynamics processing*. The most common type of dynamics processing is compression, although in this case it has nothing to do with reducing file size. Unlike normalizing, which raises the entire audio signal, compression involves both raising and lowering certain parts of the signal to create a compact, or more compressed, range of levels. So, practically speaking, compression typically lowers higher-level signals and raises lower-level signals. While that may not sound like much on paper, what it does from an audible perspective is make the processed signal sound "punchier" and, in some cases, more rounded. (Many compression effects are very subtle, however, so you really need to listen.)

Special effects

In addition to this basic processing, most digital audio programs provide a lot of other types of audio-processing effects as well. For example, many programs enable you to add ambience to a sound via digital reverb or digital delay-based effects, such as chorusing or flanging.

Reverb, in particular, can make audio files sound much better and more realistic because it provides a natural environment around the sound. Different types of reverbs and different reverb settings can sound dramatically different, so make sure you experiment to find what you like.

Effects such as chorusing or flanging, which basically combine the original signal with a slightly delayed version of the signal, can make sounds fatter and more lively. Again, experiment and listen.

Some audio-editing programs also enable you to do things such as shorten or lengthen the amount of time that a certain file takes to play back, without affecting the pitch. This is called *time compression/expansion*.

If you don't find exactly the effects you're looking for, many audio-editing programs, such as certain image-editing applications, enable you to add effects or different versions of these types of effects through audio plug-ins. Plug-ins are pieces of software that work in conjunction with the host application to bring additional features or capabilities to the program. Under Windows, the most popular plug-in format is DirectX, so if you want the most flexibility, find a program that supports DirectX plug-ins.

Making Music

If you long to extend beyond simple audio recording on your PC, then you can find a wide variety of creative music applications. The audio-editing programs I just described, for example, can be used in place of a multitrack recorder to record original compositions or any music you want to record. In addition, programs are available for creative people without traditional musical skills who want to remix existing audio. Finally, many different types of music software take advantage of the MIDI standard.

Audio remixing

One of the more interesting developments in music over the last few years has been the popularization of music that essentially reuses previous audio material. While many legal and ethical questions about this practice still haven't been resolved, it's undoubtedly had a major impact on the market. Not surprisingly, then, several companies have come up with applications that use the concept (and some clever technology) to help you create your own remixed music.

You can start with some basic music patterns, or "riffs," and combine them to create your own music. For example, you can start out with a repeating drum pattern and then add a previously recorded bass line and various prerecorded guitar parts and so on, until you get what you want. Some programs even enable you to record the result as a standard audio file. The beauty of them is that you don't have to be able to play an instrument to use them (see Figure 16-7).

Figure 16-7: Remixing your own
With a program such as Mixman Studio, you can combine and remix existing musical "riffs"

CD

A demo copy of Mixman Technology's Mixman Studio is on the CD accompanying this book.

MIDI basics

Before getting into any details on different MIDI programs, you need to understand a couple of important concepts about MIDI. (If you already know this stuff, feel free to skip ahead.) As I mentioned before, MIDI is not an audio format but a command language that provides a means for capturing and playing back musical performances.

MIDI consists of a series of different "messages" that are used to describe many aspects of a musical performance, such as what notes to play (sometimes referred to as the *MIDI Note Number*) and how loud to play them (*MIDI Velocity*). In addition, MIDI messages can be used to do such things as select different sounds on a synthesizer (MIDI Program Change), adjust the overall volume level of a section of music (MIDI Volume Control), which is just one of many types of Continuous Controller messages), and much more. MIDI messages are sent on one of sixteen different MIDI channels, all of which can be used simultaneously. Each channel works independently of the other and can carry its own musical "part."

If you're interested in creating your own MIDI files, you typically have a program on your PC called a *MIDI sequencer* whose basic purpose is to record and play back MIDI events. When you hit Play on the sequencing program, the sequence of MIDI events that were recorded and/or specifically added to the file are sent to a device capable of responding to them. This receiving device, which could be built into a sound card or in the form of an external sound module or even a MIDI-equipped musical keyboard, then plays back those messages, and you hear music as the result.

Virtually all receiving devices are referred to as *synthesizers* (or at least the synthesizer portion of a sound card) because they electronically generate, or synthesize, sounds through one of several different methods. Common synthesis methods include FM, or frequency modulation synthesis, wavetable synthesis, and sound modeling synthesis.

Cross-Reference

See Chapter 5, "Sound Cards, Speakers, and Modems," for more on synthesis methods.

The best way to understand MIDI is to think of an old player piano roll, which has a pattern of holes cut into paper. Like MIDI events, those holes "tell" the piano what notes to play and when. In fact, most MIDI sequencing programs feature a piano roll editing mode, where you can view and change the notes that make up a MIDI file. Figure 16-8 illustrates the concept.

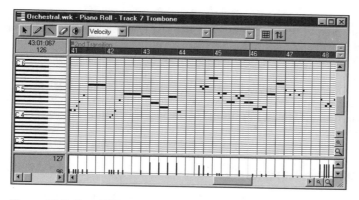

Figure 16-8: How MIDI works
Like a player piano roll, the MIDI events stored in a MIDI file describe the notes that are to
played in order to perform a piece of music.

Despite popular thinking to the contrary, MIDI files do not "sound" a
particular way—they just contain a list of events to play. The sound of
a MIDI file is actually determined by the playback device. For example, a
MIDI file played back through a cheap sound card with a very basic MIDI
synthesizer may sound quite bad, but if the exact same file is played back
through an expensive professional synthesizer, it sounds very good. (In truth,
many elements affect the overall sound quality, some of which I explain a bit
later in this chapter.)

A digital audio file of the same music, on the other hand, essentially always
sounds the same because it is the recording of a specific performance of that
music. (One way to think of the difference between the two is to imagine MIDI
being a piece of sheet music and digital audio being a recording of musicians
playing that music.) The overall quality of the sound card and/or speaker's
audio circuitry also has some impact on a digital audio file, as does any
compression that may be applied to the file, but the basic sound is identical
from computer to computer. The problem is that uncompressed digital audio
files take up tremendously more space than MIDI files, which are quite
compact. For example, a stereo digital audio file made at the CD recording
standard of 44.1kHz consumes about 10MB a minute, whereas a MIDI file that
lasts a minute long could be as little as a few kilobytes—a factor of about
one thousand less! The popular MP3 audio format compresses digital audio
files by a factor of 10:1 or 12:1, but that's still about 100 times larger than
MIDI files.

For this reason and others, MIDI and digital audio files continue to coexist. In fact, the most important trend over the last few years has been the combination of MIDI and digital audio. For music recording applications, in particular, the capability of generating the musical parts via synthesizers and recording and playing back the other parts, such as vocals, acoustic guitar, and electric guitar, and so on, as digital audio has been a very important breakthrough. As a result, most music applications now available for computers support both MIDI and digital audio. The most important of these applications are referred to as *sequencing programs*.

MIDI sequencing

As mentioned earlier, sequencing programs are used to record and play back a sequence of MIDI events, hence their name. What makes them interesting, however, is they enable you to edit your performance to clean it up (or even enter music one note at a time), and as with a multitrack tape recorder, you can build up a complete musical arrangement a piece at a time.

Tracks vs. channels

One of the most confusing parts of sequencing for MIDI newcomers is figuring out the differences between tracks and MIDI channels. A track refers to an individual music part that is recorded separately but then combined with others to create a complete song. For example, in a typical pop song, the guitar part is normally recorded on one track, the drum part on another, the vocals on another, and so on. The MIDI channel, on the other hand, is simply the means used to deliver the track information to the MIDI sound device.

In most cases you assign one track per MIDI channel, but it's possible to record several tracks' worth of data that are all assigned to a single channel. For example, you might want to have your drum kit sounds assigned to MIDI channel 10 but use separate tracks for each different type of drum sound, such as snare drum, bass drum, tom-toms, cymbals, and so on. In this case, all the drum tracks would be assigned to MIDI channel 10. Note that it's also possible to have access to more than 16 MIDI channels. The MIDI specification permits only 16 independent channels per MIDI out port, but if you have multiple MIDI outs, then you can send 16 different channels to each port, and again, they all operate independently.

Operation

Most sequencing programs operate like a tape recorder. You select a track onto which you want to record, select an instrument sound you want to use, hit the Record button, and then play the part. When you're finished, you hit Rewind and then Play. That's all there is to it. Figure 16-9 shows a main screen from Cakewalk Home Studio as an example.

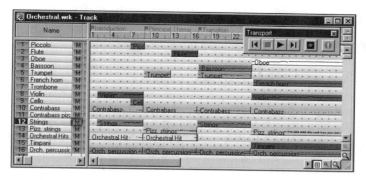

Figure 16-9: MIDI sequencing
Most MIDI sequencers offer familiar, tape transport-like controls that you can use to record and play back individual MIDI parts, or tracks.

Unlike a tape recorder, however, a sequencer enables you to do things such as record at a much slower tempo (for example, if you can't play a particular musical part very quickly) and then play back at a faster tempo without affecting the pitch of what you've recorded. In addition, you can switch the instrument sound (commonly called a *synthesizer patch*, or just *patch* for short) you recorded with to something else after the fact. For example, if you record a part with a flute-like sound and then want to hear what the part sounds like with a more electronic-sounding clarinet-like patch, you can easily do that. When you hit the Play button, the sequencer simply sends out the same series of MIDI note events to the newly selected sound.

Tip

In fact, as mentioned previously, there's a type of MIDI message called a *Program Change* that's usually inserted at the very beginning of a track to make sure that the appropriate programs, or patches, are ready to play. So, in this example, you could simply insert a MIDI Program Change message that called up the clarinet-like sound at the beginning of the sequence. Then, when the sequence was played back, the receiving instrument would respond to the MIDI Program Change by automatically switching over to the correct patch (if it wasn't already selected).

The other characteristic that sequencers share with multitrack tape recorders and digital audio-editing programs is the capability to take advantage of a technique known as *overdubbing*. As described in the digital recording section earlier in the chapter, overdubbing means that you can listen to a previously recorded part (or all the previously recorded parts) while recording a new part. For example, you could build up a complete song by yourself by recording, say, a guitar part first, and then while listening to that part play back, recording a bass guitar part, and then while listening to those two play back, recording an instrumental line, and so on. In addition, if you're making music along with someone else, you can record multiple tracks at once and then add even more tracks on top of those until you get the final musical arrangement that you want.

MIDI connections

The way sequencers typically work is they record incoming MIDI events from the MIDI input port of a MIDI interface onto a particular track, and then they play those MIDI events back out through the MIDI output port on the MIDI interface when you hit Play. The MIDI interface, in turn, is typically connected to your sound card's MIDI/joystick port, although standalone MIDI interfaces are also available that attach to your PC's USB, serial, or parallel ports.

If you have nothing more than a sound card, you can still take advantage of MIDI software by entering notes one note at a time through your computer keyboard or with your mouse. Playback can also be routed directly to your sound card's built-in synthesizer. Under Windows, to see where MIDI data is being routed, open the Multimedia control panel, and click the MIDI tab.

To make your musical data entry more efficient, however, you're better off investing in some type of MIDI controller, which is an instrument that generates MIDI commands, and attaching it to a MIDI interface. Most MIDI controllers come in the form of keyboards, but many other types correspond to lots of different instruments including MIDI guitars, MIDI wind controllers (which are somewhat similar to electronic soprano saxophones), MIDI drum pads, and a lot more.

Note

Many MIDI controllers, particularly keyboards, also generate sounds, but not all MIDI controllers do. Many guitar, wind, and drum controllers, for example, generate only MIDI data and so must be used in conjunction with a sequencer and/or a MIDI sound source (such as a synthesizer) to generate music. Similarly, several companies sell inexpensive MIDI keyboards designed for use with computers that generate only MIDI data—think of them as an alternative input device for your PC. If you have one of these MIDI-only controllers, or if you simply want to have access to more sounds, you can hook them up with a MIDI sound module, which is a box whose sole purpose is to receive MIDI data and generate sounds.

Secret

Keyboard synthesizers with their own sounds essentially combine the capabilities of a MIDI controller and a MIDI sound module into a single device. If you want, however, you can usually disconnect those two by taking advantage of a feature called "Local Off." When you select the Local Off option on your keyboard, any notes you play still generate MIDI data and are sent out the keyboard's MIDI output jack, but they won't play the keyboard's internal sounds. This feature can come in handy while you're doing MIDI sequencing with a PC because at times you want to control other MIDI devices and not hear the internal sounds when you play.

To give you a better idea of a typical example, take a look at Figure 16-10, which shows a typical MIDI sequencing setup.

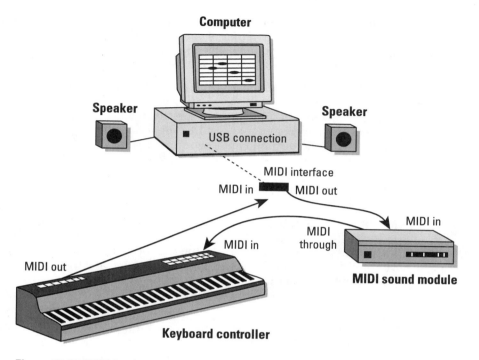

Figure 16-10: MIDI hookup
To use a sequencing program with external MIDI devices, you need some type of MIDI interface for your PC. In this example, the MIDI keyboard is being used as the controller, and its output is connected to the USB-based MIDI interface's MIDI input. The MIDI output from the MIDI interface, in turn, is connected to the MIDI sound module's MIDI input. Finally, the MIDI Through connection on the sound module is connected back to the keyboard's MIDI input.

MIDI Through is a special type of connector found on some MIDI devices that passes along an exact duplicate of the MIDI messages received at the MIDI input onto another MIDI device. In the example in Figure 16-10, you could have reversed the last two connections between the sound module and the keyboard if the keyboard also had a MIDI Through jack. (If it didn't, of course, then you couldn't.) Either way, the same MIDI messages get sent from the MIDI interface to both the sound module and the keyboard.

Another option is that some MIDI interfaces include multiple MIDI outputs. Depending on how the device and your MIDI software are configured, you could connect each device to its own dedicated MIDI output on the MIDI interface. As mentioned earlier, this is how you can get around the limitation of 16 MIDI channels.

Finally, if you want to record digital audio along with your MIDI sequences, you simply connect the output of your audio sound source (for example, a microphone, electric guitar, audio mixer output, or what have you) into the audio inputs of your sound card or other audio input device.

To hear everything you need to connect the audio outputs of your sound card/audio output device to a set of speakers. If you want to hear both the sound from your MIDI devices and the digital audio from the same set of speakers, you may need to invest in a separate audio mixer. As its name implies, an audio mixer combines, or mixes, the signals from multiple sources down into a single stereo output, which you can then plug into your sound card. Some speakers and/or sound cards have a separate audio input (commonly called a *line input*) that you may be able to use for this purpose, but not all do.

In addition to all the cables you need to make this connection, you may have to deal with connector issues and adapter plugs. In most cases you need some kind of adapter plug to take the RCA or quarter-inch jack outputs from your MIDI device into the stereo eighth-inch mini-plug that's commonly found on computer speakers. Check your local Radio Shack or similar electronics store if you have trouble tracking one down.

If you do end up needing an audio mixer, then you plug the audio outputs of all your MIDI devices as well as the audio output of your sound card/audio output device into the mixer's audio inputs. Then you can take the audio output of the mixer and either plug it back into your sound card/audio input device's line input in order to hear it on your computer's speakers, or invest in a separate set of higher-quality speakers. Figure 16-11 shows a layout with both audio and MIDI connections.

Editing

Recording and playing back MIDI sequences is all fine and dandy, but, ultimately, not that practical. What really makes sequencing programs powerful tools are the editing tools they provide. And because MIDI sequences are nothing more than a big series of individual events, editing sequences is often a fairly straightforward process. With a sequencer, for example, you can copy and paste small portions of a single track to create a repeating pattern or move large chunks of multiple tracks to completely rearrange your song. You can also quickly find and delete a clunker or two from your performance, or do such things as increase the volume, length, and/or pitch of a specific note or an entire range of notes.

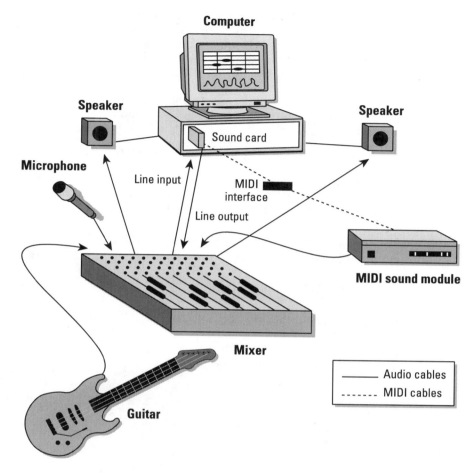

Figure 16-11: MIDI and digital audio
If you want to record and mix digital audio signals along with your MIDI tracks, the setup can get a bit more complicated. In particular, it's very common to require an audio mixer in order to be able to hear your MIDI and audio parts from the same set of speakers (which is important to do).

Editing Views

The most important thing to understand about MIDI editing is that you can view the same MIDI sequence data in numerous different ways, and different views are better suited for different types of editing. In some cases these views are designed to work on multiple tracks at once, but they're most commonly used to work on tracks individually. Most programs, for example, include both a piano roll view (sometimes called a "graphic-editing view") and an event list view. A piano roll view is great for transposing notes upward or downward, or lengthening or shortening a particular note. Event lists and event filters, which enable you to select a specific group of events based on parameters, or filters, that you enter, on the other hand, are good for performing global operations such as increasing the MIDI velocity on all the notes in a particular region. (As mentioned previously, MIDI velocity refers to a particular characteristic of each MIDI note that determines how loud the note is to be played.)

If you read music, then you should find a music program that also enables you to view the parts you've recorded (as well as edit them) in standard music notation. Not all programs can, by the way, so make sure you specifically look for this feature if you want it. Figure 16-12 shows an example of all three different types of views.

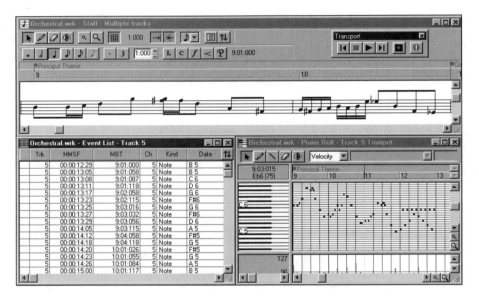

Figure 16-12: Multiple editing views
Most MIDI sequencing programs enable you to view your data in one of several ways including notation view, event list view, and piano roll view. In all cases, they're simply different ways to view and edit the same data.

If your sequencer program supports digital audio and you're also working with digital audio tracks, the program also offers a waveform editing view for each of them that's similar to what you find in standalone digital audio-editing programs.

In addition to all these individual track views, most programs also offer several global views of all the different tracks. The main view typically enables you to see and organize large sections of the piece, and a console view enables you do things such as mix, or adjust the overall volume levels, of each of the different individual tracks.

Quantization

One of the most important types of MIDI editing is typically not done in an edit window at all. *Quantization*, which basically means to move notes in time toward a user-definable grid, is commonly used to clean up the timing of notes in an imperfect performance. For example, if you're creating a drum pattern by using the keys of a MIDI keyboard controller, there's a good chance that all of your notes won't exactly be in tempo. (By the way, most programs provide a metronome sound that you can listen to while you record.) To fix those timing imperfections, you can tell the sequencer that you want to quantize that track (or even just a portion of it) by choosing Quantize from the program's Edit menu — or wherever you happen to find it.

Think of quantizing as a snap-to-grid feature in a graphics program, and you get the basic idea. By selecting a note resolution that you want to quantize to, you determine the resolution of the grid. For example, if you quantize to eighth notes, every note you play is moved to the nearest half a beat (which is one-eighth of a standard 4/4 measure). If you quantize to sixteenth notes, however, they are moved to the nearest quarter of a beat. Depending on the quality of your original performance, those two different settings may end up moving the notes to the same spot, but there can be differences as well.

Tip

As helpful as quantizing can be, it can also be overdone and overused. Most music performed by humans has some timing imperfections so if you quantize too strictly, you end up with lifeless sounding music. To compensate for this effect, most programs offer partial quantizing or swing quantizing options that move the notes a certain percentage toward the quantize grid, but not necessarily all the way there. While this concept wouldn't work for graphics, it's often very effective in music because it can improve the timing on a particular track without making the music sound robotic. Figure 16-13 compares straight quantizing with partial quantizing so that you can see the difference.

As with most music-editing operations, you need to listen to the results of any quantizing that you do to see if it gives you the results you want. Some programs can actually make quantization adjustments while the music is playing so that you can hear the effects of your edits in real time. Other programs need to stop before you can make any changes to the quantizing parameters.

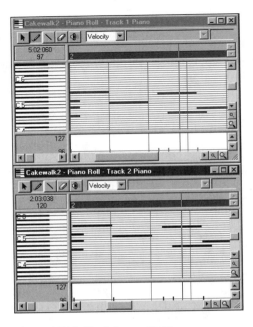

Figure 16-13: Partial quantization
The top track of this screen shows a track that has been strictly quantized to sixteenth notes, whereas the bottom shows a copy of the same original track that's been only partially quantized. Notice how the notes don't exactly start and end on the beat markers.

The final mix

The bulk of the work in using MIDI sequencers is typically done in recording and editing the individual tracks. But once you've finished that part, you can do other manipulations to complete your performance. For example, you can make adjustments to the song's tempo by slowing up or speeding down certain sections to give it a more human feel. (As with all these types of manipulations, however, this effect can be overdone, so be careful. Just use your ears, listen to what you've done, and make sure you like the way it sounds.)

Tempo changes are typically made through something called the "Tempo Map," which is a listing of all the time signatures and tempos used in a particular song. In most cases you have to manually enter any changes you want to make to the Tempo Map, but it's usually not much different than inserting any other MIDI event into a sequence.

The most important step you want to do is referred to as the *final mixdown*. This step occurs when you listen to all the different parts together and make adjustments to the volume levels of the different tracks. Many sequencers provide a mixer-like console view specifically for this purpose. When you make adjustments to the onscreen faders, which is the specific name for the volume controls used to adjust each track, the sequencer typically records those adjustments as a series of MIDI Volume Control messages. As with MIDI note messages, you can edit those as you see fit. In fact, some programs enable you to draw curves of MIDI controller messages in order to do things such as program in a fade-in or fade-out. See Figure 16-14 for an example.

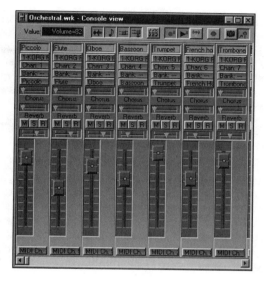

Figure 16-14: Making the mix
Most MIDI sequencers offer a mixer-like console view where you can record MIDI Volume and other types of MIDI controller messages. In addition, you can often use a graphic-editing view to quickly edit a whole series of MIDI volume messages, such as when you want to create a fade-out for your song.

When you're finally done with your musical arrangement, you can save it either in the program's default file format or in the more generic Standard MIDI file (.mid) format. If you plan on sharing the sequence with a friend or using it on the Internet, use Standard MIDI File format because it is the generic interchange format that's typically used with MIDI sequences.

There are three types of Standard MIDI Files: Type 0, Type 1, and Type 2, with Type 0 combining all data into a single track. Type 1 offers support for up to 256 tracks, and Type 2, which is rarely used, offers the equivalent of multiple Type 0 sequences in a single file. Most sequences that are shared on the Internet are stored in Type 0 format, so keep that in mind as you prepare your files. One limitation with Standard MIDI Files is that they currently don't support combining MIDI and digital audio in a single file — they are for MIDI data only. If you want to share a combination MIDI/digital audio file, you have to use a different format, such as the QuickTime streaming format. Also, Microsoft's DirectMusic API supports this capability by taking advantage of the DLS (DownLoadable Samples) 2 specification. (See the next section for more on DLS.)

General MIDI

In addition, if you're sharing your work with others, you want to make sure your sequence conforms to the General MIDI specification, which is a standard that defines a common set of synthesizer patches (among other things). There are two important steps you need to do to achieve this. First, make sure you insert a special MIDI System Exclusive event (a general type of MIDI message) that turns GM mode on at the very beginning of your sequence. This ensures that the receiving device is ready to play back a GM sequence.

Tip

To make sure everything works properly, add one measure of silence at the beginning of your GM sequences. This gives the receiving devices time to switch to GM mode.

The second thing you have to do is select patches that conform to the General MIDI standard. As I mentioned at the beginning of this section, MIDI files do not necessarily determine how a particular piece of music sounds. They can, however, include a selection of Program Change messages that tell a connected MIDI device what patches to play for a particular song. But what happens if patch 53 on your sound module is a violin, and the same patch number is a trombone on my sound card? I definitely won't hear what you intended, that's for sure.

To get around this problem, a group of musical instrument manufacturers called the MIDI Manufacturers Association (MMA) developed a set of 128 standardized patches, grouped into 16 banks of 8, and made them part of the General MIDI (GM) specification. By using sequences files that conform to GM, as well as a sound source that has a set of General MIDI patches, you can be assured that the sounds you're getting are at least close to what the creator of the piece intended (or that whomever listens to your work hears something close to what you intended). The result won't be identical because each synthesizer creates, say, a trumpet sound in a slightly different way, but at least it will be similar. If you try to play the same sequence with a different set of patches that don't conform to General MIDI, on the other hand, you could end up with a *very* strange set of results.

Note

To determine if your sound-generating device is compatible with General MIDI, look for the official General MIDI logo on its packaging or the device itself (see Figure 16-15).

Figure 16-15: General MIDI logo
If your sound card or other MIDI sound source displays the official General MIDI (GM) logo, then you know that it works with sequencer files that conform to the GM spec.

Table 16-2 lists the patches that make up the General MIDI specification.

Table 16-2	General MIDI Patches	
Patch Group	*Patch Name*	*MIDI Program Change #**
Piano	Acoustic Grand Piano	1
	Bright Acoustic Piano	2
	Electric Grand Piano	3
	Honky-tonk Piano	4
	Electric Piano 1	5
	Electric Piano 2	6
	Harpsichord	7
	Clavichord	8
Chromatic Percussion	Celesta	9
	Glockenspiel	10
	Music Box	11
	Vibraphone	12
	Marimba	13
	Xylophone	14
	Tubular Bells	15
	Dulcimer	16

Continued

Table 16-2 *(continued)*

Patch Group	Patch Name	MIDI Program Change #*
Organ	Drawbar Organ	17
	Percussive Organ	18
	Rock Organ	19
	Church Organ	20
	Reed Organ	21
	Accordion	22
	Harmonica	23
	Tango Accordion	24
Guitar	Acoustic Guitar (nylon)	25
	Acoustic Guitar (steel)	26
	Electric Guitar (jazz)	27
	Electric Guitar (clean)	28
	Electric Guitar (muted)	29
	Overdriven Guitar	30
	Distortion Guitar	31
	Guitar Harmonics	32
Bass	Acoustic Bass	33
	Electric Bass (finger)	34
	Electric Bass (pick)	35
	Fretless Bass	36
	Slap Bass 1	37
	Slap Bass 2	38
	Synth Bass 1	39
	Synth Bass 2	40
Strings	Violin	41
	Viola	42
	Cello	43
	Contrabass	44
	Tremolo Strings	45
	Pizzicato Strings	46
	Orchestral Harp	47
	Timpani	48

Patch Group	Patch Name	MIDI Program Change #*
Ensemble	String Ensemble 1	49
	String Ensemble 2	50
	Synth Strings 1	51
	Synth Strings 2	52
	Choir Aahs	53
	Voice Oohs	54
	Synth Voice	55
	Orchestra Hit	56
Brass	Trumpet	57
	Trombone	58
	Tuba	59
	Muted Trumpet	60
	French Horn	51
	Brass Section	62
	Synth Brass 1	63
	Synth Brass 2	64
Reed	Soprano Sax	65
	Alto Sax	66
	Tenor Sax	67
	Baritone Sax	68
	Oboe	69
	English Horn	70
	Bassoon	71
	Clarinet	72
Pipe	Piccolo	73
	Flute	74
	Recorder	75
	Pan Flute	76
	Blown Bottle	77
	Shakuhachi	78
	Whistle	79
	Ocarina	80

Continued

Table 16-2 *(continued)*

Patch Group	Patch Name	MIDI Program Change #*
Synth Lead	Lead 1 (square)	81
	Lead 2 (sawtooth)	82
	Lead 3 (calliope)	83
	Lead 4 (chiff)	84
	Lead 5 (charang)	85
	Lead 6 (voice)	86
	Lead 7 (fifths)	87
	Lead 8 (bass + lead)	88
Synth Pad	Pad 1 (new age)	89
	Pad 2 (warm)	90
	Pad 3 (polysynth)	91
	Pad 4 (choir)	92
	Pad 5 (bowed)	93
	Pad 6 (metallic)	94
	Pad 7 (halo)	95
	Pad 8 (sweep)	96
Synth Effects	FX 1 (rain)	97
	FX 2 (soundtrack)	98
	FX 3 (crystal)	99
	FX 4 (atmosphere)	100
	FX 5 (brightness)	101
	FX 6 (goblins)	102
	FX 7 (echoes)	103
	FX 8 (sci-fi)	104
Ethnic	Sitar	105
	Banjo	106
	Shamisen	107
	Koto	108
	Kalimba	109
	Bag Pipe	110
	Fiddle	111
	Shanai	112

Patch Group	Patch Name	MIDI Program Change #*
Percussive	Tinkle Bell	113
	Agogo	114
	Steel Drums	115
	Wood Block	116
	Taiko Drum	117
	Melodic Tom	118
	Synth Drum	119
	Reverse Cymbal	120
Sound Effects	Guitar Fret Noise	121
	Breath Noise	122
	Seashore	123
	Bird Tweet	124
	Telephone Ring	125
	Helicopter	126
	Applause	127
	Gunshot	128

*Some devices default to 0-127 instead of 1-128. If so, you may need to adjust the device's settings to get the right sounds.

The General MIDI spec consists of more than just patches, including esoteric topics such as specified controller mappings and more, but the patches are the most important. By the way, not all GM-compliant devices use the exact names shown in Table 16-2, so don't be surprised if Patch 89 isn't called Pad 1 (new age). The basic sound, however, will conform to the general requirements of the specific GM patch.

As helpful as General MIDI is, it still suffers from limitations, particularly if composers want to create a more exact replication of certain sounds or want to use something that isn't among the available choices. To help in this regard, a specification called Downloadable Samples, or DLS, was also developed by the MIDI Manufacturers Association. DLS, which is now known as DLS-2, enables you to take advantage of either the onboard RAM that many sound cards have or the system memory that sound cards can access to load specific sounds into that memory and then play them back.

For example, if you need a particular sound effect, a piece of spoken dialog, a vocal line, or a unique instrument sound to be part of your overall musical piece, you can save that sound as a downloadable sample and use it along with a standard MIDI file. Then, when that MIDI sequence is loaded, the audio information is loaded into the memory available to the sound card, and that customized sound can be played, or triggered, just as any other instrument sound can be. The benefit is that you can create different sounds for different songs (or for different games, if you're creating music for a computer game).

Tip

You can find out more about both the General MIDI and Downloadable Samples specifications at the MIDI Manufacturer's Association Web site at www.midi.org.

Music notation

MIDI sequencing programs are undeniably powerful tools, but if you're a classically trained musician (or at least took piano lessons as a kid), then you may be more comfortable working with music in standard notation form. As I mentioned in the previous section, many sequencers offer a basic notation view for simple editing, but they're not always ideally suited for those who want to compose on an electronic form of musical manuscript. Also, not all sequencing programs support music notation printing, or if they do, the output is relatively crude. For example, you may not be able to put in dynamic markings or other elements that are essential to high-quality printed music.

To address these issues, many companies have developed software that's generically referred to as "music notation software." As their name implies, these programs are primarily designed to generate high-quality musical printouts that you can share with other musicians. Some notation programs are designed solely for creating printed music; in essence, they're like desktop music publishing programs. These programs don't work with MIDI at all. Other programs support MIDI recording and playback, á la a sequencer, but are primarily designed to work with music in traditional form. These types of programs basically use MIDI input as a faster form of data entry and playback as an audible means of "proofing" your work.

One of the dilemmas with music sequencing and notation that you're bound to come across is that music notation is essentially an interpreted language, whereas a MIDI sequence is a very exact description of events. For example, a piece of music with four quarter notes on it is played slightly differently by each person that reads it, with each note a slightly different length than the others. In a sequenced file, however, four precisely measured quarter notes are always exactly the same length. The problem is that if a ordinary person plays those four quarter notes into a sequencing program set to display the notes in notation, you might actually see three double-dotted eighth notes, 32nd note rests, and one quarter note, instead of four quarters. The reason is that the sequencer expects the notes to be a certain number of ticks long, and if they're not within a tight window of tolerance, you end up with confusing notation. And as soon as you start to play more complicated music, the situation gets much worse (see Figure 16-16).

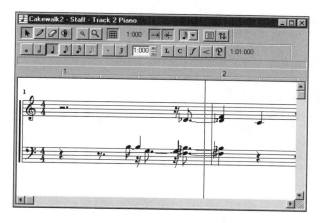

Figure 16-16: Messy music notation
Depending on how your sequencing or notation software is set, playing even a simple set of notes could lead to a very confusing bit of notation, full of short rests and notes of unusual lengths.

To compensate for this, some sequencing programs and virtually all notation programs have a setting that enables you, in effect, to "quantize" the notation, without actually affecting the imprecise, but human-sounding, MIDI data you recorded. As a result, the exact same set of MIDI data that caused the messy notation in the previous example can give you the four quarter notes you expected to see. When you play it back, however, the notes maintain the minute differences in length you originally recorded.

In addition to basic notes, some notation programs enable you to assign specific sets of MIDI commands to certain types of musical markings. For example, some programs do such things as automatically lower the MIDI velocity of all the notes in a section of music that's marked with the pp (short for *pianissimo*, which means to play very softly) or any other dynamic marking. In addition, adding a crescendo can generate a series of increasing MIDI volume commands, which can be effective in simulating the sound of the music you've composed.

Generally speaking, MIDI sequencers are better suited for musicians who are relatively competent players, whereas MIDI-based notation programs are better for composers who may not be particularly adept at performing.

Other MIDI software

In addition to MIDI sequencers and notation programs, other types of MIDI software are available that you can use for a variety of useful applications. Two of the most popular are patch editor/librarians and auto-accompaniment programs. Patch editors and the related sample-editing programs enable you to create and manage custom sounds for your MIDI synthesizers, and auto-accompaniment programs provide an instant backup band that you can play along with at any time of the day or night.

Patch editor/librarians

Modern synthesizers, both standalone keyboards and the synthesizer capabilities built into most sound cards, are sophisticated devices and use a variety of different sound-generating techniques to create their different sounds, or patches. In fact, it's not uncommon to have several hundred different parameters, or control settings, that go into making each different patch.

Many synthesizers have limited displays, however, which makes it difficult to look at or edit all of those parameters. As a result, many companies have developed software programs that can display (and enable you to adjust) all the parameters for a synthesizer's patches on your PC. These patch editors enable you to easily change existing or create new patches. They also typically enable you to store thousands of different patches, more than can be stored inside the synthesizer's limited patch memory, and then load new sounds into the synthesizer as banks of new patches. In addition, these programs incorporate librarian-like features, much like a simple database, that enable you to organize and find patches.

Editor/librarian programs use MIDI System Exclusive, or SysEx, commands to send and receive both individual patches as well as entire banks, or groups, of patches between the MIDI synthesizer/sound card and your PC. System Exclusive commands are used to send information back and forth between your PC and synthesizer (or between any two MIDI-equipped devices) about things such as the different types of parameters that are available to change in a particular sound. Because of this "exclusive" nature, they are unique to the individual type of synthesizer. As a result, you need to have either a different patch editor for each MIDI device you want to edit on your PC or, if you're using a universal editor/librarian, a unique profile for each device. A universal editor/librarian is a program that can work with a variety of different MIDI devices by plugging in different software "profiles" that show the proper controls onscreen (and send the appropriate MIDI SysEx commands when you adjust them). To work with different devices, you just load the different "profiles." Some sequencing programs offer somewhat similar capabilities for editing synthesizers via custom-created graphical front panels. Figure 16-17 shows an example.

In addition to various types of synthesis, many sound cards and other MIDI sound sources include the capability to play back short digital audio files called *samples*. Devices that have this capability are called *samplers* or, if they're used together with other synthesis methods, *synthesizer/samplers*. And just as patch-editing programs enable you to edit and create new sounds for true synthesizers, sample-editing programs are used to edit the digital audio samples used by these devices. Because samples are really not much different than regular digital audio files, however, many audio-editing programs also function as sample editors.

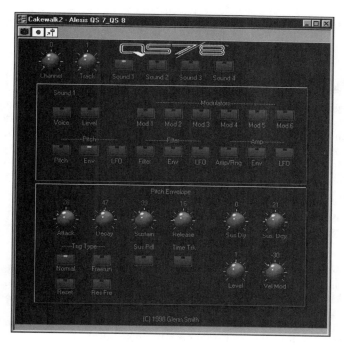

Figure 16-17: Patch editing
You can edit the many available parameters of certain synthesizers via graphical front panels, such as this StudioWare panel created for Cakewalk Home Studio.

Auto-accompaniment software

Another popular kind of MIDI software is auto-accompaniment software. Programs such as Band-in-a-Box and others that offer this capability automatically create background accompaniment that you can play along with. For example, if you want to learn a new song, or just play for fun, you can set these programs to play back particular songs, particular chord changes, or just particular styles. They generate a sequence of MIDI data that gets sent out to any MIDI devices you have attached (or straight to certain sound cards) and voilá — instant backup band!

These programs are particularly helpful for people who play solo instruments, such as saxophone, trumpet, trombone, and so on, but they're also fun for guitarists, pianists, drummers, and other musicians because you can always turn off the instrument part you want to play.

Tip

By the way, you can achieve a similar effect by simply downloading and/or purchasing Standard MIDI files of songs that you want to learn or play and loading them into your sequencer. Unlike this method, however, which sounds the same each time you play it, auto-accompaniment programs generate their music dynamically, which means it's somewhat different every time. This, in turn, makes it more like playing along with a real band (and more fun as a result).

A demo copy of Cakewalk In Concert automatic accompaniment software is included on the CD accompanying this book.

Putting Sound Files on the Web

Regardless of how you create your audio files and regardless of whether or not you use MIDI, digital audio, or both, tools and techniques are available for adding those files to your Web site (or any other sites you might work on). In most cases the process simply involves converting or saving the files in the proper format, uploading them to the Web server that hosts your site (and also holds all your HTML pages), and then pointing to the files from your Web pages.

By the way, the exact same principles hold true for adding video or any other media files to your site.

Converting files

The most important step is figuring out which formats you want to use. Depending on the intended application and audience, you've got a number of different choices that affect the size and quality of the files, as well as the requirements that users visiting your site must fulfill.

If you want to share your musical creations with the world, MP3 is probably a good choice, although not everyone has an MP3 player. Another choice might be the Liquid Audio format. On the flip side, virtually everyone has an audio player that can handle .wav files, but using .wav files means a long, slow download that most users aren't willing to wait through. MIDI files, on the other hand, download extremely quickly and are almost universally supported, but their audio quality depends entirely on the quality of the synthesizer that the site visitor's computer has. If that's okay with you, then fine, but if not, you need to think of something else.

One of the streaming media formats is probably best for general-purpose audio because they support compressed files, and a lot of people now on the Web have some type of streaming player. Of course, because several competitive standards exist, you're still stuck with a file format that isn't always ubiquitous. You can get around this limitation somewhat by offering a link to a compatible player near any links to your audio files, but this solution isn't ideal.

If you use a streaming media format, you also have to determine what bandwidth levels you want to support. So, for example, if you want to support only 56Kbps modem connections and faster, you get a higher-quality sound file because less compression is necessary to squeeze it into the available bandwidth of a 56Kbps modem than would be necessary to support 28.8Kbps modem connections. On the other hand, users who come to your site with only a 28.8Kbps modem or even less, won't be able to listen to the file because they won't have enough bandwidth to handle the rate that the audio file is streamed to them.

Another consideration with certain types of streaming media files is that you may also need to install or have access to a streaming media server program on your Web server. That can add a lot of cost and complexity to the project, and there's a good chance your Web hosting company won't permit it (unless you're hosting your own site, of course). If you don't expect a whole lot of traffic on your site, this limitation isn't usually a problem, but it is something you need to consider.

Once you've decided on a format, the next step is getting your audio files into that format. In many cases, this may be as simple as doing a Save As or Export in your MIDI sequencer or digital audio-editing program. If the program you created the files in doesn't support the format you want, you may need to look for a conversion utility to do the dirty work for you.

Adding them to your pages

With all the files in the right format, you can move on to adding them to your site's pages. The way you do that depends on if you want to just put a link to the audio files that either starts the downloading or streaming process, or if you want the files to start playing automatically as soon as someone loads a page.

In the case of downloading, say, an MP3 or MIDI file, all you need to do is put in an FTP (File Transfer Protocol) link to the file itself, just as you would normally put in an HTTP (HyperText Transport Protocol) link to another Web page. You also, then, need to make sure that the file is located in the FTP folder on your Web server that your link is pointing to and that the Web server hosting your site supports file transfer via FTP (not all have this capability turned on). For example, to get to a file MySong that's saved in MP3 format, you put in a link such as `ftp://www.mysite.com/mysong.mp3`.

To get someone to start playing a streaming audio file from a regular Web server (and not a dedicated streaming media server), you often just need to create a normal HTTP link that site visitors can click. Some streaming media formats also require an interim document called a *metafile* that contains nothing more than a pointer to the actual audio content, but most programs that encode the audio into the streaming format can help create this file for you.

Finally, if you want a file to start playing as soon as you download a page, you need to embed the file into the top of the page with an HTML Embed tag. Because these files won't start playing (and sometimes the page won't even appear) until the file has been completely downloaded, it's only practical with small .wav, .au digital audio files, or MIDI files.

Cross-Reference

For more on HTML tags, see the section "Building Your Own Web Site" in Chapter 13, "Connecting to and Using the Internet."

Summary

In this chapter I covered how to work with sound on your PC, including both digital audio and MIDI.

▶ Digital audio files come in many different formats, and playing back these different sound files requires the right type of player application.

▶ Streaming audio files differ from standalone files in that you can start listening to them almost instantly.

▶ You can create your own customized CDs with a recordable CD drive, CD recording software, and some room on your hard disk.

▶ Recording audio on your PC is no harder than doing it with a cassette recorder, but you've got a tremendously larger degree of flexibility with your PC.

▶ Digital audio-editing programs enable you to easily optimize the quality of your recorded audio and apply a wide range of audio-processing effects.

▶ Even if you don't have any musical skills, you can create your own original music with programs that enable you to remix existing musical patterns.

▶ MIDI is a technology that's used to capture musical performance data, as opposed to an audio signal.

▶ MIDI sequencing involves recording and editing a variety of different MIDI messages. Those messages can be generated by certain types of musical keyboards or any other MIDI-equipped instruments.

▶ General MIDI is a standard that defines an agreed-upon set of synthesizer sound patches.

▶ Music notation programs enable you to lay out and print traditional music notation.

▶ Auto-accompaniment programs use MIDI to provide musicians with an instant backup band.

▶ Using audio files on Web sites involves saving the files in the right format, uploading them to your Web server, and then pointing to them from within your site's pages.

Part V

Fixing Your PC

Chapter 17: Troubleshooting Techniques

Chapter 18: Solving Common PC Problems

Chapter 17

Troubleshooting Techniques

In This Chapter

▶ You will learn how to develop a troubleshooting strategy so that you can focus in on the problem (or problems) your computer is experiencing.

▶ You will learn how to check for common problems.

▶ You will learn the basic techniques for fixing hardware-related problems, including IRQ conflicts.

▶ You will learn the basic techniques for fixing software-related problems, including software conflicts and DLL problems.

▶ You will learn how to create and/or use some important diagnostic and troubleshooting tools.

▶ You will learn how to wipe the slate clean and start over fresh with your PC.

As powerful and ennobling as computers may be, so too, can they be incredibly frustrating. In fact, if you ask most people to describe their experience working with computers, you probably get an earful about all the problems their system is having, or how much time they lost recently trying to fix a problem, or any number of other assorted computer-oriented woes.

The unfortunate fact is that computers today are still too hard to use and too difficult to understand, and they break down way more often than they should. The promise of today's PCs is tremendous, which is why we put up with all this junk, but the reality of today's computing experience simply does not match the hype that the computer industry is so good at generating. Hence the next two chapters.

PC users of all levels, from novices to experts, suffer through computer problems of some sort on a semiregular, if not regular, basis. It's just part of the nature of working with these complex machines and probably will be for some time to come. As a result, it's essential for every computer user to develop some troubleshooting and problem-solving skills. The last few years have certainly seen some important improvements in the overall ease of use of computers, but when something goes wrong, it can *really* go wrong, particularly with Windows-based PCs.

In fact, though some might argue that Windows is now as easy to use as Apple's Macintosh operating system (MacOS), which has a well-deserved reputation for being user-friendly, that argument comes crashing down when problems arise and you have to troubleshoot. Because of the way the systems are designed, Macs are much easier to troubleshoot than PCs. The primary reason is when problems do happen with Windows-based PCs, all the ugly arcane technical details driving a PC's operation (which today's Windows software tries so hard to hide) come screaming up to the surface, confronting most users with concepts and terminology designed by engineers for engineers (not for ordinary people).

Still, that doesn't make the problems unresolvable; they're just a bit more challenging. The basic trick to PC troubleshooting is first to know a little about what's going on, so that you can make an educated guess on where to focus your efforts, and then to try a few straightforward procedures. You can find both background information and general step-by-step fixes in this chapter. (I think of it as the "teaching you how to fish" chapter versus some of the specific answers you can find in Chapter 18, "Solving Common PC Problems.") By applying the principles described in this chapter, you should be able to work your way through the most common problems that crop up on today's PCs.

As with most goal-oriented projects, the first step is to figure out a strategy.

Troubleshooting Strategies

Troubleshooting PCs — that is, finding and fixing problems that are keeping your computer from working, are causing you occasional glitches, or are just plain annoying — is like building a puzzle. The hard part is not attaching the appropriate piece to the section of the puzzle you've already built, it's finding the right piece. So too with troubleshooting, the procedures you need to follow to fix a problem are usually quite easy, but figuring out what's causing the problem and/or which procedure to use can be a real challenge.

To have a successful troubleshooting session, I suggest you complete the following five basic steps, all of which are explained in more detail in this chapter:

1. Define the problem.

2. Narrow in on the specifics.

3. Use available resources.

4. Keep track of what you do.

5. Test your solution.

Define the problem

The first step is to try to figure out in what general area the problem is occurring. In some instances, this step is incredibly simple; while in others, it's extremely hard. If your computer won't start up, or boot, properly, then you know you have a startup problem. If, on the other hand, your computer seems to crash on a seemingly random basis, it could be the result of any number of problems related to your computer's hardware or software. In between those extremes, if you notice that every time you use a particular peripheral, such as a printer or modem, something doesn't seem to work right, or if you have problems every time you use a particular program, then you can guess that the problem may be hardware-related in the first case or software-related in the second.

Now, the truth is, it could be the exact opposite reason in these two scenarios or even a combination of the two (that is, both hardware and software). If you recall from previous chapters about how computers are organized and how they work, PCs are made up of a complex web of dependencies. Different pieces of hardware work together as a system, different pieces of software work together as a system, and then the hardware system and the software system also have to function as an organized entity. So many cross-connections are in current PC designs, in fact, that sometimes it's a wonder that they work as well as they do. Still, many times you can at least start your troubleshooting efforts by picking an area where you think the problem may reside.

Cross-Reference

For a few suggestions on where to start, take a look at the hardware and software troubleshooting sections later in this chapter.

Narrow in on the specifics

Once you know the general area you want to pursue, then you need to do a bit more detective work to figure out exactly where within that area you want to focus. For example, if it's a startup problem, you also have to figure out where in the startup process the problem occurs. As explained in Chapter 8, many steps are involved in booting a PC, and problems at different points in that process have different symptoms and different cures. Frankly, the only way to do this detective work is to learn a bit about what's going on at the different stages. You don't need to know excruciating details, but spending a little research time up front can save you lots of time, energy, and frustration down the road.

Cross-Reference

For more details on tracking down startup problems, see Chapter 18, "Solving Common PC Problems," for more.

Similarly, if you have a problem while your system is running, or when trying to perform a particular task, it really helps to have at least a rough understanding of the principles involved. That way you can make educated guesses as to the root of the problem and have a better chance at discovering the right answer sooner rather than later. (I chose the word *guesses* very deliberately because troubleshooting PC problems is as much an art as it is a science. Yes, you can follow certain logical rules, but ultimately troubleshooting often boils down to following your instincts and making a good guess.)

Cross-Reference

Chapter 8, "How Your Computer Works," has a lot of information about the principles involved in how your computer works that can help you figure out which questions are the right ones to ask.

Use available resources

You can find a lot of the information you need to understand the important principles involved in troubleshooting PC problems and what you should do here in this book, but there's no way I can possibly cover everything. There are simply too many permutations and too many possible problems to cover them all.

To be able to solve a specific problem, you need to look for the right resources. Thankfully, the Internet and computer-oriented Web sites offer a tremendous trove of useful information. Of course, not all of it is good information, but if you go to well-established, well-respected sites, you can find an almost overwhelming amount of data.

Probably the best place to start is company Web sites, such as for the company that made your computer, any of its components, or any of the software you have loaded onto it. To find out the specific components used in your PC, such as which company made the video card or modem, you should check the documentation that came with your computer, or contact the company who sold you the PC.

Secret

Another good way to find out the specific type of components inside your computer without cracking open the case is to use the Device Manager built into both Windows 95 and 98. To get there, right-click your My Computer icon, select Properties from the context menu that appears, and in the ensuing dialog box, click the Device Manager tab. To see individual devices, click the + signs next to generic device names, and look for the listings underneath. In most cases you can find what you need there, but in others, you may need to first select the device and then choose the Properties button to get a few more details.

If you're having Windows-related problems, Microsoft's Personal Support Center (`http://support.microsoft.com/support/c.asp?M=F`) offers a wealth of information on various flavors of Windows, as well as other popular products, such as Office. Many other companies have similar online information warehouses where you can get access to lots of great information.

Another great resource for troubleshooting information is newsgroups that focus on specific computer-related subjects. You can find general computer-oriented newsgroups under the `comp.sys.xxx` label (where *xxx* is any number of different specific names) as well as from specific company newsgroup servers.

Cross-Reference

For more on using newsgroups, see Chapter 13, "Connecting to and Using the Internet."

Many programs and operating systems are also starting to build tremendous amounts of resource information into their help files (of course, that's primarily because printed documentation seems to be nearly extinct). If you select Help off the Start menu for Windows 95 or 98, for example, and select the Contents tab, you see a section on troubleshooting that lists a number of common problems such as not being able to print, not connecting to the Internet, and so on. By double-clicking one of these topics, you walk step by step through a series of screens with yes or no questions. Doing so can help you focus on a specific solution to your problem. Figure 17-1 shows an example.

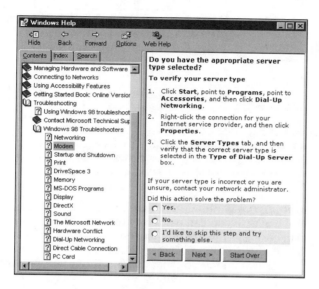

Figure 17-1: Modem Troubleshooter
As with other troubleshooters bundled into the Windows 95/98 Help files, the Modem Troubleshooter walks you through the process of solving a common problem by asking simple yes/no questions.

Tip

While they won't solve all your problems (and not all potential problems are covered), these built-in Troubleshooters are often the best place to start your Windows-based troubleshooting efforts because they can usually get you through the problem quickly.

Secret

Some of the best, but little-known resources available for Windows 95 and 98 users are the Windows 95 and Windows 98 Resource kits, both of which are included (but somewhat hidden) for free in electronic form on their respective CDs (see Figure 17-2). The Resource Kits are essentially extensive technical documentation (the equivalent paper copies are around 1,500 pages each!) on the ins and outs of the different Windows flavors and include all kinds of helpful information on solving both simple and complex problems. The Windows 98 version also includes troubleshooting and diagnostic tools that are organized under the Tools Management Console.

On the Windows 95 CD, you can find the Windows 95 Resource Kit under the Admin\Reskit directory. To use it, you can either just double-click the win95rk.hlp file inside the helpfile folder or copy it to your hard disk and run it from there.

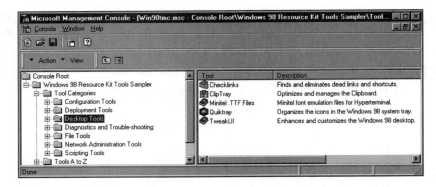

Figure 17-2: Windows 98 Resource Kit Tools
One of the best-kept secrets of the Windows 98 CD is the freely bundled Resource Kit and accompanying Tools Sampler. Once you've installed the Resource Kit, you can access these helpful utilities through the Tools Management Console.

On the Windows 98 CD, the Windows 98 Resource Kit is inside the Tools\Reskit folder. If you want to, you can just copy the help files to your hard disk (you can find the necessary win98rk.hlp, win98rk.cnt, and rk98book.chm files inside the Tools\Reskit\Help folder), but because of the additional tools that are included, I highly recommend you just use the Setup program inside the Reskit folder. That way everything is put where it belongs (although be aware that some of the utilities still need to be installed separately, as the documentation explains).

Secret

Other little-known resources you can take advantage of are all the .txt files inside your main Windows folder. Most of these files are "readmes" and are full of very useful information about various aspects of the operating system and its interactions with your PC's hardware and software. For example, the typical Windows 98 installation has files such as Display.txt, General.txt, Hardware.txt, and Printers.txt.

Finally, when it comes to finding even more current information, don't forget traditional media resources, such as computer magazines, television shows, and radio programs. They are often good sources of troubleshooting-related facts and news. In fact, you can find out more about a computer radio talk show I host called "O'Donnell on Computers" by visiting my Web site at www.everythingcomputers.com. (You can also find information about updates and corrections to this book there as well.)

Keep track of what you do

I have mixed feelings mentioning this step because when I am in the throes of troubleshooting, I don't always keep the best records (and I don't really like being hypocritical, but, well . . .). However, if you really want to be thorough, or if you're battling a particularly nasty problem, you really should keep a written record of the various steps you've taken to resolve your problem. At the very least, you need to make mental note of the various steps you're taking during the troubleshooting process. If you can, write down what you think the problem is, what files you've changed, added, or deleted from your system, and what procedures you've followed. Not only can this list keep you from duplicating steps, it should help you narrow in on the issue (and it could prove to be a big time-saver if you or a friend runs into a similar problem down the road).

Test your solution

Serious troubleshooters also make thorough notes about the results of their efforts and may even try the solution under various permutations to be sure that it's correct and that it hasn't introduced any new problems of its own. Frankly, I generally can't be bothered with all that, and I bet you won't either. (If you don't mind, more power to you.) I just want to get the darn thing working, so once I've tried a solution, I check to see if it fixes my problem and then I move on.

If another problem does crop up, it really does help to know what you changed to fix the first problem, but don't quickly presume that fixing the first problem caused the second. In many instances, that is the case, particularly if it pops up right away, but computers have problems often enough that sometimes two, or even more, problems in a row are simply coincidences.

Tip

If you're trying to solve more than one problem, which is a not uncommon scenario, then limit yourself to dealing with one at a time. You'll have better luck if you fix one and then let the system stay stable for a few days. That is, don't add or remove *any* hardware or software to it before tackling the next problem. In some cases the problems are intertwined so this method isn't feasible, but as a general rule, you don't want to change too many things on your system at once. With most Windows-based PCs, that's a sure recipe for disaster.

Basic Troubleshooting Checks

Before we dive into the nitty-gritty of troubleshooting, it's important to point out that many computer-related problems turn out to be rather simple issues. So before you start freaking out about your computer dying right before your very eyes, calm down, take a deep breath, and check the simple stuff. (And if you're in the middle of a deadline and are really going crazy, take a coffee break, and walk away from the machine for a few minutes. You need a clear head to be an effective troubleshooter.) A lot of seemingly unsolvable problems turn out to be bad connections and other simple maladies.

Physical connections

The first thing you have to check are the physical connections both outside and, if necessary, inside your PC. Check the power outlets and power cables, unplug and replug any external hardware you may have connected to your computer, and look for signs of damage in the cables or connectors themselves. I once solved a frustrating SCSI problem when, after about two hours of wasted, fruitless effort, I noticed that one of the tiny pins inside the SCSI cable had been bent so far out of the way that the connector could still connect but that pin was not doing its job. A quick replacement of the SCSI cable fixed everything.

Cross-Reference

See Chapter 3 "Hard Disks and Removable Drives," for more on SCSI.

I came across the same type of problem again with a PC card modem for a laptop that had an external dongle connector for the phone line. Fortunately I checked for bent pins early in the process (I had learned something after all) and was able to solve that problem quickly.

Connections inside your PC can also be a problem, particularly if you move the computer or if you recently added a new internal component, such as more memory, an upgraded video card, or what have you. Oftentimes pulling out and then reseating memory chips and add-in cards is all it takes to fix obtuse, seemingly random problems, as well as those cases where something isn't recognized or just doesn't work.

Secret

Moving memory chips or plug-in cards to different open connectors on the motherboard is another good trick to try for stubborn problems because sometimes the different memory banks or expansion slots are treated differently. Some expansion slots, for example, are assigned to different IRQs or different internal PCI interrupts, and moving cards into or out of these slots can overcome some confusing conflicts. Also, moving these components from one location to another often retriggers the Windows Plug and Play mechanism the next time you start the computer, and that can help with juggling resources to overcome resource conflicts.

Cross-Reference

See the section "Hardware Troubleshooting Concepts," later in this chapter, for more on resource conflicts. Also, see Chapter 8, "How Your Computer Works," for more on IRQs.

Updates and upgrades

In addition to physical connections, particularly items you've recently added to your PC system, it's also good to suspect (and check) any recent software updates or upgrades you've installed. In many cases, problems that suddenly crop up on your system are due to whatever was just added to your system. Because of this, by the way, it's usually best to install only one thing at a time and then test both it and the rest of your system before moving on to another addition. I realize that this method often takes a lot longer, but if you want to maintain a stable system, the extra time is worth it. (Remember, patience is a virtue.)

Note that these types of issues can occur even if whatever you installed doesn't seem to have anything to do with where the problem shows up. For example, if you've just installed a new game and now you can't print from your word processor, there may actually be a connection. The game may have replaced or upgraded certain system files that are also somehow involved with the printing process, for example. Or new system files added by the game may be causing a conflict with other system files that happen to be used during printing. A more obvious example is if you've upgraded your printer driver and then you can't print.

As a general rule, if you start noticing problems right after you've installed something, either hardware or software, you should remove the hardware (including any drivers) or uninstall the software and see if the problem still exists.

Cross-Reference

See Chapter 9, "Adding, Upgrading, and Removing Software," for more on uninstalling software and Chapter 10, "Adding and Removing Hardware," for more on removing hardware.

If the problem goes away, then you know that the new item or one of its related files was the culprit. In many cases, you need to contact the manufacturer of the hardware or software to find out if they have an update, or if they are aware of known conflicts with other devices or software. If they don't have any relevant information, then keep reading, and look for ideas on how to solve the problem in some of the following sections of this chapter.

If the problem still exists, it may be due to the recently installed and then uninstalled hardware or software. Depending on how effective the program or driver's uninstallation process is, it still may have left a few fragments behind that might be causing the problem. If that's the case, you probably have to contact the manufacturer to find out what's left and how to get rid of it.

Another possible scenario is that the problem existed before the install and removing and/or uninstalling the new addition didn't make any difference. If that's the case, you're better off trying to fix the problem first, before adding another factor to the equation. Again, read the next few sections to get some more ideas on where to start your hunt.

Hardware Troubleshooting Concepts

Problems with your computer's hardware can be the scariest and most confusing because they often mean that the computer won't even start up properly, or a particular device won't function. Fortunately, they're usually the easiest to solve because they tend to have very straightforward causes and solutions.

The reason is that PC hardware is a lot simpler than PC software. While a lot of pieces go into an overall PC system, it's nowhere near the number of components that make up the complex web of modern operating systems and applications. In addition, the relationship between various hardware devices is much more tightly defined and controlled than the wild and woolly world of software.

How do you know if you have a hardware-related problem? In most cases, one of the components in your PC stops working: your printer stops printing, your modem no longer dials out, your monitor is blank, or your computer won't even turn on. In some instances, these problems may be because the device has failed, but complete hardware failures are actually fairly rare on PCs. Most of the components used in today's system are pretty robust and will last as long as you own the computer (if not longer). Even hard drives, which used to fail on a regular basis on older computers, are much less prone to complete physical breakdowns. (They're still probably the most common component to fail, however, because they are one of the few components with moving parts and they are used so extensively.)

In fact, most hardware-related problems actually stem from the interactions between hardware and software, or hardware and the design of the system overall. Of course, sometimes it's not very easy to tell what the real problem is. But before you buy a replacement for the component you think may have died, I suggest Windows users spend a little time with the Device Manager, which you can find as part of the System control panel. When it comes to troubleshooting hardware problems, the Device Manager is your friend.

Not only does the Device Manager provide an inventory of all the components it finds in your PC, it also enables you to deal with the two most common source of problems that affect PC hardware: drivers and resource conflicts.

Drivers

A driver is a piece of software that communicates between a hardware component inside your PC and the operating system controlling your computer. Each device inside your PC needs its own driver (some use several) in order to function. The way drivers work is that when the operating system needs to access a particular component to do something, such as write data to a removable drive, draw windows on the screen, or what have you, it uses the driver to "talk" back and forth to the device.

Note

By the way, if you use more than one operating system, each device needs a driver designed to work with the particular operating system you're using. For example, if you run Windows 98 and Linux, you need both Windows 98 and Linux drivers for each component in your system. (One important exception is that Windows 98 and Windows 2000 share the same driver architecture, which means that drivers written for one should also work on the other — although you still need a separate copy for each OS.)

Thankfully, one of the main tasks of modern operating systems is to figure out and install the drivers that your system needs automatically when the OS is installed. (Good thing too, because modern systems have *lots* of drivers.) The Plug and Play (PnP) feature first touted by Microsoft for Windows 95 and then subsequent versions of Windows is one of the main technologies used to find these devices (technically it's called *enumerating them*), although other operating systems use other methods. When these types of techniques work, they simplify things tremendously, but it's not uncommon for them not to work and for operating systems to make mistakes as a result. If that happens, either the wrong driver can be installed for a particular device or nothing may get installed, in which case the device either won't work properly or at all.

Another common problem with drivers is that they often run into conflicts with other drivers or other operating system files. For example, if you add a new printer, upgrade your Web browser, install an operating system Service

Pack, or do any number of other things that might change your existing operating system files, those changes may interfere with the operation of one of your existing drivers. In addition, it's not unheard of for drivers (or any other files on your PC, for that matter) to become corrupted, which basically means the file on your hard disk was somehow altered. These changes can occur because of a conflict with another piece of software, a virus, a sudden power surge, or any number of other issues.

Device Manager

Regardless of how driver problems occur, you can often confirm their existence in the Device Manager. If you open it up and see either a yellow exclamation point or a red international No symbol (you know, the circle with the slash through it) next to a particular device, you know there's a problem. (Note that the problem may be related to the driver or the resource, which I explain later in this chapter.) In most cases, if your system has a problem, the outline-like structure of the Device Manager automatically opens to the location of the problem, but you may want to click the plus sign (+) next to the various device headings to be sure. Figure 17-3 shows an example.

Figure 17-3: Find hardware problems in the Device Manager
You can both find information about and resolve many hardware-related problems through the Windows 95/98 Device Manager, which is part of the System control panel. In this example, the exclamation point signifies that the COM port isn't working properly.

In addition to providing information, the Device Manager also provides the means to fix many common problems. The easiest and typically most effective solution is to force the system to try to reload the driver. All you need to do is click the problem device, and then hit the Remove button.

What this process, which is sometimes referred to as "logically" removing the device, does is removes references to the driver files in the Windows Registry, which is what tracks all this information for the Windows OS. The practical result is that the system thinks it's gone. To reload the driver, just hit the Refresh button, and that forces Plug and Play to start working. As long as the device being found is Plug and Play compatible, the system can find the device and try to reload the driver for it, either from the repository of drivers that are stored on the Windows 95 or 98 CD or, if you copied the installation CAB files onto your hard drive, as I recommended in Chapter 9, "Adding, Upgrading, and Removing Software."

If the operating system can't find the driver in either place, it may ask you to install the driver yourself, so be prepared either with the driver disks that came with the device, or know where any updated driver you may have downloaded from the Internet is stored on your hard disk so you can browse to it in the Open dialog box. In many, many cases, this installation (and then restarting) is all you have to do to solve hardware-related problems.

If the device isn't found when you hit Refresh, either because it isn't Plug and Play or just wasn't recognized, I suggest you restart your system (sometimes that works) and, if necessary, launch the Add New Hardware control panel, which walks you through the process of finding the device and installing the driver.

If reloading the driver doesn't work (and I suggest you try that technique first because it's fast and easy and it won't hurt your system), then try to upgrade the driver. In fact, in most instances, it's best to keep all your drivers up to date, even those that aren't causing any problems, because there's a good chance that down the road, one of your older drivers will eventually cause you problems.

Windows Update

If you're using Windows 98 or Windows 2000, you can stay at least somewhat up to date by using the Windows Update feature, which you can find off the Start menu and in several other places. What Windows Update does is launches your Web browser, connects to the Internet, and then goes to a special Windows Update site Microsoft maintains. From there, the Windows Update feature can compare a list of available updates against the operating system files and drivers you have installed on your PC so you can see what updates might be available for your specific system. Then you can choose the files you want to download, and they will be automatically installed onto your system.

Secret

When it works, Windows Update is a great feature, but the problem is the only driver updates that are included on the site are the ones that the manufacturers have gotten around to sending to Microsoft and that Microsoft, in turn, has added to their site. In many situations, even Windows 98 and Windows 2000 users probably find that, if they really want to keep their entire system current, they need to use the same manual techniques for finding and downloading the latest drivers that Windows 95 users need to use. If you go to the Web sites of the companies that made your PC and any peripherals, and look for driver updates, you can download from there.

Thankfully, the process of installing updated drivers you've manually downloaded is easy under both Windows 95 and Windows 98. In fact, it works the exact same way under both operating systems.

STEPS:

Installing an Updated Driver

Step 1. Open the Device Manager (part of the System control panel), and select the device whose driver you want to upgrade from the list. You may have to click one of the plus signs (+) next to device headings to find what you want.

Step 2. Click the device, and then choose the Properties button (or just double-click the device as a shortcut).

Step 3. Click the Driver tab. Select the Update Driver button, and follow the instructions of the step-by-step wizard that appears (see Figure 17-4).

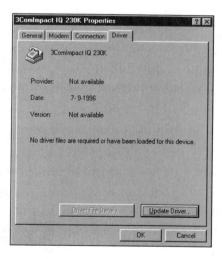

Figure 17-4: Driver updates
Updating driver software for a particular device is simple. Just double-click it from the Device Manager, select the Driver tab, click the Update Driver button, and a step-by-step process walks you through it.

Note that under Windows 95, you may incorrectly see the message, "No drivers are required or have been loaded for this device" on the Driver tab of some devices. Just ignore it, and continue with your upgrade.

One caveat you need to be aware of is that upgrading one driver can break something else. So don't be terribly surprised if you briefly find yourself in a vicious cycle that forces you to upgrade driver after driver to get your system working.

Real-mode drivers

If you regularly use DOS or have upgraded your system from Windows 3.1 to either Windows 95 or 98, you may come across driver problems that are related to 16-bit, real-mode drivers. *Real-mode* refers to an operational mode used with the original 8088 and other x86-compatible processors when they run DOS. It's the main reason DOS suffers from the infamous 640K memory limit.

With DOS and Windows 3.1, which are 16-bit operating systems, drivers were typically added to the system by putting references to them in the Config.sys (and sometimes Autoexec.bat) startup files. When you upgrade to Windows 95 or 98, many of those drivers are also upgraded to the 32-bit versions so that you can use your devices with the best possible performance and best possible compatibility under Windows 95 or 98 (which are both 32-bit operating systems).

In some instances, the drivers aren't upgraded, however, or references to the old versions are left in the startup files and still load when you start up your PC. As a result, you can run into hardware problems that are caused by the real-mode driver.

Unless you specifically need the driver to run a particular application under DOS, you're better off without it. By the way, removing old drivers doesn't mean you won't be able to use these devices with a DOS application, as you might presume. You can open a DOS Prompt window under Windows 95 or 98 and launch a DOS application from there, and still have access to all your devices under DOS through the Windows 95 or 98 drivers. The only problem is if you loaded only DOS and got a command prompt at startup.

If you have a particularly stubborn DOS game that does require you to start up in DOS, then you should create a DOS boot floppy that has all the necessary real-mode drivers on it. That way they won't interfere with the rest of your system when you're not running the game, and you can start up your PC with that floppy whenever you want to play that particular game.

I recommend you go through your startup files and either delete the lines that refer to the old drivers, the ones that typically start out **device=**, or simply remark them out, which tells the operating system to ignore them. You can manually remark individual lines out of your Config.sys or Autoexec.bat files by typing a semicolon character (;) at the beginning of the line, or you can type the letters **rem** (short for "remark") and then a space at the beginning of the line. If you're using Windows 98, an easier way to do the same thing is to use the System Configuration Utility, which enables you to turn off lines by clicking a box. See the section "Troubleshooting Tools," later in this chapter, for more.

Cross-
Reference
To find out more about fixing startup problems, see Chapter 18, "Solving Common PC Problems."

Resources

In addition to drivers, the other major hardware-related problem has to do with system resources. As I explained in Chapter 8, early PCs were designed with a variety of different mechanisms for communicating between different components. In several instances, these critical mechanisms became known as a computer's *resources*.

The most well-known example of computer resources are IRQs, or Interrupt Requests, which are used to communicate between the processor and other components of a computer system. Other resources are DMA (Direct Memory Access) channels, which are used by certain devices to bypass the processor and store and retrieve certain data directly to and from the computer's memory, and Memory Ranges, which are specific locations in memory used by DOS, Windows 3.1, Windows 95, and Windows 98 to store certain pieces of software.

Secret
Memory Ranges are the only Windows–specific computer resource. In other words, if you run other operating systems on your PC, you don't have to worry about Memory Ranges, but you still do need to worry about IRQs and DMA channels.

Over time, some of the limitations that were designed into these mechanisms have proven to be problematic. Specifically, most PCs are limited to 16 IRQs (numbered 0–15) and 8 DMA channels (numbered 0–7) and, in many cases, that simply isn't enough. A related problem is that certain devices that use IRQs or DMA channels can work only with certain ones. For example, some plug-in cards can use only IRQs 9, 10, and 11. This means that even if extras are available, you can run into a situation where a hardware device won't work because it can't get access to the computer resources it needs.

The computer industry has been scrambling over the last few years to solve these often inane problems by introducing technologies that take much better advantage of the existing PC architecture. With USB and IEEE 1394, for example, you can attach numerous devices to their high-speed buses, but all the devices can share a single IRQ. This is an enormous improvement over the one device/one IRQ model that serial ports, parallel ports, and other older PC hardware has saddled PC systems with for years. Eventually, there will need to be an entirely new PC architecture that forgoes these types of limitations, but in order to maintain backward compatibility with an enormous range of existing hardware and software, we're stuck with these limitations for now.

To find out more about the resources in use on your Windows 95/98 system, we can turn to the Device Manager once again. (You can also use the System Information utility if you're running Windows 98. See the section

"Troubleshooting Tools," later in this chapter, for more information.) Simply double-click the computer icon at the top of the Device Manager list, and you are presented with a listing of the IRQs in use on your system, as well as a quick way to look at other resources in use (see Figure 17-5).

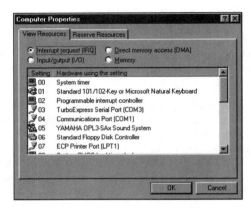

Figure 17-5: Finding resources
You can view IRQs, DMA channels, memory ranges, and input/output addresses in use on your system through the Device Manager.

Again, if there's a resource-related problem, typically called a *resource conflict,* for a particular device, you usually see the yellow exclamation point or red international No sign next to it. The red No symbol means the device is present but has been turned off to enable the system to boot, and the yellow exclamation point means the device is turned on but isn't working properly.

The basic issue with resources, with a few important exceptions, is that they cannot be shared. In other words, two devices that require, say, IRQ 5 or DMA Channel 3 cannot both use it, or you'll end up with problems with one or both devices. The important exceptions are the devices that use your computer's PCI slots usually can share IRQs with one another, and devices that attach externally to your PC typically don't require any resources. Almost all devices that require resources are internal to your PC.

Cross-Reference

To find out more about which devices need and which don't need IRQs, see Chapter 10, "Adding and Removing Hardware."

If devices are capable of sharing resources, you typically won't see a problem symbol in the Device Manager. Also note that the IRQ Holder for PCI Steering is used by every PCI device that also uses a standard IRQ, so you're bound to see both a Holder and a device sharing an IRQ. In some situations, you see multiple Holders and multiple devices sharing an IRQ.

In most cases, you don't need to worry about assigning resources such as IRQs on your computer system. In addition to recognizing or "enumerating" devices, as explained in the previous section on drivers, one of the main features of Plug and Play is to automatically arrange the available resources within a computer. In fact, part of the process of figuring out what's in your computer is also determining what resources the different devices need and what resources the system has available. With that knowledge in hand, the system can usually configure itself to make everything work right.

Plug and Play isn't perfect, however, so resource problems do occur. If you find that you do have a resource conflict, you can use several different techniques to resolve them, some of which vary according to whether it's an ISA-based device or a PCI-based device and whether or not it supports Plug and Play.

Cross-Reference

To find out more about the differences between PCI and ISA, see Chapter 8, "How Your Computer Works."

In either case, the goal is to juggle the available resources with the available devices by changing the devices' configuration settings so that you can match the resources you have with what you need. If possible, you should keep a printed list of what devices are currently assigned to what resources (specifically IRQs) and what resources are free. It makes life much easier when you try to piece this puzzle together. Once you've done that, see if you can develop a plan ahead of time that lists the resources you want each device to take. That way, all you have to worry about is changing the resource requirements of some devices in order to solve your problem.

Be forewarned that while many resource problems are fixable, some are not. Because of limitations in certain pieces of equipment or combinations of equipment that your system has, you may run across a situation where you cannot get a particular device working because it cannot be given the resources it requires. Or you may find that to make it work, you have to remove or disable something else from your system (see Figure 17-6).

Secret

Note that if you disable a device for troubleshooting purposes, you may have to do more than just uncheck the Disable in this hardware profile box to reenable it. For example, if you disable a device that is controlled by your computer's BIOS, such as a serial port or USB controller, you may have to first reenable this device in the BIOS before it is recognized by the system. This is true even if you did not disable the device in the BIOS.

Another point to be aware of is that if you disable a device under Windows 95/98, you automatically create a new hardware profile, which essentially just contains a list of what drivers to load on startup. Once you're done troubleshooting, you can just delete the profile you no longer need. Hardware profiles can be accessed from the System control panel.

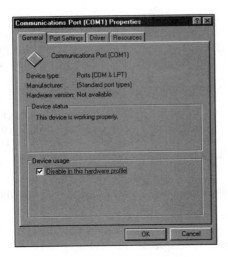

Figure 17-6: Turning a device off
To disable a particularly problematic device in software, you can use the Device Manager. Just select the device, hit Properties, and then put a check mark in the Disable in this hardware profile box on the General tab.

Fixing resource conflicts with ISA devices

Most resource conflicts are due to problems with ISA devices, particularly those that don't support Plug and Play. The reason is that these types of devices are like big stones stuck in the road: everything else has to work around them and sometimes that isn't always easy.

To manually change the settings of many older cards, you have to push some tiny DIP switches or use some other physical mechanism on the card itself. In many cases this forces you to pull the card out of the PC, which is a real pain. Other cards come with software-based configuration tools (commonly called ICU, short for ISA Configuration Utility) that enable you to make the changes with DOS-based software.

Some devices, including both ISA- and PCI-based ones, have their resource settings made in the BIOS, or CMOS Setup program. (CMOS stands for Complementary Metal Oxide Semiconductor, a type of material commonly used to create the chip that holds your PC's BIOS settings.) Serial and parallel ports typically do, for example, as well as other devices built into the motherboard, such as the USB controller. To make changes to these types of settings, you have to enter the Setup program when your computer first boots (often by holding down the Esc, F2, or Del key).

Cross-Reference

See Chapter 8, "How Your Computer Works," for more on the BIOS Setup program.

Once you've made the changes with this, or any other method, you need to restart the system and make sure everything works. (Don't forget to check the Device Manager for yellow exclamation points!) If it doesn't, you may need to force Windows 95 or Windows 98 to reserve a particular resource for the device. Here's how.

STEPS:

Reserving Resources

Step 1. Open the Device Manager, and double-click the computer icon at the top of the list.

Step 2. Switch to the Reserve Resources tab, and click the Add button (see Figure 17-7).

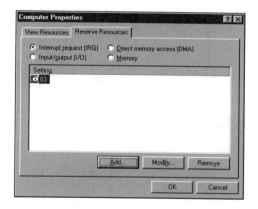

Figure 17-7: Reserving resources
You can reserve an IRQ or any other resource for a particularly problematic device that your system refuses to recognize.

Step 3. Use the scroll buttons to select the IRQ you want set aside for a particular device, and then hit OK. If you want to reserve an additional resource, select the appropriate radio button, and hit Add again. When you're finished, hit OK twice, and restart your computer.

In order to use this procedure, you're going to have to know what resources the particular device can work with. You should be able to find that in the device's documentation. Also, you need to make sure that the device's hardware settings, which you often set on the card itself, match the new software settings you just created.

One last point to be aware of is that any device that uses a reserved resource has a blue "I" next to it in the Device Manager. This doesn't signify a problem; it's just meant as a visual reminder.

If the ISA card supports Plug and Play, you should be able to make any changes to its settings through the Device Manager. Note that the same technique also works for all PCI cards (which, by definition, have to support Plug and Play).

STEPS:

Changing Resources on Plug and Play Cards

Step 1. Open the Device Manager, and double-click the device whose settings you want to change.

Step 2. Click the Resources tab, and turn off the Use Automatic Settings check box.

Step 3. Check what predefined configurations are available by choosing from the list of choices next to the Setting Based On line. If more than one choice is available, switch between various settings, and check to see if the Conflicting Device list box at the bottom of the dialog reports no conflicts (see Figure 17-8).

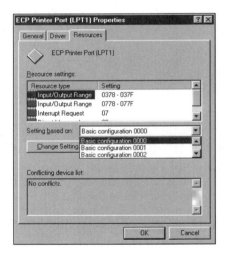

Figure 17-8: Device Manager Resources tab
With many devices, you can switch between several predefined settings of various resources by choosing between different basic configurations.

Step 4. If you find a setting that works without conflicts, click OK twice, and you're done. If not, you need to select the particular resource type that's still causing a problem, and hit the Change Setting button. Note that some devices do not enable you to adjust certain settings. If that's the case, you have to try changing the settings on the other device that's also currently using the resource you need.

Step 5. In the Change Setting dialog, make any changes you need to, and then check to see if it removes any remaining conflicts from the Conflicting Device list box. If it does, hit OK twice, and then restart your machine to make sure everything works and that the conflicts have all been resolved.

The challenge you may find yourself running into is having to change the resources of multiple devices in order to make one work. For example, if you have a plug-in SCSI controller that can work only with IRQ 10, and IRQ 11 is your only available IRQ, the obvious thing to do is to move whatever was currently on 10 over to 11. However, if the device on 10 can work only on 9 and 10, then you may also have to move whatever was on 9, and so on, and so on.

Fixing resource conflicts with PCI devices

PCI-based resource conflicts are rare, but not unheard of, particularly IRQ problems. Unfortunately, they can be a real bear to fix because, theoretically speaking, such conflicts are not supposed to happen.

In theory, PCI devices should be able to share IRQs and avoid all the mess of resource conflicts. In reality, however, because of limitations in a computer's BIOS, in the driver for the device, or in the operating system, resource conflicts can and do occur. (I know, because I've experienced one.) Notebook computers with docking stations are particularly prone to them.

You can try some of the same techniques used to resolve ISA Plug and Play card conflicts on PCI cards, but they don't always work. In addition, sometimes moving PCI cards from one slot to another can make a difference. Other things you may need to investigate include getting an updated BIOS for your PC or installing a new driver for the device.

Secret

One other trick you can try is to enable (or disable) PCI IRQ Steering, which is available through the PCI Bus Properties page in the Device Manager. PCI IRQ Steering involves communication between the computer's BIOS and Windows to determine what PCI devices get assigned or "steered" to particular IRQs. Playing with the IRQ Steering settings can sometimes resolve some thorny hardware problems. To get there, look under the System Devices section for PCI Bus, double-click it, and then click the IRQ Steering Tab. Under Windows 95 OSR2 or later, the default is for PCI IRQ Steering to be off, but with Windows 98 the default is to have it on. (Early versions of Windows 95 don't have this feature at all.) Figure 17-9 shows what to look for.

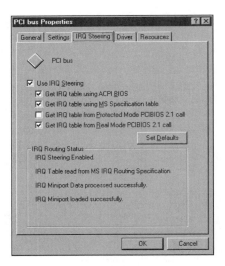

Figure 17-9: PCI IRQ Steering
The rather obscure PCI Bus Properties page includes a tab for enabling or disabling various types of PCI IRQ Steering. In some instances, changing these settings can help solve IRQ problems with PCI-based plug-in cards.

Software Troubleshooting Concepts

The most common and most troublesome problems that crop up on today's PCs are software-related issues. Software problems can be as obvious as an application that keeps crashing to something as miniscule as an error message that tells you a file is missing but doesn't stop you from doing anything.

The challenge is to figure out what's causing the problem. While it's relatively simple in some situations, such as an error message that tells you the specific name of the file causing the problem, most of the time it's pretty tough. Many software-related problems show no obvious symptoms other than crashing or locking up your machine — two frustrating outcomes that aren't very helpful in narrowing down the problem.

Of course, sometimes these very symptoms can provide the clues you need to figure out where to start your search. For example, if a problem happens every time you launch a particular program, use a specific combination of applications, or select a particular menu item or other feature within a particular program, and then you can use that info in your troubleshooting efforts.

The frustrating part about software problems, however, is that even if you're able to narrow down when and where the problem occurs, this doesn't necessarily tell you what's causing it. To continue the previous example, if you're able to determine that a problem consistently happens when you're using a specific program, you would logically assume that the problem is with that program. In many cases this might be true, but it's also possible that the problem is actually due to another piece of software that's running in the background on your computer, causing a conflict with that program. In other words, the program by itself may be fine, but when used in conjunction with this other "hidden" application running in the background, the problem occurs.

So the best solution in a case such as this is actually to remove or update that hidden application. But, of course, you first have to figure out what hidden applications you have running and then figure out which of them is the culprit, which leads you off into yet another round of mystery solving.

Shared files and DLLs

To make more sense of this situation, it's helpful to quickly review how software works on your PC. At any given moment while you're using your PC, numerous files are loaded into your computer's memory, with a certain percentage of them in active use and another portion that are just sitting there waiting to be called on. Even if you don't have any applications open, numerous operating system files are working, keeping something on your screen and enabling your computer to function. Some of these files are core operating system files, some are drivers, and still others are tiny applications or other "services" that the operating system uses to perform certain functions or that it requires in case you choose to do certain things.

Files that perform these types of functions, as well as functions that are specific to applications, typically come in the form of Dynamic Link Libraries, or DLLs. (You can tell that you're dealing with one because their filename typically ends in .dll.) As confusing as that name may sound, it actually provides a reasonable description of what they are and do — that is, as long as you're a software engineer. For the rest of us, what it means is that it's a library, or package, or software code that's called upon, or linked to, on an as-needed, or dynamic, basis.

Other files that perform operating system services are actually little applications, but not in the sense you're used to. Most have no user interface of any sort to interact with. They just get loaded into memory and do whatever they're programmed to do. As a result, in most cases you never see these files or know that they're active, they just do their work silently in the background. That's why they're sometimes considered "hidden."

If you also have traditional applications open on your PC, then another set of files come into play, including the program's main files, any shared files that it may use to perform certain functions, and some additional shared operating system files that the application requires to be available. The reason for this is that in addition to providing certain overall features, such as access to a mechanism for launching applications (like the Windows Start menu, for example), operating systems provide certain basic capabilities to applications that run on top of them. They do this so that application developers don't have to constantly reinvent the wheel and so that multiple applications can work together simultaneously (among other reasons). For example, instead of having to figure out their own way to display dialog boxes or connect to the Internet, applications can ask the operating system to provide these basic services for them. In order to do so, however, the operating system has to load, or at least activate, certain files that can perform some of these core functions.

Software conflicts

The end result of this situation is that many, many different files are at work, or at least loaded into memory, on your system, and if they don't all fit together just right, then you can have problems. Sometimes the problems are due to two or more of these files being unable to "communicate" with each other, or to their providing similar or overlapping capability. Either way, these types of problems and other similar ones are generically referred to as *software conflicts* because one or more files are interfering with the operation of another.

Software conflicts can happen whenever you introduce any new software to your system, whether it's through installing a new application, upgrading a driver, downloading an operating system update, or any other way that new software can become part of your system. Note, however, that simply downloading or copying a file onto your PC's hard drive won't necessarily cause this problem. Unless you actually install the files or they get automatically installed (which, admittedly, can sometimes be hard to tell) and become part of your active system, then merely having a file on your hard disk won't cause a problem.

Sometimes the impact of the conflicts can be obvious, but again, oftentimes it's not. For example, one common problem is that when you install a new application, it may install an updated version of a shared DLL file. Other programs that also use that shared DLL may not be able to work with the new version, however, with the practical result being that installing a new application breaks an old application that used to work fine.

Uninstalling

If you think the problems you're having with your PC are due to a software conflict, then you have to go through the often-tedious process of trying to track down the culprits. Several software programs that are explained in more detail in the section "Troubleshooting Tools," later in this chapter (such as Windows 98's System Information and System Configuration utilities or the shareware SANDRA program) can be extremely helpful in trying to figure out what's going and which files are at fault.

Once you've made that determination, which is clearly the hardest part of the job, then you can try a few different techniques to resolve the problem. First of all, you may simply be able to remove the file or prevent it from loading. To do this, you can uninstall offending applications, remove drivers, edit your startup files, (again, see the section "Troubleshooting Tools," later in this chapter, for more on how to do this) or, in some cases, just delete the file.

Caution

If you delete the file, make backups of the files in question and/or your startup files first because sometimes making these types of changes can make the problem even worse.

Unfortunately, sometimes uninstalling the problem application doesn't always work because some uninstallation mechanisms don't always take everything out (which, in my opinion, is shockingly bad software design). In addition, some poorly written uninstallers may remove shared files that other applications depend on. You'll know that's the case if after removing a particular program, something else that used to work fine stops working. Solving this type of problem often requires you to reinstall what you just removed—whether or not you want to.

Cross-Reference

For more on uninstalling and removing software, see Chapter 9, "Adding, Upgrading, and Removing Software.

Updating

Another common solution to software conflicts is to get updates to the applications or files that you think are affected by the problem. In fact, this is the best and most convenient solution for fixing many software problems. Sometimes it's the only solution because in some situations, the only way to get two applications to work together or to get a new device to work with your existing software is to get and install an updated version of the application, driver, or other file.

Tip

Don't forget to look for updated versions of certain operating system files as well. In some situations, they're the ones at fault.

Secret

Windows 95 users (only) can find out what versions of any operating system upgrades they have by using the little-known QFECheck program. Off the Start menu, select Run, and type in **qfecheck** to launch it. See Figure 17-10.

Both Windows 98 and many applications now include features that automatically check for updates on a regular basis to help avoid potential problems. In most cases, these automatic updates are quite useful, but be aware that in some situations, they can actually create new problems. The issue is that, as with drivers, updating an application can cause another previously working program to break because of new shared files that are included in the automatic update. In addition, sometimes the new files can create software conflicts that didn't used to exist. If you run into this, you may need to get multiple updates for different products to get everything working again.

Another possible scenario you may run into is that two different companies may point the finger of blame at each other. The unfortunate end result is that you get stuck in the middle with a system that doesn't work (or at least, a certain part of it may not work the way it should). As you can imagine, there's no easy way around this type of problem other than to push the issue with manufacturers or just choose a different product.

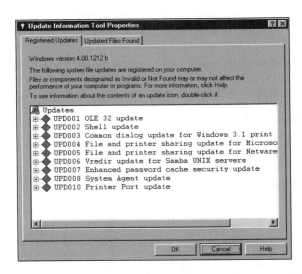

Figure 17-10: QFECheck tracks Windows 95 system updates
The QFECheck program buried inside your Windows folder can help Windows 95 users figure out which operating system updates have been installed onto their computer.

File corruption

Sometimes the problem isn't with the versions of the files you have, but a particular file itself. It's not at all uncommon for files on your hard drive to somehow get corrupted as the result of problems with other programs, a sudden power surge, or any number of other reasons. If you think that may be the case (there typically isn't any easy way to tell) then all you may need to do is reinstall the file. In most cases that means installing the application it's part of, or even the operating system itself, because installing individual files isn't always very straightforward. You need to know exactly where to put it, for example. Nor is installing files always effective. It may be necessary to adjust a Registry setting that points to the file as well, for example.

Tip

The catch here is that even if you know the name of the problem file, it's not always easy to tell where a particular file belongs. If you know the problem is with a particular application, go ahead and reinstall that program. If you don't know what it belongs to, you can sometimes decipher a bit more by finding the file, selecting it, right-clicking it, and then choosing Properties from the context menu that appears. If you click the Version tab, you might be able to find out what company made the file or even what program it belongs to.

Another possible solution to this dilemma is to use a utility that tracks which DLL files are associated with which application. Microsoft's System

Information tool for Windows 98 and SiSoft's SANDRA shareware utility, both of which are described in the section "Troubleshooting Tools" later in this chapter, may be helpful in this regard.

Moving DLLs

Speaking of DLLs, another common solution to solve DLL-related conflicts is to move some of them around. Most applications are designed to look for the DLL files they need in one of several different places, a capability you can exploit to your own good. For example, most applications first look inside the folder where the main program is located, then the Windows/System folder, and finally the main Windows folder. If the application finds what it needs in its own folder, then it stops looking.

Unfortunately, most software installation programs are lazy about where they put files and almost inevitably shove everything inside the Windows/System folder. The result, in fact, is that the Windows/System folder has become a dumping ground for all kinds of stuff. (Why they do this is beyond me.)

The problem is that if a new application upgrades a shared DLL (or even overwrites a newer version with an older one) stored in the Windows/System folder, then you're likely to run into a conflict. The solution involves tricking your system into maintaining two similar, but different versions of the same shared DLL. That way, the existing applications can use the DLL that's been in the Windows/System folder, and the newly installed application can use the version it needs.

To make this work you need to figure which DLL is the culprit — again, that's the hardest part — and then move that shared DLL out of the Windows/System folder and into its own Program folder. For example, if the application you just installed is 3D Rendering Pro, you move the DLL into the 3D Rendering Pro folder.

You probably also need to reinstall one of the applications that uses the conflicting version of the DLL so that it gets restored inside the Windows/System folder. When you do, you should be able to use each application without incident because the existing program has access to the version of the DLL that it needs via the Windows/System folder and the new application has access to the version it needs via its own folder. (You can even run them together without a conflict — or at least, you *should* be able to.)

Bugs

The most infamous type of software problem is bugs, which is just another name for problems within a program's own internal logic or operation. Some bugs are fairly obvious, but many are not. In fact, many times it's hard to tell if a problem you run across is actually a bug in a program or the result of a software conflict.

The best way to find out is to check with the manufacturer of the program you think has the problem and see if they have any updates that include bug fixes. If they do and you download and install it, then the problem should go away. If it doesn't, it's probably the result of a software conflict of some sort.

If the problem does turn out to be a bug but the company doesn't have an upgrade yet, you're stuck, because updates are the only way to fix bug-related problems.

Viruses

The final thing to consider when tackling software-related problems is a software virus, which is a small bit of software that somehow makes it way onto your system and intentionally causes havoc. Viruses are commonly suspected as the source of lots of different computer problems, but the truth is, while viruses are a very real threat, they are also relatively rare. Consequently, they're blamed for a lot more problems than they really cause. Still, they can be a factor, particularly if you're experiencing odd types of problems. (Some virus writers seem to think that this shows that they have a sense of humor.)

Tip

The only way to effectively deal with viruses and remove them from your system is with an up-to-date anti-virus program. I heartily recommend that every single computer user purchase and install one and, most importantly, keeps the virus definitions files up to date. Many new viruses are written and released every day, and if you don't keep the files that keep track of current viruses and how to get rid of them (which is what the virus definition files are), then even though you have an anti-virus program installed, you can still get a virus. So be vigilant about doing it manually, or take advantage of the built-in update features that most anti-virus programs now include.

CD

A demo copy of Norton's Anti-Virus application is on the CD-ROM accompanying this book.

Troubleshooting Tools

In addition to a plan of attack, and knowledge of what's going on, to be successful at troubleshooting, you need to be equipped to handle the job. Just as a plumber requires a good selection of tools and knowledge of how to use them to get the job done, so too does a PC troubleshooter need the appropriate tools to assist in troubleshooting efforts.

In most instances, the troubleshooting tools you should get (and get to know) are readily available software programs. However, the first tool I'm going to describe you can create yourself.

Boot disk with CD or DVD-ROM driver and utilities

The most important tool you need for troubleshooting is a boot floppy disk for your computer. But not just any boot floppy can do: you need to have one that includes a driver for your system's CD or DVD-ROM drive.

A boot, or startup floppy (as they are sometimes called), is a disk that contains both some basic operating system files, as well as a few essential utilities. With a boot floppy, you can run your system without ever needing access to your hard drive because all the files required to start the computer are on the floppy. The CD or DVD-ROM driver is critical because without it, you won't be able to "talk" to your CD or DVD-ROM drive, and without that capability, you generally can't read any discs you put into the drive. And if you can't read the discs, you can't install any applications or reinstall the operating system.

One of the great things Microsoft introduced in Windows 95 was the capability to automatically create a startup floppy by clicking a single button. Unfortunately, they did only a half-baked job because that floppy disk lacks a critical file: a real-mode (or DOS) CD-ROM driver. As a result, if you boot your computer from that disk, you can't access your CD-ROM drive. If you need to reinstall Windows 95 or 98 from the CD, that's a big problem. (Some PCs can boot from a CD-ROM — it depends on the version and type of BIOS your computer has — but many do not.)

Thankfully, there's a couple of ways to solve this problem. Frankly, the easiest one is to find someone with a copy of Windows 98 and have them make a startup disk for you. As with Windows 95, all you have to do is open the Add/Remove Programs control panel, click the Startup Disk tab, and then click the Create Disk button (see Figure 17-11).

Secret

As it turns out, the Windows 98 startup disk includes a generic CD-ROM driver for both IDE/ATAPI and SCSI CD-ROM drives that boot Windows 95 machines without a problem. You do not need to have Windows 98 installed on your computer for this boot floppy to work. It works just fine on machines with any version of Windows 95 installed.

If you don't have easy access to a Windows 98 startup disk or if the Windows 98 boot disk doesn't work on your computer, you can also create one manually. The following steps take you through the process of creating a disk with an IDE/ATAPI CD-ROM driver (which is what most, though not all, computers need).

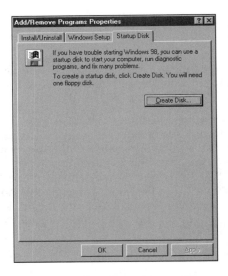

Figure 17-11: Creating a startup disk
Windows 95 and 98 make it easy to create a basic startup disk inside the Add/Remove Programs control panel, but the generic disk may not have everything you need.

STEPS:

Creating a Windows 95/98 Disk with a CD-ROM Driver

Step 1. Create a basic Windows 95/98 startup disk by going to the Add/Remove Programs control panel, clicking the Startup Disk tab, and then clicking the Create Disk button.

Step 2. Leave the completed disk in the floppy drive, and copy Mscdex.exe from the C:\Windows\Command folder on your hard drive onto the floppy. (If the file is not on your hard drive, you may have to copy it from the Windows 95/98 CD.)

Step 3. Copy the Format.com utility from the C:\Windows \Command folder on your hard drive onto the floppy as well. Also, confirm that the Fdisk.exe program is on the boot floppy, and if it isn't, copy it from the same location on your hard drive onto the floppy. These two DOS programs, FDISK and Format, are used to partition and format hard drives, two tasks that are often required if you need
to reinstall your operating system.

Step 4. Find a copy of the real-mode or DOS CD-ROM driver for the CD-ROM drive on your computer, and copy it to the floppy disk as well. Most real-mode driver files end with the extension .sys and have names such as nec_bm.sys (this is for an NEC-made CD-ROM drive).

Some systems come with this file on a separate floppy disk, but many do not. You may have to visit your computer manufacturer's Web site or contact them some other way to get a copy of this file. If that still doesn't work, you might try searching for the drivers via the Internet.

Cross-Reference

See the section "Installing Drivers" in Chapter 10 for more tips on how to find drivers.

Step 5. Simply copying the driver isn't enough. You also have to get it and the Mscdex.exe application to load and run when the computer is started by making some additions to the floppy's startup files. First open the Config.sys file on the floppy drive — not your C: drive! — and add one line that basically tells the computer to load the driver. (You know you're working with the basic Config.sys on the floppy if only one other line in it refers to Himem.sys. If you see other stuff, you might accidentally be working on the Config.sys file from your hard drive, which you don't want to do.)

Use the Edit.com application on the floppy, or any other text editor, and type in the following line at the end of the file:

```
Device=A:\<name of your CD-ROM driver> /D:MSCD001
```

Obviously you need to replace <name of your CD-ROM driver> with the actual name of the file. For example, it might say Device=A:\nec_bm.sys /D:MSCD001 (see Figure 17-12).

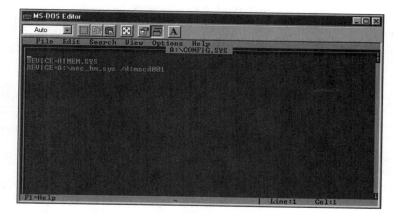

Figure 17-12: Adding a CD-ROM driver
You need to add only one line to your Config.sys file, and then create an Autoexec.bat file and put one line into it to get your DOS CD-ROM driver file to work. The second line shown here in the Config.sys file is the one that refers to a DOS CD-ROM driver.

Continued

STEPS

Creating a Windows 95/98 Disk with a CD-ROM Driver

(continued)

If you're starting with a Windows 98–created floppy, you already have Config.sys and Autoexec.bat on the disk, but you need to edit them and make changes that refer to the specific driver that you copied to the disk in the previous step.

If for some reason the Windows 95 (or 98) floppy doesn't have a Config.sys file, you can create one in the Edit program by creating a new file, typing in **device=himem.sys** on the first line, then the CD-ROM driver line referred to previously on the second line, and then saving it as Config.sys. (Note however, that the more likely problem is that you didn't create the boot floppy disk with the exact directions I provided previously.)

Step 6. The default startup disk does not typically create an Autoexec.bat file, so the next step is to create that file and add one line to it that causes the Mscdex.exe application to launch at startup. (If you already have an Autoexec.bat file on the floppy, just add the line that follows this step to the end of it.) Using Edit.com, or whatever text editor you just used to, adjust the Config.sys file, create a new file, and type in the following line:

```
MSCDEX.EXE /D:MSCD001
```

Save the file as Autoexec.bat on the A:\ drive, close it, and quit the application. The Mscdex application enables the computer to see and understand the files on a CD-ROM, and the matching reference in the Config.sys ensures that it will use your specific CD-ROM driver to do so.

Step 7. Make sure your new CD-ROM driver–equipped startup disk works by restarting the computer with the disk in the floppy drive. You should see a message about loading Mscdex.exe during startup and then be delivered to an A:\> prompt. Put a disk in your CD drive, and type:

```
D: [Return]
```

If everything works right, you should switch to a D:\> prompt. (If you have multiple hard drives in your system, your CD or DVD drive may be at a different letter, such as E:.) Just to double-check, type in the DIR command at the prompt to ensure that you can read the contents of the CD. (It doesn't matter what CD you use to test this.)

If it doesn't work, or you get a message about Invalid Drive Specification, double-check your Config.sys and Autoexec.bat files for typos.

Step 8. Once you've got everything working properly, put a label on the disk identifying it as a "Windows 95/98 Boot Disk with CD (or DVD)," and store it in a safe, nearby place.

Tip

If you're using Linux or another operating system in addition to or in place of Windows, you need a boot disk for that OS as well. In some instances, the boot disk to load the OS is different than the boot disk necessary to install (or reinstall) it, so make sure you have the right ones.

To use the boot floppy, all you have to do is start the computer with the boot disk in the floppy drive. When the disk works properly, you are left at a DOS A:\ prompt. If for some reason, the computer doesn't use the floppy drive to boot (you can tell by seeing if the floppy disk access light keeps going on during the boot process and if you boot into Windows), then you may have to adjust the boot order settings in your computer's BIOS setup program. The default setting on most machines is to check for the floppy drive first and then go to the hard drive, but you may find that some machines are set up to use the hard drive first, which means they just ignore your boot floppy.

STEPS:
Adjusting Your PC's Boot Settings

Step 1. Restart your computer, and look for the key that you need to hold down to enter the BIOS setup program — often F2 or Del. (On some computers you may have to hit the Esc key first, before you see the option for entering Setup.) Hit that key on your keyboard.

Step 2. Once you've entered Setup, look for something called Boot Order or simply Boot settings. Confirm that the floppy drive is first and the hard drive is second (or sometimes third, after the CD- or DVD-ROM drive).

Step 3. If the order isn't as described in the previous step, change it by highlighting the currently selected choice and hitting the Enter key. (Some BIOS setup programs use a different key to show available options, so you might need to use something else — hitting arrow up and down keys, or whatever your particular BIOS setup program uses.) From the available options that appear, select the choice required to make the floppy first. In some instances you may have to adjust the hard drive and CD- or DVD-ROM boot order settings as well.

Step 4. Exit the BIOS setup program, saving your changes. You can do so by hitting the Esc key a few times and then selecting from either exiting saving changes or exiting discarding changes. Make sure you choose saving changes.

Once you've completed these steps, your system will reboot, and it should use the boot disk you have in the floppy drive to start up.

Secret

If you have both the Windows 98 CD and a PC that enables you to boot from your CD- or DVD-ROM drive, one other technique you can use is to start up with the Windows 98 CD. The Windows 95 CD is not bootable, but the Windows 98 CD is, which basically means it has the startup files located in the right places. Again, you may have to adjust your PC's boot order to make this work, but it is another option to keep in mind.

Diagnostic programs

In addition to a well-equipped boot disk, it helps to familiarize yourself with some basic diagnostic programs that can help you in your troubleshooting efforts. Many third-party companies sell fix-it utilities that are supposed to solve many types of common problems, and in some cases, they can. But in many cases I've come across, they actually cause more problems than they solve (which is unbelievably infuriating!). As a result, I'm not a big fan of them.

The truth is, most of what you really need is probably already installed on your system, or at least it's readily available (and free) on your operating system CD (such as the Windows 98 CD), on the CD accompanying this book, or via the Internet. The problem is finding the tool and knowing how to use it.

Tip

By the way, Windows 98 offers a significantly better set of troubleshooting utilities than Windows 95 does, so if you're looking for a justification to make the upgrade, this could be it. Ironically, the Windows 98 utilities seem to function under Windows 95, but unfortunately there's no straightforward way to install just the Windows 98 troubleshooting tools onto a Windows 95 system.

One important point to bear in mind with these types of troubleshooting tools is that there are many different ways to achieve a similar end. As a result, you may find that any one of several different tools can be used to help resolve the same problem — sometimes one is just a bit easier to use than other.

CD

Some of the troubleshooting utilities on the CD-ROM accompanying this book include Trouble in Paradise (TIP) and Norton Zip Rescue.

Windows 98 utilities

Though they don't receive a lot of coverage, Windows 98's troubleshooting tools are quite extensive and can be helpful in overcoming many common problems. Most focus specifically on fixing operating system issues, but some can also be used to solve problems that crop up when installing application programs as well.

System Information

The most useful Windows 98 tool is Microsoft System Information, which you can get to via the Start ⇨ Programs ⇨ Accessories ⇨ System Tools.

Secret

The undocumented shortcut to launch System Information is to simply type **msinfo32** into the Run command window off the Windows 98 Start button.

System Information provides a wealth of information about three critical aspects of your system:

- The hardware and the resources it uses.

- The software components that are installed as part of your Windows system.

- The software that's currently loaded and running on your PC, which System Information refers to as the "Software Environment," when you launch the utility.

Each of the different sections is broken down into different categories, organized into an outline form. To look at the different areas, you simply click the plus sign next to the main heading. To view the particular information available within a specific section, you simply click the section name, and the info is displayed in the right pane of the program. Figure 17-13 shows an example.

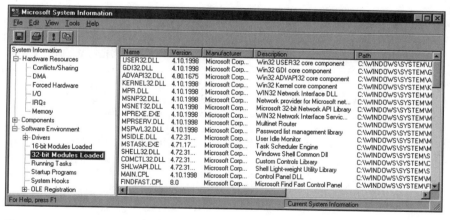

Figure 17-13: System Information
You can use Windows 98's System Information utility to do such things as see what IRQs are in use and which are free, or look at what software is currently running on your PC.

A lot of what is available in System Information is difficult to decipher and useful only for computer technicians, but you can find some useful nuggets buried there. For example, the Hardware Resources section offers a more straightforward and informative way to find out what system resources are used (or not) than the Device Manager. As I explain in the section "Hardware Troubleshooting Concepts," earlier in this chapter, having that information readily available makes a big difference when trying to fix hardware problems.

The "Components" section is useful for finding out which versions of drivers you have installed on your system. In addition, the "History" subsection can provide a detailed list of drivers that have changed since you last installed Windows 98, or in the last seven days. This type of information is valuable for troubleshooting both hardware and software problems.

Finally, the "software environment" is enormously helpful in figuring out the cause of software conflicts, which I explain in the section "Software Troubleshooting Concepts," earlier in this chapter. The list of Running Tasks, for example, can help you figure out what's really running on your system other than just open applications. In addition, the "Startup programs" subsection tells you all the things that automatically start up when Windows 98 starts, including those "hidden" elements that are loaded from the Registry.

In addition to its own features, the System Information utility also serves as a launchpad for all the other utilities bundled with Windows 98. By using the program's Tools menu, you can quickly launch any of the other major Windows 98 utilities, including the System Configuration Utility, System File Checker, Registry Checker, and Dr. Watson.

System Configuration Utility

One of the most common problems that people run into involves their startup files — that is, the files that are loaded when Windows first starts up. Oftentimes people need (or are told) to make some changes to those startup files to prevent certain things from loading along with Windows. Windows 3.1 and Windows 95 had a utility called "System Configuration Editor" (or "Sysedit," for short — see the text that follows for more information) that made this process somewhat easier by loading five important files, but the System Configuration Utility is a huge improvement (see Figure 17-14).

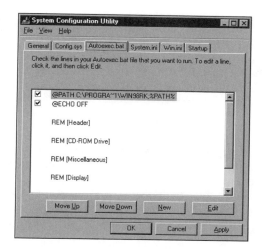

Figure 17-14: System Configuration Utility
You can easily edit your common startup files and save and try various settings for those files and more with Windows 98's System Configuration Utility.

The System Configuration Utility enables you to turn on and off individual lines in the basic startup files (Config.sys, Autoexec.bat, System.ini, and Win.ini) with simple check boxes, as well as enabling or disabling the loading of other Startup files, including most programs loaded from the Registry. The one exception (which you may be able to see listed through the System Information utility's Startup subsection, which is available under Software Environment, but not be able to turn off with the System Configuration Utility) are static VxDs (virtual device drivers). Some anti-virus programs and other utilities load this way, and they have to be disabled by editing the Registry.

Cross-Reference

See Chapter 18, "Solving Common PC Problems," for more on fixing startup problems.

Another capability of the System Configuration Utility is that it enables you to easily make some otherwise confusing to changes to your startup files through the Advanced button off of the General tab. You can also create and store different settings for all your startup files, which can be handy in trying to figure out which files are causing the problem. Finally, through its View menu, it also enables you to quickly jump to a few other common places for making adjustments during troubleshooting, such as Display Settings, the Device Manger, and more.

All in all, it's an extremely handy tool for dealing with startup problems.

System File Checker

As I explained in the section "Software Troubleshooting Concepts," earlier in this chapter, the software running inside your PC is typically made up of a complex puzzle of different pieces that work together as a system. Many of these pieces are DLLs, or Dynamic Link Libraries. The benefit of using DLLs is that programs can be smaller and the system can be more efficient — at least, in theory.

The problem with them, however, is that if one of these shared files is changed by a new application or operating system update that you install, then all the other pieces of software that also use that shared piece may break. The result is commonly referred to as "DLL hell." A practical outcome of this situation is that Windows 98 breaks, and certain elements don't work properly.

To help try and avoid some types of DLL hell, the System File Checker utility enables you to track the core Windows 98 system files and updates that have been made to them. More importantly, it also enables you to replace any problematic changed files with the original versions that shipped with Windows 98 (see Figure 17-15).

When you run System File Checker, it verifies that all system files are present and accounted for and that none have been corrupted. If it finds a problem, it replaces what it considers to be the problem file by copying over the original Windows 98 files, either from the CD or, if you copied them over to your hard disk, from there.

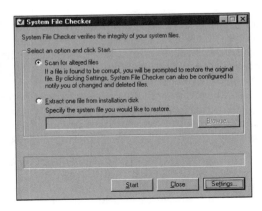

Figure 17-15: System File Checker
You can restore operating system files that have been changed or corrupted with the System File Checker utility. By clicking the Settings button, you can adjust what files the utility should look for and view a log file that lists any changes that are, or have been, made.

System File Checker works by using a reference file Default.sfc (normally found in your Windows folder) to keep track of what files were originally installed, which have been added, and which have been changed or updated. It does not track changes dynamically, however. You have to run the program manually for it to work (although a default file of the original Windows 98 installation is created automatically for you). What this means is, if you install a new piece of hardware, upgrade an existing driver, or add a Windows

98 Service Pack, you should run System File Checker and upgrade that default file so that the reference against which it compares is up to date.

Secret

One potentially powerful feature of System File Checker is that by running it after installing new applications, you can also find out what system files (if any) the application has changed or installed. This is a very common source of software conflicts and other problems.

Version Conflict Manager

A somewhat related tool that works in almost the exact opposite way is Version Conflict Manager, or VCM. VCM enables you to revert to newer versions of certain files that are replaced when you install (or reinstall) Windows 98 (see Figure 17-16).

By default, the Windows 98 installation overwrites certain DLLs and other files, even if the files on your hard disk are newer than the ones installed by Windows 98. The end result, again, can be DLL hell, because certain applications that require those newer versions may stop working, but this time it's caused by the operating system instead of the applications (which is what usually causes problems that System File Checker can fix).

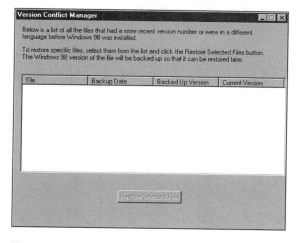

Figure 17-16: Version Conflict Manager
To restore files that are overwritten by a Windows 98 installation or reinstallation, use the Version Conflict Manager utility.

By running VCM after installing (or reinstalling) Windows 98, you can selectively restore the newer DLLs that Windows replaced and get your applications working again.

Dr. Watson

As its name suggests, Dr. Watson is an investigative tool that's useful in tracking down clues that may be helpful in solving software-related mysteries. Longtime Windows users may recall that Dr. Watson was bundled as part of Windows 3.1, disappeared from Windows 95, and then reappeared in Windows 98.

Dr. Watson can be launched either from within System Information or by typing **drwatson** into the Run command. Unlike the other utilities, when you launch Dr. Watson you won't see a main screen or dialog box; instead it just places an icon in your Windows 98 System Tray (usually located in the bottom-right corner of your screen). To see the program's user interface, you have to right-click that icon and choose Dr. Watson from the context menu that appears.

In doing so, you force the program to generate a system snapshot, which is a collection of system information it uses to try to diagnose software problems. If you select Advanced View from the utility's View menu, you see a series of tabs that list this information. As it turns out, it's essentially a subset of some of the more important content areas that you can also view via the System Information tool (see Figure 17-17).

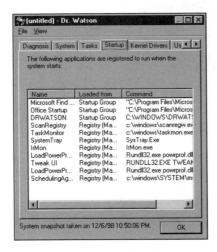

Figure 17-17: Dr. Watson, I presume
In the Advanced View, Dr. Watson gives you quick access to critical information about your system that can be useful in finding the causes of many software-related conflicts or other problems.

While this information can be somewhat helpful, what you really need to find out when you're troubleshooting is what's causing some of your applications to crash or your system to lock up. Because you may not always know when those lockups are going to occur, Dr. Watson should be running in the background at all times in order to be an effective troubleshooting tool. The default Windows 98 installation doesn't do this, however, so if you want to troubleshoot with Dr. Watson's help, you have to make it load at startup. Here's how: (Note that the same procedure can be easily adapted to load any program when Windows starts by simply selecting a different file in Step 3.)

STEPS:

Loading Dr. Watson at Startup

Step 1. Click the Start button, and select Taskbar & Start Menu under the Settings command.

Step 2. Click the Start Menu Programs tab, and click Add (see Figure 17-18).

Step 3. Click Browse, and then locate the drwatson.exe file inside your main Windows folder. Note that it is *not* inside the Drwatson folder (that's where the utility's settings and log files are kept), but should be at the root, or main, level of the Windows folder.

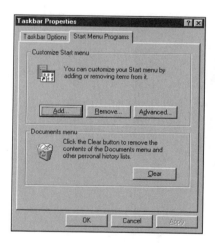

Figure 17-18: Adding programs to the StartUp Folder
You can easily place a shortcut to Dr. Watson, or any other program, inside your Windows StartUp folder by using the wizard that's available through the Taskbar Properties dialog box when you click the Add button.

Step 4. Click Next, then locate and click the StartUp folder, and click Next again.

Step 5. If you want to, you can change the name of the shortcut. When you're done, click Finish, and then OK in the Taskbar Properties dialog.

Step 6. Restart your PC for the change to take effect and for Dr. Watson to load.

Once Dr. Watson is running in the background, the utility goes to work trying to decipher the problem when a crash occurs on your computer. You can easily see it because when you click the Details button inside a dialog box saying that a crash has occurred, you get a somewhat meaningful error message instead of being confronted with the completely useless programming-related information about where the problem occurred in hexadecimal messages. Figure 17-19 shows an example.

Anytime Dr. Watson encounters an error, it automatically creates a log file that's saved in the Dr. Watson folder, which is located inside the Windows folder. If you want to add your own notes about what happened, you can do so in the open textbox at the bottom of the Dr. Watson dialog box. Note that you have to use the Save command off the File menu in Dr. Watson for those comments to be saved.

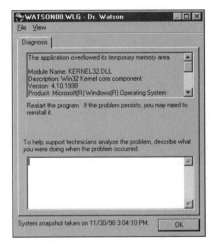

Figure 17-19: Helpful error messages
With Dr. Watson installed and running, the typically oblique information you get about program crashes is replaced by a message that explains in English what happened and, in some cases, what you may be able to do about the problem.

Tip

While it isn't a perfect answer, I think Dr. Watson's helpful explanations are useful enough that you should install it inside your StartUp folder and leave it there, even if you aren't trying to fix a particular problem.

If after fixing a problem, you want to prevent Dr. Watson from loading every time you start Windows, the easiest way is by launching the System Configuration Utility (described previously), selecting the Startup tab, and simply disabling the program by clicking off the check mark next to its name.

ScanDisk

In addition to software-related problems, some issues that can keep your PC from running properly are related to hardware. The most common of these are on your hard disk. To address these possible problems, Windows 98 (like Windows 95 before it) includes the ScanDisk utility, which is designed to look for physical errors on your disk (or disks) as well as problems with file structures and filenames for the files stored on the disks (see Figure 17-20).

ScanDisk comes in both Windows and DOS versions, so you can run it either way. ScanDisk can be run separately by launching it from the System Information utility's Tool menu, or it can be run automatically by using it as part of the Maintenance Wizard or Scheduled Task features built into Windows 98. (You can find them both off the Start menu under Programs ⇨ Accessories ⇨ System Tools.)

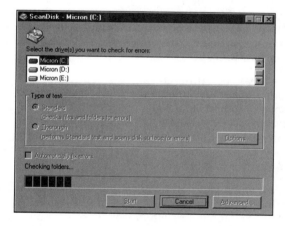

Figure 17-20: Cleaning up disk and file problems
The ScanDisk utility is an essential part of any troubleshooter's repertoire. You can use it to solve a variety of disk and file-related problems.

Registry Checker

The Registry, which actually consists of both the System.dat and User.dat files, is probably the most important software entity in your Windows setup. It stores an enormous amount of details about driver, operating system, and application settings. As a result, if problems occur in the Registry, you're bound to have trouble getting your system to work at all. In recognition of that fact, the Registry Checker utility automatically runs every time Windows 98 loads and maintains, by default, five recent backups of the Registry files (typically one for each of the last five times your system started up, although it's not supposed to save more than one copy per day).

If you want to check your Registry since you last started up, perhaps because you just installed an application and are concerned it may have caused some Registry-related problems, you can also launch Registry Checker manually through the System Information's Tool menu, or by typing **scanregw** into a Run command window.

If the utility does find a Registry problem, you need to restart your computer to a DOS command prompt and run the DOS-based version of the program (**scanreg** without the *w*) to fix it. The Windows-based version of Registry Checker can only look for problems — it can't fix them.

When you run the DOS version of Registry Checker, by typing **scanreg** and then hitting Enter at a C:\> prompt, you can restore any of your previous Registry backups, which should enable you to return your system to a stable, functioning state.

Automatic Skip Driver Agent

One of the most frustrating parts of trying to get past startup problems is figuring out which software driver is preventing your system from booting properly. To help you resolve that issue, the Automatic Skip Driver Agent (ASD) can help you determine which driver is having problems loading and can provide advice on how to fix it.

To use it, make sure you've gone through two consecutive restarts where the same driver won't load (sometimes simply restarting again can resolve intermittent problems), and then launch the program by either selecting it from System Information's Tool menu, or by typing **asd** into a Windows Run command prompt. Any drivers that haven't loaded should be listed there, along with advice on what you should do. In most cases, you need to reinstall or update the driver to get around the problem.

If you try to launch ASD when you don't have any driver problems, you get a simple dialog box that says, "There are no current ASD critical operation failures on this machine," which in English means there's nothing wrong. (Go ahead and try it.)

Update Wizard Uninstall

One of the potentially nice but also potentially problematic features of Windows 98 is the Windows Update feature, which enables you to download and install operating system patches (such as Service Pack 1 for Windows 98) as well as driver upgrades from Microsoft's Web site. The upside is that you can make sure your system stays up to date, but the downside is that upgraded drivers can cause problems with other elements in your system. In recognition of this, Windows Update also enables you to uninstall any updates you've previously made, but you have to be able to connect to the Windows Update Web site to do so. If you can't because, say, your modem driver was upgraded and now you're unable to connect to the Internet, you're out of luck.

Well, not really. The Update Wizard Uninstall also enables you to uninstall any update packages you've downloaded, but it does so without having to connect to the Internet. Fortunately, Windows Update keeps a backup of the files it upgrades, and by using this utility, you can return your system to the state it was in before you made the update.

Signature Verification Tool

If you want to verify that some of your critical system files or driver files haven't been tampered with by a destructive virus or some other problem, you can use the Signature Verification Tool utility to find signed (or unsigned) files and view the certificates associated with them. Figure 17-21 shows an example.

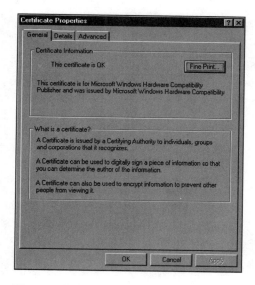

Figure 17-21: Signature certification
By using the Signature Verification Tool, you can view the Security Certificates associated with various files and ensure that they haven't been tampered with.

Windows Report Tool

If you feel like sharing your frustrating troubleshooting experiences with Microsoft, you can use this simple utility to send an e-mail message to a Microsoft support engineer.

Windows 95 diagnostic tools

If you're using Windows 95, there are some helpful tools available to you as well, and most of them are also included with Windows 98.

Secret

By the way, some Microsoft applications for Windows 95, such as Office 97, come with a simplified version of Windows 98's impressive System Information tool. You can get to it via any Office 97 program's About box (which you can get to from the application's Help menu).

System Configuration Editor

Windows 95 users who want quick access to their important startup files (and those Windows 98 users who may want an alternative to the System Configuration Utility) can use the System Configuration Editor, which you can launch by typing **sysedit** into a Run Command window (see Figure 17-22).

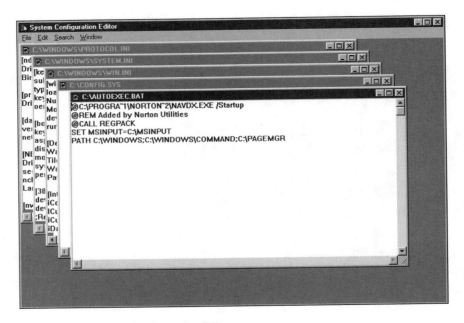

Figure 17-22: System Configuration Editor
Windows 95 users who need to edit their startup files can use the System Configuration Editor, or sysedit, which automatically opens their Autoexec.bat, Config.sys, Win.ini, System.ini, and Protocol.ini startup files in five overlapping windows.

It's nowhere near as elegant or powerful as Windows 98's similarly named System Configuration Utility, but it's better than nothing.

Disk Defragmenter

While not, strictly speaking, a diagnostic tool, the Disk Defragmenter utility included with Windows 95 and 98 can be used to help overcome certain problems. As explained in Chapter 3, over time, the files on Windows-based hard disks can get broken up into many pieces and scattered all over a hard drive. If this file fragmentation gets bad enough, it can cause all sorts of strange problems.

Consequently it's a good idea to defragment your hard drive, which unites all the separate pieces back into a contiguous group of files, on a regular basis, such as every month or so.

Tip

After you run the Disk Defragmenter utility included with Windows (or a third-party utility program), it's generally a good idea to run ScanDisk, which is also included with both Windows 95 and 98, to make sure all the freshly reorganized files are in good shape.

You can find the Defragmenter under Programs ➪ Accessories ➪ System Tools in both Windows 95 and Windows 98 — if it's been installed that is. The default installation of Windows 95 does not include it, so you have to go to the Add/Remove Programs control panel, click the Windows Setup tab, double-click Disk Tools, and then check Defrag to install it. (Have your Windows 95 CD ready if your CAB installation files aren't on your hard drive.)

If you're using Windows 98, you can automatically defragment your hard disk on a regular basis by using the Maintenance Wizard or Scheduled Tasks feature, both of which are available off the Start menu via Programs ➪ Accessories ➪ System Tools. One other benefit of the Windows 98 defragmenter is that it can help speed up the launch time of some of your applications by keeping track of what files are needed to start them and arranging those files on your hard disk in the most efficient way possible.

System Monitor and System Resource Meter

If you find yourself running into memory problems or system slowdowns, or if you want to find how efficiently your modem or network connection is transferring and receiving data, you're a good candidate to check the System Monitor utility. As its name suggests, System Monitor measures the performance and usage of certain components in your system.

A much simpler, but related utility is the System Resource Meter (sometimes just called "Resource Meter"), which tracks Windows resources currently in use. These resources are software only and have nothing to do with hardware resource issues (which are explained earlier in the section "Hardware Troubleshooting Concepts," earlier in this chapter). Essentially, Windows has limits on how much memory it can set aside for system-related files, user-related files, and the graphical display it creates for your monitor, and Resource Meter tracks their levels.

Before you can launch System Monitor or System Resource Meter under either 95 or Windows 98, make sure they're installed. Again, go to the Add/Remove Programs control panel, and click Windows Setup. Under Windows 98, you can find them both under the System Tools section, and under Windows 95 they're both under Accessories. Once they're installed, you can open either program under either operating system by going to Programs ➪ Accessories ➪ System Tools off the Start menu.

In its default state, System Monitor tracks only Processor Usage, which tells you how busy your system is at any given moment, but you can easily customize it to track a whole variety of different parameters (although only a few of them are really meaningful to normal people). To do so, go the Edit menu, select Add, and choose from a wide range of different options. You can get explanations of what the different parameters are by clicking an item and then clicking Explain, but to be honest, most of the explanations aren't very helpful.

Some useful options you may want to try under Windows 95 and 98 are Unused Physical Memory, under the Memory Manager section, which tells you if you are using up all your available RAM, and Swapfile Size, also under the Memory Manager section, to see how much of your hard disk is being used for virtual memory disk swapping. Under Windows 98 you can also check out Bytes Received/Second or Connection Speed under Dial-Up Adapter to see how fast and efficient your Internet connection is (see Figure 17-23).

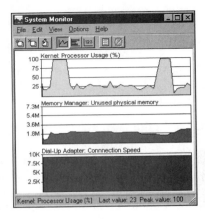

Figure 17-23: Monitoring your system
The System Monitor utility included with Windows 95 and 98 can be helpful in trying to determine if your system is running as efficiently as possible, or if any recent changes to your system have altered its performance.

WinTop

Windows 95 users who want to see all the different things that are running on their computer can use a little-known utility WinTop, which is part of Microsoft's Kernel Toys (and is available from the company's support Web site at http://support.microsoft.com). WinTop shows all the processes (explained later) that are currently running on your system, how long they've been running, and what percentage of your CPU's capacity they're using. (This last feature also makes it handy for figuring out what programs may be causing your system to slow down.) Figure 17-24 shows a typical screen.

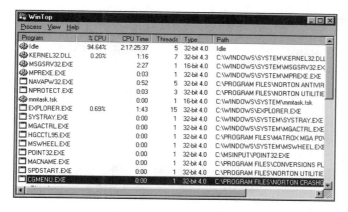

Figure 17-24: WinTop monitors processes
The WinTop utility is useful in figuring out what software is actually loaded and running on your computer.

A *process* is the technical name for each separate program that's currently loaded into memory on your system. Each process, in turn, consists of one or more *threads*, which are the subelements used by the program to do its work. By looking at the processes, and the paths where the programs were loaded from, you can get a much better idea of what's actually running on your system than you can by hitting Ctrl+Alt+Del to get to the Close Program dialog box.

Secret

Speaking of which, you can also use WinTop to close down processes by selecting a process from the list, right-clicking it, and selecting Properties from the menu that appears. Click the Priority tab, and select the Terminate Process Now button to do so (see Figure 17-25).

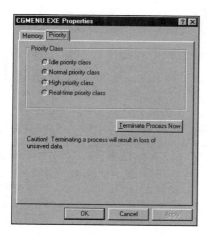

Figure 17-25: Close programs down
If you need to turn off individual applications or other programs that are currently running on your system in order to do some troubleshooting or while installing another application, you can use WinTop's Terminate Process Now feature.

SANDRA

One utility that isn't included with either Windows 95 or 98 but can be extremely useful, particularly for Windows 95 users, is SiSoft's SANDRA, or System Analyzer, Diagnostic & Reporting Assistant (see Figure 17-26).

CD

You can find a copy of SANDRA 99 Standard on the CD accompanying this book.

SANDRA is organized around a series of modules, each of which provides different types of information about the hardware and software in your system. (Note that some of the modules are unavailable in the freeware Standard version. To get to those modules, you need to register for the shareware Professional version.) Some of the modules also provide simple benchmarking utilities to test the performance of different components inside your PC.

Figure 17-26: SANDRA provides system analysis
SiSoft's SANDRA can provide a great deal of diagnostic information about your system, including both the hardware and software. Some of its modules offer Windows 95 users similar types of information to what Windows 98 users can find in the Microsoft System Information program.

One of the more useful modules is the Processes Information module, which can offer you more info about what programs are running on your computer and what files they use (see Figure 17-27).

One other handy feature of SANDRA is that, like System Information, it provides an easy way to launch other common Windows utilities via its Tools menu. In addition, you can quickly view a variety of critical system files, such as your startup files, by clicking the appropriate icon.

Table 17-1 summarizes all the Windows diagnostic programs listed in this section, noting in particular what operating system they're included with and what their primary application is.

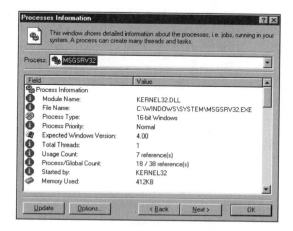

Figure 17-27: Programs and files in use
The Processes Information module offers another good way to view all the programs currently running on your system. In addition, it enables you to see which DLL files are associated with which processes, which can be handy in solving DLL problems.

Table 17-1 Windows Troubleshooting Tools

Program Name	Included in Windows 95	Included in Windows 98	Primary Application
System Information	Simplified version included with Office 97	X	Determining hardware conflicts, driver versions currently installed, and all the software currently running (including DLLs)
System Configuration Utility		X	Editing startup files
System File Checker		X	Verifying changes to system files and, potentially, shared files for applications, restoring system files

continued

Table 17-1   Windows Troubleshooting Tools *(continued)*

Program Name	Included in Windows 95	Included in Windows 98	Primary Application
Version Conflict Manager		X	Restoring newer DLLs replaced by Win98 install or reinstall
Dr. Watson		X	Looking for possible causes to software conflicts; providing advice
ScanDisk	X	X	Checking for hard disk and file corruption problems
Registry Checker		X	Checking for Registry problems and restoring previous copies
Automatic Skip Driver Agent		X	Determining which drivers won't load at startup
Update Wizard Uninstall		X	Removing problematic updates downloaded via the Windows Update feature
Signature Verification Tool		X	Checking for alterations to signed files by viruses or other security holes
Windows Report Tool		X	Sending information to Microsoft
System Configuration Editor	X	X	Editing startup files
Disk Defragmenter	X	X	Organizing files on disk
System Resource Meter	X	X	Checking for usage of software-based resources
System Monitor	X	X	Checking for a variety of system parameters including available memory
WinTop	Part of Win95 Kernel Toys (available via MS Web site)		Monitoring all the software currently running, seeing how much processing effort it takes
SANDRA			Diagnostic information on system hardware and software, including what software is currently running, benchmarks, and easy access to critical system files

Other programs

In addition to the applications listed here, you can find hundreds of other useful utilities on various shareware sites across the Internet, including Shareware.com and Download.com. Depending on your specific needs, you may find that other programs offer specific functions that are even more useful to your troubleshooting efforts. Ultimately, it doesn't matter what tools and techniques you use, as long as you get the job done.

Starting Over

If you've struggled for a while to solve a problem or if a problem just seems to keep coming back again and again, here's an important piece of advice that you need to keep in mind: sometimes it's not worth it. In other words, at times it's just not worth trying to heal all the ills that are ailing your PC. If you have reached a point where you seem to run into problem after problem and are wasting a lot of time trying to deal with them, I heartily suggest you simply start over.

I don't mean throw out your existing PC and get another (though I know that, if you've reached this point, you may be sorely tempted), but instead to start fresh with your existing PC by wiping the hard disk clean and reinstalling everything from scratch.

While I realize some may consider this notion sacrilegious, the practical reality is that sometimes, because of the horribly complex nature of the relations between PC hardware and software systems, starting over really is the best route. Let me put it this way, would you rather spend two and a half days trying to resolve a particular vexing problem, pushed forward by your stubborn nature to do whatever takes, or would you rather just decide to accept the situation and set aside a day to redo everything?

If you're the type of person who regularly adds and/or removes a lot of software to or from your system, you're the ideal candidate for just starting over. In fact, I've talked with many computer professionals who swear by the technique of reinstalling everything fresh every 6–12 months (some go so far as to say it's the only way to keep a Windows system stable). While this last notion may be a bit severe, I do know that reinstalling can magically make a lot of annoyances (as well as more serious problems) disappear.

That's not to say you should take it lightly, however, because starting over is a big job. In most cases it takes a good portion of a day. It also requires that you do some important homework ahead of time, including backing up your files, finding all the original CDs and/or floppy disks for the operating system (or systems), programs, drivers, and other software you have installed, and backing up any updates or other software you've downloaded from the Internet.

Tip

This last suggestion—backing up all your application and driver updates—is the one that most people forget about, but it can make a big difference in how quickly you can get your system back to a good working version of the state it was in before you started this process.

One other cautionary point you need to be aware of is that sometimes reinstalling can introduce new problems of its own. In particular, if you don't make sure you have all the latest driver updates, operating system service packs, application bug fixes, and what have you, you could end up worse off than before you started. If, on the other hand, you have the latest updates, you'll probably find that reinstalling everything brings you back to the near pristine state that most every computer has when you first bring it home and turn it on (and that's a beautiful thing).

Speaking of which, many computer manufacturers now include CD-ROMs (and the associated startup floppy) that make the process of starting over again much easier. In fact, many of them make it nearly automatic to reinstall both the operating system and the applications that were originally installed on the machine at the factory. If you have access to one of those CD-ROMs, I recommend using that first. If not, here are the specific steps involved in starting over with your PC.

Doing the following steps completely erases all the data on your computer's hard drive. Do not do so unless that's what you intend!

Caution

STEPS:

Repartitioning, Reformatting, and Reinstalling

Step 1. Back up all your data and application upgrades. Don't go any further until this is done.

Step 2. Restart the computer with a Windows 95/98 startup floppy disk that includes an MS-DOS, or real mode, CD-ROM driver. (See the instructions on how to make one in the section "Troubleshooting Tools," earlier in this chapter.)

Step 3. After the computer reboots and you get to an A:\> prompt, run the DOS FDISK partitioning utility by typing:

```
fdisk C: [Enter]
```

Step 4. Follow the directions on the screen to divide your hard drive into partitions of various sizes, if that's what you want. If you just want a single partition, however, select Option 2 "Set active partition," and select your C: drive (see Figure 17-28).

Step 5. When that's finished, hit Esc to quit FDISK, and run the DOS Format utility by typing:

```
format C:
```

at the A:\> prompt and then hitting Enter.

```
                    Microsoft Windows 95
                  Fixed Disk Setup Program
          (C)Copyright Microsoft Corp. 1983 - 1995

                       FDISK Options

Current fixed disk drive: 1

Choose one of the following:

1. Create DOS partition or Logical DOS Drive
2. Set active partition
3. Delete partition or Logical DOS Drive
4. Display partition information


Enter choice: [2]




Press Esc to exit FDISK
```

Figure 17-28: FDISK creates partitions
The DOS-based FDISK program enables you to create and manage partitions on your computer's hard disk.

Step 6. The next step is to switch to the CD drive and install either Windows 95 or 98 from scratch. If you haven't already done so, place the Windows 95 or Windows 98 CD into your CD-ROM drive. Then switch to the CD-ROM drive by typing:

```
cd D: (or whatever drive letter your CD-ROM happens to be)
[Enter]
```

Step 7. Once you get the D:\> prompt, type:

```
Setup [Enter]
```

Then just follow the on-screen directions to complete the installation of either Windows 95 or Window 98, as the case may be.

Tip

By the way, if you're going through the effort of starting over, it's also a good time to think about how you want to organize your hard disk via partitioning. For example, if you haven't yet converted to the more efficient FAT32 file system (File Allocation Table, 32-bit), now is a perfect time to do so. Simply make sure that when you partition the drive, you set it up to be a FAT32 partition. To do so with the FDISK utility that's bundled with Windows, simply answer yes to the question that first appears when you run FDISK on a hard drive that's larger than 2GB. (Confusingly, the question never says anything about FAT32, but instead asks if you want to enable support for large disks.) If you're using a different partitioning program, check the documentation or online help files for how to enable FAT32 support.

Note

You can use FAT32 (and FDISK only asks this question) only if you have Windows 95 OSR2 or later, or Windows 98, and the version of FDISK that comes with these respective operating systems. Earlier versions don't support FAT32.

If you prefer, you can also do the initial partitioning with a third-party program, such as PowerQuest's PartitionMagic, which offers more features and is easier to use than FDISK. For example, if you're planning to add more partitions or want to install another operating system in addition to Windows, you'll definitely find it easier to use something other than FDISK.

CD

A demo copy of PartitionMagic is on the CD-ROM accompanying this book.

Be aware that if you change the size of your partitions, such as making them larger than 8.4GB, you may run into problems with your computer's BIOS (and Windows 95 or 98 as a result) not recognizing anything beyond 8.4GB (or sometimes only 2.1GB). If that's the case, you need to update your BIOS before you can take advantage of larger partitions.

Cross-Reference

See Chapter 3, "Hard Disks and Removable Drives" for more on disk and partition limitations. See Chapter 11, "Upgrading Your PC," for more on upgrading your BIOS.

Summary

In this chapter I've described how to troubleshoot problems on your PC by developing a strategy, learning hardware and software troubleshooting concepts, and using troubleshooting software tools.

▶ Dealing with computer problems is, unfortunately, a nearly unavoidable part of using a PC, so it's important to have good troubleshooting skills.

▶ The most challenging part of troubleshooting isn't fixing the problem, but figuring out what's causing the problem.

▶ Many computer problems are like mysteries, waiting to be solved. To troubleshoot successfully, you need to know what resources are available to help you. Some of the best are the little-known Resource Kits included on the Windows 95 and 98 CD-ROMs.

▶ A large percentage of PC problems are caused by relatively simple things, such as loose or broken cables or recent software upgrades.

▶ Many hardware-related issues are due to driver problems. Fixing them often entails removing and reinstalling the driver or upgrading to a new version of the driver.

▶ Despite the advancements of Plug and Play, resource problems such as IRQ conflicts still occur. With the help of the Device Manager in Windows 95/98, most all of them can be solved with a minimum of effort.

▶ Many software problems are due to conflicts between shared DLL files. While much more difficult to fix than hardware problems, they too can be fixed with the help of the right tools.

▶ Software problems due to bugs or viruses do occur, but they're less common than most people think.

▶ One of the most useful troubleshooting tools you can have is a boot disk with a CD- or DVD-ROM driver.

▶ Windows 98 includes a wealth of useful troubleshooting tools, including the System Information utility, System Configuration Utility, and System File Checker.

▶ Windows 95 users can also use some built-in diagnostic tools to help solve their problems.

▶ Sometimes the best solution to fixing problems is to simply wipe everything off your hard disk and start all over.

Chapter 18

Solving Common PC Problems

In This Chapter

▶ You will learn how to diagnose and fix startup problems by figuring out where in the startup process the error occurs and applying the right solution.

▶ You will learn how to fix several types of hardware problems, including video display and hard disk–related issues.

▶ You will learn how to fix problems with external peripherals, such as printers and mice.

▶ You will learn how to fix problems with internal peripherals, such as modems and sound cards, as well as how to solve problems in connecting to the Internet.

▶ You will learn how to fix many types of software problems, including both consistent and random crashes and low memory–related problems.

▶ You will learn how to deal with common Web- and e-mail-related problems, such as viewing attachments.

In addition to knowing how to troubleshoot computer problems in general, it's helpful to have specific answers to common issues. In this chapter you can find advice on how to diagnose and fix many common PC ills, including those that affect your computer's capability to start up and to use certain pieces of hardware, certain kinds of software, and the Internet and e-mail. You won't necessarily find a whole lot of background information explaining why you should do what's suggested (plenty of that is in Chapter 17, "Troubleshooting Techniques," as well as throughout the book's other chapters), but you will find some procedures that can help make your computer work again.

As I mentioned in Chapter 17, there are way too many problems to address everything, so you may not find the specific answers you need to fix your problem. But if your PC is suffering from one of many different common maladies, you should find what you need here.

Fixing Startup Problems

Without a doubt, the most frustrating and confusing computer problems are those that keep your computer from starting up, or booting, properly. In many cases they involve scary-sounding error messages that make you wonder if you'll ever get your PC working again. The good news is that by following a few straightforward procedures and taking advantage of some of the troubleshooting tools bundled with Windows, most of the problems can be fixed relatively quickly.

The first step in the process is to figure out where in the boot process the problem occurs. Depending on where your computer stops working or at what point in the startup procedure you see error messages, you need to take one of several different next steps.

To help figure out which step, you need to know a little bit about what happens when you turn on your PC's power switch. The first thing that occurs is that a piece of software called the BIOS (Basic Input/Output System) is loaded into memory and starts the processor to work. The BIOS is actually stored inside a chip on your PC's motherboard, and it works completely independent of any operating system (or systems) you have on your hard disk. In fact, the BIOS loads and runs even if you don't have a hard disk in your computer at all.

The BIOS performs some tests on your system, called *POST* (Power On Self Test), looks for attached hardware, and then looks to the first section of your hard disk (called the *master boot record*) to see what to do next. Inside the master boot record are some critical files that start the process of booting your operating system (OS), typically some flavor of Windows. If you have multiple operating systems (such as Windows 98 and Windows 2000 or Windows 95 and Linux), the master boot record probably has a special program called a *boot loader* that enables you to pick from the various operating systems you have installed on your hard disk.

Once the main boot files for whatever OS you've selected (or the only one that's there) are read into memory, your computer loads and processes several different startup files, the specifics of which vary from OS to OS. In the case of Windows 95 and 98, which is what I'm focusing on, it's typically the Config.sys, Autoexec.bat, Win.ini, and System.ini files, followed by the Windows Registry. Inside each of the files, which are normally loaded while the Windows splash screen is displayed, are instructions to load many additional files, such as device drivers and other core system files. Once the Registry loads, files in your Startup folder are also loaded, and finally, you reach the standard Windows desktop.

For more details on what's involved in the startup process, see Chapter 8, "How Your Computer Works."

Cross-Reference

Secret

To find out all the different files that are loaded when you turn on your PC and boot Windows, take a look at the Bootlog.txt file, which is a hidden file that's typically stored at the root directory of your hard drive (usually C:\). If you can't see it, go to the View menu inside Windows Explorer, select Folder Options, hit the View tab, and turn on the Show all files radio button. Look at the file's modification date to determine when it was created. If you want to create a more recent version, restart your computer, and hold down the F8 key until you see a text-based menu of startup choices. Select Option 2, Logged, and a new Bootlog.txt file that includes all your most current drivers and other software is created.

With this information on how the boot process proceeds in mind, you need to closely watch your PC's screen as it starts up (presuming you can see the screen, of course — if not, see the section "Video Display Problems," later in the chapter) and try to figure out where in the process the problem occurs. Unless your PC has a power problem due to a bad outlet, frayed cord, or something else that keeps the system from even turning on, most startup issues boil down to BIOS settings or startup file settings. (If it doesn't turn on and you're sure the power from the outlet is fine, then the PC needs a new power supply or some other serious work that probably requires taking it to a repair shop.) BIOS settings are made in your computer's BIOS or CMOS (Complementary Metal Oxide Semiconductor, a type of material used to create the chip that stores your BIOS settings) Setup program (commonly just called *Setup*), and startup file adjustments can be made with one of several different utilities.

But before you make any changes to your system, it's helpful to remember that sometimes weird glitches just happen. So if your PC won't boot up one day or just after you've upgraded something and gives you some kind of error message, just shut it down, walk away for five minutes, and then try it again. Believe it or not, sometimes that really does work.

BIOS setup

If you get an error when first booting up about an invalid system disk (or the more obscure "No ROM Basic, System Halted"), or if one of your hard drives or other internal removable drives, such as your CD-ROM or DVD-ROM drive, isn't being recognized, you probably need to make some changes in BIOS Setup. (That is, of course, unless you forgot to remove a nonbootable floppy disk from your floppy drive when you restarted your computer. If that's the case, just pop it out, hit a key on your keyboard, and slap yourself for being so silly.)

Presuming that the physical connections within your PC are solid, which should always be checked first, you may have to enable a new hard drive or other internal removable IDE drive in order for it to be recognized. Most BIOS startup screens list the IDE devices they find connected to the PC's built-in IDE controller (often right after the keyboard and mouse), so if one of your devices isn't listed, you know it hasn't been enabled (or again, the physical connections are bad). The initial BIOS screens and the BIOS Setup program do not concern themselves with drive partitions, only physical drives.

To make any changes to your BIOS, you have to enter the Setup program by holding down the appropriate key that your computer uses (often F2, Esc, or Del) to launch Setup. Once you're there, the specifics of how to enable drives or switch settings varies from BIOS to BIOS (different PCs have different versions made by different companies), but most of them can be found on the main setup screen.

Adjustments for hard disks and removable drives

In most instances, the main hard drive should be set to be the master on the primary adapter (sometimes called *adapter 0*), and the CD- or DVD-ROM can either be the slave on the primary adapter or the master on the secondary adapter (sometimes called *adapter 1*). Additional removable drives, such as Zip drives, recordable CDs, and what have you, can also take either position or the slave on the secondary adapter slot. If you add a second IDE hard drive, it should be the master on the secondary adapter, and the other devices should be moved around accordingly. If you're still having problems, you might want to change the settings to move the devices around yet again. Some drives are very finicky about where they get placed.

Cross-Reference

For more on hard drive adapters and their settings, see Chapter 3, "Hard Disks and Removable Drives."

In addition to making these settings, you also have to be sure that all the drives' configuration settings are accurate. Unless you're working with an older computer and/or an older hard drive, you should be able to use the Auto configure options, which take care of making these rather arcane settings for you. (If you can't use Auto, then you need the drive's documentation to be able to type in things such as the number of cylinders, heads, and sectors.) If you want to intentionally disable a drive for troubleshooting purposes, you can also do that via the Setup program.

One final drive-specific setting you may want to look at or adjust is your boot delay. If, for some reason, your hard drive isn't spinning up quickly enough, when your BIOS finishes and looks for boot files on your hard disk's master boot record, it may not find them. By adding a brief delay, you may be able to get around some occasional boot problems. (Note that doing so delays how long it takes to boot your system.)

Other BIOS setup adjustments

You occasionally have to make other changes to your system's settings via the Setup program in order to get your PC to boot (or to solve other problems). For example, it's common to have to turn on and off or make resource settings adjustments to other peripherals in your system, such as USB (Universal Serial Bus) and IEEE 1394 controllers, serial and parallel ports, or built-in modems, video adapters, sound circuitry, and other devices. In most instances, you can find the important settings in the Peripheral Configuration section under the Advanced menu of your BIOS. On many BIOSes, you have to use the arrow keys to select Peripherals, and then hit Enter to get to a new page with the specific settings.

Once you're in there, you can enable and disable various devices to turn them on and off, as well as make changes to their resource settings, such as their IRQ (Interrupt Request), DMA (Direct Memory Access) channel, and I/O (Input/Output) Address.

Cross-Reference

For more on hardware resources, see Chapter 17, "Troubleshooting Techniques."

SCSI adapter BIOS

If you have a SCSI (Small Computer Systems Interface) adapter inside your PC and you're using a SCSI hard drive either as the main boot disk or as a second (or third) disk inside your system, you may also have to make changes to the SCSI adapter's BIOS. (To make a SCSI drive the boot disk, your main system BIOS has to support this feature and have it turned on.)

To do that, wait until the SCSI adapter's BIOS message appears. It should be after the main BIOS messages but before the startup files begin loading from the hard disk. Then look for the key combination you need to hold down. (In many cases it is Ctrl+A.) As with your system's onboard IDE controller, the SCSI adapter recognizes and displays all the SCSI devices it finds attached, so if you recently added a SCSI peripheral and you don't see it listed, then check the physical connections and/or look for a SCSI termination problem.

Cross-Reference

See the section "SCSI problems," later in this chapter, for more on SCSI termination issues.

Startup files

If your PC makes it through the BIOS display settings but still won't boot, there's a good chance that you've got a problem with one of your startup files. Startup file problems take many forms, however, so just knowing that it's a startup file issue isn't really that helpful. The hard part is figuring out which file or files are causing the problem.

Boot files

If you're still stuck with an Invalid System Disk message, for example, that may mean the very first boot files stored in your hard drive's master boot record have been corrupted, deleted, or altered by a boot virus. (If you just changed the partitioning on your hard drive, it may also mean that you forgot to set the partition as active.) If the problem is related to the master boot record, here's an undocumented procedure for reinstalling the main boot files.

STEPS:

Fixing Your Master Boot Record

Step 1. Boot your PC with a startup floppy disk that includes the Fdisk.exe and Sys.com utilities (both the standard Windows 95 and Windows 98 boot floppies that you create via the Add/Remove Programs control panel will work).

Step 2. When you reach the A:\ prompt, type:

```
Fdisk /mbr [Enter]
```

Step 3. When that operation is complete and you get to another A:\ prompt, type:

```
Sys C: [Enter]
```

Step 4. When that's complete and you get the System Transferred Successfully message, take out the boot floppy and hold down the Ctrl+Alt+Del keys simultaneously to restart your computer.

Note

If you previously installed a boot loader program that enables you to choose among several different operating systems, you have to reinstall it after this procedure to get access to the other OSes because it will have been deleted. The other operating systems are still there (don't worry), but you have to reestablish a connection to them, which is what a boot loader program provides.

Config.sys and Autoexec.bat

If you reach the point where your system starts to boot from the hard drive and you get a message about Starting Windows 98 (or 95) and then it locks up, then the problem is with one of several other startup files, such as your Config.sys or Autoexec.bat. Sometimes you get an error message that specifically tells you what file is causing the problem. If you do, make sure to write down the filename because you need that information for later.

Many times, however, the system just locks up while the Windows 95 or 98 splash screen is being displayed and the little blue bar across the bottom stops moving. If that's the case, try restarting your system and hitting the Esc key as soon as the Windows logo appears. This hides the splash screen logo and enables you to watch as some of the initial startup files are loaded. If the boot process stops at a particular line, then you can start narrowing in on the problem.

On some systems, particularly newer ones, you may not see anything on the screen when you do this because some of the startup files that display messages on the screen while they load, specifically your Config.sys and Autoexec.bat files, may be blank. That doesn't mean nothing is going on, however; it's just that other startup files and the Windows Registry do not display any messages as they load files.

Bootlog.txt

The next place to look for your problem file (or files) is in the Bootlog.txt file referred to earlier. This file logs all the drivers loaded by your system at startup. If you haven't already, you need to make a current version of Bootlog.txt by restarting your PC, holding down F8, and selecting Logged from the menu that appears.

If your system boots to Windows, you can open Bootlog.txt with Notepad or WordPad to view it. If not, boot to a DOS command prompt (C:\), and type **edit bootlog.txt**. You need to make sure you are at the root C:\ directory for this command to work; otherwise, just a blank screen opens. If you're at the C:\Windows prompt, type **cd..** to move back down to the C:\ directory.

Once you have Bootlog open, you want to look for Error, Fail, or LoadFailed messages and make note of the specific files with which they occurred. Note that LoadFailed messages, which simply indicate that a driver hasn't loaded, are common even on systems that work fine. It may just mean that your system doesn't need that particular driver so it wasn't loaded. Error and Fail (and some LoadFailed) messages, however, typically indicate a problem with the file.

Once you've done your research in determining what file (or files) may be preventing your system from starting up (if any — sometimes hardware resource problems prevent systems from booting), then you can use several different tactics to address the problem.

Using safe mode

In most all instances, your first step in trying to solve the problem is to boot into Windows 95 or 98 using Safe Mode. To do so, restart your computer, and hold down the F5 key (if you're using Windows 98, you can also hold down the Ctrl key and then select option 3 Safe Mode from the Startup menu that appears).

Safe Mode bypasses your startup files and loads only a minimal set of drivers from the Windows Registry, but it still enables you to troubleshoot from a familiar Windows interface and use available Windows troubleshooting software tools.

If your system can successfully boot into Safe Mode, then the problem is likely due to a specific file or system setting referenced in one of your startup files, or to a hardware conflict. To see if it's the latter, you need to use the Device Manager (part of the System control panel) to see what device is causing the problem and then work on resolving that problem using the techniques described in the section "Hardware Troubleshooting Concepts" in Chapter 17, "Troubleshooting Techniques."

To see if the problem is due to a specific file or system setting (or to try and find the problem file that you discovered from following the previous suggestions), you can use one of several tools. If you're running Windows 98, you can use the System Configuration Utility to individually look through your main startup files, and if you have Windows 95, you can use the similarly named System Configuration Editor to do the same.

Cross-Reference

For more on troubleshooting tools, see Chapter 17, "Troubleshooting Techniques."

If you discovered a problem in the Bootlog.txt and you're running Windows 98, you can use the Automatic Skip Driver Agent utility to find out more about the problem file and what to do about it. In fact, if you boot at least two times in a row with the same problem, Windows 98 should automatically disable the problem driver. Again, you use Automatic Skip Driver to find out which files were disabled and what to do about them.

If you're running Windows 95, things aren't quite so easy. You need to figure out where the problem driver came from and reinstall the device, update the driver, or in some instances, reinstall Windows 95.

Cross-Reference

See Chapter 17, "Troubleshooting Techniques" for more on reinstalling or updating drivers.

If your system can't boot in Safe Mode, then try the Safe Mode-Command Prompt Only setting. This bypasses all your startup and Windows files and brings you to a DOS C:\ prompt. In this case, you're probably going to need to reinstall Windows in order to get your system back into working order. Before you do, however, you need to double-check your BIOS Setup settings, and you should also restore the basic system files to your Master Boot Record, as described in the list of steps, "Fixing Your Master Boot Record," earlier in this chapter. In addition, try running the DOS version of ScanDisk from your boot floppy to verify that you don't have any hard disk problems. To do so, just type **scandisk C:** and then hit Enter at any command prompt, such as A:\ or C:\.

Turning certain files off

In many cases, solving startup problems involves disabling or ignoring certain lines in one of your startup files. Windows 98's System Configuration Utility makes this easy by providing check marks next to each line. Simply uncheck the lines that you think may be causing the problem, and they are automatically "remarked" out, which tells the system to ignore them (see Figure 18-1).

Figure 18-1: Editing startup files with Windows 98
Windows 98's System Configuration Utility makes it easy to edit your startup files. All you have to do is select the problem line and disable it by unchecking the box next to it.

Under Windows 95, you can use the System Configuration Editor to get quick access to your startup files, but you still have to edit them manually. Here's how.

STEPS:

Editing Startup Files Under Windows 95

Step 1. Open the Run window off the Start menu, and type **sysedit**.

Step 2. Select the startup file you think has the problem via the Window menu, and then look through the file to find the line that refers to what you think is causing the problem.

Step 3. Place your cursor at the beginning of that line, and type either a semicolon character (;) or the letters **rem** and then a space (see Figure 18-2).

Continued

STEPS
Editing Startup Files Under Windows 95 *(continued)*

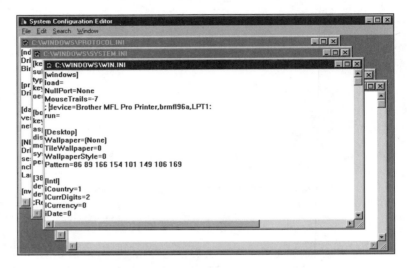

Figure 18-2: Manually editing startup files
The trick to tweaking your startup files is to get your computer to ignore certain lines by typing a semicolon or **rem** at the beginning of the line.

Step 4. Save your changes, exit the program, and then restart your computer to see if they worked. If not, start over in Safe Mode, and go through the process again until you're able to solve the problem (or just run out of patience).

In some cases the problems you run across may not be with your startup files but with other programs or services that also start up when Windows 95 and 98 boot. These files can be loaded from either the Windows Registry or the Startup folder. Under Windows 98, again, the System Configuration Utility makes it very easy to individually disable each of these items, regardless of where they start (see Figure 18-3).

Under Windows 95, again, you have to make a bit more effort. Finding the things in the StartUp folder and turning them off is easy. Just locate the folder (it's typically at C:\Windows\Start Menu\Programs\StartUp), and temporarily move any items you want to prevent from loading onto the desktop. Getting to the files loaded from the Registry is a bit more work. Here's how.

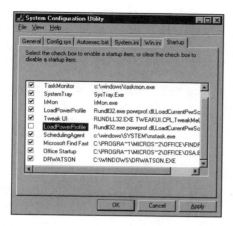

Figure 18-3: Turning off startup programs
By selecting the Startup tab under Windows 98's System Configuration Utility, you can turn off any file or service that's automatically started when you boot Windows 98, even those loaded "secretly" from the Registry.

Caution

Editing the Windows Registry is a potentially dangerous task that can screw up your system if you make a mistake, so proceed slowly and with caution. To be safe, before you get started, make backups of your System.dat and User.dat files, which go into making the Registry. You can find them inside your Windows folder. They're usually hidden, so you have to enable viewing hidden files first by going to Windows Explorer's View menu, selecting Folder Options, clicking the View tab, and then selecting the Show all files radio button.

STEPS:

Turning Off Programs That Start from the Registry

Step 1. Open the Run window, and type **regedit** to load the Registry Editor.

Step 2. Open the HKEY_LOCAL_MACHINE key by clicking the plus sign (+) next to it, and maneuver your way down until you get to HKEY_LOCAL_MACHINE\Software\Microsoft\Windows\Current Version.

Step 3. Once you're inside that level, scroll down and select the Run, RunOnce, RunOnceEx, RunServices, and RunServicesOnce folders, and see what items are listed in the right window (see Figure 18-4).

Continued

STEPS

Turning Off Programs That Start from the Registry *(continued)*

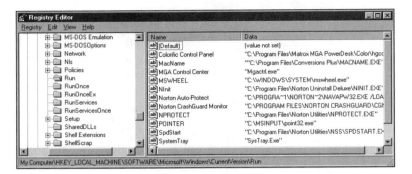

Figure 18-4: Programs launched from the Registry
To manually turn off applications that are loaded from the Registry, you have to edit the Registry and remove the keys that refer to these "hidden" programs.

Step 4. To prevent a particular application from loading, you need to select the key in the right window, right-click it, and select Delete from the Context menu that appears. Doing so does not delete the application, just the command that automatically starts it at boot time.

Step 5. If you have set up multiple users on your machine, you also have to check the HKEY_USERS\.Default\Software\ Microsoft\Windows\CurrentVersion section of the Registry and look for other Run folders there.

Step 6. When you're finished, exit the Registry Editor (all changes occur as soon as you make them and do not have to be saved), and restart your computer to see if that fixes your problem. If it doesn't, you have to go through the procedure again.

If you decide you want any programs whose Registry keys you deleted to be loaded automatically again (such as after you fix your startup problem), you have to reinstall the applications that put them there. As a result, you should keep track of what you delete and what programs they belong to. You can usually tell by looking at the Data setting in the Registry Editor window, which tells you from which folder the files are being loaded.

Note

In general you don't need nor shouldn't want to edit items from the RunOnce or RunServicesOnce folders because, as their name implies, they get run only one time and then are removed from your system. (Many program registration reminders are run this way.)

Restoring/reinstalling files

Some startup problems are due to files being changed or deleted. Under Windows 98 you can use the System File Checker utility to verify that all your critical system files are there and that they haven't been corrupted. If System File Checker does find a problem, or you know that you have a missing file based on an error message your system displayed, the program also provides an easy way to extract and reinstall a specific file from the compressed Windows 98 CAB files. This can save you from having to reinstall the entire operating system just to fix a file or two (see Figure 18-5).

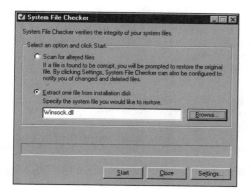

Figure 18-5: Restoring system files
Windows 98's System File Checker enables you to decompress and reinstall individual system files easily.

If you're running Windows 95 and you come across what you believe to be a missing or corrupted system file, you can extract and reinstall it manually, but it's not always straightforward. Here are the steps involved:

STEPS:

Extracting a System File

Step 1. Create a boot floppy disk with a CD-ROM driver, and copy the Extract.exe utility from your Windows\Command folder onto the floppy. If it's not there, copy it from the Windows 95 CD (it should be in the Win95 folder).

Cross-Reference
See Chapter 17, "Troubleshooting Techniques" for more on how to create a boot disk with a CD-ROM driver.

Continuued

STEPS

Extracting a System File *(continued)*

Step 2. Put your Windows 95 CD into your CD-ROM drive and the boot floppy disk into your floppy drive, and then restart your computer.

Step 3. When you get to the A:\ prompt, type:

```
extract /a <CD-ROM>:\win95_02.cab <xxx>
```

Replace <CD-ROM> with the letter assigned to your CD-ROM drive and <xxx> with the name of the file you need extracted. If you know where you want to extract the file to, you can add:

```
/l <destination>
```

to the end of the line, where <destination> is the specific folder on your hard drive where you want the file to go, such as C:\Windows\System or C:\Windows. For example, the completed command might look like this:

```
extract /a D:\win95_02.cab winsock.dll /l C:\Windows
```

Step 4. When the operation is done, remove the floppy, restart your computer by holding down the Ctrl+Alt+Del keys simultaneously, and see if it fixed your problem.

Note

If you're unable to boot into Safe Mode under Windows 98, you can use the same technique described here, but the Extract utility is already located on the Windows 98 boot disk. An even easier option is to use the simplified Ext.exe program that's also found on the Windows 98 boot disk. (This program is stored in the Ebd.cab file and is available only when the boot disk is loaded and the temporary RAM disk is created by the startup files. You can find Ext.exe and other applications inside the Ebd.cab file. Read the Readme.txt file on the Windows 98 boot disk for more information.)

Under Windows 95 you can sometimes restore certain system files by running the Windows 95 Setup program and then selecting the Verify option. In many cases you have to do this by restarting your system with a boot floppy that has a CD-ROM driver and running the Setup program again from the CD-ROM. Verify is supposed to automatically appear as an option in one of the initial Setup screens if the program notices an existing Windows 95 installation. I've come across cases when it doesn't, however. If you run into that situation, you can simply reinstall Windows again on top of your existing installation, which can solve problems as well (but takes a lot longer).

Fixing the Registry

The most critical part of your Windows system is the Registry, which is made up of two main files, System.dat and User.dat, as well as information that is created and maintained dynamically when your PC is turned on and running. If your Registry is corrupted by a software conflict, incomplete installation, or other issue, you're almost guaranteed to have problems with your computer. In some situations, the problem generates an error message when you start your computer, and in others, you may not be able to boot at all.

In recognition of its importance, as well as the fact that Registry problems can be very daunting, Windows 98 includes a new Registry Checker utility that automatically checks your Registry for errors every time you boot your system. The DOS-based Registry Checker (Scanreg.exe) runs silently in the background as your computer boots up and automatically makes a backup of your Registry on a daily basis.

Secret

The default setting is to maintain five recent copies, although you can adjust those settings from anywhere between 1 and 99 by editing the Scanreg.ini file, which is typically located in the Windows\System folder.

You can also run a Windows-based version of Registry Checker via the System Information Utility's Tools menu. This can be helpful if you think that a recent software installation may have caused a problem with the Registry.

If Registry Checker does find a problem either through its automatically run DOS-based version, or if you manually run the Windows version, you need to restore a previous copy of the Registry. You can do this only through the DOS-based version of Registry Checker, which means if you've run the Windows version first, you'll be prompted to restart your computer in MS-DOS mode (the same as Command Prompt Only). Once you restart in DOS mode, type **scanreg /restore**, and you can select from the previous backups you've made. (They're typically stored as compressed CAB files in the Windows/Sysbckup folder with the names rb000.cab, rb001.cab, and so on.)

In most cases you can select the most recent backup based on the date, but do that only if your system was stable the last time you booted your computer. If you've been dealing with the problem for the last few days, you may want to select an older backup.

It's also possible to restore a previous version of the Registry under Windows 95, but the process is much more tedious. Plus, Windows 95 generally keeps only one backup copy of the two Registry files (which it names System.da0 and User.da0), and like Windows 98, it creates a new backup every time you reboot and it successfully reaches the Windows desktop. As a result, you have to restore your old Registry settings before you can get Windows 95 to boot (which can happen even with some lingering problems in the Registry), or your fully functional Registry backup files are overwritten by a newer, possibly less-functional set. Here are the steps involved.

As always, tread cautiously when messing with Registry files.

Caution

STEPS:

Restoring Windows 95 Registry files

Step 1. Restart your computer in MS-DOS mode either by holding down F8 and then selecting Command Prompt Only from the list of startup options that appear, or by using a boot floppy disk.

Step 2. If you started with a floppy, type:

```
C: [Enter]
```

Step 3. Switch to the Windows directory by typing:

```
Cd Windows [Enter]
```

Step 4. Change the attributes of and then rename the existing Registry files by typing:

```
Attrib -r -h -s system.dat [Enter]
Attrib -r -h -s user.dat [Enter]
Ren system.dat system.xxx [Enter]
Ren user.dat user.xxx [Enter]
```

Step 5. Restart your computer by holding down the Ctrl+Alt+Del keys simultaneously. Windows should find and rename the System.da0 and User.da0 files automatically to System.dat and User.dat and use that previous Registry configuration to start your PC.

In some situations you may also find slightly older System.bak and User.bak files. If you want to try them as another Registry backup, you first need to rename them to System.dat and User.dat using the commands listed in Step 4, and then restart your machine.

Another option is to rename and use the System.1st and User.1st files, which are created when you first install Windows 95. The problem with them is that they won't have any changes you've made to your system since then. As a result, you have to reinstall all your software because applications write certain settings to the Registry, and without them, the programs won't work.

Cross-Reference

For more on reinstalling software, see Chapter 9, "Adding, Upgrading, and Removing Software."

Another Registry tool you can try is Microsoft's own RegClean, which you can find at Microsoft's support web site at `http://support.microsoft.com`.

Secret

Shutdown problems

In addition to problems starting up your computer, some people come across problems when they try to shut down their computer. In most cases these problems are due to out-of-date or conflicting drivers for one of your PC's hardware components. Unfortunately, it's not easy to tell which driver is at fault (although video card drivers are often the culprit — so check those first). Consequently, you need to find out what version of the driver you have for each of your main devices and see if you can get updates. You can use the Device Manager to get access to most driver version information.

If you're using Windows 98, the problem may also be related to that operating system's Fast Shutdown feature. To disable that feature, launch the System Configuration Utility (via the System Information Tool), and on the General tab, click the Advanced button. Click the Disable fast shutdown check box, hit OK twice, and restart your PC to see if that works (see Figure 18-6).

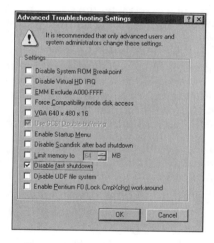

Figure 18-6: Windows 98 shutdown problems
You can fix many common shutdown problems by turning off Fast Shutdown in the System Configuration Utility. A better long-term solution is to upgrade the driver that's causing the problem.

Fixing Hardware Problems

Once you've gotten your PC to boot up, then you can move on to dealing with other issues. (Ah, aren't computers grand?) Some of the most troublesome problems that people have to deal with are those that affect different hardware components of their PC. In many cases the problems can be solved by removing the problematic device from the Device Manager and then restarting your PC, which forces it to reinstall the drivers and initialize certain settings. In other cases, a driver upgrade is the answer. Both of these solutions are described in detail in the section "Hardware Troubleshooting Concepts" in Chapter 17, "Troubleshooting Techniques." In some cases, that's not enough, however, so if you're looking for additional device-specific information and advice, keep reading.

Video display problems

Having problems with your monitor has got to be one of the most annoying computer problems there is because without a working display, you can't do anything (which makes discussions of troubleshooting pretty pointless). The trick here is to figure out where the fault lies. If when you turn on your computer and monitor, you see absolutely nothing, then either your monitor or video card has died, or you have a bad connection. Double- and triple-check the power, the physical connectors on the monitor and video card, and if necessary, try pulling out and reseating the video card. If none of that works, it's off to the shop (or computer store) you go.

If you see at least some initial BIOS messages, but your screen goes black or the display is all screwy (that's a *technical* term, by the way) when Windows or another operating system starts to load, then the hardware itself is probably fine, but you have a driver problem. Either the wrong driver was installed or the video card settings don't match the monitor. Under Windows the easiest way to solve this problem is to launch into Safe Mode and then either reinstall a new driver for the video card, or use the Display control panel's Settings tab to adjust the settings. Try a lowest common-denominator such as 640 × 480 resolution and 16 colors first, and then once you're sure that works, jump your way up to higher resolutions and more colors.

One other trick you can use if you're getting strange screen anomalies is to decrease the hardware acceleration settings. Click the Advanced button in the Display control panel's Settings tab, switch to the Performance tab, and move the Hardware acceleration slider back a notch or two (see Figure 18-7).

If things get a bit better after restarting, but aren't totally fixed, try it again, but move the slider all the way to the left. This essentially turns off any hardware acceleration your video card may support, but it may enable you to use it for a while. The long-term solution to this problem is to get an updated driver.

If your monitor suddenly goes dark in the middle of playing a game or doing something else on your PC, you may want to check the Screen Saver section of the Display control panel. If you set a relatively short time before the screen saver is supposed to kick in and you set it to a blank screen, it might look as if your system suddenly died or went to sleep. The reason is some games and other entertainment titles have long stretches of video that don't require any input from you (other than watching) and the system may interpret that as no activity. And if the system thinks there's no activity, the screen saver kicks in. Your power management settings may also be affected in a similar way.

Figure 18-7: Fixing screen anomalies
Turning down the hardware acceleration features can fix a lot of strange and annoying display problems in both Windows 95 and 98.

To fix these types of issues, just increase the time before the screen saver or power management features kick in, or temporarily turn them off.

See the section "Power management problems," later in this chapter, for more information.

Cross-Reference

Hard drive problems

Hard drive–related issues can result in all kinds of different problems on your PC, including random crashes, corrupted files, the inability to start up and more. To check for problems under Windows 95 or 98, run the ScanDisk utility. If you're running Windows 98 and you really want to make sure your hard disk stays in tip-top shape, you can even have ScanDisk run on a regular schedule by using either the Maintenance wizard or the Scheduled Tasks wizard. Both are available via Programs ⇨ Accessories ⇨ System Tools off the Start menu.

If you're really having bad problems, restart with a Windows 95 or 98 boot floppy disk, and run the DOS, or real-mode version of ScanDisk by simply typing **scandisk C:** when you get to an A:\ prompt. If you have multiple hard drives or have set up multiple partitions on a single partition, you have to check them separately.

To make ScanDisk automatically fix any problems it comes across, just type **scandisk C: /all**.

Tip

In addition to running ScanDisk on a regular basis, or other third-party disk utilities such as Norton Utilities, Nuts & Bolts, and so on, it's also a good idea to defragment your drive via the Disk Defragmenter utility on a similar schedule. You can either do this manually or, again, use Windows 98's Maintenance wizard or Scheduled Tasks wizard to automate the process for you.

Cross-Reference

See Chapter 14, "Working with Documents and Files," for more tips on disk maintenance.

CD

A demonstration copy of Gibson Research's Trouble In Paradise utility, which is for Zip and Jaz drives, is on the CD.

Bad sectors

One problem that ScanDisk or other disk utilities may find with one of your hard drives is called a *bad sector* or *bad block*. This basically means that a tiny area of your hard drive is no longer able to reliably store information. If left uncorrected, a bad block could cause big problems because a portion of a file could be written to that block and then not be readable, which would corrupt the entire file. As a result, ScanDisk and most other disk utilities block or hide bad sectors, which prevents them from being used.

Caution

It is not at all uncommon for hard disks to develop a few bad sectors, so if yours does, don't worry. However, if you start to see messages about multiple bad sectors on a regular basis, that's almost a sure sign that your hard disk is on its last legs. Back up all your data using the backup program included with Windows 95 or 98 or some other utility, and start shopping for a new hard drive.

Cross-Reference

To find out how to install a new hard drive, see Chapter 11, "Upgrading Your PC."

Partitions and drive letters

Some of the more confusing problems associated with hard drives revolve around partitions, which are logical divisions of physical disks. Under DOS and Windows, most partitions are treated as individual volumes, and each is assigned a different drive letter, which makes them "appear" as different disks.

Cross-Reference

For more on disk partitions and how they affect drive letters, see Chapter 3, "Hard Disks and Removable Drives."

If you create new partitions or remove existing partitions (after upgrading to the FAT32 file system, for example, or installing a new hard drive), you may end up "breaking" your applications because they may get confused about where some of their support files are located.

For example, adding or removing a partition typically raises or lowers the letter assigned to your CD- or DVD-ROM drive, and applications that regularly require access to the original program CD (such as for accessing clip art collections) may stop working properly or generate an error message the first time you run them after you make partition changes. Similarly, if in the process of creating partitions and reorganizing your hard disk, you move some application folders from one partition (or drive letter) to another, there's a good chance the programs won't work from the new location. Oftentimes they generate error messages that say something about not being able locate certain files.

In some situations you can simply redirect the program to the new location of the CD and everything works fine, but in others, it's not so easy. The location where the program knows to look for the CD is typically stored in the Registry and to change it manually requires finding the proper key and making the appropriate change to its value. A much simpler solution is to look for and use an application such as PowerQuest's PartitionMagic, which has an AppMover feature that takes care of fixing these types of problems for you.

A demo version of PowerQuest's PartitionMagic is on the CD.

CD

A related problem is that if you use a removable storage device, you may find that its drive letter changes depending on whether or not you start your PC with a cartridge in the drive. This can lead to the same type of frustrating problems. One solution that works for a variety of scenarios is to reserve a higher letter for the removable drive (or any drive that may be affected by this issue), such as I:, where you know it won't be affected by partition changes. To do so, you need to double-click the drive in the Device Manager, select the Settings tab, and in the bottom of the dialog, choose the driver letter you want. Figure 18-8 shows the settings.

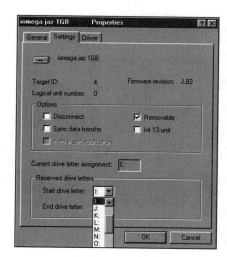

Figure 18-8: Reserving a drive letter
You can fix some confusing drive letter problems with removable cartridges as well as hard drive partitions by forcing the drive to a specific letter that you select via the Device Manager.

Note

If the drive whose letter you're adjusting has multiple partitions itself, you need to assign enough letters to cover all those partitions by changing the End drive letter setting as well.

If you've set up your drive with multiple primary partitions in order to have multiple operating systems available, you can also have problems "seeing" certain partitions, but most of those problems are simply due to the fact that not all operating systems can read all the possible file format types (such as FAT32 and so on).

**Cross-
Reference**

See Chapter 9, "Adding, Upgrading, and Removing Software," for more on working with multiple operating systems.

Compression

One final problem that often crops up with hard drives revolves around compressed disks and disk compression software. Both Windows 98 and Windows 95 (with the addition of the Windows 95 Plus Pack) support DriveSpace 3 compression, which is a means for squeezing more data into a fixed amount of space on your hard drive.

Tip

In theory, drive compression sounds great; after all, you basically get more disk space for free. In the days when hard disk space was expensive, it made certain economic sense. However, I strongly discourage the use of any type of drive compression today because of the performance penalty it puts on your computer, the potential problems it can lead to, and frankly, because plain, uncompressed hard disk space is so cheap and plentiful. If you really want to increase the usable capacity of your hard drive, you're much better off converting it to FAT32, which simply makes more efficient room of your available disk space without using compression. (DriveSpace 3 compresses only FAT16 partitions, by the way.)

The way DriveSpace and other disk compression mechanisms work is that they depend upon a piece of software that's constantly running in the background on your PC to compress data in memory before it gets written to disk, and to read and then decompress any data that has to be transferred from disk to memory. Because of the way Windows and Windows applications operate, however, those processes are going on all the time, which slows down your PC. In addition, if your computer won't boot, getting to and working with the compressed data on your hard drive is a lot harder than it is to retrieve and troubleshoot data that isn't compressed. As far as I'm concerned, it's a lot more trouble than it's worth.

Mouse, keyboard, and joystick problems

Most problems that affect mice, keyboards, trackballs, joysticks, and the like are due to faulty connections (including shorts inside cables), driver problems, or resource problems (all of which are dealt with in Chapter 17,

"Troubleshooting Techniques"). But regardless of how they occur, they can make using your PC pretty difficult, especially if you lose access to your mouse.

Navigating Without a Mouse

Most people are so dependent on their mouse when it comes to getting around their computer that if they do have a problem where their mouse doesn't work, they feel paralyzed. Believe it or not, you can make it through lots of situations with just a keyboard, but there are several tricks you need to know.

First of all, most keyboard-based navigation is done through your arrow keys, Tab key, and various modifier keys, such as Shift, Alt, and Ctrl. In addition, if you have the Windows logo key on your keyboard, you can use that for a number of useful shortcuts. In most instances, you have to hold down any and all modifier keys at the same time you hold down another key for the keyboard command to work. For example, Ctrl+Esc (which makes the Windows Start menu appear) means you have to hold down both the Ctrl and Esc keys simultaneously.

If you're stuck in DOS or in a DOS-based utility, the first trick you have to know is that to access a program's menus and features you need to hold down the Alt key, and then select either a letter key to choose a specific function (the letter that's underlined or highlighted in the word is the keyboard shortcut that invokes it) or an arrow key. Choosing an arrow key enables you to open a particular menu (and then scroll down it) or move from menu to menu.

The Tab key enables you to move from button to button or option to option in both DOS- and Windows-based applications. Shift+Tab moves the cursor backwards in the chain of options.

If you make it to Windows 95 or 98, you can use the Windows logo key (or the aforementioned Ctrl+Esc combo) to make the Start menu appear and then move along from there via the arrow keys. To switch between applications, you use Alt+Tab, and to move among tabs in a tabbed dialog box, you use Ctrl+Tab.

One little-known trick that starts the System control panel, where you can get to the Device Manager with a quick Ctrl+Tab, is the Windows Logo Key+Break (which is usually labeled "Pause"). Other Windows logo shortcuts include the key+E to launch Windows Explorer, +F to launch Find File, +R to open the Run command window, and +C to open the Control Panel folder.

If you haven't removed the Accessibility Options control panel from your system, an incredibly handy trick you can use is MouseKeys, which enables you to control the position of your pointer via the arrow keys on your numeric keypad and even simulate a mouse click. To turn on MouseKeys without a mouse, you first need to have enabled the keyboard shortcut that makes it possible for you to turn the feature on via the keyboard. (Unfortunately, you have to enabled it before you run into the problem because you can't use the keyboard to turn it on!) See the figure below.

Continued

(continued)

Settings for MouseKeys   `? X`

Keyboard shortcut
The shortcut for MouseKeys is:
Press <Left Alt+Left Shift+Num Lock>

☑ Use shortcut

Pointer speed

Top speed: Low ——————ˈ—————— High

Acceleration: Slow —ˈ—————————— Fast

☑ Hold down Ctrl to speed up and Shift to slow down

Use MouseKeys when NumLock is: ⊙ On   ○ Off
☑ Show MouseKey status on screen

                              [OK]   [Cancel]

Let your keyboard do the mousing
By enabling the MouseKeys shortcut in the Accessibility Options control panel, you can remotely turn on this handy feature for moving the mouse pointer via your keyboard.

As long as the shortcut has been enabled, you turn MouseKeys on by holding down the Alt and Shift keys on the left side of the keyboard along with the Num Lock key. If you're using a notebook, you may have to also hold down a Fn, or Function, key to get to Num Lock. Once it's on, you move the pointer around by using the number keys surrounding the 5 on your numeric keypad. Again, notebook users typically need to have turned on the Num Lock key for this to work. To click something, you select the 5 key itself, and to double-click, you use the plus sign (+). If you need more accuracy, you can hold down the Shift key while you're moving the cursor around.

If you're using a serial port–based device, such as a graphics tablet or serial mouse, the problem may not be with the device, but the port it's connected to so be sure to check for driver or resource-related problems there as well. Joysticks and other game-based peripherals must often be calibrated to work properly, so run any calibration test you can find either in a Joystick or Gaming Controllers control panel, or in software that came with the device.

One final input device issue you need to be aware of is that if you're using a USB keyboard and mouse, you won't have access to those devices until Windows 98 starts if your BIOS has not been upgraded to support USB legacy peripherals (the fancy name for USB mice and keyboards). If that's the case, you need to borrow a standard keyboard, use (or remove) a standard PS/2 keyboard cable-to-USB adapter, or get an upgraded BIOS to work through your problems.

Printer problems

Printing-related problems are often due to a combination of hardware and software. If you're using a parallel port–based printer, one of the first things you should check (and possibly change) is the mode that your parallel port is set to in you computer's BIOS or CMOS Setup program. The fastest setting is usually ECP (Enhanced Capabilities Port), but some printers work only with the normal or bidirectional modes. If you make changes in your BIOS, you may also have to make changes in the Device Manager to get everything working properly. Typically that means removing the existing LPT port from the Device Manager, and either manually reinstalling a traditional parallel port driver or enabling the system to find it automatically through Plug and Play. By the way, if you have a newer printer that supports bidirectional communications, as most do, make sure you use an IEEE 1284 (that's different than IEEE 1394) cable.

Many printers do not work at all (or just not very well) if you attempt to use them through a parallel port pass-through connection on another device, such as a scanner or removable drive. If your system is set up that way, disconnect the other device, plug the printer directly into your PC's parallel port, restart your computer, and see if the problem goes away. If you need to share the parallel port, you may have more luck with a parallel port switch, although some printers won't work well with those either. Another good option is to get a USB-to-parallel adapter cable or a USB hub with a built-in parallel port.

Windows 95 and 98 have a simple built-in diagnostic check to see if the connection between the computer and printer are working. Just open the Printers folder, right-click the printer you want to check, and select Properties from the context menu that appears. On the General tab, click the Print Test Page button to see if you get anything. If you don't, you probably have either a driver or connection problem. If you can print the test page, the problem may be with the applications you're trying to print from and/or your print spooling settings. Try clicking the Details tab and then the Spool Settings button. Inside that dialog box, try turning spooling off or on and adjusting the Spool data format from RAW to EMF (or vice versa). See Figure 18-9.

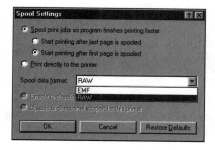

Figure 18-9: Printer spooling
Some printer problems can be fixed by changing the printer spooling between the RAW and EMF (Enhanced Metafile Format) settings.

If you're having problems seeing or printing to a printer on a small network from within one of your applications, you should confirm the settings under the Sharing tab, and you might try the Capture Printer Port button on the Details tab. This maps a network printer to a specific port, which the application may be able to "see" and print to.

Modem and Internet connection problems

Internet connection problems due to analog modem-related issues are all-too-common with many PC users. The difficulty in figuring these issues out is determining what part is causing the trouble, because many different elements go into making a dial-up Internet connection.

The first thing you have to do is check the modem itself and see if it's functioning and can dial out. Open the Modems control panel, and confirm that your specific brand and model of modem are selected. If not, click the Add button, and work your way through the Install New Wizard modem. When that's complete, you may need to remove the setting for the modem that the system previously thought was yours.

To test your modem, switch to the Diagnostics tab button, select the modem (and associated port) you want to test, and click the More Info button. This tells you how good the connection between the PC and the modem is (see Figure 18-10).

Figure 18-10: Checking your modem
The More Info button on the Diagnostics tab of the Modem control panel can help determine if you have good communications between your modem and the rest of your PC.

Note that even if you see error messages in the resulting dialog, that doesn't mean there's a problem with the modem. In most cases, it just means that a particular modem command isn't recognized or is being ignored by the modem.

Secret

If you need to make additions to your modem's initialization string to turn on or off a particular feature inside your modem via standardized modem commands, you do so in the Extra Settings box, which you get to via the

Modem control panel. Select the modem you want to adjust and click the Properties button; then select the Connection tab, and the Advanced Settings button to find it (see Figure 18-11).

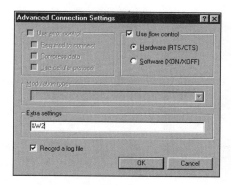

Figure 18-11: Modem initialization strings
You can make additions to your modem's initialization string by typing it into the Extra Settings line of the Advanced Connection Settings dialog. While you're there, you can also try turning on and off hardware flow control to see if that helps with your connection problems.

Once you're sure the modem connection is okay, you should next check to see that the modem can dial out. The easiest way to do so is with the HyperTerminal program bundled with both Windows 95 and 98. If it's installed, you can find it under Programs ⇨ Accessories in Windows 95 and Programs ⇨ Accessories ⇨ Communications Tools under Windows 98. If it's not installed, you need to install it via the Windows Setup tab in the Add/Remove Programs control panel. Here are the steps you need to take to use it.

STEPS:

Testing Your Modem with HyperTerminal

Step 1. Select HyperTerminal from the appropriate location on the Start menu, and in the folder that appears, double-click Hypertrm.exe to launch it.

Step 2. Type a name for the Connection you're going to make. You can use anything you want (I use "Test").

Step 3. Type the phone number you want your modem to dial. Generally speaking, it doesn't matter what you use because you just want to see if the modem can dial out, but if you know the number of a computer bulletin board service or something similar, use that. When you're done, hit OK (see Figure 18-12).

Continued

STEPS

Testing Your Modem with HyperTerminal *(continued)*

Figure 18-12: HyperTerminal connections
You can use the bundled HyperTerminal to see if your modem's driver enables you to successfully dial out.

Step 4. If necessary, make any adjustments to where you're calling from in the Connect dialog box, and then hit the Dial button when you're done.

If your modem dials the call, then the problem is probably not with the main modem driver. If doesn't dial out, however, there's a good chance that it is a driver-related problem.

Modem speed and line quality problems

In some situations, you may find that while you're able to connect to the Internet, the connection speed isn't up to what you thought it would be. Numerous factors can influence this speed, including the quality of the connection on a particular call, how busy the modems at the ISP or online service you're dialing into are, and more. Another common reason is that your phone lines simply may not be up to the task. Some modems, 56K modems in particular, are a bit fussy about the quality of the phone connection. Depending on how old the lines in your house or business are, how the phone company routes them through their switches, and other factors that are generally out of your control, you may not ever get much faster than a 33.6K connection. It's possible in some situations to get the phone company to install a new phone line that overcomes this speed limitation, but it usually costs you money, and they generally won't do it.

Secret

If you want to find out whether your connection speed problems are related to your phone lines, you should try 3Com/US Robotics' 56 Line Test tool, an explanation of which you can find on their Web site at `http://www.3com.com/56k/need4_56k/linetest.html`. You can use this simple test with any modem (it doesn't need to be a USRobotics modem nor does it have to support 56K) to see if the phone lines you have available are even capable of supporting 56K transfer rates. Note that you need to make multiple different phone calls to the number they provide to ensure an accurate result — one or two phone calls can often give a false reading.

Dial-up networking problems

Once any modem and phone line issues are settled, it's time to move onto dial-up networking issues. Windows 95 users can resolve problems in some cases by upgrading to the latest version of Dial-Up Networking that Microsoft makes available on their Web site. Both Windows 95 and 98 users may also have luck by removing and then reinstalling the Dial-Up Networking software (which you do via the Windows Setup tab in the Add/Remove Programs control panel — look under the Communications folder). Another possible solution is to delete and then recreate the individual dial-up networking "connectoid" documents that you create by using the Make New Connection wizard.

To check for problems with your specific connection, right-click the Dial-Up Networking Connection document, and select Properties from the context menu that appears. Check the Server Types to make sure that the server type matches the type used by your ISP (most use PPP). See Figure 18-13.

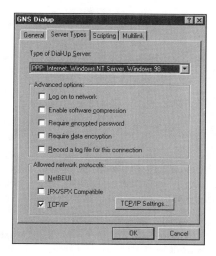

Figure 18-13: Dial-up server types
Internet connection problems can be caused by selecting the wrong settings on the Server Types tab of a Dial-Up Connection Properties sheet. Most ISPs use PPP.

Tip

You may need to make other adjustments in this dialog as well. One tip that can help you log onto your ISP more quickly is to disable the Log on to Network check box, which is usually on by default. This change can shave several seconds off the time it takes to connect.

In order for dial-up networking to work, several components have to be installed on your machine in addition to the Dial-Up Networking software itself. Specifically, you need to have a Dial-Up Adapter, Client for Microsoft Networks, and the TCP/IP protocol installed inside your Network control panel. (Connecting to the Internet is a form of networking, after all.) So another thing you can do is check your Network control panel to confirm they're there, and if necessary, click the Add button to install them.

Cross-
Reference

See Chapter 12, "Setting Up a Small Business or Home Network" for more on networking software-related issues.

The last important thing to check when troubleshooting an Internet connection is your TCP/IP settings, which you can get to from the Server Types tab (see Figure 18-14).

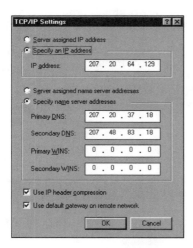

Figure 18-14: TCP/IP Settings
You need to have the right TCP/IP settings in order for your computer to connect to and "communicate" with your ISP's server. Most ISPs handle assigning IP address information automatically via one of their servers, but some require you to enter a specific address.

In most cases, you need to make sure that you adjust the TCP/IP settings that are associated with each dial-up connection and not the overall TCP/IP settings found in the Network control panel. The overall settings are generally used for network connections, whereas each dial-up connection, if you have more than one, stores its own unique settings that override the general settings when you use it.

If you can connect to the Internet but can't visit any Web sites, you might have a problem with your ISP's DNS (Domain Name Services) server, which is what converts names such as www.everythingcomputers.com into numbers such as 207.20.37.115. To find out, try typing a known IP address, such as the one for my site that I just gave, into your Web browser's address line, and see if doing so connects you to my Web site. If it does, then the DNS server is temporarily down, or you may have it incorrectly entered its settings. If it doesn't, then the problem may again be with your TCP/IP settings.

Another little trick you can try to see if your TCP/IP settings are correct is to use the DOS-based Ping utility bundled with Windows 95 and 98. You can run it either in a MS-DOS window or at a command prompt, such as the Run window, by typing **ping xxx.xx.xx.xxx**, where the *x*'s are a TCP/IP address. If it works, the Ping program sends a tiny message to the Web site and receives a reply saying how long the process took. If it times out, either you typed the TCP/IP address incorrectly, or your settings are wrong.

Secret

Along somewhat similar lines, the little-known TraceRoute (tracert) program, which is DOS-based and comes with both Windows 95 and 98, enables you to see both how long and what path your request for a particular Web site's home page takes. This can be very handy for such things as seeing why a particular site is slow, if all your ISP's traffic is being routed through a particularly slow spot, and much more (see Figure 18-15).

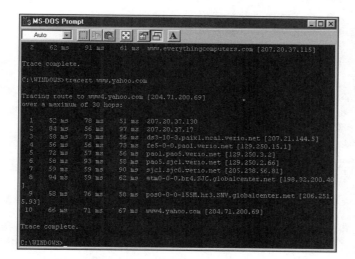

Figure 18-15: TraceRoute follows the path of your page requests
By opening an MS-DOS prompt window and typing **tracert** and then the address of any Web site, you can see how your data requesting the page travels all over the Internet before it reaches its final destination.

Sound card/audio problems

Not being able to hear music or any other audio from your computer system may not be the most devastating problem (unless you're an audio professional, that is), but it sure can be annoying. Many sound-related problems are due to driver issues, but some can also be due to improper settings.

The first thing you should do when troubleshooting sound problems is open the Multimedia control panel and confirm that both the preferred Audio Playback and Audio Recording Devices are selected correctly (see Figure 18-16).

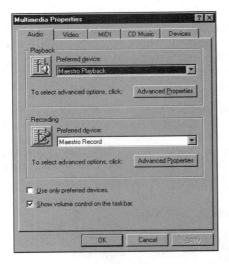

Figure 18-16: Fix sound card settings in the Multimedia control panel
You can adjust most of the important settings related to audio and your sound card here in the Multimedia control panel. First check that the proper device (or devices) is set for Audio Playback and Audio Recording.

The control panels differ slightly between Windows 95 and 98, but most of the critical settings are the same.

Tip

One thing you can do in both operating systems is to ensure that a volume control is present in the taskbar (it shows up as a speaker icon). That way you can double-click the speaker to launch the audio mixer–like Volume Control application and either raise or lower the volume levels of different audio components, or turn off, or mute, individual elements. In fact, sometimes audio problems are simply the result of the volume level being too low or the sound being muted (see Figure 18-17).

If you can hear certain types of audio files but not others (for example, if you can hear digital audio .wav files but not MIDI [.mid] files), then the problem may also be that you don't have the proper driver installed or assigned to play back those files. Check the Devices tab of the Multimedia control panel to see what drivers you have installed.

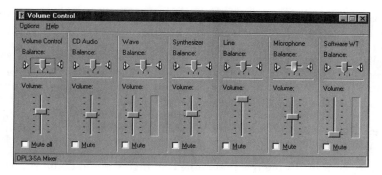

Figure 18-17: Volume adjustments
You can use the Volume Control to mute either individual elements or all the audio coming from your PC, as well as adjust volume levels for each of them.

In the case of MIDI-related problems, one common issue is assigning MIDI files to be played back via an MPU-401 device. What this means is you're routing all the MIDI data to a MIDI interface to be played back by an external MIDI device. If you don't have either a MIDI interface or an external MIDI sound module, however, you won't hear anything. To fix this, click the MIDI tab, and make sure the MIDI output is assigned to your soundcard's FM (sometimes referred to as "OPL-3") or wavetable section or to a software-based wavetable synthesizer (see Figure 18-18).

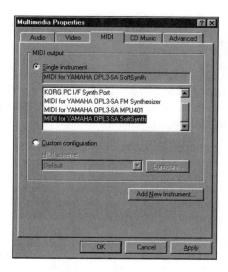

Figure 18-18: Fixing MIDI problems
One easy way to fix problems with MIDI files is to make sure you aren't assigning MIDI files to be played back with an MPU-401 device. This setting works only if you have an external MIDI sound module attached to your computer.

If your system has USB speakers that take advantage of a digital audio connection (sometimes mischaracterized as "digital speakers"), then you may need to consider several other issues. First of all, Windows 98's Multimedia control panel has a CD Music tab where you can enable digital playback of audio from either CD- or DVD-ROM disks. This works only if your CD- or DVD-ROM player has a digital audio output and that output is connected to your system's motherboard. (You may need to check your system's documentation for more information on whether or not this affects you.) If you're having problems playing back audio CDs, you should try disabling this function.

Secret

A more serious problem is that some USB digital audio connections suffer from pops and other audio glitches that in many situations are unfixable. The problem has to do with the way certain USB controllers handle *isochronous* data, which is a fancy word for a continuous stream (which is what a piece of music or other digital audio is). Because USB controllers are integrated onto your motherboard, you can't easily replace them, short of buying a new motherboard or getting a whole new system. The only possible fix in this case is to use the speaker's standard analog audio connections.

Power management problems

Problems with your notebook or desktop computer not being able to properly go into or come out of "sleep" mode, as well as some shutdown problems are all related to power management issues. *Power management* refers to how your system deals with low-power modes, typically used in notebook computers to save battery life and on both desktops and notebooks to conserve energy.

The problems often arise because of conflicts between your computer's BIOS and the operating system essentially "fighting" for control. Consequently, solving them sometimes involves making changes in both your BIOS (or CMOS) Setup program as well as in the Power Management (or just Power under Windows 95) control panel. In general, I recommend making changes to your control panel first, but if that doesn't work, try the BIOS Setup program. In some instances, you may also have to make adjustments to the control panel after you've changed settings in your BIOS Setup.

To see if the problems you're experiencing are power management–related, try adjusting the control panel settings so that the system never goes into sleep mode. Figure 18-19 shows what to look for in Windows 98's Power Management control panel.

If you're running Windows 95, go to the Power control panel, and click off the Allow Windows to manage power use on this computer check box. Another thing you can try is to click the Advanced button and then the Troubleshooting tab, and turn on the Use APM (Advanced Power Management) 1.0 compatibility mode check box (see Figure 18-20).

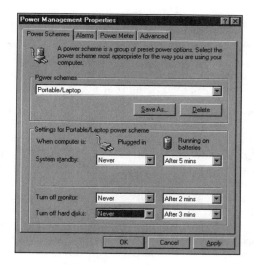

Figure 18-19: Turning off power management
By setting all your computer's different components to never go into low-power mode, you can find out if any problems you have are due to power management issues.

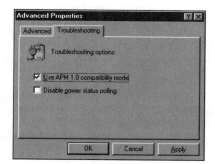

Figure 18-20: Windows 95 APM mode
Windows 95 has less power management features than Windows 98, but one possible workaround for problems you run into is to turn on APM compatibility mode.

Regardless of which version of Windows you have installed, you may also need to adjust your monitor's energy conservation settings in addition to your system's settings. Open the Display control panel, click the Screen Savers tab, and then under the Energy Star section of the dialog, select the Settings button under Windows 98, or just make changes directly under Windows 95. With a notebook computer running Windows 98, this actually takes you to the main Power Management control panel (which includes a setting for your monitor).

USB problems

Some problems you experience with specific devices attached to your PC may actually be due to the characteristics or limitations of the connection mechanism, or bus used to attach the device. In addition, the problems may be caused by other devices that are also using that bus.

As handy as USB, or Universal Serial Bus, can be, for example, it can also suffer from its share of frustrating problems. One problem is just enabling it in the first place. Many PCs that include USB ports have them turned off in the BIOS, which means that initially they won't appear to work. You can fix this easily by entering your BIOS Setup program and enabling your USB ports under the Peripherals section. However, if you've added other devices to your system, doing so may create a resource conflict between the USB controller and other elements on your system. In fact, you may even run into a situation where there are no more available IRQs, which means you have to physically remove or disable another component of your system to get the USB ports to work. (I know because I had this very problem on one system I worked on.)

Cross-Reference

See Chapter 17, "Troubleshooting Techniques" for more on dealing with resource conflicts.

Power issues

One of the great features of USB is that it can supply power to many types of attached devices, which saves you from having to deal with yet another power cord. Many USB device problems are power-related, however, for one of several reasons.

The first issue is just terminology. If a USB hub (either standalone or built into another device, such as a monitor) is bus-powered, that really means that it *receives* the power it needs from the USB bus. It cannot provide any power to USB devices that attach to it; it only passes along whatever power is remaining on the bus. Consequently, if you attach a USB device that needs power to one of those types of hubs, it may not work properly because it isn't receiving the power it needs. The answer to this problem (and the way to avoid it) is to get a powered hub, which doesn't drain any power from the bus and, in fact, provides additional power for those USB devices that may need it (and are plugged into its connectors).

Secret

You also want to make sure that any USB hubs you buy comply with USB 1.1 specification or higher. Changes were made to the standard's 1.0 Version specifically to deal with some hub-related problems.

Even with a powered hub, you can run into USB problems if too many devices are draining two much power from a particular USB port. Rearranging the devices so that the power needs are more evenly distributed can sometimes solve this problem.

Tip

The Windows 98 Resource Kit included on the Windows 98 CD includes a handy USBView utility as part of the Tools Management Console. You can use it to look at all the USB connections on your system and troubleshoot problems, including power-related issues, you may be having with a specific device (see Figure 18-21).

Figure 18-21: USBView provides power info
USBView, which is available on the Windows 98 CD as part of the Resource Kit, enables you to troubleshoot common USB problems by looking at power settings and requirements for various devices.

One final power-related tip is that some devices don't work properly when they're plugged in while your system is on. While the USB spec says that any devices should be able to use this hot-swapping capability, the reality is often different. So if you try to plug in a new USB device while your system is on and it doesn't work, try turning off your PC first. Conversely, I've also heard of some devices that work only if they're plugged in while the system is on. In some instances, that may mean unplugging and replugging the device nearly every time you use it (that is, until a driver update fixes the problem!).

Compatibility

USB is supposed to be a universal standard, which means that any USB device should work with any USB-equipped computer. Unfortunately, however, I've encountered situations where certain USB devices just won't work (or won't work properly) with some USB ports. The issue boils down to there being two main types of USB controllers (Universal Host Controller Initiative, or UHCI, versus Open Host Controller Initiative, or OHCI), and because of some minor differences between them, a limited number of devices can work only with one or the other. In addition, some early implementations of USB apparently didn't adhere to the specification as well as they should have, which can also lead to some devices not working on slightly older systems with USB.

In some situations, you can overcome these types of compatibility problems with driver upgrades. But if you suspect it is an issue and you want to find out what type of controller your system uses, open the Device Manager, click the plus sign (+) next to the Universal serial bus controller section, and look to see what type of controller is listed. Be aware that your only recourse in some situations is to return the USB device you bought and get an equivalent device that does work with your system.

SCSI problems

The Small Computer Systems Interface, or SCSI, bus is an ideal way to attach high-performance hard drives, scanners, and other peripherals to your PC system. But like USB, it too has it share of foibles.

The most common SCSI problem is termination. In order for a chain of SCSI devices to work properly and share the SCSI bus, the devices at the beginning and end of the SCSI chain must be terminated, but all devices in the middle should not be terminated. Most SCSI devices have simple switches that enable you to turn termination on or off and many newer SCSI devices feature automatic termination, which senses where in the chain they are and turns on or off its internal termination accordingly. Some SCSI devices do not offer their own termination circuitry, however, so if you have a device such as a scanner, rearrange it so that it sits in the middle of the SCSI chain (and so won't need to be terminated), or you need to buy and attach a separate SCSI terminator. (Most terminators look like the plug end of a SCSI cable.)

The SCSI controller inside your PC almost always acts as the beginning (or end) of the chain, and so it is virtually always terminated. If you add a single external SCSI device to the controller, it too needs to be terminated. But if you later add a second device and attach it to the first, then you need to unterminate the device in the middle, and make sure the new device is terminated.

The same rules hold true for any internal SCSI chains. Both the first device and the last device need termination, but the others don't. Things can get confusing if you have both internal and external SCSI devices attached to the same SCSI controller. Some controllers maintain two separate chains — one for internal and one for external. So they need to be terminated at both the ends of the internal chain and the external chain. Some controllers, however, make both internal and external devices part of the same chain. In that case, the SCSI controller sits in the middle of the chain, and so needs to have its termination turned off (typically via the SCSI BIOS Setup program), but devices at both ends still need termination turned on.

Another common problem revolves around SCSI IDs. Each device in a chain needs to have its own number typically between 1 and 7 (the controller is usually assigned to ID 0). Again, if you have separate internal and external chains, two devices could both have the same ID number, but on a single chain, each number must be unique.

The last thing to consider when dealing with SCSI problem is that SCSI connections are notoriously finicky about the quality of the cables you use. Many strange problems with SCSI devices can, in fact, be traced back to using cheap cables. I highly recommend the best SCSI cables, though they can cost a lot more.

Network problems

If you've created a small home or business network, you probably will run into some issues when you first try to get it going. It's a fairly complicated process, and it's very easy to make mistakes when first setting it up. Luckily, most of these types of problems can be fixed by just checking and making corrections to your various configuration settings. (Either that, or making sure that any network cards you've installed haven't created resource conflicts, which is another common issue.)

For example, you not only need to make sure you have network clients, adapters, and protocols installed on your system, via the Network control panel, you also have to check that you have matching protocols and that the protocols are "bound" to the adapters. If you've enabled file and print sharing, you need to make sure each computer is assigned a computer name and, in some cases, a workgroup name as well via the Network control panel's Identification tab. In addition, you need to make sure that the information or printers you want to make available to other users on the network have been shared. Just creating the connections doesn't automatically make everything visible to other computers connected on the network.

Cross-Reference

See Chapter 12, "Setting Up a Home or Small Business Network" for more information on setting up network-related software.

Fixing Software Problems

Dealing with software problems is really more of an art than a science, and in most cases, you'll want to follow the software troubleshooting techniques I describe in Chapter 17 first. But, in addition, you can try some other procedures to help you solve common software problems.

Uninstalling software

One mistake that a lot of relative newcomers to computers make is to try and uninstall software by just deleting the folder with the program's name. As I explained in Chapter 9, "Adding, Upgrading, and Removing Software," that's a real no-no because not only does it not get rid of all a program's components, it can actually cause other problems with your system.

If you, or someone else who used your PC recently, accidentally did this, you need to reinstall the program and then remove it via either the Add/Remove Programs control panel or the program's own uninstaller. This should remove the program completely from your system (although in some cases, some tiny pieces still get left behind, as the section "Removing Software" in Chapter 9 explains).

Consistent and random crashes

If you run into the same problem with the same application over and over, then either the version of the program you have has a bug in it, or you have a specific conflict with other software on your system. Either way, you need to contact the manufacturer of the problematic program and get an update. That's the only way you're going to fix this kind of issue.

Secret

If you're running Windows 98 and want to get a more specific answer about what's causing the problem, launch the Dr. Watson utility (via the System Information Tool), and then recreate the problem. When the problem or error message occurs, click the Details button to see what Dr. Watson has to say. If you can, print the log file it creates so that you can give specific information to the software vendor. If you can't print it right then, you can restart your computer, find the log in the Dr. Watson folder inside the Windows folder, open it, and print it from there.

If you're experiencing random crashes, try to determine if they always happen in the same program or in any number of different programs. If you make conscientious records of when the crashes occur, you might begin to see some kind of pattern that can point you in the right direction.

If you don't notice any type of pattern, more than likely you have some type of hardware problem, such as RAM that's starting to fail or electrical power-related problems. To rule out power, try using a line conditioner, which is an electronic device that provides a rock-steady 117 volts, no matter how much the voltage from the wall may vary. Many uninterruptible power supplies (UPSes) include line conditioning, but not all do.

Cross-Reference

See Chapter 7, "Input Devices and Power," for more information on line conditioners and uninterruptible power supplies.

You may need to check and/or replace your computer's power supply and its RAM. The only way to do so (unless you have specific testing tools) is to bring your PC into a repair shop that has the right equipment. While you're there, you might also want to have them check your motherboard to see if it might be the cause of your problems.

I'm warning you now, however, that it won't be easy to track down the answer because random crashes are the most bedeviling problems that a computer user can face. So try to keep a positive attitude, back up your data, and remember that, if worse comes to worse, you can always just wipe the slate clean and start all over.

Cross-Reference

See Chapter 17, "Troubleshooting Techniques," for details on how to repartition and reformat your hard drive and reinstall your software.

Running out of memory

Now that most computers include at least 32MB of memory (and many have a lot more), error messages about not having enough memory to perform certain operations are a lot less common than they used to be. However, they can still crop up, particularly if you're trying to run DOS-based games or other applications.

Windows memory problems

As long as you do have at least 16 or 32MB of memory in your computer, a low memory message in Windows 95/98 or from a Windows application is often a sign that you're running out of room on your hard drive.

While I realize that sounds confusing, the issue is that the message usually signifies a problem with virtual memory, or your Windows swap file, which uses space on your hard drive to store data and "trick" the system into thinking you have more physical RAM than you do. So first you need to make sure you have at least 100 or 200MB of free space on your hard drive. Anything less than that, and you're starting to ask for trouble. If you don't, start looking for files and applications you can remove, but remember not to just drag applications folders to the trash — that will give you problems down the road.

Cross-Reference

See Chapter 9, "Adding, Upgrading, and Removing Software," for details on how to remove your applications.

If you want to, another thing you can look at is your Virtual Memory settings, which are part of the Performance tab of the System control panel. In most cases, you should leave the default setting of enabling Windows 95 or 98 to manage your virtual memory settings, but in some situations you may need to adjust them manually, such as when you're using a program that requires an extremely large amount of working memory. (See Figure 18-22.)

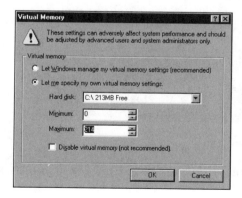

Figure 18-22: Adjusting virtual memory
By clicking the Virtual Memory button on the Performance tab of the System control panel, you get to a dialog box where you can adjust virtual memory settings. If a Windows application complains of not having enough memory, you might try increasing the maximum amount of virtual memory space available.

DOS memory problems

The much more common type of memory problem comes from trying to use DOS-based applications, particularly games, under Windows 95 or 98. Even on systems with 64MB or much more RAM, you might get an error message about not having enough RAM in order to run a particular program. What it's referring to is not enough free memory available in the 640K real-mode world of DOS. This 640K is also commonly referred to as *conventional memory*.

Cross-Reference

See Chapter 8, "How Your Computer Works," for more on conventional memory, real mode, and the infamous first megabyte of memory under DOS.

The trick to solving this problem is figuring out how much free conventional memory your system has, what's using it, and then removing some items so that you have all the room you need. Finding out what you have is easy. Just go to an MS-DOS prompt window or boot to a command prompt, and type **mem**. You get a quick summary of your system's memory under one megabyte (see Figure 18-23.)

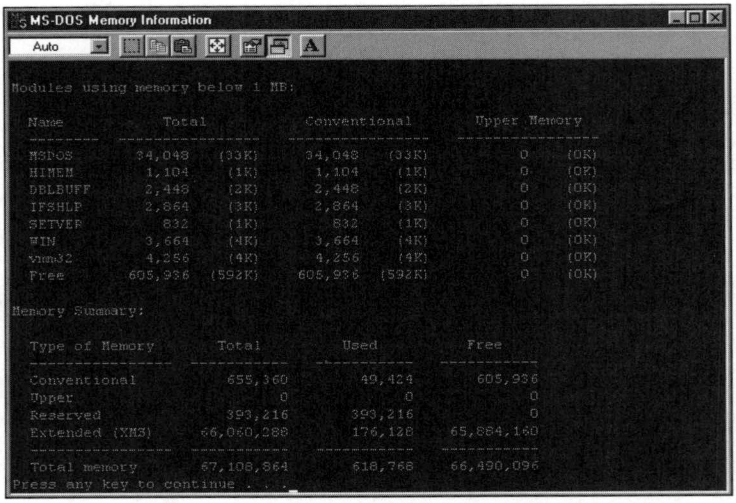

Figure 18-23: DOS memory map
You can use the DOS Mem utility to see how much free conventional, or real-mode memory you have available for games and other DOS applications. This system uses 48K, leaving 592K free.

To make more room, you need to prevent certain items from loading into conventional memory. To do so, you need to edit your computer's Config.sys and Autoexec.bat startup files. These files are where you tell your system what real-mode drivers and other DOS programs you want loaded when your system starts up. Following the guidelines on how to edit your startup files from earlier in this chapter (see the section "Fixing Startup Problems"), you should remark out anything except the drivers you know you absolutely need.

Generally speaking, you don't want to have much of anything referenced in these two files if you're running Windows 95 or 98, so there shouldn't be much there anyway. The only exception is if you consistently use DOS applications that require certain real-mode drivers.

Once you've remarked out unnecessary lines from your startup files, save them, restart your computer, and run the Mem utility again to ensure you have enough free conventional memory. If you don't know how much memory an application needs, just try to launch it, and see if it works.

DOS games

Some of the most problematic software you run across for your PC is DOS-based games. In fact, they typically lead to the DOS memory problems I just discussed. Other common problems you run into with DOS games are the inability to use your mouse and CD-ROM drive, and sound cards that seem to stop working.

In virtually all cases, the issue is drivers being loaded (or not) into conventional memory. DOS applications, like many games, have different types of requirements than typical Windows programs, and they basically need some special care — that is, if you're trying to run them from a true MS-DOS, or command prompt mode. If you plan to play the game through an MS-DOS prompt window inside Windows 95 or 98, everything is taken care of for you because the CD-ROM, sound card, mouse, and joystick drivers are all available from the operating system.

Not all games work this way, however, so if you need to start (or restart) your computer in MS-DOS mode to play a game, you need to have drivers for all those devices loaded from your startup files, specifically Config.sys and Autoexec.bat. Otherwise, you won't be able to access them to play the game.

Tip

Because of these issues, I highly recommend you create a special boot floppy that you can use to start your PC whenever you want to play these types of games. That way you won't have to worry about messing up your main boot files, and you can easily adjust the boot disk as necessary. Plus, if the real-mode boot drivers get installed into your main Autoexec.bat and Config.sys files, they are loaded into your system's memory every time you boot up, whether or not you need them.

PIFs

Another option is to customize the PIF (Program Information File) file that Windows 95/98 creates for all DOS applications. You can have blank or near-blank Autoexec.bat and Config.sys files as part of your main startup files, but run customized ones that load the necessary drivers only when you launch a particular game that needs them. Here's how to do it.

STEPS:

Loading DOS drivers only as needed

Step 1. Right-click any DOS application you have installed on your hard drive, select Properties from the context menu that appears, and click the Program tab on the resulting dialog box (if it isn't already selected). See Figure 18-24.

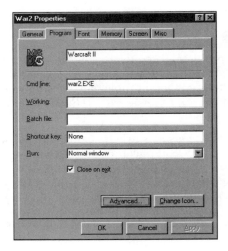

Figure 18-24: PIF power
You can customize the environment that you want DOS games to have by using the PIF (Program Information File) configuration settings available in either Windows 95 or 98.

Step 2. Click the Advanced button, and then turn on the MS-DOS mode check box. Be sure the Warn before entering MS-DOS mode check box is also selected.

Step 3. Assuming that your primary Config.sys and Autoexec.bat startup files don't have references to the real-mode drivers you need for your CD-ROM, mouse, and sound card, check the Specify a new MS-DOS configuration box as well.

Step 4. Make any necessary changes in the startup files you want to load when you launch the application or game whose settings we're now adjusting (see Figure 18-25).

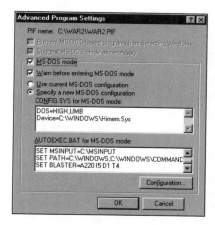

Figure 18-25: Editing the startup files
In the Advanced Program Settings dialog, you can customize the startup files you want loaded when you launch a particular DOS game.

Step 5. If you want, you can also click the Configuration button to make a few automatic adjustments to your startup files, although most of them probably won't be relevant for games. When you're done, click OK.

Now, the next time you run this program, it will warn you that it's going into MS-DOS mode; it will then quit all open applications and then start a DOS session. It will also load and process the startup files you created in Step 4. When you quit the application, Windows will automatically restart, and when it gets to the point where it loads your Config.sys and Autoexec.bat files, it will use the (hopefully) near-empty ones located at the root level of your hard drive.

Customized startup files

Whether you create the startup floppy or use the PIF method, you need to create special Autoexec.bat and Config.sys files that you can use to set up your system and load the necessary drivers. The specifics of how to do this varies, based on the components in your system, but it essentially boils down to tracking down the real-mode drivers for your CD-ROM, mouse, and sound card, as well as any other applications or special settings those devices may need. Then you need to make references to these drivers and settings in your startup files so that they get loaded into memory and any games you run have access to them.

To load driver files (which typically end in .sys) in your Config.sys file, you use the line Device= and then type the name and location of the driver. If it's on the boot floppy, you might end up with something such as Device=mouse.sys, whereas if it's on your hard drive, it might be Device=C:\Windows\System\ Mouse.sys.

To load application-like drivers via Autoexec.bat, you typically just type the filename (including its location, if necessary). So again, if the file is on the floppy, it might say something such as MSCDEX.EXE /D:MSCD001, or if it's on your hard drive, it might be C:\Windows\Command\Mscdex.exe /D:MSCD001. (The /D:MSCD001 in this example is a switch that provides some additional settings to the MSCDEX program.)

Another thing you may have to do in Autoexec.bat is to set certain variables for the device by using the Set command. The syntax for this is usually something such as Set Device= and then type the specific device settings. With Sound Blaster-compatible sound cards, for example, you commonly see the line SET BLASTER=A220, I5, D1, T3, which, in this example, sets the Sound Blaster to work at I/O Address 220, IRQ 5, and DMA channel 1, among other things.

For the CD-ROM drive, you should use the same driver (or drivers) and support files you need to create a boot floppy with CD-ROM support. If you have Windows 98, you can use the generic drivers on the Windows 98 boot floppy. (In fact, you can use the boot floppy with CD-ROM support as the starting point for a "games" boot floppy.)

Cross-Reference

For more on creating boot floppies, see the section "Troubleshooting Tools" in Chapter 17, "Troubleshooting Techniques."

For the mouse, you can either load a driver in the Config.sys file, reference a mouse driver application that loads a driver in your Autoexec.bat file, or point your system to where it can find the necessary files with a Set command. For the sound card, you often need to both load a driver in Config.sys and put some settings into a line of your Autoexec.bat. In addition, many sound cards require you to put in another driver to your Config.sys that handles assigning the card to the proper resources.

Putting this all together, you might end up with Config.sys and Autoexec.bat files that look somewhat such as those shown in Table 18-1. (Remember, though, the specifics vary based on what equipment you have. The ones in Table 18-1 do not work in real life!)

Table 18-1 Game Startup File Examples
Config.sys
Device=A:\Cdrom.sys /D:MSCD001
Device=A:\Mouse.sys
Device=A:\Ctsb.sys /UNIT=0 /BLASTER=A:220 I:5 D:1 H:5
Device=A:\Ctmmsys.sys
Autoexec.bat
MSCDEX /D:MSCD001
SET SOUND=C:\AWE32
SET BLASTER= A220 I5 D1 H5 P330 E620 T6
SET MIDI=SYNTH:1 MAP:E MODE:0

In order for a floppy drive that had startup files such as those shown in Table 18-1 to work, you need to make sure it has the basic MS-DOS system files, as well as the individual driver files referenced in Config.sys and Autoexec.bat. Either that, or make sure that the references in the startup files go to the places on your hard disk where the driver files are located.

Web browser/Internet problems

Once you're connected to the Internet, browsing around from site to site is usually not a big deal. Occasionally, though, you may come across sites that simply aren't there or don't look right. In many cases, these are problems with the sites themselves. If the server hosting the site has gone down or if there's an error in a script or other element they've included on one of their pages, there isn't anything you can really do about it. (Actually, if you think there's a problem with the site itself, you can send a note to the site's Webmaster. You can often find an e-mail link to them at the bottom of the home page, or even every page, to tell them about your experience. It may not fix the situation right away, but the Webmaster will certainly appreciate it and will probably try to get to a fix as soon as possible.)

Other times the problem can be the result of Web sites using features that your current browser doesn't support. For example, if you're using an older browser that doesn't support Cascading Style Sheets or some other recent addition to the HTML (HyperText Markup Language — the "language" of Web pages) specification, then you may not see a site in the way the site's designers intended. If you want the full effect, you need to upgrade to a more recent version of Internet Explorer, Netscape Navigator, or any other browser that supports the latest Web standards.

Tip

As a general rule, it's a good idea to keep up to date with Web browsers, not only so you don't run into these types of display problems but also so you don't run into security issues. Security "holes" that could conceivably be taken advantage of by unscrupulous hackers to do such things as wipe out your hard disk or copy your data are being discovered in browsers all the time. Only by downloading and installing the most recent versions can you insure yourself against problems.

A related problem is that some Web sites require the use of certain helper, or plug-in applications in order to be viewed or interacted with properly. Most sites that do this make it clear and provide links to where you can download the necessary plug-ins. If you don't feel like downloading and installing some new software, you can just move on, but if you really want to see the site the way it was intended, the only thing you can do is get the plug-in.

Tip

If you're visiting a news-related site or some other site that gets updated on a regular basis, another problem you may run into is not being able to refresh the page to get the absolute latest version. Oftentimes hitting your browser's Refresh button won't do the trick. Instead you should try holding down the Shift key and clicking Refresh (this works for both Internet Explorer and Netscape Navigator). This tells your browser to ignore whatever it has in its cache and forces it to reload the entire page. Not only does this give you the freshest version of the page, in some cases it can help fix some strange scripting or Java errors you may run across on certain sites.

E-mail problems

Electronic mail messages, or e-mail, has transformed the way people communicate and become one of the primary motivations for people buying and using computers. Perhaps for that reason, people can get very feisty if they're unable to retrieve or read their messages, including any and all file attachments that may be included along with them.

Most retrieval problems, other than mixed up usernames and passwords, are due to configuration issues or other problems at your Internet Service Provider (or Web-based mail service). So before you go changing things on your system because you can't read your mail, make sure you check with your e-mail provider to see if their servers are down (a not-uncommon situation, unfortunately) or if they're suffering from some other problem. If they aren't, double-check your e-mail account details, such as the username and password, to make sure they haven't been changed.

Message formats

As for reading messages, most problems center around figuring out the file format of the main message, either plain text or HTML, as well deciphering file attachments that turn into nothing more than long strings of text. Most current e-mail packages can automatically decipher between plain text and HTML messages and display each type of message appropriately, but you may need to turn on certain options in older packages if you want to view graphical HTML-based mail (or just upgrade to a newer version of the e-mail program). If you're having problems getting a message through to someone, switch to plain text format. Oftentimes that's all it takes.

Cross-Reference

For more on e-mail formats, see Chapter 13, "Connecting to and Using the Internet."

Similarly, sometimes copying images into an e-mail so that it becomes an embedded part of the message—which you can only do if the message is not in plain-text format—causes more problems than simply attaching the image to the message.

Decoding file attachments

Reading file attachments is the big bugaboo of e-mail and probably the most common problem on the Internet. The basic problem is that the Internet was originally designed to handle only text messages, and so, to enable the transfer of data files (which are in binary format), most types of file attachments must be converted from binary into ASCII text form. This process is usually referred to as *encoding* the file, and the opposite process of converting from text back to binary is called, logically enough, decoding.

In an ideal world, all this encoding and decoding of file attachments is supposed to happen behind our collective backs and just work. And, in many cases, it does, and an e-mail message with an attachment looks no different on the receiving end than it does on the sending end. The MIME (Multipurpose Internet Mail Extensions) standard, for example, is supported in many different e-mail programs so that if you enable MIME support in your program and send an attachment, it is automatically converted to a MIME format using Base64 encoding when it's sent. (Base64 is an algorithm or method for encoding the data in a MIME message.) A MIME-compliant e-mail package on the receiving end then recognizes it as being in MIME format, decodes the Base64 data, and presents it to the receiver as a regular attached file. In fact, both parties may never even know the file was encoded and decoded.

In many situations, however, the file is encoded but never decoded, for a number of odd reasons. Oftentimes the fault typically lies with the sender's or receiver's ISP's router settings and the type of equipment they have, which is obviously out of your control. Regardless of the reason, however, the end result is that the recipient gets a confusing bunch of text where they thought there'd be a file. In some cases, there's still an attachment, but the contents of the attachment are a huge text mess.

Luckily, the process of manually decoding the text message and getting the file attachments you want isn't that hard. You need to save the attachment as a file and then convert it using any number of different utilities that can do the decoding process. (If the attachment contents are not scrambled, you obviously don't need to decode it.) If the encoded attachment text is part of the e-mail message, you first need to select it and then save that as a plain text-only file, and then decode it with a decoding utility.

The only tricky part of saving the text inside the message is that you have to make sure you get what's called the "header information" at the beginning of the attachment, because this header is what tells the decoding utility what format it is in. For MIME messages, you can usually see that information in plain text: you usually see a MIME type, encoding type, and so on. Uuencoded files (another algorithm used for encoding) typically have the word "begin" on a separate line right above the string of characters. Make sure you include that when you copy it over into a plain-text message.

Tip

By the way, you're much better off using Notepad or a plain text editor to save the file, because if you paste it into Word or another word processor, that program may add some subtle formatting changes that can make the file unreadable by the decoding utility. Also, if you get a really big attachment this way, it may get broken up into several different messages. If that's the case, you have to copy and paste the different pieces into a single file and then save it before you can decode.

To decode the file, you can use WinZip or any number of other utilities. In most cases you just need to launch the utility and then open the encoded file from within the program.

CD

A demo copy of WinZip 7.0 is available on the CD accompanying this book.

One final problem you may come across with regard to file attachments is that the file format of the attached file may not be something that any of your computer's applications is capable of opening. In that case, you need to figure out a way to convert it into a format that you can use.

Cross-Reference

See Chapter 14, "Working with Documents and Files," for more on converting files from one format to another.

Summary

In this chapter I've provided solutions for fixing a number of common problems that happen on PCs, including startup problems, hardware-related problems, and software-related problems.

▶ The trick to fixing startup problems is figuring out where in the startup process they occur.

▶ Some startup problems can be fixed only by making changes to your computer's BIOS or CMOS Setup program.

▶ Many startup problems can be fixed by turning off individual lines in one of several different startup files.

▶ The Bootlog.txt file provides tons of information about which drivers successfully load when Windows 95 or 98 starts and which ones don't.

▶ Some startup problems require restoring or reinstalling files that were accidentally deleted or somehow corrupted.

▶ Many shutdown problems are due to incompatible or out-of-date drivers.

▶ If you create new partitions and volumes on your hard drive and then try to move applications from one volume to another, you'll probably run into problems.

▶ If your mouse ever stops working, there are ways to move around with your keyboard only.

▶ Problems with Internet connections can be due to one of several factors, including the modem's setup and dial-up networking settings.

▶ USB can be handy for attaching new devices to your PC, but it also has its share of gotchas, particularly with regard to power-related issues.

▶ Most memory problems are due to DOS games not having enough conventional memory. You can fix them by editing your Config.sys and Autoexec.bat startup files.

▶ E-mail attachments that come across as a huge string of text can be converted into something useful by decoding them.

Appendix A

What's on the CD-ROM?

The *Personal Computer Secrets* CD that is bound inside the back cover of the book is designed as a companion to the book's text. Like the book, it's also meant to be a comprehensive, useful resource on its own. As a result, it's full of neat stuff to help you get more out of your PC, troubleshoot problems, do creative applications, and, in general, encourage you to try some new things.

On it, you can find both the complete text of the book in electronic form, as well as over 35 programs, organized into six categories, that can help you apply the principles you've learned here. Some of the programs are freeware, which means they can be used for as long as you like at no cost to you. Others are shareware, which you can try for free, but for which you are eventually expected (or need) to pay a small registration fee to the program's creator if you continue to use it. Finally, the CD also includes several demonstration versions of commercial products.

In many cases, the shareware and "demoware" have a limited-time usage, which means you can use all the features of the program for a limited amount of time, after which the program no longer works (that is, unless you pay the shareware registration fee or decide to purchase the full version of the commercial demo). In other instances, the shareware and demoware programs disable certain critical functions, such as save and print, but still enable you to try the basic capabilities of the program. In all cases, the programs come as is, without technical support. If you do have any questions about them, please contact the specific program's publisher. Neither I, nor anyone at IDG Books, can answer any questions about the software on the CD.

Interface

The CD is designed to be easy to navigate, with an HTML-based interface that should automatically open as soon as you insert the disc into a Windows 95-, 98-, or 2000-based system. (If it doesn't open automatically, you can just open the Start Here.htm file with any Web browser.) On the main screen you'll find buttons for The Software, The Book, and About the CD-ROM.

Under The Software, you'll find that the programs are organized by category, and are also listed in their entirety under The Complete Software List. To get to any category, simply click the category. Once you're on an individual category page, you can get back to the main page by clicking the *Personal Computer Secrets* CD-ROM logo or back to The Software Categories page by clicking on The Software button.

On each category page you'll find a table that lists the program's name, a brief description of what it does, the type of software it is (for example, freeware or shareware), and a link to a Web site that includes more information and/or an even more recent version of the specific program. All of the programs can be installed by clicking on the program's name and then choosing the Run this program option from the dialog box that appears. What should happen then is you should launch into the setup program for each specific application.

Most programs only require this step, but some require other support files in order to work properly. In most cases, installing Internet Explorer 5.0 first is all you need to do because it will update all the operating system files that these other applications need. (You can find more detailed installation instructions in the Readme file located at the root directory of the *Personal Computer Secrets* CD-ROM).

Clicking on The Book button takes you to a page where you can get to an electronic version of the book stored in Adobe's PDF (Portable Document File) format. PDF files require Adobe's Acrobat Reader to read and this page also includes a button that lets you install Acrobat Reader 4.0 (if you don't already have it on your system). The PDF file of *Personal Computer Secrets* has been electronically indexed, which means you can quickly search for any word or phrase from the entire book within the Acrobat Reader application. In addition, it includes all the book's line art and screen shots. You can either view the Acrobat file directly from the CD or, if you want to, you can copy it onto your hard drive, and then have easy, electronic access to its contents whenever you need it (at the cost of some hard disk space).

Finally, the About the CD button provides some of the same background information on how the CD is organized as I've written here.

Contents

The six categories of software on the CD are:

- Audio/music software

- Graphics/video software
- Internet software
- Networking software
- Utility software
- Web site software

The audio/music section has a MIDI sequencer, as well as digital audio-editing software, audio-remixing software, and more. Chapter 16, "Working with Audio and Music," explains all the things you can do with them.

The graphics/video section includes a wide range of graphics programs, including several image editors. You can use any and all of them to try out the tips discussed in Chapter 15, "Working with Pictures and Video."

The Internet section features browser plug-ins, Internet utilities, and other useful Web and e-mail tools that are discussed in Chapter 13, "Connecting to and Using the Internet."

The Networking section includes the software you need to share a single Internet connection across a network of computers, as discussed in Chapter 12, "Setting Up a Small Business or Home Network.".

The Utility section offers a host of different programs that can help diagnose problems with your PC, overcome annoying limitations, provide detailed technical information about your PC, convert between file formats, scan for viruses, and more. Many of these issues are discussed in Chapter 14, "Working with Documents and Files," as well as Chapter 17, "Troubleshooting Techniques" and Chapter 18, "Solving Common PC Problems."

Finally, the Web site section includes a variety of different tools you can use to build a Web site, as explained in Chapter 13, "Connecting to and Using the Internet," including HTML authoring programs and Web graphics programs.

Table A-1 is an alphabetical list of all the programs on the CD, along with a brief description of the program, the chapter it is mentioned in, the category and type of software, and finally, a Web address where you can get more information and/or look for even more recent versions.

Table A-1 Personal Computer Secrets CD

Program*	Description	Mentioned in Chapter	Category	Type	Web Site
Adobe Acrobat Viewer 4.0	Utility for viewing PDF files over the Internet and on your PC's hard disk.	13, 14	Internet	Freeware	http://www.adobe.com/prodindex/acrobat/readstep.html
Adobe ImageStyler	Program for creating graphics for Web sites.	13, 15	Web site	Demo	http://www.adobe.com/prodindex/imagestyler/main.html
Adobe PageMill	Web site authoring program	13	Web site	Demo	http://www.adobe.com/prodindex/pagemill/main.html
Adobe PhotoDeluxe, Home Edition 3.0	Image editing program that includes built-in projects.	15	Graphics/video	Demo	http://www.adobe.com/prodindex/photodeluxe/main.html
Adobe Premiere 5.0 program	Video recording and editing.	13	Graphics/video	Demo	http://www.adobe.com/prodindex/premiere/main.html
Allaire HomeSite	Web site authoring program.	13	Web site	Demo	http://commerce.allaire.com/download/
Cakewalk Guitar Studio 1.0	A MIDI Sequencer program complete with built-in digital audio editing that's specifically designed for guitarists.	16	Audio/music	Demo	http://www.cakewalk.com/Products/GS/GS1.html

Program*	Description	Mentioned in Chapter	Category	Type	Web Site
Cakewalk Home Studio 7.0	A MIDI sequencer program with integrated digital audio recording and editing.	16	Audio/ music	Demo	http://www.cakewalk.com/ Products/HS/HS8.html
Cakewalk In Concert 1.0	A MIDI accompaniment program that automatically generates a back-up band that you can play along with in a variety of different musical styles.	16	Audio/ music	Demo	http://www.cakewalk.com/ Products/IC/IC1.html
JASC Paint Shop Pro 5.0	Image editing program with sophisticated feature set.	15	Graphics/ video	Demo	http://www.jasc.com/ download.html
Macromedia DreamWeaver	Web site authoring program.	13	Web site	Demo	http://www.macromedia. com/software/downloads/
Macromedia FireWorks	Program for creating graphics for Web sites.	13, 15	Web site	Demo	http://www.macromedia. com/software/downloads/
Microsoft Internet Explorer 5.0	Web browser and e-mail package.	13	Internet	Freeware	http://www.microsoft. com/ie
Microsoft PowerPointer Viewer 97	Utility for viewing PowerPoint presentation files.	14	Utility	Freeware	http://www.microsoft. com/office/
MIRC	Internet Relay Chat (IRC) client program.	13	Internet	Shareware	http://www.mirc.co.uk/
Mixman Studio 1.0	A digital audio remixing program that lets you use original or existing audio clips to create new musical pieces.	16	Audio/ Music	Demo	http://www.catalog. mixman.com/mixman/ demo/studiodem.html

Continued

Table A-1 *(continued)*

Program*	Description	Mentioned in Chapter	Category	Type	Web Site
MusicMatch Jukebox 3.05	An MP3 audio player and recording program.	16	Audio/ Music	Demo	http://www.musicmatch. com/jukebox/
NetMedic	Utility for tracking down performance problems with your Internet connection.	13	Internet	Demo	http://www.vitalsigns. com/netmedic/index.html
Netscape Communicator 4.5	Web browser and e-mail package.	13	Internet	Freeware	http://www.netscape.com/ computing/download/ index.html?cp=hom03prt1
PowerQuest Boot Magic	Boot Loader.	9	Utility	Demo	http://www.powerquest. com/ product/bm/index.html
PowerQuest Drive Image	Hard disk backup program.	11	Utility	Demo	http://www.powerquest. com/product/di/ index.html
PowerQuest Lost & Found	Hard disk data recovery utility.	14	Utility	Demo	http://www.powerquest. com/product/laf/index.html
PowerQuest Partition Magic	Hard disk partitioning software and OS boot loader.	9, 11, 17	Utility	Demo	http://www.powerquest. com/product/pm/index.html
QuickView Plus 5.1	File conversion and viewing utility.	12, 13, 14	Utility	Demo	http://www.jasc.com/ download.html
RealPlayer G2	RealAudio and RealVideo streaming media player for listening to audio and watching video over the Internet.	13	Internet	Freeware	http://www.real.com
SANDRA	System analysis and troubleshooting utility.	9, 17	Utility	Demo	http://www.sisoftware.demon. co.uk/sandra/index.htm

Program*	Description	Mentioned in Chapter	Category	Type	Web Site
ShareClean	Utility for turning off file sharing.	12	Networking	Freeware	http://www.nsclean.com/sclean.html
Socklock	Utility for preventing the Happy 99 virus from damaging your WinSock files.	13	Utility	Freeware	http://www.nsclean.com/socklock.html
SurfWatch	Utility for restricting access to objectionable Web sites.	13	Internet	Freeware	http://www1.surfwatch.com/download/free.html
Symantec Anti-Virus	Anti-virus utility.	17	Utility	Demo	http://shop.symantec.com/trialware/
Symantec Norton Zip Rescue	Utility for creating a bootable Zip Disk for fixing hard disk problems.	14, 17	Utility	Freeware	http://shop.symantec.com/trialware/
Symantec Y2K BIOS Fix	Utility for fixing Y2K-related date problems with PC BIOS.	11	Utility	Freeware	http://shop.symantec.com/trialware/
Trouble in Paradise	Utility for "Click of Death" problems associated with Zip and Jaz removable drives.	18	Utility	Freeware	http://www.spinrite.com/default.htm
WinGate 3.0	Proxy server software that allows you to share a single Internet connection.	12	Networking	Demo	http://www.wingate.com/index.htm
WinZip 7.0	File compression and decompression utility.	13, 14, 17, 18	Utility	Shareware	http://www.winzip.com
WS_FTP LE	FTP utility for transferring files over the Internet.	13	Internet	Freeware	http://www.ipswitch.com/cgi/download_eval.pl?product=main

*Note that these programs are subject to change and may differ from what actually comes on the CD.

I hope you enjoy the CD and its contents. If you want to get updated information about the CD or the book in general, head over to `http://www.everythingcomputers.com/book.htm`, which is the Web site for *Personal Computer Secrets*.

Glossary

Numeric

100Base-T

A computer network that uses the Fast Ethernet, or 100Mbps, network architecture. As the name implies, it is ten times faster than standard 10Base-T Ethernet networks, although it uses the same type of RJ-45 connectors as a 10Base-T network. *See also* Ethernet, 10Base-T, and 10Base-2.

10Base-2

A computer network that uses the standard 10Mbps Ethernet network architecture but uses BNC connectors and coaxial cable to make the physical connections between PCs. Sometimes also called "Thinnet." *See also* Ethernet, BNC, 10Base-T, and 100Base-T.

10Base-T

A computer network that uses the standard 10Mbps Ethernet network architecture and uses telephone-like RJ-45 connectors. This is the most common type of PC network. In some instances, 10Base-T is also used to describe the type of physical connectors used on devices that include support for Ethernet. *See also* Ethernet, RJ-45, 10Base-2, and 100Base-T.

16-bit

A reference to the number of individual bits that make up one discrete chunk of data, the number of different levels that those bits can represent, or the width of a particular data channel, or bus, inside your PC. Practically speaking, 16-bit color or 16-bit audio, for example, offer 2^{16}, or 65,536 different levels that each bit of data can be assigned to. *See also* Bit, Byte, and Digital Audio.

24-bit

A reference to the number of individual bits that make up one discrete chunk of data, the number of different levels that those bits can represent, or the width of a particular data channel, or bus, inside your PC. In most instances, 24-bit is used in reference to the number of colors that your video card is currently displaying or the amount of colors used in a digital photograph. Numerically speaking, 24-bit color translates into 2^{24} or 16.7 million different colors. *See also* Bit, Byte, and Resolution.

32-bit

A reference to the number of individual bits that make up one discrete chunk of data, the number of different levels that those bits can represent, or the width of a particular data channel, or bus, inside your PC. In most instances, 32-bit refers to the width of a bus that moves data around different areas of your PC, or the size of data chunks that the microprocessor can work on. In some cases, 32-bit refers to color images that also take advantage of an alpha channel. *See also* Alpha Channel, Bus, and Microprocessor.

3DNow

A set of additional processing instructions used in AMD's K6 and K7 family of processors that are optimized for rendering 3D graphics and performing other floating-point calculations. *See also* Instructions, Microprocessor, MMX, and Streaming SIMD.

56K

A shortened name for the 56Kbps data transfer rates supported in modems that support the V.90 standard as well as other modems that predate the ratification of the standard. 56K modems are the fastest analog modems currently available. *See also* V.34, V.90, and Modem.

64-bit

A reference to the number of individual bits that make up one discrete chunk of data, the number of different levels that those bits can represent, or the width of a particular data channel, or bus, inside your PC. In most instances, 64-bit refers to the width of a bus that moves data around different areas of your PC, or the size of data chunks that the microprocessor can work on. *See also* Bus and Microprocessor.

8-bit

A reference to the number of individual bits that make up one discrete chunk of data, the number of different levels that those bits can represent, or the width of a particular data channel, or bus, inside your PC. In the case of 8-bit, the term is frequently used to describe the color setting of the video card. Eight-bit color offers support for 2^8 or 256 colors. *See also* Bit, Byte, and Resolution.

8086

The name of Intel's first generation 16-bit processor. The 8086 serves as the basic foundation for all later processors up to and including the various types of Pentiums. Processors that conform to or are compatible with this basic 8086-driven architecture and the instructions included in the processor are referred to as "x86" or "x86-compatible processors." The 8086 was used in the IBM XT. *See also* X86 and Processor.

8088

The name of Intel's 8-bit processor that served as the basis for the first IBM PC. The 8088 was limited to accessing 1MB of memory. All later x86-compatible processors are capable of emulating the 8088 via real mode. *See also* Real Mode.

80286

The name of Intel's second generation 16-bit processor. It's also commonly referred to as a "'286." The 80286 was used in the IBM AT and compatibles.

80386

The name of Intel's third-generation processor, it was the first to operate in 32-bit mode. It's also commonly referred to as a "'386." There were several types of '386s available, including the '386DX and the '386SX.

80486

The name of Intel's fourth-generation processor. It's also commonly referred to as a 486. Like the 386, several types of 486s were available, including the 486DX, the 486SX, and the 486SL.

A

Accelerator

A component in your PC, typically hardware, that enables your PC to perform a function more quickly and/or efficiently than the computer could without it. In most cases, accelerators refer to video cards, which are sometimes called "graphics accelerators," because most video cards have features that accelerate the display of 3D graphics or motion video. In some instances, the term is also used with other devices within a system, such as sound cards or processors. *See also* Video Card.

Access Time

The amount of time it takes for a storage device, typically a hard drive or a CD- or DVD-ROM drive to get to the next chunk of data it needs to read. Specifically, it refers to how long it takes for the drive's media to spin around and for the drive's head to move into position over the particular sector that is to be read. Access times are commonly quoted specifications for storage devices, but because there are several different types of access time, such as average access time, peak access time, and so on, they can be misleading. *See also* Sector and Seek Time.

ACPI

An acronym for Advanced Configuration Power Interface, also called "OnNow" under Windows. A power management specification, in which the operating system can put a computer and its various components into one of several low-power sleep modes. This can be useful because instead of having to shut down and then boot your computer every time you want to use it again, you can just bring it out of sleep mode, which takes much less time. ACPI is a later-generation power management system than APM, which is more dependent on the computer's BIOS than the operating system. *See also* APM, OnNow, and Power Management.

Active Matrix

A type of display system used in the LCD monitors found in notebooks and flat-panel displays used with desktop computers in which every pixel dot on the LCD can be individually addressed and refreshed. The tangible result is a brighter, crisper picture than other display systems and one that offers faster refresh rates, which makes it better suited for displaying animation, video, and other moving elements. Sometimes also referred to as "TFT," or "Thin Film Transistor," technology. *See also* Dual Scan, LCD Panel, and Passive Matrix.

ActiveX

A type of software found in Windows that's commonly used to create small programs called *ActiveX controls* that are used on Web sites or within HTML-based documents. Specifically, ActiveX is a programming model that's designed to create reusable software components that can be used individually or put together to make larger programs. *See also* Java and JavaScript.

Adapter

A device within your computer that serves as a bridge between two different types of components. In many instances, an adapter is a type of plug-in card that links external components with your PC's basic architecture. For example, a SCSI host adapter is a plug-in card that enables you to attach SCSI-based devices to your PC and connects them through your PC's PCI bus. Similarly, with a video adapter or Ethernet adapter, you can connect monitors and other Ethernet-based devices, respectively. In some cases, the term also refers to a small device that enables you to mate two dissimilar types of physical connectors. *See also* Host Adapter.

ADC

An acronym for Analog-to-Digital Converter, a component found in many sound cards and video digitizing cards that converts an analog signal into digital form. *See also* Analog, DAC, and Digital.

ADSL

An acronym for Asymmetric Digital Subscriber Line, a type of digital connection that offers the potential of very fast 1.5Mbps (or even higher) connections to the Internet using existing copper phone lines. ADSL also supports the capability to simultaneously make a data connection and a voice call on a single line. High-speed ADSL connections often require a splitter, to separate the voice and data calls, but lower-speed ADSL does not require this hardware and is said to be "splitter-less." To use ADSL, you need access to ADSL service on your existing phone line and you need to use an ADSL modem, which often connects to your PC via an Ethernet card or connection. Internal ADSL modems come in the form of a plug-in card and do not require an Ethernet card. A common form of ADSL that offers a maximum transfer rate of 1.5Mbps and a minimum of 384Kbps is sometimes called "UADSL" (Universal ADSL) or "ADSL Lite," and modems that support this service conform to the G.Lite standard. Like a network connection, ADSL Internet connections are always on, so you do not have to dial in. ADSL is one of several different types of DSL, with the "Asymmetric" part of the name meaning that the transfer rates for uploading are different from (and typically slower than) the transfer rates for downloading. *See also* DSL and G.Lite.

AGP

An acronym for Advanced Graphics Port, a type of connection used in PCs to connect certain types of video cards directly to the computer's system bus. The term refers both to the standard that certain video cards use to transfer data and the physical connector on the PC's motherboard. By moving the bandwidth-intensive video card off the PCI bus, AGP theoretically enables a system to work faster and more efficiently. In addition, AGP enables a video card to use part of the computer's main memory to temporarily store graphics images, such as large bitmapped images found in computer games, which can help reduce the need for lots of dedicated video memory on the video card. Standard AGP supports a dedicated 66MHz, 32-bit bus, and AGP 2x and 4x offer two and four times the standard throughput, respectively. *See also* Bandwidth, PCI, and Throughput.

AIFF

An acronym for Audio Interchange File Format, a type of digital audio file format that's commonly used on the Macintosh and other platforms, particularly for professional audio-recording applications. It is also sometimes found on the Internet. *See also* Digital Audio.

Algorithm

A highly defined process, typically in the form of a complex mathematical equation, used to complete a particular task. Applications and other software commonly use different algorithms to perform certain functions.

Alpha Channel

A portion of a digital image file that can be used to set various levels of transparency. Not all image file formats support an alpha channel, but some, such as PNG (Portable Network Graphics) do. *See also* PNG.

Analog

A continuously varying signal that is typical of how things occur in nature. Analog sound, for example, is defined as a continuously varying waveform and, in fact, is the type of sound our ears hear emanating from a speaker or other sound source. Analog video consists of a continuously changing video signal. Media that we can see and hear exists in an analog state, but to use it with a computer, it must be converted into digital form, a process called *digitizing*, *sampling*, or in the case of video, *video capturing*. Doing so converts the continuously varying analog signal into a series of discrete steps that can be represented numerically. To understand the difference, think of a regular analog clock with a continuously sweeping second hand, versus a digital clock where the display updates in discrete steps. *See also* Digital, Sampling, and Video Capture.

Anti-aliasing

A technique used to improve the appearance of graphics and type on a computer screen by slightly changing the color of some pixels at the edge of the graphic or particular character. By adding and/or changing a few pixels to various shades of gray, for example, the sharp edges of black text on a white background can be softened, making the text look smoother. *See also* Font.

AO/DI

An acronym for Always On/Dynamic ISDN, a capability found in certain ISDN modems that enables the modem to maintain a consistent low-bandwidth connection. Like traditional analog modems, most ISDN modems, or adapters, require you to dial up to make a connection and disconnect to end a connection, but with AO/DI you can have some of the same benefits of an always on connection found with DSL and cable modems. *See also* ISDN.

API

An acronym for Application Programming Interface, a mechanism used by programmers to enable one program to work along with or take advantage of the capabilities of another. For example, by taking advantage of, or "hooking" into an existing API, programmers may be able to use features found in another program or operating system function to make their programs work better or do things they couldn't otherwise do.

APM

An acronym for Advanced Power Management, a mechanism for automatically controlling the computer's on and off states. On notebook computers it helps preserve battery life. APM is an older technology than ACPI and primarily driven by a computer's BIOS. *See also* ACPI, OnNow, and Power Management.

Application

A piece of software that performs a particular function. Sometimes also called a "program." A word processor, for example, is a common type of application.

ASCII

An acronym for American Standard Code for Information Interchange, a standard used to define text characters, punctuation marks, and other symbols as a number between 0–127. ASCII text is typically the lowest common denominator file format among different computer platforms and applications and is used to exchange text-based data between different programs. *See also* Binary File, Document, and RTF.

AT Commands

A set of standardized modem functions that are used to configure a modem to dial out, using specific connection rates and error correction methods, among other things. Originally developed by now-defunct modem maker Hayes, they are used by telecommunications programs and recognized by virtually all analog modems. ATDT, for example, is an AT command that's used to tell the modem to dial a phone number. *See also* Modem.

ATA

An acronym for AT Attachment, a standard that defines how hard drives connect to and communicate with IDE-based hard disk controllers. The name stems from a connection method used on the IBM AT, one of the earliest personal computers. Several enhancements and extensions have been added to the ATA standard, including ATAPI, ATA-2 (sometimes called "EIDE" or "Fast ATA"), ATA-3, UltraATA, and ATA/66, all of which are designed to add additional features and increase the speed of the interface. *See also* IDE and SCSI.

ATAPI

An acronym for AT Attachment Packet Interface, an extension to the ATA standard that added support for CD-ROMs, tape drives, and other removable storage devices. *See also* ATA and IDE.

Attachment

A file or program that is packaged along with an e-mail message. Attachments are separate documents that you must first detach from the e-mail message (usually by just double-clicking) before you can open and use them. Attachments represent the easiest way to send a file or group of files from one person or one computer to another. *See also* E-mail.

ATX

One of several different standard-sized and -shaped motherboards. ATX format motherboards are probably the most common size now available. If you're replacing a motherboard or building your own computer, you need to make sure you purchase one in a shape, or form factor, that fits into your computer's case. A more compact version of the ATX is called the "MicroATX" or "MiniATX." *See also* NLX and Motherboard.

Autoexec.bat

One of the two most well-known types of startup files used by DOS and early versions of Windows. Autoexec.bat is a batch file that automatically executes (hence the name) whatever programs or commands are in it every time the computer is first started. It is commonly used to set certain configuration settings, sometimes called "environmental variables," as well as to load certain pieces of software. Later versions of Windows, from 95 on up, do not require an Autoexec.bat, but they typically include one for backwards compatibility. *See also* Config.sys, BAT File, and Startup Files.

B

Backwards Compatible

A characteristic of certain types of hardware, software, and technical standards in which newer versions are able to be used alongside older versions. If something is not backwards compatible, then it cannot work with older versions of the file format or technology.

Bandwidth

The amount of data that a particular connection is capable of transferring in a given amount of time. Specifically, the bandwidth of a connection is determined by the width of the connection, in bits, times the speed of the connection, which is typically expressed in MHz. For example, the PCI bus on many PCs is 32 bits (or 4 bytes) wide and runs at 33MHz, which translates to an overall bandwidth of 132Mbytes/second. Different types of connections within a PC and between a PC and other devices offer different amounts of bandwidth, which makes them suited for different types of applications and purposes. *See also* Throughput.

BAT File

A shortened name for batch file, a type of text file that uses the extension .bat and includes a set, or batch, of instructions that are supposed to run whenever the file is opened. The instructions inside a batch file work like macros to quickly and automatically perform certain functions. The most well-known type of batch file is Autoexec.bat, which is automatically run whenever a Windows-based computer that has an Autoexec.bat file is turned on. *See also* Autoexec.bat and Macro.

Benchmark

A type of application that measures the performance of a computer system, or one of its components. Benchmarks are used to differentiate the speed of different computer systems or different individual pieces, such as the hard drive or video card.

BeOS

An alternative operating system available for x86-compatible PCs that focuses on supporting audio, video, MIDI, animation, and other media-related features. BeOS offers a graphical interface and supports symmetric multiprocessing and other advanced hardware technologies.

Beta

A software program that isn't completely finished yet but is generally close enough to be usable. In the normal process of software development, the first version of the program that is created is called an *alpha*, and the version that is supposed to be nearly complete is referred to as a *beta*. Companies used to release their beta versions to a limited group of beta testers, who would run the software through all kinds of various tests in order to find bugs and other problems. Recently, however, most companies have begun to release beta versions to the general public. While, on the one hand, this provides users with the opportunity to try a new version of a program sooner than they would otherwise be able to, many beta versions still have significant problems and can crash on a regular basis. As a result, it's best to avoid beta versions if you want to keep your computer system as stable as possible. *See also* Bugs and Crash.

Binary File

A generic term for a file that is stored in a format made up of binary numbers, as opposed to ASCII text. Most applications as well as many proprietary file formats use binary format. As a result, they cannot be opened with a text-editing program such as a word processor, whereas text-based or text-only files can be. *See also* ASCII.

Binary Math

Also known as "Base-2 math," the type of mathematics used in computers and many other digital devices. Binary math reduces all data to a series of ones and zeros. These ones and zeros, in turn, can be represented by a simple switch that stores on or off. The benefit of binary math is that it enables calculations to be done by a series of on/off switches, which greatly simplifies how microprocessors, memory, storage devices, and other computer peripherals work.

Binding

In a networking environment, the connection made between a network service, such as file sharing, and a network protocol. The protocol tells the network service how to communicate with computers on a network. Devices and protocols that are connected in this way are said to be "bound." *See also* Network and Protocol.

BIOS

An acronym for Basic Input/Output System, the first and lowest level software that runs on your PC as soon as you turn it on. The BIOS is stored on a chip that's attached to your computer's motherboard, and when it runs, it performs several functions including directing the computer to perform some diagnostic tests called *POST*, finding what hardware is attached to the motherboard, and then loading whatever operating system or other software it finds on the first sector of the computer's first hard disk (called the *Master Boot Record*). You can make changes to your computer's BIOS settings by entering the Setup program (sometimes also called "BIOS Setup" or "CMOS Setup") as soon as your PC turns on. Your settings are typically stored in CMOS, which is why BIOS and CMOS are sometimes used interchangeably. *See also* CMOS, Master Boot Record, POST, and Setup.

Bit

The smallest measurement of digital data, equivalent to a single one or zero in a binary number. There are eight bits in a byte, and four bits are sometimes called a *nybble* (or *two quarters*, depending on who you ask). *See also* Byte.

Bitmapped Graphics

A family of graphics formats, typically used with digital photographs or other exact representations of the computer screen, where the image is made up of numerous independent dots, or pixels, of different colors. This is in contrast to vector-based graphics, where the image is made of lines, shapes, or other mathematically defined symbols. As a consequence, bitmapped graphics tend to be much larger in file size than vector graphics and cannot be easily resized without distorting the image. Programs that generate bitmapped graphics are generally referred to as "paint programs," whereas vector graphics are created by drawing programs. Many popular graphics file formats including BMP, GIF, JPEG, and others use some type of bitmapped graphics. *See also* Vector Graphics.

BMP

A popular Windows file format for simple bitmapped graphics. Files that are in BMP format use the extension .bmp. *See also* Bitmapped Graphics, Extension, and File Format.

BNC

An acronym for British Naval Connector, or Bayonet-Neill Concelman or Baby Nevel Connector (depending on whom you ask), a round-shaped locking connector used with coaxial cables. BNC connectors are found on 10Base-2 Ethernet cards and some types of video equipment.

Bookmark

A mechanism used by Web browsers to remember the addresses of your favorite Web sites. By creating a bookmark, called a "Favorite" in Internet Explorer, you automatically save the name of the page and its URL (Universal Resource Locator) so that you can quickly revisit the page by simply selecting the bookmark from a menu. *See also* URL.

Boot

Short for "bootstrap," or pulling yourself up by your bootstraps, it's the process that happens when you first turn a computer on and it starts to load the operating system. Sometimes also used to describe the process of loading or starting up a particular application. *See also* Operating System and Startup Files.

Boot Loader

A special-purpose program that enables you to select from one of several different operating systems that you have installed on your computer when you first turn on the PC. A boot loader, which is used only on computers that can dual boot, is typically stored in your hard drive's Master Boot Record, or MBR. *See also* Dual Boot and Master Boot Record.

Browser

An application that you can use to view Web sites on the Internet or any other documents stored in HTML (HyperText Markup Language) format. The most popular browsers are Microsoft's Internet Explorer and Netscape's Communicator/Navigator. *See also* HTML.

Bugs

A generic term for problems with an application (or the operating system) that prevent it from performing a particular function as it's supposed to, or that cause it to stop working completely—a situation known as a "crash." Bugs are not a fault of the user, but a problem in the software code that the programmer created. The only way to fix a bug is to get an upgraded version of the program that includes corrections for the problem—known as a "bug fix." *See also* Crash and Service Pack.

Bus

A path for connecting two or more components inside your PC and transferring data between them. All computers have several different buses, including the PCI bus, Universal Serial Bus (USB), and system bus, each of which runs at different speeds and offers different bandwidth. *See also* Bandwidth, PCI, System Bus, and USB.

Bus Master

A device that's connected to a particular bus that can independently take command of that bus without interrupting the computer's processor. Many computer components can function only with input from the processor, but devices such as hard drives, controllers, and other plug-in cards that support bus mastering can do so without the processor's help. This enables the processor to keep working and should, therefore, make the system more efficient.

Byte

The most popular measurement of digital data, a byte consists of eight bits. Virtually all computer measurements are made in multiples of bytes such as kilobytes or KB (1,024 bytes), megabytes or MB (1,048,576 bytes), gigabytes or GB (1,073,741,824 bytes), and even terabytes or TB (1,099,511,627,776 bytes). *See also* Bit, Gb/GB, Kb/KB, Mb/MB, and Tb/TB.

C

Cable Modem

A device that enables you to connect to the Internet via existing cable TV lines you have installed in your home or business. Many cable modems support the DOCSIS standard and offer download transfer rates of up to 38Mbps, although rates between 1.5 and 8Mbps are more typical. Like other asymmetric systems, such as ADSL, however, upload rates are typically much slower and, in some cases, are limited to as little as 128 or 384Kbps. *See also* ADSL and DOCSIS.

Cache

A quickly reachable temporary storage area, or buffer, used to hold recent data. Many computer components need to reuse data soon after it's been first accessed. By using a cache to hold that data, they can speed up their overall performance. On a processor, for example, the cache holds recently used data and instructions that it can get to and reuse much more quickly than if it needed to get to them in normal memory. A disk cache is an area of memory set aside by the operating system that stores data that was recently retrieved from the hard disk. Many types of software use caches as well, such as Web browsers, which use a cache to stored recently visited Web pages. *See also* L2 Cache.

CardBus

An updated, 32-bit, 33MHz version of the bus used to connect a notebook computer's PC card (sometimes also called "PCMCIA") slots to the computer's system bus. *See also* System Bus and Zoomed Video.

Cat5

An acronym for Category 5 cabling, which is the type of cable recommended for use with most types of data networks, including Ethernet-based home networks. Category 5 cabling supports frequencies up to 100MHz, which commonly translates to transfer rates of 100Mbps.

CCD

An acronym for Charge-Coupled Device, an electronic component that's found at the heart of many computer and video peripherals, including scanners, digital cameras, video cameras, and camcorders. A CCD senses various degrees of light and dark, as well as various shades of color, and passes that information along to other electronics in the device that converts that information into digital color data. *See also* Digital Camera and Scanner.

CD-R

An acronym for Recordable CD, a type of CD-ROM drive that enables you to record data onto a specially formatted CD-R disc, as well as read from normal CD-ROMs. Unlike CD-RW, which enables you to record onto a disc multiple times (much like a floppy drive), CD-R supports writing to a disc only one time (although it can sometimes be done in multiple sessions). CD-R is ideally designed for creating master copies, such as audio CDs and archives of critical data. Discs created on a CD-R can be read by most, but not all, CD-ROM and DVD-ROM drives. *See also* CD-RW and DVD-R.

CD-ROM

An acronym for Compact Disc, Read Only Memory, a type of storage device that can read optical discs, such as data CDs or audio CDs, that can store up to about 650MB of data. Also used to refer to the discs themselves. *See also* CD-R, CD-RW, and DVD-ROM.

CD-RW

An acronym for Rewritable CD, a type of CD-ROM that enables you to record data over and over onto a specially formatted CD-RW disc, as well as read from normal CD-ROMs. CD-RW discs can be written, erased, and overwritten thousands of times, which makes them kind of like a huge floppy. CD-RW drives can also create CD-Rs if used with CD-R media. CD-RW format discs created on a CD-RW drive can be read only on some recent CD-ROM and DVD-ROM drives, which makes it more difficult to use them for exchanging data than CD-R discs. *See also* CD-R, DVD-RAM, DVD-R/W, and DVD+RW.

Celeron

A low-cost x86-compatible processor that is similar to the Pentium II and Pentium III but features less L2 cache and a few other feature limitations. Original Celerons came packaged on a small circuit board with an SEPP (Single Edge Processor Package) connector, but later versions came in the form of 370-pin PPGA (Plastic Pin Grid Array) chip. *See also* Pentium and SEPP.

Certificates

A mechanism used by certain Web sites to reassure site visitors that the programs, such as ActiveX controls, they include on their pages are safe because they come from a respected source. A certificate is essentially a digital statement of authenticity that says, "Yes, the programs on this page come from XYZ Corporation." Based on this information, you can then decide whether or not to accept the certificate and download the page with the embedded programs (meaning they are part of the page and are automatically downloaded and run through the process of visiting the page in your browser). *See also* ActiveX.

Chip

An integrated circuit that plugs into a circuit board and provides a particular function or set of functions.

Chipset

A set of, typically, two chips found on a computer's motherboard that integrate a number of core PC functions and therefore determine a number of the PC's capabilities. Chipsets such as the Intel 440BX, for example, determine the speed of the computer's system bus, the type of memory that the system can use, and lots more.

CISC

An acronym for Complex Instruction Set Computing, a technology used in processors that enables them to work with instructions of different sizes. Most x86-compatible processors are primarily based on CISC. *See also* RISC.

Client

In a networking environment, the software needed on a PC in order to be able to connect to other computers on the network. In addition, the name for computers that attach to others in a network. *See also* Client-Server, Network, and Server.

Client-Server

A type of networking structure in which a central computer called a *server* sits at the logical center of a group of other computers called *clients*, which all attach to it. This is in contrast to a peer-to-peer network, which doesn't use a centralized server. *See also* Client, Network, Peer-to-Peer, and Server.

Cluster

The smallest individually addressable region on a hard drive. The individual platters in a hard drive are divided up into circular tracks, and each of those tracks is broken up into sectors. A computer's operating system, particularly the file system, doesn't normally work with sectors, however, but clusters, which are groups of sectors. The number of sectors in a cluster is determined by the file system as well as, in many cases, the size of the drive. The FAT-32 file system supported in Windows 98, Windows 2000, and later versions of Windows 95, for example, is more efficient than the older FAT-16 and, as a result, can have less sectors per cluster. This is important because if a data file uses only a portion of the sectors in a cluster, the rest go unused and are wasted. By having smaller clusters, file systems can take better advantage of the available space. *See also* FAT, FAT-32, Hard Drive, Sector, and Track.

CMOS

An acronym for Complementary Metal Oxide Semiconductor, a type of material that used to be used only in an area of the computer that stored the BIOS settings but is now used for many types of components. Technically, CMOS still refers to the battery-backed memory that stores the BIOS settings, but some people use it almost interchangeably with BIOS and refer to a computer's BIOS Setup program as "CMOS Setup." *See also* BIOS and Setup.

CMYK

An acronym for Cyan, Magenta, Yellow, and Black (K), the official name for four-color printing that uses inks in each of these colors. Some three-color inkjet printers that don't include the capability to print black along with the other three colors are referred to as "CMY printers." *See also* RGB.

Codec

A contraction for compressor/decompressor, typically used when referring to various types of video capture and compression technologies, such as MJPEG or MPEG. The codec is the software responsible for doing the actual compression and decompression of the video signal. With most computer video standards, such as AVI and QuickTime, you can choose from among several different codecs. *See also* Compression, Encoder, MJPEG, and MPEG.

Color Management

A type of system-level software that's designed to ensure that the colors you see in a photograph you scan, and/or view on your monitor, look the same when they are printed. Without color management in place or in use, you can run into problems such as an image that has a vivid green onscreen turning into a yellowish, chartreuse-like green when you print it.

COM

Short for "Communications Port," it's the naming convention used by PCs to assign physical connectors such as a serial port to a "virtual" software port that your applications send data to. For example, you can assign your computer's only external serial port to be COM1, COM2, COM3, or COM4, depending on the settings and needs of your software. *See also* LPT and Serial.

Command Prompt

A text-based user interface that you interact with by typing in commands. The most common example is a DOS prompt, such as C:\, but other operating systems also offer command prompt or command-line interfaces.

CompactFlash

A type of storage device used on digital cameras and other handheld computing devices that can store images and other data in special battery-backed memory. CompactFlash is a physically smaller form of Flash memory, which typically comes in PC Card format, but it can be used in conjunction with a PC Card adapter to fit into standard PC Card slots. On a digital camera it essentially works as one of several different types of digital film. *See also* Digital Camera, Flash Memory, PC Card, and SmartMedia.

Component Video

A type of very high-quality analog video signal that's separated into several components, including one each for red, green, blue, and a separate synchronization signal. Component video is typically found only on professional quality video-recording and -editing equipment and can often be identified through the use of several BNC connectors to carry the signal. *See also* Composite Video and S-Video.

Composite Video

A type of analog video signal that combines all the different portions of a signal into one. Composite video is the standard type of video signal used by NTSC-compatible devices, such as regular analog TVs, and comes from a video device's RCA jacks. *See also* Component Video, NTSC, and S-Video.

Compression

A technique used to squeeze a given amount of data into a smaller space. Using one of several different algorithms, or mathematical instructions for processing data, compression can reduce the size of image files, to improve the throughput on low-bandwidth connections, and to store more data onto a given storage device. Some compression methods, called *lossy compression*, reduce the size of a file by throwing away certain data, while others, called *lossless compression*, do so without losing any data. The process of returning compressed data to its regular, larger form is called "decompression." In audio applications, compression can also mean a technique for reducing the overall dynamic range of an audio signal by making the softer sections louder and the louder sections a bit softer. *See also* Codec and Normalize.

Config.sys

One of the two most well-known types of startup files used by DOS and early versions of Windows. Config.sys is a system file that's primarily used to load real-mode drivers into the first 640K, or sometimes first megabyte, of a computer's memory when the computer is first turned on. Later versions of Windows, from 95 on up, do not require a Config.sys, but they typically include one for backwards compatibility. In addition, most devices no longer require a real-mode driver, unless they are used in a completely DOS environment. *See also* Autoexec.bat, Real Mode, Startup Files.

Continuous Tone

The capability of a printer to produce any one of 16.7 million colors at any point on a page with a single dot. Most printers require several dots and use halftones to create the impression of a full range of colors, but continuous tone printers can generate prints that look identical to photographs. In fact, they're the kind of printers used to create many photographs. *See also* Halftone and Dye Sublimation.

Controller

A device that's used to communicate between a computer's processor and another component inside a PC. A hard disk controller, for example, acts as an intermediary between the processor and a hard disk, converting commands from the processor into a format that the hard disk can understand. Similarly, a SCSI controller enables a PC system to communicate with SCSI-based devices. *See also* Adapter.

Conventional Memory

Under DOS, the infamous first 640K of memory, which is typically used for applications and the operating system itself. In order for DOS applications, such as games, to get access to more memory, you need to use expanded memory and/or extended memory. Conventional memory is also sometimes referred to as "low memory." *See also* DOS, Expanded Memory, Extended Memory, and Upper Memory.

Cookies

A tiny text file used by certain Web sites to help keep track of where you have been on the site and any preferences you may have selected. Unless you specifically request to see them, cookie files are typically transferred from the Web server to your PC's hard drive without your knowledge. While this sounds somewhat nefarious, the vast majority of cookies are innocuous, and many can actually be useful. For example, cookies can do such things as remember your username and password or any other settings you may have made, which makes it easier for you the next time you visit the site. The Web site checks to see if you have a cookie file that it had previously sent, and if it finds one, it uses the settings associated with that file. If it doesn't find one, you simply have to make the settings again.

CPU

An acronym for Central Processing Unit, which is used both as another name for the computer's processor and as a name for the main computer case on a desktop PC. *See also* Microprocessor.

Crash

A situation that occurs when an application on your computer, or the operating system, stops working properly. When your computer stops responding, for example, it's said to have "crashed." Crashes can occur for a wide variety of reasons, including problems with the program itself, or more likely, interactions between that program and other software currently running on your system. *See also* Bugs.

CRT

An acronym for Cathode Ray Tube, the type of display mechanism used in traditional monitors. The term "CRT" is used interchangeably with "tube-based monitor." *See also* Dot Pitch, LCD Panel, and Monitor.

Cursor

The onscreen pointer, typically in the shape of an arrow, used to interact with graphical user interfaces. Many applications use multiple cursor shapes that change depending where in the program's screen the pointer is located.

D

DAC

An acronym for Digital-to-Analog Converter, a component found in many sound and video cards, as well as USB-based speakers, that converts a digital signal back into analog format. *See also* ADC, Analog, and Digital.

Daughtercard

A small circuit board that attaches to a larger board as an accessory. *See also* Motherboard.

DB25

A D-shaped connector with 25 pins that is typically used with a PC's parallel port but is sometimes also used with certain SCSI devices. *See also* Parallel Port and SCSI.

DB9

A D-shaped connector with 9 pins that is typically used with a PC's serial port. *See also* Serial Port.

DDC

An acronym for Display Data Channel, a communications method used by Plug-and-Play monitors to communicate their capabilities, such as maximum refresh rates and resolutions supported, to the video card and computer to which it is attached. Sometimes referred to as "DDC-2" or "VESA DDC." *See also* PnP and Resolution.

DDR SDRAM

An acronym for Double Data Rate SDRAM (Synchronous Dynamic Random Access Memory), a type of high-speed memory that sends information twice as fast as normal SDRAM by sending data on both the rising and falling edges of the clock signal. *See also* SDRAM and Virtual Channel Memory.

Decoder

A piece of hardware or software that converts a signal or file from a compressed, or encoded, format into a normally viewable or usable format. *See also* Encoder.

Demoware

A type of software made available by commercial software vendors that enables you to download and/or install a program for free and try it out for a limited period of time. Sometimes "demoware" refers to programs with certain features, such as saving and printing, disabled. *See also* Freeware and Shareware.

Desktop

The primary feature of an operating system's graphical user interface, the desktop serves as a home base for getting access to your computer's files and programs. Also used to describe a computer that is primarily designed to be used on a desk, as opposed to a mobile or notebook computer.

Device Bay

A connection mechanism that enables you to add devices such as hard drives, CD-, or DVD-ROM drives into a computer by simply sliding it into a special slot. Device Bay takes advantage of both USB and IEEE 1394 to provide fast, hot-pluggable connections. Three different Device Bay sizes can fit a variety of different peripherals into both desktops and notebooks, and an Eject button makes it as easy to remove a device as it does to install one. *See also* Hot Plugging, IEEE 1394, and USB.

DFP

An acronym for Digital Flat Panel, a type of digital video connection mechanism used with certain LCD monitors. DFP is essentially a simplified version of the more robust P&D (Plug & Display) standard and only supports a digital connection between the monitor and video card. The DVI (Digital Video Interface) standard incorporates elements of both DFP and P&D. *See also* DVI, LCD Panel, LDI, and P&D.

DHCP

An acronym for Dynamic Host Configuration Protocol, a method for automatically assigning IP addresses to computers that attach to a network. DHCP is commonly used by Internet Service Providers (ISPs) and online services to give your PC an IP address when you make a dial-up connection via an analog modem. Unlike fixed IP addresses, which never change, DHCP gives you a different IP address every time you connect. *See also* IP Address.

Dialog Box

A mechanism used by applications to request information or other input from the user. You use dialog boxes to do things such as save or open a file or adjust certain settings.

Digital

A means of describing information as a series of discrete steps in the form of ones and zeros. Before a computer can work with any type of information, it must be in digital form. *See also* Analog and Binary Math.

Digital Audio

A format that describes an audio signal as a series of ones and zeros. Digital audio is essentially a recording of an existing sound or piece of music, whereas MIDI, with which it is commonly associated and confused, is a language for describing the characteristics of a musical performance. *See also* MIDI, Sampling, and S/PDIF.

Digital Camera

A device that typically looks and functions as a regular film-based camera but stores its images either in memory or on a digital storage device, such as a floppy disk, CompactFlash, or SmartMedia card. *See also* CompactFlash, Megapixel, and SmartMedia.

Digitizing

The process of converting an analog signal into the digital form that computers require. In the case of video signals, this is often referred to as "video capture," and in the case of audio signals, it's typically referred to as "sampling." *See also* Sampling and Video Capture.

DIMM

An acronym for Dual Inline Memory Module, a type of miniature circuit board with a 168-pin connector that holds memory chips. DIMMs essentially combine two SIMMs (Single Inline Memory Modules) into one and feature a 64-bit connection to the computer's system bus. Because the Pentium and later processors use memory 64 bits at a time, you can add DIMMs to a PC one at a time, whereas SIMMs must be added in pairs. Most current desktop PCs feature DIMM slots on the motherboard as their primary type of memory chip connection. DIMMs can come in one of several different memory types, including SDRAM and DDR SDRAM. *See also* RIMM, SIMM, and SODIMM.

DIP Switch

A type of tiny on/off switch found on some motherboards, older plug-in cards, and storage devices that you use to change the device's configuration. Most newer devices can be configured via software, but you still occasionally need to change some DIP switch settings.

Directory

Another name for a folder in a computer's storage hierarchy. A computer's root directory is the lowest (or highest, depending on you perspective) level available. In DOS or Windows, the root directory is usually C:\, and in Linux it's just /. *See also* Path, and Root.

Distribution

A collection of software that's bundled and sold as a single package. A Linux distribution consists of the core Linux kernel files, utilities, applications, electronic documentation, and whatever else the company selling the distribution believes adds value. *See also* Kernel and Linux.

Dithering

A technique for simulating a wider palette of colors than are available in a digital image by using other colors and patterns in certain combinations. You typically need to worry about dithering only if you're dealing with an image in 8-bit color. *See also* 8-bit.

DLL

An acronym for Dynamic Link Library, a type of software component that exists as a separate file and performs a particular function or set of functions. DLLs are not applications on their own but provide specific capabilities to an application, the operating system, or both. DLLs are also sometimes called "shared libraries" because they are often used by several different applications simultaneously. Some applications actually consist of a small umbrella program and numerous DLLs that each perform different functions for that program. You can run into DLL Hell if you find that one application has been updated or changed a DLL that other applications depend on and causes them to break. *See also* Libraries and Shared Files.

DLS

An acronym for Downloadable Samples, a standard for transferring customized sampled sounds into the RAM available to a sound card (either on the card itself or a specified area of main memory) and making them available as a MIDI sound source. DLS, which is incorporated into Microsoft's DirectMusic API, provides a way for games and musical applications to expand the sonic palette of a wavetable synthesis-based sound card by adding new sounds, sometimes called *sound fonts*, from which you can choose. DLS2 is an updated version of the standard. *See also* MIDI and Wavetable Synthesis.

DMA

An acronym for Direct Memory Access, a mechanism for sending information directly to and from memory, without passing through the processor. Also, a computer resource used by certain devices to perform this function. Most PCs have eight DMA channels, labeled 0–7. UltraDMA is a type of higher-speed, 33MB/sec ATA or IDE connection for hard drives and other storage devices. UltraDMA is used interchangeably with UltraDMA/33, UltraATA, ATA/33, and other variations. *See also* ATA, IDE, and Resources.

DNS

An acronym for Domain Name Server, a computer that performs the task of converting text-based Web addresses into numerical IP addresses and back again. A DNS essentially looks up the address, or URL, you type into your Web browser in a huge database, finds the IP address, and then routes your request to the computer at that IP address. *See also* Domain Name, Hosts File, IP Address, and URL.

DOCSIS

An acronym for Data Over Cable Service Interface Specification, a standard for cable modems developed by an industry consortium known as MCNS (Multimedia Cable Network System) that enables devices that support the standard to communicate with one another. DOCSIS-compliant cable modems offer transfer rates of up to 38Mbps. *See also* Cable Modem.

Document

An organized body of data that's given a name and also called a "file." A document is the most basic type of structure in a computer's storage system. Most documents are created and/or opened from within an application.

Domain Name

The first part of a Web address. For example, in the address `www.everythingcomputers.com/books.htm`, the domain name is everythingcomputers. When creating your own Web site, you can register for your own domain name at `www.internic.net`. Also used to provide a name for a particular segment, or domain, in a larger network. *See also* DNS.

DOS

An acronym for Disk Operating System, a text-based operating system that was the first used on IBM-compatible PCs and is still available through various versions of Windows. The most common type of DOS is MS-DOS, which is the version sold by Microsoft, but other types include IBM DOS and DR-DOS, which was originally developed by Digital Research. DOS suffers from a number of well-known limitations — including a maximum of eight-character filenames (with a three character extension — a combination known as 8.3) and a 640K usable memory limit — many of which still have an impact on modern operating systems and PC design. *See also* Autoexec.bat, Config.sys, and Real Mode.

Dot Pitch

A measurement used with CRT-based monitors that describes how far apart the individual elements that create an image on the screen are. The lower the dot pitch (typical numbers are around .26 mm or .28 mm), the closer the elements are and the sharper the image that can be created. Monitors with high dot pitches are often blurry and difficult to read. *See also* CRT and Monitor.

Download

The process of copying files over a network connection, such as the Internet, from one computer to another. Also used to signify the difference between receiving information over an Internet connection, which is downloading, versus sending it, which is uploading.

DPI

An acronym for Dots Per Inch, a common measurement used to describe the resolution of printer, scanners, digital cameras, and other devices that work with images. *See also* Resolution.

DRAM

An acronym for Dynamic Random Access Memory, the main type of memory used in computer systems. DRAM needs to be refreshed on a regular basis in order to function and can remember its contents only when power is supplied to it, which means it is a type of volatile memory. This is another way of saying that when the power gets turned off or the batteries run out, everything currently loaded in DRAM is lost. *See also* DDR SDRAM, EDO, Flash Memory, FPM, RDRAM, SDRAM and SRAM.

Driver

A piece of software that communicates between the operating system and particular device inside your PC, typically a piece of hardware. Every single hardware component inside your PC needs a driver in order for it to function properly. Sometimes also called "device driver." *See also* VxD.

DSL

An acronym for Digital Subscriber Line, a family of different digital connection standards that uses regular copper phone lines. All the various types of DSL, sometimes generically referred to as "xDSL," support simultaneous voice and data calls and maintain a constant high-speed network connection, typically to the Internet. Some of the more well-known types of DSL are ADSL and UADSL. To use DSL, you need to have access to DSL service over your existing phone lines, and you need to use DSL-compatible modem, some of which conform to the G.Lite standard. *See also* ADSL, G.Lite, SDSL, and UADSL.

DSTN

An acronym for Dual Super Twist Nematic, another name for "dual scan technology" used in LCD monitors that support passive matrix screens. *See also* Active Matrix, Dual Scan, HPA, LCD Panel, and Passive Matrix.

DSVD

An acronym for Digital Simultaneous Voice and Data, a technology found in some analog modems that enables them to simultaneously support both a low-speed data connection and a phone call on a single phone line.

Dual Boot

The capability to choose from two (or more) operating systems to be loaded onto your machine when you first turn on, or boot, your computer. In order to support dual-booting, a PC has to be specifically set up to support it, typically through a boot loader program and the creation of several different active partitions. *See also* Boot Loader and Partition.

Dual Scan

An enhancement to passive matrix display technology used in LCD panels in which the screen is divided in two and both halves are updated simultaneously. Dual Scan is sometimes also referred to as "DSTN" (Dual Super Twist Nematic), which is the technology used in the screen. The practical result is a brighter screen with better contrast and higher refresh rates, although it still doesn't produce as sharp or as bright a picture as active matrix technology. *See also* Active Matrix, DSTN, HPA, LCD Panel, and Passive Matrix.

Duplex

The capability to communicate over a particular connection, such as a telephone line, in both directions. With a full-duplex system, both parties can be speaking simultaneously back and forth, but in a half-duplex system only one party can be speaking at a time, which creates a walkie talkie–like effect.

DV

An acronym for Digital Video, a format used in most digital camcorders. You can typically send DV footage straight into a PC through an IEEE 1394 connection, all within the digital domain. *See also* FireWire, IEEE 1394, and NTSC.

DVD

An acronym for Digital Video Disc or Digital Versatile Disc, an optical disk format that holds from 4.6GB up to 17GB of data. Many full-length movies, encoded in MPEG-2 format, now come on DVD. *See also* MPEG.

DVD-R

An acronym for Digital Versatile Disc Recordable, a type of storage device and media that can read standard CD- and DVD-ROMs, as well as write to specially formatted DVD-R discs. Like CD-R, DVD-R is designed only to record masters or archives of files; it cannot be written over. *See also* CD-R, DVD-RAM, DVD-R/W, and DVD+RW.

DVD-RAM

An acronym for Digital Versatile Disc Random Access Memory, one of several competitive standards for a recordable and rewritable DVD. Rewritable discs created with a DVD-RAM typically cannot be read by other rewritable DVD formats, such as DVD+RW and DVD-R/W, nor can they typically be read in a DVD-ROM drive. *See also* CD-RW, DVD-R, DVD-R/W, and DVD+RW.

DVD-ROM

An acronym for Digital Versatile Disc Read Only Memory, a type of storage device that can read both DVD and CD-ROM format discs. Most DVD-ROM drives can also read CD-R discs. *See also* CD-ROM, DVD, DVD-R, DVD-RAM, DVD-R/W, and DVD+RW.

DVD-R/W

An acronym for Digital Versatile Disc Read/Write, one of several competitive standards for a recordable and rewritable DVD. Rewritable discs created with a DVD-R/W, which is different from a DVD+RW, typically cannot be read by other rewritable DVD formats, such as DVD-RAM and DVD+RW, nor can they typically be read in a DVD-ROM drive. *See also* CD-RW, DVD-R, DVD-RAM, and DVD+RW.

DVD+RW

An acronym for Digital Versatile Disc Rewritable, one of several competitive standards for a recordable and rewritable DVD. Rewritable discs created with a DVD+RW, which is different from a DVD-R/W, typically cannot be read by other rewritable DVD formats, such as DVD-RAM and DVD-R/W, nor can they typically be read in a DVD-ROM drive. *See also* CD-RW, DVD-R, DVD-RAM, and DVD-R/W.

DVI

An acronym for Digital Video Interface, a new industry standard for providing direct digital connections between a video card and a digital LDC-based monitor. DVI is a compromise standard that incorporates some of the elements of DFP and P&D. *See also* DFP, LDI, and P&D.

Dye Sublimation

A type of printing technology in which sheets of color dye–filled plastic ribbons are turned into a gaseous state (a process called *sublimation*) and then transferred onto the paper. While it's much more expensive and slower than most inkjet printers, it can offer extremely high-resolution, continuous tone prints. *See also* Continuous Tone, Inkjet, and Resolution.

E

ECC

An acronym for Error Correcting Code, a technology used with certain types of memory chips that enables them to determine if any errors have been introduced into the memory's contents. ECC is a more sophisticated version of error correction than that found in parity memory. You can use ECC memory only on computers that support it. *See also* Parity.

ECP

An acronym for Extended Capabilities Port, an enhanced mode for standard parallel ports that supports bidirectional communication and increases the port's bandwidth. ECP also enables the port to work more efficiently with a wide variety of devices including scanners and removable drives, and you can print more quickly if your printer supports this mode. ECP differs from the similar EPP primarily in that ECP is designed to use DMA transfers. *See also* DMA, EPP, Parallel Port, and SPP.

Editor/Librarian

A type of MIDI application that enables you to store and edit sounds created by sound cards and MIDI synthesizers. *See also* MIDI and Synthesizer.

EDO

An acronym for Extended Data Out, a type of memory technology that improves the performance over traditional FPM (Fast Page Mode) RAM by including the capability to start accessing the next block of data while it is still sending the previous block to the processor. *See also* FPM, RAM, RDRAM, and SDRAM.

E-IDE

An acronym for Enhanced IDE (Integrated Drive Electronics), a type of controller built into the motherboards of most PCs that includes support for up to four different IDE devices and transfer rates of up to 16Mbps. Sometimes also referred to as "ATA-2." *See also* ATA, IDE, PIO, and SCSI.

EISA

An acronym for Extended Industry Standard Architecture, a faster 32-bit version of the ISA bus that was intended to compete with the PCI bus, but lost. As a result, it is rarely seen in computers today. *See also* Bus, ISA, and PCI.

E-mail

Also known as "electronic mail," a method for exchanging information between computer users over a network connection, typically the Internet. You can use e-mail to send text messages, as well as pictures, documents, or any other type of file from your computer to another person's computer by sending it to their unique e-mail address. *See also* Attachment, IMAP4, LDAP, POP3, and Spam.

EMF

An acronym for Enhanced Metafile Format, a common means of packaging files that are sent to printers. The default setting for many Windows programs is to send their files to the printer as EMF files, but you can also select RAW, which sends an unformatted raw stream of binary data.

EMS

An acronym for Expanded Memory Specification, a standard used under DOS and early versions of Windows to provide access to memory from 1MB up to 32MB. Sometimes also referred to as "LIM" (Lotus-Intel-Microsoft) 4.0, after the companies who developed it, EMS is designed to work with any type of

Intel processor from the 8088 on up. EMS basically fools the processor into thinking that the extra memory is available within the 1MB limit of the 8088 and DOS by using small blocks of memory known as *page frames*. *See also* Expanded Memory, Real Mode, and XMS.

Encoder

A piece of hardware or software that compresses a file or continuous stream of data into a different and typically smaller format. *See also* Codec and Decoder.

Encryption

The process of scrambling the contents of a file for security purposes so that it cannot be read and/or opened by someone for whom the file was not intended. Files are typically encrypted by one of several different algorithms and require keys of different length (in bits) before they can be decrypted and used. The longer the key, typically, the more secure the encryption method. Encrypted files are sometimes decrypted automatically and in some cases require passwords. (The password length is not related to the key length used to encrypt or decrypt the file, however.)

Enumerate

The process of listing what hardware is found in a computer system. Both the BIOS and the operating system typically perform enumeration in order to determine what hardware is installed and, therefore, what driver software for that hardware must also be installed. Plug-and-Play technology is based around enumeration. *See also* PnP.

EPP

An acronym for Enhanced Parallel Port, an enhanced mode for standard parallel ports that supports bidirectional communication and increases the port's bandwidth. *See also* ECP, Parallel Port, and SPP.

EPROM

An acronym for Erasable Programmable Read Only Memory, a type of memory chip used with computers and other electronic devices, which can store software that is automatically run when the device is turned on. Software stored in this matter is typically called *firmware*. A computer's BIOS, for example, is stored in an EPROM. Because an EPROM is erasable, that also means it is upgradeable. A Flash EPROM is a specific type of EPROM that uses Flash memory and can be easily upgraded, typically by running an upgrade program from your PC's floppy disk. An EEPROM is an Electrically Erasable Programmable Read Only Memory chip. *See also* BIOS and Flash Memory.

Error Correction

A general technique for finding errors that may occur in memory due to minor electrical fluctuations or other types of problems. Also used in modems and communications protocols to ensure that data is properly sent and received. *See also* ECC and Parity.

Ethernet

A type of network architecture, sometimes referred to as part of IEEE 802.3, that defines how data can be transferred over a network. Ethernet is, by far, the most popular type of networking system. Standard Ethernet runs at a rate of 10Mbps; Fast Ethernet, sometimes also called 100 Megabit Ethernet, runs at 100Mbps; and Gigabit Ethernet runs at 1Gbps. *See also* 10Base-T, 10Base-2, 100Base-T, and Network.

Executable

Another name for an application or other software program that can be launched, or executed. Sometimes also referred to as a ".exe file."

Expanded Memory

A type of memory used under DOS and early versions of Windows that exists above the 1MB limit imposed by DOS and early Intel processors, specifically the 8088. Expanded memory, sometimes also called "EMS," basically fools the processor into thinking that the extra memory is available within the 1MB limit of the 8088 and DOS by using small blocks of memory known as *page frames* and mapping data from the expanded memory into those page frames. *See also* Conventional Memory, EMS, Extended Memory, Real Mode, and XMS.

Export

The process of moving data from one application's format into another. Exporting a file is essentially the same thing as saving it as a different format. *See also* Format.

Ext2

The type of disk partitioning system used under the Linux operating system. *See also* Partition and Linux.

Extension

Under Windows and some other operating systems, the period (.) and three (or more) characters found at the end of a file's name. A file extension, such as .doc, or .exe, identifies what type of file it is and/or what program it is associated with. Practically speaking, this means what program automatically launches when you double-click the file. *See also* Format.

Extended Memory

A type of memory used under DOS and most versions of Windows that exists above 1MB. Unlike the somewhat similar expanded memory, extended memory does not pretend to exist under the 1MB limit and, as a result, can be accessed only by the 80286 processor and later versions that support Protected Mode operation. Both extended and expanded memory are only an issue for DOS and DOS applications. Other operating systems that use an x86-compatible's Protected Mode "see" all of a computer's memory as one contiguous chunk. *See also* Conventional Memory, EMS, Expanded Memory, Protected Mode, Real Mode, and XMS.

F

FAQ

An acronym for Frequently Asked Questions, a type of document that attempts to answer the most common questions about a particular subject or product. FAQ documents can be found all over the Internet and cover virtually any subject imaginable. They are typically an excellent resource if you're trying to research a particular product or technology.

FAT

An acronym for File Allocation Table, the disk partitioning system used under DOS and early versions of Windows. The basic version of FAT is sometimes also referred to as "FAT-16" because it uses a 16-bit file to keep track of where files are located on a hard disk. This limits FAT, or FAT-16, to working with a maximum partition or volume size of 2.1GB. *See also* FAT-32, Cluster, and Partition.

FAT-32

An acronym for File Allocation Table 32-bit, which is a more advanced disk partitioning system that's supported in later versions of Windows 95, Windows 98, and Windows 2000. FAT-32 uses a 32-bit file to keep track of where files are located on a hard disk. As a result, FAT-32 can work with individual partitions that are up to 2TB (terabytes) in size. *See also* Cluster, FAT, and Partition.

FDISK

The name of a DOS-based disk-partitioning program. It's also sometimes used as a verb to refer to the process of erasing existing partitions and creating new ones. *See also* Partition.

File Format

The particular structure of a computer document and the way the information inside a document is stored. Different applications use different file formats and, consequently, store the data inside a file in slightly different ways. As a result, you can't always read one program's files inside another similar type of program, unless the program you're opening a file into has a filter for that file type that can understand how the data is stored and can convert it into the program's own native format. *See also* Document and Extension.

File

The generic name of individual documents used within a computer. Files may be documents associated with a particular program, an application itself, or other software components that are part of the operating system. *See also* Document.

Firewall

A mechanism for blocking certain types of data or any types of messages from certain IP addresses from entering into a network. Firewalls, which can be implemented with hardware and software or just software, are used as a security measure to prevent intruders from getting into a network, and to prevent a network from getting overloaded with incoming data. *See also* IP Address and Network.

FireWire

Another name for the IEEE 1394 connection standard, which offers transfer rates of 400Mbps, supports hot plugging, and provides power to connected devices. *See also* IEEE 1394.

Flash Memory

A type of memory that can maintain its contents without electrical power (although it often includes a tiny voltage from a battery or other power source). Flash memory is typically used with EPROMs to store a computer's BIOS and is also used in memory cards for digital cameras, PDAs, notebooks, and other devices.

FlashPix

An image file format with an extension of .fpx that stores photographs as a series of tiles. The benefit of this approach is that images can be opened very quickly and stored in multiple resolutions. In addition, by using this file format over the Web with a technology called IIP (Internet Imaging Protocol), it enables you to use a single high-resolution image that can be zoomed in on. *See also* Extension and Photo CD.

Flat Panel

Another name for LCD-based monitors. *See also* LCD Panel.

Floating Point

A type of mathematical calculation that uses noninteger numbers where the decimal point can float. In other words, there's an integer number plus an exponent. In real-world terms, floating point math is often used in image, audio, and video editing, as well as other multimedia-type applications. Some types of processors offer better floating point performance than others, making them better suited to these types of tasks. Other processors offer better integer performance, which is typically important in office-type applications such as word processing and spreadsheets. *See also* Microprocessor.

Floppy Drive

A storage device found inside most computers that can read and write to magnetic media that are referred to as "floppy disks." The "floppy" name stems from the fact that early disks, such as the 8-inch and $5^{1}/_{4}$-inch varieties, did not come in a hard plastic case and, therefore, were flexible and, well, floppy. All modern floppy drives read $3^{1}/_{2}$-inch disks of various capacities.

FM Synthesis

An acronym for Frequency Modulation Synthesis, a sound creation method that uses combinations of sine waves and other simple waveforms to create a variety of different timbres, or sounds. Many older sound cards, including the original Sound Blaster, use FM synthesis to generate sounds. *See also* OPL3, Sound Card, Sound Modeling, Synthesizer, and Wavetable Synthesis.

Font

A set of text characters and symbols that conform to a particular design or look and have specific spacing measurements associated with them. There are thousands of different fonts, sometimes also called "typefaces." The most popular font formats are TrueType and Type 1. *See also* TrueType Font and Type 1 Font.

Force Feedback

A mechanism found in joysticks and other game controllers that provides a physical sensation to the person holding or using the device. Playing a game that supports force feedback (not all do) on a force feedback–enabled joystick, for example, you actually feel the sensation of running a car into a wall, flying an airplane, or being shot at by a bad guy. The sensation is created by tiny motors inside the device that basically push back against your hand, or whatever you're using to hold the device, in a variety of different ways.

Form Factor

Another name for the shape that a particular component or device comes in. A computer's form factor, for example, might be a mini-tower or notebook with a fold-over screen.

Format

The particular method for storing data inside a document or file. A file's format reflects what type of file it is. Also used to describe the process of preparing a storage device, such as a hard drive or floppy disk, for first use or reuse. Formatting a disk typically erases any existing data that's stored on it (or, at the very least, the file that keeps track of where all the other files are located) and enables you to copy new data onto the disk. *See also* Extension, File Format, and Partition.

FPM

An acronym for Fast Page Mode, a type of memory that enables you to read an entire page, or section, of data at once. FPM RAM is the most basic type of RAM available and is typically found only on older computers. *See also* EDO, RDRAM, SDRAM, and Virtual Channel Memory.

FPS

An acronym for Frames Per Second, a measurement of how fast a video signal is capable of being played back or recorded on a PC. Film runs at a rate of 24 FPS, and television runs at a rate near 30 FPS (29.97 to be exact), so to get a high-quality image that is free from jerky motion you usually want a frame rate of 25–30 FPS. NTSC video uses two interlaced fields per frame, which translates to about 60 fields per second. *See also* Interlaced, MPEG, and NTSC.

Fragmentation

A characteristic of hard drives and other storage devices in which the files stored on the disk get scattered across the disk. In the course of normal usage, files are constantly being read from and written to the disk, often in small chunks, and as a result, pieces of files end up getting placed all over the disk. If the disk has enough fragmentation, its performance can slow down because it has to find all the different pieces of a file on different areas of a disk in order to read the file into memory. To resolve this problem, you can run a utility program called a "disk defragmenter," which finds all the scattered pieces of files and combines them back into contiguous chunks. After a while, the same problem arises, and you have to do the same thing over again.

Frame Buffer

The memory set aside on a video card for storing the image that is to be sent to the monitor. Video cards are constantly creating a new image to be sent to the monitor, and the frame buffer is the place it's briefly stored before being transferred. On most video cards, particularly those that accelerate 3D graphics, the frame buffer is only a portion of the total memory on the card. Cards that support double- and triple-buffering, for example, have a second and third buffer, respectively, to store images, which means they use two or three times as much memory. This is important for applications such as games with 3D graphics because the additional buffers are used to render, or draw, the next frame or two while the previous frame is sent to the frame buffer. The practical result of this is that the frame rates for video games can be much higher, resulting in a more realistic display. *See also* Z-buffer.

Frame Grabber

A device that can capture a still image, or frame, from a video signal. Some frame grabbers come as external computer peripherals that you plug a video signal into, and others are incorporated into video capture cards, which can capture both still images as well as a continuous stream of video. *See also* Video Capture.

Freeware

A type of software that you can install and use for free for as long as you like. These types of programs are essentially provided to the public as a service by the program's author. *See also* Demoware, Open Source, and Shareware.

Frequency

A measurement of how quickly a signal oscillates, or changes from one state to another. Frequencies are measured in hertz (Hz). In audio signals, which are quoted in kilohertz (KHz), the frequency determines the pitch at which we hear a sound, with higher frequency sounds having a higher pitch and lower frequency sounds having a lower pitch. Clock signals used inside a PC to drive the operation of certain devices or buses are usually quoted in megahertz (MHz), which is millions of cycles per second, well beyond the audible range. See also GHz and MHz.

FTP

An acronym for File Transfer Protocol, a method used to send files back and forth across the Internet or any other network that uses the TCP/IP protocol. When you FTP a file, you basically copy it from one computer to another.

G

G.Lite

A standard used in modems that support the UADSL, or ADSL Lite method of communication. G.Lite modems typically support transfer rates of up to 1.5Mbps for downloading and 384Kbps for uploading, although this can vary. G.Lite, which is sometimes also referred to as "G.992.2," offers an upgrade path to the faster transfer rates of full-blown ADSL but enables a "splitter-less" installation, which means it can be used without the addition of a device called a *splitter* (which true ADSL requires). External G.Lite modems connect to a PC via a 10Base-T Ethernet connection, and internal ones come in the form of PCI cards. *See also* ADSL and UADSL.

Gamma

A measurement used to describe a computer monitor's ratio of dark to light. By adjusting a monitor's gamma, a process called *gamma correction*, you can adjust the contrast and brightness of images it displays. PCs and Macs typically use different gamma settings with the practical result being that the same image file viewed on a PC typically looks darker than it does on a Mac.

Gateway

A hardware device or software program that serves as a connecting point between two networks. When configuring a connection to the Internet, you often need to supply the IP address of a computer that can serve as a gateway between your computer or your home network and the Internet. An e-mail gateway is typically a software program that enables e-mail messages to be sent from one type of messaging system to another. *See also* Router.

Gb/GB

Acronyms for gigabit and gigabyte, respectively. (A small "b" always represents bits and a large "B" always represents bytes.) Giga means one billion, so a gigabyte is approximately one billion bytes, or 1,000 megabytes. Technically speaking a gigabyte is 2^{30} or 1,073,741,824 bytes. Gigabytes are commonly used as specifications for storage devices, signifying how much data the device can hold. *See also* Bit, Byte, Kb/KB, and Mb/MB.

Gbps/GBps

Acronyms for gigabits per second and gigabytes per second, which is a speed measurement for how quickly data is transferred over a connection. *See also* Kbps/KBps and Mbps/MBps.

GDI

An acronym for Graphical Device Interface, the standard mechanism for displaying graphical images under Windows. It's also the name of one of the three core Windows system files.

General MIDI

A standard that defines a number of important parameters that enable Standard MIDI Files (SMFs) to play back on a variety of different General MIDI, or GM-compatible hardware with a relatively similar sonic result. Specifically, the GM spec defines 128 different instrument sounds, organized into 16 groups of 8, and assigns them to specific MIDI Program Change commands. As a result, musicians and composers for computer games can be assured that music that was intended to be played by a violin sound, for example, will be played by a violin patch, and not a bass drum sound. *See also* MIDI, Patch, and SMF.

GHz

An acronym for gigahertz, a measurement in chip or bus performance that's expressed as billions of cycles per second. *See also* Frequency and MHz.

GIF

An acronym for Graphics Interchange Format, a very common image file format used on Web sites and inside other HTML documents. GIF files are compressed with a lossless compression algorithm but are limited to only 256 colors. As a result, they are best suited for simple illustrations and color graphic elements, but not photographs. *See also* Compression, JPEG, and PNG.

Gigabit/Gigabyte

A unit of measurement for storage devices, memory, and files, expressed in terms of billions of bits or bytes. Typically referred to as Gb and GB, respectively. *See also* Bit, Byte, Kb/KB, Mb/MB, and TB.

Graphics Tablet

An input device on which you can write or draw with an electronic version of a pen, called a *stylus*. A graphics tablet is a great way to bring freehand drawings into a computer.

Grayscale

A means of displaying an image with only black, white, and shades of gray. Converting a color image to grayscale basically turns it into a black and white image.

GUI

An acronym for Graphical User Interface, a means of interacting with a computer by using icons, shapes, and other visually attractive elements, as opposed to a character-based display. Most modern operating systems and applications use a GUI to make the process of using a computer easier and more intuitive. *See also* Command Prompt.

H

H.323/H.324

An International Telecommunications Union (ITU) standard for setting up and using audio and videoconferencing over dial-up or network connections. Two or more people can create a videoconference using different applications, as long as the applications being used are all H.323-compliant. The H.324 standard is specifically for doing videoconferencing over dial-up analog modem connections, using the V.80 standard for receiving streaming media over this type of connection. *See also* Streaming Media and Videoconferencing.

Halftone

A type of image that uses a series of tiny dots to try to create the illusion of a continuous tone image. The process of creating a halftone is done by using a screen, which is typically measured in lines per inch (LPI). The screen breaks the image up into a series of tiny dots. Halftones typically use *dithering*, which is a technique for simulating a wider range of gray shades or colors than your printer can generally support, by arranging the dots in different types of patterns. Because most inkjet printers cannot generate continuous tone images, they typically use halftones or other similar techniques for generating color photographic images. *See also* Continuous Tone, Dithering, and LPI.

Handwriting Recognition

A technology that enables you to write text and numbers with an electronic pen-like device called a *stylus* onto an input device, such as a graphics tablet or a touch-sensitive screen, and have those handwritten characters be converted into editable text on your computer's (or the device's) screen. Handwriting recognition is common on small devices such as PDAs that don't have room for a keyboard, but it can also be used with computers as well. *See also* PDA.

Hard Drive

The most common type of storage device in a PC. A hard drive consists of a number of magnetic platters called *cylinders* that spin at very high speeds and a read/write head that can quickly store data onto or read data from those platters. Many hard drives come with IDE connectors, but you can also get them with SCSI and IEEE 1394 connections. *See also* Access Time, Cluster, Floppy Drive, IDE, IEEE 1394, RAID, SCSI, Sector, Seek Time, and Track.

HFS

An acronym for Hierarchical File System, the type of disk partitioning system used on a Macintosh. Like the FAT system on PCs, HFS is limited in the maximum size of partitions it can support (up to 4GB, in this case), so HFS+ was developed to raise that limit to 2TB, just like FAT-32. *See also* FAT, FAT-32, and Partition.

HiFD

A type of alternative floppy drive that can read and write traditional $3^1/_4$-inch 1.44MB disks, as well as special higher-capacity floppies that support up to 200MB on a single disk. Another type of high-capacity floppy drive is called the "LS-120." To use either of these types of floppy drives on your system, you typically require a BIOS that supports them. *See also* BIOS, Floppy Drive, and LS-120.

Histogram

A bar chart tool available in image-editing programs and TWAIN (Technology Without An Interesting Name) scanning software that displays the range of light and dark colors in a scanned image. By adjusting a Histogram's Level settings, you can increase the effective contrast resolution of your scanner and thereby improve the overall quality of a scanned image. *See also* TWAIN.

Host Adapter

Another name for a controller plug-in card, particularly those that attach to hard drives. A SCSI host adapter, for example, is another name for a SCSI controller. *See also* Adapter and Controller.

Hosts File

A file used in certain types of TCP/IP networks that keeps track of the computers on the network and their respective IP addresses. Specifically, it associates a computer's name with its IP address, which enables computers on a small network to connect to each other by name instead of number. In this regard, it is similar to a mini-DNS server. *See also* DNS, IP Address, Network, and TCP/IP.

Hot Plugging

The capability to plug in or remove a peripheral device while a computer is turned on. Hot plugging first appeared with PC cards that plugged into notebooks but is now also available with USB, IEEE 1394, and Device Bay (which uses USB and IEEE 1394). The capability to hot plug a peripheral makes it much faster and easier to install because instead of having to turn off your machine, you can simply plug in the peripheral. When you do, the system recognizes it and then starts the process of either automatically installing any necessary drivers or requesting that you install them manually. Hot plugging is what many people thought (or at least hoped) Plug-and-Play would be all along. *See also* Device Bay, IEEE 1394, PnP, and USB.

HPA

An acronym for High-Performance Addressing, an enhancement to passive matrix LCDs that increases the rate at which the screen's pixels are updated and therefore increases the response rate of the display. The practical result is a brighter screen with better contrast and faster refresh times (which is particularly important for things such as playing back a digital video file), though it still isn't as good as the more expensive active matrix, or TFT screens. *See also* Active Matrix, Dual Scan, LCD Panel, Passive Matrix, and TFT.

HPFS

An acronym for High Performance File System, the type of disk partitioning system used in IBM's OS/2 operating system. *See also* OS/2.

HTML

An acronym for HyperText Markup Language, a common, text-based file format that uses tags to assign attributes to different elements in a document. HTML is the primary format of pages used on Web sites and is quickly becoming the *lingua franca* of the computer world. Many applications on a variety of different platforms can read and write HTML files, which makes it an extremely good way to transfer information from one computer to another. Most e-mail programs, in fact, offer the capability to send and receive e-mail messages in HTML format. *See also* Metatag, Tag, and XML.

HTTP

An acronym for HyperText Transport (or sometimes Transfer) Protocol, the mechanism used to request and send messages and files over the World Wide Web. HTTP works on top of the TCP/IP protocol, which is the lower-level language used to send packets of data across the Internet. A Web browser is considered an HTTP client because it sends an HTTP command to a Web server when you type in an URL (Universal Resource Locator) and then receives an HTTP reply from that server. *See also* Protocol, TCP/IP, and URL.

Hub

A device that serves as a central connecting point for multiple devices. An Ethernet-based network hub, for example, enables you to connect all the devices on the network to a single point, which makes it easy to pass messages from one device to the next. The connectors on a hub are referred to as *ports*. A USB hub expands the number of available USB ports by taking one input and turning it into several outputs. *See also* Router and Switch.

Hyperlink

A means defined by the HTML standard to provide a connection between one HTML document and another or between predefined sections within a single document. On a Web page, hyperlinks commonly show up as colored, underlined text that you can click to get to another page. Hyperlinks can also be embedded into graphics, and multiple hyperlinks can be defined within a single graphic to create an image map.

I

I/O

An acronym for Input/Output, a generic term for devices and ports that can bring data into and/or out of your computer, such as USB (Universal Serial Bus) ports. I/O also refers to address settings assigned to each piece of hardware within your computer. I/O addresses, which are considered a computer resource, are used to distinguish between different devices so that information or data intended for a particular device or component is sent to the right place. *See also* Resources.

Icon

A small picture that's used to represent something, such as a file, a particular function within a program, or a component that's attached to your PC. Icons are an essential part of a graphical user interface, or GUI. *See also* GUI.

IDE

An acronym for Integrated Drive Electronics, a type of connection mechanism commonly used on hard drives, CD- and DVD-ROM drives, and other types of storage devices. Because of limitations in the way IDE works, all IDE devices must be internal to the PC. Most computers offer support for up to four IDE devices on two channels (two per channel). The two channels are commonly called *primary* and *secondary*, and the devices on each of those channels are referred to as *master* and *slave*. Some PCs feature an enhanced version of the standard called "EIDE" or "Enhanced IDE." In addition, all ATA standards, including ATA-2, UltraATA, and ATA/66 are simply faster versions of the normal IDE connection, which typically feature 40-pin connectors. *See also* ATA, EIDE, and SCSI.

IEEE 1284

A standard for bidirectional communications over a PC's parallel port endorsed by the Institute of Electrical and Electronics Engineers (IEEE). Devices, including peripherals and parallel cables, that support the IEEE 1284 standard include proper support for this bidirectional communication. *See also* ECP, EPP, and SPP.

IEEE 1394

A standard endorsed by the Institute of Electrical and Electronics Engineers (IEEE) for high-speed bidirectional communications that supports data transfer rates of up to 400Mbps in the original version of the spec and is expected to offer even faster rates (such as 800Mbps) in later iterations. As a result, it's ideally suited for applications that require high-bandwidth connections, such as high-performance storage devices, printers, digital camcorders, and more. Sometimes also referred to as FireWire or i-Link, IEEE 1394 uses a six-pin connector that supplies both data connections and power to peripherals (although some still require a separate power supply). Like USB, IEEE 1394 supports hot plugging for instant recognition and use of your peripherals. In addition, with appropriate hubs, IEEE 1394 supports chaining together multiple devices over a single connection. (The limit for IEEE 1394 is 63 devices versus 127 for USB.) Some PCs include an IEEE 1394 controller in their chipset or in other chips on their computer's motherboard, but you can add IEEE 1394 support to any PC by installing an IEEE 1394 controller plug-in card. IEEE 1394 is also used in the Device Bay standard. *See also* Device Bay, Hot Plugging, and USB.

Image Editor

A type of application that enables you to open and edit digital photographs and other images.

IMAP4

An acronym for Internet Message Access Protocol Version 4, a standard found in e-mail programs that includes many useful capabilities for retrieving messages. For example, IMAP4 provides the capability to read an e-mail message off a mail server and still leave a copy of it there, or search through your messages on the server and choose which messages you want to download onto your machine. (Previous e-mail standards automatically downloaded a message onto your PC and deleted it off the server as soon as you started to read it.) *See also* POP3 and SMTP.

Import

The process of taking data from a file and bringing it into a program. Importing a file typically involves converting from its existing format into the program's native format. *See also* Export and File Format.

INF File

Short for Setup Information File, a type of text-only file with an extension .inf that is used to store certain parameters used by setup or installation programs. With some simple Windows programs, you can simply right-click the program's associated .inf file and select Install to install the program on your system. *See also* Setup.

INI File

Short for Initialization File, a type of text-only file with the extension .ini that is used by some applications and early versions of Windows to store configuration settings that are unique to the program or operating system. Under Windows 95 and later, most application and operating system settings are stored in the Windows Registry, although the System.ini and Win.ini files are still present for backwards compatibility with applications that use them. INI files are typically broken up into sections, which are denoted by bracketed headings, and each section includes separate entries, with one entry per line. *See also* File Extension and Registry.

Inkjet

A type of printer that sprays tiny dots of liquid ink onto a page. Color inkjet printers are, by far, the most popular type of printer because they offer tremendous resolution and print quality for a reasonable price. *See also* Dye Sublimation and Laser Printer.

Input Device

A generic name for any type of peripheral that enables you to bring data into your PC. Typical examples include keyboards, mice, and scanners.

Instructions

When it comes to microprocessors, instructions are the fundamental mathematical operations that it uses to perform its calculations. Different processors and different generations of processors support different instruction sets. Pentiums with MMX support, for example, offer 57 additional instructions that processors without MMX support don't have. Similarly, AMD's K6-2 line introduced 3DNow instructions. More recently, the Pentium III added 70 new instructions called "Streaming SIMD" Extensions, or SSE, to those found in the Pentium II line. The term *instructions* is also used to describe the "directions" that applications send to the processor when the application is used. *See also* 3DNow, Microprocessor, MMX, and Streaming SIMD.

Int13

An acronym for Software Interrupt 13 (this is different from Hardware Interrupts or IRQs), a low-level mechanism used by a computer's BIOS to communicate directly with a hard drive. Int13 extensions are used by many current operating systems to enable them to recognize and communicate with large hard drives. Specifically, complete support of Int13 extensions enables a computer to work properly with drives larger than 8.4GB. (The original Int13 extensions help break the infamous 504MB hard disk barrier.) *See also* LBA.

Interface

A means through which two things, such as a person and an application or two pieces of software, can communicate with one another. An operating system or application's interface refers to how the product is designed and how easy it is for you to find your way around. Different types of software also use interfaces as a way to transfer and/or share information between them.

Interlaced

A type of video signal that consists of two separate parts that appear quickly after each other but that our eyes perceive as a single image. The analog NTSC video signal used with TVs, for example, consists of two fields per frame, with the first field filling in all the screen's odd lines and the second field filling in all the screen's even lines. Most computer monitors are noninterlaced, which means they draw in all the lines on the screen in a row, before moving onto the next frame. Noninterlaced screens suffer from less flicker because of this and are easier to look at for long periods of time, particularly up close. *See also* FPS and NTSC.

Interleave

The process of combining two or more entities into one. In certain systems, for example, you can interleave two banks of memory and have them essentially work as one, which can provide a minor boost in performance.

Internet

A global information network that includes, but is not limited to, the World Wide Web. All communication over the Internet occurs via the TCP/IP protocol, and each device that is connected to the Internet has a unique IP address. *See also* IP Address, TCP/IP, and World Wide Web.

Interrupt

A mechanism used by hardware and software to send a signal to the processor that it needs attention. The most common type are hardware interrupts, and they're referred to as IRQs, or Interrupt Requests. IRQs are one of several important (and limited) computer resources. Most PCs have only 16 interrupts, labeled 0–15. *See* Resources.

Intranet

A network that uses the same technologies and standards as the Internet, including TCP/IP and HTML but exists within the walls of a company and is typically inaccessible by outsiders. Many companies build in-house intranets to share important information with their employees.

Io.sys

The name of the startup file used by Windows 95 and Windows 98 that basically contains all of the critical features of DOS. Io.sys is the first boot file that your PC runs after the BIOS program executes, and it is commonly found in a hard drive's master boot record (unless you have installed multiple operating systems and a boot loader). Io.sys, which is normally hidden, is a critical file that a Windows-based computer cannot start up without. *See also* BIOS, Master Boot Record, and Startup Files.

IP Address

A set of numbers that are used to uniquely identify every computer that's connected to the Internet or to a network that uses the TCP/IP protocol. IP addresses take the form of 000.000.000.000 (although some use less than twelve digits), where each of the four different three-digit placeholders is filled in with a number between 0 and 255. IP Addresses identify where a particular message or request was sent from and where the reply was received. Some TCP/IP networks have fixed IP addresses that are assigned once to a particular computer and then stay there, but many assign addresses dynamically whenever the computer connects to the network. The technology for making these assignments is referred to as "Dynamic Host Configuration Protocol," or DHCP. Dial-up modem connections, for example, use DHCP, which means every time you sign onto the Internet your computer has a different IP address. *See also* DHCP and TCP/IP.

IPX/SPX

An acronym for Internetwork Packet Exchange/Sequenced Package Exchange, a protocol that's used on Novell NetWare-based networks and with some networkable computer games.

IRC

An acronym for Internet Relay Chat, a standard for real-time text-based messaging software. By using an IRC client and connecting to an IRC server, you can join in a live chat, which is typically an ongoing text-based discussion, where you can communicate with other chat participants by typing in messages and reading the messages they've typed. As long as your chat software conforms to the IRC standard, you can interact with other chat participants, regardless of what program they're using.

IRDA

An acronym for Infrared Data Association, an organization that created a standard for short distance (one meter) wireless communication between PCs and other peripherals that also bears the IRDA name. The original IRDA standard, sometimes called "SIR" for Standard Infrared, supports transfer rates of up to 115Kbps, and the Fast IRDA standard, sometimes called "FIR" for Fast Infrared, supports transfers of up to 4Mbps. Even faster versions of the standard that support 16Mbps are expected in the future. IRDA ports are commonly found on notebook computers and PDAs and are increasingly being found on printers, desktop computers, and peripherals. With IRDA enabled, you can send a file wirelessly to a printer or between computers by pointing one device's infrared port at the other. *See also* Bandwidth.

IRQ

An acronym for Interrupt Request, a mechanism used by hardware devices inside x86-compatible-based PCs to signal to the processor that they need attention. Not all hardware components inside a PC require an interrupt, but many do. Most PCs have only 16 interrupts, numbered 0–15, and several of these IRQs have predefined functions within the standard PC architecture and cannot be changed. Generally speaking, two devices cannot share an interrupt or they create an IRQ conflict, with the result being that one or both of the devices won't function properly. One important exception is with devices that attach to a computer's PCI bus; many, though not all, of them can safely share an IRQ with other PCI-based devices. *See also* Interrupt and PCI.

ISA

An acronym for Industry Standard Architecture, a type of data bus — first found in the IBM AT — that became an industry standard. ISA is typically used to signify the format of slots built into a PC's motherboard that accept plug-in cards as well as the format of the cards that plug into those slots. Until recently, most computers offered several ISA slots, most of which were 16-bits wide and supported a maximum speed of 16MHz. However, the PC98 and PC99 industry specifications codeveloped by Microsoft, Intel, and several major PC vendors are attempting to eliminate the ISA bus from modern PC designs because of its slow speed and the drain it places on overall system performance as a result. The process has gone more slowly than expected, however, because of the enormous number of existing ISA cards in use (which people don't want to just throw away). The ISA/X-Bus, sometimes just called "X-Bus," is a little-known extension of the ISA bus that handles communication with basic peripherals, such as the system clock and keyboard. Newer PCs that don't support ISA use LPC (Low Pin Count), as a means to communicate with these components. *See also* Bus, LPC, PCI, and X Bus.

ISDN

An acronym for Integrated Services Digital Network, a type of communication service that uses special digital phone lines to offer transfer rates of up to 128Kbps. Though it was one of the first high-speed access methods available to many PC users, it is quickly being replaced by various types of DSL and cable modems, which offer much faster performance at even lower prices and don't require special lines. *See also* AO/DI, Cable Modem, and DSL.

ISP

An acronym for Internet Service Provider, a company that provides individuals and businesses with access to the Internet through their computers. ISPs maintain a variety of servers and other equipment that are constantly connected to the Internet and provide users with accounts they can use to get onto the Internet.

J

Java

A programming language commonly used on Web sites but also used for standalone applications that offers the promise of "write once, run anywhere." What this means is the exact same application can be run on a variety of different platforms, including Windows, Mac, and Linux. Most programs have to be written specifically for the type of operating system on which it will be run, but Java uses a generalized method that creates software code that is run, or interpreted, by a Java Virtual Machine, or JVM. JVMs, which are unique to each platform, essentially function as a computer inside your computer and interpret the platform-neutral Java code in a way that makes sense to your specific platform. Most Web browsers include a built-in JVM for running Java applications, but it's also possible to use a different standalone version. *See also* ActiveX and JavaScript.

JavaScript

A platform-neutral macro language that, despite the similar name, is different from Java in how it functions but is similar to Java in that it is commonly used on Web pages and in standalone HTML documents. JavaScript is a relatively simple way to add some interactive or dynamic elements to a Web page, such as buttons that change colors as you roll the mouse over them. As with Java, most Web browsers include support for reading and running JavaScript macros when you load a page that includes them. *See also* ActiveX, Java, and Macro.

Joystick

A type of input device typically used with computer games that consists of several buttons and a stick-like controller that you can move in one of several directions. More sophisticated joysticks now include support for Force Feedback technology. *See also* Force Feedback and Input Device.

JPEG

An acronym for Joint Photographic Experts Group, an association that developed a similarly named common image file format used on Web pages and in other HTML documents. Like GIF, JPEG can reduce the size of images, but unlike GIF, JPEG typically uses a "lossy" compression method to achieve its results. Generally speaking, JPEG is better suited for digital photographs and other complex images because it supports 24-bit color, and GIF is better suited for color illustrations, logos, and line art, because it's limited to 256 colors. *See also* Compression, GIF, MJPEG, and PNG.

K

Kb/KB

Acronyms for kilobit and kilobyte, respectively. (A small "b" always represents bits, and a large "B" always represents bytes.) *Kilo* means one thousand, so a kilobyte is approximately 1,000 bytes. Technically speaking it is 2^{10} or 1,024 bytes. Kilobytes are often used to describe the size of individual files or the amount of memory in a particular device. *See also* Bit, Byte, Gb/GB, and Mb/MB.

Kbps/KBps

Acronyms for kilobits per second and kilobytes per second, which are speed measurements for how quickly data is transferred over a connection. Modem transfer rates are often specified in Kbps. *See also* Gbps/GBps and Mbps/MBps.

Kernel

The core files at the heart of most operating systems. An OS kernel often performs the most critical tasks, such as interacting with software applications and communicating with device drivers. Kernel32 is also the name of one of the three core Windows system files. *See also* Operating System.

Kilobit/Kilobyte

A unit of measurement for a file or memory, expressed in terms of thousands of bits or bytes. Typically referred to as Kb and KB, respectively. *See also* Bit, Byte, Kb/KB, Megabit/Megabyte, and Gigabit/Gigabyte.

L

L1/L2 Cache

A special type of high-speed memory used by the processor to store recently used instructions and data. The smaller L1, or Level 1 cache, is always found within the processor itself, and the larger L2, or Level 2 cache, can be found either as a separate chip located on the motherboard near the processor (such as with original Pentium systems), on the processor daughtercard (such as with Pentium IIs and some Pentium IIIs), or in the processor itself (such as with Celeron A and later Pentium IIIs). Some systems, such as those based on the AMD K6-3, also use a third L3 cache. The amount of L1 and L2 cache varies from processor to processor, as does the speed with which the processor communicates with the larger L2 cache. With early Pentiums, the processor-to-L2 cache connection ran at the speed of the system bus; with Pentium IIs and early Pentium IIIs, it ran at half the speed of the processor; and with Celeron As and other chips that integrate the L2 cache into the processor, it runs at the full speed of the processor. The amount and speed of a computer's L2 cache can make a large difference in the computer's overall performance. *See also* Cache, Processor, and System Bus.

LAN

An acronym for Local Area Network, the name used to describe small networks that typically exist within a single building. *See also* Network.

Laptop

A type of portable computer that's small enough to use in your lap. Also called a "notebook."

Laser printer

A device that creates images on paper by charging areas of a rotating drum with a laser, running that drum past toner particles that are electrically attracted to the charged areas, and then fusing those charged particles onto paper. While color laser printers exist, most laser printers print black and white and are ideally suited for high-volume printing of text-based documents. *See also* Dye Sublimation and Inkjet.

Latency

Another word for delay. In memory and storage devices, latency often refers to how long it takes to reach the next bit of data that needs to be read. On hard drives, for example, latency involves how much time it takes for the drive to spin around to the spot where the next chunk of data is located.

LBA

An acronym for Logical Block Addressing, a means of accessing all the available data on large hard drives by renumbering the cylinders, tracks, and sectors found on a hard disk. LBA support typically needs to be made available through a computer's BIOS. *See also* BIOS and Int13.

LCD Panel

An acronym for Liquid Crystal Display Panel, the type of screen used in notebooks and flat-panel monitors. While generally more expensive than traditional tube-based CRT monitors, LCD panels typically offer brighter, crisper displays, take up much less space, and are lighter and easier to move around. LCDs usually use either active matrix, also called "TFT," technology or some type of passive matrix technology, such as Dual Scan or HPA (High-Performance Addressing). Standalone LCD monitors offer either standard analog VGA connections or one of several incompatible digital connections, including DFP DVI, and P&D. *See also* Active Matrix, DFP DVI, Passive Matrix, and P&D.

LDAP

An acronym for Lightweight Directory Access Protocol, a standard means for looking up e-mail addresses over the Internet. LDAP is typically used in conjunction with Web sites that offer directory services.

LDI

An acronym for LVDS (Low Voltage Differential Signaling) Display Interface, one of several incompatible standards used to send a digital video signal direct to a flat-panel display that offers a digital signal input. LDI and a variation called "OpenLDI" were originally developed to provide a digital connection between notebook computer video cards and their displays but is now also used for some desktop flat-panel monitors. *See also* DFP, DVI, LCD Panel, and P&D.

Legacy

A reference to older technology, such as the ISA bus or the memory limits imposed by DOS, that is still found in some computer systems or is used by some computer peripherals or software. The need to continue supporting legacy technologies is one of the main reasons for holding back the progress of PC development.

Libraries

A type of software component that is typically made available to other pieces of software that may also want to use it. Software libraries often perform specific functions that both the operating system and specific applications can benefit from. Software libraries encourage a building block approach to creating software, where applications actually consist of many different pieces. The benefit of this approach is that it can save disk and memory space because you don't need to include the same code in each program but can simply link to one copy of it from multiple programs. The problem with it is that if the library is replaced or upgraded when you install a new application, the new version of the library may cause all (or some) of the other programs that also use that library to break. The most common type of shared libraries under Windows are called DLLs. *See also* DLL.

LILO

An acronym for Linux Loader, a boot loader program included with most distributions of Linux that enables you to select from Linux or any other operating systems you may have installed on your PC. *See also* Boot Loader and Linux.

Line Conditioner

A standalone device, or capability within another device, that can take a varying electrical voltage from a wall electrical socket and turn it into a steady 117-volt signal. Most line voltages in homes and businesses actually vary a few volts in either direction on a regular basis, particularly in rural locations, and this variation can lead some particularly sensitive devices to function somewhat erratically. A line conditioner, or the line conditioning portion of a device such as a UPS (Uninterruptible Power Supply), fixes this problem by conditioning the line and generating a steady, nonvarying voltage. Line conditioners can also help overcome brownouts, which are relatively severe but typically short-lived voltage fluctuations that can lead to things such as a brief dimming of the lights (and which can play havoc with PCs and computer peripherals). *See also* Surge Suppressor and UPS.

Linux

A variation of the Unix operating system, developed by Linus Torvalds (hence the name), that runs on x86-compatible PCs (as well as other types of processors). One of the most distinguishing characteristics of Linux is that both the operating system and the source code, which is the actual lines of software code written by the programmer, are freely available. This type of free software is known as *open source*. While powerful and flexible, Linux can also be confusing to install and use. In addition, you cannot run Windows applications in their native form under Linux. Instead you need to download and/or purchase Linux applications, although many of them are freely available as open source as well. The most common way to get Linux is through what's called a *distribution* — several different types of which are sold by different companies. Linux distributions include the core Linux kernel files, applications, utilities, documentation, and other helpful materials that justify the cost of software that is otherwise available for free. *See also* Distribution, Ext2, LILO, and UNIX.

LIon

An acronym for Lithium Ion, a type of chemical combination used in notebook batteries (as well as other types of batteries). Lithium ion batteries tend to run longer than other types and don't suffer from a memory effect, where a battery needs to be completely discharged before it can be properly recharged. Partially as a result, they also tend to be more expensive than others. *See also* NiCAD and NiMH.

Log

A type of file that keeps track of various events associated with a particular program or device. A log file can include events such as when and how a particular program or hardware component, such as a modem, were used.

Logging In/Out

The act of signing into and out of a secure operating system, network connection, or Web site by providing a username and password. The process of logging in/out, which essentially establishes your identity on the system, is also sometimes referred to as *authentication*. Not all operating systems, network connections, or Web sites require you to log in, but those that do typically provide a more secure environment. Operating systems that require you to log in force you to do that before you can do anything on the PC.

LPC

An acronym for Low Pin Count, a bus used on PCs (not including the ISA bus) that enables the system to communicate with older types of peripherals, such as the system clock and keyboard. These devices have traditionally been connected via the ISA/X-bus, or just X-bus for short. LPC is a transitional technology that will be used only until PCs are built completely around the PCI bus. *See also* Bus, ISA, PCI, and X-Bus.

LPI

An acronym for Lines Per Inch, a measurement that signifies the resolution of screening methods used to create halftones on many types of color printers. Most printers' LPI resolution is only a small fraction (such as $1/6$) of their DPI (dots per inch) resolution, but it often provides a more accurate picture (no pun intended) of the printer's capability to print color photographs. Determining LPI resolution is difficult, however, because it can vary on the same printer depending on the settings you use for printing a particular image. *See also* DPI and Halftone.

LPT

An acronym for Line Printer Terminal, the term is used to identify the parallel port to which a device, such as a printer, is attached. Most computers include only a single parallel port, which is typically referred to as "LPT1." *See also* COM and Parallel Port.

LS-120

An acronym for Laser Servo 120, the generic name for a type of alternative floppy drive that can read and write traditional $3^1/_4$-inch 1.44MB disks, as well as special higher-capacity floppies that support up to 120MB or more on a single disk. Another type of high-capacity floppy drive is called "HiFD." To use either of these types of floppy drives on your system, you typically need to have a BIOS that supports them. *See also* BIOS, Floppy Drive, and HiFD.

M

Macro

A series of simple text commands that are stored as a file and can be replayed again at another time. Macros, which provide a useful, time-saving way to repeat certain operations, are often used within programs, but also can be used across applications via the operating system or a special macro utility.

Mapping

The process of assigning a letter or name to a hard drive that is attached to a computer on a network so that you can more quickly and easily attach to that drive at another time. If you regularly need access to a particular PC's hard drive in a Windows-based network, for example, you can map that drive to a particular drive letter on your PC so that the drive appears to be part of your system.

Master Boot Record (MBR)

The first sector on the first hard drive in a computer. The Master Boot Record is a particularly important place because that's where a computer's BIOS points to when it finishes running and that's where an operating system's boot files are stored. If you have set up your system to dual boot to any one of several different operating systems, a program known as a *boot loader* typically takes the place of a single operating system's boot files. The importance of the MBR, unfortunately, hasn't been lost on virus writers either because if your PC's master boot record is deleted or otherwise altered, then your system typically won't boot. As a result, boot sector viruses, sometimes just called *boot viruses* for short, are some of the most common types of computer viruses. *See also* BIOS, Boot Loader, Startup Files, and Virus.

Mb/MB

Acronyms for megabit and megabyte, respectively. (A small "b" always represents bits, and a large "B" always represents bytes.) Mega means one million, so a megabyte is approximately one million bytes, or 1,000 kilobytes. Technically speaking it is 2^{20} or 1,048,576 bytes. Megabytes are commonly used as specifications for memory, storage devices, and file sizes, signifying how much RAM is available, how much storage space is available, or how large the file is. *See also* Bit, Byte, Kb/KB, Gb/GB, and TB.

Mbps/MBps

Acronyms for megabits per second and megabytes per second, which are speed measurements for how quickly data is transferred over a connection. Network transfer rates and some high-speed modem transfer rates are often specified in Mbps. *See also* Kbps/KBps and Gbps/GBps.

Media

A type of physical device on which you can store or record data. A Zip cartridge, for example, is a type of media, as is a floppy disk and a hard drive.

Megabit/Megabyte

A unit of measurement for storage devices, memory, and files, expressed in terms of millions of bits or bytes. Typically referred to as Mb and MB, respectively. *See also* Bit, Byte, Gigabit/Gigabyte, Kilobit/Kilobyte, and Terabyte.

Megapixel

A term used to describe the resolution of digital cameras that include over 1 million pixels per image. Cameras that offer a resolution of 1,280 × 960, for example, include 1,228,800 pixels. *See also* Digital Camera, Pixel, and Resolution.

Memory

An electronic circuit that can store data. Also used to describe the working area that a computer or other electronic device uses to load software into and perform its calculations. The most common type of memory is called RAM, or random access memory. There are several different varieties of RAM but almost all of them are volatile memory because they all lose their contents whenever power to them is turned off. Certain components inside PCs and in PDAs use nonvolatile memory, which is able to store the contents even when power is turned off, typically through a small charge provided by a battery. Flash Memory and SRAM are two examples of nonvolatile memory. Another type of memory called ROM, or read-only memory, is used to store information that cannot be altered. *See also* Flash Memory, RAM, and ROM.

Metatag

A type of HTML tag that's usually used to define a page or document's characteristics but isn't visible when viewed within a Web browser or other HTML-compliant application. Metatags are often used to provide a description of a page as well as keywords that are reflective of the page's content. They are typically used by search engines to classify the page and its contents. *See also* HTML, Search Engine, and Tag.

MFD

An acronym for Multi-Function Device, a unit that typically combines the capabilities of a printer, scanner, fax machine, and copier into a single box. MFDs can be handy in small home offices.

MHz

An acronym for megahertz, a measurement in chip or bus performance that's expressed as millions of cycles per second. The higher the MHz rating, the faster a chip or bus operates. *See also* Frequency and GHz.

Microprocessor

A chip that performs the calculations that are at the heart of a computer's operation. Sometimes called simply a "processor" or "CPU" (central processing unit) for short, the microprocessor provides the computer's brain. In addition, the entire computer is organized around the microprocessor, with most data inside a PC being either sent to or received from it. Microprocessors, such as the Pentium family of chips, contain a set of core internal instructions that they use to manipulate, or process, the data and software instructions they are fed from the computer's memory. Microprocessors that can emulate the instructions found inside Intel's x86 family are said to be x86-compatibles. Microprocessor chips consist of several different components, including the ALU (Arithmetic Logic Unit), which is the main mathematical engine, and areas of high-speed temporary memory storage known as "L1 cache" (and sometimes "L2 cache"). *See also* x86, CPU, Instructions, L1/L2 cache, Pipelining, Processor, and Speculative Execution.

MIDI

An acronym for Musical Instrument Digital Interface, a command language typically used to describe a musical performance or to send data between musical devices. MIDI consists of a series of different messages that are generated by devices called *MIDI controllers* on any one of 16 different MIDI channels and responded to by devices generically referred to as *MIDI slaves*. In some instances, both the controller and the slave are a single device. MIDI messages can be sent to and from a PC through the use of a MIDI Interface. MIDI, in and of itself, doesn't sound like anything — the sound quality of a MIDI file is determined by the quality of the MIDI sound source, typically a sound card or synthesizer. *See also* Digital Audio, Editor/Librarian, MPU-401, Sequencer, and Synthesizer.

Millisecond

One thousandth of a second. The access time of hard drives and other storage devices is often measured in milliseconds. *See also* Nanosecond.

MIME

An acronym for Multipurpose Internet Mail Extensions, a standard mechanism for sending different types of files over the Internet as e-mail attachments without converting them to text format. Many common file formats already have predefined MIME types, but new types are being added all the time. S/MIME is a newer version of the format that adds security through various types of automatic file encryption. As a result, when you send files with an S/MIME-compliant e-mail package, the files can be automatically encrypted by the sender and automatically decrypted by the receiver. *See also* Attachment, E-mail, File Format, and UUencoding.

MJPEG

An acronym for Motion JPEG (Joint Photographic Experts Group), a type of video compression method that's based on the JPEG still image compression techniques. With MJPEG, each individual frame is compressed into a JPEG image file. This technique, which is known as *intra-frame compression*, is significantly different than other video compression methods, such as MPEG, which do a great deal of inter-frame compression. With inter-frame compression, the compressor takes advantage of the fact that, for example, the background in a scene doesn't always change much, so it doesn't have to be digitized every frame. Instead, only the changes between frames are recorded. While this frame differencing technique can save a great deal of space, it makes it extraordinarily difficult to use for editing purposes. The reason is because certain frames don't exist per se and have to be rebuilt based around the differences between a reference, or key, frame. As a result, MJPEG is commonly used with video-editing programs. *See also* Codec, JPEG, and MPEG.

MMX

An acronym that "officially" stands for nothing but is commonly recognized as meaning Multimedia Extensions. MMX is a series of 57 processor instructions that Intel added to its Pentium line of processors several years ago and was subsequently adopted by most x86-compatible microprocessor makers shortly thereafter. MMX was designed to improve the processor's overall performance with multimedia-related applications, such as computer games, but it offers benefits only to applications that were specifically written to take advantage of the 57 instructions. Unfortunately, not many applications were, so MMX ended up making a fairly tiny impact on the market. The Pentium III family of chips added 70 more new instructions, called *Streaming SIMD Extensions* (SSE), to the x86 processor core, but again, only applications that specifically take advantage of them benefit. Similarly, the 3DNow instructions that AMD added to their K6 and K7 line of processors are beneficial only to programs that take specific advantage of them. Many of the instructions found in MMX take advantage of a processing technique known as *SIMD* (Single Instructions, Multiple Data), which enables the processor to perform the same operation on several bits of data at once. In the case of MMX, the SIMD operations were directed toward integer data, whereas the Streaming SIMD instructions introduced in the Pentium III perform this technique on floating point data. *See also* 3DNow, Floating Point, Instructions, Microprocessor, and Streaming SIMD.

Modem

Technically, an acronym for modulator-demodulator, but more commonly a device used to connect a PC to the Internet or another PC. A modem functions as an adapter that makes a connection over a specific type of communication line to another computer (which, in turn, may be directly connected to the Internet). Analog modems, which typically conform to the V.90 56K standard, enable you to make a low-speed connection over standard copper phone lines. DSL modems, on the other hand, which often conform to the G.Lite standard, enable you to make a high-speed connection over standard copper phone lines, but with the important caveat of only if DSL service is available in your area. Cable modems, which often conform to the DOCSIS standard, enable you to make high-speed connections via the coaxial cable used to provide cable TV service into your home. Technically speaking, both DSL and cable modems don't provide dial-up connections as traditional analog modems do, because DSL and cable connections are always on. Nevertheless, the term *modem* is used to describe them because it provides a familiar, comfortable metaphor. *See also* 56K, DOCSIS, G.Lite, and V.90.

Monitor

A device used to display the signal from a computer's video card. In fact, it's also called a *display*. Monitors come in two basic forms: the traditional, tube-based CRTs, and the LCD-equipped flat panel monitors. *See also* CRT, DDC, and LCD.

Motherboard

The main printed circuit board that sits at the center of your computer and to which all the components in your PC are attached. The motherboard, or mainboard, houses connections for the processor(s), memory, storage devices, and plug-in cards. It is housed inside a computer's case.

Mouse

An input device used with graphical user interfaces that enables you to interact with the computer by pointing and clicking. Mice typically come in one of several formats including serial mice, which attach to the serial port; PS/2 mice, which attach to the dedicated PS/2 mouse port; and most recently, USB mice, which attach to a PC's USB port (or a USB keyboard with a built-in USB hub). Systems that use a USB mouse must have it supported in the BIOS; otherwise, you won't be able to use the mouse until an operating system that supports USB is loaded. *See also* Cursor, Trackball, and Trackpad.

MP3

A shortened name for MPEG Audio Layer 3, which is an increasingly popular sound format used on the Internet and in some electronics devices that provides high-quality sound but compresses the digital audio file size by a factor of about 10 or 12:1. In order to playback MP3 files on your PC, you simply need to have an application that supports them. *See also* Digital Audio and MPEG.

MPEG

An acronym for Moving Picture Experts Group, an association that developed several similarly named standards for compressing video files on a computer. To store files in MPEG format, you need to encode them with an MPEG encoder, and to play them back, you need an MPEG decoder, which can come in the form of a hardware plug-in card or a piece of software. MPEG-1, which is often used in games and CD-ROM titles, offers a resolution of 352 × 240 pixels and a maximum frame rate of 30 frames per second (FPS), which is a little less than standard VHS quality. MPEG-2 offers a resolution of 720 × 480 or 1,280 × 720 at 60 FPS, which is equivalent to DVD (Digital Video Disk) standards. In fact, DVD video discs store the movies in MPEG-2 format. The most current version is MPEG-4, which is based on Apple's QuickTime technology and adds the capability to stream the signal over an Internet connection in real time. *See also* DVD, FPS, and MJPEG.

MPU-401

The name of a MIDI interface made by Roland Corporation that was one of the first available for the PC and quickly became a default standard. Many PC-based MIDI interfaces include an MPU-401 compatibility mode. *See also* MIDI.

Multimedia

A type of information that combines several independent media, such as sound, pictures, and video. Generally speaking, multimedia refers to a software program that uses these type of media or a computer that provides support to play back these type of media files.

Multitasking

The capability to run multiple programs at once. All operating systems except DOS support the capability to multitask, although some have better multitasking capabilities than others.

Multitimbral

A characteristic of synthesizers, including those built into sound cards, that enables them to play several different sounds, or timbres, at once. A 16-part multitimbral sound card or synthesizer can play 16 different sounds, or patches, at once, each on a separate MIDI channel. *See also* MIDI, Patch, Polyphony, and Synthesizer.

N

Nanosecond

Billionths of a second. Many operations that occur on a computer are measured in nanoseconds. *See also* Millisecond.

NetBEUI

An acronym for NetBIOS (Network Basic Input/Output System) Extended User Interface, an enhanced version of NetBIOS that's commonly used as a protocol in basic Windows peer-to-peer networks. Unlike the TCP/IP or IPX/SPX protocols, NetBEUI does not require assigning a numeric address to each PC on the system, which makes it easier to set up and use, particularly for simple file and print-sharing applications. *See also* IPX/SPX, NetBIOS, Network, Peer-to-Peer, Protocol, and TCP/IP.

NetBIOS

An acronym for Network BIOS (Basic Input/Output System), a type of basic networking software built into Windows and other operating systems. NetBIOS functions like an extension of a PC's system BIOS in a manner that enables your PC to communicate with other devices on a network. Practically speaking, when you assign your computer a name in the Network control panel of Windows 95 and later, it is NetBIOS that enables other computers on the network to see the name. *See also* BIOS, NetBEUI, and Network.

Network

A group of two or more computers that are connected via some type of physical media and that each include some basic software that enables them to communicate with one another. Networks provide a fast, easy way to share data, peripherals, and services among multiple computers, including printers, modems, Internet accounts, and more. Networks consist of a basic network topology or layout; a type of network architecture, which determines how messages are packaged and sent across the network; and a basic network structure or type. Most home networks, for example, use a star layout, with an Ethernet architecture, and are structured as a peer-to-peer network. The three critical pieces of software you need to make a network work are clients, protocols, and services. Network client software determines what capabilities the computers connected to the network have, protocols determine the "language" used to send messages back and forth on the network, and services provide the actual features, such as file and print sharing, that make using a network worthwhile. *See also* Client, Client-Server, Ethernet, Peer-to-Peer, Protocol, Server, and Topology.

Newsgroup

An Internet-based threaded discussion group, or bulletin board, that you can read messages from or post messages to via a dedicated newsreader program, or an e-mail application that also supports newsgroups. There are newsgroups, like Web sites, on virtually any subject matter. The most well-known newsgroups on the Internet are the Usenet newsgroups. Some programs enable you to subscribe to specific newsgroups you may be interested in, which enables you to keep up to date with all the messages that are posted in that newsgroup. Newsgroups typically have names such as "comp.pc.windows".

NIC

An acronym for Network Interface Card, a plug-in card for a desktop computer or PC card for a notebook computer that enables you to attach your PC to a network. Most NICs support one of several different Ethernet standards, which is the most popular type of network architecture. *See also* Ethernet and Network.

NiCAD

An acronym for Nickel Cadmium, a type of chemical combination used in notebook batteries (as well as other types of batteries). NiCAD was the primary battery technology for many years, but it has started to fall out of favor because most NiCAD batteries suffer from something called a *memory effect*. The battery essentially "remembers" how much of a charge it had left before it is recharged and then enables the battery to be charged up only to the point where it used to be. The only real way around this is to completely discharge the battery before it's recharged. NiCADs also don't last as long as other technologies, although they're usually less expensive. *See also* LIon and NiMH.

NiMH

An acronym for Nickel Metal Hydride, a type of chemical combination used in notebook batteries (as well as other types of batteries). NiMH batteries don't suffer from the memory effect commonly found in NiCAD batteries, but they also don't usually last as long as LIon batteries, placing them in the middle of the battery performance pack. *See also* LIon and NiCAD.

NLX

A type of motherboard that's used in compact tower computers and some smaller desktops. The main differentiating factor of NLX motherboards is that they use a riser card to attach expansion cards to the system. *See also* ATX and Motherboard.

Normalize

The process of expanding the dynamic range of a recorded digital audio file by raising its peak volume to the highest level possible before distortion. *See also* Digital Audio.

NOS

An acronym for Network Operating System, a type of software used to control the interactions on a network of computers, typically client-server networks. In many cases, the NOS, such as Novell's NetWare or Microsoft's NT Server, is installed on a server, and then special client software that "talks" to that particular NOS is installed on each PC attached to the network. Because Windows 95, 98, and 2000 include basic networking support, they can be considered a simplistic type of NOS. *See also* Client-Server, Network, and Server.

Notebook

Originally the term meant a type of portable computer that, when closed, approximated the size of a pad of notebook paper. Now, however, the term is used generically to describe virtually all portable PCs. It is used interchangeably with the word *laptop*. *See also* Laptop and Subnotebook.

NTFS

An acronym for NT File System, the native disk partitioning system of both Windows NT and Windows 2000 Professional. Windows NT 4.0 actually uses NTFS 4.0, and Windows 2000 Professional uses NTFS 5.0, an enhanced version. *See also* FAT, FAT-32, and Partition.

NTSC

An acronym for National Television Standards Committee, an organization that developed a standard of the same name that defines how television signals in the United States and a few foreign countries, including Japan, are to be sent and the format they are to use. With computers, NTSC typically refers to a normal television-like composite video signal (in contrast to the video signal that's normally sent to a computer monitor, which is in a different format) that can be plugged straight into a television or other video monitor. Many notebooks include an NTSC output to ease the process of doing presentations in conference rooms and other places where large television screens are available. In addition, video digitizing cards often include analog NTSC inputs (and outputs), so that you can send a normal video signal from a camcorder or other source into (or out of) your PC. *See also* Composite Video, DV, FPS, and Interlaced.

O

OnNow

The name of a feature available in Windows 98 and 2000 that takes advantage of the ACPI (Advanced Configuration Power Interface) power management system in order to enable both desktop and notebook computers to be instantly available. Basically, OnNow works by never really shutting off the computer and all its components, but instead putting it into a sleep mode that can be quickly gotten out of by touching the Power button again. *See also* ACPI and Sleep.

Open Source

A type of software licensing system in which the software is not only freely available and free to use, but so is the source code used to generate the software. (Source code is the original lines of software written by the programmer that are compiled into a standalone application.) The benefit of open source software is that anyone with the skills or interest is welcome to make changes and additions to the source code, and the entire community of users can benefit as a result. The downsides are that it's not always clear who to turn to for support, nor is it clear how long people and/or companies can continue to develop products for which they make little or no money. The most well-known example of open source software is the Linux operating system. *See also* Linux.

Operating System

A type of software that works directly with a computer's hardware and creates an environment in which applications can be run. Operating systems, or OSes, are large, complex beasts that provide a PC with its fundamental personality and determine the way a computer works. Operating systems also define how applications work with them and how files are to be stored on the disk, which is why applications written for one operating system cannot run on another (with a few minor exceptions) and why different operating systems use different disk partitioning systems. Most operating systems consist of hundreds of different files, but the core files are typically referred to as the *kernel*, or *kernel files*. Various types of Windows and Linux are two examples of operating systems you can run on a PC. Only one operating system can be run at once, but you can install multiple operating systems onto your computer's hard drive and then choose which one you want to use for a particular session with the help of a program called a *boot loader*. *See also* Application, BeOS, Boot Loader, Dual Boot, Linux, OS/2, Partition, and Windows.

OPL3

The name of a Yamaha chip used on many sound cards that can create sounds via FM synthesis. Some sound cards offer an OPL3-compatible chip. The lesser-known OPL4 includes both FM synthesis and wavetable synthesis. *See also* FM Synthesis, Synthesizer, and Wavetable Synthesis.

Optical Resolution

The physical capabilities of an imaging device, such as a scanner or digital camera, in capturing an individual image. Most scanners, for example, have specs for their optical resolution (which is the device's "real" resolution) and another higher number for their interpolated resolution. An interpolated image, however, is created by automatically filling in colors between two adjacent pixels, so the end result is rarely better and often worse than the original. The optical resolution is what the device can actually "see." *See also* Digital Camera, Pixel, Resolution, and Scanner.

OS

An acronym for Operating System. *See also* Operating System.

OS/2

An operating system originally conceived by IBM and Microsoft but now developed and marketed solely by IBM. Recent versions are often referred to as "OS/2 Warp," or just "Warp" for short. At one point, OS/2 was a reasonable competitor to Windows, but over time its influence has faded considerably. As a result, a limited number of applications are available for OS/2, and it has a relatively small (though usually vocal) group of users. *See also* HPFS.

OSI

An acronym for Open Systems Interface, a standardized framework, or model, that enables computers of different types to communicate over a network. The OSI model divides network communications into seven layers, each of which performs a specific task. Network hardware devices and/or software components may perform one or several of the different layers. *See also* Network.

OSR

An acronym for OEM (Original Equipment Manufacturer) Service Release, a name that Microsoft gives to various versions of the Windows operating system that it releases to computer vendors, or OEMs. Windows 95, for example, went through several OSR releases, the most well-known of which is OSR2. In addition, the most recent version of Windows 98 is sometimes called OSR1. *See also* Service Pack.

P

P&D

An acronym for Plug & Display, a digital connection standard for flat panel monitors that was developed by VESA (Video Electronics Standard Association — the same people who originally developed the VGA standard). P&D incorporates not only the digital display signal, but also support for USB, IEEE 1394, and an analog video signal (for backwards compatibility) in a relatively compact package. By incorporating these extra elements, P&D simplifies connections between a monitor that incorporates built-in speakers and a video camera, for example. Unfortunately, some video card and monitor manufacturers felt the standard was too robust and decided to develop and/or use other incompatible digital display standards such as DFP (Digital Flat Panel), which is essentially a simplified version of P&D, and LDI (LVDS Display Interface). *See also* DFP, DVI, LCD Panel, and LDI.

Parallel

A technique for sending multiple blocks of data simultaneously over a connection, in contrast to serial connections, which send one block at a time. Another way to think of it is that parallel connections are often wider, though serial connections are often faster. Sometimes also used to describe multiple operations that occur simultaneously, as in parallel processing. *See also* Serial.

Parallel Port

A type of physical connection found on many PCs that's used to connect printers, scanners, and removable storage devices, among other types of peripherals. Parallel ports, which typically use DB25 connectors, offer transfer rates of up to 3MBps if you use certain high-speed modes, such as ECP or EPP, but are often limited to only 300KBps if you use the standard or SPP mode. *See also* DB25, ECP, EPP, IEEE 1284, LPT, Serial Port, and SPP.

Parity

A simple type of error correction mechanism found in certain types of memory in which individual data bytes are added and the result is checked to be either odd or even. The result of this parity check is stored in a parity bit. Instead of having eight individual memory chips, many parity memory modules have nine in order to store these parity bits. A more sophisticated form of error correction is provided by ECC (Error Correction Code) memory. Parity is also used as a simple form of error correction in some dial-up modem connections and the protocols they use. *See also* ECC and Error Correction.

Partition

An individually addressable segment of a hard disk (or other storage device) that is treated as an independent disk. In DOS and Windows, partitions are also referred to as *volumes* and assigned individual drive letters, such as C:, D:, and so on. The structure, or format, of a partition is typically determined by the file system of the operating system that first created it, such as a FAT-32 partition under Windows 98, an NTFS 5.0 partition under Windows 2000 Professional, or an Ext2 partition under Linux. In most instances, hard drives do not have to be broken up into partitions; they can be treated as one large partition. Some situations do require multiple partitions, or multiple partitions may provide an easier way to organize a disk's contents. There are two main types of partitions: primary partitions, which are limited to a maximum of four per disk, and extended partitions, which are limited only by the availability of drive letters (at least under Windows). Primary partitions can store any kind of files, including operating system boot files, and extended partitions can hold any kind of files except operating system boot files. By using a boot loader program, you can select which of your primary partitions you want to make active for a particular session, and the operating system files located on the active partition are the ones that are loaded. Disks can be broken up into partitions through a disk partitioning program, such as FDISK. A list of partitions used on a particular hard disk are stored in a partition table. *See also* Ext2, FAT, FAT-32, FDISK, NTFS, Operating System, and Volume.

Passive Matrix

A type of display technology used on LCD panels in which the pixels are refreshed on a row-by-row basis. The tangible result is a screen that isn't as bright or as crisp as active matrix, or TFT-based, screens, but one that is much less expensive. Early passive matrix screens, sometimes also called "CSTN (Color Super-Twist Nematic) displays," suffered from ghosting problems, where a shadow-like image of an item (such as the mouse pointer) remained on the screen while it was moved, but several developments have improved the quality of passive matrix screens. One of the most well known is Dual Scan (sometimes also referred to as "DSTN"), which divides the screen in two and updates each half simultaneously. Another is called "High-Performance Addressing," or HPA, which also increases how often the screen's pixels are updated. In both cases the end result is a screen that is much better than older passive matrix displays, although still not as crisp as an active matrix. *See also* Active Matrix, DSTN, Dual Scan, HPA, LCD Panel, and TFT.

Patch

Another name for a particular sound program in a synthesizer. The term comes from the early days of synthesizers where, to create different types of sounds, you had to use patch cables to connect various parts of the synthesizer. Also used to describe a software upgrade that fixes a bug. *See also* Bug, General MIDI, Multitimbral, and Synthesizer.

Path

The address for a given file or set of files within the operating system's file system. A path tells you where a file is located on your hard drive by listing the folders and subfolders in which it is stored. For example, the path C:\Windows\System tells you that the file is located on the C: drive inside the System folder (or directory), which is inside the Windows folder. A path statement is sometimes used by DOS and early Windows applications to "remind" the program where to look for particular files. *See also* Directory.

PC98/PC99

Specifications created by Intel, Microsoft, Compaq, and several other major PC vendors that define the types of components and capabilities that they believe should be included in modern PC systems. The specs are not requirements but merely suggestions of what these companies think is important. However, in order for computers or hardware peripherals to gain Microsoft's "Designed for Windows 98" or "Designed for Windows 2000" logos, they must meet the requirements listed in the specs. PC98 is actually geared for systems sold in 1999, and PC99 is geared for systems sold in 2000. The first PC system spec was called "PC95" and was developed in conjunction with the release of Windows 95, as an attempt to enable system designers to know what type of basic features should be included in PCs designed to run Windows 95. An updated version called "PC97" was released about a year and a half later. The current specs define five different categories of computers: Consumer PCs, Business PCs, Entertainment PCs, Workstation PCs, and Portable PCs, each of which has different types of recommendations, depending on their intended applications.

PC Card

A format for credit card–sized peripherals and expansion cards that plug into notebook computers and other small electronic devices. The term is also used to describe the slots into which these devices are plugged. PC cards can be used to add a wide variety of things including memory, input/output devices such as modems and network interface cards, as well as hard drives. PC cards come in three basic sizes or types, the primary difference being the width of the cards. Type I cards are 3.3 mm thick and are typically used for adding memory; Type II cards, the most popular by far, are 5 mm thick and are used for a wide variety of purposes; and Type III cards are 10.5 mm thick and often used for miniature hard drives. Type I and II cards can fit into any standard PC card slot, and Type III cards essentially fill the space of two PC card slots (which is why most notebooks come with two stacked PC card slots). Additional sizes and formats called "Small PC Card" and "Miniature Card" have also been defined. Early versions of PC cards and PC card slots were often called (and sometimes still are) "PCMCIA" (Personal Computer Memory Card International Association), after the association that developed the standard. *See also* CompactFlash, PCMCIA, and SmartMedia.

PCI

An acronym for Peripheral Component Interconnect, the name of the primary bus used in PCs today. The term is also used to describe the type of slots into which expansion cards that support the standard are placed. Unlike ISA format expansion boards, many (though not all) PCI devices are capable of sharing an IRQ. In addition, PCI cards use their own set of PCI-specific interrupts, which are different from and have no bearing on IRQs. The original version of PCI defined a 32-bit-wide, 33MHz bus, but later versions of the spec, including PCI-X, call for a 64-bit-wide bus that runs at up to 66MHz, which is four times faster than the original. PCI is often called a "local bus," because it has a direct, or local, connection to the processor. *See also* Bus, Interrupt, IRQ, and ISA.

PCL

An acronym for Printer Command Language, a standard developed by Hewlett-Packard for transferring data from an application to a printer. Most printers designed for use with PCs support PCL. *See also* PostScript.

PCMCIA

An acronym for Personal Computer Memory Card International Association, an organization that defines the standard for small, rugged plug-in cards that are typically used on notebook computers and other electronic devices. The most well-known standard they have developed is the PC Card standard, which is sometimes still referred to as the PCMCIA standard. They have also helped develop the SmartMedia and CompactFlash standards, which are often used with digital cameras and PDAs. *See also* CompactFlash, PC Card, and SmartMedia.

PCX

A common Windows bitmapped graphics file format that uses the extension .pcx. PCX is the default file format of the Paintbrush application bundled with Windows. *See also* BMP, Bitmapped Graphics, and Extension.

PDA

An acronym for Personal Digital Assistant, a term that was originally used to describe Apple's Newton but has since come to mean any electronic organizer-type device, as well as several different types of handheld computers.

PDF

An acronym for Portable Document Format, the file format used by Adobe's Acrobat software. PDF files, which also use .pdf as their file extension, enable you to create an exact electronic duplicate of a printed page's layout that is resolution-independent, complete with the same typefaces and all the embedded graphics, yet still has searchable text. You can create PDF files from any application by basically "printing" to the PDF format, but you need special PDF software in order to do that. PDF files can be read only by a PDF reader, such as Adobe's freely available Acrobat Reader. *See also* Extension and Format.

Peer-to-Peer

A type of network structure in which all the connected PCs have an equal, or peer-level, status. Technically speaking, each of the computers on a peer-to-peer network functions as both a client and server, which means each of them can easily send files to or receive files from any other computer on the network. Peer-to-peer networks, which are generally recommended for small networks of up to ten computers, are the simplest to set up, and so they're the most common type used for home networks. *See also* Client, Client-Server, Network, and Server.

Pentium

The name of Intel's fifth generation processor. Since the introduction of the original Pentium, the company has used the name for several other generations of processors, including the Pentium Pro, Pentium with MMX, Pentium II, and Pentium III. Processors from other companies that support the main Pentium instruction set are sometimes referred to as "Pentium compatibles." *See also* 8086, Processor, and X86.

Peripheral

A device that attaches to or plugs into a computer system and adds some additional capabilities to the system—in other words, an accessory. Common peripherals are printers, modems, and scanners.

Photo CD

A graphics file format created by Kodak that stores scanned digital photos in five different resolutions, including one high-resolution image. Also the name for the disc that holds those images. Photo CD files, which have the extension .pcd, typically come from a Photo CD (as redundant as that may sound), which can be created only via a photo-finishing lab that offers the service. Photo CDs can hold up to 100 high-quality images but do not include any image-editing software. *See also* PictureCD.

PictureCD

A CD-ROM disc that stores scanned digital photos in a single resolution on a CD. Photo files stored on Picture CDs are in the JPEG format. Like Photo CDs, PictureCDs are created by photofinishing labs, but unlike Photo CDs, PictureCDs include basic image-editing software on the CD. *See also* JPEG and Photo CD.

PIF

An acronym for Program Information File, a type of file used in Windows that uses the extension .pif and that contains information and/or configuration settings about a DOS application that you want to run from within Windows. Under Windows 95 and later, for example, you can store all of the following (and more) within a PIF file: the icon associated with the program, its location, whether to run it in an MS-DOS prompt window or in MS-DOS mode, and program-specific Autoexec.bat and Config.sys files that you want to run whenever you launch the application. You can get to all of these types of settings by right-clicking a PIF file and selecting Properties from the context menu that appears. *See also* Autoexec.bat, Config.sys, and DOS.

Ping

An acronym for Packet Internet Groper, a common type of Internet utility program that's used to verify the connection between your PC and another out on the Internet (or any other TCP/IP-based network). A Ping utility sends a message out to a destination that you choose and then waits to receive a response from that destination. The process of testing a connection to a particular IP or Web address is called "pinging" a server. *See also* IP Address.

PIO

An acronym for Programmed Input/Output, a type of data transfer method used with hard drives that support the EIDE or ATA-2 standard. There are several different PIO modes, with the higher numbered modes supporting faster data transfer rates. *See also* ATA and EIDE.

Pipelining

A technology used in microprocessors in which several different execution paths, or pipelines, are created so that the processor can perform multiple operations at the same time. *See also* Microprocessor.

Pixel

A unit of measurement in digital images, monitors, and other image-related devices. A pixel is equivalent to a single dot in a picture or on the screen. In fact, specifications for certain devices sometimes use PPI (pixels per inch) interchangeably with DPI (dots per inch). The term is a shortened version of *picture element*. *See also* DPI.

Platform

A generic term used to describe the type of computer and the operating system it is running. For example, a PC with an x86-compatible processor running Windows is using the Windows platform, whereas the same hardware running Linux is using the Linux platform. The term is often used when referring to technologies that work with multiple types of computers. The Java language, for example, is said to be cross-platform. *See also* Operating System.

Plug-In

A piece of software that can be used in conjunction with an application to add features to the "host" program. Plug-ins, which are like software accessories, often can't run on their own but must be used as part of, or within, the main program. *See also* Application.

Plug-In Board

A circuit board that you can attach, or plug into, your computer's motherboard to add additional capabilities to your system. Sound cards, network cards, video cards, and internal modems, for example, are all types of plug-in boards, which are sometimes also called *expansion cards*.

PNG

An acronym for Portable Network Graphics, a relatively new graphics format used on Web pages that offers several benefits over GIF and JPEG, including support for alpha channels and gamma correction. Like GIF, PNG uses lossless compression techniques, but like JPEG, it also includes support for 24-bit color. The 4.0 and later versions of both Internet Explorer and Netscape Navigator/Communicator include the capability to display PNG graphics. *See also* Alpha Channel, Compression, Gamma, GIF, and JPEG.

PnP

An acronym for Plug and Play, a technique introduced in Windows 95 in which the operating system automatically recognizes what hardware is installed or attached to a PC and then automatically installs (or requests that you manually install) the necessary drivers and sets the various resource settings the devices need. In order for Plug and Play to work properly, your computer needs both a BIOS that supports it (because the BIOS lists the hardware it finds and the requirements that hardware has and passes that information along to the OS), as well as peripherals that are Plug andPlay compliant, so that they can announce their presence and requirements to the OS as well. If PnP doesn't work (the fact that it's nowhere near 100 percent effective is sometimes why it's referred to as Plug and Pray), then you may have to manually install some drivers and adjust things such as IRQ, DMA, and I/O settings in the Windows Device Manager. In some instances, you may even have to undo the settings that Plug and Play has created to make a particular device work. A more effective implementation of Plug and Play is offered by the USB and IEEE 1394 buses, because they enable you to literally plug a device into your PC and then, shortly thereafter, begin to use it. *See also* BIOS, Driver, and Resources.

Polyphony

A measurement of how many individual notes a synthesizer can play at one time. A sound card with 128-note polyphony, for example, includes synthesizer circuitry that can generate 128 different notes simultaneously. This is different from its multitimbral capabilities, which refers to how many different timbres it can make. For example, if you play 64 notes with a piano timbre, another 32 with a violin-like timbre, and 32 more with a flute timbre, you're using three timbres, but 128 notes of polyphony. *See also* Multitimbral and Synthesizer.

POP3

An acronym for Post Office Protocol Version 3, an older Internet mail standard that defines the guidelines for how e-mail programs (called "clients") can retrieve messages from e-mail servers. *See also* IMAP4 and SMTP.

Port

Another name for a physical connector which you use to connect to another device. In programming, the process of converting a program from one platform to another. *See also* Parallel Port, Platform, and Serial Port.

POST

An acronym for Power On Self Test, a diagnostic procedure that most computers go through every time they're turned on or are restarted. The most well-known part of POST, which is run by a computer's BIOS, is the memory check that quickly counts up how much RAM is installed in your system. *See also* BIOS and RAM.

PostScript

A text-based language developed by Adobe that's primarily used for printing. PostScript enables a computer to describe vector-based graphics as a series of commands that the printer can "interpret" and use to generate the image. In order to use PostScript, you need to have both an application and a printer that supports it. PostScript also defines a format for fonts, the most well known of which is Type 1 Fonts. *See also* PCL, Type 1 Font, and Vector Graphics.

POTS

An acronym for Plain Old Telephone Service, another name for a regular voice line. The term is used to distinguish normal phone lines from various types of data lines or services.

Power Management

A technique used to automatically control the on and off settings of a computer, particularly notebooks. Support for power management (or not) is what enables you to put a computer into a sleep mode, which can save battery life, in the case of a portable computer, and give you quicker access than rebooting, in the case of a desktop PC. Power management is typically implemented via one of two main standards: APM (Advanced Power Management) or the newer ACPI (Advanced Configuration and Power Interface). The capability to take advantage of power management is dependent both on the computer's BIOS, as well as any peripherals that are added to the system. *See also* ACPI, APM, BIOS, and Sleep Mode.

PPM

An acronym for Pages Per Minute, a measurement of how quickly a printer can generate a page. Most printers have several PPM ratings depending on what mode you may be using and whether or not you're printing in color (which always takes longer) or just black and white. Really slow or really high-quality modes on certain printers are rated with MPP (minutes per page), which means they can print only a portion of a page within a minute's time.

PPP

An acronym for Point-to-Point Protocol, a means of sending information between two computers that are directly connected, such as when you make a dial-up connection between your computer and an ISP (Internet Service Provider) through a modem. PPP is a higher-level protocol through which you can send other protocols, such as TCP/IP or NetBEUI. *See also* Protocol.

Processor

A shortened version of the word *microprocessor*. Also, any integrated circuit, or chip, that has the capability to perform calculations on data. Some video cards, SCSI controllers, and other types of expansion cards include their own dedicated processors, for example, that perform specific functions. *See also* Microprocessor.

Protected Mode

One of two main modes of operation found in x86-compatible processors (the other being real mode). In protected mode, which became available starting with 80286, a processor can set aside, or allocate, a certain amount of memory for each application, and that memory is protected from being interfered with by other applications (at least in theory, that is). Protected mode also enables support for extended memory, which is the memory beyond 1MB, virtual memory, and multitasking. Operating systems that use a processor's protected mode — which is every one except DOS — have no problems accessing additional memory. In addition, they don't treat the memory below the 1MB level any differently than any other memory. In real mode, on the other hand, which is what DOS uses, the processor works within the limitations of the original 8088 processor and is therefore limited to directly accessing only the first megabyte of memory. *See also* DOS and Real Mode.

Protocol

An agreed-upon format or "language" for communicating between two or more devices. Protocols define how messages are sent as well as things such as the size of individual messages. Some protocols work at higher levels than others, so it's not uncommon to use several different protocols at once. For example, if you request a Web page from a PC using an external DSL modem, you send a message using HTTP (HyperText Transport Protocol), which is wrapped by a general purpose TCP/IP message in order to travel over the Internet, and that, in turn, starts out wrapped in an Ethernet protocol message because DSL modems typically connect to PCs via Ethernet connections. In order to use a protocol, you need to have software for it installed on your system. Most operating systems now include support for the most common types of protocols, but if you're putting together a home network, for example, it's common to have to install, say, the NetBEUI protocol. *See also* NetBEUI, Network, and TCP/IP.

Proxy Server

A piece of hardware or software that acts as an intermediary between one network and another, typically between a LAN and the Internet. Proxy servers funnel the requests of everyone on a network through a single point of connection and also provide a means to prevent unwanted messages from getting into a network. Many proxy servers incorporate a firewall, for example, to prevent security attacks and, in some cases, to filter out certain types of material. A hardware proxy server functions as a network version of a browser's cache by storing Web pages requested by users on the network and then sending pages directly to other users who may request the same page, instead of having to retrieve the pages again over the Internet. A software-based proxy server doesn't necessarily provide the caching functions of a hardware server, but it does enable a small network of computers to share a single Internet connection. The way it works is all the computers on the network send their Internet-bound messages to the proxy server and it, in turn, forwards them onto the Internet. When it receives Web pages or other data back, it forwards them to the appropriate machine, based on the IP address of the original request. *See also* Firewall and IP Address.

PS/2

A dedicated port for connecting your mouse that first appeared on IBM's PS/2 line of computers.

Q

Quantization

The technique of adjusting the placement of notes stored in a MIDI sequencer so that they line up with a user-definable time grid. *See also* MIDI and Sequencing.

R

RAID

An acronym for Redundant Array of Inexpensive Disks, a type of storage system that consists of several hard drives that work together as a system. There are several different RAID Levels, the most well known of which are Level 0, 1, and 5. RAID systems generally offer better performance and/or security than single hard drives. In RAID Level 0, two or more hard drives are treated as a single disk, and the data is striped across the drives, meaning a portion is written to one drive and another portion to the next. In RAID Level 1, the data is mirrored across two drives, which means the identical information is written to two or more drives simultaneously. In RAID Level 5, data is striped across multiple drives, but some sophisticated error correction techniques also copy special data onto multiple drives so that if any single hard drive stops working, all the data that it stores can be recreated from pieces found on other drives. In addition to these security features, many RAIDs, which tend to be pretty expensive, include things such as redundant power supplies and support for hot-swapping hard drives. RAIDs are typically used only on servers, although they're occasionally used for professional video- and audio-editing applications as well. *See also* Hard Drive.

RAM

An acronym for Random Access Memory, the main working area that a computer or other electronic device uses to load software into and perform its calculations. Most RAM comes in the form of Dynamic RAM, which is a type of memory whose contents are refreshed on a regular basis. Even within the genus of DRAM, there are several species including FPM (Fast Page Mode) DRAM, EDO (Extended Data Out) DRAM, SDRAM (Synchronous DRAM), and RDRAM (Rambus DRAM), each of which operate somewhat differently. Another general type of memory called "SRAM" (Static RAM) can maintain its contents without being constantly refreshed. SRAM is commonly used for L1 and L2 cache in microprocessors as well as in Flash Memory cards. *See also* DRAM, Memory, and SRAM.

Rambus

The name of a company and a memory technology it created that offers a narrow, high-speed connection (a RAM bus) between a processor and memory. Rambus memory comes in the form of RDRAM (Rambus DRAM) and is packaged in RIMMs (Rambus Inline Memory Modules). *See also* RDRAM and RIMM.

Raw

A type of printing file format used under Windows that sends a stream of raw binary data to the printer. *See also* EMF.

RCA

A type of physical connector, originally developed by the old RCA company, that's commonly used with audio and video equipment.

RDRAM

An acronym for Rambus DRAM (Dynamic Random Access Memory), a type of high-speed memory that takes advantage of a high-speed connection between the processor and memory to offer throughput of 1.6Gbps or higher, which is even faster than SDRAM. RDRAM, which is typically found only on later Pentium III and K7-equipped systems, comes in the form of RIMMs (Rambus Inline Memory Modules), which use the same basic type of connector as SDRAM DIMMs but are packaged differently. *See also* DIMM, RIMM, and SDRAM.

RealAudio

A popular type of streaming audio file format found on the Internet that enables you to do things such as listen to live radio broadcasts as well as listen to large audio files without having to first download the entire file. RealVideo offers similar capabilities for video files, such as television broadcasts. The two together are sometimes referred to as "RealMedia." In order to play these types of files on your computer, you need to install a program that supports the RealAudio or RealVideo file formats. *See also* Streaming Media.

Real Mode

A mode of operation in x86-compatible processors that essentially emulates the original 8088 processor, including its limitation of being able to directly access only the first megabyte of memory. DOS was designed for the 8088, and in order to enable DOS and DOS applications to work on later processors, they need to be able to operate in real mode. Under DOS and real mode, the first megabyte of computer memory is divided into 640K of conventional memory and 384K of upper memory (remembering that 1MB equals 1,024K). In order to get access to memory beyond this 1MB limit, the notion of expanded memory was developed, which basically tricks the processor into thinking that the extra memory is actually part of the 640K of conventional memory. In addition, with the addition of extended memory that the 80286 and later processors' protected mode enabled, techniques were developed to "convert" extended into expanded memory (which in turn was an extension of conventional memory). *See also* Conventional Memory, DOS, Expanded Memory, Extended Memory, Protected Mode, and Upper Memory.

Registry

A software entity used by Windows 95 and later versions (including NT 4.0) that stores configuration and preference settings. The Registry is made up of two main files, System.dat and User.dat, as well as some information that's created in real time, as the computer is running. The Registry, which plays a critical role in Windows, is meant to take the place of the many INI files that previous versions of Windows used for storing this type of information. The Registry is organized into a set of six main keys, called "Hkeys," which are further subdivided into hundreds of categories and thousands of individual keys. Only three of the main keys actually contain unique information, the other three are simply shortcuts that provide easier access to subcategories under those main keys. When programs are installed, they typically create new keys in the Registry and/or update values of existing keys to store those settings. If the Registry is ever damaged, your programs won't work because they won't be able to find the settings they need inside the Registry. As a result, you typically need to reinstall your applications so that those settings can be restored. *See also* INI File.

REM

An acronym for Remark, a command used in certain DOS and Windows startup files that tells the computer to ignore the information on the line that begins with the command. The process of "REMing" something out means to type REM at the very beginning of a particular line so that the computer won't load whatever software is listed there. The semicolon character (;) can be used for the same purpose. *See also* Autoexec.bat, Config.sys, Startup Files, System.ini, and Win.ini.

Removable Drive

A type of storage device that enables you to remove the media from the drive. A floppy drive, for example, is technically a removable drive because it enables you to remove the floppy disk. However, the term is typically used with larger-capacity drives such as Zip and Jaz drives. *See also* Media.

Resolution

A means of measuring the amount of detail offered by a device or within the contents of a file. Also, a means of expressing the degree of accuracy that a device can support, with higher numbers translating to better accuracy. Resolution refers to how many dots, typically within a given area, a device is capable of creating or displaying. Printers, for example, can generate x number of dots per inch, with x being considered the device's resolution. Some devices, such as monitors, offer support for multiple resolutions, which means they can provide different numbers of dots per inch, according to their settings. The resolution of an image file refers to the number of dots stored per inch when the image is viewed or printed at its original (100 percent) size. *See also* DPI.

Resources

On a computer, components of the machine's architecture that are available in limited supply. Typically, computer resources refer to IRQs (Interrupt ReQuest Lines), DMA (Direct Memory Access) channels, I/O (Input/Output) addresses, and under certain versions of Windows, UMBs (Upper Memory Blocks). When you run out of available resources or if two devices try to share certain types of resources, you can create a resource conflict. A resource conflict often keeps a particular component, or sometimes the entire machine, from working properly. *See also* DMA, I/O, IRQ, and UMB.

RGB

An acronym for Red Green Blue, the format, or color model, used to display colors on monitors. On a system that supports 24-bit color, each of the three primary colors have eight bits of resolution, which enables them to display 256 different shades. When you combine the three in various combinations, however, you increase the palette of possible colors to 16.7 million. RGB is different from the CMYK color model used to create colors on paper, which is why colors on the screen don't always appear the same when they are printed. This also explains why you need color management software in order to convert from one color model to another. *See also* 24-bit color, CMYK, and Color Management.

RIMM

An acronym for Rambus Inline Memory Module, the name for the physical packaging used with RDRAM (Rambus DRAM). RIMMs feature a 168-pin connector that is similar to DIMMs, but the chips can only be used with RIMM slots. *See also* Rambus and RDRAM.

RISC

An acronym for Reduced Instruction Set Computing, a technology used by certain types of microprocessors in which the number of possible instructions entering into the processor is reduced to a simple set and they are all of the same, fixed size. This is in contrast to CISC (Complex Instruction Set Computing)-based processors, which support a larger set of instructions that can be of various sizes. The argument in favor of RISC is that a processor's design can be optimized to work with instructions of a certain length, whereas the argument for CISC is that it provides a more flexible environment for software developers. Most x86-compatible processors are based on CISC technology, but Intel's 64-bit Merced chip is expected to primarily use RISC. *See also* CISC.

RJ-45

A type of connector used with 10Base-T networking products that looks like a slightly fatter version of a typical phone cord jack (which is called an RJ-11 jack). *See also* 10Base-T.

ROM

An acronym for Read Only Memory, a type of storage device, or chip, that can be read from but cannot be written to or changed. Various types of ROM chips are used to store software that is automatically loaded when a computer or other electronic device is turned on. Your computer's BIOS, for example, is stored in a ROM chip, as is the operating system for small handheld electronic devices. *See also* EPROM, Memory, and RAM.

Root

The name given to the lowest (or highest, depending on your perspective) directory on a storage device. Under DOS or Windows for example, C:\, which is the lowest storage level of your first hard drive, is also referred to as the "root" directory. (Technically, it's just the backslash (\).) Under Linux or other versions of UNIX, the root directory is often referred to as just the forward slash character (/). With Linux or other versions of UNIX, root also refers to the primary account available to the OS, through which you can perform administrative functions and configure your system. *See also* Directory and Linux.

Router

A device that directly connects two networks together and handles the process of directing, or routing, traffic to the proper destination, typically through IP addresses. Some high-speed modems, such as cable modems and DSL modems, actually function as routers because they connect one network (the Internet) with another, which may only consist of a single PC (but is still considered a "network" because it has a unique network address). You can also connect a router to a small network of a few PCs (if, for example, you have a home network). This is different than a modem because a router provides a direct, always-on connection that is treated like a network link, as opposed to the occasional dial-up links made by modems. *See also* IP Address and Network.

RTF

An acronym for Rich Text Format, a text-based file type that extends beyond basic ASCII text by including many types of formatting information as well. RTF files, which have the extension .rtf, are commonly used to transfer moderately formatted word processing documents between different applications or across different platforms. Some e-mail programs also support the RTF format. *See also* ASCII.

S

S/PDIF

An acronym for Sony/Philips Digital Interface, a type of digital audio connection standard that typically uses either RCA plugs or optical connectors. Unlike analog audio, S/PDIF carries a stereo signal over a single cable. *See also* Digital Audio and RCA.

Sampling

The process of converting an analog audio signal into digital form. The sampling rate, typically measured in KHz, is the frequency with which the digitizing process occurs. CD-quality audio has a sampling rate of 44.1KHz. A *sample* is a digital audio file that has been captured through this process. *See also* Digital Audio.

Scanner

A computer peripheral that converts a traditional photograph or other graphic material into digital form, commonly a TIFF (Tagged Image File Format) file. Like a copy machine, a scanner essentially takes a high-resolution digital picture of the item it is scanning and transfers the results to a computer. Scanners are available in several different forms, the most common of which is called a "flat-bed" scanner because it features a flat surface onto which you place your originals. Different scanners offer different resolutions and most scanners offer two types of resolution: optical and enhanced. Scanners communicate with applications via the humorously named TWAIN (Technology Without An Interesting Name) interface. *See also* CCD, TIFF, and TWAIN.

SCSI

An acronym for Small Computer Systems Interface, a high-speed parallel connection standard used to link peripherals such as hard drives and scanners to PCs. There are many different types of SCSI, each of which offers different data transfer rates and some of which use different-sized connectors. Common examples include Fast SCSI (sometimes also called "SCSI-2"), Wide SCSI, UltraWide SCSI, Ultra2 SCSI, and Ultra3 SCSI. Most PCs don't come with built-in SCSI support, so to use SCSI devices you often need to install a SCSI controller. SCSI devices can be hooked together in chains of either 7 or 15 devices, depending on the type of controller being used, with each device requiring its own SCSI ID and both ends of the SCSI chain requiring termination. You can mix and match devices and controllers that use different types of SCSI, but the type and speed of controller determines the maximum transfer rates possible, regardless of what the devices connected to the chain support.

SDRAM

An acronym for Synchronous DRAM (Dynamic Random Access Memory), a type of high-speed memory commonly used on PCs and commonly packaged in the form of DIMMs. Synchronous DRAM derives its name (and speed) from its capability to transfer data at every click of (or synchronously with) a computer's system bus clock. Because of this, several different types of

SDRAM are available that vary according to the speed of the system in which they are used. PC100 SDRAM, for example, is designed for systems with 100MHz system buses, PC66 SDRAM is for systems with 66MHz system buses, and PC133 is for systems with 133MHz system buses. *See also* DRAM and System Bus.

SDSL

An acronym for Synchronous Digital Subscriber Line, a type of DSL that supports the same rates for uploading data as it does for downloading data. *See also* ADSL and DSL.

Search Engine

A service available on the Internet that maintains the addresses of millions of Web sites and individual Web pages. To use a search engine, you simply visit a Web site that offers one, type in the word or phrase you're interested in researching, and it responds with the names and Web addresses of all the pages that it's aware of that match your search request. Search engines use special software called *robots* or *spiders* to look for new and updated Web pages to add to their database of available choices, but even with these special techniques, the search engines can't possibly include all the Web sites that are actually available on the Internet.

SECC

An acronym for Single Edge Cartridge Connector, a generic term for the type of slot connectors, such as Slot 1, Slot 2, and Slot A, found on many microprocessors, such as the Pentium II/III and the K7. *See also* Microprocessor, SEPP, Slot 1, and Slot A.

Sector

A tiny segment of a hard drive or other storage device. Most storage devices offer several cylinders, each of which are divided into tracks, and those tracks, in turn, are divided into sectors. A group of sectors that can be individually addressed by the computer's file system is called a *cluster*. A bad sector is a tiny section of the disk that is no longer able to reliably hold data and is therefore blocked off and prevented from being used. *See also* Cluster, Hard Drive, and Track.

Seek Time

The amount of time it takes for a hard drive or other storage device to move its read/write head from one section of the disk to another (technically, to a specific sector). Though they're often used interchangeably, the seek time is only one part of a storage device's access time. *See also* Access Time.

SEPP

An acronym for Single Edge Processor Package, a type of physical connector used to connect some Celeron processors to desktop computer motherboards. SEPP is similar to Slot 1, which is also called SECC (Single Edge Cartridge Connector), except that Celerons don't come wrapped in the plastic cartridge that Pentium IIs and some Pentium IIIs use. *See also* Celeron, SECC, and Slot One.

Sequencer

A type of MIDI (Musical Instrument Digital Interface) application that stores MIDI messages and plays them back, much like an audio recorder. MIDI sequencers also enable you to edit the messages they record, and most now enable you to record and edit digital audio along with MIDI. *See also* Digital Audio and MIDI.

Serial

A type of connection in which data is transferred one bit at a time. This is in contrast to parallel connections, which can send multiple blocks of data at once. *See also* Parallel and USB.

Serial Port

A type of physical connection found on many PCs that's used to connect a wide variety of different peripherals including modems, mice, and graphics tablets. Most serial ports, which typically use DB9 connectors, are limited to a maximum transfer rate of 115Kbps. *See also* DB9 and Parallel Port.

Server

A computer that sits at the logical center of a network and provides services to the client computers connected to it. At minimum, most servers provide a central place to store files that can be easily accessed by any other computer on the network, but servers can also provide a centralized place to offer printing services and certain types of network applications, such as e-mail. *See also* Client, Client-Server, and Network.

Service Pack

The name that Microsoft gives to upgrades to its operating systems and applications. Most Service Packs contain only bug fixes, but some also contain a few new features. *See also* Bugs and Upgrades.

Setup

The name of the installation program used by most Windows applications. You use the Setup program (usually by double-clicking it) that comes with each application to install that application onto your computer's hard drive. The term is also used to generically refer to a computer's BIOS Setup (or CMOS Setup) program, through which you can set a number of your PC's most basic settings, including turning on and off controllers and ports. *See also* BIOS and INF File.

SGRAM

An acronym for Synchronous Graphics RAM (Random Access Memory), a type of Synchronous DRAM that's used on video cards. *See also* Memory, SDRAM, and VRAM.

Shared Files

A type of software that is used by multiple applications or by both the operating system and applications. *See also* DLLs and Libraries.

Shareware

A category of software that is made available to try for free by the program's author, but for which you are supposed to pay a registration fee (typically $25 or less) if you continue to use the program. Some shareware programs stop working a certain number of days after you've installed them if you haven't paid the registration fee, while others, sometimes called "nagware," continue to work but continually remind you that if you keep using it, you should pay the fee. In some cases, the shareware version of a program offers a more limited set of features, but paying the registration fee gives you access to additional features. *See also* Demoware, Freeware, and Open Source.

SIMM

An acronym for Single Inline Memory Module, a type of miniature circuit board with either a 72-pin or 30-pin connector that holds memory chips. Thirty-pin SIMMs are found only on older PCs, while 72-pin SIMMs are found on some more current machines. SIMMs can include several different types of DRAM, including FPM DRAM and EDO DRAM. 72-pin SIMMs use a 32-bit path to the computer's system bus, which means that if they're used on a computer that has a 64-bit path to memory, such as the Pentium and later processors, they need to be added to your system two at a time. *See also* DIMM, RIMM, and SODIMM.

Sleep

An operational state used on notebook computers and some desktops in which the computer appears to be off, but in fact is in a low-power state from which it can be "awoken" relatively quickly. In Sleep mode, the contents of a computer's memory is stored to the hard disk, and when you bring a machine out of Sleep mode, that information is read back into memory. Using Sleep mode enables you to conserve battery life on a notebook and provides the convenience of enabling you to quickly pick up where you left off on either a notebook or desktop. *See also* ACPI, APM, and Power Management.

Slot 1

A type of physical connector with 242 pins that's used to connect Pentium II and some Pentium III processors to a desktop computer's motherboard. Originally an Intel proprietary specification, Slot 1 is now used by some other companies as well and is sometimes referred to as "SECC." The similar but larger Slot 2 is used by some Pentium II and Pentium III Xeon processors found in servers. *See also* SECC.

Slot A

A type of physical connector used by AMD's K7 processor that is physically similar to, but not compatible with, Slot 1. *See also* Slot 1.

SmartMedia

A type of memory device used on digital cameras, PDAs, and other electronic devices that comes in a form that isn't much larger than a postage stamp. On digital cameras, it is essentially used as a form of digital film. SmartMedia can also be used with notebook computers through the use of a PC card adapter, which plugs into a standard PC card slot. *See also* CompactFlash, Digital Camera, and PC Card.

SMF

An acronym for Standard MIDI File, a type of file format used to store MIDI sequences. *See also* General MIDI, MIDI, and Sequencer.

SMTP

An acronym for Simple Mail Transfer Protocol, the mechanism commonly used by e-mail programs to send messages from your PC to your ISP's e-mail server. When setting up an e-mail account, many programs require you enter information about an SMTP server. *See also* IMAP4 and POP3.

Socket 7

A type of physical connector used to connect Pentium-class processors to desktop computer motherboards. The less common Socket 8 was used for the short-lived Pentium Pro processor. *See also* Pentium, Slot 1, and Slot A.

SODIMM

An acronym for Small Outline DIMM (Dual Inline Memory Module), a smaller 72-pin DIMM that's designed for use in notebook computers. Unlike traditional DIMMs, which offer a 64-bit connection to the system bus, SODIMMs use a slower 32-bit connection, making them more like SIMMs. *See also* DIMM, SIMM, and System Bus.

Sound Card

A component inside many PCs that's designed to generate and record audio signals. Sound cards include both the circuitry required to record and play back digital audio files as well as a synthesizer, which can be used to play back MIDI files. Different sound cards include different types of synthesizers, which support different methods of sound generation, or synthesis. The most common types are FM synthesis, wavetable synthesis, and sound modeling synthesis. On some computers that don't have sound cards, the digital audio and synthesis circuitry is built straight onto the computer's motherboard. *See also* Digital Audio, FM Synthesis, MIDI, Sound Modeling, Synthesizer, and Wavetable Synthesis.

Sound Modeling

A technique for generating sounds found on some sound cards that uses models, which are complex mathematical equations that describe the characteristics of different musical instruments. For example, a model of a trumpet may enable you to create the equivalent of a trumpet with a 20-foot long bell, by adjusting parameters of the model that pertain to the bell. Sound modeling attempts to combine the realistic emulations of acoustic instruments that wavetable synthesis offers, with the more expressive capabilities enabled by pure synthesis techniques, such as FM synthesis. *See also* FM Synthesis, Synthesizer, and Wavetable Synthesis.

Spam

A nickname given to unsolicited, and generally unwanted, e-mail messages. It's the electronic equivalent of junk mail.

Speculative Execution

A technique used by microprocessors in which they try to "guess" or speculate as to what operations the software programs running on them will need to have performed in the near future. By performing those calculations while they're waiting for additional instructions and/or data to arrive, the processor can work more efficiently. *See also* Microprocessor.

SPP

An acronym for Standard Parallel Port, the old parallel port standard that supports a maximum transfer rate of 300KBps and unidirectional communications. Many PCs offer an SPP mode for backwards compatibility with older peripherals. *See also* ECP, EPP, and Parallel Port.

SRAM

An acronym for Static RAM (Random Access Memory), a type of memory chip that can retain its contents without being refreshed. Because of this, SRAM can access and retrieve data more quickly than DRAM (Dynamic Random Access Memory), and it can maintain its contents with small trickle of power, such as from a battery. Unfortunately, it's much more expensive than DRAM, which is why it isn't used for all of a system's memory. The fast type of SRAM is commonly used for things such as L1 and L2 cache, which are very dependent on high performance. The low power SRAM is typically used in Flash Memory and for things such as handheld electronics devices that have to be turned on and off all the time. *See also* DRAM, Flash Memory, and L1/L2 Cache.

Startup Files

A group of files that an operating system needs in order to be able to boot, or start up, properly. Under DOS and early versions of Windows, startup files such as Config.sys and Autoexec.bat were also used to configure settings for your PC and applications, as well as automatically load certain types of software. If your computer is unable to boot properly, the problem probably has to do with one of your startup files. *See also* Autoexec.bat, Config.sys, Io.sys, System.ini, and Win.ini.

Storage

A generic term for devices that can serve as a long-term repository for data, such as hard drives and removable media drives.

Streaming Media

A type of real-time data, such as audio or video signals, that are sent, or streamed, across a network connection, typically the Internet. Streaming media, such as RealAudio, enables you to listen and/or watch large prerecorded audio and video files without having to first download the entire file. In addition, streaming media enables you to listen and/or watch live broadcasts on your PC. In order to use these files, you need to have software that understands these file formats. *See also* RealAudio.

Streaming SIMD

The name of 70 additional processor instructions first introduced with the Pentium III. Streaming SIMD (Single Instruction Multiple Data) Extension are often referred to as SSE, particularly focused on improving the processor's floating point performance and are designed to enable applications such as software decoding of MPEG-2 video, 3D graphics, and more. Like MMX (which also used SIMD) and 3DNow, however, Streaming SIMD Extensions are beneficial only to applications that specifically take advantage of them. While MMX uses SIMD techniques on integer data, Streaming SIMD uses SIMD techniques on floating point data. *See also* 3DNow, Floating Point, Instructions, Microprocessor MMX, and Pentium.

Subnotebook

A type of very small portable computer that, while larger than a handheld computer, is smaller and thinner than a traditional notebook. There are no hard and fast rules that distinguish a notebook from a subnotebook, although generally speaking, subnotebooks weigh less than four pounds and are around an inch thick. *See also* Notebook.

Subwoofer

A type of speaker that's designed to reproduce very low frequency audio signals, such as low bass rumbles. Many speaker systems designed for computers include two (or more) satellite speakers, which are like traditional stereo speakers, as well as a subwoofer. Unlike the satellites, whose placement affects how the speakers sound, subwoofers are not directional, which means it doesn't matter where in the room they are placed or in what direction they are pointed.

Surge Suppressor

A device that's designed to protect equipment plugged into it from surges of electrical power, such as can occur during a storm. Different surge protectors provide different levels of protection, but in all cases, once a surge protector has blocked a surge (or taken a "hit"), it must be replaced. Some devices, such as UPSes (Uninterruptible Power Supplies), include surge suppression as a feature. *See also* Line Conditioner and UPS.

SVGA

An acronym for Super VGA (Video Graphics Array), a standard video resolution for video cards and monitors that extends beyond the capabilities of the original VGA standard. In most cases, SVGA now refers to a resolution of 800 × 600 pixels. *See also* VGA and XGA.

S-Video

A shortened name for Super Video, a type of high-quality analog video signal that's separated into two components: luminance and chrominance. Luminance is basically the lightness and darkness portion of the signal, and chrominance is the color portion of the signal. Because of this separation, S-Video provides a better quality picture than traditional composite analog video signals, which combine the two into one. Composite signals are available from a video device's RCA jack, whereas S-Video signals can be transferred only via a special S-Video jack, which is a circular plug with five pins. *See also* Component Video and Composite Video.

Swap File

A type of temporary file used by operating systems and some applications to support virtual memory, which basically tricks your computer into thinking it has more memory than it actually does. Swap files serve as containers on your PC's hard disk for information that doesn't fit into RAM or is temporarily not needed. *See also* Virtual Memory.

Switch

With certain DOS-based applications, a type of command that enables you to run a program with specific settings. As a result, it's often referred to as a "DOS switch." Switches can be used only when programs are run from a command prompt, and they are separated from the main command or application with a forward slash, such as /s. For example, running the format program with the /s switch, which you do by typing **format /s**, means to run the format command (which is actually a tiny DOS application) and also copy basic system files to the disk being formatted. Some applications support the use of several switches. To find out which ones are available for a specific program, you can often type the program's name and then **/?**. In a networking environment, the term *switch* is short for *switching hub*, which is a device that offers a full-bandwidth connection to each computer or other device that is connected to it. In a 10Base-T hub, for example, all the devices connected to the hub share the 10Mb of available bandwidth, whereas with a switch, each device has a full 10Mb of dedicated bandwidth. *See also* Command Prompt and Hub.

Synchronization

The process of making two or more devices or signals work in unison, typically through the use of a shared clock or timing signal. In video editing, for example, it's important to make sure that audio and video signals are in sync.

Synthesizer

A device or integrated circuit that electronically generates, or synthesizes, sounds. Most computers include a synthesizer, either as part of a sound card or integrated into the system's motherboard. Different types of synthesizers use different techniques, or synthesis methods, for creating sounds, each of which results in different kinds of sounds. Popular synthesis techniques include FM Synthesis, Wavetable Synthesis, and Sound Modeling Synthesis. *See also* FM Synthesis, Sound Modeling, and Wavetable Synthesis.

System Bus

The main data highway around which a PC's internal structure is organized. Specifically, the system bus connects the microprocessor to memory (RAM) and to the main peripheral buses, such as PCI. The speed of a computer's system bus determines how quickly information can be transferred to and from the processor, as well as into and out of memory. Common system bus speeds are 66MHz, 100MHz, and 133MHz, although even slower and faster speeds are also possible. *See also* Bus, Microprocessor, PCI, and RAM.

System.ini

A startup initialization file for Windows that is used to store overall system settings and parameters. System.ini was required in early versions of Windows but is included in Windows 95 and later versions solely for backwards compatibility for those applications that may still need it. Most settings geared for INI files, including System.ini, are now stored in the Windows Registry. *See also* INI Files, Registry, Startup Files, and Win.ini.

T

Tag

In HTML (HyperText Markup Language) files, a short text command enclosed in arrow brackets (<>) used to define particular characteristics, or attributes, of a piece of text or section of the document. You can use the bold tag , for example, to signify that you want the subsequent piece of text in your HTML document to be in bold. Most all HTML tags require both a beginning and an ending, with the ending tag always including a forward slash (/) character in front of the command's name. So, for example, an ending tag for the bold attribute is . *See also* HTML and Metatag.

TB

An acronym for terabyte, which is approximately one trillion bytes, or 1,000 gigabytes. Technically speaking it is 2^{40} or 1,099,511,627,776 bytes. Terabytes are sometimes used as specifications for really large storage devices, signifying how much data the device can hold. *See also* Bit, Byte, Gb/GB, Kb/KB, and Mb/MB.

TCP/IP

An acronym for Transmission Control Protocol/Internet Protocol, the format, or language, used to send messages and data over the Internet. Technically speaking, TCP and IP are two separate protocols: TCP handles making connections between two computers and transmitting data, and IP breaks up data to be sent into individual packets. Together, TCP/IP forms a very robust protocol that may not always be the fastest way to get data from one point to another, but is very reliable and forgiving of problems that may occur on the network. *See also* Protocol.

Temp

A shortened name for Temporary, a generic name given to certain files or folders that are used to hold short-lived data. A temp folder, or directory, for example, is often used to hold files that are used during the installation of an application but then no longer required. Similarly, temp files are often created by applications while they are working on a particular document (sometimes as a backup of that document). In most cases, the contents of any temp folders and all temp files are supposed to be automatically deleted when the program that created them is done with them, such as when you quit the application. If the program or operating system crashes, however, sometimes the temp files remain. Generally speaking, you can get rid of most temp files you come across.

Terabyte

A unit of measurement for storage devices, memory, and files, expressed in terms of trillions of bits or bytes. Typically referred to as "TB." *See also* Bit, Byte, Kilobit/Kilobyte, Gigabit/Gigabyte, Megabit/Megabyte, and TB.

TFT

An acronym for Thin Film Transistor, a type of technology used on LCD panels in which each pixel on the screen has its own set of transistors that can be individually addressed. The result is a bright, crisp picture with excellent contrast and fast refresh rates (which is important for such things as playing back video files). TFT is also referred to as "Active Matrix." *See also* Active Matrix and LCD Panel.

Thread

A specific section, or branch, of software that is loaded and operating in your computer's memory. Most applications, when run, generate or "spawn" several independent threads, each of which performs a different function. The term also refers to a branch of a multipart online discussion, such as are found in newsgroups and other online bulletin boards. A multithreaded discussion is one that includes several different branches.

Throughput

A reference to how much data can be passed along a particular bus or network connection. Sometimes also referred to as "bandwidth." *See also* Bandwidth.

TIFF

An acronym for Tagged Image File Format, a standard bitmapped graphics file format that's commonly used by scanners. TIFF images, which are recognized by the extension .tif, are often uncompressed and therefore take up a large amount of space. *See also* Bitmapped Graphics and Scanner.

Topology

A fancy name for the layout of a network. The three main types of network topologies are a bus network, in which all the computers are connected in a line; a ring network, in which all the computers are connected in a circle; and a star network, in which all the computers connect through a central point. The most common type is the star network. *See also* Network.

Tower

A type of desktop computer system in which the case (and the motherboard inside it) stand upright. Mini-towers and micro-towers are smaller versions of the same basic design.

Track

A circular section of a hard drive or other storage device. On a hard drive, for example, each platter, or cylinder, is divided into many separate tracks. A track is analogous to a groove in a record. *See also* Sector.

Trackball

An input device that's basically equivalent to a mouse turned upside down. Instead of moving a mouse with a ball inside it around a tabletop, with a trackball you directly roll a ball to move your cursor around the screen. Trackballs are particularly handy mouse replacements when space is tight. *See also* Cursor and Mouse.

Trackpad

An input device, commonly found on notebook computers, that enables you to move the cursor by moving your finger across a small area of conductive material. The material tracks your finger's motion and essentially turns your finger into a mouse. Sometimes also called a *touchpad. See also* Cursor, Mouse, and Trackball.

TrueType Font

A standard font format supported in Windows and other operating systems that describes font outlines or shapes. As a result, TrueType enables type characters to be made bigger or smaller (sometimes referred to as *scaling up* or *scaling down*) yet still maintain smooth edges both onscreen and when printed. (This capability to maintain a high-quality image at multiple sizes is sometimes referred to as *resolution independence*.) *See also* Font and Type 1 Font.

TWAIN

An acronym for Technology Without An Interesting Name (really!), a standard interface for communicating between scanners (and other imaging devices, such as digital cameras) and applications, such as image-editing programs. Most scanners come with TWAIN-compliant software, which can be used to scan an image either on its own or from within another program as a plug-in. *See also* Plug-In and Scanners.

Type 1 Font

A standard font format, described in the PostScript printing language, that uses font outlines. As a result, like TrueType fonts, Type 1 fonts can be scaled up and down and yet still print smoothly. In order for this to work properly, however, you need a printer that supports PostScript and/or a piece of software that can do the font smoothing, both onscreen and while printing. The most well-known program for this purpose is Adobe Type Manager, or ATM. *See also* Font, PostScript, and TrueType.

U

UADSL

An acronym for Universal ADSL (Asymmetric Digital Subscriber Line), a type of DSL connection that trades off a bit of performance for ease of installation and compatibility. Sometimes also referred to as "ADSL Lite," UADSL typically supports a maximum download rate of 1.5Mbps and an upload rate of 384 Kbps. Unlike true ADSL, which offers even higher data transfer rates, UADSL doesn't require the installation of a splitter, which is a hardware device that separates the voice and data calls that can be shared on a single copper phone line when using DSL. As a result, it's said to be "splitter-less." UADSL connections typically require modems that conform to the G.Lite standard. *See also* ADSL, DSL, and G.Lite.

UDP

An acronym for User Datagram Protocol, a method for transmitting data over a network connection that doesn't require an acknowledgment from the receiving end. UDP and other similar "connection-less" standards, including RTP (Real-Time Transport Protocol) and RTSP (Real Time Streaming Protocol), are often used in place of TCP over the Internet for applications, such as streaming media, where it's more important to send a continuous stream of data than to know whether or not each packet of IP data was received. TCP, on the other hand, has stringent requirements about making sure that each packet is received and acknowledged, which is why it is a robust, reliable protocol but not suited for real-time delivery. *See also* Protocol, Streaming Media, and TCP/IP.

UMB

An acronym for Upper Memory Block, an area of memory used by DOS to store drivers and other types of software. There are six UMBs, and each of them are 64K in size. With the use of an expanded memory manager utility, such as EMM386, you can convert a UMB into a window through which you can access expanded memory. Under Windows, UMBs are considered a resource and can be managed through the Device Manager. *See also* DOS, Expanded Memory, and Upper Memory.

UNC

An acronym for Universal Naming Convention, a standard way of naming computers or peripherals on a LAN (Local Area Network). You use UNC names to connect to other PCs on the network. To map a network drive to a drive letter on your system, for example, you can use the computer's UNC name, which comes in the form *//computer name/resource name*. The resource name can be a directory and file name or the name of a printer or other peripheral that can be shared over the network. *See also* Directory and Mapping.

UNIX

A multiuser operating system originally developed by Bell Laboratories that's based around the notion of user accounts, where the same computer may be used by multiple people. UNIX was originally designed for networked workstations that were used by engineers, and its interface and architecture often reflects that technical heritage. There are many varieties of UNIX, but the most popular type for PCs is Linux. *See also* Linux and Operating System.

Upgrade

A more recent and (hopefully) improved version of an application or other piece of software. Some upgrades are made available for free, while those that add many new features cost money. The term also refers to the process of installing these new versions.

Upper Memory

Under DOS, a 384K area of memory that exists between the 640K ceiling of conventional memory and the 1MB, or 1,024K, limit of DOS. Upper memory, which is divided into six Upper Memory Blocks (UMBs) of 64K each, is typically used to hold things such as DOS drivers, TSR (Terminate and Stay Resident) programs, and the video card BIOS; it is not typically available to applications. However, you can also use upper memory as a means to get access to expanded memory through an expanded memory manager program. *See also* Conventional Memory, DOS, and Expanded Memory.

UPS

An acronym for Uninterruptible Power Supply, a device that includes a backup battery that keeps any equipment plugged into it powered, even in the event of a power loss, or blackout. Different UPSes include different-sized batteries, which enable them to keep power supplied to plugged-in devices for various amounts of time. Some UPSes also include other power-related features, such as surge suppression and line conditioning, but not all do. *See also* Line Conditioner and Surge Suppressor.

URL

An acronym for Universal Resource Locator, the format used for finding Web sites and other types of data on the Internet. A typical URL, such as `http://www.everythingcomputers.com`, includes the type of Internet protocol used to access the resource at the beginning of the URL (`http://`, in this case), as well as the address of the resource itself (`www.everythingcomputers.com`, in this example). URLs are also sometimes referred to as *Web addresses. See also* Domain Name and HTTP.

USB

An acronym for Universal Serial Bus, a high-speed serial port connection that supports data transfer rates of up to 12Mbps in its original incarnation. Version 2.0 of the USB specification support speeds of up to 240Mbps. USB supports up to 127 devices and can provide power to certain types of low-power peripherals. In addition, USB supports hot swapping, which enables you to connect and disconnect devices while your PC is turned on and have your system automatically compensate for that, such as by installing a driver. USB does not, however, support daisy-chaining. Instead each device has to be connected to a separate connector or port on a USB hub or other device that integrates a USB hub, such as a monitor. Most PCs now feature USB support on the motherboard, but it's also possible to add a USB controller via a plug-in card. USB is also used in the Device Bay standard. *See also* Device Bay, Hot Plugging, IEEE 1394, and Serial.

Uuencode

A technique for converting binary files into a text-only format so that they can be sent over the Internet. Some e-mail systems cannot (or do not) enable binary files to be passed through them, so uuencoding was developed to enable binary files to look like ASCII text files. To make them usable again, these files have to be decoded on the receiving end. Oftentimes uuencoding and decoding is done in such a way that's completely transparent to the two parties sending and receiving the file. In other words, they never even know it happens because the encoding process occurs on a mail server after the message is sent and the decoding process occurs on the receiving party's e-mail server before it's received. Some e-mail client programs, however, enable you to specifically turn uuencoding on so that the e-mail package takes care of converting any attached binary files. In some cases, files that are uuencoded are not automatically decoded, which results in receiving an e-mail message that appears to contain a bunch of odd-looking text. Sometimes you can salvage the file by selecting the text and running it through a uudecoding utility. Unlike file compression techniques, uuencoding often makes a file larger (because binary is often a more efficient means of storing data than a text format). *See also* ASCII, Binary Files, Decoding, Encoding, and MIME.

V

V.34

The name of an analog modem standard supported by the ITU (International Telecommunications Union) that supports transfer rates of up to 33.6Kbps. With V.34, both uploading and downloading occur at the same rate. *See also* V.90.

V.90

The name of an analog modem standard supported by the ITU (International Telecommunications Union) that supports transfer rates of up to 56Kbps. Because of the limitations of most phone lines, however, the real maximum rate is 53Kbps. The uploading and downloading rates for V.90 are different from those of V.34. V.90 supports a maximum download rate of 56 Kbps and an upload rate of 33Kbps. V.90 is the culmination of a compromise between two older, incompatible 56K modem standards: X2 and K56Flex. Older modems that support one of these two standards can typically be upgraded to V.90. *See also* V.34.

Vector Graphics

A family of graphics formats, typically used with illustrations and line drawings, in which the elements of the image are defined by a series of lines, or vectors. This is in contrast to bitmapped graphics, where the image is made of numerous independent dots, or pixels, of different colors. Programs that generate vector graphics are generally referred to as *drawing programs*, whereas bitmapped graphics are created by paint programs. One of the benefits of vector graphics is that drawings made in this type of format can be resized without distorting the image and print at whatever resolution(s) an attached printer supports. Popular graphics formats that are based on vector graphics include CGM (Computer Graphics Metafile) and EPS (Encapsulated PostScript). *See also* Bitmapped Graphics.

VGA

An acronym for Video Graphics Array, a video signal output standard devised by VESA (Video Electronics Standards Association) that, technically speaking, supports a resolution of 640 × 480 pixels with 16 colors. Nowadays, however, it's typically understood to mean a monitor resolution of 640 × 480 pixels at any color depth (in other words, with any amount of colors). VGA is considered the baseline default standard for PCs, and some people still prefer to design documents designed to be viewed onscreen, such as Web pages, to the VGA screen. (Personally, I think the 800 × 600 resolution of SVGA is a safe choice.) Common extensions to the VGA standard include SVGA and XGA. The acronym "VGA" is also used to refer to the standard 15-pin port found on video cards that provides an analog video connection to traditional CRTs and analog flat panel monitors. *See also* DFP, LDI, P&D, SVGA, and XGA.

Video Capture

The process of converting an analog video signal into digital form and storing the result on a computer's hard drive or other storage device. *See also* Digitizing and Frame Grabber.

Video Card

A critical component inside a computer that generates a visible image that can be displayed on a computer's monitor. A typical video card includes chips that accelerate the display of 2D and 3D graphics, and TV-style video signals, as well as dedicated memory, called a *frame buffer*, that's used to store the image before it's sent to the monitor. The amount of memory on the card, which, like a computer's main memory, comes in many varieties, determines the resolutions and color depths that the card is capable of supporting. For example, a card with 4MB of memory can display 24-bit color at a resolution of 1,280 × 1,024 pixels, or 16-bit color at a resolution of 1,600 × 1,200 pixels. Video memory is also used to store such things as textures for complex graphics in computer games. Most newer video cards connect to a computer via the AGP (Advanced Graphics Port) slot, although some still use the PCI (Peripheral Component Interconnect) bus. Some computer systems don't include a separate video card at all, but instead incorporate the graphics acceleration chips and frame buffer onto the motherboard. *See also* Acceleration, AGP, and PCI.

Videoconferencing

A communications link that incorporates both audio and video signals — in other words, a video phone call. Videoconferencing can be done on a point-to-point basis but is now more commonly done over a network connection, such as the Internet. Many videoconferencing products comply with H.323 or H.324 standards. *See also* H.323/H.324.

Virtual Channel Memory (VCM)

A type of memory technology that basically adds the equivalent of a small amount of cache memory to a typical RAM (Random Access Memory) chip. One of the main problems with most types of memory, including SDRAM

(Synchronous DRAM) and RDRAM (Rambus DRAM), is that getting the first bit of data is always slower than getting subsequent bits. VCM attempts to address this limitation by providing a small amount of cache, or buffer memory, that stores recently requested data on a standard DRAM (Dynamic Random Access Memory) chip so that the initial chunk of memory can be retrieved quickly. This, in turn, speeds the overall performance of the memory subsystem, which makes the entire computer run faster. VCM can be used in conjunction with other types of DRAM, such as SDRAM and RDRAM. *See also* Cache, DRAM, RDRAM, and SDRAM.

Virtual Memory

A technology that essentially fools your computer into thinking it has more memory, or working area, than it actually does. The way virtual memory works is that your PC's operating system creates a swap file on your hard disk and when it fills up all the available physical RAM, it starts moving parts of the software and data currently loaded in memory into the swap file (a process called *paging*), thereby freeing room in traditional memory. Applications that are loaded into memory never know that they're being moved out of "real" memory. They just think the computer has more memory than it really does, which is why it's called "virtual" memory. The only drawback to virtual memory is that it is much slower than real memory because data has to be written to and read from the hard disk, which is several orders of magnitude slower than accessing data that's in memory. In fact, if your system has to use virtual memory too often, then your hard disk will be constantly paging data to and from the hard disk, which slows it down. This is why it's important to have enough memory. *See also* Swap File.

Virus

A destructive type of software that is designed to intentionally destroy data, or otherwise cause problems with your system. Like a regular virus, a computer virus can infect your system by coming into contact with it, such as by inserting a disk that's been infected, running a program that's been infected, or opening a file that's been infected. There are many different types of viruses, some of which are visible programs that cause problems, and others of which are hidden inside files or programs. A Trojan Horse is a type of virus that, like the infamous gift after which the category is named, hides something bad inside something that appears good (or at least innocuous). Two of the most common types of viruses are macro viruses which are hidden inside word processing and spreadsheet documents, and boot sector viruses, which damage or overwrite your hard drive's master boot record (MBR), thereby preventing your computer from booting. The only way to get rid of viruses is to run an up-to-date anti-virus program. *See also* Master Boot Record.

VL-Bus

An acronym for VESA (Video Electronics Standards Association) Local Bus, a now obsolete bus that provided a dedicated, high-speed (at the time) connection between the video card and the system bus. In many ways, the AGP standard is similar to an updated version of VL-Bus. *See also* AGP.

Voice Recognition

A software technology that enables you to speak into a microphone attached to your computer and have the computer understand what you say and respond to your words. Early voice recognition products, sometimes also called *speech recognition*, offered command and control features, which meant you could tell your computer to perform certain actions (such as launching a program) instead of using your mouse to achieve the same end. Most voice recognition products now also offer dictation, where the program translates your spoken words into typed text on the screen. The most popular type of voice recognition is called *continuous speech recognition*, because it enables you to speak in a normal, continuous manner. Early systems used discrete speech recognition, which forced you to speak one word at a time in an awkward, halting fashion.

Volume

Another name for a hard disk partition that is formatted and usable within the operating system you are running. *See also* Partition.

VRAM

An acronym for Video RAM (Random Access Memory), a special type of memory that's commonly used on video cards. Unlike traditional DRAM, most VRAM is dual-ported, which means that information can be going in one way at the same time that other data is leaving through a different "exit." This type of structure is well suited to a video card, which has to rapidly update the contents of its frame buffer, which is where the image headed for the monitor is temporarily stored. *See also* SGRAM.

VxD

An acronym for Virtual Device Driver or Virtualization Driver, a generic term for various types of 32-bit Windows drivers that use the .vxd file extension. (Under Windows 3.1, these type of files used the .386 extension.) The "virtual" part of the name means that the driver enables multiple programs to access the device at once. Each program can connect to its own "virtual" version of the device. The "x" in the name is generally replaced with another letter that refers to what type of device it is, so that, for example, a VPD is a virtual printer driver, and so on. *See also* Driver.

WAN

An acronym for Wide Area Network, a type of network that typically extends beyond a single building, and often across the country, or even the world. *See also* LAN.

WAV

A standard type of digital audio format, primarily used under Windows, that uses the file extension .wav. Wav(e) files can be 8- or 16-bit format, mono or stereo, at one of several different sampling rates. *See also* Digital Audio and Sampling.

Waveform

A visual representation of signal, typically an audio signal. Programs that permit waveform editing enable you to edit digital audio by looking at and manipulating the sound's waveform. *See also* Digital Audio.

Wavetable Synthesis

A technique for generating sounds, found on some sound cards, that uses short samples, or wavetables, of real acoustic instruments. Wavetable synthesizers and sound cards typically include a certain amount of samples in a sound ROM, and some even include RAM where you can load your own samples, such as through the DLS (DownLoadable Samples) standard. They generate sounds by playing back the wavetables, which are typically short recordings of individual notes, and slightly speeding up or slowing down the playback rate to adjust the sound's pitch. Wavetable synthesizers are known, in general, for their realistic emulations of traditional instruments, but the quality of different versions varies according to the quality of the sampled sounds stored in ROM. *See also* DLS, FM Synthesis, ROM, Sound Modeling, and Synthesizer.

Web site

Traditionally, a collection of HTML (HyperText Markup Language) documents that are available at a particular Web address or URL (Universal Resource Locator). Many current Web sites have much more sophisticated mechanisms for generating pages than simple HTML. *See also* HTML, URL, and World Wide Web.

Win.ini

A startup initialization file for Windows that is used to store configuration information for the operating system and some Windows applications. Win.ini was required in early versions of Windows but is included in Windows 95 and later versions solely for backwards compatibility for those applications that may still need it. Most settings geared for INI files, including Win.ini, are now stored in the Windows Registry. *See also* INI Files, Registry, Startup Files, and System.ini.

Windows

A family of operating systems, produced by Microsoft, that are the most popular and widely supported ones available for PCs. Windows can be found in many different guises, ranging from the older Windows 3.0 and 3.11 (also called Windows for Workgroups), up through Windows NT, Windows 95, Windows 98, and Windows 2000. There's also always a Windows CE available for handheld computers and other electronic devices. Each version of Windows has important differences with the others, but all the current versions share a similar interface, which makes it relatively easy to move from using one type to another.

WINS

An acronym for Windows Internet Naming Service, a technique for converting IP addresses into specific computer names on a Windows-based LAN or Intranet that is running TCP/IP. WINS is essentially like a version of DNS (Domain Name System) that's ideally suited for business LANs. *See also* DNS, Intranet, and IP Address.

Wizard

A step-by-step process in which you complete a particular task or function. Wizards are commonly used in Microsoft's operating systems and many Windows-based applications. In virtually all cases, you can get the same task done without using the wizard, but the wizard process makes it easier (and can help teach you what's involved).

Workstation

A type of computer system that's typically equipped with powerful components and is often used for engineering applications. In the early days of computers, workstations were often a clearly defined category versus regular PCs, but that distinction has gotten blurry over time. The word is also sometimes used to signify a single computer connected to a network. *See also* Client-Server.

World Wide Web (WWW)

Networked computers that hold collections of HTML (HyperText Markup Language) documents known as Web sites. Though it's commonly interchanged with the Internet as a whole, the World Wide Web — or just the Web, as it is typically known — is actually only a segment of the Internet (albeit the biggest, most well-known one). *See also* Internet, HTML, and Web Site.

WYSIWYG

An acronym for What You See Is What You Get, a means of describing a program or feature in which the visual display on screen approximately matches what you see when you print the file.

X

X Bus

A portion of the ISA bus that's connected to the floppy drive, keyboard port, system clock, and other stalwart old parts of the PC architecture. The X-bus items on some systems are starting to be moved to a new interface called "LPC" (Low Pin Count) and are expected to eventually be connected directly to the PCI bus. *See also* LPC and PCI.

X86

A shortened name for x86-compatibles, or microprocessors that are compatible with Intel's family of processors that began with the 8086 and continues up through the numerous iterations of Pentiums. X86 is often used to refer to processors that are capable of running software that is written for the PC platform. *See also* 8086.

XML

An acronym for Extensible Markup Language, a sophisticated text-based file format that extends beyond HTML in several important ways. Like HTML, XML uses tags, but XML enables you to create your own tags for your own purposes. In addition, with XML you can assign not only visual attributes to tags, but also object attributes, so that you can interact with the data. With XML, you can essentially turn Web pages into interactive applications. *See also* HTML and Tags.

XMS

An acronym for Extended Memory Specification, a technique for accessing memory above the 1MB limit of DOS. XMS is available only on the 80286 and later processors and is made available through the use of the Himem.sys driver in the Config.sys file. (Windows 95 and 98 automatically load Himem.sys.) XMS differs from EMS in that the computer isn't fooled into thinking that the extra memory is within the 1MB limit of DOS. *See also* Conventional Memory, EMS, Expanded Memory, Extended Memory, and Real Mode.

XGA

An acronym for Extended Graphics Array, an extension to the VGA standard that technically includes support for many resolutions but is commonly used to signify a resolution of 1,024 × 768 pixels. SXGA, or Super XGA, extends that to a resolution of 1,280 × 1,024 pixels, and UXGA, or Ultra XGA, signifies a resolution of 1,600 × 1,200 pixels. *See also* SVGA and VGA.

Y

Y2K

A reference to the Year 2000 problem, in which computer hardware and/or software may not recognize the date properly, and may stop functioning or may function erratically. On most PCs, Y2K will probably have little or no impact, but it's still worthwhile to check that your computer's BIOS, operating system, and applications are updated to be Y2K-compliant or Y2K-compatiable. *See also* BIOS.

Z

Z-Buffer

A dedicated amount of memory used by video cards that support 3D graphics acceleration in which the depth, or z, coordinates for each object in a 3D scene are stored. By setting aside this memory, which typically comes from the video card's frame buffer, the card can keep track of what objects should be in front of or behind one another so that the scene is created properly. *See also* Frame Buffer.

Zip

A common type of removable storage device made by Iomega. Zip disks are roughly similar in size to, but incompatible with, normal floppy disks. The term *Zip* also refers to a common compressed file format that uses the extension .zip.

Zoomed Video

A bus found on notebook computers with PC card slots that enables video peripherals, such as video capture cards, to send data directly to the computer's video card. Sometimes also referred to as the "ZV Port." *See also* CardBus and PC Card.

Index

Symbols & Numbers

100Base-T, 815
10Base-2, 447, 815
10Base-5, 447
10Base-T, 815
16-bit data, 815
24-bit data, 815
32-bit data, 815
3D audio, 168-169, 176
   head-related transfer functions (HRTFs), 168
   speaker support, 176
3D mouse, 236
3D speakers, 176
3DNow, 54, 816
56K, 816
56K modems, 181-184, 193
64-bit, 816
8-bit, 816
80286, 816
80386, 816
80486, 817
8086, 816
8088, 816

A

accelerated graphics port (AGP), 126, 131-132
accelerated graphics port (AGP) bus, 64, 266-268, 818-819
accelerator, 817
access time, 83, 87-89, 111, 817
   CD-ROM drives, 111
   DVD-ROM drives, 111
active matrix, 817

active matrix screen, 150-151
ActiveX, 526-528, 529, 530, 531-532, 533-534, 818
actuator, 89
adapter, 818
ADC, 818
additional call option (ACO), 190
address bus, 262
ADSL, 818
advanced configuration and power interface (ACPI), 244, 817
advanced power management (APM), 244, 820
AGP. *See* accelerated graphics port (AGP).
AGP bus. *See* accelerated graphics port (AGP) bus.
agreements, license, 905-907
AIFF, 819
algorithm, 819
all-in-one unit, 30
alpha channel, 123, 819
analog modem, 181-187
   voice-enabled, 184-186
analog signal, 819
anti-aliasing, 819
anti-virus application, 528-529
AO/DI, 820
API, 820
applet, 526
AppleTalk, 448
application, 5, 258, 302-305, 590-592, 820
   launching procedure, 302-303
   launching process, 258
   software layers, 281-282
   upgrading, 323-326
   virtual memory in, 302
   Web-based, 525-536

application sharing, 568-570
architecture, 52-56
areal density. *See* density.
ARPAnet, 504
articles, newsgroup, 558
ASCII, 820
AT commands, 820
ATA, 820
ATA standard, 97-98
ATA-2 standard, 97-98
ATAPI, 821
attachment, 821
ATX, 821
audio archives, 661
audio decoding, 169
   Dolby Digital, 169
   for DVD, 169
audio extraction, 170, 662
audio interference, 149
audio mixer, 169-171
audio outputs, 169-171
   digital, 170-171
   mixer function, 169-170
   multiple, 170
   using S/PDIF, 171
audio problems, 786-788
audio processing, 3D, 167-169
audio remixing, 669-670
autoexec.bat, 296-297, 760-761, 799-801, 821
automatic private IP addressing, 468-469
automatic skip driver agent (ASD), 741, 749

B

backbones, 510
backside bus, 51
backwards compatibility, 821
bad sectors, 774
bandwidth, 263, 264, 660-661, 821
basic input/output system (BIOS), 57, 66, 84-85, 286-287, 411, 756, 823
   in booting process, 288-289

CMOS, 289
   settings, 411
   setup, 211, 288-289, 411, 434, 757-759, 788
   upgrading, 420-423, 430
BAT file, 822
batteries, 243
   uninterruptible power supply (UPS), 247
benchmark, 67, 822
BeOS, 822
beta, 822
bicubic resizing, 638
bidirectional communications, 210-211, 212
binary file, 822
binary math, 822-823
binding, 463-464, 823
BIOS. *See* basic input/output system (BIOS).
BIOS Setup program, 211, 411, 434, 788
bit, 7, 823
bit depth. *See* color depth.
bit width, 128-130
bitmapped graphics, 823
BMP, 823
BNC, 824
bookmark, 524-525, 824
Boolean logic, 540
boot, 824
boot disk, 725-730
boot drive, 415
boot files, 759-760
boot loader, 332, 756, 824
boot settings, adjusting, 729-730
boot viruses, 290
   master boot record, 289-290, 756
booting, 288-297. *See also* startup problems.
   BIOS setup, 288-289
   BIOS software, 288
   DOS memory problems, 294-296
   involving partitions, 290
   master boot record, 289-290, 756
   Power-On Self Test (POST), 288

startup files, 292-297
bootlog.txt, 761
bridge, 473
bridge chips. *See* chipset.
brownout, 246
browser. *See* Web browser.
bugs, 723-724, 824
bus master, 825
bus mastering, 94-95
bus network, 445
bus speed, 263, 264-265, 274
buses, 62-64, 261-263, 824
   AGP, 267-268
   bandwidth, 263, 264
   chipset, 261-262
   connection system, 262
   I/O, 269-271
   ISA, 266
   as logical construct, 263
   PCI, 262, 267
   peripheral, 266-274
   speed, 263, 264-265, 274
   system, 261-262
   Universal Serial Bus (USB), 269-270
byte, 7, 825

C

cable modem, 190-191, 825
   DOCSIS standard, 190
   Ethernet card, 190
   potential problems, 191
cables, 409-410, 457-459
   network, 457-459
cache, 48-52, 89-90, 536-539, 825
   buffer, 89-90
   hard drive, 89-90
   L1, 49-51
   L2, 49-52
   Web browser, 536-539
cache, hit, 49
cache miss, 49
CAD. *See* computer aided design.

cardBus, 825
cascading style sheets (CSS), 574
case, 400-404
   installing, 401-404
   opening, 400-401
Cat5, 825
cathode ray tubes (CRTs), 144, 830
CCD, 826
CD-R, 826. *See* recordable CD drive.
CD-ROM, 107-108, 826
CD-ROM drive, 20, 107-112, 418-420
   access time, 111
   adding or upgrading, 418-420
   physical connections, 111-112
   rotation speed, 108-110
   variable speed, 109-110
CD-ROM driver, 725-730
CD-RW. *See* recordable CD drive.
Celeron, 51-52, 826
Celeron A, 51-52
central processing unit (CPU). *See*
   microprocessor.
certificates, 826-827
chat. *See* live chat.
chip, 827
chipset, 64, 261-262
CISC, 55-56, 827
client, 450, 460-461, 827
client-server, 827
clipping, 666
cluster, 827
CMOS (complementary metal oxide
   semiconductor), 289, 827. *See also*
   basic input/output system (BIOS).
CMOS battery, 422-423
CMYK, 828
codec, 828
color depth, 124-126, 218
   resolution and, 125-126
color management, 828
color printing, 204-207
   color management, 205-206, 828
   dithering, 206

continued

color printing (*continued*)
  halftone process, 206
  options, 205
  process, 204-205
color profiles, 644-645
COM, 828
command prompt, 828
CompactFlash, 828
component video, 828-829
composite video, 829
compression, 776, 829
  hard drives, 776
computer, 3-42, 397-435
  activities, 5
  basic concept, 253-254, 273-274
  basic operation, 10-11
  buying, 3-42
  components, 11-14
  CPU (central processing unit), 256
  data, 256-257
  display subsystem, 121-154
  form factor, 27-30
  general operation process, 257-260
  hardware, 260-281
  hardware/software relationship, 254-255
  operating principles, 253-260
  operating system (OS), 254-255
  purchase planning and research, 36-37,
    37-38, 39-41
  refurbished PCs, 41-42
  resources, 275-281
  service, 41
  specifications, 19-21, 22-26
  subsystems, 14-18
  system cost, 26
  system type, 38-39
  typical I/O paths, 256
  upgrading, 397-435
computer aided design, 134
computer games. *See* games.
computer peripherals, 195-196, 874
consumables, in printing, 201-203
conference, 568-569

config.sys, 760-761, 799-801, 829
connection
  speeds, 363
  troubleshooting, 703-704
  video, 648-650
connection utilities, 539-540
connectoid, 511
connector, 362-364
continuous tone, 829
  imaging, 198-199
control bus, 262
controller, 93-104, 268-271, 362, 367, 829
  as drive interface, 268-269
  and I/O buses, 269-271
  types of, 96
conventional memory, 830
conventions, used in this book, xi
cookies, 830
copyrights, 905-907
core OS components, 286
CPU. *See* microprocessor.
crash, 794, 830
creative computer work, 34
cursor, 830-831

D

data bus, 262
data input and output (I/O), 255-257
daughtercard, 831
DB25, 831
DB9, 831
DCC. *See* Direct Cable Connection (DCC).
DDR DRAM, 75
DDR SDRAM, 831
decoder, 831
decoding, e-mail, 803-804
decompiling, 905
demoware, 831
density, 90-91
desktop, 27-28, 30, 831
Device Bay, 92-93, 362, 377-378, 832
device driver. *See* driver.

Device Manager, 275, 385-386, 388-389, 390, 700, 706, 707-708
DFP, 832
DHCP, 832
DHCP server, 513
diagnostic programs, 730
dial-up connection, 513-517
dial-up network problems, 783-793
dial-up server, 497-498
dialog box, 832
digital audio, 158-163, 655-694
   versus analog, 666
   digitizing process, 159
   editing, 666
   equipment, 656
   file formats, 660-662
   hooking up, 664-665
   MIDI and, 158, 659-662
   normalizing files, 667-668
   recording, 664-668
   sampling rates, 159-161
   special effects, using, 668-669
digital audio format, 832
digital camera, 196, 215-216, 222-226, 832
   benefits, 222-223
   camera issues, 226
   compression, 224-225
   features, 223
   pixels per image, 223-224
   printer connections, 215-216
   related digital imaging devices, 226-228
   resolution, 223-224
   selection recommendations, 228
   storage media, 225-226
digital data, 7-8
digital ID, 555-556
digital image storage, 225-226
digital pictures, 624-647
   cleaning, 640-641
   cropping and resizing, 637-638
   editing, 635-637, 638-642
   file formats, 625-626
   printing, 643-645

   resolution, 631-635
   scanning, 629-638
   sharpening, 638-639
   sources, 626-628
   special effects, 642-643
   using in other programs, 645
   using on the Web, 646-647
digital processing, 832
digital subscriber line (DSL) technology, 191-193, 835
digital versatile disc (DVD), 122, 836
digital video, 140-142, 836
digital-to-analog converter (DAC), 167, 831
digitizing, 832-833
DIMM, 68-72, 399-400, 401, 833
   installing, 404
DIP switch, 833
direct cable connection (DCC), 458-459
direct memory access (DMA), 97, 711, 834
   channels, 276-277
directory, 833
directory services, 546-548
DirectX services, 284-285
disk defragmenter, 743-744, 749
disk recovery, 612-613
display data channel (DDC), 147-148, 153, 831
   Plug and Play support, 147-148
display subsystem, 121-154
   monitor, 144-154
   video card, 121-144
distribution, 833
dithering, 833
DLL, 321-322, 719-720, 723, 833
DLS, 834
DNS. *See* domain name server (DNS)
DOCSIS, 834
document, 834 *See also* file.
Dolby Digital, 169
domain name, 834. *See also* Web address.
domain name server (DNS), 467, 507-508, 834

DOS, 834-835
  conventional memory, 294
  DOS/Windows memory map, 294
  expanded memory (EMS), 295
  extended memory (XMS), 294, 295
  himem.sys requirement, 295
  management with Emm386.exe, 295
  memory, 294-296
  problems, 796-797
  upper memory blocks (UMB), 294
dot pitch, 835
dots per inch (dpi), 199-200, 835
downloading, 835
downloading/uploading transfer rate, 179
Dr. Watson, 736-739, 749, 794
DRAM, 71-76, 835
drive bays, 408
drive interfaces, 268-269
  controller, 268-271
drive letter problems, 775-776
drive mapping, 483-485
drive sharing, 482-485
drive speed, 87
driver, 286-287, 384-393, 419, 706-711,
    797-801, 835
  DOS, 797-801
  extending BIOS, 286-287
  installing, 384-385, 419-420, 709-710
  real-mode, 710-711
  removing, 389-393
  troubleshooting, 706-711
  updating, 709-710
  upgrading, 385-389
dropping out, 661
DSL, 835
DSL modems, 191-193
  universal ADSL, 192
DSTN, 836
DSVD, 836
dual boot, 836
dual scan, 836
dual-ported memory, 128
duplex systems, 836
DV. *See* digital video.

DVD. *See* digital versatile disc (DVD).
DVD-ROM, 107-108, 419, 837
DVD-ROM drive, 20, 107-112, 418-420
  access time, 111
  adding or upgrading, 418-420
  physical connections, 111-112
  rotation speed, 108-111
  variable speed, 109-110
DVD-ROM driver, 725-730
dye sublimation printing, 198-199, 837
  continuous tone images, 198-199
dynamic link libraries (DLLs), 285
dynamic RAM. *See* DRAM
dynamics processing, 668

E

E-IDE, 838
e-mail, 541-556, 838
  account editing, 543-546
  account establishment, 541-543
  attachments, 552-555
  decoding file attachments, 803-804
  finding addresses, 546-548
  message formats, 802-803
  message types, 548-551
  problems, 802-804
  security, 555-556
  signature, 551-552
ECC, 78, 837
ECC memory, 405
ECP, 838
editing, online versus offline, 649-650
editor/librarian, 838
EDO, 838
EDO RAM, 74
EIDE, 95, 97
EISA, 838
electronic document format, 609-610
EMF, 838
EMS, 838-839
encoder, 839
encoding, 553-555

encryption, 555-556, 839
end-user license agreement, 905-907
enhanced resolution, 218
enumeration, 839
EPP, 839
EPROM, 839
equalization, 667
ergonomic keyboard, 234-235
error correction, 77-78, 839
Ethernet, 446, 447, 448, 456, 458, 840
   adapters, 456
   cable, 458
   connections, 447
Ethernet card, 192
Ethernet network card, 190
executable file, 840
expandability, 32-33
expanded memory, 840
expansion card, installing, 380-383
expansion card upgrades, 32
exporting, 840
Ext2, 840
extended data out RAM. *See* EDO RAM.
extended memory, 840-841
extension, 592-594, 840

F

FAQ, 841
fast page mode RAM. *See* FPM RAM.
FAT, 85-87, 330, 413, 483, 841
favorite. *See* bookmark.
FDISK, 841
file, 478-481, 841
   backing up, 612-615
   changing associations, 596-598
   compressed, 317-319, 617-618
   converting, 606-608
   corruption, 722-723
   creating, 598-602
   finding, 316-317
   format, 660-662, 841
   managing, 611-621

   moving, 617
   opening, 602-604
   opening with other applications,
     604-608
   restoring/reinstalling, 767-768
   security, 481
   sharing, 478-481, 608-609
   standardization, 591-592
   templates, 600-602
   turning off, 762-766
   types, 594-598
file allocation table. *See* FAT.
final mix downs, 680-682
firewall, 842
FireWire, 842
firmware, 424-425
flames, 562
flash BIOS, 421-422
flash memory, 842
FlashPix, 626, 842
FlashPix CD, 627, 628
flat panel, 842
flat-panel monitors, 145, 146, 147, 152-153.
     See also liquid crystal display
     (LCD).
   connection methods, 152-153
flat-panel speakers, 176
flight simulator games, 240
floating point calculations, 842
floppy drive, 105, 107, 842
flopticals, 107
FM synthesis, 163-164, 843
font, 610, 652, 843
force feedback, 843
form factor, 843
format, 843
FPM, 843
FPM RAM, 73-74
FPS, 843
fragmentation, 844
frame buffer, 121, 126, 128, 844
frame grabber, 227, 844
freeware, 312-313, 844
frequency, 844

FTP (File Transfer Protocol), 504, 582-583, 845

G

G.Lite, 845
game controllers, 239-240
  accessories, 240
  head-mounted displays, 240
  pad, 240
gamepad, 240
games, 135, 491-492, 797-801
  DOS, 797-801
  and entertainment, 35
  multiplayer, 491-492
gamma, 845
gateway, 473, 845
Gb/GB, 845
Gbps/GBps, 845
GDI, 846
general MIDI, 846
  standard, 162-163
GHz, 846
GIF, 626, 646, 846
gigabit/gigabyte, 846
gigabyte, 9, 82
Gopher, 504
government-restricted rights, 907
graphic tablets, 238-239, 846
graphics, 652
grayscale imaging, 846
grounding strap, 379
GUI, 846-847

H

H.323/H.324, 847
halftone usage, 847
halftoning, 199
handwriting recognition, 847
hard disk. *See* hard drive.
hard disk controller. *See* controller.
hard drive, 10, 82-104, 406-418, 847
  adding, 406-418
  adjustments, 758
  care, 618-620
  configuring settings, 407
  connections, 83-84, 407-411
  copying Windows CD files, 337-338
  defragmenting, 620
  dimensions, 91-92
  freeing up space, 615-617
  interfaces, 93-104
  operation, 82-83
  partitions, 84, 290-292, 413-414
  preparing for use, 413-414, 414-415
  problems, 773-776
  recommendations, 104
  reinstalling, 750-753
  size limitations, 84-87
  size problems, 417-418
  specifications, 87-93
  speed, 87
  testing the connection, 412
hardware, 260-281, 361-394, 771-793
  adding, 371-383
  buses, 261-263
  drive interfaces, 268-269
  external, 371-378
  internal, 378-383
  overall structure, 260
  problems, 771-793
  processor, 264
  removing, 393-394
  resources, 275-281
  troubleshooting, 705-718
hardware accelerator, 133
hardware resources
  conflicts, 279-280
  device manager control, 275
  DMA channels, 276-277
  I/O addresses, 277
  IRQs, 276-277
  levels of, 275-281
  memory ranges, 277
  Plug and Play, 280-281
head-mounted displays, 240

head-related transfer functions (HRTFs), 168
header, 627
HFS, 847
HiFD, 848
himem.sys, 295
histogram, 636-637, 848
home networking, 475-478. *See also* network.
home office, 33-34
HomePNA, 476
HomeRUN, 476
host adapter, 373, 848
hosts file, 469, 848
hot plugging, 92, 371, 848
HPA, 848
HPFS, 849
HTML, 520, 548-551, 849
  basics, 574-579
  tags, 576-578
http, 449, 849
hub, 473, 849
hyperlink, 849
HyperTerminal, 781-782

I

I/O, 849
I/O addresses, 277
I/O buses, 269-271
icon, 850
IDE controllers, 93-95, 410, 418, 850
IEEE 1284, 850
IEEE 1394, 93, 95, 103-104, 362, 647-648, 850. *See also* controller.
IIP (Internet imaging protocol), 627
image compression, 224-225
image editor, 850
images. *See* digital pictures.
IMAP4, 850-851
import, 851
industry standard architecture (ISA) bus, 266-267

X bus, 272
industry standard architecture (ISA) connector, 156, 854
INF file, 851
information, 6
information movements. *See* data input and output (I/O).
Infrared wireless (IrDA), 215
INI file, 851
inkjet, 851
  cartridges, 202-203
  printing, 196-199
input device, 16, 231, 232-241, 851
  built-in pointing devices, 237
  features, 232
  game controllers, 239-240
  graphic tablets, 238-239
  keyboard, 232-234
  mice, 235-237
  purchase recommendations, 240-241
  significance of, 231
  wireless, 236
instructions, 851
Int13, 852
interface, 852
interlaced signal, 852
interleaving, 852
International Standardization Organization (ISO), 453
Internet, 503-585, 852
  application sharing, 568-570
  connection to, 488-491, 510-518
  downloading programs, 311-319
  finding information on, 540-541
  operation, 504-518
  phone calls, 565-568
  problems, 780-785, 801-802
  security, 528-541
  videoconferencing, 568-570
Internet Service Provider. *See* ISP.
InterNIC, 467-468
interrupt, 852
interrupt request. *See* IRQ.
intranet, 492-496, 852

IO.sys, 292-293, 853
IOsubsys, 391
IP address, 507-508, 513, 853
IPX/SPX, 448, 853
IRC (Internet relay chat), 563-564, 853
IRDA, 853
IRQ, 32, 276-277, 711-712, 854. *See also* resources.
    device limits, 368
    users, 369-370
ISA. *See* industry standard architecture.
ISDN, 854
ISDN modems, 187-190, 193
    additional call option (ACO), 190
    AO/DI technology, 188-189
    home office, 189
    multiple phone lines connections, 189-190
    plain old telephone service (POTS), 189
isochronous data, 104, 788
ISP, 558, 854-855

J
Java, 526-528, 529, 855
    turning off, 531-532
Java Virtual Machine, 527
    turning off, 531-532
JavaScript, 526-528, 529, 855
Jaz drive, 112-113
joystick, 855
    problems, 776-778
JPEG, 626, 646, 855-856
jumpers, 280

K
Kb/KB, 856
Kbps/KBps, 856
kernel, 856
keyboard, 16, 232-234
    ergonomic, 234-235
    feel, 234
    notebook, 234
    problems, 776-778
    repetitive stress injuries (RSIs), 234
    USB version, 241
    Window keys, 232-233
    wireless, 236
kilobit/kilobyte, 856
kilobyte, 8-9

L
L1/L2 cache, 856
label printers, 210
laptop. *See* notebook.
laser printer, 857
laser printing, 196-199
    printing function, 197-198
latency, 857
LBA, 857
LCD. *See* liquid crystal display (LCD).
LCD panel, 857
LDAP, 857
LDI, 857
legacy, 858
level 2 (L2) cache, 264-265
libraries, 858
license agreement, 905-907
LILO, 858
limited warranties, 906
line conditioner, 245-246, 858
line input, 676
Linux, 31, 858-859
    creating new user accounts, 353-354
    hardware recognition, 352
    installing, 348-353
    logging in, 353
    partitions, 351
LIon, 859
liquid crystal display (LCD), 122, 149-153
    active matrix, 150-151
    color and resolution limitations, 151-152
    connection methods, 152-153
    passive matrix, 151

live chat, 563-565
local area network (LAN), 442, 857
log, 859
logging in/out, 859
low pin count (LPC), 273
LPI, 859
LPT, 860
LS-120, 860
lurkers, 561-562
LVD signaling, 102

M

Macintosh, 470-472
  adding to your PCnetwork, 470-472
MacOS, 31
macro, 860
Magic Wand, 641-642
mainboard. *See* motherboard.
mapping, 860
masking, 641
master boot record (MBR), 289-290, 756, 860
  partition table, 290-292
Mb/MB, 860-861
Mbps/MBps, 861
media, 861
megabit/megabyte, 861
megabyte, 8-9
megapixel, 861
memory, 68-79, 399-405, 425, 861
  adding, 399-405
  connection speed, 264
  level 2 (L2) cache, 264-265
  printer, 425
  problems, 794-797
  RAMBus DRAM, 265-266
  range, 279, 711
  recommendations, 78-79
  reconfiguring, 404-405
  specs, 72-73
  standard, 264

  testing, 405
  types, 71-76
  upgrades, 32-33
  video card memory, 126-130
  Windows, 278
metatag, 861
MFD, 862
MHz, 862
microphone, 171-172
  electret, 172
  omnidirectional, 171-172
microprocessor, 12, 44-68, 256, 425-430, 830, 862
  alternatives, 56-57
  architecture, 52-56
  cache, 44-45
  connection types, 425-427
  electrical specs, 62
  installing, 428-430
  logical connections, 62-64
  operation, 44-45
  physical connections, 60-62
  recommendations, 66-68
  speed, 47-48
  types, 45-46
  upgrading, 425-430
MIDI (Musical Instrument Digital Interface), 162-163, 655, 862
  auto-accompaniment software, 691-692
  basics, 670-672
  connections, 674-676
  controller, 674
  differences from digital audio, 659-662
  editing views, 677-679
  final mix downs, 680-682
  joystick port, 172-173
  music notation software, 688-690
  note number, 670
  operation, 672-674
  patch editor/librarians, 690-691
  problems, 787
  quantization with, 679-680

continued

MIDI (Musical Instrument Digital
    Interface) *(continued)*
  sequencing programs, 672-688
  sound cards, 659-662
  standard, 163, 682-688
  standard file types, 681-682
  tracks versus channels, 672
  velocity, 670
millennium bug. *See* Y2K problem.
millisecond, 862
MIME, 522, 553-554, 803, 862-863
mini-tower, 30
mixing down, 666
MJPEG, 863
MMX, 53, 54, 863
mobile module, 59
modem, 16-18, 21, 178-194, 864
  56K, 181-184
  analog, 181-187
  basic function, 178-179
  cable connected, 190-191
  DSL technology, 192-193
  features, 179
  high speed access, 180
  improving access, 193-194
  Integrated Services Digital Network
      (ISDN), 187-190
  ISP connection, 179
  line quality, 782-783
  problems, 780-785
  speed, 179-180, 182, 782-783
  standards, 182
  terminal adapters, 178
  testing, 781-782
  transfer rate, 179
  voice-enabled, 184-186
  wireless, 186-187
modulation, 17
monitor, 16, 144-154, 864. *See also* screen.
  audio interference, 149
  built-in components, 148-149
  CRT-based, 144-149, 153
  features, 144, 148-149
  flat-panel, 145, 146

LCD-based, 145, 149-153
  resolutions, 146-147
  sizes, 145
  speakers, 148-149
  USB hubs, 149
Moore's Law, 37
motherboard, 12, 380, 431-436, 864
  installing, 434-436
  removing, 432-433
  replacing, 431-436
Motion Picture Export Group (MPEG),
      formats, 138, 863, 865
motion video acceleration, 138-139
  compression, 138-139
  MPEG formats, 138
  zoomed video, 139
mouse, 16, 235-237, 864
  3D, 236
  cleaning, 237
  features, 235-236
  navigating without, 777-778
  pointing alternatives, 237
  problems, 776-778
  PS/2, 235
  trackballs, 237
  USB, 235, 241
  wireless, 236
MP3, 864
MPEG. *See* Motion Picture Export Group
      (MPEG)
MPU-401, 865
MTUSpeed, 539
multibank DRAM, 125
multichannel audio, 176-177
multifunction printing devices, 207-208
multimedia, 865
multiprocessor systems, 59-60
multispeaker systems, 176-177
multitasking, 865
multitimbral synthesizers, 865
music, 655-694
  adding files to Web pages, 693-694
  audio remixing, 669-670
  converting files from the Web, 692-693

digital music applications, 668-692
  MIDI basics, 670-672
  MIDI sequencing programs, 672-688
  MIDI software options, 689-692
  music notation software, 688-690
  putting sound files on the Web, 692-694

N

nanosecond, 865
NASA FAR supplement, 907
NetBEUI, 448, 461-462, 866
NetBIOS, 465, 866
NetMedic, 539
NetMeeting, 568-569
Netscape messenger, 545-546, 547, 550,
    552, 554, 559-560, 561
NetWatcher, 500-502
network, 439-502, 866
  architectures, 446-448
  basic concepts, 440-455
  binding, 463-464
  building, 455-474
  client-server, 450-451
  clients, 459, 460-461
  data, 441-442
  expanding, 472-474
  home, 474-478
  messaging, 499-500
  monitoring, 500-502
  names, 464-466
  Open Systems Interconnection model,
    451-455
  operating systems, 451-452
  peer-to-peer, 450-451, 460-461, 479-481
  problems, 793
  protocols, 448-449, 459, 461-463
  software, 459
  structure, 442-446
  types, 449-451
  using, 478-502
  wireless, 477-478

network connection, 518
network control panel, 460
Network Interface Cards, 442
newsgroup, 557-563, 866
NIC, 866-867
NiCAD, 867
NiMH, 867
NLX, 867
non-parity memory, 77-78
normalizing, 867
NOS, 867
notebook, 27-30, 32-33, 234, 383, 857, 867
  keyboards, 234
  power supply, 243
NTFS, 868
NTSC, 868

O

OnNow, 868
open source, 868
operating system (OS), 31-32, 254-255,
    451-452, 868-869
  installing, 328-354
  network, 451-452
  software layers, 281-282, 282-283
  using more than one, 329-330
OPL3, 869
optical character recognition (OCR), 221
optical resolution, 218, 869
OS/2, 31, 869
OSI, 869
OSI model, 452-455
OSR, 870
Outlook, 543-544, 545, 547, 549-550, 552,
    554
Outlook Express, 543-544, 545, 547,
    549-550, 552, 554, 558-559, 561,
    562-563
output devices, 16
overclocking, 428-429
overdubbing, 666, 673-674

P

P&D, 870
packets, 447, 508
page description language, 204
parallel connections, 870
parallel port, 18-19, 211-213, 372-373, 870
  pass through, 212
  switch box connections, 213
  types, 211
parity, 870
parity memory, 77-78, 405
partition, 290-292, 330-332, 871
  active, 292
  adding or removing, 774-775
  creating, 331-332
  multiple, 292
  types, 331
Partition Magic, 331
passive matrix, 871
passive matrix screens, 151
patch, 323, 871
path, 872
PC 98, 22-26
PC 99, 22-26
PC Card, 111-112, 383, 872
PC98/PC99, 872
PCI. *See* peripheral component
    interconnect (PCI).
PCI IRQ Steering, 717-718
PCMCIA, 873
PCX, 873
PDA, 873
PDF, 609-610, 873
peer-to-peer networks, 874
Pentium, 874
peripheral, 874
peripheral buses, 266-274
  accelerated graphics port (AGP) bus,
    266-268
  I/O buses, 269-271
  industry standard architecture (ISA)
    bus, 266-267
  peripheral component interconnect
    (PCI) bus, 266-267

universal serial bus (USB), 269-270
video card connections, 266-268
peripheral component interconnect (PCI),
    132, 873
  bus, 131, 262, 266-267
  connectors, 156
  steering, 717-718
personal Web Server, 493-495
phone lines, 476
photo CD, 626, 628, 874
photo collages, 641-642
photo printers, 208-209
photo scanners, 220-221
physical modeling synthesis, 166
  software-based approach, 167
picture CD, 626-627, 628
Picture Disk, 627, 628
Picture Disk Plus, 628
PictureCD, 874
pictures. *See* digital pictures.
PIF (program information file),
    customizing, 797-799, 874-875
ping, 875
PIO (programmed I/O), 97, 875
pipelining, 875
pixel, 123-124, 875
pixel doubling, 218
plain old telephone service (POTS), 189,
    877
platform, 875
Plug and Play, 280-281
plug-in, 520-524, 875
PNG, 626, 646, 876
PnP, 876
point-to-point protocol (PPP), 442
pointing devices, 237
pointing stick, 237
polyphony, 156, 162, 876
POP3, 876
port, 18-19, 876
positional audio. *See* 3D audio.
POST (power-on self test), 288, 756, 877
PostScript, 877. *See* Page description
    language.

POTS. *See* plain old telephone service.
power, 231, 241-248
    batteries, 243
    key issues, 241-242
    line conditioners, 245-246
    management, 244
    notebook, 243
    portable, 243
    recommendations for perpherals, 248
    significance of, 231
    supplies, 242-244
    surge protectors, 245
    uninterruptible power supply (UPS),
      247
power connectors, 409
power lines, home networking, 476-477
power management, 244, 877
    ACPI (Advanced Configuration and
      Power Interface), 244
    Advanced Power Management (APM),
      244
    OnNow, 244
    problems, 788-789
power supply, 242-244
    redundant, 244
    wattage, 243-244
powerline-based networking, 246
PPM, 877
PPP, 877
print quality, 200
print resolution, 199-200
    dots per inch (dpi), 199-200
print server, 451
print speed, 201
printer, 26, 195-196, 96-216, 425, 478,
    485-487
    bidirectional communications, 210-211,
      212
    BIOS setup program, 211, 212, 215
    color printing, 204-207
    connections, 210-216
    consumables, 201-203
    cost per page, 201-203
    digital camera, 215-216

    digital photo, 208-209
    driver, 210
    dye sublimation technology, 198-199
    features, 196
    infrared wireless (IrDA), 215
    inkjet, 196-199, 202-203
    labels for, 210
    laser, 196-199
    memory, 425
    OS support, 204
    page description language, 204
    paper size, 203-204
    parallel ports, 211-212
    print quality, 200
    print speed, 201
    problems, 778-779
    resolution, 199-200, 631-632
    selection, 216
    sharing, 478, 485-487
    specialty papers, 203
    switch boxes, 213-214
    USB port, 215
printing, 305, 609, 643-645
    digital pictures, 643-645
    software function, 305
    specialty, 609
printing control language (PCL), 873
private key, 555-556
problem definition, 698-699
problems, 755-804. *See also*
    troubleshooting.
    audio, 786-788
    e-mail, 802-804
    hard drive, 773-776
    hardware, 771-793
    Internet, 780-785, 801-802
    joystick, 776-778
    keyboard, 776-778
    memory, 794-797
    modem, 780-785
    mouse, 776-778
    network, 793
    power management, 788-789

continued

problems *(continued)*
  printer, 778-779
  screen, 772-773
  SCSI, 792
  shutdown, 771
  software, 793-804
  sound card, 786-788
  startup, 756-770
  USB, 790-791
  Web browser, 801-802
process, 746
processor. *See* microprocessor.
program, 5, 311-319, 326-328, 730
  change, 673
  diagnostic, 730
  downloading off the Internet, 311-319
  reinstalling, 326-328
protected mode, 878
protocol, 442, 448-449, 459, 461-463, 878
protocol stacks, 449
protocol wrapping, 449
proxy server, 488-491, 878-879
PS/2, 879
public key, 555-556
Publisher 2000, installation, 319-321

Q
quantization, 679-680, 879
Quick View, 602-603

R
RAID, 102, 142, 879
RAM. *See* random access memory.
Rambus, 880
RAMbus DRAM, 265-266
RAMDAC. *See* random access memory
    digitial-to-analog converter.
random access memory (RAM), 8-10,
    71-76, 880
  speed, 74-75
random access memory digital-to-analog

converter (RAMDAC), 128, 130-131
ratings functions, 529
raw, 880
RCA, 880
RDRAM, 75-76, 880
read only memory (ROM), 106, 286-287
  storing BIOS, 286
real mode, 881
Real Video, 653
RealAudio, 880
recordable CD drive, 113-117, 826, 836
recordable DVD drive, 113-117
recording CDs, 663-664
  legality of, 664
recycle bin, 357
Red Book audio, 662
redundant array of inexpensive disks. *See*
    RAID.
redundant power supplies, 244
refresh rates, 130
  RAMDAC speed, 130
  video card support, 130
registry, 285, 299-300, 881
  changing settings, 300
  cleaning, 357-358
  file organization, 299-300
  fixing, 769-771
  Windows startup role, 299
Registry Checker, 739-740, 749, 769
REM, 881
remote access server (RAS), 496-499
removable drive, 881
removable storage device, 105-119
  adjustments, 758
  costs, 116-119
  recommendations, 117-118
  sharing, 482-483
repetitive stress injuries (RSIs), 234
resampling, 635
resolution, 123-124, 147, 217-218, 631-635,
    882
  charge-coupled device (CCD), 223-224
  color depth, 125-126
  CRT-based monitor, 146-147

digital camera, 223-224
dot pitch, 147
dot-per-inch (dpi) rating, 147
enhanced, 218
image size and, 633
interpolation, 218
noninterlaced operation, 147
optical, 218
scanner, 217-218
resource, 364-371, 711-718, 882
changing, 716-717
limits, 365
reserving, 715
troubleshooting, 711-718
resource conflict, 712
ISA devices, 714-717
PCI devices, 717-718
reverse engineering, 905
RGB, 882
Rich Text Format (RTF), 548-551
RIMM, 68-72, 399-400, 404, 882
ring network, 445
RISC, 55-56, 882-883
RJ-45, 883
ROM, 883
root directory, 883
rotation speeds, 89
router, 473, 488, 508, 883
RTF, 883-884
RTP, 567

S

S-RIMMs, 72
S-Video, 890-891
S/MIME, 555
Sony/Philips Digital Interface Format
(S/PDIF), 171, 884
safe mode , 761-762
sampling, 884
SANDRA, 322, 746-748
satellite modem connections, 187
satellite speakers, 175

scan disk, 618-619
ScanDisk, 739, 749
scanner, 7, 16, 195-196, 217-222, 487,
629-638, 884
bundled software, 221
color depth, 218
enhanced resolution, 218
features, 217
flatbed scanners, 217
interface types, 219
optical resolution, 218
ORC program, 221
parallel port, 219
pixel doubling, 218
quality, 217
resolution, 631-632
SCSI-based, 219
selection recommendations, 221-222
sharing, 487
sheet-fed, 217
size and speed, 219-220
specialty types, 220-221
USB connections, 219
screen, 772-773
problems, 772-773
resolution, 633-635
SCSI. *See* Small Computer Systems
Interface (SCSI).
SDRAM, 75, 884-885
SDSL, 885
search engine, 540-541, 584, 885
SECC, 885
sector, 885
seek time, 83, 885
Send To command, 605-606
SEPP, 885
sequencer, 886
sequencing programs, 672
serial connection, 886
serial port, 18-19, 886
server, 450, 886
service pack, 886
setup, 886
SGRAM, 127, 886

shared files, 719-720, 886
shareware, 312-313, 887
shutdown problems, 771
signature verification tool, 741-742, 749
SIMD, 54
SIMMs, 68-72, 399-400, 402-403, 405, 887
single-ported memory, 128
sleep, 887
slot, 60-62, 430, 887
slot cover, removing, 381
Slot One system, 430, 887
Small Computer Systems Interface, (SCSI),
      219, 373-374, 648, 792, 884. *See also*
      controller problems.
  adapter, 759
  controllers, 93-94, 95, 412, 419
  connection testing, 412
SmartMedia, 887
SMF, 888
SMTP, 888
sneakernet, 155
socket, 60-62, 888
SODIMM, 68-72, 888
software, 281-287, 416-417, 459-466,
      718-724
  basic connections, 281-282
  conflicts, 720
  copying, 416-417
  inside Windows, 283-287
  installing, 308-355, 459
  layers, 281-283
  network, 459-466
  problems, 793-804
  troubleshooting, 718-724
  uninstalling, 720-721, 793
  updating, 721-722
software layers
  application programs, 281-282
  interconnections, 281-282
  operating system, 282-283
software synthesis, 167
software operation concepts, 287-305
  BIOS setup, 288-289
  booting, 288-297

printing, 305
running applications, 302-305
Windows startup, 298-302
sound card, 155, 156-174, 888
  audio outputs, 169-171
  audio processing effects, 167-169
  capabilities recommended, 173-174
  DAC in, 167
  digital audio, 158-163
  duplex support, 161
  features, 156-157
  microphones, 171-172
  MIDI/joystick port, 172-173
  modems and, 161, 184, 185
  polyphony, 162
  problems, 786-788
  synthesized sound, 158, 162-167
  synthesizer, 158
sound files
  playing back, 657-658
  on the Web, 692-694
sound modeling, 888
sounding technologies
  liquid audio, 660
  perceptual audio coding, 660
  psychoacoustic modeling, 660
spam, 562, 888
speakers, 148-149, 153, 174-178
  3D, 176
  flat panel, 176
  key specifications, 174-175
  multispeaker systems, 176-177
  powered versus unpowered, 175-176
  purchasing tips, 177-178
  satellites and subwoofers, 175
  traditional, 176
  for USB-based audio, 177
special effects, 642-643, 652, 668-669
specialty papers, 203
specialty printers, multifunction devices,
     207-208
speculative execution, 889
SPP, 889
SRAM. *See* static RAM.

SSL (Secure Sockets Layer) connection, 529
star network, 444, 446
startup files, 292-297, 759-771, 889
  autoexec.bat, 296-297
  customized, 799-801
  DOS memory problems, 294-296
  editing, 763-764
  IO.sys, 292-293
startup floppy. *See* boot disk.
startup problems, 756-770
static electricity, 378-379
static RAM, 71-76, 889
stereo speakers, traditional, 176
storage, 10, 889
streaming, 653
streaming audio, 660-661
streaming media, 889
streaming SIMD, 890
subnotebook, 890
subwoofer, 175, 890
surge protectors, 245
surge suppressor, 890
SVGA, 890
swap file, 891
switch, 891
switch box function, 213-214
switching hub, 473
synchronization, 891
synchronous DRAM. *See* SDRAM.
synchronous graphics random access memory. *See* SGRAM.
synthesized sound, 158, 162-167
  FM synthesis, 163-164
  hardware versus software synthesis, 166-167
  MIDI (musical instrument digital interface) music, 158, 162-163
  physical modeling synthesis, 166
  polyphony, 162
  wavetable synthesis, 164-165
synthesizer, 670, 891
synthesizer patch, 673
system bus, 62-64, 261-262, 891

System Configuration Editor, 742-743, 749
System Configuration Utility, 732-733, 748
System File Checker, 733-735, 748
system file extracting, 767-768
system information, 731-732, 748
System Monitor, 744-745
System Resource Meter, 744-745, 749

T

tag, 892
tape drive, 115-116
TB, 892
TCP/IP, 448, 462, 467-470, 567, 892
  protocol, 511
  setting up, 467-470
  settings, 784-785
technical support, 41
Telnet, 504
temp, 892
terabyte, 893
terminal adapters, 178
TFT, 893
thread, 558, 746, 893
3D graphics, 134-137, 143-144
  acceleration, 134-137, 144
  computer games, 134-135
  image creation, 135-136
  image quality, 137
  speed, 136
throughput, 90, 893
  sustained, 106
TIFF, 626, 893
time compression/expansion, 668
titles, 652
topology, 893
touchpad. *See* trackpad.
tower, 30, 893
TraceRoute, 785
Tracert, 539-540
track, 893
trackball, 237, 894
trackpad, 237, 894

transfer rates, 96-97
Trojan horse, 528
troubleshooting, 697-753
   basic checks, 703-705
   connections, 703-704
   documentation, 702-703
   hardware, 705-718
   resources, 700-702
   software, 718-724
   solution testing, 703
   strategies, 698-703
   tools, 724-753
   updates, 704-705
   upgrades, 704-705
   Windows 95 tools, 742-753
   Windows 98 troubleshooting utilities,
     730-742
TrueType font, 894
TV tuner card, 139, 140
TWAIN, 629-630, 894
2D graphics acceleration, 133, 144
type 1 font, 894

U

UADSL, 894-895
UDP, 567, 895
UltraATA. *See* UltraDMA.
UltraDMA, 95, 97-98
UMB, 895
UNC, 895
unified memory architecture (UMA), 127
uniform resource locator (URL), 505-507,
   896
uninstaller program, 356-359
uninterruptible power supply (UPS), 247
universal serial bus (USB), 375-377, 896
   audio, 177
   compatibility, 791
   hub, 149, 215, 376-377
   port, 18, 215
   power issues, 790-791
   problems, 788, 790-791
   speakers, 177

user profiles, 33-36
UNIX, 348, 895
unpowered speakers, 175
Update Wizard Uninstall, 741, 749
updates, 424-425
   and troubleshooting, 704-705
upgrade, 895. *See also* expandability.
   automatic, 324-325
   removing, 325-326
   troubleshooting and, 704-705
upgrading, 397-420
   applications, 323-326
upper memory, 896
Uunencode, 553, 896-897

V

V.34, 897
V.90, 897
vCard, 552
vector graphics, 897
verify, 335
Version Conflict Manager (VCM), 735, 748
VGA, 898
video, 647-653
   compression, 650-651
   editing, 649-650, 651-652
   graphics, 652
   saving, 653
   special effects, 652
   titles, 652
video acceleration, 133-139
   hardware accelerator, 133
   motion, 137-139
   2D graphics, 133
   3D graphics, 134-137
video adapter. *See* video card.
video camera, 227-229
video capture, 898
video capture card, 227, 648
video card, 12-13, 20, 121-144, 258, 898
   accelerated graphics port (AGP), 126,
     131-132
   acceleration, 133-139

color depth, 124-126
frame buffer, 121, 126
interfaces, 131-132
memory, 126-130, 144
peripheral bus connections, 266-268
purpose, 121-122
refresh rates, 130-131
resolution, 123-124
specifications, 122
TV inputs, 139-140
video recording, 140-143
video card memory, 126-130, 144
bit width, 128-130
dual-ported, 127-128
types, 127-128, 144
unified memory architecture (UMA), 127
video circuitry, 122. *See also* video card.
video recording, 141-143
videoconferencing, 568-570, 898
virtual channel memory (VCM), 76-77, 898-899
virtual machine, 392, 527
virtual machine manager, 391-392
virtual memory, 303, 899
virus, 724, 899
VL-bus, 899
VMM32, 391-392
voice modem. *See* modem.
voice recognition, 900
volume, 900
volume control, 786
VRAM, 900
VxD, 900

W

WAN, 900
warranties, 906
WAV, 900
wave audio. *See* digital audio.
waveform, 901
waveguide. *See* physical modeling synthesis.

wavetable synthesis, 164-165, 901
process, 164
RAM storage, 164-165
sound quality, 165
Web address, 581-582. *See also* uniform resource locator (URL).
Web applications, 525-536
Web browser, 505-506, 518-519, 536-539, 824
e-mail, 35-36
performance, 536-539
problems, 801-802
Web page
adding files to, 693-694
creating, 572-581
graphic design, 573-574
posting, 582-583
testing, 580-581
Web ring, 585
Web server, 492-495, 583
Web site, 901
building, 570-585
connecting with, 505-510
navigation, 580
publicizing, 584-585
updating, 584
Web TV, 36
Win.ini, 901
window keys, 232-233
Windows, 31-32, 794-797, 901
Windows 2000
installing, 347-348
Windows 3.1, upgrading, 338-345
Windows 95
CD upgrades, 343-345
diagnostic tools, 742-753
installing, 332-334, 345-347
reinstalling, 335-345
upgrading, 334, 338-345
version history, 341-343
Windows 98, 332-334, 335-347
installing, 332-334
reinstalling, 335-345
troubleshooting utilities, 730-742
upgrading, 334

Windows CE, 29
Windows Report Tool, 742, 749
Windows Resource kits, 701-702
Windows software, 283-287
    basic input/output system (BIOS), 286-287
    core OS components, 286
    DirectX services, 284-285
    drivers, 286-287
    dynamic link libraries (DLLs), 285
    layers structure, 283
Windows startup, 298-302
    files summary, 301-302
    initialization files, 298
    registry function, 298
    registry storage, 298
Windows update, 324-325, 325-326, 708
WINS, 901
WinTop, 745-746
wireless modems, 186-187
    cellular phones, 187
    satellite link, 187
wizard, 902
word size, 54-55

workstation, 902
World Wide Web (WWW), 505, 902
WYSIWYG, 902

X

X bus, 272, 902
x86 processors, 52-53, 56-57, 902
XGA, 903
XML, 575, 902-903
XMS, 903

Y

Y2K problem, 420

Z

Z-Buffer, 903
ZIF (zero insertion force) socket, 429
Zip drive, 112, 903
zoomed video, 138, 903

IDG BOOKS WORLDWIDE, INC.
END-USER LICENSE AGREEMENT